Medieval and Renaissance Manuscript Books in the Library of Congress

A Descriptive Catalog

by Svato Schutzner

Volume I

Bibles, Liturgy, Books of Hours

LIBRARY OF CONGRESS
WASHINGTON 1989

Library of Congress Cataloging-in-Publication Data

Library of Congress.
Medieval and Renaissance manuscript books in the Library of Congress.
Bibliography: p.
Includes indexes.
Contents: 1. Bibles, liturgy, books of hours.
Supt. of Docs. no.: LC 4.2:M46
1. Library of Congress—Catalogs. 2. Manuscripts, Medieval—Washington (D.C.)—Catalogs. 3. Manuscripts, Renaissance—Washington (D.C.)—Catalogs. I. Schutzner, Svato, 1923- . II. Title.
Z6621.U58M64 1988 091'.09753 85-600260
ISBN 0-8444-0516-7 (v. 1)

∞ The paper used in this publication meets the requirements for permanence established by the American National Standard for Information Sciences "Permanence of Paper for Printed Library Materials" (ANSI Z 39.48-1984).

For sale by the Superintendent of Documents,
U.S. Government Printing Office, Washington, D.C. 20402

Contents

Manuscripts Described in This Volume

Foreword

This is the first volume of a projected three-volume catalog that will describe the medieval and Renaissance manuscripts held by the Library of Congress. This collection of early handwritten books is not the result of a systematic acquisitions program. In the years before the First World War, the Library of Congress occasionally purchased pre-1601 Western manuscripts, often as part of a large collection containing only a few early manuscripts. In the last fifty years a number of particularly beautiful manuscripts came to the Library as gifts, most prominent among these being the manuscripts in the Lessing J. Rosenwald Collection. The resulting mix of slightly fewer than two hundred pre-1601 manuscript books includes several stunning works of art that over the years have attracted the attention of art historians (e.g., items 6, 8, 46, and 52 in this volume of the catalog). One or two were once beautiful but suffered, before coming to the Library, from neglect, mistreatment, mutilation by miniature collectors, and mishandling by overzealous scholars. Some of the books are quite utilitarian: copies of important standard texts (Bibles, liturgical books) or collections of texts newly assembled by a nonprofessional scribe for his own use (e.g., MS 33). All document some aspect of cultural history.

This first volume treats sixty-four Bibles and liturgical and paraliturgical texts. Volume 2 will be devoted to canon law and theology. Volume 3 will describe secular manuscripts. Volume 2 is scheduled for publication in 1990 and the third volume three years later. The catalog's scope is limited to "Western" manuscripts, excluding fragments, documentary material, correspondence, and manuscripts written wholly or in substantial part in the Semitic languages and those of the Far East.

In Seymour de Ricci's 1935 *Census of Medieval and Renaissance Manuscripts in the United States and Canada,* many of the manuscripts described in this catalog are listed as being in the Manuscript Division's care. All of these passed to the custody of the Rare Book Room following the issuance of a November 29, 1937, memorandum of Librarian Herbert Putnam, directing their transfer. The change of custodial responsibility is recorded in C. U. Faye and W. H. Bond's 1962 *Supplement* to the De Ricci *Census*. Inquiries about the manuscripts described in the catalog should be directed to the Rare Book and Special Collections Division. Most music manuscripts (items 9, 10, 11, 16, 19, 36, and 38–43 in this volume of the catalog) are housed in the Music Division, which cares for and services its own rare book collection of printed and manuscript music material.

The particular need for this catalog grew from my discovery in January 1980 that the Library's cataloging divisions were no longer using the designation "Ms." in assigning call numbers to manuscripts. Fearing that the identity of the Library's manuscript books would be lost, I proposed that rare book cataloger Svato Schutzner be assigned the task of preparing a catalog of the pre-1601 Western manuscripts, the most directly affected portion of the manuscript book collection. Mr. Schutzner's studies at the theological faculties of Prague and Strasbourg had given him the needed background in medieval texts, art history, the history of liturgy, and languages. He commenced work on the catalog in July 1980.

In the launching of a time-consuming project such as this, many factors come together. Following the death in 1979 of the Library's great benefactor Lessing J. Rosenwald and the 1980 transfer of his collection from the Alverthorpe Gallery in

Jenkintown, Pennsylvania, to the Library of Congress, serious scholars—textual students, art historians, and codicologists—increasingly made their way to the Rare Book and Special Collections Division. The inadequacies of the De Ricci *Census*, the advances in the study of early manuscripts, and the recognition that a unified catalog of American manuscripts would almost certainly never be published, given the immense expense of such an undertaking, created a climate in which a number of institutions—among them Yale, the Newberry Library, the Huntington Library, and the Library of Congress—undertook the preparation of catalogs of manuscript collections which are now being—or shortly will be—published.

The presence on its shelves of the largest collection of incunabula outside Europe made it particularly appropriate that the Library of Congress should publish a catalog of a body of material so directly a part of the same social, cultural, and aesthetic context. In proposing this catalog in 1980 I noted that its publication, "describing vitally important material for which the control is either inadequate or non-existent, [would be] exactly in line with [Librarian of Congress, Daniel J. Boorstin's] interest in establishing the Library of Congress as a center for scholarship." All of us involved in the catalog's preparation hope that it will encourage the use of collections, here and elsewhere, which through their direct link with the past have such rich potential for further study.

William Matheson
Chief, Rare Book and
Special Collections Division

Preface

The format of the manuscript descriptions that follow is eclectic (in some respects idiosyncratic)—developed independently but with helpful advice from many persons. The influence of recent British and other catalogs will be noticed. I do not view the result as ideal; possible improvements in the volumes yet to come are under study. The format is largely self-explanatory, but a few notes are in order:

Provenience, i.e., where the manuscript originated: the place name (often an area) given first in the first line after title. Sometimes the line reads "Written and decorated in . . ."; but such precision was not always possible.

The statement of the number of leaves as printed in the opening paragraph of the description corresponds, unless otherwise stated, to the foliation found in the book, mostly added in pencil in recent times by owners, dealers, or librarians. The foliation is always explained further and complemented by information concerning end-leaves, and so forth, in the first paragraph after the contents.

Sins of Omission: The kind reader will do well not to draw conclusions from the mere absence of a statement. Musical notation may have been caught every time it appeared but other things have certainly remained unmentioned in some cases and stated in others. Inscriptions by former owners are noted, but it is possible that some have been missed.

Sins of Commission: In the quotations that introduce each section of contents I have departed from the fairly common practice of silently expanding contractions. The transcriptions are, however, not full-fledged critical transcripts. The very numerous brackets are used rather in the way they appear in transcripts of early book titles in Library of Congress rare-book cataloging as adapted to automated retrieval machinery. Since this seemed far from satisfactory, another compromise was struck: abbreviations such as *scī, epī, dn̄i*, and, in particular, *xp̄i* have been (largely) retained, with macrons fairly imitating the contraction marks of the source. In some other cases, this style seemed to show more of the flavor of the original. The choice of method has often been subjective and the gods of consistency have not been adhered to as much as the spirit of variety.

Bracketed "[et]" means the tironian note. In the volumes to come it may be possible to have the note printed as such (in some legal materials from Leon & Castille the sign stands sometimes for "et" and sometimes for "e," perhaps even for "y").

Italics are used primarily for "rubrics," more exactly for those parts of a quoted text which in the source are written in red (or blue, or gold, in some); assuming the normal case in which the text is black and red. But sometimes the italics mean a "rubric" created in the source by red underscoring of black text; an attempt has been made to give some warning when that case arises. Not all manuscripts are "normal," among them the Archieraticon, LC MS 37. I tried to treat such cases individually and to be as clear and explicit as practicable.

Illuminated initials (even the calligraphic ones in a book which relies heavily on them for its *ordinatio textus*, as the MS 28) are indicated by parentheses around the letter, with a superscript numeral indicating the height of the letter in terms of text lines. In some cases this information is given, instead, in a parenthesized statement. An initial letter in parentheses without a superscript means ordinarily an illuminated initial one line high, noted only where this seemed to be important. (A superscript "1+" is meant to signal an initial almost but not quite two lines high. In texts with music, superscript "1+1" means an initial reaching vertically from the top of the musical staff to the base of the text line.)

Our choice of color plates attempts a compromise between aesthetic value and informativeness; the black-and-white reproductions are meant chiefly to show samples of the script. The short paragraphs of individual bibliography given at the end of each description list such reproductions found elsewhere as I am aware of.

Of the five indexes, the general one (first) includes some Greek titles or phrases in romanized form; one should apologize to the Greeks for this but it makes simpler both the alphabetizing and the printing. In the index of *initia*, those in Greek follow the end of the roman alphabet. The index of initia omits some very commonly available or necessarily present texts (e.g., beginnings of individual Psalms); and, alas, it is probably not fully consistent in this and other respects. Of all the indexes, that of the "2° folio" seems to puzzle most nonspecialists; it is an old identifying device somewhat akin to the modern "fingerprint" concept in cataloging: the opening words of the second recto of a manuscript do not, as a rule, make much sense but they do help to recognize a book which may otherwise have been given new covers, a new number, or new identification.

The cost of book production and (therefore) the need to avoid duplication of catalogs makes it unlikely that this country would in the foreseeable future produce a work analogous to the *Manuscrits datés.* (See "*MSS datés*" in the Abbreviations for the French model product; here the term serves also for similar undertakings in other countries.) The several descriptive catalogs produced in and by the various institutions of learning will have to serve the purpose. Hence, a summarization of what is also discussed in the individual descriptions: Of the manuscripts in this volume, expressly dated are the MSS 8 (the Giant Bible of Mainz, 1452–53), 26 (a Missal from the Netherlands, 1451), and 52 (the *Horae* Rosenwald 10/14, of 1524). A fairly narrow time span could be assigned on the basis of internal evidence to the production of MSS 6 (at least as regards the decoration), 7, 15, 29, 45, 46, and 53. Cumulative evidence of liturgical history and paleography has made it possible to revise the dating of several items previously poorly identified, notably the two Carthusian homiliaries, MSS 13 and 23; this, as some other new opinions advanced in this catalog, is largely due to the considerable progress of liturgical scholarship in our time.

A stranger to the Library of Congress may find it surprising that the manuscripts described here are not located in the Manuscript Division. Almost all books discussed in this volume are now in the custody of the Library's Rare Book and Special Collections Division and can be seen, with due restrictions, in its reading room; queries or requests for further information should be directed to that division. Most music items are cared for by the Library's Music Division, specifically MSS 9–11, 16, 19, 36, and 38–43 in this book.

Acknowledgments

This project was first suggested by Renata V. Shaw of the Library of Congress Prints and Photographs Division. Special thanks are due to William Matheson, chief of the Rare Book and Special Collections Division, for his initial approval and continuing support; to David Smith, head of the Special Materials Cataloging Division, who has provided both encouragement and logistical assistance; and to my colleagues in Rare Book Cataloging, in particular to its coordinator Nicoletta Marketos, for tolerating in the small office we share an activity which contributes nothing to production statistics and instead takes up shelf space for esoteric reference works.

Expert assistance with an individual codex or in a specific problem is acknowledged in footnotes to the description involved; I hope I have always given proper credit, but I may have failed to make a record of advice communicated orally. This is especially true of many discussions with my colleagues inside the Library. Opinion, advice, or (in the area of art history) expertise have been frequently sought from Kathleen T. Mang *née* Hunt, curator of the Library's Rosenwald Collection; to her and other members of the Rare Book and Special Collections Division thanks are due also for their unfailing patience and helpfulness in all kind of practical problems. I often had the honor and pleasure of meeting in the Rare Book Reading Room visiting scholars and experts in various fields, and sometimes profited from their willingness to share their experience; among these: Adelaide Bennett-Hagen, Marvin L. Colker, Charles Faulhaber, Lotte Hellinga-Querido, A. Dean McKenzie, Marie-Claire Mangin, Nigel Morgan, Paul Needham, Jeremy Noble, Myra D. Orth, Joseph Sonderkamp, Laetitia Yeandle. The wide experience of Thomas C. Albro of the Library's Restoration Office has often been required in matters pertaining to bindings. In working with the music manuscripts, invaluable help has come from Rembert Herbert, the medieval music specialist of the Library's Music Division.

In or out of the Library, the catalog *in statu nascendi* was discussed with Lilian Randall, curator of manuscripts at the Walters Art Gallery; Robert Maloy, director of Smithsonian Institution Libraries; Richard H. Rouse of the University of California, Los Angeles; Donald A. Yates of Michigan State University; Michael Gullick; and others. None of these should be blamed for whatever may be found wrong with the volume.

An essential contribution to this project, particularly in its early stages, was provided by the organizational know-how, diplomacy, friendly criticism, and professional awareness of Thomas Daniel Burney, former assistant chief of what then was called simply the Rare Book Division. Mr. Burney's participation was generally that of a manager and liaison; but for his optimistic attitude, the project could have ground to a halt at some point.

A prominent supporting role was that of Barbara Killian of the Library's Collections Development Office, who repeatedly managed to get through special orders for reference books, once recovering in person a whole set of Hauréau's *Initia* from the abandoned office of a staff member who had died. A lion's share in inputting several years' worth of typewritten descriptions on magnetic disks was taken by Lisa Cockran. George Von Rautenfeld's reading has speeded up my work on proofs. A number of others, sometimes without my knowledge of it, have contributed by their decisions before or behind the scene.

The catalog belongs to the Library of Congress and to this country's people whom it serves; may my part in this effort be dedicated also to the memory of my father, Dr. Josef Schützner, before World War II head of the Comenius University Library in Bratislava. The library was then just reaching its first million titles, and as a boy I was much more aware of its contemporary treasures—including a very up-to-date collection of American and English philosophy—than of its manuscripts, of which, I later learned, the holdings were quite important. But our family lived in the building; the medieval walls of the former Poor Clares' convent where the library was then located were decorated with frescoes. For me, their spell and that of the volumes I have now been privileged to examine speak the same language of home.

Works Quoted in Abbreviated Form

AH
(G. M. Dreves *et al.*, eds.) *Analecta hymnica Medii Aevi* (Leipzig, 1886–1922) (normally cited by volume and item number)

Berger, *Hist. Vulg.*
S. Berger, *Histoire de la Vulgate pendant les premiers siècles du moyen âge* (Paris, 1893; repr. Hildesheim, 1976)

Berger, *Pref.*
S. Berger, "Les préfaces jointes aux livres de la Bible dans les manuscrits de la Vulgate," in: Académie des inscriptions et belles-lettres, Paris. *Mémoires présentés par divers savants.* 1e série, t. 11, 2e pt. (Paris, 1904)

Bonniwell, *Hist. Dom. lit.*
W. R. Bonniwell, *A history of the Dominican liturgy, 1215–1945.* 2nd ed. (New York, 1945)

Branner
R. J. Branner, *Manuscript painting in Paris during the reign of Saint Louis* (Berkeley, 1977)

Bri.
(F. E. Brightman and/or C. E. Hammond, comp.) *Liturgies, eastern and western: being the texts, original or translated, of the principal liturgies of the church* (Oxford, 1965)

Briquet
C. M. Briquet, *Les filigranes: dictionnaire historique des marques du papier . . . 1282 jusqu'à 1600* (Paris, 1907) (also reprint)

CCSL
Corpus Christianorum. Series Latina (Turnhout, 1953–)

Cappelli
A. Cappelli, *Cronologia, cronografia e calendario perpetuo* (3. ed., Milano, 1969)

Cath. encycl.
Catholic encyclopedia: an international work of reference . . . (New York, 1907–22)

COLLECTANEA O.C.R.
COLLECTANEA ORDINIS CISTERCIENSIUM REFORMATORUM (Rome, 1934–)

Cottineau
L. H. Cottineau, *Répertoire topo-bibliographique des abbayes et prieurés* (Maçon, 1935–70)

Delaissé
L. M. J. Delaissé, *Illuminated manuscripts: the James A. De Rothschild collection at Waddesdon Manor* (Fribourg, 1977)

De Ricci
S. de Ricci, *Census of medieval and Renaissance manuscripts in the United States and Canada* (New York, 1935–40)

Dict. d'archéologie chrétienne
F. Cabrol, *Dictionnaire d'archéologie chrétienne et de liturgie* (Paris, 1907–)

Dict. mon. cisterc.
(M. Cocheril) *Dictionnaire des monastères cisterciens* (Rochefort, Abbaye Notre-Dame de St-Rémy, 1976–)

Du Cange
C. D. Du Cange, *Glossarium mediae et infimae Latinitatis* (Paris, 1840–50)

EEFL
(E. Lodi, ed.) *Enchiridion euchologicum fontium liturgicorum* (Roma, 1979)

Faye and Bond
C. U. Faye and W. H. Bond, *Supplement to the Census of medieval and Renaissance manuscripts in the United States and Canada* (New York, 1962)

GW
Gesamtkatalog der Wiegendrucke (1925–)

Grotefend
H. Grotefend, *Zeitrechnung des deutschen Mittelalters und der Neuzeit* (Hannover, 1891–92)

Haebler
K. Haebler, *Rollen- und Plattenstempel des XVI. Jahrhunderts* (Leipzig, 1928–29)
Hauréau-Schmeller, *Initia*
B. Hauréau, *Initia operum scriptorum Latinorum Medii potissimum Aevi . . . Accedit Schedarium initia amplectens ab A. G. Schmeller et G. Meyer . . . collecta* (Turnhout, 1973–74)
Horae Eboracenses
Horae Eboracenses: the Prymer or Hours of the Blessed Virgin Mary, according to the use of the illustrious Church of York . . . [Christopher Wordsworth, ed.] (Durham, 1920) (The Publications of the Surtees Society, vol. 132)
Hughes, *Medieval manuscripts*
A. Hughes, *Medieval manuscripts for Mass and Office: a guide to their organization and terminology* (Toronto, 1982)

Illuminated books . . . (1949)
Illuminated books of the Middle Ages and Renaissance: an exhibition . . . organized by the Walters Art Gallery . . . (Baltimore, 1949)

Ker, *Med. mss. in Brit. libs.*
N. R. Ker, *Medieval manuscripts in British libraries* (Oxford, 1969–)
Kyriss
E. Kyriss, *Verzierte gotische Einbände im alten deutschen Sprachgebiet* (Stuttgart, 1951)

Leroquais, *Brév.*
V. Leroquais, *Les bréviaires manuscrits des bibliothèques publiques de France* (Paris, 1934)
Leroquais, *LH*
V. Leroquais, *Les livres d'heures manuscrits de la Bibliothèque nationale* (Paris, 1927-43)
Leroquais, *Psautiers*
V. Leroquais, *Les psautiers manuscrits latins des bibliothèques publiques de France* (Maçon, 1940-41)
Leroquais, *Sacramentaires et missels*
V. Leroquais, *Les sacramentaires et les missels manuscrits des bibliothèques publiques de France* (Paris, 1924; suppl. 1943)
Lex. f. Theol. u. Kirche
Lexikon für Theologie und Kirche. 2. Aufl. (Freiburg i.B., 1957-67)

Lundén, *Officium parvum*
(T. Lundén, ed.) *Officium parvum / den heliga Birgitta och den helige Petrus av Skänninge* (Uppsala, 1976)

MSS datés (sometimes with added specification "(France)")
(C. Samaran) *Catalogue des manuscrits en écriture latine portant des indications de date, de lieu ou de copiste* (Paris, 1959-)
Meertens, *Godsvrucht*
M. Meertens, *De Godsvrucht in de Nederlanden naar handschriften van gebedenboeken der XV*[e] *eeuw.* (v. 1–3 and 6) (Brussel, etc., 1930–34) (Leuvense studiën en tekstuitgaven)

Nomenclature des écritures livresques
Nomenclature des écritures livresques du IXe *au XVI*[e] *siècle: premier colloque international de paléographie latine . . .* (Paris, 1954) (Colloques internationaux du Centre national de la recherche scientifique. Sciences humaines; 4)

OMRL
S. J. P. Van Dijk, *The origins of the modern Roman liturgy* (Westminster, Md., 1960)

PG
(J. P. Migne, ed.) *Patrologiae cursus completus. Series Graeca* (Paris, 1857-66)
PL (sometimes not italicized for clarity)
(J. P. Migne, ed.) *Patrologiae cursus completus. Series Latina* (Paris, 1844-80)
Parkes, *Med. mss. Keble College*
M. B. Parkes, *The medieval manuscripts of Keble College, Oxford* (London, 1979)
Perdrizet, *Calendrier parisien*
P. Perdrizet, *Le calendrier parisien à la fin du Moyen Âge* (Paris, 1933) (Publications de la Faculté des lettres de l'Université de Strasbourg, fasc. 63)
Piccard, *Ochsenkopf-Wasserzeichen*
(G. Piccard) *Die Wasserzeichenkartei Piccard im Hauptstaatsarchiv Stuttgart, 2: Ochsenkopf-Wasserzeichen* (T. 1-3) (Stuttgart, 1966)

Rep. der griech. Kopisten
Repertorium der griechischen Kopisten, 800–1600 (Wien, 1981–)

SMRL
(S. J. P. Van Dijk, ed.) *Sources of the modern Roman liturgy* (Leiden, 1963) (Studia et documenta Franciscana, 1–2)

Sonet
J. Sonet, *Répertoire d'incipit des prières en ancien français* (Genève, 1956)

Stegm.
(F. Stegmüller, ed.) *Repertorium biblicum Medii Aevi* (Matriti, 1950–77; repr. 1981)

Strubbe, *Chronologie*
E. I. Strubbe, *De chronologie van de middeleeuwen en de moderne tijden in de Nederlanden* (Antwerpen, 1960)

Szövérffy, *Annalen*
J. Szövérffy, *Die Annalen der lateinischen Hymnendichtung* (Berlin, 1964–65)

Thieme-Becker
U. Thieme and F. Becker, *Allgemeines Lexikon der bildenden Künstler . . .* (Leipzig, 1907–50)

Van Wijk('s edition of Geert Grote's Getijdenboek)
Het Getijdenboek van Geert Grote : naar het Haagse handschrift 133 E 21 (Leiden, 1940)

Walther, *Initia*
H. Walther, *Initia carminum ac versuum Medii Aevi posterioris Latinorum* (Göttingen, 1959)

Wilmart, *Aut. spir.*
A. Wilmart, *Auteurs spirituels et textes dévots du moyen âge latin* (Paris, 1932; repr. 1971)

Zender, *Räume und Schichten*
M. Zender, *Räume und Schichten mittelalterlicher Heiligenverehrung in ihrer Bedeutung für die Volkskunde* (Köln, 1973)

LITURGICAL ABBREVIATIONS (used chiefly in appendices to descriptions):

(For elements of the Office:)

a, aa	antiphon, -s
V_1	first Vespers (= for the evening before the feast)
Hy	hymn
Cap	*capitulum* (short reading)
ad M	antiphon to *Magnificat*
Suffr	*suffragium* (mostly consisting of an antiphon, a versicle with a response, and a formal prayer)
ad N D	antiphon to *Nunc Dimittis*
Invit	Invitatory
I Noct	first Nocturn (section of Matins)
II Noct	second Nocturn
III Noct	third Nocturn
a_1, a_2, a_3 . . .	first, second, etc., antiphon of Matins (for the psalms of the Nocturns)
R_1, R_2, R_3 . . .	first, second, etc., responsory of Matins; also any other responsory
L	Lauds
ad B	antiphon to *Benedictus*
P, T, S, N	Prime, Terce, Sext, None
V_2	second Vespers (= for the evening of the feast day)
/ . . .	versicle in a responsory, or following an antiphon

(For elements of the Mass:)

Intr	Introit
IntrPs	Psalm verse in the Introit
Coll	Collect (formal prayer which precedes the readings)
Ep	Epistle (the first reading)
Grad	Gradual (the choral item between readings, not the book)
All, AllV	Alleluia, Alleluiatic verse
Seq	sequence (the liturgical/poetic genre)
Gos	Gospel (the pericope read in Mass, not one of the four books in the New Testament)
Off	Offertory antiphon
Comm	Communion antiphon
Postcomm	Formal prayer after Communion

Color Plates

II **MS 5, f. 1r** The letter *I* of the beginning of Genesis, thought to be by a Parisian-trained artist operating in England. (Actual size of the leaf: 17.9 × 11.5 cm)

III **MS 6, v. I, f. 5v (detail from lower left corner)** A perhaps identifiable church structure is being offered to the Lord; Christ's face as seen by Master Hertul? (cf. note 24 of description).

IV **MS 7, f. 35v (detail)** Moses on his knees. ▶ The portable Bible was written in Bohemia around the time John Huss was preaching in Prague; later, it surfaced not far from the place of his execution.

Explicit lib Leuitic Incip[t] liber Numeri

Incipit liber Exodi quem hebrei Ellesmoth dicunt.

Capitulum Primum

[H]Ec sunt nomina fili-
orum Israhel qui ingres-
si sunt in Egiptum cum
Jacob. singuli cum do-
mibus suis introierunt.
Ruben. Symeon. Levi.
Judas. ysachar. Zabu-
lon et Benyamyn.
Dan et Neptalim.
Gad et Aser. Erant
igitur omnes anime eorum qui egressi sunt de fe-
more Jacob septuaginta quinque. Joseph autem
erat in Egipto. Quo mortuo. et universis
fratribus eius. omnique cognacione illa. filii Israhel creverunt. et quasi germinantes multiplicati sunt. ac roborati nimis. impleverunt terram.
Surrexit interea rex novus super Egiptum.
qui ignorabat Joseph. et ait ad populum suum.
Ecce populus filiorum Israhel multus et forcior nobis est. venite sapienter opprimamus eum. ne
forte multiplicetur. et si ingruerit contra nos bellum. addatur inimicis nostris. expugnatisque
nobis egrediatur a terra. Preposuit itaque eis
magistros operum. ut affligerent eos oneribus.
Edificaveruntque urbes tabernaculorum Pharaoni
Phiton et Ramasses. Quantoque opprimebat
eos. tanto magis multiplicabantur et cresce-
bant. Oderantque filios Israhel Egipcii. et
affligebant illudentes eis. atque ad amaritudinem perducebant vitam eorum operibus duris.
luti et lateris. omnique famulatu quo in terre o-
peribus premebantur. Dixit autem rex obstetricibus hebreorum. quarum una vocabatur Sef-
fora. altera Phua. precipiens eis. Quando ob-
stetricabitis Hebreas. et partus tempus adve-
nerit. si masculus fuerit interficite illum. si fe-
mina reservate. Timuerunt autem obstetrices deum. et non fecerunt iuxta preceptum regis.
Egipti. sed conservabant mares. Quibus ad
se accersitis rex ait. Quid nam est hoc quod facere voluistis. ut pueros reservaretis. Que responderunt. Non sunt Hebree sicut Egipcie mulieres. ipse enim obstetricandi habent scienciam. et
priusquam veniamus ad eas pariunt. Bene
ergo fecit deus obstetricibus. Et crevit populus.
confortatusque est nimis. Et quia timuerant
obstetrices deum. edificavit illis domos. Pre-
cepit autem Pharao omni populo suo dicens.
Quicquid masculini sexus natum fuerit in
flumen proicite. quicquid feminei reservate.

Capitulum Secundum.

[E]Gressus est post hec vir de domo Levi. accepit uxorem stirpis sue. Que
concepit et peperit filium. Et videns
eum elegantem. abscondit tribus mensibus.
Cumque iam celare non posset. sumpsit fiscellam
scirpeam. et linivit eam bitumine ac pice. po-
suitque intus infantulum. et exposuit eum in car-
recto ripe fluminis. stante procul sorore eius. et
considerante eventum rei. Ecce autem descende-
bat filia Pharaonis ut lavaretur in flumine.
et puelle eius gradiebantur per crepidinem al-
vei. Que cum vidisset fiscellam in papirione.
misit unam e famulabus suis. et allatam ape-
riens. cernensque in ea parvulum vagientem. mi-
serta eius ait. De infantibus hebreorum est hic.
Cui soror pueri. vis inquit ut vadam et vocem
tibi hebream mulierem. que nutrire possit infantulum. Respondit. Vade. Perrexit puel-
la. et vocavit matrem eius. Ad quam locuta
filia Pharaonis. accipe ait puerum istum et nutri
michi. ego tibi dabo mercedem tuam. Suscepit
mulier et nutrivit puerum. adultumque tradidit
filie Pharaonis. Quem illa adoptavit in locum filii. Vocavitque nomen eius moyses. dicens.
Quia de aqua tuli eum. In diebus illis postquam creverat Moyses. egressus ad fratres su-
os. vidit afflictionem eorum. et virum Egipcium per-
cucientem quendam de Hebreis. fratribus suis.
Cumque circumspexisset huc atque illuc. et nullum
adesse vidisset. percussum Egipcium abscondit
sabulo. Et egressus die altero. conspexit duos Hebreos rixantes. Dixitque ei qui faciebat
iniuriam. Quare percutis proximum tuum.
Qui respondit. Quis constituit te principem
et iudicem super nos. Num occidere tu me vis.
sicut occidisti heri Egipcium. Timuit Moyses.
et ait. Quomodo palam factum est verbum istud.
Audivitque Pharao sermonem hunc. et quere-
bat occidere Moysen. Qui fugiens de conspectu
eius. moratus est in terra Madian. et sedit iuxta puteum. Erant autem sacerdoti Madian
septem filie. que venerunt ad hauriendas aquas.
Et impletis canalibus. adaquare cupiebant
greges patris sui. Supervenere pastores. et eie-
cerunt eas. Surrexitque moyses. et defensis puel-
lis. adaquavit oves earum. Que cum rever-
tissent ad Jethro patrem suum. dixit ad eas. Cur
velocius venistis solito. Responderunt. Vir
Egipcius liberavit nos de manu pastorum.
Insuper et hausit aquam nobiscum. potumque
dedit ovibus. At ille. Ubi est inquit. quare
dimisistis hominem. vocate eum ut comedat
panem. Iuravit ergo moyses quod habita-
ret cum eo. Accepitque Sephoram filiam eius
uxorem. Que peperit ei filium. quem vocavit
Gersan. dicens. Advena fui in terra aliena.
Alterum vero peperit quem vocavit Eliezer dicens. Deus enim patris mei adiutor meus. et eripuit me de manu Pharaonis. Post
multum vero temporis. mortuus est rex Egipti.
Et ingemiscentes filii Israhel propter opera
vociferati sunt. Ascenditque clamor eorum ad
deum ab operibus. Et audivit gemitum eorum.
ac recordatus est federis quod pepigerat cum
Abraham ysaac et Jacob. Et respexit dominus filios Israhel. et liberavit eos.

Capitulum Tercium.

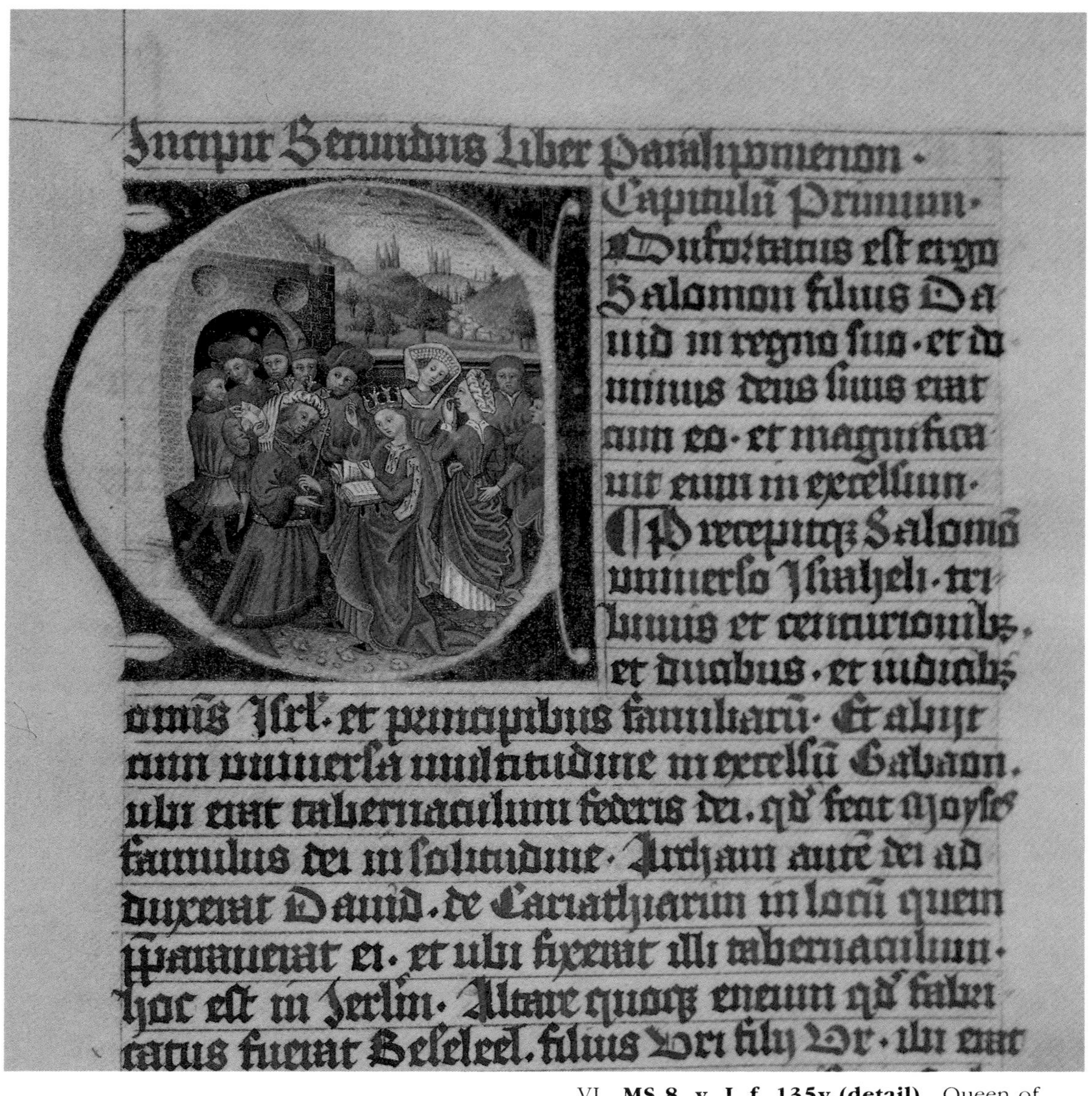

VI **MS 8, v. I, f. 135v (detail)** Queen of Sheba visiting Solomon: one of two miniatures added very early to the Giant Bible of Mainz by other artists than its primary Master. It is open to speculation why the ten books between Leviticus and the Second Chronicles were by-passed.

◀ V **MS 8, v. I, f. 18r** Giant Bible of Mainz: the beginning of Exodus. One of five pages in this codex decorated by one master artist, possibly identical with the "Master of the Playing Cards." (Actual size of the leaf: 57.6 × ca. 40.5 cm)

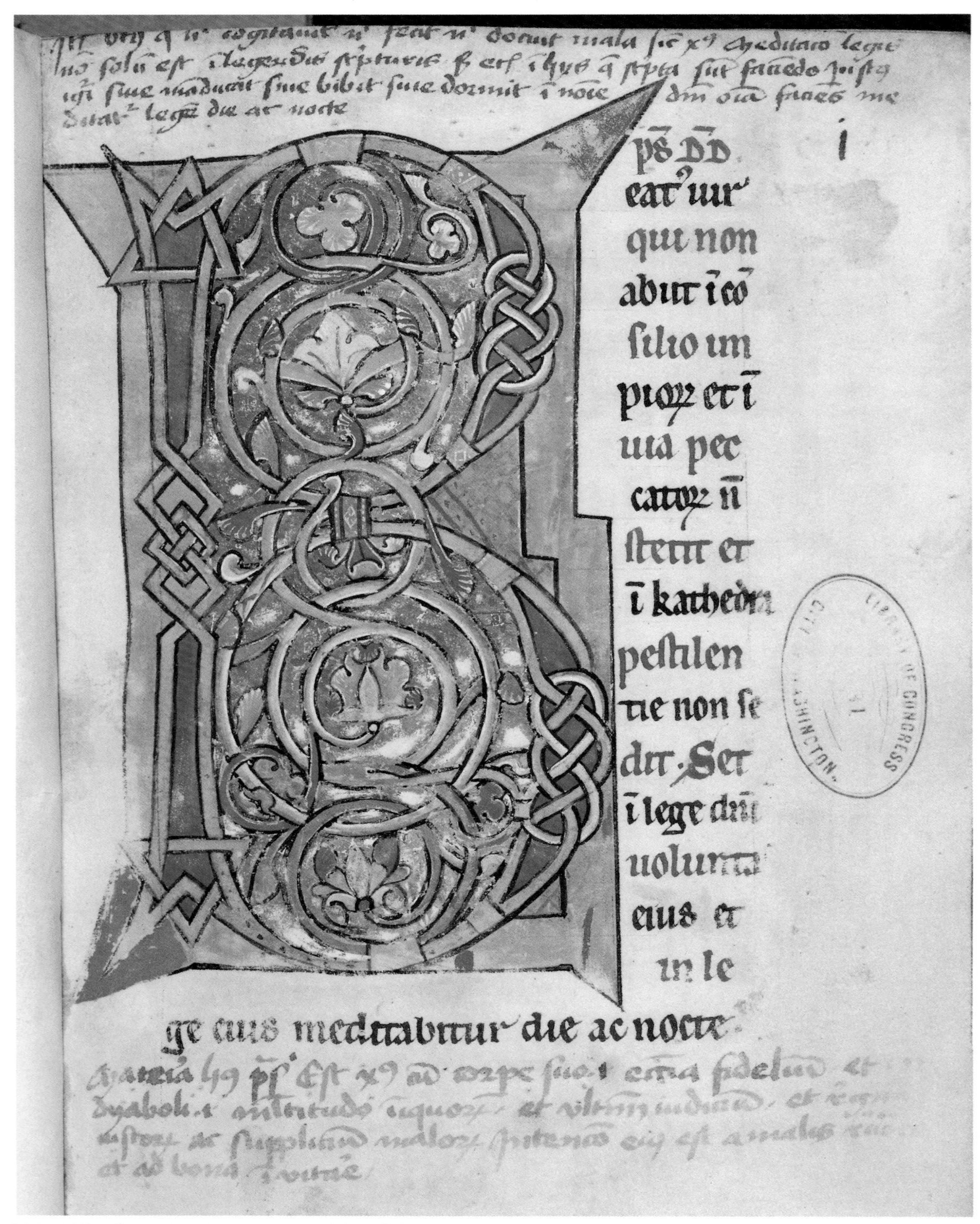

VII **MS 14, p. 1** Opening initial (*B* of the "Beatus vir qui . . .") of the Psalter; thought to be from Southern Germany, first half of 13th century. (Actual size of the leaf: 19 × 15.8 cm)

VIII **MS 15, neighboring columns of ff. 380v and 381r** Two of the very few preserved initials in the breviary believed made for Robert of Vendôme, son of Louis IX. (Actual height of the leaves: 18.8 cm) ▶

m epm 7 dixerit
udia tua i dno
o sit posita. 7
na tz de diuina
e glorie: scim
sulem deme
fuisse germanu.
s soror [lc. scda.
tella in famulos
uiit. Et tunc qn
o aplo uerbu
ens credidit bap
nos simul secu
sua domicella
mare 2secrauit
no 7 dns petr
rona martyru
d xpm 7 plan
is terrenum
uit. lectio. iij.
ella uo filia
aurelianum
hret sponsum
uitate credidit
n. q nos exore
unus. qr uir
more dni i uir
seruat. xpm
e sponsum cu
rnis delicijs 7
perseueret. De
. Totum require

supra in festo sci georgij. fient
lc. de cõi unius mris. Oratio.
Da qs omps ds: ut q
beati urbani martyris
tui atqz pontificis sol
lempnia colimus. eius
apud te intercessionibz ad
iuuemur. p. oro. Pstª qs
omps. Sancti germani ad
vs. super pslos. A. Simila
bo eu. cu cetis q sequuntur: cap.
Ecce sacerdos magnus. R. Lau
demus dnm in beati antistitis
germani meritis glosi ~~mirificate~~
ad sepulcru eius egri ueniut
7 sanantur. V. Vere mirabilis
ds in scis suis qui assiduus be
atum germanu epm miraclis
choruscare facit. Ad sepulcrum.
hy. Iste 2fessor. V. Ora p nob be
germane. A. Suscipiamus ergo
tanta sollempnitate huili de
uocione qua beatus germanus
carnis nexibz absolutus meru
it penetrare secreta celi habitacla
alla alla. ps. Magnif. Oratio.
Deus qui es scor
tuor splendor
mirabilis qui
qz hunc diem
beati germani confessoris
tui atqz pontificis depositione consecrasti. da ecclie
tue de eius natalicio semp
gaudere. ut apud miam
tuam exemplis eius pte
gamur 7 meritis. p. do. Ea
dem die fit memor. bi cerauni. A.
filie ierlm. ad compl. vt. s. Inuit.
xpm omf. ps. Venite. hy. Jhesu
redemptor. In .i. n. A. Beatus
germanus parisior pontifex pre
sciuit uirtute qua ex matris utero
nasceretur. ps. Beatus uir. A. Cer
tabat mat cu paruulo renitebatur infans ab utero. erat ergo con
flictus int mulierem 7 uiscera. ps.
Quare frem. A. Ledebatur matro
na nec nocebatur infancia obluc
tabatur sarcina nec genitrix fiet
parricida. ps. Dne quid multi.
Iustum deduxit ds p ui. lc. i.
Beatus gma
nus igitur
parisiorum
pontifex au
gustu du
nensis idi
gena patre eleutherio. mre
quoqz eusebia. honestis
honoratis qz parentibz pcre
atus est. Cuius genitrix p
eo qr hunc post aliu intra
breue spatium 2cepisset in

uto p
bu ca
infar
accep
tuui
n pos
tem.
n ual
manu
august
nesis p
fecit un
nascer
mis ille
reddidit
O
infan
pugn
Ledeba
nocebat
luctab
nitrix
Ledebatu
tur inf
sarcina
cida ipe
matre n
tabat m
batur in
conflictu
Ipse illet

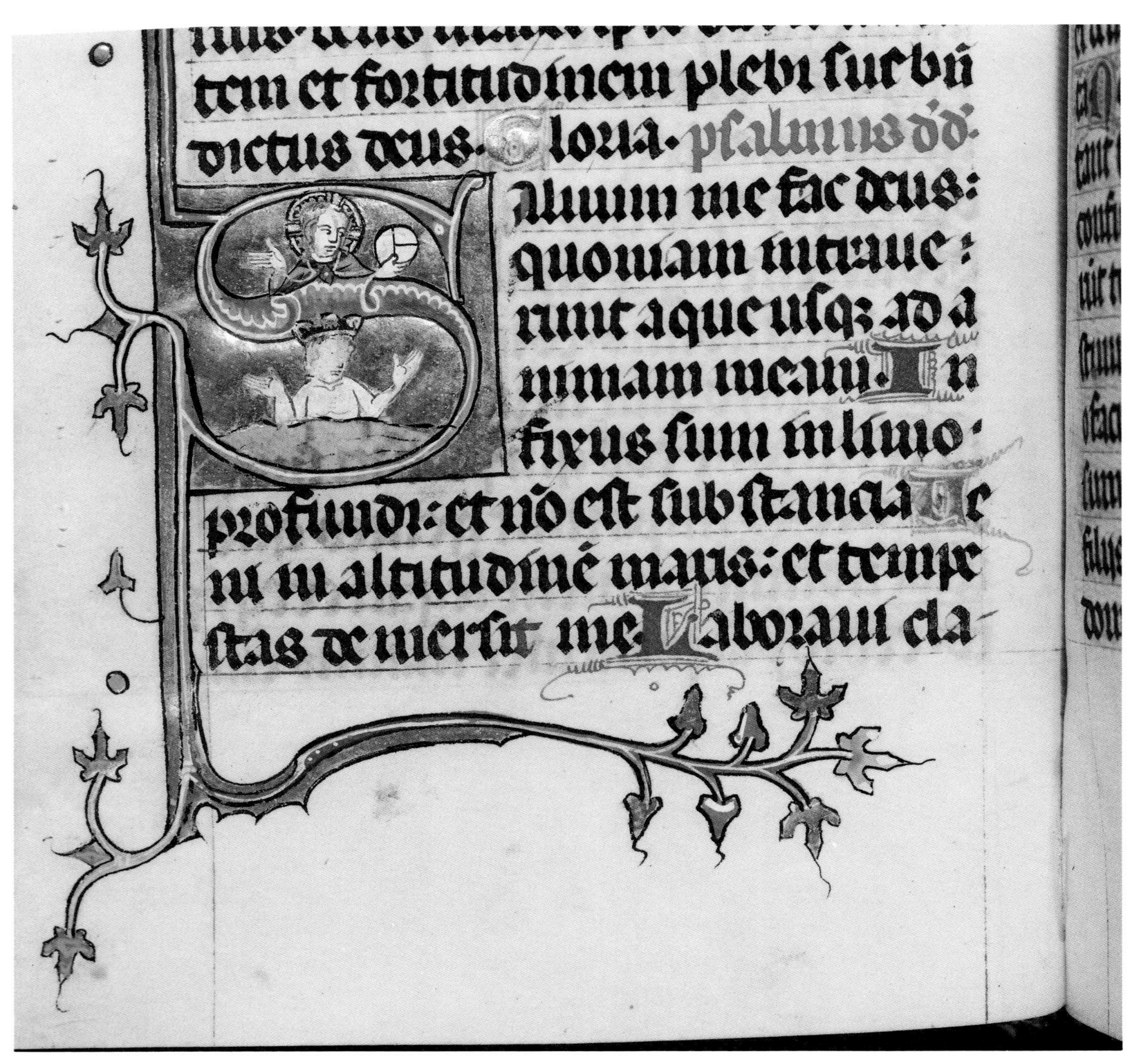

IX **MS 17, f. 83v (lower two-thirds of the page)** Christ and David in the initial *S* of Psalm LXIX which opens one of the liturgical divisions of the Psalter.

X **MS 25, f. 28v (detail)** Nativity initial from a late-medieval North Italian choir book. Note white penwork (words?) in purple stems of the letter. (Actual size of the initial: 14.3 × 17 cm)

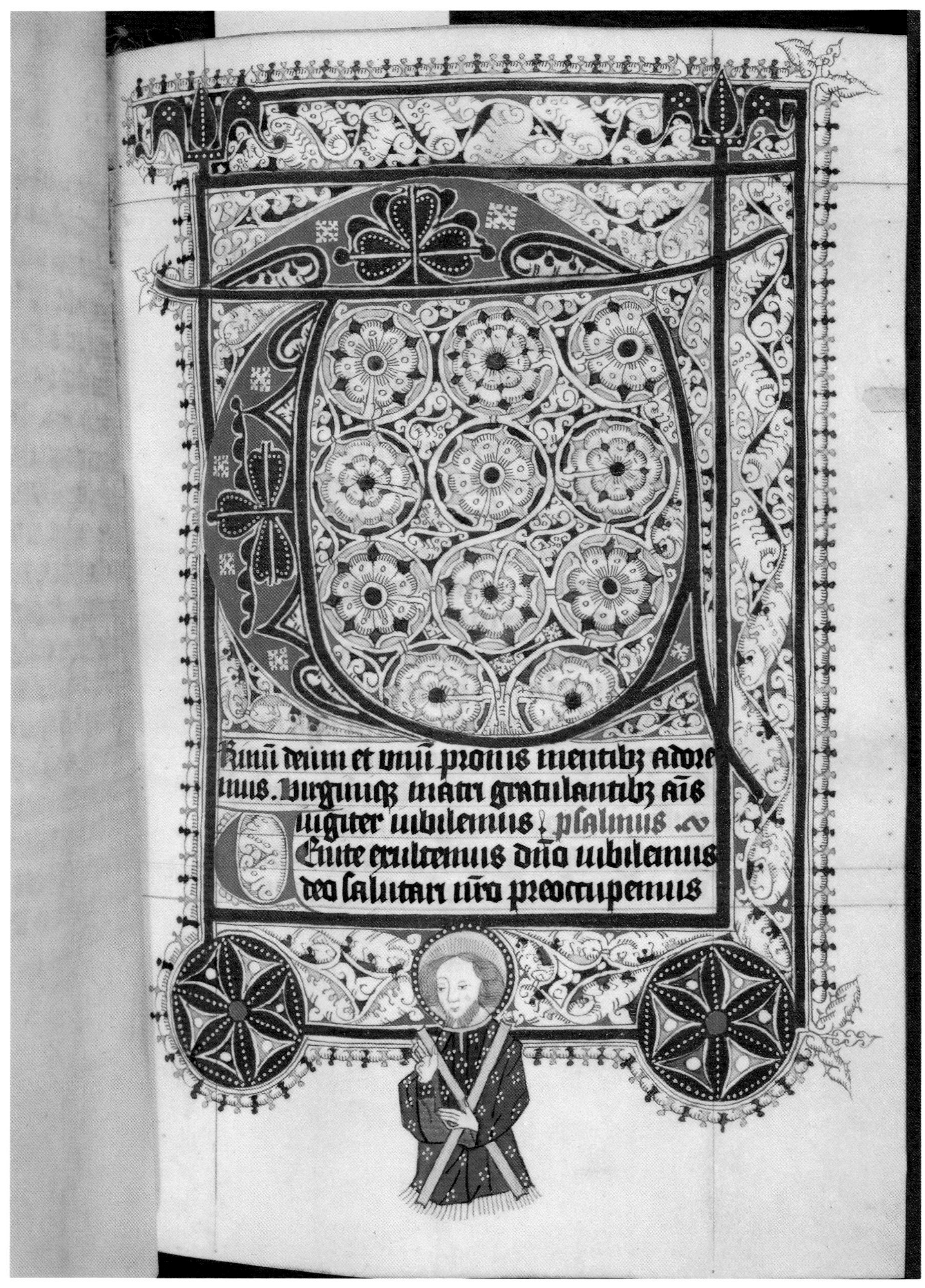
rinū deum et unū pronis mentibz adore
mus. Virginiqz matri gratulantibz aīs
iugiter iubilemus. psalmus
enite exultemus dn̄o iubilemus
deo salutari nr̄o preoccupemus

XII **MS 30, f. 243v (detail)** The grotesque, even surrealistic side of the artist of plate XI.—Women's convents were not always free of difficulties with the local bishop.

◀ XI **MS 30, f. 165r** Brigittine breviary of Sister Jutke: the *T* of Sunday invitatory. From Marienwater Abbey in North Brabant, mid-15th century. Luxurious work by a woman religious denied the goldleaf of early monks. (Actual size of the leaf: 19.5 × 13.3 cm)

Beatus vir qui nō abiit ī cōsilio
impiorū et in via peccatorū nō
stetit; et ī cathedra pestilencie
non sedit. Sed in lege dn̄i volū
tas eius: et ī lege eius meditabit
die ac nocte. Et erit tāq̄ lignū

◀ XIII **MS 34, f. 15r** Samson and the Lion. Not high art, the "historiated" initial nevertheless possesses considerable energy which matches the strong hand of the text. (Actual size of the leaf: 19.2 × 13.3 cm)

XIV **MS 37, f. 54r** Sample page of the once sumptuous book used by a high dignitary of the Greek Church. Color contrasts have suffered from primitive preservation measures. (Actual size of the page: 22.7 × 18.4 cm)

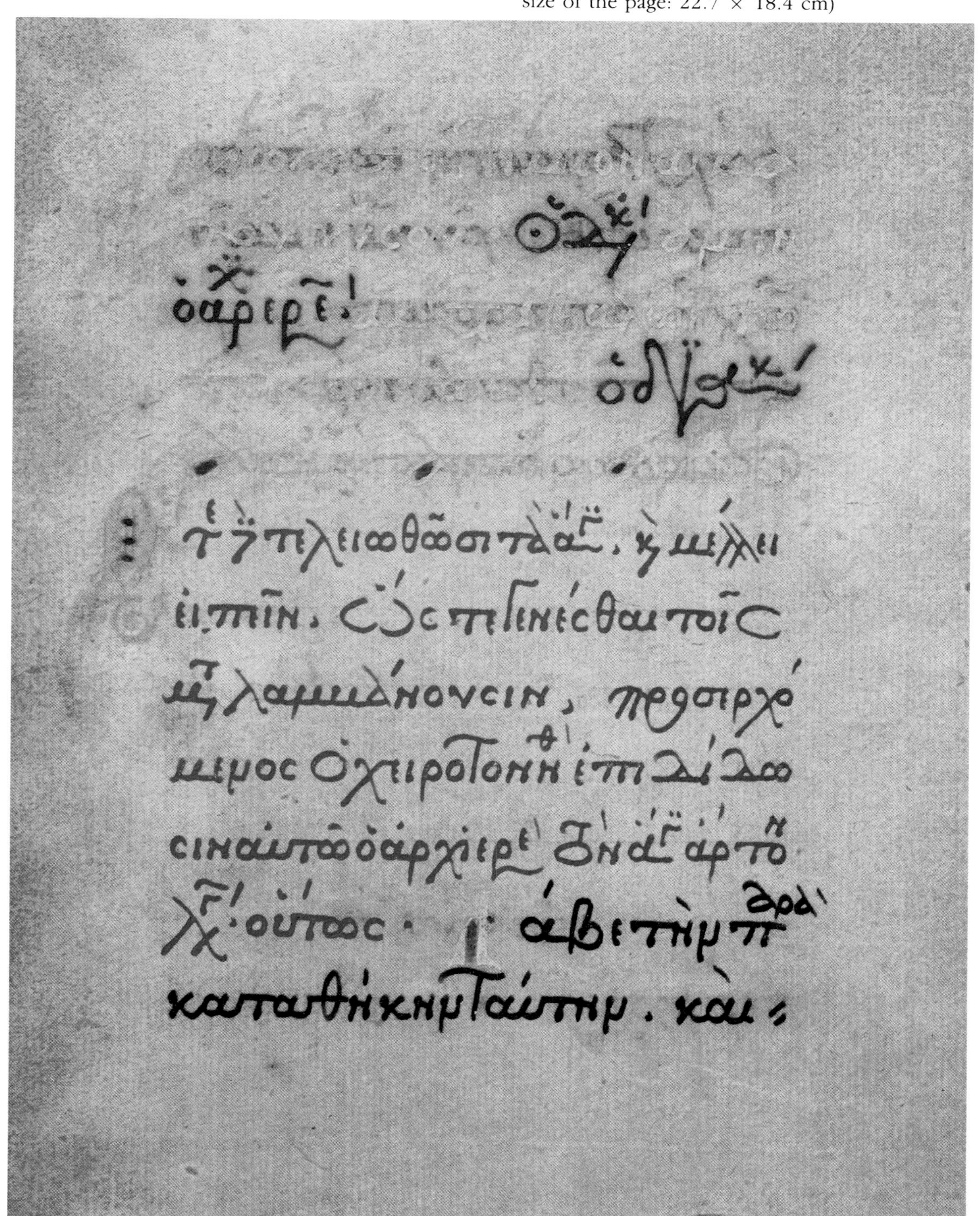

onuerte nos
deus salutaris
noster.
t auerte iram tuam

XVII **MS 45, f. 17r** Saint Christopher, patron of travelers; one of a series of nine prefatory illustrations in the gem-like miniature book (see bibliography at end of the description for other published reproductions). (Actual size of the leaf: 6.6 × 4.8 cm)

◀ XVI **MS 44, f. 65r** Coronation of Mary in Heaven; without the usual explicit representation of the Trinity. Note blue peacock, the border artist's favorite. (Actual size of the leaf: 14.7 × 9.9 cm)

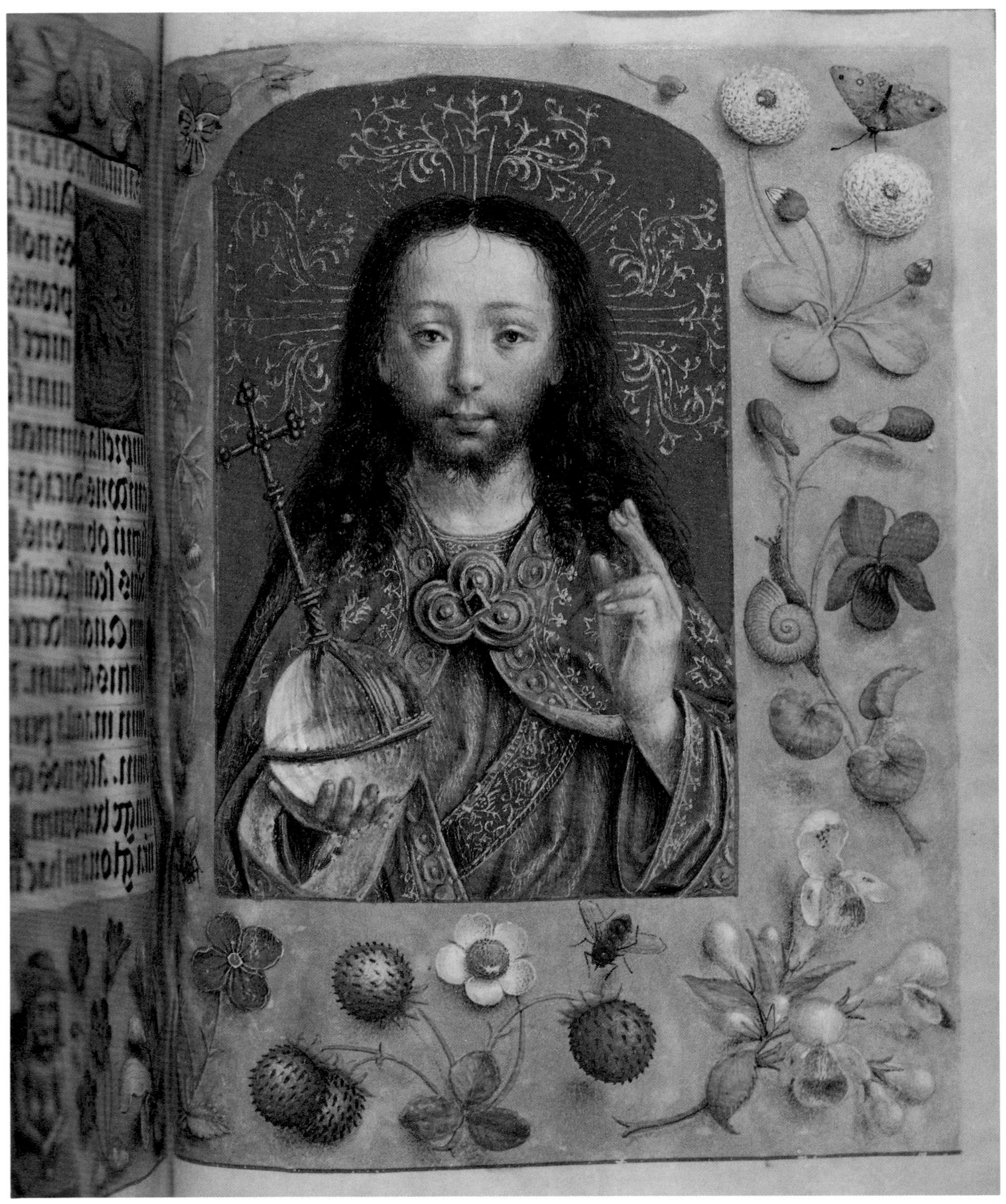

XVIII **MS 46, f. 16v** "Salvator Mundi" (Christ portrayed with the world-globe in his hand). The striking physiognomy recurs on f. 112v of the manuscript. Note the "Ghent-Bruges" border. (Actual size of the leaf: 10.5 × 7.8 cm)

XIX **MS 50, f. 17r** Page shows the several kinds of display and text lettering used in this outstanding product of early 16th-century calligraphy. (Actual size of the leaf: 13.8 × 8.4 cm) ▶

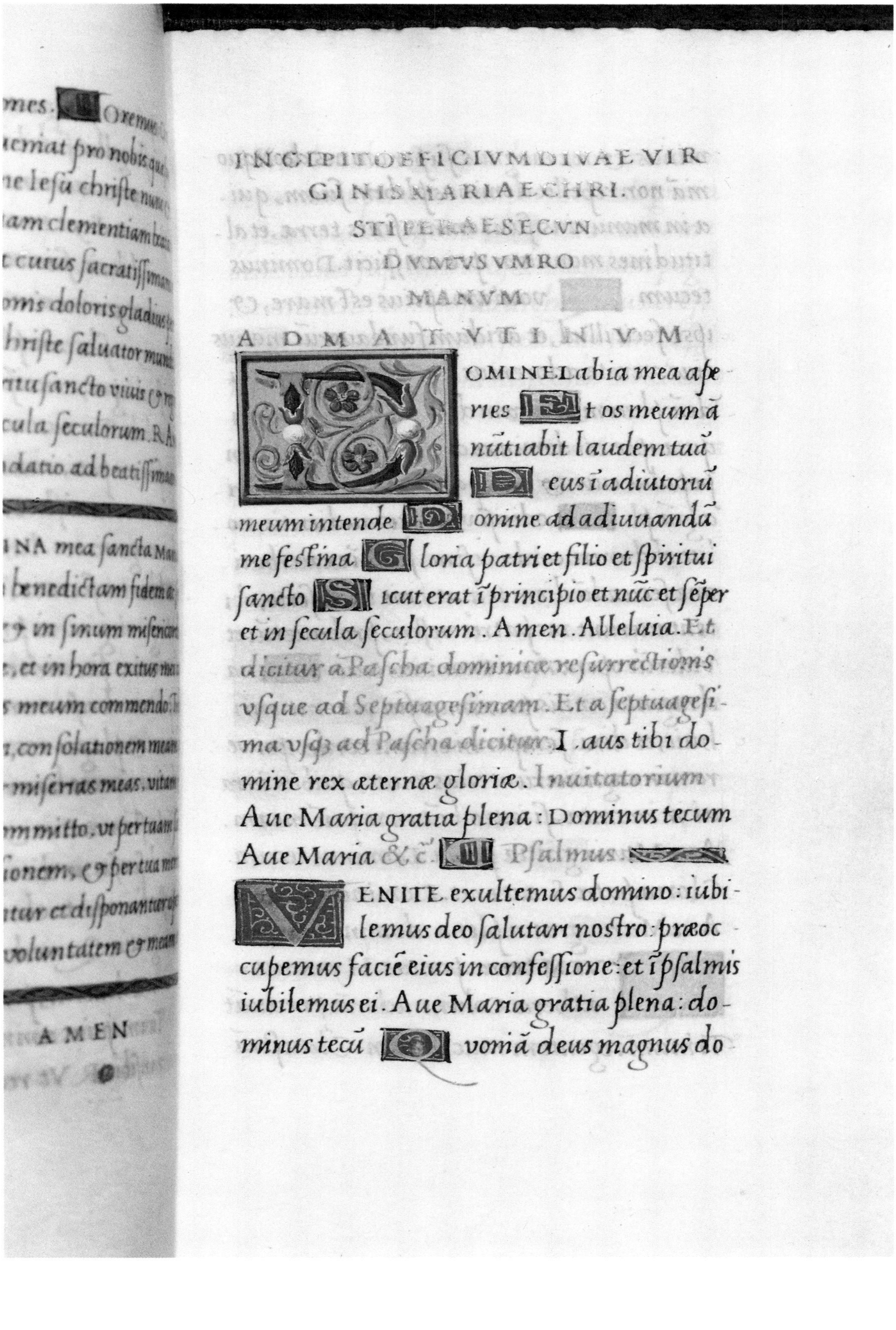

INCIPIT OFFICIVM DIVAE VIR
GINIS MARIAE CHRI.
STIPERAE SECVN
DVM VSVM RO
MANVM

AD MATVTINVM

DOMINE Labia mea aperies Et os meum annũtiabit laudem tuã Deus ĩ adiutoriũ meum intende Domine ad adiuuandũ me festina Gloria patri et filio et spiritui sancto Sicut erat ĩ principio et nũc et sẽper et in secula seculorum. Amen. Alleluia. Et dicitur a Pascha dominicæ resurrectionis vsque ad Septuagesimam. Et a septuagesima vsqȝ ad Pascha dicitur Laus tibi domine rex æternæ gloriæ. Inuitatorium Aue Maria gratia plena: Dominus tecum Aue Maria &c. Psalmus.

VENITE exultemus domino: iubilemus deo salutari nostro: præoccupemus faciẽ eius in confessione: et ĩ psalmis iubilemus ei. Aue Maria gratia plena: dominus tecũ Quoniã deus magnus do-

XX **MS 51, f. 75r** Jesus healing a leper; one of twenty-one large illustrations (by the "Gebetbuchmeister um 1500"?) in these *Horae* from Flanders. (Actual size of the leaf: 15.1 × 10 cm)

XXI **MS 52, f. 60r** The Veronica incident on the Way of the Cross. The scene (Veronica's face recurs several times in the book) seems to have been used here in preference to the Crucifixion, which would be the theme expected. (Actual size of the leaf: 22.6 × 14.1 cm) ▶

Ad Magnificat
gnum hæreditatis
ctus est vterus nesci
ex ea carnem assu
t dicentes gloria ti
vesperis sabbati sā
domini dici offici
sicut ante aduentū
ad Magnificat, et

lleluia. Quia quē
Resurrexit sicut
obis deum, alleluia.

VMDECRV
INOS
VC

abia mea aperies.
neum annuntiabit
am Deus in ad

Domine ad adiuuandum me festina.
Gloria patri Sicut erat. hymnus.
PATRIS sapientia veritas diui
na. Deus homo captus est hora
matutina. A suis discipulis cito derelictus

De sancto Ioanne baptista. ã.

Inter natos mulierum nõ surrexit maior Ioanne baptista. V. Fuit homo missus a deo. R. Cui nomen erat Ioannes. Oratio.

Præsta quæsumus omnipotens deus: ut familia tua per viam salutis incedat & beati Ioannis præcursoris christi hortamenta sectando ad eum quem prædixit secura perueniat dominum nostrum Iesum christum filium tuũ. Qui tecũ. v.

De sancto Ioanne euangelista. Añ.

Ioannes apostolus & euangelista virgo electus est a

XXIII **MS 55, f. 67r** The Shepherds; the only surviving illustration from what seems to have been a whole series. (Actual size of the leaf: 18.2 × 13.5 cm)

◀ XXII **MS 53, f. 124v** Showing the two miniatures used repeatedly in this cryptically coded book of hours made at Bourges about the time of Leonardo da Vinci's stay there. (Actual size of the leaf: 13.3 × 7 cm)

XXIV **MS 56, f. 94r** Heavenly and hellish powers struggle for a Dead man's soul: opening the Office for the Dead. Workshop of the Boucicaut Master. (Actual size of the leaf: 13.2 × 9.5 cm)

XXVI **MS 59, f. 13r** Annunciation, Wilson Hours. Northern France, ca. 1430? (Actual size of the leaf: 16.4 × 11.4 cm) ▶

Bibles

(MSS 1–8)

None of the eight medieval handwritten Bibles in the Library's possession antedates the year 1200. The first five, LC MSS 1–5, were all produced in the 13th century and are small, more or less the size of the Gideon Bibles found in American hotel rooms: they attest the need for multiple copies of what was the basis of much of the intellectual activity in the rising universities. The other three are each different: the princely Hungarian 14th-century Nekcsei-Lipócz Bible (MS 6); the Giant Bible of Mainz, handwritten just a year or two before Johannes Gutenberg began work on his 42-line edition, and facing permanently one of that edition's copies on the first floor of the Library's Thomas Jefferson Building (MS 8); and the MS 7, of the early 1400s, written in Bohemia, much more modest in decoration but fascinating by its historical setting.

All these Bibles are Latin Vulgates; any variations in their primary content pertain to the history of textual transmission of Jerome's version. Other aspects are displayed in tables A (comparing the prologues) and B (listing, by theme, the historiated initials which constituted the traditional décor of luxury Bibles).

◀ I **MS 3, f. 4r** The *I* of the beginning of Genesis with representations of the Days of Creation. Mid-13th century; Mathurin atelier in Paris? (Actual size of the leaf: ca. 14 × 9.5 cm)

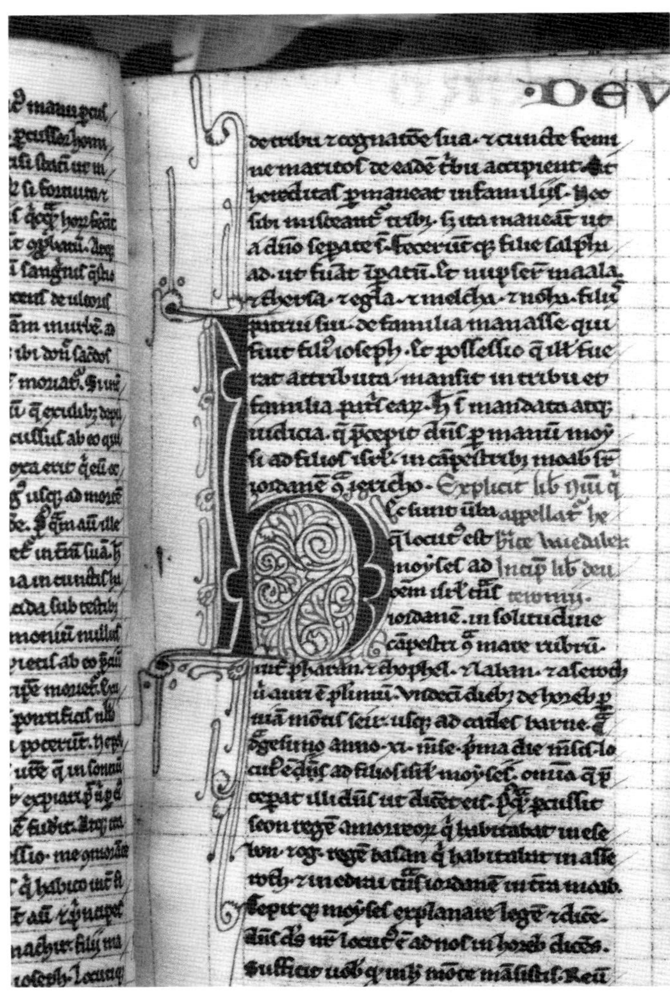

MS 1, f. 61ra (with the beginning of Deuteronomy)
(actual size of area shown: ca. 95 × 65 mm)

MS 1

(Faye and Bond 72)

BIBLE IN LATIN XIIIth c., 1st half

Written in England? Parchment. 454 leaves, ca. 163 × ca. 110 mm (bound volume: 176 × 130 mm) 2 columns. 49 lines.

f. 1r (in 3 columns, without ruling; a roughly contemporary ADDITION, in *notula*:) i D[omi]nica adue[n](tus) Scie[n]tes q[uia] hora e[st]. ro. xiij. . . . [end not legible]

Order of liturgical Epistles and Gospels for the seasonal cycle, each reading identified by its initium and book-and-chapter Bible reference. Altogether 53 sets, including one (*Multifariam, In principio*) for Christmas and that for Ascension; for "hepy[phania]," the readings are those of the Sunday after (*Obsecro vos, Cum factus esset Ihesus*); the four Sundays which follow are numbered *i, ij, iiij* [!], *v*; after Pentecost, "*j*ª p[ost] pe[n]teco[sten]" through "*xxiiij*"; in this series, the disposition originally noted underwent several corrections in a different though not much later hand; when so corrected, the readings agree with the Curia Missal.[1] As originally written, the list had for the 4th Sunday after Pentecost the Gospel *Estote misericordes*; for the 5th, *Cum irruerent*; for the 6th, *Nisi abundaverit.* — After a space (with remnant of erased ownership inscription of a later date), an interesting series for weekdays ("feria *ij*" through "Sabbato," plus yet another "feria *ij*"); for the first Monday, it gives "Stans Petrus in medio" and "Exeuntes duo ex discipulis."[2]

1va–4va: *I[n]cip[it] ep[isto]la scī jero[nim]i p[re]sb[ite]ri ad paulinu[m] d[e] o[mn]ib[us] diuine ystorie libris.* (12/49-line initial F:) (F)Rater ambrosius . . . (4ra:) . . . *Explic*[*it*] *epl'a* . . . *Incip*[*it*] *p*[*ro*]*logus* . . . *sup*[*er*] *genesin:* (8-line initial D:) (D)Esiderij mei desideratas . . . (ends in 4va:) . . . inst[itu]ere sermone[m]. vale *Explic*[it] *p[ro]log[us]. Incip[it] liber geneseos.* (rest of the page, i.e., all but 6 lines of first column, originally blank; now contains the next item)

Jerome's introductory letter (Stegmüller 284) and *Praefatio in Pentateuchum* (Stegm. 285). Chapter numbers in the letter are within the text columns. The Greek words which Jerome occasionally used are romanized and corrupted (2va, lines 9–10: "metolene" for *μέθοδον*; "emetrani" for *ἐμπειριαν*).

4v (in 3 columns, a roughly contemporary ADDITION in *notula*, probably by same hand as f. 1r:) I[n] festo scī a[n]dree . . .

MS 1 Order of liturgical Epistles and Gospels for saints' days: 53 sets, including several entries now barely legible, perhaps owing to frequent use for liturgical reference:[3] Andree, Nicolai, Lucie, Thome Ap., Stephani, Johannis, Innocentium, Silvestri, Fabiani & Sebastiani, Agnetis, Vincencii, Conv. Pauli, Purificationis, Agathe (?), Cathedre Petri, Matthie, Gregorii, Benedicti, Annunciationis, (illegible name of a *confessor pontifex*), Georgii, Marci, Philippi & Jacobi, (Inv.) S. Crucis, Johannis ante Portam Latinam, Barnabe, Gervasii et Prothasii, Joh. Baptiste, Petri & Pauli, Pauli, Margarite, Magdalene, Jacobi, Ad Vincula Petri, (Inv.) Stephani, Dominici (!), Laurencii, Bte. Marie (= Assumptio), Bartholomei, Augustini, Decoll. Joh. Bapt., Nativitas B. Virginis, Exalt. Crucis, Matthei, Michaelis, Jeronymi, Luce, Simonis & Jude, Martini, Omnium Sanctorum, Cecilie, Clementis, Katerine. — After the last entry, another line obscured, with obvious intent, by heavily written "s. nōei" (= ?) followed by a scribble which fails to obscure initial capital *W* and final *f* (?) — Except for the name of St. Dominic, the list gives little clue to its origin. Dominic was canonized in 1234.

5ra–445vb: (ca. 30-line, partly cropped initial *I*:) (I)N p[ri]ncipio c[re]auit d's . . . (5ra–159rb, Genesis through 2 Chronicles, without the Prayer of Manasseh; 159rb-168ra, Ezra, Nehemiah; 168rb-172va, Esther (!); 172va-176ra, Tobit; 176ra-180vb, Judith; 180vb-190va, Job; Psalms wanting, though no doubt originally present; 191va-224rb, Proverbs, Ecclesiastes, Song of Solomon, Wisdom, Ecclesiasticus, with the Prayer of Solomon at end as part of the book;[4] 224va-268vb, Isaiah, Jeremiah; 268vb-271vb, Baruch (!); 271vb-274rb, Lamentations (!); 274va-308ra, Ezekiel, Daniel; 308rb-328rb, Minor Prophets; 328va-329rb, "Capitula in libro [*i*°] machabeorum";[5] 1 Maccabees; 343rb-vb, capitula[6] and 343rb-352va the text of 2 Maccabees; 352va-399ra, the Gospels of Matthew, Mark, Luke, and John, each preceded by "breues" or "capitula";[7] 399ra-410va, Acts;[8] 410va-415vb, Catholic Epistles, each with its own set of "capitula";[9] 416vb-440rb, the Pauline letters;[10] 440vb-445vb, Revelation[11])

Vulgate Latin Bible (imperfect: Psalms wanting), with archaic features distinguishing it from the Parisian Vulgate: The order of the books is nonstandard in both Testaments;[12] the choice of the prologues differs considerably;[13] the *capitula*, here included with all New Testament books except the Acts, had gone out of style with or before the Parisian revision;[14] and although the modern, originally Parisian chapter division is more or less conspicuously added in the margins, it is obvious

MS 1, f. 4v, 3rd column, lines 21–27 (actual size of area shown: ca. 25 × 40 mm)

that the original scribes knew nothing of it. The original chapter numbering, uniform in style and size with the script of the text and corresponding to colored versals within it, is found written in the margin in red roman numerals; some of these have been variously corrected, crossed through, or deleted; they permit us, however, to determine that to the original scribes, Genesis had 82 chapters; Exodus, 139; Leviticus, 89; Numbers, 74; Deuteronomy, 155; Joshua, 34; Judges, 18; no old numbering is found in Ruth.[15] Absence of the First Book of Esdras (see next item) from the original sequence should be noted. — A cumulative chapter count (in red lowercase roman numerals) appears in the tail margins of many leaves, often (intentionally?) washed off. The count is based on modern chapter division; it was done after removal of the Psalms. It reaches 1166 at the end of Revelation; same hand added "M.clxxv" on f. 452r (see next item).

446ra–452vb: Et fecit iosias pasca . . .

The First Book of Esdras[16] (Stegmüller 94, apparently the version 94,1, although the word *rege* is omitted in ch. II,1). Added by a contemporary hand conspicuously different from that which had written the Revelation. Uncaptioned. Versals suggest 21 chapters (the last beginning with verse VIII,26 of the now accepted count).

453ra: (in upper margin, partly cropped blank caption:) [con]tinu(acio?) (narracionis?) .viij. cpl'o luce eu. (in text column:) f[a]ctū e[st] au[tem] i[n] una die[rum] . . . (= Luke VIII,22-30)

Supplying part of text of the Gospel of Luke omitted through error on f. 380ra; there, a note in inner margin refers to "ultimum folium libri."

453rb: (ADDITION in a different hand; blank space reserved for 2-line initial *D* not filled) omine d[eu]s om[n]ip[o]t[ens] . . .

Oratio Manasse (Stegmüller 93,2)

453v: (6 long lines; a LATER ADDITION:) [contra] ster[ilitate]m falsa[m]. [primum] [recipe] cupparosa[17] . . . d[e] pip[er]e puluericato quarta[m] libra[m]

A recipe for, it seems, an aphrodisiac.

453va-454rb: (ADDITION by a different hand; 2-line blank space for initial *O* not filled) [O]Mnes qui pie uolu[n]t . . . [et] p[ar]abole salomonis.

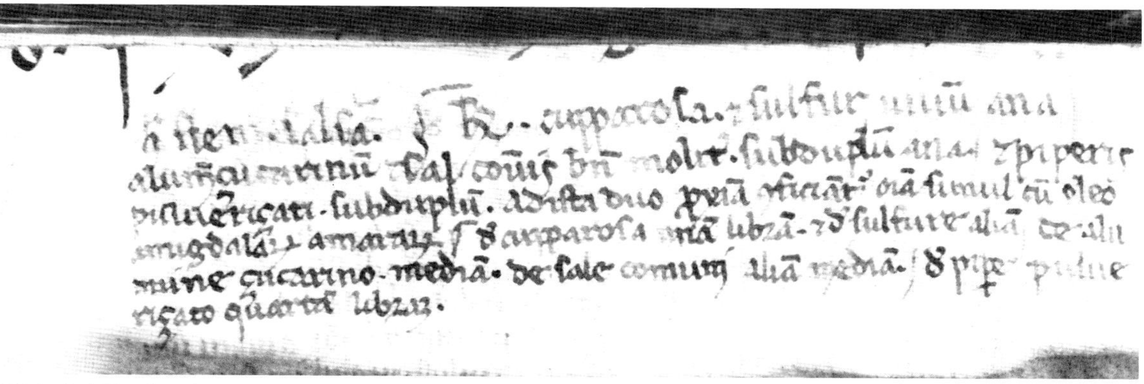

MS 1, f. 453v, head margin (the aphrodisiac recipe) (actual length of the lines: average 80 mm)

Stegmüller 839, the prologue to Revelation by Gilbertus Porretanus standardly included in Parisian University Bibles.

* * *

Foliated in modern pencil. One free vellum endleaf in front, one at end, both from the same unidentified ms.;[18] the one in front has pasted on verso a late (16th?-century) engraving (ca. 77 × 55 mm) of the Crucifixion. — Written area ca. 130–37 × ca. 80 mm. — Ruled fully in lead or crayon (bluish lines); in the last quires (ca. 50 leaves at end) the ruling was done in blind or came otherwise to be, by now, invisible. There are 8 vertical lines per page.[19] The (red/blue) running titles above the text columns, in many cases cropped, had not been ruled for. First line of text above the top ruled line. Three horizontals at the top, three in center, and three lowest ones tend to go all the way to edges. — Written by several hands in an extremely small (ca. 700 words per page) *littera textualis currens*[20] with numerous contractions. The ink varies from black to brown. — Red captions, by various hands, within the text columns, in spaces provided by the scribes; their layout (and formulation) varies. — Thin parchment (ca. 10 mm per 100 leaves). — Chapter numbers according to the Parisian revision (in this case, entirely identical with those now commonly used) are added in the margins; red or blue *litterae notabiliores* within the text, reflecting an older division, correspond to a series of red numbers written in the margins at an earlier point and later subjected to various corrections. The Parisian chapter numbers in the margins were added in alternately red and blue roman uncial-type numerals through ch. XXIIII of Leviticus; in later parts, in red or black cursive, with varying degree of care and skill.

Collation (medieval signature numbering in center of tail margin of first recto of each gathering): 0^{4}(= f. 1–4) i–xiv^{12} xv^{10}(= ff. 173-182) xvi^{12}(wants $\text{xvi}_{9\text{-}12}$ = 4 leaves after f. 190 = beginning of Psalms?) (probably two 12-leaf gatherings, with the Psalms, wanting; removed prior to signature numbering) xvii–xxi^{12} xxii^{12+1}(= ff. 251-263; f. 253 a singleton?) xxiii-xxxvii^{12} xxxviii^{12}(wants xxxviii_{12}; no text loss)

Decoration: Most individual books (but not single apostolic letters) and some of the prologues are signaled by a large calligraphic initial in divided red and blue, with flourishes in one or both colors; that of the beginning of Genesis (5r), partly cropped, is ca. 30 lines high, while the stem of the *F* of "Frater Ambrosius" (1v) runs the whole height of the column, with the penwork of the flourishes considerably more creative, ending in the lower margin with a wolf-like head. These major (mostly 6-line or more) initials are rather uniformly skillful[21] work, with penwork infilling in two colors, chiefly from Exodus (23v) through Job (181v) inclusive; those which follow may be by other hands. Those on ff. 297v, 298r, 440v, and 446r, are green and red, not skillful work. — Small initials, in one color, with contrasting flourishes, are used occasionally, notably (2-line) in Job (181v-190v). Alternately red or blue *litterae maiores* indicate old chapter divisions (see above); versals of alternating color are used in most of the sets of *capitula* found in the last fourth of the book. Capitals beginning a sentence and some other letters are touched with red throughout. — The running titles in head margins, written, as usual, in alternating red and blue uncials, run across each two-page opening ("DEVTERO" on verso, "NOMIVS" on recto) through f. 76v ("IO"); on 77r, the "IO/SVE" is complete on one page, divided only between the two text columns, and this method is then continued through the rest of the Bible; in its second half, the titles tend to be cropped off; while maintaining the 49–line count, the text columns had expanded upward (to ca. 137 mm height) and the titles were placed higher up. Toward the end, the color or scheme becomes less regular (on 412v, whole title red). The First Book of Esdras, added on 446r sqq., seems not to have had running titles at all.

Binding: probably German, 16th century, yellowish pigskin over wooden boards with beveled edges, over 3 bands. Covers and spine blindtooled with stamps, covers also with rolls (not in Haebler, Kyriss). Two back-to-front brass clasps, perhaps more recent; the roughly triangular fixed leaves of the hinges do not fit into the rectangles mortised in the lower cover. — Both covers have paper pasted to their inner surface, over stubs conjugate with the free vellum endleaves. On the inside of the upper cover, small label of B. Westermann (firm in New York) and several markings in pencil ("Temp. no.5," "14"), some more or less erased. On recto of the free vellum endleaf in front: Ac. 4560(3) no. 3; £ 12 12 0; ms. 72; etc. In top margin of f. 1r, written (or stamped?) in display-type capitals: A.L.S. Mounted on the paper pastedown of the lower cover, a clipping from a British dealer's catalog in which the present ms. was no. 409, with price given as £ 12 12s.

Erased ownership inscription (of a German monastery?) on f. 1r. — Prior to purchase by LC in 1916 the Bible belonged to the collection of Rev. E. A. Dalrymple of Baltimore.[22]

2° fo.: hortat[ur] ([inserted:] ad) studiū l[e]ct[i]oīs. ne . . .

Bibl.: De Ricci, *Census* (1935), p. 229, no. 100; Faye and Bond, *Suppl.* (1962), p. 119, no. 72.

APPENDIX: *CAPITULA* TO NEW TESTAMENT BOOKS IN MS 1

Gospels (in the capitula to the four Gospels, individual items within each set are marked, generally, by red or blue versals, or by red underscoring of key words):

for Matthew, 28 items; incipit: Natiuitas Christi . . .
for Mark, 42 items; incipit: De iohanne baptista et uictu et habitu eiusdem.
for Luke, 69 (?) items; incipit: Zacharias angelo non cedens obmutuit . . .
for John, 48 items; incipit: Phariseorum leuite interrogant iohannem (= the set for John ignores the Johannine Prologue!)

(Acts: no capitula)

Catholic Epistles: each item of the summaries begins on a new line, with a red or blue *D*. There are:

for James, 20 items; incipit: De inimicorum inuectionibus risui deputandis.
for 1 Peter, 20 items; incipit: De regeneracionis inuicta potentia.
for 2 Peter, 11 items; incipit: De sanctis quos in hoc mundo interfectos . . .
for 1 John, 20 items; incipit: De uerbo uite quod erat antequam mundi machina principium sortiretur.
for 2 John, 5 items; incipit: De diligendis cultoribus ueritatis.
for 3 John, 5 items; incipit: De filiis apostoli rigore tenentibus ueritatem.
for Jude, 7 items; incipit: De falsis doctoribus necatoribus . . .

Pauline letters:

(Romans: no capitula)
1 Corinthians: 25 items; incipit: Obsecro itaque uos fratres. (Rather than summaries, these are all opening phrases of what must have been 26 chapters: in the text, as in the capitula, these phrases are marked by colored versals. The modern division into 16 chapters is noted in the margins.)
2 Corinthians: 20 items; incipit: Benedictus Deus et pater . . . (system similar to that used for 1 Corinthians)
Galatians: 12 initia-type capitula; incipit: Miror quod sic tam cito . . .
Ephesians: 31 genuine summary-type capitula; incipit: De sanctis qui ante constitutionem mundi . . .
Phillippians: 8 initia-type items; incipit: Gracias ago Deo meo . . .
Colossians: 10 initia; incipit: Gracias agimus Deo . . .
1 Thessalonians: 10 initia; incipit: Gracias agimus Deo . . .
2 Thessalonians: 7 initia; incipit: Gracias agere debemus . . .
1 Timothy: 12 initia; incipit: Sicut rogaui te ut remaneres . . .
2 Timothy: 7 initia; incipit: Noli itaque erubescere . . .
Titus: 6 initia; incipit: Huius rei gracia . . .
Philemon: 4 summary-type capitula, each beginning "De . . ."; incipit: De Phylomone *(sic)* et Apia et Archippo . . .
Hebrews: 22 initia; incipit: Multifarie multisque modis . . .

(Revelation: 25 initia, see note 11)

NOTES

1. Cf. *SMRL* II (Ordo Missalis)

2. = ? (The book-and-chapter quotation has become illegible.)

3. 1r and 4v are outside pages of the first gathering; both show much wear in lower outside corners. — N.B. I have to an extent standardized the saints' names; "Katerine" is spelled with *K* in the manuscript.

4. The "Parisian" or "University" Vulgates generally include the Prayer of Manasseh (at end of 2 Chronicles), do not include the Prayer of Solomon (the text "Et declinavit/inclinavit Salomon . . . vir iuxta te," printed as ch. LII or *Liber Iesu Filii Sirach* in the Stuttgart critical ed. of the Vulgate [1969, 1975]).

5. 61 summaries, beginning: Ubi euersa Ierusalem consenserunt Iudei . . .

6. 54 items; incipit: Ubi occisus est rex Antiochus . . .

7. "Capitula" and "breves" meant (with possible regional preferences for one or the other term) the same thing; i.e., a set of short summaries; they reflected the various pre-13th-century chapter divisions. — For some details on the N.T. *capitula* in MS 1, see appendix at end of the description.

8. Acts without summaries; following the prologue Stegm. 631, the rubric says: *Explicit prefacio. Incipit textus libri* . . .

9. Only some are captioned. — See appendix at end of this description for more detail.

10. To Romans, no capitula, only "Argumentum in epistola ad Romanos" = prologue Stegm. 651, etc. (cf. table A); the other letters have both the prologues, sometimes called "argumentum," and capitula (for the latter, see the appendix).

11. The (uncaptioned) set for Revelation consists of 25 initia, beginning with "Iohannes vii ecclesiis que sunt in Asia."

12. In no case is this owing to misplacement of gatherings or leaves: the unusually placed books begin generally within a column. — Particularly interesting is the sequence Gospels-Acts-Catholic Epistles-Pauline Epistles-Revelation. (Cf. Berger, *Hist. Vulg.*, p. 340, no. 2; order of the whole as in Bib. nat. ms. 11932, cf. Berger, *op. cit.*, p. 335, IV/104).

13. Of the 64 prologues standard in the Parisian revision Bibles (from ca. 1230 on), our ms. includes 38; it has, apart from the "capitula," 14 other prologues not used in the revision (cf. our table A).

14. Cf. J. P. P. Martin, "Le Texte parisien de la Vulgate latine," *LE MUSÉON* 8 (Louvain, 1889), p. 444 sqq., and 9 (1890), p. [55] sqq. — For the canonic Parisian order of Bible books and prologues, see first column of our table A. — Cf. also *The Cambridge History of the Bible*, v. 2 (1969), p. 145 sqq.

15. The numbers are identical with those found (in the form of "capitula") in certain ms. Bibles of Spanish, Italian, and Carolingian provenience grouped by the editors of the Roman critical edition of the Vulgate (1926, etc.) under the symbol Λ : cf. vol. 1 of that edition, prolegomena, etc.

16. The book was "Esdre II" to the Parisian Bibles, "Ezrae III" to the Clementine Vulgate which relegated it to its small collection of books not considered inspired, printed "ne prorsus interirent."

17. = copperas ("green vitriol," heptahydrate of ferrous sulfate)?

18. Visible parts of its text are from John XVII, 23–24. The script is large (minims ca. 9 mm) and elegant; characterized by *o* pointed at top and bottom, and cursive *a*, somewhat similar to the fragment Dijon Bib. munic. 161 (from Heilsbronn Abbey, dated 1473; cf. *MSS. datés* (France) 6, pl. CXXXIX).

19. Spaced, in a typical sample: 7, 3.5, 36, 3.5, 36, 3.5 (mm).

20. Cf. *Nomenclature des écritures livresques* (1954), fig. 16. — The *y* is dotted throughout. The prologues on ff. 1va–4va have single-lobed *a* throughout; the rest of the book occasionally.

21. Rather like those in the Bible of Norwich Cathedral, lot 68 in Sotheby's (London) sale of Dec. 7, 1982 (their *Catalogue of Western manuscripts and miniatures* for the sale, with black-and-white reproductions).

22. Information from De Ricci; Rev. Dalrymple's usual ownership label is not in the book.

MS 2

(Faye and Bond 71)

BIBLE IN LATIN mid-XIIIth c.

Written in Paris? Parchment. 556 leaves, ca. 145 × ca. 95 mm (bound volume: 154 × ca. 106 mm) 2 columns. 47 lines.

f. 1rv: (LATER ADDITIONS:) *Incipit diuisio sacre sc[ri]pture s[e]c[un]d[u]m q[uod] ext[ra]bit[ur] ex v[er]bis b[eat]i Ieronimi de p[ro]logo galeato . . . [et] ex p[ro]logo breuiloq[ui] Bonaue[n]ture . . . Explicit di[ui]sio o[mn]i[u]m libroru[m] biblie* (following 4 words are by another hand, over erasures:) p[er] ffr[atr]em B. sel (?) (first hand resumes; initial:) *(I)ncipit ordo siue num[er]us libro[rum] qui co[n]tine[n]t[ur] i[n] biblia scdm̄ t[ra]nslac[i]o[ne]m bī. Jeronimi p[ro]ut et[iam] ponu[n]t[ur] i[n] biblia sequenti* . . . (1rb-vb, list of books, indicating for each the number of chapters; followed by:) Est t[ame]n no[ta]ndu[m] q[uod] aliqui p[re]dictor[um] libror[um] n[on] su[n]t de canone biblie . . . *Explicit Num[erus] lib[ro]r[um] siue ordo eor[um] . . . [et] i[n] lib[r]o sequenti.*

In a cursive script of the *anglicana* type; written probably in 14th century, perhaps by the same owner who also added the text on 556r (*q.v.*). — The list of books, with chapter count in arabic numerals, agrees with the main contents of the manuscript in assigning to Esther only 6 chapters, 4 to Lamentations, and 12 to Hebrews;[1] it also calls for 9 chapters for the *Canticum* (the Song of Solomon), agreeing, it seems, with the misnumbering found on f. 265v (where "VIII" and "IX" follow the correct "VI" on 265r). For the First Book of Maccabees, the list has "15"; the text as originally decorated and numbered had 16 chapters but the "XVI" (397ra) was at some point erased. — The note (lvb) concerning the Apocrypha seems to draw a distinction between the group commonly found in the Vulgate and the apocryphal books, "liber de infancia Salvatoris et cetera huiusmodi." — Added in the outer margins alongside the list of books, in red ink and a rather formal secretary script, group classifications: *libri historiales, legales, sapienciales, prophetales*.

2ra–501vb: *Incip[it] p[ro]log[us] in bibli[a?]* (F)Rater ambrosius . . . (5va:) . . . *Incip[it] lib[e]r bresith .i. gen[esi]s* (historiated intial *I* with the "Seven Days"[2] and Crucifixion) (I)N p[ri]ncipio . . . (Bible text ends on f. 501v:) . . . cu[m] o[mn]ib[us] amen.

The 13th-century Parisian revision of the Vulgate, with the then usual order of books and the standard set of 64 prologues;[3] in our copy, with the following features: In the first prologue (Frater Ambrosius . . .),

Greek words are (poorly) romanized;[4] for Genesis, Exodus, Leviticus, and Judges, the red captions include quasi-romanizations of the Hebrew titles ("bresith," "yelesmoth," "uagecra," "cethim").[5] At end of 2 Chronicles (186va), without special markings, the Prayer of Manasseh. Nehemiah (191ra–196va) is divided into 15 chapters (ch. XV begins with XIII,23 of later standard division); the apocryphal First Book of Esdras ("ESDRE II," ff. 196va–201vb), into 27;[6] Esther (212ra sqq.) has 6 numbered chapters, the ch. VI comprising standard Vulgate's Esther X,4–XVI,24. — The Book of Psalms is captioned (228ra:) "Incipit liber hymnorum et soliloquiorum prophete Dauid de Christo"; the Psalm numbers[7] are noted in lowercase roman numerals in the tail margin; the semibiblical Psalm headings are in red; the (eight) liturgical divisions are marked by (4-to-6-line) initials; on 252va, "Explicit Psalterium." — Ecclesiasticus (271vb–287ra) is accompanied, in the margin, by red indication of subjects (*De honore parentum, De pupillis et viduis* . . .); the script is similar to that of other captions. Prayer of Solomon is not included. — The verse Isaiah XXXVIII,9 (Scriptura Ezechie . . . infirmitate sua) is written in red as a caption (f. 299ra). — The spurious verse which in the Clementine Vulgate introduces the Lamentations (Et factum est . . . et eiulans dixit) is included, written as end of Jeremiah (f. 330rb-va); a red caption on f. 332rb signals the *Oratio Ieremiae,* not numbered as ch. V of the Lamentations; in Baruch, the last chapter (*Exemplum epistolae* . . . , ff. 334rb–335ra) is treated similarly. — The spurious verse Daniel XIV,42 (Tunc rex ait . . . leonum) is included.[8] — The beginning of New Testament material, on 406ra, is not signaled as such; the Gospel of Matthew itself, beginning on 406va, starts with a 7-line, otherwise ordinary (rinceaux) initial *L.* Mark is erroneously captioned (419ra) "Incipit ma[t]th[e]us euangelista." Luke I,1–4, taken (as commonly in Parisian Bibles) as one of the prologues, is captioned "Incipit argumentum secundum lucam"; same term ("argumentum sancti euangelii") is used with Jerome's prologue to John (Stegm. 624, on f. 439vb). John has the standard 21 chapters. — The prologue to Colossians (467ra) includes the part bracketed in Stegm. 736; that to (First) Thessalonians (468ra) matches only inexactly the texts offered by Stegmüller (his 747 or 748).[9] — In Hebrews (472vb–476rb), the beginning of ch. XIII is unmarked, making the total number of chapters 12. — The prologue to Acts begins (476rb) as Stegm. 637, in other respects agreeing with the (normally expected) Stegm. 640. In the present ms., this is followed (476va-477ra) by: *Item p[re]fac[i]o.* Ubi p[re]cepit ih[esu]s discip[u]lis ab ier[usa]l[em] ne disced[er]ent petr[us] de iuda cum discipulis suis loq[ui]tur u[t] p[ro] eo unu[m] ex duob[us] elig[er]ent . . . i[n] [n]auem alexandrina[m] q[ue] [in] i[n]sula hiemau[er]at nauigau[er]unt.[10]

501vb–539va: (A)Az app[re]he[n]de[n]s . . . zuzim consiliantes eo[rum] uel [con]siliatores eorum.

The vocabulary known as *Interpretationes Hebraicorum nominum* (= Stegmüller, *Repertorium* 7709, in v. 5 and 9) sometimes attributed to Remigius or to Stephen Langton; often present in the Parisian Bibles.

539vb–550va: *Incip[it] L[iber] 3. Esdre v[el] [etiam] 2.* . . . Liber esdre p[ro]ph[et]e filii sarei . . . (ends, 550va:) . . . [et] nutritur ad deuorationem ignis. (rest of column and page blank)

The apocryphal Second Book of Esdras.[11] Chapters (variously not coinciding with those of later editions) are numbered and marked by 2-line blue or red initials through ch. "XXXI" on f. 546ra (the chapter begins with verse 37b of ch. X of later standard); from that point on, the text is written continuously without initials or numbering.

551r–555rb: D[omi]nica p[ri]ma in Aduentu. Epistola ad romanos .xiii.c°. Scientes e[st] hora . . . (553rb:) . . . fi[nitur:] q[ui] uent[ur]us [est] in mundum. *Incipit titulus epistolar[um] et euuangelior[um] que eueniunt in festis sanctorum.*

Scī siluestr[i] . . . (555ra:) *In nathali apostolor*[um] . . . (555rb:) . . . IN anniu[ersario] eccl[es]ie[12] . . . facere q[uod] p[er]ierat. (rest of column originally blank; 4 lines added in later, probably English hand:) Leg[er]e assidue . . . (see next item)

Liturgical lectionary, i.e., a program of Mass readings (Epistles and Gospels) for the liturgical year, with the temporal first, from the 1st Sunday of Advent to the 25th Sunday after Pentecost. The pericopes are identified by their incipits and explicits. — The temporal numbers 5 Sundays as "post Epiphaniam"; after Pentecost, it specifies "De scā Trinitate," with readings *Gaudete* (2 Cor XIII,11–13) and *Cum venerit* (John XV,26-XVI,4), followed by "ii post pent."; this and further Sundays through the 24th are assigned combinations of epistolary and Gospel readings identical with those called "famille B" by A. Chavasse (*REVUE BÉNÉDICTINE* 62[1952], p. 13); the 25th Sunday differs, given in our ms. the readings *Ecce dies veniunt* (Jeremiah XXIII, 5[-12?]) and *Cum sublevasset* (John VI, 5–14). — The sanctoral lists 115 feasts; among them: William (apparently the archbishop of York[13]), Cuthbert, "Robertus Abbas," Egidius, Lambertus, Mauritius, Remigius, Denis, Edward conf., Malachias ep., Quattuor Coronati, Eadmundus archiep.,[14] Hugo ep., Eadmundus rex; ending with Thomas the Apostle. Orientation toward the British Isles seems obvious but the absence of Thomas à Becket (Cantuariensis) is puzzling.[15]

555rb, lines 28–31 (14th(?)-century ADDITION in anglicana-type cursive): leg[er]e assidue sac[ra]m sc[ri]pturam // magis on[er]at(?) dyabolu[m]. q[uam] o[mni]a relinq[ue]re et sequi xp̄m̄ // h[ec] Criso[stomus]. sup[er] jo[annem]. om[ili]a. 3.a.

The words seem to paraphrase, in a questionable manner, the rather more orthodox ideas recorded in *PG* 59, col. 38. — A corrector, apparently contemporary, attempted to save the situation by adding in the margin "Non," as an insertion.

(555v blank)

556r (recto of a singleton leaf; one column, 29 lines, in hybrid cursive script;[16] a 14th?-century ADDITION): (L)ector obs[er]ua q[uod] d[ictio]nes q[ue]da[m] . . . Explic[i]t r[egul]a vtilis ad rege[n]du[m] ho[m]i[n]em i[n] [con]cordanciis sup[er] bibliam.

The "regula"[17] explains a system of numerical and alphabetical signs used or to be used in a biblical concordance to indicate the case and gender of a noun, the tense and person of a verb, etc. It may have been a preface to an existing concordance or a guide in preparing one.

* * *

Foliated in modern pencil. — Three free endleaves (paper) in front, three at end (all added in 18th-century rebinding). — Written area ca. 103 × ca. 65 mm. — Fully ruled in crayon or similar tool, generally only on one side of the very thin parchment (ca. 7.3 mm per 100 leaves), making the ruling show through; in addition, frame-ruled in diluted ink: this includes a line in the head margin below which the running titles were written across each opening, in alternately red and blue letters (some are partly cropped). Pricking for the vertical framing lines preserved on some leaves. — Written in very small (up to 700 words a page) text hands varying from *rotunda* to *quadrata*: later (14th-century?) additions on ff. 1 and 556 in a hybrid script based on the *anglicana*. — Primary text in very good black ink. — Red captions[18] in blank spaces provided by the black-text scribe, sometimes in the descending-triangle pattern, sometimes also protruding into the margin. — Chapter numbers, variously combining red and blue, were placed into the text block where last line of the preceding chapter left sufficient blank space, otherwise in the margin.

Collation: f. 1 singleton (14th-century addition) 1^{24}(= ff. 2–25) 2^{22}(= ff. 26–47) $3^{24?}$(= ff. 48–71, but sewing line between 62 and 63?) $4–7^{24}$(= ff. 72–167) 8^{26}(= ff. 168–193) 9^{24}(= ff. 194–217) $10–11^{22?}$(= ff. 218–261) 12^{26}(= ff. 262–287)

MS 2 13–21^{24} (= ff. 288–503) 22^{22}(= ff. 504–525) 23^{20}(= ff. 526–545) 24^{10}(= ff. 546–555) — f. 556 singleton (14th-century addition). — In gatherings 2–4, 6(?), 8, 9, 12–14, 16–18, and 20–24, the first half of the leaves are sequentially marked (on rectos, in centers or outside corners of tail margins) with hybrid-script lowercase alphabet ranging from *a* (often omitted) to *l, m, n,* or *o*; the letters are very faded, some to the point of invisibility; some are cropped.[19] — Remnants of what may have been catchwords are barely visible on bottom edges of some leaves.

Decoration: of the scribal type (rinceaux) except for the initial *I* at the beginning of Genesis (f. 5v) which is historiated, with 7 vesica-form compartments containing scenes symbolic of the Creation, followed, in a square at bottom, by Crucifixion. The sequence does not correspond to the "days" of the scriptural account:[20] the 1st (topmost) scene appears to stand for the general beginning, the 2nd for the creation of light; the meaning of the next two (3rd and 4th) scenes is rather unclear, resembling what in other Bibles of probably same origin[21] more obviously stood for the Firmament/Division of waters and Sun/Moon days; the next (5th) compartment pictures plants, followed by (6th) birds, and (7th) Man. — The scribal initials beginning the text of individual Bible books are generally 4 to 8 lines high, with the vertical bars of some letters going far beyond that (27 lines for the *P* which begins the Book of Judges, f. 96v); those introducing the prologues tend to be 3 to 4 lines in height. Both kinds use combinations of blue and red for the body of the letter as well as for the flourishing. The initial *T* of Tobit (202vb) and the *A* of Judith (206vb) differ in style from the rest.

Binding: 18th-century, French, over 4 bands; covers straight-grain bright red morocco, simply decorated with straight framing lines in gilt; spine stamped more richly. On it, in gilt: BIBLIA SACRA // MSS: VELIN. Edges all gilt. Endpapers marbled, French-style. — Kept in a pull-off case (19th-century?) with rounded back and raised bands, covered in dark brown, now much worn calf; on the spinelike back of the case, gold-stamped: BIBLIA.// MSS.

On pastedown of upper cover: label of B. Westermann & Co., New York; clipping from an (early 20th-century?) catalog in which the Bible is no. 410; and tipped-on LC label ("Temp. no. 4"; "Ms. 71"). — On verso of the first free endleaf, inked numbers ("no. 412"; "1372(?)"). On recto of the next leaf, in pencil: Ac. 4560 (3), n.2; £ 14.14.0; 463. — On pastedown of lower cover, ownership label of Rev. Edwin A. Dalrymple, D.D.

Inscriptions: on f. 145r, in (parallel to) the outer margin: Edwardus Regens dei gr[ati]a Angl[ie] Ffrancie;[22] on 194r (similar position, different hand; partly cropped; end possibly erased): feyt known to all men by these p[re]sens that I John pers of Milton// next graueysend in the Comitye of Kent (. . . ? . . .);[23] on 219r, in tail margin, inverted: De te (space of ca. 15 mm) Iste liber per[tinet]//Joh[n]i gamble (?).[24] Repeatedly, i.e., in the tail margin and inverted on 307r and 359r, in outer margin on 473r, 478r, 492r, and 546r: Thomas Sylvester (followed by slightly varying: "owneth thys book(e)").[25] — Scribbles, apparently meaningless, fill parts of the margin space on ff. 49v and 50r, 92v and 93r.

2° fo.: (running title:) PROLOGVS — (text column, red:) *Incip[it] p[ro]log[us] in bibli[a?]*

Bibl.: De Ricci, *Census* (1935), p. 229, no. 99; Faye and Bond (1962), p. 119, no. 71. — R. Branner, *Manuscript painting in Paris during the reign of Saint Louis* (c1977), p. 78 and 216; also black-and-white reproduction of the Genesis initial, fig. 179.

APPENDIX: TEXT OF THE *REGULA UTILIS AD REGENDUM HOMINEM IN CONCORDANCIIS SUPER BIBLIAM*, MS 2, f. 556r (contractions expanded)

Lector observa quod dictiones quedam secundum suas obliquationes variantur, et pro huiusmodi dictionibus litere ponuntur et aliquando ad earum declarationes signa premittuntur. Cum siquidem dictio concordancialis sit nomen seu pronomen seu participium si loco ipsius ponatur "p" litera significat quod dictio illa est masculini generis; si "s" litera quod feminini, si "t" litera quod neutri. Si vero in margine preponatur vnitas algorismalis significat quod dictio est nominativi casus; si "2" quod genitivi; si "3" quod dativi, si "4" quod accusativi, et sic de ceteris casibus. Et ubi numero algorismali non superponatur punctus significat quod dictio est singularis numeri, ubi vero superponatur quod pluralis. Cum autem dictio concordancialis fuerit verbum si loco ipsius ponatur "p" litera significat quod dictio illa est prime persone; si "s" litera quod secunde persone, si "t" litera quod 3^e^ persone; si vero in margine preponatur vnitas algorismalis significat quod dictio illa est presentis temporis; si "2" quod preteriti imperfecti; si "3" quod preteriti perfecti; si 4^or^ quod preteriti plusquamperfecti; si "5" quod futuri. Si autem preponatur senarius, sic "6", significat quod dictio est imperativi modi; si "8" quod optativi modi; si "9" quod coniunctivi modi. Si vero preponatur talis caracter "[a somewhat H-like shape]" significatur quod est coniunctivi modi futuri temporis, et aliquando se extendit ad futurum optativi modi. Et ubi numero algorismali non superponatur punctus significat quod dictio est singularis numeri; ubi vero superponatur quod pluralis; si autem numerus non preponatur sed loco numeri ponatur virgula, eque iacens sic "—" significat quod est infinitivi modi. Explicit regula vtilis ad regendum hominem in concordanciis super bibliam.

NOTES

1. Standard for later Vulgates is 16 chapters for Esther, 5 for Lamentations, 13 for the Letter to Hebrews (8 for the Song of Solomon, 16 for the First Maccabees).
2. Actually, it seems, Six Days of Creation preceded by an introductory medallion and followed by the Crucifixion: the Creation of Man is in the seventh compartment. (See further details in paragraph on decoration, following contents.)
3. See table A. — The prologues (commonly identified by their number in F. Stegmüller's *Repertorium biblicum Medii Aevi* [Madrid, 1950–77, also repr. 1981; the prologues primarily in v. 1]) may be counted variously; cf. Ker, *Med. mss. in British libraries* 1 (1969), p. 96–97.
4. In some Parisian Vulgates (e.g., LC MS 5) the Greek expressions are translated.
5. None of this in, e.g., LC MS 5, another bona fide Parisian Vulgate.
6. In the Clementine Vulgate, in which it is added at end, as an apocryphal ("ne prorsus interirent") "Liber III Esdrae," the number of chapters is 9. — N.B. This is the book beginning "Et fecit Josias Pascha . . ." and ending "secundum testamentum Domini Dei Israel," apparently the version Stegmüller 94,1.
7. The numbers are, of course, those of the Vulgate/Septuagint system.
8. The only source listed as having this verse in the Stuttgart critical edition of the Vulgate (2nd ed., 1975) is the 16th-century printed Sixto-Clementina: the Stuttgart apparatus for the O.T. does not include the 13th-century Parisian Bibles (the "Ω" family). The verse is found in all ms. Vulgates in LC except the MS 1 written probably in England (cf. table A).
9. It reads: Thessalonicenses sunt macedones in xristo ihesu qui accepto uerbo ueritatis persistiterunt in fide et in persecutione ciuium suorum. Preterea nec receperunt falsos apostolos nec ea que a falsis apostolis dicebantur. Hos collaudat apostolus scribens eis ab athenis per titicum et onesimum. — LC MS 5 (Faye and Bond 19) has same text without the "in xristo ihesu." — See table A for other variations in the prologues.
10. A summary rather than prologue, the text appears, among other mss., in the ms. Bonifatianus 1 of the Landesbibliothek in Fulda, written in 547 (cf. S. Berger, *Hist. de la Vulgate* [1893], p. 312 and 356–357). The version found in our ms. seems to be the shorter one, with 40 items, as in Bib. nat. 93?
11. This is the "Liber IV Esdrae" in the appendix to the Clementine Vulgate (= Stegm. 96 + 95 + 97).
12. This caption black. — N.B. The "lectionary" does not appear to be a later addition.
13. Meant is, I think, the feast of translation of his relics, Jan. 8; another William, once bishop of Bourges, was celebrated on Jan. 10. The notice in our ms. places the feast between Sylvester (Dec. 31) and Felix in Pincis (Jan. 14). (The ms. does not give any month-and-day information.)
14. Archbishop of Canterbury (but died among Cistercians in France); canonized in 1247. This provides a *terminus a quo* for at least this part of the manuscript (on its face, roughly contemporary with the rest).
15. Unless, e.g., an ignorant scribe decided not to duplicate the name "Thomas."
16. The *a, b, c, d, e* (circular), *l, r* (long, forked), *s* (sigma-like in initial and final positions), and *t* (shaft not yet above the head stroke) as in the *anglicana* of 14th century; *g* different, similar to non-cursive form.
17. Not successfully identified. See full text in appendix at end of this description.
18. Incl. the semi-biblical Psalm headings in the Book of Psalms.
19. Our partly conjectural collation of the very tightly bound book is based on these markings.
20. Genesis (I,3–II,3) gives for day 1: light; 2: firmament/division of waters; 3: dry land/plants; 4: Sun/Moon; 5: fish, reptiles, birds; 6: quadrupeds, Man; 7: Day of Rest.

MS 2

21. R. Branner (d. 1973) in his *Manuscript painting in Paris* . . . (c1977) has identified the initial in our ms. as a work of the "Soissons atelier" (located in Paris and named after a Bible which is now in Soissons). The unscriptural order of the "days" (especially the sequence Sun/Moon — plants — birds — man) prevails, judging from reproductions op. cit. fig. 174–184, in all Bibles decorated by that atelier (unlike many others), e.g., in Yale MS 433 in which, however, the Creation of Man is followed by Day of Rest.

22. Ending abruptly although space was available. The script is a mixed cursive with forms suggesting court hand of (2nd half of) 15th century — N.B. It is not at all likely that this would indicate royal provenience.

23. Inscription datable (on paleographical grounds) to ca. 1400. — Milton, Kent, between London and Canterbury; now, it seems, no more on the map (having merged into Gravesend).

24. Script of mid-15th century? — The page contains Job V,13–VII,10; perhaps the "De te" refers to a part of these texts.

25. Close to 1500?

MS 3

(Rosenwald 31/3)

BIBLE IN LATIN mid-XIIIth c.

Paris.[1] Parchment. 551 leaves, 140–142 × ca. 95 mm (bound volume: 153 × ca. 111 mm) 2 columns. 48 lines.

ff. 1ra–4rb: *I[n]cipit epi[stola] scī ieronimi p[res]b[iter]i ad [paul]inu[m] de o[mn]ibus diuine historie libris* (7-line historiated initial *F*, with Jerome represented as a brown-clad monk:) (F)$^{7+}$Rater ambrosius . . . (3vb:) Desid[er]ij mei . . . (prologue ends, 4rb:) . . . sermonem.

The usual preliminary texts, Stegmüller 284 and 285. The red "Incipit . . ." caption is largely faded or rubbed off. Greek words in Jerome's letter distorted (except for "logos") beyond recognition (2vb: oronatytim theodocti lactri; 3ra, in c. VI: . . . in doctrinam thologmaten . . .)

4rb–505vb: (on 4r, in the central area between the text columns, page-high historiated *I* with 8 quadrilobe compartments containing representations of the Six Days of Creation, the Day of Rest, and the Crucifixion; text begins in 32nd line of column *b*:) (I)$^{48+}$N principio creauit . . . (Bible text ends on f. 505vb:) . . . cu[m] om[n]ib[us] uobis amen. Explicit bibliotheca (remainder of column blank)

Text[2] of the Vulgate in the Parisian "University Bible" form, with the then standard selection and order of books and with the then usual set of 64 prologues.[3] Chapter division and numbering generally as in later standard editions, with some exceptions: 2 Chronicles (running title "PA[RA]LI-[POMENON] II," ff. 168r–183r) shows evidence of many corrections or changes in its numbering before the standard 36 was achieved, with the Prayer of Manasseh (f. 183ra) written, unmarked, as part of the last chapter; Nehemiah ("NE[E]MIE," ff. 187v–193v) has 14 chapters; it is followed, as customarily in Parisian Bibles, by the apocryphal First Book of Esdras (Stegmüller 94,1; here on ff. 193v–199v, with running title "ESDRE II"). Judith (203v–209r) has 15 chapters, the standard ch. XV and XVI forming but one. In Esther (209r–214v) the versals had originally signaled 6 chapters; the 16-chapter division was later noted in the margins (in black ink; partly cropped). The Psalms (ff. 226r–251v) carry the usual Parisian caption "Incipit liber hym(p)norum vel soliloquiorum prophete David de Christo"; the usual liturgical divisions of the books are marked by 3–4-line-high illuminated initials;[4] the Psalm numbers (not normally found in Parisian Vulgates of the time) have been added in lowercase roman numerals (black ink) in the margins (and later, for the most part, cropped). After the end of the Psalms, the column 251vb (= end of gathering L) is left blank, and the beginning of the Proverbs (252r–261v) has the appearance of the opening page of a major section, perhaps meant as the beginning of the second half of the whole Bible: the prologue to Proverbs is introduced by a column-high illuminated initial *I*. Wisdom (266v–273r) was originally copied with a chapter division different from that displayed now.[5] Ecclesiasticus doesn't have at end the Prayer of Solomon. — The introductory statement to Lamentations ("Et factum est . . . eiulans dixit") is written (f. 332vb) as end of Jeremiah LII; the Incipit rubric of the Lamentations follows it. — Daniel XIV includes at end the verse numbered as 42 in the Clementine Vulgate ("Tunc rex ait . . ."). Prologue to Matthew begins in the same column (408va) where the Second Book of Maccabees ends. Luke I,1–14 is used (429vb) as first prologue to the Gospel, with Stegm. 620, another prologue, interposed before the actual Gospel text. John (443v–453v) has 22 chapters, the verses 15–25 of ch. XXI marked as ch. XXII. — As is usual in Parisian Vulgates, the order of New Testament books is Gospels — Pauline Epistles — Acts — Catholic Epistles — Revelation.

506ra–551vb: ***Incip[i]u[n]t int[er]p[re]tat[i]o[n]es hebraicor[um] no[m]i[num]*** **. . . (A)$^{5+}$az app[re]hendens . . . [con]siliantes eos vel consiliatores eorum. Expliciunt interp[re]tationes.** ***Orate p[r]o me scriptore [et] p[rio]re*** **(or** ***p[at]re?) n[ost]ro bernbardo***

The vocabulary (known under the title given in the incipit) attributed sometimes to Remigius of Auxerre or to Stephen Langton (cf. Stegmüller, *Repertorium,* vol. 5, no. 7709, and 9, no. 7709); a usual ingredient of the Parisian Bible copies. — The red-ink words at end are unfortunately very faded or rubbed off, especially what follows the word "scriptore." Whether the request concerns the scribe and his superior or (in very odd phrasing) the scribe's spiritual father, Bernard of Clairvaux, Cistercian affiliation is likely. In the Paris area, books were being copied in the 13th century at the Cistercian abbey Royaumont.[6]

* * *

No foliation. — Four free parchment endleaves, of recent origin, in front, four at end. — Written area ca. 93 × ca. 65 mm (right margins quite irregular). — Four vertical ruled lines per page, done in diluted ink, visible to varying degree; of the horizontal lines, those for the running titles are present but rarely any other. Some pricking has been preserved, all of it for the vertical lines. — The script is a small (ca. 600 words per page) utilitarian *littera textualis currens, semiquadrata*, rather irregular. Very good black or brownish black ink. — Very thin parchment (ca. 9 mm per 100 leaves). — Chapter numbers (in roman capitals, generally within text columns) and running titles (variously abridged and generally divided between the two pages of an opening) are written in various combinations of blue and red (basically, alternating red and blue digits or letters). — Captions of individual Bible books (in "Incipit . . ." form) are red. Capitals are touched with red throughout.

Collation: A^{24} (wants A_1, probably blank, and $A_{12.13}$ following f. [10], with loss of text) $[B]^{30}$(wants $B_{1.22}$ following f. [21] and [49] respectively, with text loss) C^{24} D^{24-1}(= ff. 74–96; apparently no text lost) E^{26} $F\text{-}H^{24}$ I^{24-1}(= ff. 195–217; apparently no text lost) K^{24} L^{10} $M\text{–}P^{24}$ Q^{22} R^{24-1}(= ff. 370–392; apparently no text lost) $S\text{–}T^{24}$ V^{22} X^{24} Y^{20}(wants Y_1 following f. [486], with loss of text) Z^{24} $[AA]^{22}$(= ff. 530-551). — Gatherings A–Z are so marked on last versos, except [B] which lacks the last leaf. — (The lost texts: following f. [10], Gen. XIX,38b–XXIV,49a; following f. [21], Gen. XLVIII,4a–L,17a; following f. 49, Lev. XXVI,24a–Num. I,22a; following f. [486], Acts XIII,11a–XV,7b)

Decoration: Individual Bible books are introduced by illuminated initials of Parisian style, with square-shape letters ca. 4–6 lines high, the vertical bars of the *P*'s, *F*'s, etc., reaching 15–25 lines, and with mostly moderate extensions. Eight of the initials are historiated:

f. 1r (Ad Paulinum) Jerome, in brown and gray (silver?) monkish garb, at his desk: *F*

f. 4r (Gen.) Six days of Creation, Day of Rest, Crucifixion: the seven days' scenes in rounded quadrilobe compartments in the central column, the Crucifixion protruding into the lower margin: *I* (see plate I, p. x1)

f. 103v (1 Sam.) Elkana and Anne praying: *F*

f. 226r (Psalms) David harping: *B*

f. 252r (Proverbs) Solomon instructs (tonsured) Rehoboam: *P*

f. 290r (Isaiah) The prophet sawn asunder: *U/V*

f. 409r (Matthew) The Tree of Jesse: *L*

f. 453v (Romans) Paul with sword: *P*

The illuminator missed Esther (209r). — A ferret-like (or perhaps cat-like) white zoomorphic head appears frequently in the decorative initials or in their extensions: variously placed, often at end of a serpent-like body or vine. Prevailing color of the illuminated initials is blue, with the usual pinkish magenta, white, and moderately used gold.

The 64 prologues are signaled by two-color (red and blue) calligraphic initials, average height 4 lines, with two-color flourishes; the chapters, by alternately red or blue ca. 2 1/2-line versals, with flourishes always in the other color. — The blue used in the calligraphic initials, versals, running titles, and in chapter numbering is of two different kinds: a very light blue (rather like ultramarine with added opaque white) or a rather saturated ultramarine; in any particular section of the book, one or the other is used for all the purposes named and the two do not appear together.

Binding, etc.: modern light brown morocco covers over probably older boards, gold-stamped (decorative fleurs-de-lys) and blind-tooled. Pastedowns replaced by vellum framed in gold-tooled reddish morocco. On spine, in gold: BIBLIA SACRA// LATINA//SOEC. XIV. Gilt edges. — Kept in an elaborate pull-off case of 20th-century manufacture, covered in red morocco, with rounded back and raised bands.

On recto of first free endleaf, penciled numbers: 590615; 1750/7L; in lower half, pasted-on label with: THE GIFT OF//LESSING J. ROSENWALD//TO THE LIBRARY OF CONGRESS. On second free endleaf, on recto, ink inscription: Alexander Campbell, Harriette Campbell, August 20, 1855. On f. [1]r, in tail margin, in ink: A.iiij. biblia.

2° fo.: dit[ur] que[m] si ded[er]is ho[min]i scienti lit[e]ras ut legat.

Bibl.: R. Branner, *Manuscript painting in Paris during the reign of Saint Louis* (c1977), p. 214 (among works of the Mathurin atelier; N.B. the ms. is listed as Jenkintown, Pa., Lessing J. Rosenwald Collection 31), also in tables of O.T. subjects, p. 184–190 (as Rosenwald 31). — *The Lessing J. Rosenwald collection : a catalog of the gifts* . . . (Library of Congress, 1977), no. 3 (lists also the old shelflist number of the manuscript in LC, "Rosenwald Collection ms. no. 31")

Illuminated initials in this Bible resemble in various respects[7] the products of the Mathurin atelier which operated in Paris in mid-13th century and apparently specialized in decoration of the Vulgates. Not unlikely, this one, while copied by a Cistercian monk perhaps at Royaumont, was then professionally illuminated in Paris.[8]

NOTES

1. Decorated in Paris; written in the area (see concluding comment).

2. Imperfect: wanting parts of Genesis XIX-XXIV and XLVIII-L, the end of Leviticus and the beginning of Numbers, and Acts XIII,11-XV,7. (See also the notes to collation, following the contents)

3. See table A.

4. The Ps. XCVIII (Vulg. XCVII, Cantate Domino canticum novum) on f. 243r is not so marked; confirming, perhaps, the monastic origin of the copy. Cf. A. Hughes, *Medieval manuscripts for Mass and Office* (1982), p. 227 sqq.

5. Corrections have made it rather impossible to determine the original division.

6. Ca. 30 miles north of Paris; founded in 1228. — Cf. R. Branner, *Manuscript painting in Paris . . .* (c1977), p. 9.

7. Among them: the rounded quadrilobe compartments of the Genesis initial, and the choice of its Seventh Day's theme; Christ's body on the cross, in the same initial, disposed in an inverted-S curve; the choice of theme for the First Book of Samuel; the whitish catlike heads in the ornamental initials. — Cf. Branner, *op. cit.*, esp. the Genesis initials from other Mathurin atelier Bibles, reproduced as fig. 166-168.

8. About this practice, cf. Branner, *op. cit.*, p. 9.

MS 4

(Faye and Bond 19)

BIBLE IN LATIN XIIIth c., 2nd half

Written in Paris. Parchment. 551 (originally ca. 575?) leaves, 167 × ca. 110 mm (bound volume: 174 × 120 mm) 2 columns. 47 lines.

ff. 1ra–513 rb: *Incipit p[ro]log[us] b[eat]i Ieronimi In tota[m] bibliam* (F)[6]rater ambrosius . . . (3vb:) . . . *Incipit p[ro]l[ogus] Ieronimi In libro Genesis.* (D)Esiderij mei . . . (Bible text, imperfect at the beginning and with some further lacunae, ends on f. 513rb:) . . . cum omnibus vobis. Am[en]

The Vulgate, in the form most commonly accepted from the 13th to the 16th century, known as the Parisian revision;[1] with the standard choice of prologues and also in other respects not significantly departing from the norm. — The text is now incomplete owing to missing leaves. Wanting: last two-thirds of the prologue *Desiderii mei* and the beginning (I,1–II,13) of Genesis (lost leaf after f.3); Genesis XLVI,32–XLIX,1 (lost leaf after f. 22); almost half of Leviticus (XIII,55–XXVII,34) and the first two-thirds (I,1–XXIV,7) of the Book of Numbers (ca. 18 leaves missing after f. 46); most of the prologue *Si septuaginta* (Stegmüller 328) and the beginning (I,1–II,23a) of 1 Chronicles (missing leaf after f. 146); Judith IX,17–XII,17a (torn-out leaf following f. 197); the *Prologus in libris Salomonis* (Stegm. 457) and Proverbs I,1–III,17 (lost leaf after f. 243); Hebrews XI,33–XIII,25, the prologue to Acts (Stegm. 640), and Acts I,2a (lost leaf after f. 484). — The First Book of Samuel is called (as commonly in Vulgates) "primus liber Regum"; 2 Samuel and 1 Kings are not captioned, although marked by large initials. Uncaptioned although signaled by initials is also 2 Chronicles (the Prayer of Manasseh is included at end as part of the text). Ezra is divided into 9 chapters, Nehemiah into 14; they are followed by uncaptioned First Book of Esdras (Et fecit Josias Pascha . . . = Stegm. 94,1) with running title "ESDRE II." Jerome's note concerning the deuterocanonical parts of Esther (203rb) isn't differentiated from the text which is divided into altogether 9 chapters. The Psalms (217rb–243vb) are captioned "Incipit liber hymnorum et soliloquiorum prophetae David de Christo; psalmus David"; the semi-biblical psalm titles are in red; Pss. XXVII, XXXIX, LIII, LXIX, LXXXI, XCVIII, and CX begin with large initials;[2] after the end of the last Psalm (CL) the remaining lines of f. 243v have been left blank. Ecclesiasticus

(263v–281v) ends with LI,38 (i.e., the "Prayer of Solomon" is not included). — New Testament is not signaled as such: the prologue to Matthew (Stegm, 590) begins in the column (f. 406ra) which contains the end of 2 Maccabees.[3] Luke I,1–4, captioned "Incipit prologus libri Luce euangeliste," is additionally separated from the Gospel by another prologue (Stegm. 620) introduced as "alius prologus." — The order of New Testament books is, as usual in the Parisian revision Bibles: Gospels — Paul — Acts — Catholic Epistles — Revelation.

The absence of captions with some of the prologues and some of the Bible books themselves is to some extent compensated for: large initials and running titles convey the needed information. In several cases, spaces left blank for captions have remained unfilled, and sometimes a later hand supplied the caption,[4] in red or black. The general phrasing of the captions is "Incipit . . ." — Chapter division differs occasionally from that standard today; apart from cases of scribal error, conspicuous differences appear in Ezra, Esther, in the Gospel of John (John XXI,15–25 is marked as ch. XXII), and in the Letter of Jude (verses 11–25 are styled as ch. II). The numbers differ from both the modern count and (except for the division of Jude into two chapters) from that introduced (perhaps) by Stephen Langton and said to be characteristic of Parisian Vulgates.[5]

513rb: (the end of the Revelation is immediately followed by:) [A]az apprehendens . . . (but after 15 lines, this is discontinued and the rest of the page is blank; the text is taken up anew on next page:)

513va–551vb: AAz apprehendens . . . (ending imperfectly, at end of 551 vb:) Zebida . . . fortitudo u[e]l dotacio m[e]a.

The vocabulary known as *Interpretationes Hebraicorum nominum,* sometimes attributed to Remigius of Auxerre or to Stephen Langton (= Stegmüller, *Repertorium*, v. 5 and 9, no. 7709). Ending imperfectly owing to loss of one or more leaves at end.[6]

* * *

Foliated in modern pencil. Not included in the numbering: one free endleaf (18th–century paper) in front, one at end. — Written area ca. 115 × ca. 75 mm. — Fully ruled in pencil or a similar medium, generally on one side of the very thin material, making the ruling show through; in some cases, some of the lines seem to have been drawn again on the other side. The ruling includes lines for the running titles; the titles are written across each two-page opening, in alternating blue and red letters; some are partly cropped. Pricking for the vertical lines is preserved on some leaves. — Written in a very small (ca. 590 words per page) *littera textualis* by professional scribes not easy to distinguish. Black ink of excellent quality. — Parchment thickness ca. 42–43 mm for the text block (= ca. 7.7 mm per 100 leaves). — Red captions frequently fill a descending triangle of left-out blank space. Chapter numbers, written in combinations of red and blue, are within the text column where space permitted (not always adequately planned for). Many capitals within the text are touched with red.

Collation: impracticable in detail; the basic pattern was 24 leaves per gathering but some gatherings have more, sometimes unevenly divided by the visible sewing lines.[7] No catchwords; no signatures (unless lost due to cropping when the book was being rebound). — Ca. 25 leaves are missing: lacunae of probably one leaf each after ff. 3, 22, 146, 197, 243, 484, and 551 (cf. contents); ca. 18 leaves have disappeared following f. 46, apparently before the 18th–century rebinding; irregular stubs after the ff. 197 and 484 indicate those leaves have been torn out more recently.[8] — An unidentified malefactor using a sharp blade has cut out major portions of the tail margin of ff. 120, 121, 181, 187–192, 196, 442–451, and 547–551; integrity of the biblical text was, however, preserved.[9]

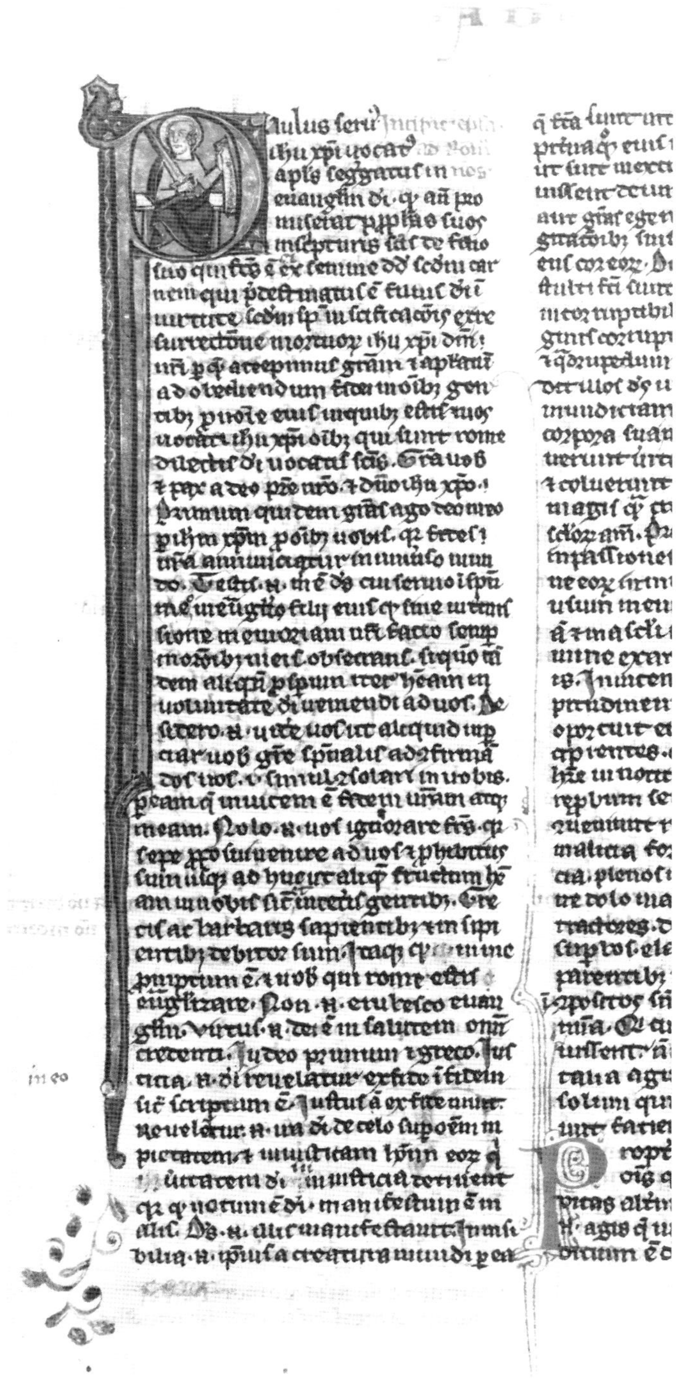

MS 4, f. 455va (beginning of the Letter to the Romans) (actual dimensions of the column: 115 × ca. 36 mm)

MS 4 Decoration consists of red, blue, and purple pen flourishes and of initials, mostly of the calligraphic kind; also preserved are seven historiated initials in the 13th–century Parisian style;[10] their letters are silvered blue or pink on pink or blue grounds, extending into cusped-branch pendants; very little gold is used (e.g., in David's crown). They are:

f. 1ra: Jerome standing at his desk in a brown hooded cape over white (?) robe, inside the 6-line high upper portion of an *F* with a column-high stem

68ra: Head of God, three men by the water; in the 6-line *E* which begins the book of Joshua

217rb: David playing harp, in a 6-line *B* (beginning the Psalms)

281vb: Isaiah being sawn asunder: in a 6-line *U* (beginning the book of Isaiah and thus the whole group of Prophets)

362ra: Seated prophet, in a 6-line *U* beginning Hosea (the first of the Minor Prophets)

406va: Tree of Jesse, in an *L* which extends over 20 lines; beginning the Gospel of Matthew[11]

455va: St. Paul with the sword, in a *P* with stem running along most of the column (begins the Letter to the Romans)

The large calligraphic initials are red, blue (often purplish), or a combination of both colors. They are filled with filigree decoration drawn with pen, mostly in red ink, with some green ground. The largest of these initials (*F* or *P* with ca. 12-line stems; *J* even higher) are used at the beginnings of the biblical books but sometimes also to start a prologue. In the Psalms, the liturgical divisions are marked by 7-line initials of this kind.

Of the missing leaves only that wanting after f. 3 is fairly certain to have included important decoration (the Days of Creation), although the loss of the opening passages of Numbers, Chronicles, Proverbs, and Acts is also best explained by presence of visually appealing matter.

The state of preservation of the historiated initials is rather poor; the recto of f. 1 and verso of f. 551 are badly stained by water or other agents.

Binding: covers are 18th–century brownish orange calf, possibly American, modestly gold-tooled. On spine, dark leather label with: HOLY BIBLE//M.S.S. Upper cover detached. On its pastedown, in ink: Ac. 1241, with penciled "(4)"; other numbers in pencil: #96; C.32; (no. 3); 175238; MS. 19; (on recto of free endleaf in front:) ff. 45. Also on the pastedown, traces of lost, once pasted-on ownership label; a smaller LC label is pasted upside down on pastedown of the lower cover. A paper slip (95 × 126 mm) with partly inexact typed information ("An early English Bible . . .") is laid in.

Former owners: Obtained by LC in 1911 through Dr. V. G. Simkhovitch.

2° fo.: (in running title position:) LO — (in the text column:) d[e]i gl[ori]am [con]templemur. Liber in epoca

Bibl.: De Ricci, *Census* (1935), p. 189, no. 32; Faye and Bond, *Suppl.* (1962), p. 117, no. 19. — R. Branner, *Manuscript painting in Paris during the reign of Saint Louis* (University of California Press, c1977), p. 112, 231, and fig. 315.

NOTES

1. Table A lists in its second column the prologues and some other details characteristic of the "University Bibles" produced in large quantity in Paris from ca. 1229 on. — On the Parisian revision, see *The Cambridge history of the Bible*, v. 2 (1969), p. 145 sqq. Cf. also Branner, *Manuscript painting in Paris* (c1977), p. 16 (with bibl.). (N.B. Branner's listing of books and prologues constituting the standard Parisian text, *op. cit.*, p. 154 sq., includes several errors.)

2. Marking the eight liturgical divisions of the Psalter. — N.B. In the Vulgate system of Psalm numbering (used until recently in Roman Catholic liturgy) the divisions begin with Pss. 1 (Beatus vir), 26 (Dominus illuminatio mea), 38 (Dixi custodiam vias meas), 52 (Dixit insipiens), 68 (Salvum me fac Deus quoniam intraverunt aquae), 80 (Exsultate Deo adiutori nostro), 97 (Cantate Domino canticum

novum), and 109 (Dixit Dominus Domino meo). (The manuscript itself contains no Psalm numbering.)

3. The beginning of the first Gospel itself is, however, signaled prominently (historiated initial on 406va, cf. the paragraph on decoration).

4. In column *b* of f. 194v, the supplied caption, in black, reads: Incipit prologus in libru[m] iudit/ /apocrypha.

5. Cf. *The Cambridge history of the Bible*, v. 2 (1969), p. 147; J. P. P. Martin, "Le texte parisien de la Vulgate latine," *LE MUSÉON* 8 (1889), 9 (1890). Where Martin noted a difference in the number of chapters between the present system and that ascribed to Langton, our ms. agrees with Langton in only one case, the Letter of Jude.

6. Full text would end with "Zuzim consiliantes eos vel consiliatores eorum."

7. The thread is visible between leaves 11/12, 34/35, 63/64, 87/88, 111/112, 133/134, 154/155, 178/179, 202/203, 226/227, 254/255, 278/279, 302/303, 326/327, 349/350, 373/374, 441/442, 488/489, 535/536.

8. N.B. The missing leaf with the beginning of Genesis (and very likely major decoration) following f. 3 must have been originally a singleton inserted after the initialist had done his part: a small stub conjugate with the stub of the missing leaf is visible between the leaves 19 and 20 where no loss occurred.

9. Was this act (excision of undesired marginal matter?) done in this country, only subsequent to the 18th–century rebinding? Some leaves adjacent to the affected areas suffered cuts which almost but never quite reach the gutter, suggesting that the book was already bound when the excising took place; it is also unlikely that the bookbinder would have left the damaged leaves in their present state.

10. Cf. Branner, *op. cit.*, p. 112, 231, and fig. 315. — Branner ascribes the initials in this Bible (= his "Library of Congress 19") to the "St. Louis group" (so called after the ms. Bib. nat. 10426 said to have belonged to St. Louis) of the Aurifaber atelier which was active in Paris from ca. 1250 to at least 1292 (*ibid.*, p. 115). — N.B. His list (p. 231) of historiated initials in our ms. missed the one on f. 1r.

11. The initial is reproduced (in black and white) in Branner, *op cit.*, fig. 315.

MS 5

(Rosenwald 5/2; Faye and Bond 160)

BIBLE IN LATIN   XIIIth c., 3rd quarter

Written in England. Parchment. [563] leaves, ca. 179 × ca. 115 mm (bound volume: 188 × ca. 128 mm) 2 columns. 42 lines.

f. [i] r–v:[1] (in an English 14th?-century hand:) Ordinac[i]o Biblie p[er] libros. Genes[is] h[abe]t L. cap[itu]la . . .

The *Ordinatio* gives for both Deuteronomy and Joshua the number of chapters as 33;[2] for Ezra, 9; for Lamentations, 4; for Letter of Jude, 2.[3] — "Esdre II" was originally omitted, entry supplied later in faint orange ink, adding "alias Neem(ie) vocat[us]," thus avoiding confusion with the First Book of Esdras which, under whatever name, is absent both from these preliminary listings and from the primary text of this Bible as originally written.[4] — Ecclesiasticus is listed before Wisdom (and so placed also in this Bible's text, ff. 266–289).

[ii]r(a–b): (another English hand of same period:) Ge[nesis] qui[n]q[ua]ginta capitella dat, Ex[odus] q[ua]draginta . . . Ap[ocalypsi]s ter septe[m] dat [et] vnu[m].

In rhythmic Latin. Not in Walther, *Initia*; not in Hauréau-Schmeller, *Initia*. — Tobit, Esther, Judith are named in that order; Psalms and Isaiah omitted (the latter due to a homoeoteleuton). Nehemiah is so called ("Neemi[a]"); no First Book of Esdras; Ecclesiasticus is called "Sira" and given 52 chapters (meaning that the author of the summary counted with the presence of the Prayer of Solomon). The Second Book of Samuel is ascribed 34 ("bis duo terque decem") chapters; Micah, 8; Malachi, 3. — New Testament books are listed in the then common order of Gospels, Paul, Acts, Catholic Epistles, Revelation. The Letter to Hebrews is said to have 14 chapters (Jude has 1, as in the later standard).

[ii] rb–va: (perhaps by same scribe as the preceding:) [C]Anon[5] sc[ri]ptura[rum] hijs lib[ri]s [con]ti[n]et[ur]. qui[n]q[ue] moyses [id est] genesi, exodo, leuitico . . . *Hec Augustin[us] 2º De doct[rin]a x'ana*

Cf. *PL* XXXIV,41 (slightly abridged). — N.B. The part on f. [ii] verso is written on lines 10–22; it is preceded by the following:

[ii] va, lines 1–9 (in a cursive script of similar character but by a different writer; no doubt written before the quote from Augustine): P[ro]log[us] e[st] ex[er]c[i]c[iu]m artis [et] respicit t[ra]nslatore[m]

O[ritur] e[ni]m a prothos p[ri]mu[m] [et] logos s[er]mo [id est] p[ri]m[us] s[er]mo / P[ro]hemiu[m] est de c[ar]encia artis [et] respicit [con]ditore[m] In quo tangit[ur] in gen[er]ali q[uo]d in tractatu ins[e]q[ui]t[ur] in sp[eci]ali. P[er] p[ro]hemiu[m] remouet[ur] ab auditore ignorancia neg[aci?]o[n]is. P[er] tractatu[m], ignorancia disposicio[n]is etc.

A rhetorical and etymological note. The text is underscored in faint black ink. — Its writer provided also some of the marginal notes further on (that in tail margin of 28v? One of two on 144r?).

[ii] va, line 23–[ii] vb (probably same scribe as that of the Augustine quote): Hic genesis h[uius] genesis v[e]l genesios *[sic]* q[ui]da[m] lib[er] vet[er]is testa-[men]ti i[n] quo . . . [vb:] Hic exod[us] di, q[ui]da[m] lib[er] q[ui] . . . Hic leuitic[us] ci . . . Hic num[er]us [blank space for continuation of incomplete note] Hoc deut[ero]nomiu[m] i . . . Paralipomeno[n] d[icuntur] a para . . . su[m]mati[m] [et] b[re]uit[er] explica[n]t[ur] (rest of column blank)

Grammatical, etymological, and content notes. — Notes of similar scope appear sporadically in the margins throughout the book.

(WHAT FOLLOWS, THROUGH f. 558ra, IS IN 13TH-CENTURY *LITTERA TEXTUALIS:*)

[iii] ra–1ra: *Incipit ep[istola] b[eat]i ieronimi ad paulinu[m] de om[n]ib[us] di[uin]e historie lib[ri]s.* (F)$^{5+42+}$rat[er] a[m]b[ro]si[us] . . . (f. [v] va:) . . . (D)^{3}esiderii mei . . . (ends in column *a* of f. 1r:) . . . s[er]monem.

The usual preliminary material of Vulgate Bibles, Stegm. 284 and 285. — Jerome's letter to Paulinus is here written without interruption or chapter division. — Some effort was made to copy what, at some remove, had been Greek words in Greek alphabet ([iv] ra, in the would-be Greek equivalents of "in doctrinam, . . . rationem, . . . et usum, . . ." the result resembles the forms found in the 12th-century Bib. nat. ms. lat. 53[6]).

1ra–522rb: (the eight-compartment initial *I* runs along the whole height of the text column)[7] (I)$^{42+}$ (the original scribe had left blank space for the first two words but the initialist failed to fill them in; supplied in a later unskilled hand:) n p[r]incipio (the next and the further lines are by the original scribe:) creauit d's celū [et] t'rā . . . (Bible text ends on f. 522rb:) . . . Gr[aci]a dñi n[ost]ri ih'u xp̄i cū o[mn]ib[us] uob[is] amen. (See plate II, p. xvii)

The Vulgate, in a copy rather similar to the Parisian "University" Bibles but disagreeing with them in various ways.[8] — Among the notable features of the copy: In the sequence of the books, the First Book of Esdras (the apocryphal Stegm. 94) is absent; the running title "ESDRE II" is over Nehemiah (197r–203r). Ecclesiasticus (266rb–282va) precedes Wisdom (282va–289ra);[9] it doesn't include the Prayer of Solomon expected by the author of the preliminary material on f. [ii]r. — The New Testament begins without any special signal (prologue to Matthew begins in the middle of column 413rb; the Gospel itself does begin the page 413v). — Of the 64 prologues standard in the Parisian Bibles the original scribe or scribes included ca. a half, copying from their exemplar also ca. 30 prologues not expected, or unusual variants of the familiar ones.[10]

Later hands, very likely those of (Oxford?) university scholars, provided parts of the text with marginal captions and notes indicating content (e.g., on 4r: *De rixa inter pastores A. et Loth*), linguistic or archeological explanation (28v: *Gomor est decima pars ephi* . . .); also, especially in the Gospels, with scriptural cross-references; with 1 Timothy, also exhortatory or moralizing comment (with 1 Tim. V, on respect, etc., due a priest).

522va–558ra: AAz app[re]hende[n]s . . . [con]silian-tes eorum [ue]l consiliatores eo[rum].

The vocabulary known as *Interpretationes Hebraicorum nominum* (Stegm. 7709, in v. 5 and 9) produced, perhaps, by Stephen Langton and commonly included in the Parisian "University" Bibles and Bibles influenced by the Parisian model.

558rb–va: (14th-century hand, not one of those represented on ff. [i–ii]:) expo[sicio] reg[u]la[rum] tyconii p[er] hug[onem] l[ibro] 5. ditascalico[rum] .c. 4. t[un]c p[er] a[ugustinum] .1. 3. D[e] doc[trina]

.x. c. 30. u[bi] s[anctu]s ait tyconius q[ui]d[am] [contra] donatistas i[n]u[ic]tissi[m]e sc[ri]ps[i]t . . . re[gula] 1. cap[ut] n[ost]r[u]m c[um] cor[por]e iu[n]g[i]t . . . (558va:) . . . 7. re[gula] e[st] de dya[bol]o [et] e[ius] cor[por]e . . . (*ibid.*, last line:) q[uod] [con]t[ri]tu[m] e[st] ut puluis q[uem] p[ro]icit ue[n]t[us] a facie t[er]re.

A combined abstract of the hermeneutical principles developed ca. 380 in the *Liber regularum* of the Donatist theologian Ticonius Afer;[11] based on the accounts found in Augustine's *De doctrina Christiana* (*PL* XXXIV, 82–88) and in the fifth book of *Eruditionis didascalicae libri VII* of Hugo de S. Victore (*PL* CLXXVI,791–93). Some aspects of these teachings may have been of interest to the Wycliffite party at Oxford. The abstract is written in the university manner, saving space by a drastic accumulation of contractions. Rather oddly, there is a change of hands: on 558r, long *r*, two-compartment *g*, single-lobed *a*; on the verso, two-lobed *a*, short *r*, tailed single-compartment *g*.

559r (blank except for first line of column *a* which contains, out of all context, the following words): plectendu[m] [est] [et] adiudicat[us] morti appen (line ends, text broken off)

The words are from Deuteronomy XXI,22 (continuation would have been: [appen]sus fuerit in patibulo); they duplicate the identical line written on f. 79r. Perhaps poor quality of the parchment of what is now f. 559 had made the scribe discard the sheet after the first line and use another instead.

559va (written with considerable disregard for the vertical ruled lines): [III] Re. 11 [= III Regum XI] Astarten . fuit ydolum sydonio[rum] . . . .le. 20 [= Leviticus XX] Moloch . Amonita[rum] . . . [IV] Re. 17 Nebaaz [et] tharbacc [*sic*; should be "thartac", as on f. 160va] . eueo[rum]

A list of Middle Eastern deities, one per line, altogether 17 lines. Probably unfinished. In the biblical references which introduce the individual entries, the "III" and "IV" *Regum* is indicated by three or four dots over the "Re."; arabic numerals, of interesting forms, are used throughout.

* * *

Medieval foliation in old-style (14th century?) arabic numerals, written in faint brownish-black ink in upper right corners of rectos, starts on the leaf which contains the beginning of Genesis (thus disregards the prologues); altogether 9 leaves precede the f. "1": 3 paper endleaves (the first one pasted to purple silk lining) and 6 vellum leaves of which the first one is blank, the next two ([our "i" and "ii"]) contain 14th-century writing, and the three remaining ones seem to have been an integral part of the manuscript as originally conceived and written (cf. contents). The foliation ceases, for unknown reasons, with f. 464 (in the middle of the Letter to the Romans). At the end, following the unnumbered ff. [465–559], 4 free endleaves (1 vellum, 3 paper), the last of which is pasted to the purple silk lining conjugate with the silk doublure. — Written area of the main text is ca. 123 × ca. 80 mm (37 + 6 + 37 mm). — Fully ruled (incl. ruling for the running tiles) in what seems to be faint ink; the verticals are brownish throughout, the horizontals appear bluish and on some pages done in blind. The verticals do not reach all the way to the bottom edge, in spite of the cropping which clearly has occurred; some pricking is preserved in the tail margins. — Topmost line of the text is below the top-ruled line. — Main text is written in a small (ca. 840 words per page), carefully formed *littera textualis semiquadrata*, by obviously professional scribes. A peculiarity is the rather consistent use of the form of capital *N* based on the Roman monumental letter, with the (notched and/or bowed) vertical strokes (stems) joined by a horizontal, sometimes doubled. — The ink is brownish black to brown, of good quality; the writing material quite thin (text block ca. 46 mm thick = ca. 8.2 per 100 leaves), with an occasional defect. — The running titles in Lombardic letters, written across the two-page spreads, are entirely blue, with some minimal flourishing in red ink; blue are also the chapter numbers, always outside the text column, and the chapter-signaling capitals in the text to which the numbers in the margins relate. The chapters do not, as a rule, begin on a new line. — Incipit and explicit statements have never been added[12] although the scribes had provided blank spaces (graded) for them. — In parts of the book the capitals have been touched with red.

Collation: impracticable owing to tight binding.

Decoration: (a) 84 historiated initials, executed in Parisian style but with a choice of themes (see table B) found in Bibles of English rather than French origin.[13] They are for the most part 5 or 6 lines high, occasionally more (Haggai on f. 383r: 8 or 9 lines; James on 508r, 24 lines; the two compartments for the Gospel of John, on 451v, add to 25 lines); those indicating the traditional Psalter divisions, 2–3 lines. The color of the letters is purplish blue or mauve, on a lightly black-framed field of the other color, with some sparingly applied gold. Frequent extensions by variously shaped bars into the margins or between the text columns, in a matching palette, outlined in black, often include zoomorphic elements. (b) over 50 ornamental illuminated initials, similar to the historiated kind in coloring and shape preferences; height 2 to 4 lines (more for the letter *I/J*); many zoomorphic elements (including salmon-like fish, on ff. 487r and 489r). Used with the prologues.

Bound early in the 19th century in Paris by P. Bozérian Jeune (name on spine near the bottom edge): in very dark purplish blue or purplish black long-grain morocco; covers and spine stamped in gilt. On spine: BIBLIA//SACRA//MANUSCRIPTUS//IN// MEMBRANIS. — Reddish purple silk linings. Gilt edges. — Protected by a dark blue book-shape pull-off box made in the 20th century in Philadelphia; on its spine: BIBLIA SACRA//ILLUMINATED MANUSCRIPT//ON VELLUM//XIIITH CENTURY; near top, small square white label with "2" in gold.[14] — On verso of the first free endpaper (with the silk lining pasted to recto), armorial *Ex libris* of A. Brölemann (with "B 53" in ink), also recent label: "The gift of Lessing J. Rosenwald to the Library of Congress." On same page, in ink: Latina; also small label with: A/139.hx. On recto of next leaf, in pencil: K[?]–6091. — On recto of the last free endleaf at end (with verso pasted to silk lining), LC cataloger's note in pencil: "Bible. Manuscript. Latin. Rosenwald coll. ms. no. 5" (initialed: MLS 2 D 49). — On f. [iii] recto, in head margin, slightly cropped inscription in ink: Vacate et videte. Kenelme Digby.

Former owners: Sir Kenelm Digby (b. 1603, d. 1665); A. Brölemann; Mme Étienne Mallet; William Permain; W. R. Hearst; Lessing J. Rosenwald.

2° fo.: (f. [ii] r:) *Ge.* quīq[ua]ginta capitella dat — (f. 2r:) sci[enci]e fuit

Bibl.: Sotheby catalog of the Étienne Mallet sale, May 4–5, 1926 (item 2). — Faye and Bond (1962), p. 124, no. 160. — A. L. Bennett, "The place of Garrett 28 in thirteenth-century English illumination" (Ph.D. diss., Columbia U., 1973; University Microfilm DCJ 76–29050), p. 164–165, tables, and passim. — *The Lessing J. Rosenwald collection : a catalog* . . . (Library of Congress, 1977), p. 4 (no. 2)

NOTES

1. To be able to follow the medieval foliation which starts at the beginning of Genesis, I have assigned the numbers [i–v] to unnumbered leaves at the beginning which contain medieval writing (hence exclusive of the 4 leaves without text which precede them). For the unnumbered text leaves at end, I have continued the sequence of arabic numerals.

2. Cf. Berger, *Hist. Vulg.*, p. 345 (ms. Cambrai 401) for Deuteronomy; P. Martin, "Le texte parisien de la Vulgate latine," *LE MUSÉON* 9, p. [58] (Bib. nat. ms. lat. 14597) for Joshua. In both cases, the chapter division is archaic, i.e., predating Langton's 13th-century revision and the "University Bible." In our ms., the blue capitals used to indicate chapter beginnings were originally in agreement with what the *Ordinatio* commends but have been subsequently erased, corrected, or ignored when the chapter numbering was being added in the margins. That numbering agrees almost completely with what has eventually become standard.

3. In the present ms., blue capital in column *a* of f. 514v indicates the beginning of what at the time of the original writing was viewed as chapter II of the Letter of Jude.

4. The apocryphal book (Stegmüller 94, etc.; Latin incipit "Et fecit Josias Pascha") was included in the Parisian University Bibles and called in them "Esdre II"; it was not, or often not, included in the Bible copies made in 13th-century England. Cf. LC MSS 2, 4, also 7, and the MS 1 written perhaps in England; also the various Bibles described by N. R. Ker in his *Medieval manuscripts in British libraries.*

5. Two-line space left blank and a guide letter provided for an initialist to supply the capital *C* which, nevertheless, remained undone.

6. Cf. the "K" reading reported in the footnote apparatus in the Maurist edition of the Vulgate (Rome, 1926–), v. 1, p. 18.

7. See table B (Historiated Initials). — N.B. The actual biblical text begins only in the middle of the column 1ra, after the concluding lines of the prologue *Desiderii mei.*

8. For the concept of the Parisian "University" Bible see *The Cambridge History of the Bible*, v. 2 (1969), p. 1435 sqq.; also Branner, p. 16, etc.

9. The whole sequence in this ms.: Genesis, Exodus, Leviticus, Numbers, Deuteronomy; Joshua, Judges, Ruth; 1–4 "Regum" (= 1–2 Samuel and 1–2 Kings), 1–2 Chronicles (with the Prayer of Manasseh), Ezra, Nehemiah; Tobit, Judith, Esther, Job, Psalms, Proverbs, Ecclesiastes, Song of Solomon, Ecclesiasticus, Wisdom; Isaiah, Jeremiah, Lamentations, Baruch, Ezekiel, Daniel; Hosea, Joel, Amos, Obadiah, Jonah, Micah, Nahum, Habakkuk, Zephaniah, Haggai, Zechariah, Malachi; 1–2 Maccabees; (413v sqq.:) Matthew, Mark, Luke, John; Romans, 1–2 Corinthians, Galatians, Ephesians, Philippians, Colossians, 1–2 Thessalonians, 1–2 Timothy, Titus, Philemon, Hebrews; Acts; James, 1–2 Peter, 1–3 John, Jude; Revelation. — N.B. The switched order of Ecclesiasticus (Ben Sirach) and Wisdom is not caused by misbinding.

10. See table A (Prologues, etc.) for detailed listing. — Textual variants in the biblical text itself present in this copy would deserve study. I have noticed (f. 494ra, line 38) the reading "hoc donum quod . . ." in Acts II,33 (cf. LC MS 7 from Bohemia, and Berger, *Hist. Vulg.*, p. 74, footnote).

11. Cf. Stegm. 8263 sqq. (also v. 9, 8266); our text differs from all those listed there.

12. The red caption introducing Jerome's Letter to Paulinus on f. [iii] is an exception.

13. Dr. Bennett's thesis on the ms. Garrett 28 (available on microfilm, cf. bibl. at end of this description) includes comparative tables of historiated initials from a number of manuscript Bibles of English origin, incl. our MS 5 (= her Rosenwald 5). — It may be observed, on the other hand, that the eight rounded quadrilobe compartments of the Genesis initial in our ms. (not, however, the Six Days + Original Sin + Crucifixion thematic sequence) resemble the style of the Parisian Mathurin atelier, as do certain zoomorphic decorative elements (cf. Branner, p. 75–77, and illus. 166–173). Our artist seems to have learned his trade in Paris.

14. Corresponding to entry numbering in the 2nd edition of the Rosenwald Collection catalog (Library of Congress, 1977, p. 4).

MS 6

(Nekcsei-Lipócz Bible)

BIBLE IN LATIN ca. 1335–1340?

Written in Hungary?[1] Parchment. 2 volumes, 352, 394 leaves, ca. 450 × ca. 323 mm (bound volumes: 475 × ca. 348 mm) 2 columns. 33 lines.

Vol. I, recto of flyleaf (saved from the original binding) immediately preceding f. 1 (16th-century ADDITION, in current cursive): Ego Zulema[n] Qui fui orator Regis Ferdinandi Anno do[m]inj 1545 . . . (ca. 36 lines, end illegible, partly lost in repairs)

"A rambling account in Latin of the captivity among the Turks of Zuleman, envoy of King Ferdinand of Hungary"—M. Harrsen, *The Nekcsei-Lipócz Bible,* p. 41.[2] — See also our concluding comment.

Vol. I, f. 1r–vol. II, f. 394r: (vol. I, f. 1ra:) (F)[7] RATER amb[ro]sius . . . (5ra:) (D)[8]esiderij m[e]i . . . (5va:) . . . *Explicit p[ro]log[us]. Incipit biblia et p[ri]mo liber genesis.* (5vb:) (I)[33 +] N p[ri]ncip[io] c[re]auit . . . (vol. I, f. 352vb:) . . . p[ar]abolas uulgata edic[i]o p[ro]u[er] bia uocat. (vol. II, f. 1ra:) [coele]th q[uem] grece eccl[es]iaste[n].latine . . . (1rb:) (P)[8]Arabole salomonis . . . (394rb:) . . . cu[m] omnibus uobis. Amen. (394v blank)

The Vulgate Bible, with selection and order of books[3] as temporarily fixed in 13th century by the Parisian revision,[4] and a not very different apparatus of prologues.[5] — The chapter division as signaled, with extraordinary sumptuousness, by illuminated (2-line, generally ornamental) initials at the beginning of each chapter is quite standard; the numbering, apparently done last,[6] full of errors, leading to seemingly nonstandard final counts: thus, the Book of Numbers has its last chapter numbered "XXXV" (f. 96v) due to misnumbering of its ch. VII on f. 78v; in Deuteronomy, ch. XXIII is misnumbered "XIII" (f. 109r) and here, too, the error is continued to the end, making the last chapter "XXIV."[7] — The Psalms are numbered in a peculiar way, obvious errors[8] combining with the idea of counting each of the traditional sections of Ps. CXIX (in the Vulgate count, CXVIII) as another Psalm with its own number (on ff. 346v–348v: Pss. "CVII [*sic*, repeating number already used]–CXVII"). The highest-numbered Psalm is "CXLVII" (352va), being the Ps. CXLVIII of both the common and the Vulgate count; the remaining two are unsignaled and unnumbered.[9] — In vol. II, the Lamentations have their chapters numbered as a continuation of Jeremiah, through "LVII" on f. 124r.[10] —

MS 6

The Gospel of John has 23 chapters, John XIX,25–42 having been marked and numbered as "XX," and our XX,1–10, XX,11–31, and XXI,1–25 numbered as chapters "XXI" through "XXIII." — An odd division appears in the Letter to Romans: our I,13–17 is made into "II," and I,18–25 and I,26–32 are made into further chapters; in this way, the standard ch. II becomes "V" and, eventually, the last chapter, generally known as XVI, is numbered "XIX." — Greek expressions occurring in Jerome's introductory matter in v. I are handled (as they were, no doubt, in the scribe's exemplar) by attempted, mostly unsuccessful romanization and/or translation.[11] — The Hebrew book titles of Pentateuch books, found in the red captions of many medieval Bibles, are not mentioned; in vol. II, f. 1ra, "[co(h)ele]th"(?); 121 v, "Incipit lamentacio ieremie prophete quod est intitulo chinoth." — In Gen. XVIII, verses 4 and 5 have the readings "lauentur pedes uestri" and "confortetur cor uestrum"; Leviticus V,11, ". . . columbe . . ."; V,12, ". . . ex eo pugillum hauriens . . ."; Deut. II,19, "in uicinia"; Judges II,22, ". . . experiatur . . ."[12] — Joshua ends (131rb) with non-standard ". . . in monte effraim cum pace."[13] — (Judges XXI,12–24 and Ruth I,1–II,7 wanting due to missing leaves, cf. collation.) — The Prayer of Manasseh is separated from 2 Chronicles by explicit and incipit. — Ezra is called "primus liber Esdre" in its explicit; running title "ES/DS." — In Esther, Jerome's cautionary words before X,4, etc., are all written in black, as if part of text. — The Psalms (with two prologues, see note 5) are introduced by simple "Incipiunt psalmi Dauid"; individual psalms are treated as chapters and numbered (see above). The higher-grade initials (here 5- or 6-line, historiated) placed traditionally at the beginning of each liturgical division of the Psalter are found on ff. (v. I) 319v (for Ps. I, *Beatus uir*), 324v, 328r, 331r, 334r, 338r, 341v, and 345r (for the *Dixit Dominus*, with a half-length figure of Christ *en face*).[14] — The prologue to Proverbs (*Iungat epistola*, Stegm. 457) begins in the last column of v. I (f. 352vb, with a large picture of Jerome as a cardinal[15]) and continues in column 1ra of volume II. — The Prayer of Solomon at the end of Ecclesiasticus in vol. II, numbered as its ch. LII,[16] is followed (f. 54va) by *Nemo cum prophetas*, the prologue to Isaiah (Stegm. 482), erroneously understood as yet another chapter of the preceding and numbered "LIII" (!); followed further (55ra–56va) by a thoroughly unexpected list of 177 *capitula*[17] to Isaiah, written in black as if part of the biblical text, numbered as ch. LIIII, and concluded by "Explicit liber Ecclesiastici," on f. 56v. — At the beginning of the Lamentations (121va), after the incipit, the introductory "Et factum est . . . dixit." — (Daniel XIV, 15 through end and Hosea I,1 through IX,16 wanting due to missing leaves, cf. collation) — The New Testament, while not signaled with any emphasis in decoration or caption, begins (i.e., the prologues to Matthew begin) on a new page, f. 237v. Matthew has 29 chapters, due to division in two of our ch. XXVIII. Luke I,1–4 is called "ii prologus" and is separated from the Gospel by "*Explicit secundus prologus. Incipit Lucas euuangelista.*"[18] In John I,3.4, the interpretation (as communicated by interpunction, etc.) seems to be Parisian (f. 292rb, lines 6/7): ". . . est nich'.//Qd' f[a]c[tu]m e[st]. inip[s]o uita erat." (See above on the chapter division at end of John; also on the odd division of Romans.)

Location of the biblical books in detail:

(Vol. I:) Genesis (ff. 5vb–34va); Exodus (34vb–58v); Leviticus (58v–74r); Numbers (74v–96v); Deuteronomy (97r–116v); Joshua (117r–131r); Judges (131v–145v; XXI,12–24 wanting); Ruth (146r–147r; I,1–II,7a wanting); 1 Samuel (148v–169r); 2 Samuel (169r–185r); 1 Kings (185r–203v); 2 Kings (204r–221r); 1 Chronicles (222r–237v); 2 Chronicles (237v–257v), with Prayer of Manasseh (257vb–258ra); Ezra (259r–264v); Nehemiah (265r–273r); First Book of Esdras (Stegm. 94,1; 273r–282r); Tobit (282v–288r); Judith (288r–295v); Esther (295v–303r); Job (304r–318v); Psalms (319v–352v) (Last 18 lines of 352vb are from prologue Stegm. 457 which continues on what is now f. 1 of vol. II)

(Vol. II:) Proverbs (1r–13v); Ecclesiastes (13v–18r); Song of Solomon (18r–20v); Wisdom (20v–29v); Ecclesiasticus ("Multorum . . . agere" on 29v, text proper 29v–54v; includes at end the Prayer of Solomon); Isaiah (56v–85v); Jeremiah (85v–121v); Lamentations (121v–124v); Baruch (124v–129r); Ezekiel (129v–161v); Daniel (162v–174v; XIV,15-41 wanting); Hosea (175r–176r; I,1-IX,16 wanting) (176v blank) Joel (177v–179r); Amos (180r–183v); Obadiah (184r–184v); Jonah (185r–186r); Micah (186v–188v); Nahum (189r–190r); Habakkuk (191r–192r); Zephaniah (192v–194r); Haggai (194v–195v); Zechariah (196r–200v); Malachi (201r–202v); 1 Maccabees (203v–223r); 2 Maccabees (223r–237r); Matthew (238r–257r); Mark (257v–270r); Luke (270v–291v; Lk. I,1–4, separated as a prologue, on 270r); John (292r–308r); Romans (308v–316v); 1 Corinthians (316v–324v); 2 Corinthians (324v–330r); Galatians (330r–332v); Ephesians (332v–335v); Philippians (335v–337v); Colossians (337v–339r); 1 Thessalonians (339v–341r); 2 Thessalonians (341r–342r); 1 Timothy (342r–344r); 2 Timothy (344v–346r); Titus (346r–347r); Philemon (347rv); Hebrews (347v–353v); Acts (354r–375v); James (375v–377v); 1 Peter (378r–380r); 2 Peter (380r–381r); 1 John (381v–383r); 2 John (383v); 3 John (383v–384r); Jude (384rv); Revelation (385r–394r)

* * *

Modern foliation, in pencil, excludes: in vol. I, two free endleaves of thicker vellum in front and two at end, and a leaf preserved from the original binding, with 16th-century handwriting, inserted before f. 1; in vol. II, two endleaves of thicker vellum in front and two at end. — Written area ca. 314 × ca. 220 mm (two columns of ca. 100 mm width each, separated by space ca. 20 mm wide). — Fully ruled in diluted brownish ink, with 7 vertical lines per page; ruling for running titles in a different medium, crayon-like, bluish. — The script is a gothic *textura* of the Bohemian type,[19] perhaps all by one scribe who did his work in two major stages; or by two scribes distinguishable only by different form of their tironian *et*, perhaps also by interpunction.[20] Many contractions of the usual kind. — Black ink of excellent quality in vol. I, tending to brown in much of vol. II. — The rubricator's red used in the incipits and explicits, finished through the end, differs from the rather dull red and duller blue used in various combinations for chapter numbering and for the running titles, neither of which have been completed in the latter part of vol. II (from ca. 329v on); on the neglected pages, the otherwise systematic red touching-up of black capitals is also lacking. — The running titles are generally divided between the two pages of an opening, and strongly abbreviated. The *incipit* rubrics are often located at the end of the column which precedes the actual beginning of a text; the same is true about chapter numbers. — Guide numerals in cursive-style minuscule written in lead on many pages, in the margins. — Chapter beginnings clearly signaled by illuminated initials (cf. Decoration). — Rather rare paragraph-like marks, red or blue, are used exclusively to indicate that words written at the end of a line continue text from the line which precedes (at the end of chapters). — Parchment of fair quality; thickness ca. 20.6 mm per 100 leaves, color medium cream. Some medieval-style repairs; many tail margins replaced or reinforced in 19th-century rebinding.

Collation: Vol. I: i^{10}($i_{1,2}$ wanting, presumed blank) ii–xiv^{10}(= ff. 9–138) xv^{10}(xv_8 following f. 145 wanting, with text loss[21]) xvi–xxvi^{10}(= ff. 148–257) xxvii–$xxviii^{?}$(= ff. 258–273) xxix–xxxiv^{10}(= ff. 274–333) xxxv^{10}($xxxv_{10}$ detached, inserted in vol. II as its f. 1)

Vol. II: (f. 1 = $xxxv_{10}$ from vol. I) i–xvii^{10}(= ff. 2–171) $xviii^{10?}$(= ff. 172–176; $xviii_{4,5,6,7,8}$ following f. 174 wanting, with text loss[22]) xix–xxxix^{10}(= ff. 177–386) $xxxx^{10?}$(= ff. 387–394; $xxxx_{9,10}$ wanting, presumed blank). — The gatherings in both volumes have been numbered at a very early point, in red lowercase roman numerals placed in center of the lower margin on each final verso;[23] many of these have since disappeared, partly or completely, owing to cropping and repairs.

Decoration consists primarily of illuminated initials: numerous, lavish, original, and of considerable interest to art history.[24] Historiated initials (preserved are 122) introduce individual books, prologues, and the liturgical divisions in the Book of

MS 6 Psalms. Elaborate, variously inhabited borders on ff. 1r and 5v in vol. I, i.e., with the beginning of Jerome's introductory letter *Ad Paulinum* ("Frater Ambrosius . . .") and with the beginning of Genesis.[25] — There are also over a thousand illuminated initials which mark the beginning of each chapter; these are generally 2 lines high, with well-designed extensions in various colors; for the most part they are floral, quite a few, however, contain faces, perhaps portraits. Reddish laid gold has been used extensively; contrary to the usual practice it appears to have been applied after rather than before the painted artwork had been completed. — The themes of the historiated initials are partly traditional (shared with many 13th-century Bibles),[26] partly, it seems, original, taken perhaps afresh from reading the biblical texts, or at least the first few sentences of each ("Posui ori meo custodiam" with Ps. XXXIX; the "Congregans congregabo omnia" of Zephaniah I,2; *et al.*). The relatively rare use of historiated intials also with the prologues produced some unusual ideas: e.g., with the prologue to First Maccabees (vol. II, f. 203r) an image of Hrabanus Maurus writing his letter to Geroldus about that book. Elsewhere, it has made possible completing one idea with another: the book of Tobit begins with a picture of the young man's blind father; the prologue to it, with one of the young Tobias outfitted for travel (on his head, a hat which, I believe, is late medieval Hungarian, and/or Slovak). — The border on f. 1r includes, at top, a ship and a hunt; in the lower margin, St. Peter, Annunciation, Nativity, Three Kings, and St. Paul. The Genesis page (5v), with the initial words beginning the second column and the Creation series built into a page-high letter "I," has in the lower margin, perhaps to represent the Day of Rest, an (allegorical) scene dominated by enthroned Christ; it includes, together with other only tentatively interpretable elements, the representation of a church edifice which is being offered to the Lord by a man and a woman, with the assistance of an angel.[27] (See plate III, p. xviii.)

Binding: by (Charles) Hering of London, (early) Victorian; very thick (ca. 12 mm) boards covered in greyish blue-green morocco, heavily blind-stamped. In center of each cover, coat of arms of Henry Perkins, gold-stamped, with initials *HP* in the manner of a crest. On spine, in gold: BIBLIA// SACRA//LATINA//MANNSCRIPTUM *[sic]*// IN MEMBRANIS//SAECULI XIV//I(–II). — In vol. I, a clipping from a sale catalog is pasted to the vellum lining of the lower cover ("200 BIBLIA SACRA LATINA . . ."; not from the Gadsden or Quaritch lists).

2° fo.: (vol. I:) mus. Qui aūt docti fu[er]int. fulgeb[un]t q[ua]si — (vol. II:) cordis tui. [et] i[n]uenies gr[ati]am [et] discipli

Former owners: Count Demeter Nekcsei-Lipócz (d. 1338); Henry Perkins, brewer and collector (d. 1855); Algernon Perkins (son of Henry; d. ca. 1873). — Acquired by the Library of Congress at the Perkins sale (through Quaritch) in 1873.

Bibl.: (Ellis Gadsden & Co.) *Catalogue of the . . . library formed by the late Henry Perkins, Esq. : first day's sale, June 3, 1873:* p. 21, no. 174. — (B. Quaritch) *A list of the chief books and manuscripts of the Perkins library, May and June 1873:* no. 1. — (Walters Art Gallery, Baltimore) *Illuminated books of the Middle Ages and Renaissance: an exhibition . . .* (1949): no. 160 and pl. LXII (reduced black and white reproduction of f. 1r). — M. Harrsen, *The Nekcsei-Lipócz Bible : a fourteenth century manuscript from Hungary in the Library of Congress . . .* (1949) (includes slightly reduced color reproduction of f. 5v and many in black and white). — Faye and Bond (1962): p. 117, no. 1. — (F. Levárdy, ed.) *Magyar Anjou legendárium* (Budapest, 1973): passim in introduction. — Reduced color reproductions in C. A. Goodrum, *Treasures of the Library of Congress* (New York, 1980): on p. 44, (vol. II) the opening 192v–193r; p. 45, parts of (vol. II) ff. 85v, 183v, 308v.

It was M. Harrsen's conclusion (*op. cit.*) that this Bible was executed for Count Demeter Nekcsei-Lipócz, a prominent official in the court of Charles Robert of Anjou, King of Hungary (1310–1342); final judgment on this may best be left to Hungarian scholars. Our doubts: The coat of arms on f. 5v seems to have been painted into the two shields only after the rest of the decoration had been completed, including the laying of gold (which had been, contrary to the usual procedure, done last, i.e., after the artwork); and the heraldic work was done by a considerably less skilled hand than the rest: the "argent" (white) of the arms covers at one point a part of the shield-holding hand (over the left text column); the sword of the *issuant* youth over the right column is painted over the already laid gold; his face is, in both cases, drawn in a primitive manner never used by the artist of the surrounding decoration.[28] — The conjugate leaves 2 and 5 in vol. I were not written by the same scribe or at least not in the same phase of his writing activity as the surrounding leaves. The text on 2v, second column did not originally tie in with its continuation on 3r, and the chapter VI of the prologue (Videlicet manifestissima est . . .) had to be started a second time, with empty lines in between.[29] — The Bohemian-type gothic script, strangely out of step with the Bolognese early-Renaissance style of the decoration, may have been in use throughout Central Europe: one may note, though, that of the two instances of such use in what was the Kingdom of Hungary brought up by Harrsen, one (the Széchényi Library Missal Cod. Lat. 214) was written in the rather cosmopolitan Bratislava (= Pozsony = Pressburg), the other (the Esztergom Missal of the Batthyaneum in Alba-Iulia = Gyulafehérvár) in Čukárovce (now Veľké Trnie), ca. 10 miles NNE of Bratislava, by a priest of German origin. — It is not at all impossible that the book was originally written in one place and eventually decorated elsewhere.[30] — One final point concerns the whereabouts of our Bible in 16th century: the Zuleman document written on the flyleaf (at that time perhaps sig. i_1 or i_2) in vol. I in or about 1550 (Harrsen, p. 67–68) was very probably written outside of what is now Hungary. In 1550, most of what is now Hungary, including Buda and Esztergom, was under Turkish control; Ferdinand, who was also king of Bohemia and "King of the Romans" and resided in Vienna was retaining title only to what is now Slovakia plus a narrow strip of Hungary east of the Austrian border; the Archbishop of Esztergom resided in Bratislava. It is not at all likely that Zuleman would have been writing his document inside the Turkish-occupied territory; or, indeed, far from the court (in the 9 lines in the left margin not included in the translation printed in Harrsen, *op. cit.*, p. 67, he seems to be asking for merciful treatment). — None of the preceding calls into doubt, it should be observed, M. Harrsen's central thesis about the existence of a Bologna-inspired atelier in Hungary under Charles Robert of Anjou and about the provenience of the artwork in our Bible from that atelier.

NOTES

1. Decorated almost certainly in Hungary; probably also written there, or at any rate within the area then controlled by the Crown of St. Stephen. — Our description is partly indebted to the 1949 monograph by Meta Harrsen (1891–1977), *The Nekcsei-Lipócz Bible* (Washington, 1949), which seems to be in need of revision (a new study by Ferenc Levárdy has recently been announced). (N.B. Harrsen used Hungarian toponymy for the whole area in question but many of the places she mentions are in Slovakia. See also our concluding commentary.)
2. Reproduction of the document, *ibid.*, pl. I; English translation, *ibid.*, p. 67.
3. Detailed listing, with folio numbers, at end of the contents note.
4. Cf. our notes and references in descriptions of MSS 2 and 5. — The distinction drawn in M. Harrsen's study (p. 4 and 43) between the Vulgate and the Parisian version is a misunderstanding.
5. Of the 64 prologues standard in the Parisian-revision Bibles (see table A) the Nekcsei-Lipócz ms. has all but three, two of them (Stegm. 500 and 507) very likely once present and only lost with the partial disappearance of gathering *xviii*. Unexplained is the absence of the prologue to 2 Chronicles (*Quomodo Graecorum,* Stegm. 327). — Prologues not expected in a Parisian-revision Bible are the two

which precede the Psalms: on f. 319r, the "Dauid filius Yesse . . ." (= Stegm. 430; with faulty "portare" at end); quite unexpected also in vol. II the *capitula* to Isaiah (see comment above) and the additional prologue to Obadiah on 183vb (beginning in line 26)–184ra: "Esau filius Ysaac frater Iacob uocatus est eciam edom . . . contra Ydumeos ergo loquitur hic propheta" (not found in Stegmüller). Some of the standard prologues are more or less unusual variants, notably that to Joshua (Stegm. 311) in vol. I, f. 116r, here beginning "Hic tandem finito . . ." Stegm. 677 begins (vol. II, 308r): "Romani sunt partis . . ."; ignorance or fatigue produced, on f. 375v of vol. II, a pseudovariant of Stegm. 809: "Est donita [*sic*] ordo apud Grecos . . ."

6. While the illuminated initials of chapter beginnings are finished throughout, and so are the red incipits and explicits of individual books and prologues, the chapter numbering (along with running titles which, like the numbers, alternate red with blue) remained undone in much of the latter part of vol. II (beginning ca. on f. 329v); on such pages, also the red touching-up of ordinary black capitals is lacking. — In much of the two volumes, chapter numbers had been indicated by means of guide numerals written (or hastily scribbled) in the margins, in a grayish medium (lead?).

7. Similar errors in vol. II in Ecclesiasticus, Isaiah, Ezekiel, Daniel. In 1 Chronicles, the final count of 30 chapters is caused by a separation of verses XVI,8–43 as ch. XVII (ff. 230v–231r). Ezra has 9 chapters because the present ch. III is not marked.

8. "XXXI" is followed by "XXII", this continued until "CVII" for CXVII on f. 346r.

9. But present: beginning 352va, line 25 and 352vb, line 6 respectively (this corrects Harrsen, *op. cit.*, p. 42). — Both the joining of these three Psalms and the splitting of Ps. CXIX into several are vestiges of liturgical use.

10. Beginning with "LV" for our Lam. II. — The *Oratio Ieremiae* (= Lam. V) is not included in the count, given instead its own incipit and explicit statements (f. 124va).

11. Only "Logos" is correct. *θεοδίδακτοι* is rendered (f. 2ra, lines 10–11) "oronatyrim.theodoctilact' docibiles d[e]o" = rather like in Bib. nat. lat. 10431 (of XIIth c.) or even closer Bib. nat. lat. 60 (XVth c.). (Cf. the Maurist ed. of Vulgate Genesis, Rome, 1926, p. 12.)

12. I have spelled out contractions. The *u* for *v* even in initial position is characteristic of the scribe.

13. Variant not listed in the Stuttgart 1975 edition.

14. Marking the beginnings of Pss. I, XXVII (Vulg. XXVI), XXXIX (Vulg. XXXVIII), LIII (Vulg. LII), LXIX (Vulg. LXVIII), LXXXI (Vulg. LXXX), XCVIII (Vulg. XCVII), and CX (Vulg. CIX) respectively. (N.B. As mentioned, the Psalms are variously misnumbered.)

15. Harrsen, *op. cit.*, p. 45, has incorrectly "351v." The picture is damaged by water.

16. The chapter ("Et inclinauit Salomon genua sua . . . uir iuxta te") is not a usual ingredient of Parisian-revision Bibles. (Cf. table A.)

17. Not so or otherwise captioned. Inc.: "Sermo Domini super Ierusalem et Iudam . . ."; ends: ". . . et de apostolis et de populo." — The summary, an obvious relic from pre-Parisian Bibles, reflects one of the older chapter divisions of Isaiah found also in Bib. nat. lat. 15178 (cf. Berger, *Hist. de la Vulgate*, p. 351 sq.).

18. So spelled, with "*uu*" (cf. "ewangelium" and "ewangelista" in the Bible MS 7, from Bohemia).

19. "Bold, handsome, laterally compressed letters" — Harrsen, *op. cit.*, p. 6. There is a distinctive final *s* resembling our numeral 6. A similar *s* in scripts of similar type appears, e.g., in cod. 365 of the Schottenstift in Vienna, written in 1374 in Dobersberg (48°54' N, 15°19' E) (reprod. in *Katalog der datierten Handschriften . . . Österreich,* Bd. V, 1981, pl. 37); in Österr. Nationalbib. cod. 537 written in Prague in 1386 (reprod. Kirchner, *Scriptura gothica libraria,* 1966, p. 30); in Stockholm, Kungl. Bib. ms. A 155, of 1331, place of origin unknown (reprod. in *Katalog der datierten Handschriften . . . Schweden,* Bd. II, 1980, pl. 6).

20. In one form of the *et* the vertical shaft has a left-pointing bump instead of a crossline; this form is used in all of vol. I except on the (conjugate) leaves 2 and 5; also in vol. II through f. 296va. The other form has the vertical shaft crossed by a thin line; it is used on the two leaves 2 and 5 of vol. I and in vol. II on ff. 270r (or 269vb) through end.

21. Wanting: Judges XXI,12–Ruth II,7; with probably one historiated initial.

22. Wanting: Daniel XIV,15–41; (probably) prologues Stegm. 500 and 507; and Hosea I,1–IX,16. This doesn't seem quite enough to fill 5 leaves (needed would be only ca. 14 columns), and the original composition of the gathering remains unclear. The lost leaves included probably two historiated initials.

23. Where preserved, the numbers end with the superscript "*-us*" sign; they must have been read as ordinal numbers.

24. M. Harrsen seems to have been first to realize its importance and to postulate the existence of a workshop of illuminators at the court of Charles Robert of Anjou (King of Hungary from 1310 to 1342) in Buda. More recently, the artwork has been discussed (in Hungarian) by F. Levárdy in his introduction to *Magyar Anjou Legendárium* (Budapest, 1973). The Legendarium or Passionale in question (unfortunately split into the Pierpont Morgan Library's ms. 360, Vatican Lat. 8541, and further fragments) seems to share with our Bible the same principal artist, perhaps identifiable as a Master Hertul, known to have been sponsored and favored by the king. (A layman may note with interest, e.g., the striking resemblance of the face of Christ appearing in our Bible, v. I, on f. 5v in lower left-hand corner, to that in the initial to Ps. CIX on f. 345r and passim elsewhere in the Legendarium.) — Results of Dr. Levárdy's research concerning more directly our

Bible are expected in connection with a facsimile edition being considered in Hungary. — M. Harrsen's monograph includes many black-and-white reproductions.

25. This latter reproduced in color, slightly reduced, as frontispiece in Harrsen, *op. cit.* It includes in the head margin two shields with the coats of arms of Count Demeter Nekcsei-Lipócz: *argent* two bars *sable*, on a chief *azure* the head and shoulders of a youth holding in his right hand a sword in bend sinister proper. — It is, however, doubtful that the arms were done by the artist of the surrounding decoration (cf. our concluding comment). — Another coat of arms, possibly relevant, appears in the initial to Joshua (v. I, f. 117r): Paly of eight *or* and *sable* (black-and-white reproduction in Harrsen, plate IVc).

26. For a listing of the themes used for initials to the Bible books see our comparative tables at end (table B); for the whole series in the present Bible, with themes also to the prologues, cf. Harssen, *op. cit.*, p. 44–48.

27. Cf. Harrsen, *op. cit.*, p. 44. — It may be possible to identify the church. The suggestion has been made that it resembles a still-surviving structure known as "Jáki templom," near Szombathely in W. Hungary; that one was, however, built in mid-13th century.

28. None of this is very clear in the 1949 reproduction used as frontispiece in Harrsen.

29. The leaves 2 and 5 were written by whoever completed the last third of vol. II; presumably as substitutes for lost (or intentionally discarded?) original ones.

30. Demeter Nekcsei-Lipócz was made *Comes Trenchinensis* (Trenčín, Slovakia) by Charles Robert after the defeat (1312) or death (1321) of the quasi-independent ruler Máté Csák who, joining or fighting sovereigns as he himself pleased, had achieved control over much of Slovakia in the early part of 14th century. Máté did have Bohemian contacts. Cf. G. Kristó, *Csák Máté tartományúri hatalma* (1973). — Count Demeter's Aba clan had vast possessions in what is now northeastern Slovakia, in the region called Spiš in Slovak, Zips in German, Szepes in Hungarian, where town population was largely German (cf. the fresco from St. James Church in Levoča, fig. 8 in Harrsen's book). His favorite estate is said to have been Hanusfalva = Hanušovce nad Topl'ou, near Prešov; it was presumably he who granted the place its township and market rights, in 1332.

MS 7

(Faye and Bond 70)

BIBLE IN LATIN early XVth c.

Written in Bohemia. Parchment. 381 leaves, ca. 265[1] × ca. 175 mm (bound volume: ca. 280 × ca. 195 mm) 2 columns. 61 lines.

ff. 1ra–351rb: (F)[13]Rater Ambrosius . . . (3ra:) (I)[17]N p[ri]n[cipio] creauit deus . . . (351rb:) . . . cu[m] om[n]ib[us] vobis Amen

The Vulgate Latin version of the Bible, with books of the Old Testament in the usual order[2] and, in the New Testament, the Acts placed after Paul, before the Catholic Epistles.[3] — The 2 Chronicles does not include at end the Prayer of Manasseh; Ecclesiasticus ends with ch. LI (no Prayer of Solomon). — In the New Testament, Luke's Gospel begins, startlingly, with "Fuit in diebus Herodis" (f. 294rb), i.e., the introductory verses Lk I,1–4 are omitted.[4] — Of the 64 prologues which had come in 13th century to be standard equipment of the Vulgates produced in Paris and then of most copies made elsewhere, 53 are included;[5] absent are Stegm. 327, 344, 507, 510, 513, 521, 538, 547, and 553 in the Old Testament, Stegm. 699 (to 2 Corinthians) and 772 (to 2 Timothy) in the New. Peculiar to our ms. are, in the Old Testament, the prologue to Joel (f. 253ra) which is Stegm. 508b (In hoc propheta idcirco nec reges . . .) followed by the usual Stegm. 511; the variant beginning words of the prologue to Jonah (Stegm. 524, on f. 255vb, "Hunc prophetam . . ."); the employ of Stegm. 539 (In anno secundo . . .), normally prologue to Zechariah, to introduce Haggai (f. 259vb) while Zechariah is given a variant version of Stegm. 540 ("Zacharias qui nominatur memoria Domini . . . asinae subiugalis," on f. 260va). — New Testament begins (f. 278va) with the prologue Stegm. 595 ("Beatissimo pape Damaso Jeronimus: Novum opus facere me cogis . . .") followed by Stegm. 596 ("Plures fuisse qui . . . canendas," without last sentence). The prologue to Luke, Stegm. 620 (f. 294rb) has a variant beginning: "Lucas ewangelista[6] Syrus nacione Antiocensis . . ." (and the scriptural prologue is completely omitted, see above). The Second Letter to the Corinthians is introduced by Stegm. 702 (f. 318va, "Quibusdam Corinthiorum . . . elemosinas mitti") and divided into 14 chapters.[7] The prologue to 1 Thessalonians, on f. 325rb, appears closer to Stegm. 748 than to the usual 747; that to Hebrews (f. 329ra) mixes elements of Stegm. 793 and 794. The usual Stegm. 809 (Non ita est ordo . . .) before the Catholic Epistles is followed (f. 342va) by: "Quia in circumcisione ordinatus erat Jacobus . . . sic et absentes per epistolam consolari, increpare, instruere conatur" (= Stegm. 810 with a variant ending?). — On ff. 346vb–347ra (following the usual prologue to Revelation *Omnes qui pie volunt*, Stegm. 839): "Iohannes de testimonio Iesu Christi . . . testificari vobis hic in ecclesia" = 26 summarizing phrases.[8] The Greek words occurring in several passages of Jerome's letter to Paulinus (Frater Ambrosius . . .) are treated variously: in last line of f. 1rb the scribe attempted Greek majuscule (for ΛΟΓΟΣ), with mixed result;[9] for *θεοδίδακτοι*, in same column, the text gives only the supposed Latin equivalent ("docibiles deo"); "epitomen," in line 34 of f. 2rb, is successfully romanized. — No Hebrew names are offered for the books of the Pentateuch; on f. 109va, however, the red caption reads: *Incipit liber dabreiamin* [*or dabreianim*] *.i. p[ar]ali[pomenon] .i. v[erb]a dierum*. — The Psalms, ff. 157vb– 174rb, are captioned "liber hymnorum vel soliloquiorum prophete David de Cristo." Painted initials mark the liturgical divisions of the Psalter[10] except the last one; another, not much later hand noted in the margin (f. 170va) in red: *d[o]m[ini]co die ad ve[speras]*; further marginal notes in red on ff. 171–173 signal psalm sets used in the Vespers on other days of the week.[11]

On f. 187r, in tail margin, a footnote referred to by means of a three-dot symbol in red ink near the verse Wisdom XVII,2 is a translation of that and of the next verse into Old Czech, in pre-Hussite orthography.[12]

In the Gospel of John, I,4–5 (f. 304ra), the manuscript has, marked by capital *Q*, the reading "Quod factum est in eo vita erat";[13] in Acts II,33 the "Hoc donum quod," corrected (f. 332vb) in the margin to the standard "Hunc quem."[14] (Text of Acts IV,16 is standard over erasures, f. 333rb.)

351rb–381vb: *AAz* app[re]he[n]de[n]s . . . (381vb:) . . . co[n]siliatores eorum (one line omitted, then:) explicit scutu[m] fidei q[uo] pugna[n]t filij Dei (next line, in red:) *Amen zpieway kazdy dobry Amen*[15] (remaining 38 lines of the column blank)

The vocabulary known as *Interpretationes Hebraicorum nominum* (Stegmüller 7709), commonly included in 13th-century Vulgates and some later copies; followed by the scribe's explicit and the line in Czech.

* * *

Foliated in modern pencil. Two free paper endleaves in front, two at end (no watermarks). — Written area ca. 194 x ca. 127 mm. — Fully ruled in brownish diluted ink, incl. lines for running titles; the verticals are 4 to a page. Some pricking preserved.[16] — Written in a neat but somewhat crowded gothic cursive, with over 900 words to a page, by several skilled scribes. Good black to brownish black ink; some powdering-off in last two gatherings. — Good quality parchment; thickness 17–20 mm per 100 leaves. — Red running titles in somewhat larger script of same kind, sometimes one per page, sometimes divided between the verso of one leaf and recto of the next; none in the book of Psalms. Red are also the captions (explicits and incipits; not always given), Psalm titles ("in finem," *et sim.*), and the chapter numbers, which are mostly but not always within the text column, in spaces provided by the black-text scribe. Capitals and some other letters are touched with red; red also used for interpunction. Both the touching up and the interpunction remained to a large extent undone on ff. 188r–191r, 192v–198r, 199v–227r, 237v–252v, 258v–264v, 269v–278r, 300rb–308r, 348v–351r, and 352r–381r.[17]

Collation (using the medieval roman numbering found in center of the tail margin on last verso of most gatherings): i–[xxxi]^{12} [xxxii]$^{4?}$(= ff. 373–376) [xxxiii]$^{4+1?}$(f. 379 a singleton?)

Decoration: ca. 100 initials, 80 of them painted; the latter begin the books, in the

Old Testament also the prologues; also several segments of the Book of Psalms. Seven are historiated:

1r (the *F* of "Frater Ambrosius . . ."): Jerome at his writing desk, in a cardinal's red hat and garb; the letter is blue and bluish white

3r (*I* at the beginning of Genesis): standing male figure in blue robe; letter purplish pink of two shades

16v (*H*Ec sunt . . ., Exodus): a seated king (pharaoh?) in blue garb, with crown; letter is green of two shades and yellow

27v (*U*Ocauit . . ., Leviticus): standing Moses (with horns) in a garment shaded from whitish to light purple, on dark-blue ground relieved by orange hairline curves; letter green of two shades and yellow

35v (*L*Ocutus . . ., Numbers): Moses on his knees; painted landscape and sky; letter purplish pink of two shades (see plate IV, p. xix)

46v (*H*Ec sunt verba . . ., Deuteronomy): standing white-haired Moses with a group of three smaller figures, on painted-gold ground with an olive cast;[18] letter purplish pink in two shades

157v (*B*Eatus vir . . ., Psalms): David with crown and psalter, in muted purplish pink garb, on dark blue ground; letter dark green, light green, and yellow

The letters of the painted initials are generally of the Lombardic type; each is of one basic color with three-dimensionally conceived acanthine foliage in various, generally lighter shades of same hue; the whole set into an inconspicuous quasi-rectangular field of contrasting color relieved by lighter lines of white, yellow, or other color. The infilling of the area enclosed by the letter is often in a different hue than the slightly protruding rectangular field outside: the outer part may be blue lightened by white hairlines, the inside darkish red purple relieved by orange; *et sim.* — Leafy, mostly acanthiform[19] extensions of various length and curvature (no straight stems) issue from the painted letters into the margins; they are colored in different combinations of the green, purplish pink, and blue which are used for the letters; also rather skillfully shaded for three-dimensional effect.[20] Laid gold is not used at all.

Decorated calligraphic initials 2 to 7 lines in height are used for the ca. 20 prologues in the New Testament, and in two cases in the Old: at the beginning of the fifteenth chapter[21] of 2 Samuel (f. 87v, a 12-line *I/J*) and to begin the First Book of Esdras (136r). They are usually blue (on the purplish side), with skillfully done red-ink infilling and flourishing; in a few cases, the blue letter has some red within the blue; the out-of-order *I/J* on 87v is decorated with white-and-red flowers. — Two-line lombardic letters, alternately red and blue, indicate the chapters.

Binding: yellowish-white (ivory) vellum over stiff boards, probably 18th century. Reddish lettering piece pasted on spine, with title tooled in gold: BIBLIA SACRA.// Manucriptum.[*sic*]//Saeculi XII. — On inside of front cover, ownership label of Rev. Edwin A. Dalrymple, also label of B. Westermann & Co., New York; in pencil: Temp. no. 2. On recto of first free endleaf, in pencil: Ac. 4560(3), n. 1; also: MS. 70 (corrected from earlier "98"); other penciled numbers. On inside of lower cover, pasted clipping from a 19th-century English sale catalog ("408 Biblia sacra Latina, cum Prolegomena [*sic*] S. Hieronymi, Saec. XII") which gives the number of leaves as 380; it prizes the book at £ 16.16.0.

Former owners: Benedictine abbey Ochsenhausen in southwest Bavaria, perhaps until its suppression in 1803;[22] from ca. 1870 to 1916 in the collection of Rev. E. A. Dalrymple, Baltimore; acquired by LC in 1916 from Rev. Dalrymple's nephew Nathaniel D. Sollers (Ms. Ac. 4560,3,1).

2° fo.: re[m] terre de pet[ra] deserti ad mo[n]te[m] fi[lie] syon Sa

Bibl.: De Ricci, *Census* (1935), p. 229, no. 98 ("written in Germany"); Faye and Bond (1962), p. 119, no. 70.

The manuscript comes from a time of intense theological controversy in Bohemia. Two questions are particularly intriguing: Why were the not especially famous or difficult verses from the Wisdom of Solomon (cf. contents, f. 187r, and note 12) selected for Czech rendering? Could the handwriting of the gloss be identified as that of one of the Czech followers or adversaries of Jan Hus involved in his trial at the Council of Constance? — Hus was burned at the stake in Constance in 1415; the most natural explanation of the Bible's straying to the monastery of Ochsenhausen, one day's ride distant, would seem to be that it was deposited there after the grim outcome of the trial.

NOTES

1. Cut inexactly, making the vertical dimension vary from 262 to 267 mm.

2. That is, as rather generally in Vulgates of the period: the Pentateuch, Joshua, Judges, Ruth, I–IV "Regum" (= 1–2 Samuel and 1–2 Kings), 1–2 Chronicles ("Paralipomenon"), Ezra, Nehemiah, "II Esdre" (= First Book of Esdras, Stegmüller 94,1), Tobit, Judith, Esther, Job, Psalms, Proverbs, Ecclesiastes, Song of Solomon, Wisdom, Ecclesiasticus, Isaiah, Jeremiah, Lamentations, Baruch, Ezekiel, Daniel, Hosea, Joel, Amos, Obadiah, Jonah, Micah, Nahum, Habakkuk, Zephaniah, Haggai, Zechariah, Malachi, 1–2 Maccabees.

3. The order is that established in Paris in the 13th century (the Acts were not repositioned into their present place immediately after the Gospels until shortly before the Council of Trent). It is also the order found in Old Czech translations (through at least the 1498 printed edition *GW* 4324) which, however, include in the N.T. the pseudo-Pauline Letter to Laodiceans (Stegm. 233), absent from the present ms. — Cf. Berger, *Hist. Vulg.*; also V. Kyas' introduction to v. I (1981) of the Prague Academy edition of the Czech "versio antiquissima" (*Staročeská bible drážd'anská a olomoucká*, v. I, p. 16–17).

4. Same omission occurs in Old Czech translations: cf. *Staročeská bible drážd'anská* . . . (op. cit.) v. I, p. 194–195; also S. Graciotti, *La bibbia paleoboema della Biblioteca di Brera* (Milano, 1964), p. 186. — In many medieval Bibles the verses were included as one of the prologues (cf. table A, LC MSS 2, 3, 4, 6, and 8).

5. See table A. (The table includes other elements besides the 64 prologues; for a narrower listing and for explanation of the count see Ker, *Med. mss. in Brit. libs.* 1, p. 96.)

6. The manuscript uses "ewangelium" and "ewangelista" throughout; in the older Czech orthography (as in today's German) *w* stood for the voiced fricative /v/.

7. Chapter XII of the now standard division is split, making our 2 Cor. XII,14–21 a separate chapter XIII.

8. Cf. Berger, *Hist. Vulg.*, p. 362, Apocalypse, V (the codex with what seems to be the same series of *capitula* as that in LC MS 7 is identified as "Reg. Hisp.").

9. The scribe's gamma resembles lowercase roman *t*; the final sigma, an *e* (in the exemplar or even farther back it must have been *C*-form).

10. Cf. note 2 in description of LC MS 4.

11. "Feria 2ª" through "feria sexta."

12. *Nebo kdiz ssu sye zly vradili chtycze panowaty swate*[*mu*] *pokolenij tu sie gie zlybylo wiecznі*[*mu*] *obmyslenij aby byly vwrzeny wnokowy tempne dlube noczi yako zbyczy vnyczeny(?) Nebo kdyz mnye by sye vtagili wtemnych hrziessiech wtemniem przikritij swebo zapomenutye rozprasseny ssu bogiecze sie hroznye welykymy zazraky ssucze zamuczeny.* — The orthographic reform introduced by Jan Hus (his *De orthographia Bohemica* of 1406), although certainly not immediately accepted by everybody, was followed in Czech Bibles of ca. 1430. Cf. A. Novák, *Přehledné dějiny literatury české*, 4th ed. (1939), p. 66.

13. This interpretation seems to be common to the Parisian-revision Vulgates (cf. LC MS 4; but also MS 5); it was followed in the Old Czech translation (cf. *Staročeská bible drážd'anská* . . . (op. cit.) 1, p. 292–293; Graciotti, *op. cit.*, p. 186). The Clementine Vulgate (1592) and the Tridentine Missal have more or less canonized the reading ". . . quod factum est. In ipso vita erat . . ."

14. Suggesting dependence of what Berger considered the Languedoc form of Vulgate? Cf. his *Hist. Vulg.*, p. 74. — I haven't been able to check any Old Czech Bible on these points.

15. The (Old Czech) words mean: Amen Let every good (man) sing Amen.

16. Chiefly for the vertical lines; on ff. 160–167 also for some of the horizontals.

17. The neglected parts are in the last third of the Vulgate Old Testament, including the Major Prophets; in the N.T., parts of Luke and John and the end of the Revelation; most of the *Interpretationes* are neglected also in other ways. The blue or red lombardics which signal chapter beginnings have been made throughout, except in the *Interpretationes*.

18. Artwork perhaps more primitive than in the initials which precede.

19. A somewhat different shape, with (pointed) three-lobe element, enters in the New Testament (ff. 279v, 288v, 294r, 304r). — Leafy decoration ceases after the four Gospels.

20. The style resembles, on a less luxurious level, that of some better-known manuscripts from Bohemia or Moravia: e.g., the *Boskovice Bible* (Olomouc, Czechoslovakia, University Library, M III 3) of ca.

1420(?) (cf. E. Petrů, *Z rukopisných sbírek Universitní knihovny v Olomouci* (1959), p. 33)

21. The chapter tells the story of Absalom's rebellion and his end.

22. Two different stamps of the abbey appear in the tail margin of f. 1r (the more recent one, with "Sig. Biblioth. Ochsenhusan.," twice). — Relatively much is known of the Ochsenhausen library, incl. its manuscripts; a large number of them (over 40) are preserved together in the library of castle Kynžvart in Czechoslovakia (cf. F. Čáda, *Rukopisy Knihovny Státního Zámku v Kynžvartě* [Praha, 1965; with a summary in French]). I haven't found any reference to our Bible in sources seen so far.

MS 8

(Giant Bible of Mainz)

BIBLE IN LATIN

April 4, 1452–July 9, 1453

Written in Mainz? Parchment. 2 volumes, 244, 215 leaves, 576 × ca. 405 mm (bound volumes: 590 × ca. 420 mm) 2 columns. 60 lines.

Vol. I, ff. 1ra–244ra: *Incipit epistola beati Iheronimi presbiteri ad Paulinu[m] de omnibus diuine historie libris Capl'm primum.* (F)[13]Rater Ambrosius . . . (2va:) *Incipit liber Genesis qui Hebraice Bresith dicitur. Capitulu[m] Primum.* (I)[16]N principio creauit . . . (244ra:) . . . tempore suo. *Explicit Liber Ecclesiastici.*

Vol. II, ff. 1ra–215rb: *Incipit Prefacio btī Iheronimi presbiteri. In libro ysaie prophete.* (N)[7]Emo enim (i.e., cum?) prophetas . . . (215rb:) . . . cum omnibus vobis. Amen. *Explicit liber apocalipsis btī Johannis apostoli.* (followed by a colophon on mounted blank piece of vellum which replaces cut-out lower right portion of the leaf:) *Finis veteris ac noui testamenti tociusq[ue] biblie. quam Calamus fidelis anno dñi Millesimo quadringentesimo quinquagesimo secundo, quarta aprilis inchoando . nona iulij anni sequentis superno iuuamine consummauit.*

A sumptuous copy of the Vulgate, in 2 volumes: (I) Genesis (ff. 2v–17r); Exodus (18r–30r); Leviticus (31r–39v); Numbers (40r–50v; XXII,13–XXVIII,14 wanting); Deuteronomy (51r–62r); Joshua (63v–71r); Judges (72r–80r); Ruth (81r–82r); 1 Samuel (84r–94v); 2 Samuel (95r–103v); 1 Kings (104r–114r); 2 Kings (115r–124r); 1 Chronicles (125v–134r); 2 Chronicles (135v–145r + Prayer of Manasseh, 146v); Ezra (147v–150v); Nehemiah (151r–155v); "*Liber Esdre secundus*" (= Stegm. 94,1; ff. 156r–160v); Tobit (161v–164v); Judith (165v–169v); Esther (170v–174r); Job (176r–183v); Psalms (187r–207r + Ps. 151 + 14 canticles and other liturgical items, 207v–217v); Ecclesiastes ("*liber Celeth* [sic] *idest Ecclesiastes,*" 219r–221r); Song of Solomon ("*Sirasirim idest Cantica canticorum,*" 222r–223v); Wisdom (224v–229v); Ecclesiasticus ("Multorum . . . agere" on 230r, text proper 230v–244r);

(II) Isaiah (1v–17r); Jeremiah (18v–36v); Lamentations ("*Lamentaciones . . . quod est in titulo Cynoth,*" 37r–38v); Baruch (39v–41v); Ezekiel (42r–57v; wants XXXIX,14–XLI,13); Daniel (58r–65r); Hosea (67v–69v); Joel (70v–71r); Amos (72v–74r); Obadiah (75v); Jonah (76v–77r); Micah (78v–79v); Nahum (80v–81r); Habakkuk (83rv); Zephaniah (84r–85r); Haggai (86r); Zechariah (87v–90r); Malachi (91v–92r); 1 Maccabees (93v–103r); 2

MS 8 Maccabees (104v–111v); Matthew (114v–124v); Mark (125v–131v); Luke (132v–143v; Lk I,1–4 separated on 132r); John (144v–152v); Romans (154v–158v); 1 Corinthians (159v–163r); 2 Corinthians (164v–167r); Galatians (168v–169v); Ephesians (170r–171v); Philippians (172v–173r); Colossians (174v–175r); 1 Thessalonians (176v–177r); 2 Thessalonians (178v); 1 Timothy (179v–180v); (following f. 180, a lacuna: 2 Timothy, Titus, and Philemon wanting) "*Epistola Pauli ad Laodicenses*" (! = Stegm. 233; on 181r); Hebrews (182v–185r); Acts (186v–197r); James (199v–200v); 1 Peter (201v–202v); 2 Peter (203v–204r); 1 John (205v–206v); 2 John (207v); 3 John (208v); Jude (209v); Revelation (210v–215r).

The order of the books is that found in other continental Bibles of the period, with the First Book of Esdras[1] following Nehemiah in the Old Testament, and with the sequence Gospels–Paul–Acts–Catholic Epistles–Revelation in the New.[2] Less common is the inclusion of the 151st Psalm ("Pusillus eram inter fratres meos . . . ," Stegm. 105,3) and of the liturgical material[3] in v. I and, in v. II, of the Letter to the Laodiceans. — The red captions (running titles, incipits, explicits) include more Hebrew titles, however distorted, than one would expect: besides the "Bresith," "Ellesmoth," "Vagechra," "Vagedaber," "Addebar" for the books of the Pentateuch, also "Masloth" for the Proverbs, "Celeth" for the Ecclesiastes (= Koheleth), "Sirasirim" for the Song of Solomon, "Cynoth" for the Lamentations. — Ignorance of Greek is displayed, as usual, in the copying (disastrous attempt to imitate Greek majuscule) and romanization ("theodidasi" for θεοδίδακτοι, etc.) of expressions occurring in Jerome's prefatory texts (1r–2r). — The Prayer of Manasseh (Stegm. 93,2) at end of the Second Book of Chronicles is captioned as such (in last line of f. 146r: *Or[aci]o Manasse filij Ezechie*). — The "Liber Esdre secundus" is divided into 9 chapters. Some peculiarities in chapter numbering are merely a result of the rubricator's error (in Tobit, the caption "Capitulum septimum" occurs twice, making the final count 14), some correspond to the unsettled situation (Judith XV and XVI made one chapter; variously irregular numbering in Esther). — Job XXXII,1: "Amiserunt . . ." — The Psalms are captioned "*liber canticorum seu soliloquiorum prophete* ['David' is omitted!] *de Christo*"; individual Psalms are numbered, mostly in spelled-out form; the traditional liturgical divisions are marked by (unfinished) 8-line initials (ff. 190ra, 191vb, 193vb, 195va, 198ra, 200ra, 202rb). — In the Song of Solomon, rubrics suggest interpretation: "*Vox ecclesie ad Christum*," "*Vox Christi*," "*Vox synagoge*." — Ecclesiasticus has 51 chapters (no Prayer of Solomon at end). — In v. II, the first Aleph of the Lamentations is preceded by the introductory sentence "Et factum est . . . et ejulans dixit";[4] Daniel ends with the even less frequent verse numbered XIV,42 in the Clementine Vulgate, "Tunc rex ait . . . de lacu leonum." — The beginning of the New Testament (v. II, f. 112 sqq.) is not signaled as such.[5] In the Gospels, the rubricator uses the spelling "ewangelista." In Matthew XVIII, before what is in today's numbering verse 15[6] (Si autem peccaverit in te . . .) our ms. has (f. 120rb, line 12): "Et respiciens Ihesus discipulos dixit Symoni Petro." Luke I,1–4 is separated from the rest of the gospel as a prologue. John I,3–4 (f. 144va, 6th line) is written as ". . . est nichil. Quod factum est in ipso vita erat." In Acts II,33 (f. 187ra): ". . . effudit hoc donum quem vos videtis et auditis"; Acts XIII,6 (f. 191ra, last line): ". . . quod interpretatur paratus." The highly variable verses 7–8 in ch. V of the First Letter of John (f. 206rb) have, except for an "et" added or omitted, the same wording as in the Clementine Vulgate.

A conspicuous feature of this Bible is the number and prominence of its prologues.

To the 64 prologues made more or less standard in the 13th century, the Giant Bible adds 53 (marked in our listing by asterisks):

Volume I:

f.	Book	Prologue	Stegmüller no.
f. lr	General prologue	Frater Ambrosius	284 incomplete!
2r	Pentateuch	Desiderii mei desideratas	285
63r	Joshua	Tandem finito	311
		* Josue vero filius Naue . . . spiritalia regna describit. cf. Stegm.	307
83r	Samuel, Kings	Viginti et duas	323
125r	Chronicles	Si septuaginta	328
135r	2 Chronicles	Eusebius Ieronimus Dominioni et Rogaciano . . . salutem. Quomodo Grecorum . . .	327 var.
147r	Ezra	Utrum difficilius	330
161r	Tobit	Chromacio et Heliodoro episcopis Ieronimus . . . salutem. Mirari non desino . . .	332 var.
		* Thobias filius Ananihel . . . iacet in Niniue humatus. (from Isidorus Hisp., *De ortu*, with variant ending)	5190 var.
165r	Judith	Apud Hebraeos	335
		* Judith vidua filia Merari . . . inter Dothan et Balmon. (from Isid. Hisp., *De ortu*)	5191 var.
170r	Esther	Librum Esther variis	341
		Rursum in libro	343
175r	Job	Cogor per singulos	344
175v		Si autem fiscellam	357
		* In terra quidem habitasse	349
		* Job exemplar patiencie	350
184r	Psalms	* Psalterium est ut Hieronymus ait	424
		* Dum multa corpora librorum	384
		* Legi litteras apostolatus vestri	398
		* Nunc autem exposuimus originem	407
184v		* Nunc itaque exposuimus libros . . . per capita. Psalterium dicitur a . . .	406
		* Psallere qui docuit dulci moderamine sanctis . . . (10 verses, through:) . . . gratia vocis (poem once falsely ascribed to Jerome; text. ed. in *Epigrammata Damasiana*, ed. A. Ferrua [1942], p. 224–225)	
		* Nunc Damasi monitis aures prebete benignas . . . (15 verses, graphically not separated or distinguished from the preceding; ending:) . . . tuos monstrare triumphos (= pseudo-Damasian *In laudem Davidis*; text. ed. in *Epigrammata Damasiana*, p. 224–225 [no. 60])	
185r		* *De libro scī ysidori episcopi.* Liber psalmorum quamquam uno . . . ut voluit.	5193
		* Canticum psalmorum animas decorat . . . (par.) Canticum psalmorum carmen electum est . . . (par.) Qui diligit canticum psalmorum . . . mirificabit in secula seculorum. Amen. (from pseudo-Augustinian *De virtute psalmorum*) cf. Stegm. 369	
		* *Origo prophetiae regis Dauid* . . . Dauid filius yesse cum esset in regno . . . ex persona Dauid dicuntur. cf. Stegm. 414	
185v		* *Incipit inquisicio seniorum de psalterio et psalmis.* Psalterium inquirendum est in cuius lingua . . . de quo dicitur inferius Pusillus eram inter fratres meos. cf. Stegm. 426	
186r		* *Epistola Iheronimi ad Paulam et Eustochium.* Psalterium rome dudum positum [sic; for "positus"] . . .	430
		* Nudius tercius cum centesimum octauum decimum	405
186v		* *De dictis beati Iheronomi excerptum.* Qui psalmi proprie ad singulos dies feriatos . . . Joseph dicit qui corpus domini sepeliuit.	437

(207 r, rubric preceding the apocryphal Ps. 151:) *Hic psalmus Dauid proprie ponitur extra numerum ut superius in prologo dictum est.)*

f.	Book	Prologue	Stegmüller no.
210r	Proverbs	Cromacio et Eliodoro episcopis Ieronimus presbiter. Iungat epistola . . .	457
218r	Ecclesiastes	Memini me hoc ferme quinquennio	462
		* *Item alius prologus.* Petrus. Queso te quid sit quod Salomon ait, Dixi . . . spirituali veritate diffiniuit. (= ?)	
222r	Song of Solomon	* Tribus modis vocatum fuisse Salomonem . . . magister est et nescit te esse regem. cf. Stegm. 456	
224r	Wisdom	* Tres libros Salomonis	455
		Liber sapiencie	468
230r	Ecclesiasticus	Multorum nobis et magnorum . . . vitam agere.	26,(1)

Volume II:

f.	Book	Prologue	Stegmüller no.
1r	Isaiah	Nemo cum prophetas	482
18r	Jeremiah	Ieremias propheta cui hic prologus	487
		* Ioachin filius Iosie	490
		* Ieremias Anathites qui est viculus	486
39r	Baruch	Liber iste qui Baruch nomine	491
42r	Ezekiel	Ezechiel propheta cum Ioachim rege	492
58r	Daniel	Danielem prophetam iuxta septuaginta	494
66r	Minor Prophets	Non idem est ordo	500
67r	Hosea	Temporibus Ozie et Ionathe [sic]	507
		* Osee crebro nominat Effraim	506
70r	Joel	Sanctus Ioel	511
		* Ex tribus igitur generibus rethorum . . . prouocare reddidit attentos ad mirans futurum malum ut considerantes venture cladis asperitatem ocius acciperent penitenciam. cf. Stegm. 508	
		Iohel filius Fatuel	510
72r	Amos	Ozias rex cum dei religionem	515
		Hic Amos propheta non fuit tempore [sic; for "pater"] ysaie prophete . . . patribus suis.	513 var.
		Amos pastor et rusticus	512
75r	Obadiah	Iacob patriarcha fratrem habuit	519
		Hebrei hunc esse dicunt	517
		* Abdias seruus domini qui interpretatur	516

Folio	Book	Prologue	No.
76r	Jonah	Sanctum Ionam Hebrei affirmant	524
		Iona columba dolens . . . Tyberiadem.	521
		* Ionas columba pulcherrima . . . denunciat.	522
78r	Micah	Temporibus Ioathe . . . denunciat.	526 var.
		* Micheas de Morasti . . . Israel.	525
80r	Nahum	Naum prophetam . . . libri huius demonstrabitur.	528 (incomplete? var.?)
		* Naum consolator orbis	527
82r	Habakkuk	Quatuor prophete . . . invenire desiderat.	531
		* Hic in principio voluminis describit dyabolum . . . (ca. 165 words, ending in 82va:) . . . quid est nisi tropheum crucis. (=? Continuation of the prologue by Hugo a S. Caro?)	
82v		* Vocabulum autem saluatoris hic propheta proprie ponit . . . (ca. 30 words, ending:) nominare et predicare. (=? May be continuation of the preceding)	
		* Abacuc luctator fortis	529
84r	Zephaniah	Tradunt Hebrei	534
		* Sophonias speculator et archanorum domini	532
86r	Haggai	Ieremias propheta ob causam	538
		* Aggeus festiuus et letus	535
87r	Zechariah	Secundo anno Darii . . . est reuelata.	539 var.
		* Zacharias memor domini dei sui . . . subiugalis.	540
91r	Malachi	Deus per Moysen	543
		* Malachias aperte in fine . . . oblatio munda.	544
93r	1 Maccabees	Domino excellentissimo . . . Lodouico regi. Rabanus . . . salutem. Cum sim promptus . . .	547
		* Machabeorum liber licet non . . . requiescunt.	552 var.
104r	2 Maccabees	Reuerendissimo domino et omni [sic] caritatis dignissimo Geroldo . . . salutem. Memini me in palacio vuangionum . . . dignetur.	553
		Machabeorum libri duo prenotant prelia	551
112r	Gospels	* (*Incipit Epistola seu Prefacio beati Iheronimi presbiteri Ad Damasum papam in quatuor ewangelistas.*) Beatissimo pape Damaso Iheronimus. Nouum opus me facere cogis . . . papa beatissime. ora pro me.	595
112v		* Plures fuisse qui ewangelia scripserunt . . . quam ecclesiasticis viuis canendas.	596
114r	Matthew	Matheus ex iudeis sicut in ordine primus ponitur . . . non tacere.	590
		Matheus cum primum predicasset	589
125r	Mark	Marcus ewangelista electus dei et Petri . . .	607
132r	Luke	Lucas syrus nacione anthiocensis, arte medicus	620
		(Quoniam quidem multi . . . ueritatem = Luke I,1–4)	

Folio	Book	Prologue	No.
144r	John	Hic est Iohannes ewangelista . . . doctrina seruetur.	624
153r	Paul	* (*Incipit prefacio beati Ieronimi presbiteri de corpore epistolarum beati Pauli apostoli.*) Epistole pauli ad romanos . . . melior factus est.	651
153v		* (*Incipit alia prefacio in epistolas Pauli.*) Primum queritur quare . . . mànentem substanciam in celestibus.	670 var.
154r	Romans	* Romani sunt qui ex iudeis gentibusque crediderunt . . . cohortatur.	674 var.
		Romani sunt partes [sic; for "in partibus"] ytalie . . . scribens eis ab athenis siue a chorintho per timotheum et per feben dyaconissam.	677 var.
159r	1 Corinthians	* (*Incipit prologus in duas epistolas pauli apostoli Ad Chorinthios.*) Epistola prima ad chorinthios multas causas . . . acciones.	690
		Chorinthij sunt achaici et hi similiter ab apostolis audierunt . . . suum.	685
164r	2 Corinthians	* (*Incipit prologus in secunda Epistola . . .*) In secunda ad chorinthios epistola . . . sectantes.	697
		Post actam a Corinthiis . . . (23 words) . . . ostendens.	699
168r	Galatians	(*Incipit argumentum in Epistola . . .*) Galathe sunt . . . ab epheso.	707
170r	Ephesians	Ephesij sunt . . . per Tytum dyaconum.	715 var.
172r	Philippians	Philippenses sunt Macedones	728
174r	Colossians	(*Incipit argumentum in epistola Pauli ad Colocenses.*) Colosenses et hij sunt . . . ab epheso per tychicum dyaconum et onesimum acolitum ab urbe roma [sic]	736 var.
176r	1 Thessalonians	Thessalonicenses sunt macedones in xpō ihesu. Hij . . . et onesimum. Non solum ipsi perfecti erant sed alij eorum verbo profecerunt et exemplo. Laudando ergo eos apostolus ad maiora prouocat et inuitat. (cf. Stegm. 747, 749, 746)	
178r	2 Thessalonians	Ad Thessalonicenses secundam . . . notum fecit eis . . . per Tytum diaconem et Onesimum acolitum.	752 var.
179r	1 Timothy	Tymotheum instruit . . . a macedonia per Thitum dyaconum	765 var.

(Prologues to 2 Timothy, Titus, and Philemon, possibly also one to the Letter to the Laodiceans, wanting owing to missing leaves xx_{1-4} after f. 180)

Folio	Book	Prologue	No.
182r	Hebrews	In primis dicendum est cur apostolus	793
186r	Acts	(*Incipiunt prologi . . . In libro actuum apostolorum.*) *Canit psalmista, ambulabunt	633
		Lucas nacione syrus . . . medicina.	640
		* Actus apostolorum nudam . . . medicinam.	631

198r	Catholic Epistles	Non idem ordo est . . . denegabo.	809
		* Iacobus, Petrus, Iohannes, Iudas septem	807
199r	James	* Iacobus apostolus sanctum instituit clerum . . . et mendacio [! for "et de mandatione"] magistrorum.	806 var.
201r	1 Peter	* Symon petrus . . . exhortatur.	816
203r	2 Peter	* Per fidem huic mundo . . . manifestat. Amen.	817
205r	1 John	* Iohannes racionem verbi . . . occasio.	822 var.
207r	2 John	* Vsque adeo ad sanctam feminam	823
208r	3 John	* Gaium pietatis causa	824

(On 209r, an initial I without text where a prologue to the Letter of Jude would be expected; the initial would fit Stegm. 825 or 826. N.B. The text may have been written, then erased!)

210r	Revelation	*(Incipit prologus in libro apocalipsis . . .)* Omnes qui pie . . . hoc est et parabole salomonis.	839 var.
		* Apocalipsis Iohannis tot habet sacramenta . . . intelligencie.	829

Liturgical texts which follow the Ps. 151 and the explicit "*finit psalterium a beato Iheronimo presbitero emendatum*":
(207r:) *Canticum ysaie prophete* (Confitebor tibi Domine . . . = Is. XII,1–6) *Canticum Ezechie* (Ego dixi in dimidio . . . = Is. XXXVIII,10–20) *Canticum Anne* (Exsultavit cor meum . . . = 1 Sam. II,1–10) *Canticum Moysi* [sic] (Cantemus Domino . . . = Exodus XV,1–19)
(207v:) *Canticum Abbacuc prophete* (Domine audivi auditionem tuam . . . = Hab. III,2–19) *Canticum Moysi* [sic] *ad filios Israhel* (Audite caeli . . . = Deut. XXXII,1–43)
(208r:) *Ymnus trium puerorum* (Benedicite omnia opera . . . = Dan. III,57–88.56) *Canticum Zacharie prophete* [!] (Benedictus Dominus Deus Israel . . . = Luke I,68–79)
(208v:) *Ymnus sancti Ambrosii episcopi* (= Te Deum laudamus) *Canticum sancte Marie virginis* (Magnificat . . . = Luke I,46–55) *Canticum Symeonis* (Nunc dimittis . . . = Luke II,29–32) *Dominica Oracio* (Pater noster . . .) *Symbolum apostolorum* (Credo in Deum . . .) *Fides Athanasij episcopi* (Quicunque vult . . . , ending on 209r)

* * *

Foliated in ink (19th century?). — Written area ca. 348 × ca. 244 mm (two columns of ca. 105 mm width separated by ca. 32 mm). — Fully ruled in faint brownish ink, incl. the pages left blank. — Very regular *littera textualis formata*, one hand throughout (cf. the colophon quoted in contents). Ink black to grayish black. — High quality material with both sides quite uniform (split calfskin?); thickness ca. 25 mm per 100 leaves.

Running titles, complete over each page, are red with first letter blue.[7] Captions (mostly in the "incipit" form), explicits, and the (mostly spelled-out) chapter numbers are red.[8] Three-line letters which begin the chapters are alternately red or blue; so are the paragraph marks used to signal subdivisions inside a chapter.[9] Most capitals are touched with red. — The rubricator's red ink undergoes a marked change between v. I and II: it turns from the bright red mostly characteristic of red ink to a more opaque, thicker, and darker appearance the color of clotted blood (deep red).

Collation: Vol. I: a^{10}($a_{1,3,4}$ wanting, with loss of text on a_3 and a_4;[10] a_2 = f.1) b–e^{10} f^{10}($f_{1,2}$ wanting, with text loss;[11] f_3 = f.48) g–z^{10} aa^{10} (aa_9 = f. 244; aa_{10} detached, made f. 1 in v. II) (N.B. The signature alphabet in v. I clearly includes or included *p, q, r, s, t, v, w, x, y, z,* and *aa.*)

Vol. II: aa_{10}(= f. 1) bb–ff^{10} gg^{10} (gg_4 following f. 54 wanting, with text loss[12] hh–oo^{10} (= ff. 61–130)[13] qq–vv^{10} (= ff. 131–180)[14] xx^{10} (= ff. 181–186; xx_{1-4} wanting, with text loss[15]) yy–zz^{10} $[aaa]^{10}$($[aaa]_{10}$ wanting; the colophon pasted on f. 215 is probably a part of it). — Catchwords on last verso of each gathering in the tail margin, possibly written by the scribe of the text. Signatures, by a different hand, in lower right corner of first rectos and lower left of last versos; in v. I they are cropped through *r*; in v. II, fully or partly preserved are: *aa-ee, nn*(?), *qq*(?), *rr, ss, tt, vv, xx,* and *yy*.

Decoration: initials, mostly unfinished, and some borders; in part famous (cf. Bibl.). — Several historiated initials of considerable charm, probably by more than one artist, have been completed in volume I:

f. 1r (Ad Paulinum): Jerome at his desk, in a cardinal's outfit, with a lion at his feet (13/24-line *F*). — Associated with this, a richly populated and colored vine-based all-around border (unframed) with mostly realistic birds, animals, semi-naked humans or humanoids, an unidentified coat-of-arms, and in the tail margin a mask joining together the two main strands of the vine.

f. 2r (Desiderii mei . . .) Jerome in cardinal's hat and white surplice over blue robe receives letter from a kneeling messenger (8-line *D*). — Extensions of the letter into the inner and head margins support a pearl, a monkey, a jay, and a cat.

f. 2v (Genesis) God Creator in a round medallion next to the 16/28-line initial *I/J*. — The once silver-framed medallion which includes also, under a rainbow, a castle and a miniature chase scene with deer is more or less a part of an all-around multicolor border with sundry living creatures, realistic or grotesque (but no semi-naked humanoids), and flowers; like the one on f. 1r, the border is unframed and based on entwined vines.

f. 135v (2 Chronicles) Queen of Sheba visiting Solomon (11-line *C*) (see plate VI, p. xxi)

f. 170v (Esther) Ahasuerus and Esther (in an otherwise only outlined 20-line *I*).

The art (or at least the borders) on ff. 1r, 2rv, also on 18r (with the beginning of Exodus) (see plate V, p. xx) and 31r (Leviticus) where variously inhabited borders accompany ornamental (uninhabited) initials, is thought to be by a single artist, christened, on this assumption, the Master of the Giant Bible.[16] His work stopped at that point; the excellent miniatures on 135v and 170v are by others. — For the rest of v. I and most of v. II much gold leaf has been laid in and near the generous spaces left out by the scribe (11-line high for initial letters of the Bible books, 7- or 8-line for the prologues[17]). Outlines of the letters and some amount of ornamentation have also been drawn;[18] no more historiated initials seem to have been contemplated.

In v. II some colorful, not very high-grade, often garish work on the initials appears on ff. 207rv, 208rv, 209r (an initial without text, cf. contents in the listing of prologues), 209v, 210rv. Branch-like extensions, where included (207v, 208v [with a bird], 209v [with a bird and a puppy], 210v) seem in part to imitate the borderwork of v. I. — In the Revelation (v. II, 210v–215r) the 3-line Lombardic letters which start the chapters received considerable flourishing, with a not unpleasant effect.

Binding more or less contemporary: undecorated white pigskin over partly beveled wooden boards; sewn over 9 bands. Remnants of leather-hinged clasps, two per volume. Headbands have red, white, and green sections.

Pastedown of front cover in v. I is a fragment from a manuscript office book for choir use, with readings for St. Andrew and responsories with music (plainchant notation). Mounted on it, a label inscribed in ink: "No. 5–6//Bibbliorum latinorum Pars I & II, vollendet 1453.//Jacobs Beitr. II, p. 15//Falk, XVIII Beiheft zum Centralblatt fur Bibliothekswesen (1897) p. 21. u. 112f." — On f. 1r of v. I in tail margin between the text and the decorative border, inscription in ink, " Anno 1566 Henric. a Stockheim cantor mogunt. posteror. mem. prodidit"; a similar inscription is on inside of the front cover in v. II. — Pressmarks ("M.N.5") on insides of front covers, and oval stamps BIBLIOTHECA//DVCALIS//GOTHANA on rectos of first leaves (between the text columns) of both volumes.

Former owners: Heinrich von Stockheim;[19] Cathedral of Mainz (from ca. 1566 to 1631); (seized in 1631 by Gustavus II Adolphus of Sweden and given to:) Bernhard, Duke of Saxe-Weimar (d. 1639); Ducal Library, Gotha; Lessing J. Rosenwald; given by Mr. Rosenwald to LC in 1952.

2° fo.: (v. I:) *Incipit prefacio beati Ih'onimi presbiteri.* — (v. II:) (running title:) *Liber ysaie prophete.* (black text:) domini exercituum super omnem superbum

Bibl.: *BEITRÄGE ZUR ÄLTERN LITTERATUR ODER MERKWÜRDIGKEITEN DER HERZOGL. ÖFF. BIBLIOTHEK ZU GOTHA* (/ hrsg. von Fr. Jacobs u. F. A. Ukert) 3. Heft (= Bd. 2, Heft 1) (Leipzig, 1826), p. 15 sq.

— F. Falk, "Die ehemalige Dombibliothek zu Mainz," in *BEIHEFTE ZUM CENTRALBLATT FÜR BIBLIOTHEKSWESEN* 18 (1897), p. 571 and 662–663. — Faye and Bond (1962), p. 125, no. 168 (with additional bibliography) — D. Miner, *The Giant Bible of Mainz, 500th anniversary* (LC, Washington, 1952) — *The Rosenwald Collection, a catalogue* . . . (LC, Washington, 1954), p. 1 (no. 4) — *The Lessing J. Rosenwald Collection, a catalog* . . . (LC, Washington, 1977), p. 4 (no. 5)**[20]**

Black-and-white reproductions of parts of ff. (v. I) 135v, 18r, 2v, and 170v in D. Miner's 1952 study above. — A reduced-size color reproduction of f. 2v (the beginning of Genesis) in the 1977 Rosenwald Collection catalog. — A color reproduction of the lower left quadrant of f. 1r of v. I serves as frontispiece to the 1966 study *Gutenberg and the Master of the Playing Cards* by H. Lehmann-Haupt (Yale University Press) (also minor reproductions in black and white). — Several reduced-size color reproductions (all from v. I) in C. A. Goodrum, *Treasures of the Library of Congress* (New York, 1980): on p. [43], whole f. 1r; p. 42, parts of ff. 2r, 18r, 31r.

NOTES

1. = "Liber Esdre II" in the terminology of this and other medieval Bibles which (in agreement with the 13th–century Parisian redaction) included the book as an integral part of the scriptural canon (see also table A). "Liber Esdre primus" referred to Ezra.

2. The terms "Vetus ac Novum Testamentum" make their appearance only in the colophon. In some medieval Bibles, awareness of the New Testament as a distinct entity was shown by a particularly ornate or otherwise emphasized initial at the beginning of Matthew (or of its prologue). In our volume II there is an otherwise unexplained stub, neatly cut, between the ff. 111 and 112, i.e., between the O.T. and the N.T. Could something like a "special title page" have been planned? (N.B. The stub is between the first and second leaves of the apparently complete gathering *nn*.)

3. See at the end of contents.

4. The sentence is absent from most important early manuscripts of the Vulgate (cf. the Stuttgart critical ed.) but it eventually found its way into the Clementine official text of 1592. In LC Bible manuscripts it is sometimes written as the last sentence of the prophecies of Jeremiah; cf. table A.

5. But see note 2.

6. There is no verse numbering in this or other medieval Bibles.

7. The running titles, also the incipits and explicits, while all in the same script, differ sometimes from the black text in spelling (e.g., "Colocenses" vs. "Colosenses" in v. II, 174v–175r).

8. The rubricator (was there only one?) was directed by (roman) guide numerals; sometimes, especially in v. II, also by titles scribbled with lead (?) in the margins. These aids have partly survived (in v. I beginning with ca. f. 70; in v. II, more, including a directive for the running title on f. 167r).

9. In v. I, the shape of the paragraph mark changes in the vicinity of f. 100 (the convex part becomes a triangle).

10. Wanting: last two-thirds of Jerome's letter *Ad Paulinum*.

11. Wanting: Numbers XXII,13 (end of verse) through XXVIII, 14 (beginning of verse).

12. Wanting: Ezekiel XXXIX,14 (end of verse) through XLI,13 (most of the verse).

13. No loss of text although "*pp*" seems to have been, puzzlingly, skipped.

14. In v. II, the alphabet of signatures clearly did not include "*ww*."

15. Wanting: both the prologues and the texts of 2 Timothy, Titus, and Philemon.

16. Possibly (as suggested by D. Miner in her 1952 study, cf. Bibl.) identical with the Master of the Playing Cards (*Meister der Spielkarten*, cf. Thieme-Becker, v. 37 [1950], p. 316). On this question see also H. Lehmann-Haupt, *Gutenberg and the Master of the Playing Cards* (New Haven, Yale University Press, 1966).

17. For each book which has one or more prologues, at least one was to have an illuminated initial; of the fourteen prologues given to the Psalms, six are introduced in this manner. In other cases the beginning of a distinct text is shown less clearly: often by paragraph indention, sometimes by a 3-line red or blue versal; and sometimes the scribe was simply unaware that he was dealing with more than one item, e.g., in the case of the two pieces of poetry on f. 184v in v. I.

18. In a manner called by Dorothy Miner (*op. cit.*, p. 29) "paltry" and "feeble."

19. "Mainzer Domdekan und Propst von St. Alban" — H. Schneider, *Der Text der Gutenbergbibel* (Bonn, 1954), p. 32. (N.B. On that and the next page, interesting observations on the text of our Bible, more distant, in the general framework of Vulgate transmission, from that of the Gutenberg Bible than other manuscripts from Mainz.)

20. Assuming its retention the catalog notes also the number which the Giant Bible had been given in what is now referred to as the "old manuscript shelflist": "Rosenwald Collection ms. no. 28." — One of the two volumes (on a rotating basis) is always on exhibit in the Great Hall on the first floor of the Library of Congress Thomas Jefferson Building, opposite the Gutenberg Bible.

TABLE A—Prologues in Library of Congress Manuscript Bibles

	Prologues, etc., expected in Parisian Bibles (Stegm.)	(Initium)	MS 1[1] (Bond 72)	MS 2 (Bond 71)	MS 3 (Rosenwald 31/3)
(Ad Paulinum)	284	Frater Ambrosius	S 284	S 284	S 284
Pentateuch	285	Desiderii mei	S 285	S 285	S 285
Joshua	311	Tandem finito	S 311	S 311	S 311
Judges					
Ruth					
1 Samuel	323	Viginti et duas	S 323	S 323	S 323
1 Chronicles	328	Si septuaginta	S 328	S 328	S 328
2 Chronicles	327	Quomodo Grecorum	S 327	S 327	S 327
Prayer of Manasseh	93,2	Domine omnipotens	Omitted (added in another hand at end)	Included, as part of ch. XXXVI	Included, as part of ch. XXXVI
Ezra	330	Utrum difficilius	S 330	S 330	S 330
First Book of Esdras	94,1	Et fecit Josias Pascha[2]	Omitted (added in another hand at end)	S 94,1	S 94,1
Tobit	332	Mirari non desino	S 5190?[3] (Tobias filius Ananihel . . .) + S 332	S 332	S 332
Judith	335	Apud Hebreos	S 5191[3] (Judith vidua . . .) + S 335	S 335	S 335
Esther	341	Librum Esther	S 341	S 341	S 341
	343	Rursum in libro	S 343	S 343	S 343
Job	344	Cogor per singulos	S 344	S 344	S 344
	357	Si autem fiscellam	S 357 + S 350	S 357	S 357
Psalms		No prologue	(Psalms wanting: missing gatherings)	—	—
Proverbs (resp. Libri Salomonis)	457	Iungat epistola	S 456 S 455 S 457	S 457	S 457
Ecclesiastes	462	Memini me hoc ferme	No prologue	S 462	S 462
Song of Solomon		No prologue	—	—	—
Wisdom	468	Liber sapientie	S 468	S 468	S 468
Ecclesiasticus	26,1	Multorum nobis	S 26,1	S 26,1	S 26,1
Prayer of Solomon[5]	1	Et declinavit Salomon genua . . . (. . . vir iuxta te)	Included	Omitted	Omitted

MS 4 (Bond 19)	MS 5 (Rosenwald 5/2)	MS 6 (Nekcsei-Lipócz)	MS 7 (Bond 70)	MS 8 (Giant Bible of Mainz)
S 284 S 285 S 311	S 284 S 285 S 311 + S 307 Jesus filius Nave . . .	S 284 S 285 S 311 va. (Hic tandem finito . . .)	S 284 S 285 S 311	S 284 (partly lost) S 285 S 311 + S 307? (Josue vero filius Nave . . .)
S 323 S 328 S 327 Included, as part of ch. XXXVI	S 323 S 328 S 327 Included, as part of ch. XXXVI	S 323 S 328 Omitted Included, separately captioned	S 323 S 328 Omitted Omitted	S 323 S 328 S 327 Included, separately captioned
S 330 S 94,1	S 330 Omitted	S 330 S 94,1	S 330 S 94,1	S 330 S 94,1
S 332	S 332 + S 5190? (Thobias Ananihel . . .)	S 332	S 332	S 332 + S 5190 var. (Thobias filius Ananihel . . . humatus)
S 335	S 335	S 335	S 335	S 335 + S 5191 (var.?) (Judith vidua . . .)
S 341 S 343	S 341 + (unsignaled) S 342 (Rufini in) S 338 (Esther in)	S 341 S 343	S 341 S 343	S 341 S 343
S 344 S 357	S 344 S 349 (In terra quidem)	S 344 S 357	S 357 (only)	S 344 S 357 B 349 (In terra quidem) S 350 (Job exemplar)
—	—	S 414 (David filius Yesse), S 430 (Psalterium Rome dudum positus)	—	S 424 (Psalterium est ut) B 384 (Dum multa corpora) B 398 (Legi litteras) B 407 (Nunc autem) B 406 (Nunc itaque) Psallere qui docuit . . .[4] Nunc Damasi monitis . . .[4] S 5193 (Liber psalmorum) S 369? (Canticum psalmorum . . .) S 414 var.? (David filius Yesse) S 426 var.? (Psalterium inquirendum est in cuius) S 430 (Psalterium Romae) S 405 (Nudius tercius) S 437 (Qui psalmi proprie)
Leaf wanting	S 457	S 457	S 457	S 457 (with address)
S 462	S 462	S 462	S 462	S 462 Item alius prologus. Petrus. Queso te . . . (?)
—	—	—	—	B 456 var.? (Tribus modis vocatum . . . esse regem)
S 468	No prologue	S 468	S 468	S 455 (Tres libros) S 468
S 26,1 Omitted	S 26,1 Omitted	S 26,1 Included (as ch. LII)	S 26,1 Omitted	S 26,1 Omitted

	Prologues, etc., expected in Parisian Bibles (Stegm.)	(Initium)	MS 1[1] (Bond 72)	MS 2 (Bond 71)	MS 3 (Rosenwald 31/3)
Isaiah	482	Nemo cum prophetas	S 482	S 482	S 482
Jeremiah	487	Ieremias propheta cui	S 487	S 487	S 487
(Introductory sentence to Lamentations)	—	Et factum est postquam in captivitatem . . . et eiulans dixit.	Omitted (later added in tail margin)	Included, written as end of Jer. LII	Included, as end of Jer. LII
Baruch	491	Liber iste qui Baruch	Omitted (later added in tail margin)[6]	S 491	S 491
Ezekiel	492	Ezechiel propheta	S 492	S 492	S 492
Daniel	494	Danielem prophetam	S 494	S 494	S 494
verse Dan.XIV,42	—	Tunc rex ait (. . . de lacu leonum)	Omitted (later added in tail margin)	Included	Included
Minor Prophets	500	Non idem ordo	S 500	S 500	S 500
Hosea	507	Temporibus Oziae	Omitted	S 507	S 507
Joel	511	Sanctus Ioel	Omitted	S 511	S 511
	510	Ioel Filius Phatuel	Omitted	S 510	S 510
Amos	515	Ozias rex cum Dei	Omitted	S 515	S 515
	512	Amos propheta pastor	Omitted	S 512	S 512
	513	Hic Amos propheta	Omitted	S 513	S 513
Obadiah	519 + 516	Iacob patriarcha fratrem . . . Hebrei hunc esse dicunt . . . (usually written as one prologue)	Omitted	S 519 + 517	S 519 + 517
Jonah	524	Sanctum Ionam Hebrei	Omitted	S 524	S 524
	521	Ionas columba (et) dolens	Omitted	S 521	S 521
Micah	526	Temporibus Ioathae	Omitted	S 526	S 526
Nahum	528	Nahum prophetam	Omitted	S 528	S 528 va.? (expl.: . . . libri huius demonstrabitur)
Habakkuk	531	Quatuor prophetae	Omitted	S 531	S 531
Zephaniah	534	Tradunt Hebraei	Omitted	S 534	S 534

MS 4 (Bond 19)	MS 5 (Rosenwald 5/2)	MS 6 (Nekcsei-Lipócz)	MS 7 (Bond 70)	MS 8 (Giant Bible of Mainz)
S 482	S 482	S 482 (as Ecclesiasticus LIII !) + *capitula* to Isaiah as Ecclesiasticus LIIII !)		
S 487	S 487	S 487	S 487	S 487 + S 490 (Ioachin filius) + S 486 (Ieremias Anathites . . .)
Included, as end of Jer. LII	Included, as end of Jer. LII	Included at beginning of Lamentations	Included at beginning of Lamentations	Included at beginning of Lamentations
S 491	S 491	S 491	S 491	S 491
Included	Included	(Leaf wanting)	Included	Included
	S 500	(Leaf wanting)		
S 507	Omitted	(Leaf wanting)	Omitted	S 507 (Temporibus Ozie) S 506 (Osee crebro)
S 511 S 510	Omitted Omitted	S 511 S 510 var. (Joel Fatuel filius. . .)	S 508b (In hoc propheta . . .) S 511 (Sanctus Ioel)	S 511 (Sanctus Ioel) S 508 va.? (Ex tribus igitur . . . penitenciam) S 510 (Iohel filius . . .)
S 515 S 512 S 513	(S 515 omitted) S 512 (expl.: sed audiendi verbum Dei) (S 513 omitted)	S 515 S 512 S 513	S 515 S 512 (S 513 omitted)	S 515 (Ozias rex) S 513 va. (Hic Amos propheta non fuit tempore)
S 519 + 517	S 516 (Abdias qui interpretatus . . .)	S 512 (Amos pastor) S 519 + 517	S 519 + 517	S 519 + 517 S 517 (Abdias servus Domini qui interpretatur)
S 524 S 521	S 522 (Ionas columba pulcherrima)	S 524 S 521	S 524 va. (Hunc prophetas . . .) (S 521 omitted)	S 524 (Sanctum Ionam) S 521 (Ionas columba pulcherrima)
S 526	S 525 (Micheas de Morasti)	S 526	S 526	S 526 (Temporibus Ioathe) S 525 (Micheas de Morasti)
S 528	S 527 (Naum consolator orbis)	S 528 var.? (expl.: . . . libri huius demonstrabitur)	S 528	S 528 var.? (expl.: . . . libri huius demonstrabitur) S 527 (Naum consolator orbis)
S 531	S 529 (Habacuc luctator fortis)	S 531	S 531	S 531 (Quatuor prophete) + (unidentified:) Hic in principio voluminis . . . tropheum crucis + (unidentified:) Vocabulum autem salvatoris . . . et predicare. S 529 (Abacuc luctator fortis)
S 534	S 532 (Sophonias speculator)	S 534	S 534	S 534 (Tradunt Hebrei) S 532 (Sophonias speculator)

	Prologues, etc., expected in Parisian Bibles (Stegm.)	(Initium)	MS 1[1] (Bond 72)	MS 2 (Bond 71)	MS 3 (Rosenwald 31/3)
Haggai	538	Ieremias propheta ob causam	Omitted	S 538	S 538
Zachariah	539	In anno secundo Darii	Omitted	S 539 var. (Anno secundo Darii)	S 539
Malachi	543	Deus per Moysen	Omitted	S 543	S 543
1 Maccabees	547	Cum sim promptus	Capitula in libro	S 547 (with address)	S 547 (with address)
	553	Memini me in palatio	Machab. (I-LXI)	S 553 (with address)	S 553 (with address)
	551	Maccabeorum libri duo	(S 552 added later, in tail margin)	S 551	S 551
2 Maccabees	—	—	Capitula Machabeorum libri 2i(I-LIV)	—	—
(Form in which the N.T. begins:)	(No special signal except for the Tree of Jesee initial often used for the beginning of Matthew)		Prol. to Matthew begins in the column which contains end of 2 Maccabees	as in MS 1	as in MS 1
Gospels	—	—	—	—	—
Matthew	590 589	Matheus ex Iudeis Matheus cum primo	S 590 var. (Matheus ex Iudea) "Breves" [= capitula] (28 items)	S 590 var. (Matheus ex Iudea) S 589	S 590 var. (Matheus ex Iudea) S 589
Mark	607	Marcus euangelista	S 607 S 611 (Petrus apostolus . . .) Capitula (42? items)	S 607	S 607
Luke	Luke I, 1-4 written as if not part of biblical text 620	 Lucas Syrus	S 620 var. (Lucas natione Syrus)[7] "Breves" (69? items)	Lk I,1-4 as first prologue S 620	Lk I,1-4 as first prologue S 620
John	624	Hic est Iohannes	S 624 var. (Iohannes euangelista . . .) S 630 (Tres euangeliste) S 627 (Iohannes apostolus quem . . .) Capitula (48 items)	S 624	S624
Romans	677	Romani sunt in partibus	S 651 (Epistole . . . factus est) S 670 (Primum queritur quare . . .) S 674 var. (Romani sunt qui ex . . .) Capitula (25 items)	S 677	S 677 var. (Romani sunt in partes)
1 Corinthians	685	Corinthii sunt	S 685	S 685	S 685

MS 4 (Bond 19)	MS 5 (Rosenwald 5/2)	MS 6 (Nekcsei-Lipócz)	MS 7 (Bond 70)	MS 8 (Giant Bible of Mainz)
S 538	S 535 (Aggaeus festivus . . .)	S 538	S 539[!] (In anno secundo darii)	S 538 (Ieremias propheta) S 535 (Aggeus festivus)
S 539 var. (Anno secundo . . .)	S 540 (Zacharias memor)	S 539 var. (Anno secundo . . .)	S 540 (Zacharias memor)	S 539 var. (Secundo anno) S 540 (Zacharias memor)
S 543	S 544 (Malachias aperte)	S 543	S 543	S 543 (Deus per Moysen) S 544 (Malachias aperte)
S 547 (with address)		S 547 (with address)	S 551	S 547 (with address)
S 533 (with address)	no prologue	S 553 (with address)		S 552 var. (Machabeorum liber licet . . . requiescunt)
S 551		S 551		
—	—	—	—	S 553 (with address) S 551 (Machabeorum libri duo . . .)
as in MS 1	as in MS 1	Prologue to Matthew begins on new page (v.II, f. 237v)	Prologue to Gospels begins on new page (f. 278v)	Prologues to Gospels begin on new leaf (v. ii, f. 112r) preceded by stub.
—	—	—	S 595 with address (Beatissimo . . . Novum opus facere . . .) S 596 (Plures fuisse . . . canendas)	S 595 with address (Beatissimo . . . Novum opus me facere cogis . . .) S 596 (Plures fuisse . . . canendas)
S 590 S 589	S 590? var. (Matheus ex Iudea qui et Levi sicut in ordine . . .)	S 590 var. (Matheus ex Iudea) S 589	S 590 var. (Matheus ex Juda) S 589	S 590 S 589 var. (Matheus cum primum . . .)
S 607	S 607	S 607	S 607	S 607
Lk I,1-4 as first prologue S 620	Lucas nacione Syrus . . . in Achaie partibus scripsit hoc euangelium. Lk I,1-4[8]	S 620 Lk I,1-4 (at end, "Explicit secundus prologus")	S 620 (Lk I,1-4 omitted completely)	S 620 Lk I,1-4 as [second] prologue
S 624	S 624	S 624	S 624 var. (. . . unus ex duodecim discipulis . . .)	S 624
S 677	S 674 var. (Romani sunt qui ex gentibus iudeisque . . .)	S 677 var. (Romani sunt partis)	S 677	S 674 var. (Romani sunt qui ex Iudeis . . .) S 677 var. (Romani sunt partes . . . et per Feben dyaconissam)
S 685	S 683 (Corinthii sunt Achaici denominati a . . .)	S 685	S 685	S 690 (Epistola prima . . . acciones) S 685 (Chorinthii sunt Achaici et hi similiter)

	Prologues, etc., expected in Parisian Bibles (Stegm.)	(Initium)	MS 1[1] (Bond 72)	MS 2 (Bond 71)	MS 3 (Rosenwald 31/3)
2 Corinthians	699	Post actam a Corinthiis	Capitula (20 items) S 699 (omitting "a Corinthiis")	S 699 (omitting "a Corinthiis")	S 699
Galatians	707	Galate sunt	Capitula (12 items) S 707	S 707	S 707
Ephesians	715	Ephesi sunt	S 715 Capitula (31 items)	S 715	S 715
Philippians	728	Philippenses sunt	Capitula (8 items) S 728	S 728	S 728
Colossians	736	Colossenses et hi[9]	Capitula (10 items) S 736	S 736	S 736
1 Thessalonians	747	Thessalonicenses sunt	Capitula (10 items) S 747 var. (. . . Macedones in Christo . . .)	S 747 var. or 748 var.?[10]	S 747
2 Thessalonians	752	Ad Thessalonicenses	Capitula (7 items) S 752 var. (. . . ab Athenis per Titum et Onesimum)	S 752 (with the bracketed part)	S 752
1 Timothy	765	Timotheum instruit	Capitula (12 items) S 765	S 765 var. (omits "et docet," ends "a Laodicea")	S 765 (". . . a Macedonia . . .")
2 Timothy	772	Item Timotheo	Capitula (7 items) S 772	S 772 var.(". . . scribens a Laodicea")	S 772 var. (". . . scribens a Laodicea")
Titus	780	Titum commonefacit	Capitula (6 items) S 780 (. . . credunt)	S 780 (. . . a Nicopoli)	S 780 (. . . a Nicopoli)
Philemon	783	Philemoni familiares	Capitula (4 items) S 783 (. . . de carcere)	S 783 (. . . Onesimum)	S 783 (. . . Onesimum)
Hebrews	793	In primis dicendum	Capitula (22 items) S 793	S 793	S 793
Acts	640	Lucas nacione Syrus	S 631 (Actus Apostolorum . . .)	S 640 var. (S 637?) (Lucas Antiocensis natione Syrus . . . medicina) (unidentif.: Ubi precepit . . .)[14]	S 640 var. (S 637?) (Luca Antiocensis natione Syrus . . . medicina)
James (or Catholic Epistles)	809	Non idem ordo est	S 809 Capitula (20 items)	S 809 var. (Non est ita ordo . . .)	S 809 var. (Non ita est ordo . . .)
1 Peter	—	—	Capitula (20 items)	—	—
2 Peter	—	—	Capitula (11 items)	—	—
1 John	—	—	Capitula (20 items)	—	—
2 John	—	—	Capitula (5 items)	—	—
3 John	—	—	Capitula (5 items)	—	—

MS 4 (Bond 19)	MS 5 (Rosenwald 5/2)	MS 6 (Nekcsei-Lipócz)	MS 7 (Bond 70)	MS 8 (Giant Bible of Mainz)
S 699 (omits "a Corinthiis")	S 699 var.? (Post actam penitenciam . . . a Philippis)	S 699 (omits "a Corinthiis")	S 702 (Quibuadam Corinthiorum . . .)	S 697 (In secunda ad Chorinthios . . . sectantes) S 699 (Post actam . . . ostendens)
S 707	S 707	S 707	S 707	S 707
S 715	S 715	S 715	S 715	S 715 (with ". . . per Tytum dyaconum")
S 728	S 728	S 728	S 728	S 728
S 736	S 736 (bracketed part originally lacked "et Onesimum acolitum")	S 736	S 736	S 736 (with illogical addition "ab urbe Roma" at end of bracketed part)
S 747 var. or 748 var.[11]	S 748 var./749 var.? (combined?)	S 747/748? (same text as in MS 2)	S 748	S 747/749/746? (combined?)[12]
S 752 (with the bracketed part)	S 752	S 752 (with the bracketed part)	S 752 (with the bracketed part)	S 752 var. (. . . per Tytum diaconem et Onesimum acolitum)
S 765 (". . . a Macedonia . . .)	S 765 (thru "a Laodicea") + S 760 var. (Hic episcopus)	S 765 (" a Laodicia")	S 765 (". . . ab urbe Romana")	S 765 var. (". . . a Macedonia per Titum diaconum")
S 779 (". . . ab urbe Roma)	S 772 (". . . ab urbe Roma de carcere")	S 772 (. . .ab urbe Roma)	No prologue	(Leaf missing)
S 780 (. . . A Nicopoli)	S 780 (. . . credunt)	S 780 (. . . a Nicopoli)	S 780 (. . . a Nicopoli)	(Leaf missing)
S 783 (with "mittit" instead of "facit")	S 783/784 (combination, variant)	S 783 (. . . Onesimum)	S 783 (". . . per supradictum Onesimum)	(Leaf missing)
S 793	S 793	S 793 (× 794?)	S 793 var.(× 794?)	S 793[13]
(Leaf missing)	S 640 var. (S 637) (Lucas Antiochensis natione Syrus . . . medicina)	S 640 va. (S 637?) (Lucas Antiochensis nacione Syrus . . .)	S 640 (Lucas nacione . . . with, at end, "animarum saluti eius proficeret medicina")	S 633 (Canit psalmista) S 640 (Lucas nacione) S 631 (Actus Apostolorum)
S 809 var. (Non ita ordo . . .)	S 809 var. (Non ita est ordo . . .)	S 809 corrupt ("Est donita ordo . . .)	S 809 var. (Non ita est ordo . . .) S 810? var. (Quia in circumcisione . . . conatur)[15]	S 809 (Non idem ordo est) S 807 (Iacobus Petrus Iohannes Iudas . . .) S 806 corrupt (Iacobus apostolus . . . et mendacio magistrorum)
—	S 812 var. (Discipulos Salvatoris invictos . . . princeps apostolorum)	—	—	S 816 (Symon Petrus)
—	S 818 var. (Symon Petrus servus et apostolus Iesu Christi per fidem)	—	—	S 817 (Per fidem huic mundo . . . manifestat. Amen)
—	S 822 var. (Rationem Verbi . . . manifestat et delusores . . . occasio)	—	—	S 822 var. (Iohannes rationem Verbi . . . occasio)
—	S 823 var. (Usque adeo . . . perhibetur)	—	—	S 823 (Usque adeo . . . perhibeat)
—	S 824 (Gaium pietatis . . . universis fratribus)	—	—	S 824 (Gaium pietatis . . . fratribus universis)

	Prologues, etc., expected in Parisian Bibles (Stegm.)	(Initium)	MS 1[1] (Bond 72)	MS 2 (Bond 71)	MS 3 (Rosenwald 31/3)
Jude	—	—	Capitula (7 items)	—	—
Revelation	839	Omnes qui pie volunt	S 835 (Iohannes apostolus . . . servetur) Capitula (25 items) (S 839 added in another hand at end)	S 839	S 839
Interpretationes Hebraicorum nominum	7709	Aaz apprehendens . . . consiliatores eorum.	Not included	Included	Included

NOTES: 1. Order of N.T. books in MS 1: Gospels, Acts, Catholic Epistles, Pauline Epistles, Revelation. 2. Shown is presence or absence of the whole book (not a prologue). 3. Order of books: Nehemiah, Esther, Tobit, Judith. 4. Further information in the description of the manuscript. 5. Prayer of Solomon not expected in Parisian Bibles. 6. In MS 1, Baruch precedes the Lamentations. 7. Luke I, 1-4 is written as part of the Gospel. 8. Written more or less as part of the Gospel; Luke I, 5 begins, however, with (F) initial. 9. All manuscript

TABLE B—Historiated Initials in the Bibles

(MS 1 has no historiated initials. MS 2 has one, with the beginning of Genesis: the Seven Days of Creation, not in scriptural sequence, and Crucifixion: cf. details in the description)

BOOK	MS 3	MS 4	MS 5
(Ad Paulinum)	Jerome at his desk in monk's garb	Jerome at his desk	Jerome at his desk in monk's garb
(Desiderii mei)			
Genesis	Six Days of Creation, Day of Rest, Crucifixion		Six Days of Creation, Original Sin, Crucifixion
Exodus			Moses at the Burning Bush
Leviticus			Two men, one cutting wheat
Numbers			Moses and group of three
Deuteronomy			
Joshua		Three men by water, God (head)	Man, woman, partly obscured 3rd person, all kneeling
Judges			Gideon and angel
Ruth			Four narrative scenes
1 Samuel	Elkana and Anne pray		Elkana's and Anne's offering
2 Samuel			Saul's burial
1 Kings			Solomon's judgment
2 Kings			Ascension of Elijah
1 Chronicles			Solomon anointed
2 Chronicles			Men with swords follow half-naked man
Ezra			Ezra reads to the people
Nehemiah			Nehemiah presents cup to Artaxerxes
First Book of Esdras			(book not included)
Tobit			Tobias and Angel
Judith			Judith unsheathing sword
Esther			Esther, Ahasuerus (two medallions)
Job			Job on dunghill (wife present) addressed by God

MS 4 (Bond 19)	MS 5 (Rosenwald 5/2)	MS 6 (Nekcsei-Lipócz)	MS 7 (Bond 70)	MS 8 (Giant Bible of Mainz)
—	S 826 var. (Iudas frater Iacobi . . . computetur) S 825 var. or corrupt (Iudas apostolus de incorruptibilibus . . .)	—	—	? (Initial prepared for S 825 or 826; text erased? Never written?)
S 839	S 835 (Iohannes apostolus . . . servetur)	S 839	S 839 Capitula (26 items) (inc.: Iohannes de testimonio . . .)	S 839 (ending: ". . . et Parabole Salomonis") S 829 (Apocalipsis . . . intelligencie)
Included (ending imperfectly because of missing leaf)	Included	Not included	Included	Not included

Bibles here include the ending "per Tychicum diaconum et Onesimum acolitum" bracketed in Stegmüller. 10. Full text in description of the manuscript, note 9. 11. As in MS 2, except for minor omission. 12. Cf. additional information in description of the manuscript. 13. Before Hebrews, the manuscript includes the Letter to Laodiceans; prologue, if any (cf. Stegm. 800, 801) is lost with the missing leaves. 14. See further information in description of the manuscript. 15. Fuller text in the description of the manuscript.

MS 6	MS 7	MS 8
Seated teacher instructs class of 8 students, in school	Jerome at writing desk, in cardinal's garb	Jerome at desk, in cardinal's garb; lion
Jerome in cardinal's garb presents Vulgate to Damasus	J. in cardinal's hat receives letter	
Six Days of Creation, the Sin, Expulsion; and offering of a church (for Day of Rest?)	Standing male figure in blue robe	God Creator, rainbow (also castle, chase)
Moses at the Burning Bush	Sitting king (pharaoh?) in blue garb, with crown	
Aaron offering lamb, in presence of God and Moses	Standing Moses (horns) in whitish; dark blue ground	
Moses with census scroll, communing with God	Moses on his knees; landscape, sky	
God (head and hand) speaking to man (not Moses) standing in front of bush (not burning)	Moses, holding scroll, addresses 6 listeners	Standing white-haired Moses, with group of 3 (smaller) persons
(above:) Angel with sword; (below:) kneeling warrior		
Armed warriors standing		
(leaf missing)		
Presentation of child Samuel		
Saul's death		
David and Abishag in bed		
Ahaziah falling from tower		
King addresses group of six		
Solomon kneeling, praying		Queen of Sheba visits Solomon
(upper pt.:) Cyrus on throne		
(lower pt.:) Ezra looking up		
Nehemiah mourning the ruin of the Temple		
Josiah celebrates Pascha		
Tobit in bed		
Judith slaying Holophernes		
(upper pt.:) Esther and Ahasuerus		Esther and Ahasuerus
(lower pt.:) Haman hanging		
Job on dunghill, wife		

BOOK	MS 3	MS 4	MS 5
Psalms (Ps. 1)	David playing harp	David playing harp	David playing harp
Ps. XXVII			Man crowning a boy
Ps. XXXIX			Solomon's judgment
Ps. LII			Saul's suicide
Ps. LIII			Fool
Ps. LXIX			David in water
Ps. LXXXI			
Ps. XCVIII			Two singing monks
Ps. CX			Trinity
Proverbs	Solomon instructs (tonsured) Rehoboam		Solomon instructs Rehoboam
Ecclesiastes			Solomon, man, youth
Song of Solomon			Two lovers, standing
Wisdom			Three men in front of a building
Ecclesiasticus			Personified Church (?) flanked by old and young man
Isaiah	Isaiah sawn asunder	Isaiah sawn asunder	Isaiah and the Lord
Jeremiah			Jeremiah called; water
Lamentations			Half-length portrait of beardless, sad man
Baruch			Baruch reading (Jeremiah's prophecies?) to group
Ezekiel			Lord touches lips of child dressed in blue
Daniel			Daniel in the lion's pit
Hosea		Seated prophet	Man with halo speaking to 2 men
Joel			Joel preaching (to group at his feet)
Amos			Amos as shepherd, sitting
Obadiah			Three men in conversation
Jonah			God speaks to sleeping Jonah
Micah			Micah, standing
Nahum			Nahum and walls of Niniveh
Habakkuk			Habakkuk seated, writing
Zephaniah			Zephaniah, standing, with jar (?) in hand
Haggai			Haggai, standing, holds tablet with inscription: IN A[NNO?]
Zechariah			Zechariah, standing
Malachi			Malachi, holding white stick, preaches to 5 beardless faces
1 Maccabees			Apostates revering idol
2 Maccabees			Mounted combat

MS 6	MS 7	MS 8
David playing harp	David with crown and harp	
David pointing to his eyes		
David pointing to his mouth		
Fool, with club		
David in water		
Old David, holding bell		
Franciscan monks' choir		
Christ blessing (en face, half-length)		
Solomon instructs Rehoboam		
Solomon, man, youth		
Mary, enthroned, embraced by Christ Child		
Bishop and king praying (above them, in initial to prologue, Christ, en face, half-length)		
Solomon addresses the old and the young		
Isaiah sawn asunder (while suspended on a cross)		
Lord touches the prophet's lips		
—		
Baruch reading to Jeconiah and assembled group		
Ezekiel amid captives, near river, sees descending angel		
Daniel (as an adult) and the 3 other young men (as boys)		
(leaf wanting)		
Joel sitting in the woods		
Amos speaks to a lion		
Obadiah speaks to a youth, among rocks		
Jonah thrown from the boat		
God (or angel?) extending right arm over earth and sea		
God (Christ?) speaks to Nahum and disciple		
Habakkuk praying; God's hand above		
Zephaniah, with another man, watch the "congregating" (Zeph. I,2 Vulg.: "Congregans congregabo omnia . . .")		
Haggai kneeling; hand of God above		
Zechariah kneeling; hand of God above		
Lord prefers Jacob (looking young) to Esau (looking adult) (cf. Mal. I,2.3)		
An after-battle scene (victorious king lifts hand; kneeling man, fallen men)		
(?) Two men emerge from under a portico to meet 2 others (messengers?)		

BOOK	MS 3	MS 4	MS 5
Matthew	Tree of Jesse	Tree of Jesse	Jesse (?), reclining
Mark			Mark with book (in interesting architectural setting)
Luke			Luke with book
John			(above:) John sitting, Jesus above him (below:) bishop (washing someone's feet?)
Romans	Paul with sword	Paul with sword	Paul's conversion (Paul fainting on horseback)
1 Corinthians			Two haloed men, talking
2 Corinthians			Paul and penitent Corinthian
Galatians			Paul led blind to Damascus(?) (or being welcomed at door by a Galatian?)
Ephesians			Baptism of a man (in a tub)
Philippians			Paul talking to a woman
Colossians			Paul talking to a (sitting) Colossian man
1 Thessalonians			Paul and another haloed man sitting behind a (red) bar (?)
2 Thessalonians			Paul speaks to a (haloless) Thessalonian (both standing)
1 Timothy			Paul before a gate
2 Timothy			Paul sitting and writing
Titus			Paul addressed by fierce man with torch (jailer?)
Philemon			Paul's beheading
Hebrews			Peter and Paul in twin compartments of uncial *M*
Acts			Tonsured cleric unfolds scroll in front of assembly
James			St. James, standing
1 Peter			Peter, crucified head down
2 Peter			Peter holding book, pointing up
1 John			John (?) sitting, reading
2 John			Droll man sits on midsection of the *S*; wormlike creature, on its lower arm
3 John			Half-naked man carries the *S* by its midsection; over ramparts, a head
Jude			(deer, fish, dog, deer in initial *I*s of prologue & epistle)
Revelation			John on Patmos, writing

MS 6	MS 7	MS 8
Tree of Jesse (4 kings in roundels; Virgin and Child)		
John the Baptist in the desert, reading from scroll to group of 5		
Zechariah offering incense		
John (the Apostle) in pulpit, writing on scroll		
Paul (half-length figure) with sword		
Paul (half-length figure) with sword and rolled-up black scroll (?)		
Paul with sword and open book		
Paul with sword and half-unrolled scroll		
Paul with sword and scroll		
Paul, with sword, speaks to group of 4		
Paul, with sword beside him, writing; 2 men present		
Paul, holding sword		
Paul, holding sword		
Paul, holding open scroll and sword		
Paul, holding scroll and sword		
Paul, holding sword and book		
Paul holding sword (full-face)		
Paul, with sword, talks to group of 3		
The 7 deacons (cf. Acts VI,5)		
James (full-length, with pilgrim staff)		
Peter (half-length) key and book		
Peter (half-length) with with key and book		
John writing at lectern		
John speaking to woman and 2 children		
John writing, at lectern		
James (!) with book; next to him, staff; above him, cockleshell		
John (beardless) on Patmos, sitting, with scroll; angel addresses him from above		

XV **MS38, f. 1v** A Moorish-feeling frame embraces (or clashes with) the black-and-white arms of the Dominicans (bottom center) on this introductory page of a choir book from Spain. (Actual size of the leaf: 76 × 57 cm)

Liturgy

(MSS 9–43)

Any definition of what is a "liturgical book" is likely to be soft at the edges, and the grouping together of LC MSS 9 through 43 pretends to neither bibliographical nor theological exactness. Broadly speaking, one may call liturgical those texts or arrangements of texts which were used in congregational or "public" cult; thus, the only justification for including in the present group the MS 33, a prayer book, is that it could not conveniently be placed elsewhere.

The primary books used in public cult were those for the Mass (so called in the Western Church; in the Eastern Church, it is "Leitourgia," a terminological trap to beware of) and those for the Office (the "divine office," a system of prayers and readings which had developed over centuries in monastic communities, is associated with some of the best music ever produced, and became a canonical requirement affecting all clergy). An excellent guide to both groups is Andrew Hughes's *Medieval manuscripts for Mass and Office : a guide to their organization and terminology* (University of Toronto Press, 1982). A serious student of such manuscripts will have to use Hughes's book; for a fast orientation and for a reader who has absolutely no idea what a missal or a breviary might contain, pertinent articles in encyclopedias may be useful. Straight reading of our catalog may be tried, too: for the bold person willing to attempt learning by immersion, an otherwise superfluous explanation has been given here and there.

The unplanned and modest collection of liturgical manuscripts in the Library of Congress happens to include several books which are not at all common: two Carthusian homiliaries (see their descriptions with pertinent notes: MSS 13 and 23), a Netherlandish translation of the breviary (MS 27), and two items of the Birgittine (or Bridgettine) liturgy, unknown even to most liturgists until quite recently (the MSS 30 and 34). Quite rare in Western manuscript collections is also the Greek Orthodox Archieraticon, this being the correct identification of LC MS 37

If the books here assembled were to be cataloged within the framework of the *Anglo-American cataloguing rules* (2nd ed., 1978), the correct choice of main access point would be "Catholic Church" for the MSS 10–13, 15–32, 34–36, and 38–43; correct main entry heading for the MS 37 (and probably for the MS 9) would be "Orthodox Eastern Church." About the Psalter now numbered MS 14, opinion would oscillate between "Bible. O.T. Psalms. Latin" and "Catholic Church"; the prayer book MS 33 would be just "Library of Congress. Manuscript. MS 33."

A perennial linguistic difficulty which could not possibly be entered into again and again: In the context of liturgical materials, the words *proper, temporal, ordinary* are not adjectives; rather (used as technical terms in imitation of the Latin *proprium, temporale, ordinarium),* nouns. They stand for certain standard units or types of textual (or chant) material, or for the basis of certain groupings. (For more on this, see any of the larger dictionaries of the English language.) N.B. Musicologists use the terms *proper* and *ordinary* with meanings only slightly modified.

It has been said that ignorance of liturgy is ignorance of the history of Western culture. If this is not the place to ponder the validity of the statement, one must still agree, at the least, that the production of liturgical aids played a major role in the history of medieval bookmaking.

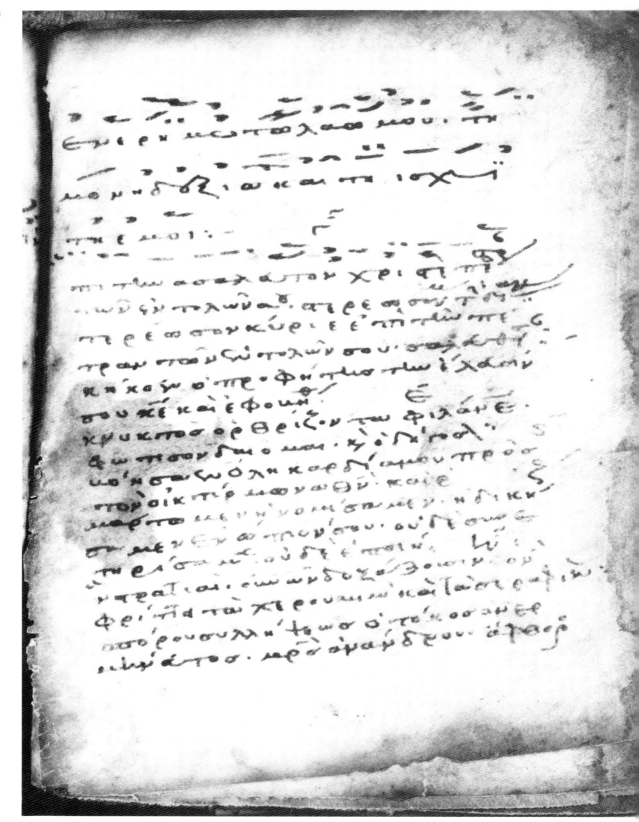

MS 9

(Music Division: M2156 XII M1 Case)

HIRMOLOGION (in Greek) XIIIth c.

San Salvatore monastery in Sicily?[1] Parchment. 110 leaves, ca. 105 × ca. 84 mm[2] (bound volume: 115 × ca. 98 mm) 1 column. 12 lines (each consisting of a line of Byzantine neumes and a line of text)

◀ **MS 9**, f. 39r (see note 13) (actual size of written area: ca. 80 × 60 mm)

f. 1r: (caption in center of head margin:) *η*ˣ[*os*] *γ*´ (1st line, centered between scribal ornamental fill-ins:) (red:) *ω*ᐞ[*η*] (black:) *α*´ (red:) T(black:)*ῆs* *θ*[*εοτο*]*κου* (red:) *ω*ᐞ[*η*] *α*´(2nd line:) (*A*)$^{1+1}$*σμα καινον ασωμεν λαοι τω* . . . (f. 72r, 4th line:) *Aρ*ˣ[*η*] *Tῶν μακαρισ*ᵘ[*ων*] . . . (f. 110, 11th line:) *σου θεον ου γινωσκομεν* :–

A very irregular copy or version of the *εἱρμολόγιον*, the Greek liturgical music book serving to indicate the tunes of the numerous hymns (*ᾠδή*, *–αί*[3]) of the *ὄρθρος*, the morning service; this is done (both here and in the more regular *hirmologia*) by giving the music, with text, of the first stanza of each ode. Nine (in principle; actual number varies; often eight) such first stanzas with music (*εἱρμοί*), numbered *α*´ through *θ*´(mostly without the *β*´, and often with one or more alternates) represent the nine odes which constitute a *κανών*.[4]

The different *kanons,*[5] normally consisting of a fairly standard sequence of certain odes, are standardly distributed among the 8 traditional musical modes (*ἦχος*, *–οι*) of Byzantine chant.

The present manuscript, a small-size, undecorated, utilitarian *Hirmologion*, shows considerable irregularities in the selection and arrangement of its contents.[6] There have been, apparently from the start, fewer kanons than usual, and other than usual combinations of odes (or more precisely of their *hirmoi*) have been used to build some of them:[7] the result being "mixed" or "composite" kanons, at least by comparison with the main line of tradition.

The book is now incomplete, with some lacunae easily ascertainable and other gaps possible. It has also suffered incorrect rearrangements.[8] The probable original order seems to have been (using and extrapolating present foliation):

MODE	
I	(lost material) 76r–88v, 97r–100r[9]
II	100v–102v, 89r–96v, 103r–110r
III	1r–10v
IV	10v–28r

MS 9

I pl.	28v–36r
II pl.	37r–45r
III pl.	46r–54r
IV pl.	55r–72r, third line

(A list of the 444 *hirmoi* preserved, in the order in which they occur within this reconstructed arrangement, will be found in the appendix.)

Macarisms: I 72r–75v II 72v–73r III 73rv IV 73v–74v I pl. 74v–75r II pl. 75r–75v (ending imperfectly)

Captions are preserved for modes II (on f. 101v) and III (f. 1r); that for IV is now invisible but space for it is signaled by (poorly drawn) pointing fingers (10v; unlike the rest, mode IV starts in mid-page, with only four lines left blank); more or less invisible have become also the captions for the plagal modes but all are signaled in similar manner and begin on a new page. It is not clear why the first plagal mode begins on a verso: 28 recto seems to have been blank until filled, as most blank areas, at a later time with non-germane writing. — The division into *kanons* is less clear: captions such as "*Τοu ἁγίου Ἠλίου ῳΔ[η] α΄ ἠχ[ου] β΄*" (f. 106r)[10] do occur but may not be meant to apply to whole sets. Elsewhere, the number "α΄" supplied in the margin (by more than one person? often but not always in the form resembling a roman lowercase **g** of the one-lobe kind) is the only indication that a new numbered series begins. — Single *hirmoi* are often though not always marked by their appropriate Greek number within a kanon, alpha through *theta*: the formal red ω$^{\Delta}$[η] (capital-type *delta* over minuscule *omega*) followed by the Greek number can be seen occasionally but may have been made only where space for it was available; for most *hirmoi*, the number, if present, seems to be a hastily made later addition, in the margin or above the first line of the item; done in faint black ink. —Some of the *hirmoi* include textual variants not noted in Follieri's *Initia.*[11]

Later ADDITIONS (15th? century):
28r (16 lines): *εφανεροσο τουσ αγγελουσ . . .*
36rv (beginning after 8 lines of original text): *τουτον δε λεγο τεκνια μου . . .* (5 + 16 lines)
45rv (after 4 lines of original text on 45r): *κορασιον εμπροσθεν του υροδου . . .* (10 + 16 lines)
54rv (beginning in 4th line of 54r): [*και*] *κραζασ //ουσουσ* [ ] *πετρε . . .* (10 + 15 lines)
100r (beginning in mid-7th line): [*και*] *εγο μετα ενοχ*[*ου*] [*και*] *υλιανος θεολογου και μαριασ μιτροσ μου* [*και*] *μετα του αγιου ιοανου του βαπτισαντοσ με* [much unused space left]
110v (full page, 19 lines): *Αγ*[*ι*]*οσ τισ περι ζισ αντιλογιασ . . . εφανισε* [breaks off abruptly at end of page; end lost]

Non-germane, preoccupied (with exception of 100r) with the Antichrist and the devil. Unidentified; partly resembling known medieval speculations on the Antichrist peril but appears syntactically disjointed, and may be manifestation of the writer's poor mental health. Non-traditional phonetic orthography; no diacritics.

* * *

Modern pencil foliation, partly very faded and apparently marking only selected leaves, is radically disturbed following f. [96]: next recto is numbered "89," either remnant of earlier more correct arrangement or else meant to indicate where the text from 88v continues; fading traces of this sequence also on several leaves which follow. — Preceding f. 1, a free endleaf (paper) and a non-original vellum leaf inscribed on recto in imitation of a modern title page:" ΤΡΟΠΑΡΙΟΝ//CODEX MEMBRANACEVS//CVM NOTIS MVSICIS//Saec. XII, exarat." At end, one free paper endleaf. — Written area ca. 80 × ca. 60 mm (the width varies). — No visible ruling, although pricking along the fore edge well preserved (in very unstraight lines 2–7 mm from edge). — Main text written throughout by one copyist, in a non-calligraphic, utilitarian hand based on the "pearl script"; preserved captions and numbers probably by a different scribe using a peculiar form of *alpha* (resembling a one-lobe **g**).[12] — The text line of each *hirmos* begins with a red capital letter set off into the margin (only a handful begin in mid-line); the red ink has often faded to the point of invisibility. — (The non-germane additions on ff. 28, etc., are by a poorly educated person

MS 9, f. 100r (with one of the inscriptions by a later hand) (actual size of the leaf: ca. 105 × 85 mm)

in a state of deep depression; his script is akin to childish printing.) — Middle Byzantine musical notation throughout except on f. 39r where text alone of several *hirmoi* (16 lines)[13] is squeezed into the space left after 4 normal lines of music with text. (No music with the non-germane additions listed at end of contents). — Parchment of, at best, just tolerable quality (unrepaired holes) but smooth on both sides; now variously stained, especially near edges. Thickness of text block: ca. 15 mm (= ca. 13.4 mm per 100 leaves).

Collation (very tentative due to restoration efforts and resewing): 1?(= missing beginning of mode I) $2^{10?}$(= ff. 76–83; $2_{5.6}$ = a bifolio[?] missing following f. 79) 3^8(= ff. 84–88 and 97–99) $4^?$(= ff. 100, 101, 102 and 89–95; stub after f. 91, no text loss) (f. 96 a singleton; conjugate stub follows f. 95) 5^8(= ff. 103–110) $6^{10?}$ (= ff. 1–8; $6_{2.9}$ wanting, with text loss) 7^8(= ff. 9–16) 8^8(= ff. 17–23; 8_4 following f. 19 wanting; no text loss?) 9–13^8(= ff. 24–63; following 13_8, singleton or inserted bifolio wanting, with text loss) 14^8(= ff. 64–69; 14_2 following f. 64 absent, no loss; 14_8 following f. 69 wanting, with text loss) 15^8 (= ff. 70–75; $15_{1.8}$ wanting, text loss with both). — No catchwords, no signature numbers.[14]

Decoration: except for the red capitals, no longer visible, and the scribe's or editor's minimal black-and-red ink doodle around the caption on f. 1r, none, or none preserved.[15]

Binding: recent spine; covers somewhat older calf, simply blind-tooled. Apparently reassembled and resewn (or even made to hold by gluing) within last thirty years.

On inside of upper cover, penciled: δο .ισ /200.00; also old LC label with penciled call number.

Former owners: Some clue to early ownership may be in the inscription on f. 100r, part of (and in the same hand as) the rest of the ca. 15th-century additions (see end of contents). — Apparently acquired by LC from J. Martini (his Cat. 13 [1917], no. 30 [not seen]).

2° fo.: (under line of music): [*T*]*ο φως σου το ανεσπερον χριστε*

Bibl.: De Ricci, p. 244, no. 166 — Mary Térey-Smith, "Analysis and musical transcription of the Washington Hirmologion" (master's thesis, University of Vermont, 1964). — M. Velimirovic, "The Byzantine Heirmos and Heirmologion," in *GATTUNGEN DER MUSIK IN EINZELDARSTELLUNGEN*, 1. Folge *(Gedenkschrift Leo Schrade)* (Munich, Francke, 1975), p. 193–244 (LC manuscript is mentioned and partly discussed on p. 212–213, esp. in footnote 69).

The small and rather unsightly codex is one of a none-too-large number of preserved and known medieval *hirmologia*; its particular interest is in its irregular character.[16] Recording of its complete content (musical and textual), not feasible here, will have to be undertaken soon if definitive losses are to be avoided: legibility of the ink seems to be decreasing with every passing year.[17]

APPENDIX: THE 444 *HIRMOI* IN MS 9

(Identified by mode, kanon, and ode numbers. The numbering is based on codex Iviron 470 [see note 5], with occasional correction. Within each mode, the kanon number always precedes the colon; the numbers in italics which follow the colon correspond to the Greek α΄, β΄, γ΄, δ΄, ϵ΄, [στιγμα], ϛ΄, η΄, θ΄. "1a, 1b, 1c" are the *hirmoi* given in the Iviron codex as the first, second, third alternates to the *alpha* hirmos given first; etc. The odd sequence of the various items reflects that of our manuscript. — The listing is very essentially indebted to M. Térey-Smith's thesis cited in the bibliography.)

Mode I (59 *hirmoi* preserved):
(beginning wanting)
ff. 76–79: (kanon) 15: (*hirmos*) *3a, 3b, 4a, 4b, 4c, 5, 6a, 6b, 7a, 7b, 8a, 8b*; 21: *8*; lacuna; ff. 80–88: 8:*4b*; ?(f. 80r):*4*; 8:*5b,6b,7b*; ?(f. 81v):*8*; 8:*9b*; 16:*3a,5*; 22:*1*; 17:*2a*; 16:*4a*; 22:*6*; 18:*9b*; 16:*1*; 17:*5*; 16:*6*; 17:*7*; 18:*8,9a*; 7:*1,3,4,5,6,7,8,9*; 6:*1*; 5:*1,3*; 12:*4*; 5:*5,7,8,9*
ff. 97–100r: 4:*1b,1a,3,4,5,6,7,8,9*; 22:*9*

The two *hirmoi* marked above by question marks instead of kanon number are not in Iviron 470:
f. 80r: 'Ακήκοε πάλαι 'Αββακούμ
f. 81v: Τέρατος ὑπερφυοῦς ἔδειξε τύπον

Mode II (73 *hirmoi*):
ff. 100v–102: (kanon) 2: (*hirmos*) *1*; 14:*2a*; 2:*3,4,5,6,7,8a,9*; 6:*1*; 8:*3*; 6:*4*;

ff. 89–96: ?(f.89r):*5*; 8:*7*; 1:*8a,9*; 12:*1*; 10:*2*; 12:*3,4,5,6,7,8a*; 17:*9a*; 10:*9*; 14:*3,4*; 10:*5a*; 14:*6,7*; 15:*9b*; 4:*9*; 8:*1,6,9d*; 10:*5b*; 7:*7*; 10:*8*; 4:*1,3,4,5,6*;

ff. *103–110*: 4:*7,8*; 5:*1,3,4,5,6,7,8,9*; 7:*1*; 12:*2*; 11:*8b*; 12:*9a*; 8:*9c*; 17:*9b*; ?(f. 107r):*2*; 15:*8b*; 8:*8b,9a,8a*; 6:*3*; 8:*8c,9b*; 14:*9*; 11:*8a*; 13:*1*; 3:*8*; 1:*5*

The two *hirmoi* not in Iviron 470:
f. 89r: 'Ο τοῦ φωτὸς χορηγός χαὶ τῶν αἰώνων
f. 107r: Προσέχετε λαοί τὰ τεραστεῖα

Mode III (45 *hirmoi* preserved):
ff. 1–10v: 2:*1,3,4,5,7*; lacuna; 13:*5*; 16:*6a*; 17:*7*; 16:*8*; 14:*9b,1,3a,4b*; 16:*5*; 10:*6a*; 13:*7*; 12:*8a*; 10:*9c*; 3:*7*; 4:*8*; 6:*9*; 17:*1*; 7:*1,3,4,5,6,7,9*; 16:*3,4*; lacuna; 6:*6,8*; 13:*3*; 17:*8*; 16:*9*; 17:*2*; 18:*2*; 17:*4*; 16:*1*; 8:*3*; 5:*4*; 4:*1,3*; 2:*6*

Mode IV (76 *hirmoi*):
ff. 10v–28r: 2:*1,2,3,4,5,6a,7,8,9*; 18:*1*; 16:*2*; 15:*3*; 11:*3*; 18:*4b*; 5:*4*; 17:*5*; 18:*7*; 11:*7*; 17:*8,9b*; 6:*9*; 5:*3,5*; 8:*1*; 14:*1*; 13:*3b,5*; 12:*6a*; 13:*7,9b*; ?(f. 17v):*4*; 15:*6,7*; ?(f. 18v):*8*; 19:*1a*; 3:*5*; 9:*6,7*; 8:*8b*; 3:*1*; 4:*3*; 13:*4b*; 3:*4,6,7,8,9b*; 9:*1*; 16:*3*; 18:*4a*; 17:*7*; 15:*8*; 7:*1,3,4,5,6,7,8,9*; 11:*1,4,5,8,9a*; 13:*1,3b*; 14:*4*; 13:*8,9a*; 18:*8a*; 17:*9a*

The two not in Iviron 470:
f. 17v:: Τί ἐκβοᾶς ὦ προφῆτα
f. 108v: Κάμινος χαλδαϊκὴ σῴζει

Mode I plagal (39 *hirmoi*):
ff. 28v–36r: 8:*1,4*; 8:*5*; 7:*6,7,8b*; 8:*9b*; 10:*1,3,4,5,6,7,8,9*; 2: *1,3a,3b,4,5,6,7,8,9*; 3:*5*; 21:*6b*; 4:*7*; 11:*8a,2a*; 15:*8a*; 7:*9*; 6:*5*; 7:*4b*; 5:*5*; 8:*8*; 7:*3*; 15:*8b*; 21:*9*

Mode II plagal (38 *hirmoi*):
ff. 37–45: 13:*1,3*; 10:*4b,5,6a*; 6:*6*; 10:*7*; 13:*8*; 10:*9b*; 14:*1*; 10:*2a*; 14:*2,3b,3a,4, 5,6,7,8,9*; 6:*1,3,4,5a,7, 8a,9a*; 7:*1,3,4, 5,6,7,8,9*; 6:*5b,8b,9b*

Mode III plagal (39 *hirmoi*):
ff. 46:54: ?(f. 46r):*1*; 2:*3,4*; 3:*5b*; 1:*5b*; 5:*6*; 6:*7*; ?(f. 47v):*8*; 2:*9*; 3:*9*; 7:*1*; 20:*3b*; 19:*4,5*; 1:*6*; 21:*7b*; 7:*8,9*; 1:*8*; 19:*3*; 7:*5,4*; 9:*1*; 7:*3*; 20:*5,6*; 9:*7,8*; 20:*9a*; 6:*1,3,4,5*; 20:*4b,9b*; 19:*8,1a*; ?(f. 53v):*6*; 21:*8*

The three not in Iviron 470:
f. 46r: Τῷ ἐκτινάξαντι Θεῷ
f. 47v: Τὸν μόνον ἄναρχον
f. 53v: Τὰ δεσμὰ σου καὶ τὸ ἑκούσιον

Mode IV plagal (preserved, 75 *hirmoi*):
ff. 55–72: 7:*1,3*; 8:*4*; 10:*5*; 7:*6,7,8,9*; 2:*1,3*; 7:*5*; 4:*5*; 1:*6*; 2:*7*; 4:*9*; 13:*1*; 10:*1*; 7:*3*; 13:*4,5*; 9:*5,6*; 12:*7*; 9:*7*; 14:*8b*; 13:*9a*; 10:*9*; 5:*6*; 3:*1*; 11:*8*; 2:*8*; 8:*1,3,5,6,7,8,9a,9b*; 3:*3,4*; 2:*5*; 3:*6,9*; 9:*1*; 3:*5*; 20:*6a*; 9:*8*; 10:*3a*; 7:*4*; 9:5a; 10:*6*; 9:*3*; ?(f. 66r):*5*; 10:*7*; 14:*1a*; 13:*3*; 14:*4,5*; 13:*6,7*; 14:*8a,9a*; 2:*4,9*; 9:*2*; 15:*1a*; lacuna; 14:*9b*; 20:*9a*; 11:*1a,7*; 9:*4*; 10:*3b*; 17:*8b,8c*

Not in Iviron 470:
f. 66r: Τῆς (ms.: Τοισ) τῶν παθῶν με ἀχλύος (ms.: αχλυωσ)

NOTES

1. I owe this suggestion to the 1964 unpublished master's thesis by Mary Térey-Smith (now professor at Western Washington University, Bellingham, Wash.) cited in the bibliography. It is based on systematic exclusion of other known scriptoria, on the impression that the manuscript comes from a fringe area of Greek language (unconventional phonetic orthography), rite (idiosyncratic composition of the kanons), and book production (format and appearance), and also on similarity of the script and format to that of a *kontakarion* known to have originated at the *Soteros* (San Salvatore) monastery: ms. M.129 of the Biblioteca universitaria in Messina (reprod. of f. 43r in *DEUTSCHE VIERTELJAHRSSCHRIFT FÜR LITERATURWISSENSCHAFT UND GEISTESGESCHICHTE*, 34 [1960], facing p. 96). — The Greek monastery stood on the Messina Strait from 12th to 16th century. Cf. *ORIENTALIA CHRISTIANA ANALECTA*, 185 (1969).

2. The leaves are cut extremely poorly, irregularly shaped; for the most part, the measurement along the fore edge is several millimeters less, and the width varies. The text block seems to have been through much vicissitude, including water and perhaps fire.

3. The term ᾠδαί is also used for the (nine) biblical canticles to which the odes = hymns, and their *hirmoi* relate. (N.B. An *alpha* ode, and *hirmos*, of a kanon relates in some way to Moses's canticle in Exodus XV; other odes and *hirmoi*, to the other canticles, the number indicating their pertinence.)

4. The text of a *hirmos* is the first stanza of an ode; the complete ode has typically four or five stanzas. Their text must be sought in several different liturgical books.

5. The codex Iviron ms. 470, a fairly regular 13th-century Hirmologion from Athos which I used for comparison has 190 kanons. (The facsimile, edited by Carsten Höeg, appeared under the title *Hirmologium Athoum* in Copenhagen in 1938 as v. 2 of the series MONUMENTA MUSICAE BYZANTINAE.)

6. Further: "The unique and astonishing feature of this manuscript is the presence of single *hirmoi* in random order between kanons." (Térey-Smith, *op. cit.*, p. 19.)

7. As a matter of fact, I am not sure that the copyist was aware, much of the time, that or where a new *kanon* begins.

8. The latest of these, it seems, in a restoration and preservation treatment applied ca. 1960; in the process, the vellum lost its former brittleness, unfortunately at the cost of, among other things, the legibility of most initial letters and of whatever else was in red ink.

9. The present f. [97] which should follow f. 88 is, in fact, numbered (in pencil) "89"; numbers of this (more correct) foliation sequence, dating probably from before the last rebinding, are more or less faintly visible on several other leaves in that part.

10. The *hirmos* so captioned is the first of the 7th *kanon* of mode II in the ms. Iviron 470: ''Ἀ̣δωμεν τῷ̣ Κυϱίω τῷ̣ ἐν θαλάσση πάλαι . . .

11. I.e., *Initia hymnorum Ecclesiae Graecae*, by Henrica Follieri (Città del Vaticano, 1960–).

12. The form seems to be rare; it occurs, nevertheless, in a manuscript from 1067 (Oxon. Auct. T. 2.2 (Misc. 202)) and in another from 1441; cf. *Rep. der griech. Kopisten* I B, p. 39 and 68 (nos. 82 and 158).

13. These sixteen lines, in the hand of the primary text, show the scribe's rather poor ability to separate words, also his accentuation practices (in the texts with music the accents seem to be integrated into the musical notation).

14. Some false sewing lines. My collation is likely to include errors.

15. Since the mildly decorated caption on 1r opens mode III and almost certainly was once preceded by the missing beginning of mode I and the present ff. 76–110, there was very likely somewhat more decoration at the beginning of the book in its original shape.

16. Cf. Velimirovic, *op. cit.*, p. 212.

17. Professor Térey-Smith's 1964 thesis included, among other information, a complete list of the initia, concordance tables comparing the contents of this manuscript to other *hirmologia*, musical analysis, and transcriptions of the music into modern notation. The author, now occupied in other areas of music history, has very kindly sent me a copy but is not, I understand, planning publication.

MS 10

(Music Division: M2147 XIV M1 Case)

CISTERCIAN ANTIPHONARY for day hours

end of XIIth c.?

From northern Italy? Parchment. 92 [i.e., 93][1] leaves, ca. 280 × ca. 197 mm (bound volume: 292 × ca. 206 mm) 1 column. 9 lines (each consisting of a staff of music and a line of text)

(2? leaves missing at the beginning)

ff. lr–3v: (begins abruptly:) ad aquas querite . . . *ad.ix.ā* (*E*)[1 +] cce ueniet p[ro]pheta magnus . . . seuouae *v'* Domine deus u[irtutum] *Hec sup[ra]dicte ant[iphone] p[er] tota[m] septimana[m] ad easdem horas repetantur. R T*u exurgens *v'* Rorate celi *F[e]r[ia] .ii. ad b[e]n[edictus] antiphonā* (*A*)[1 +] Ngelus domini nuntiauit . . . seuouae *ad.m[agnificat].* (*H*)[1 +] ierusalem respice . . . (breaks off on 3v, last line, with:) *ad.ix.ā.* (*E*)[1 +] cce dominus noster cum [expected: uirtute ueniet . . .]

Office chants for the day hours in the first two weeks of Advent. Preserved part contains: of the 1st week, the end of assembled antiphons for the minor hours and the complete set of antiphons to *Benedictus* and *Magnificat* for each weekday; of the 2nd week, all for the 2nd Sunday, and the assembled antiphons for the minor hours on weekdays. — Throughout, as in this whole book, the red caption for an antiphon, when spelled out in full, reads "antiphonam" (2v line 6, etc.). — As everywhere through f. 25v, the group of letters used for intonation of the "seculorum amen" is "seuouae" (common, and here used on ff. 26–92, is "evovae"). — Vespers seem to have only one antiphon "super psalmos."[2]

(2? leaves wanting; lacuna signaled by inserted paper leaf)

4r–5v: (beginning abruptly:) (*A*)[1 +] lleluia *ad.iii.* . . . (breaking off with last line of 5v with:) *ad mag ā'* (*E*)[1 +] leuare eleuare consurgere [expected: iherusalem . . .]

3rd Advent week, fragment: 3rd Sunday from Prime on, Monday, Tuesday. — Textual variant: *CAO,* no. 5337 "et illuminabit."[3]

(1? leaf wanting; blank paper leaf inserted)

6r–9v: proximo est dominus . . . (8r, last line:) . . . *Dom[inica] .iiii. In laudib[us] .ā.* . . . (9v, end of page:) (*L*)[1 +] eua iherusalem occulos [sic] et [expected: uide . . .]

(3rd week:) Thursday (beginning imperfectly in the ant. *ad Ben.*), Friday, Saturday. 4th week: the Sunday, the psalm antiphons common to weekdays up to Christmas

O oriens splendor lucis eterne et sol iusticie Antiph
ueni et illumina sedentem in tenebris & umbra mortis seuouae

O Rex gentium et desideratus earum lapisq: an
gularis qui facis utraq: unum ueni salua homi
nem quem de limo formasti seuouae Antiph

O emmanuhel rex et legifer noster expecta
tio gentium et saluator earum ueni ad saluandu
nos domine deus noster seuouae Quinta die ante nāt domini.

N olite timere quinta enim die ueniet ad uos

MS 10, f. 10r (actual size of the leaf: ca. 280 × 197 mm)

Vigil; and (with rubric-caption on 9r:) "Antiphone ad benedict[us] eisde[m] priuatis diebus" (broken off in that for Thursday). — *CAO,* nos. 2092 "ei," "eius"; 4144 "ueniet."

(1? leaf wanting; blank paper leaf inserted)

10r–v: (*O*)[1+] oriens . . . illumina sedentem . . . (last line of 10v:) . . . *ad.i.ā.* (*H*)[1+]odie scietis quia ueniet do [expected: minus et mane . . .]

"O antiphons," the last three of seven; the *Nolite timere quinta enim die,* and the Vigil of Christmas through Prime. — In the *O oriens,* the variant noted in *CAO* VI, p. 285 (no. 4050).

(3? leaves wanting; blank paper leaf inserted)

11r–12v: (begins abruptly:) eterne seuoae *R* Uerbum caro factum est . . . ([rubric-caption added(?) in gutter margin:]) *[In die san?]cto [ad] m[agnificat] a'* (H)[1+]odie[4] xpistus natus est . . . seuouae *Priuatis dieb[us] usq[ue] ad c[ir]c[um]cis[ionem] d'. In laud' ā.* . . . (12v:) . . . *Cōm de dominica ad bn̄* (*D*)[1+]um medium scilentium [*sic*] . . . (*P*)[u]er ihesus . . . in illo seuouae (last staff and last text line empty).

Sections of the Christmas and post-Christmas offices. Prior to 1185 (when Thomas à Becket was introduced) Cistercian office had 2 empty days between Christmas and Circumcision.[5] — *CAO,* no. 3093, "exultant"; no. 3877, var. "ubera de celo plena" (f. 12v, 1st line).

(following f. 12, blank paper leaf inserted; but nothing wanting)

13r–15v: (*U*)[1+]erbum caro factum est . . . (15v, end of last line:) *v'* Omnes de [expected: Saba uenient]

Circumcision (whole) and Epiphany (through part of Lauds). — *CAO,* nos. 3763, "id quod"; 2523, "exclamavit"; 3677, "factus" and "nesciens"; 3654, var. "viderunt" (f. 15v).

(major lacuna: 3 gatherings, of 8? leaves each, wanting; blank paper leaf inserted)

16r–24v: (begins abruptly:) [De]us ne perdas me . . . (24v ends:) (*I*)[1+]nuocabo no[men tuum]

Major fragment beginning in the 3rd Sunday of Lent (short responsory of the Vespers) and ending in the office of Palm Sunday (in the antiphon for Sext), with materials for each of the twenty days in between. — For unknown reasons, the (not prominent) captions introducing the 4th (f. 17v) and 5th (20v) Sundays leave out a space where the number should be. — Texts for the Thursdays of the 3rd and 4th week (16v, 19v) are not same as those used by Cistercians in the 20th century (see appendix). — Ant. *Aqua quam* = *CAO,* no. 1469 has "ultra"; 4982, "excitabo"; 4571, "quis" and "ut"; 4203, "audient." — In the *ad Magnificat* for Monday of the 5th ("Passion") week, variant not registered in *CAO* VI: "Quis sitit ueniat . . ." (for "Si quis sitit . . .").

(6? leaves wanting; blank paper leaf inserted)

25r–v: in galileam ibi eum uidebitis . . . (25r, in 5th line:) *In die pasche In laud' .ā.* . . . (25v ends:) . . . *v'* Et apparuit symoni

Easter Sunday: beginning imperfectly in the short responsory of 1st Vespers, breaking off in the versicle of the Sext. — The caption "*In die pasche,*" placed, as all such captions in this book, before the Lauds (25r) differs in no way from other captions (the greenish blue initial *A* of the "Alleluia" has some minimal decoration).

(1? leaf missing; blank paper leaf inserted)

26r–v: (*A*)[1+]lleluia . . . *FR.ii. ad bn̄.ā.* (*Q*)[1+]ui sunt hii sermones . . . (26v, last line:) iam tertio . . . postquam resurrexit

Fragment with Benedictus and Magnificat antiphons for Monday through Wednesday of Easter week.

(4? leaves missing)[6]

27r–57r: (beginning abruptly:) est xpistus filius dei & ut credentes . . . *Dom[ini]c[a] ad bn̄.* (*E*)[1+]go sum pastor bonus . . . (29r:) . . . *In uig[i]l[ia] ascensionis dn̄i* . . . . . . (30v:) . . . *Priuatis dieb[us] p[ost] oct' Inuit'*[!] . . . (33r:) . . . *In uigl' pe[ntecos]t[es] ad ue[s]p'* . . . (34r:) . . . *Priuati[s] dieb[us] Inuit'.* [!] . . . (36r:) *Hic ordo in feria scd'a dispositus per totam ebdomada[m] cotidie repetat[ur]*

MS 10 . . . (38r:) . . . *Sabb[ato] ant[e] do[mini]c[am] d[e) t[ri]nitate ad u[e]sp[eras] sup[er] ps[almos] a[ntiphone]* . . . (41v:) . . . *Incipiu[n]t ant[iphone] i[n] sabb[at]is p[ost] oct̄ pent[ecostes] ad mag[nificat] dice[n]de.* . . . (42v, last line:) *Antiphone ad mag̅ dicende sabb'tis a k[a]l[end]is augusti.* (43r:) (*S*)[1]+apientia . . . *Ant[iphone] de libro iob in sab'b'is a kl'is sept[embris] ad mag̅ dic[en]d[e]*. . . . (45r:) . . . . . . *in medio sept̄ ad mag̅* . . . (*N*)[1]+e reminiscaris . . . (46r:) . . . . . . *a k[alendis] oct[obris]* . . . (*A*)[1]+d aperiat dominus cor uestrum . . . (47r:) *In sabb'is a kl' nouemb[ris]* . . . (*U*)[1]+idi dominum sedentem . . . (48r:) . . . *Antiph' de euangl'iis post pent' dn̄icis dieb[us] dicende ad bn̄. [et] ad mag̅. Dōmc .i.* . . . (*H*)[1]+omo quidam erat diues . . . . . . (57r:) . . . *Dom[ini]c[a] .xx.v.*[7] . . . . . . in mundum evovae

Preserved section begins two weeks after Easter (in mid-antiphon *ad Magn.* of the Saturday after Easter octave); caption gives no number to this (the Good Shepherd) Sunday; those that follow are numbered "*.ii.*", "*.iii.*", and "*.iiii.*" (last before Ascension). — Pentecost Sunday (its Lauds begin on unfoliated [33bis]) has no caption of its own. — The Trinity[8] office gives for its 1st Vespers (captioned as "Sabbato ante," cf. above) 4 antiphons and agrees with Cistercian use of our time in everything except the (2nd) Vespers for which the antiphon "super psalmos" is only one: *Gloria et honor deo in unitate trinitatis* . . . ; there is also no commemorating of the lost Sunday. — The series of Benedictus and Magnificat antiphons for the Sundays after Pentecost (48r sqq), based on their gospel pericopes, gives for the last one *Cum subleuasset* = John VI,5sqq.[9] Their numbering shows the confusion brought in by introduction of the Trinity Sunday:[10] the numbers *ii* through *x* (ff. 48v–51v) are the result of imperfect corrections, by erasure and otherwise, from *iii* through *xi; xii* through *xxv* remained uncorrected; the actual number of sets is only 24. — Inserted between ff. 50 and 51, a piece of vellum (height ca. 97 mm, width of other leaves) with, on recto, the *ad Magn*. antiphon for the 7th Sunday which had been omitted on 51r.[11] — *CAO,* no. 1490 (?) (in short responsories, 29v–30r) with "et"; 4920 (36r) "in ipso"; 4546 (41v–42r) "tuo"; 4811, "cum"; 1980, "aliquid stultum" (44v); 4426, "dragmas decem si perdiderit"; 2682, "sicut"; 3894, "et non iudicabimini [!]" (50r); 4903, "ante"; 2202 (55v) and 4873 (56v): ". . . dicit dominus."

57v–92v: *In natali sc̄i stephani p[ro]tom[a]r[tyris] Ad uesperas commemoratio.* (*S*)[1++]TEPHANVS autem . . . . . . (59v:) . . . . . . *ioh'is eua[n]g[e]liste* . . . . . . (61v:) . . . . . . *innocentū* . . . . . . [no Thomas à Becket; no Sylvester] (63r:) . . . . . . *agnetis* . . . (*P*)[1]+ulchra facie . . . . . . (65v:) . . . . . . *uincentii* . . . *quere om[n]ia in unius mr̄is. In c[on]u[er]sio[n]e sc̄i paul[i]* . . . . . . (68v:) . . . *In purificatio[n]e sc̄e marie* . . . . . . (70r, SALVE regina . . .) . . . (72v:)*In natale sc̄e agathe uirginis ad uesp[er]as R* (*B*)[1++]eata agatha . . . (74v:) . . . *In cathedra sc̄i pet[ri]* . . . . . . (75r:) . . . [no Gregory] *In natale sc̄i benedicti ad uesp[er]as* . . . (78r:) . . . *In annuntiatione sc̄e marie* . . . (80v:) . . . *Quando fe*(81r:)*stum sc̄i ambrosii p[os]t pascha celebrat[ur] dicat[ur]* . . . . . . *xii R.* (*I*)[1]+ndiademate *Cet[er]a respo[n]soria ut in uni[us] [con]fessoris pontificis. // In nat[ali] uni[us] m[arty]ris u[e]l [con]fessoris p[er] tota]m] resurrectione[m]* . . . *Plurimo[rum] m[a]r[tyru]m p[er] resurrectione[m]* (81v:) . . . *In natale sc̄i marci euang[e]liste* . . . (83r:) . . . *In nat[ali] apl'o-[rum] phylippi [et] iacobi* . . . (84v:) . . . *In inuentione sc̄e crucis* . . . . . . (breaks off at end of page:) . . . (*H*)[1]+ymnu[m] dicam[us] [MAJOR LACUNA] (85r:)do enim infirmor . . . [= last half of *In Commemor. s. Pauli*] . . . (86r:) . . . *per octab' ap[osto]lo[rum]* . . . *In octab'*. . . . . . . *In nat'. sc̄e Marie magdalene*[12] . . . . . . (88v:) *ad uincula sancti petri* . . . . . . *In inuentione sc̄i stephani* . . . . . . (89r:) . . . *In natale sancti laurentii* . . . . . . (91v:) . . . *In assumptione s' marie* . . . . . . (breaks off at end of 92v midway in the *ad Mag*'. of 1st Vespers:) illa preclara festiuitas omnium sancto[rum] festiui[tatibus incomparabilis . . .]

The sanctoral part of this antiphonary; about half of the contents is preserved. Lost sections contained most of saints' days of May and June (the gap between leaves 84 and 85, probably one 8-leaf gathering) and all from mid-August to Stephen (= ca. 20 or more leaves missing at end).[13] — Generally four antiphons "super psalmos" in Vespers. — Beginning perhaps with f. 75r, changes in overall appearance in particular of the rubrics (a rather festive-looking caption for St. Benedict) and of the calligraphic initials (more decoration), also irregularities in content: material for *Cathedra Petri* includes (by way of initia) "*Hy[m]nus,*" "*In uitat*' " ("audete venite" [?]) and "*In i° noct[urn]°*" ("Petrus & ioh's"), "*Et cetera omnia sicut in alia festiuitate*"; in major feasts that follow, hymn is indicated several times. — On 83r, marginal ADDITIONS (in black, disciplined non-cursive *notula*; partly cropped): "Sc̄ī Rob'ti abb'is . . ." and "Petri m̄r̄is. . . .".[14]

* * *

Foliated in modern pencil; by error, the foliator omitted a leaf following f. 33.[15] Leaves 1–25 have two numbers each: the one above line corresponds to faulty order of the leaves prior to last rebinding. Unnumbered white paper leaves inserted to signal lacunae (before f. 1 and) following ff. 3, 5, 9, 10, 12 (no gap?), 15, 24, 25, 84, 92. — Written area ca. 230 mm[16] × ca. 148 mm. Four-line musical staves with the *fa* line red and *do* line yellow; the other lines, done, as all the rest of the ruling, in dry-point, are often barely visible. Ruling for the text constitutes a fifth equidistant line above the music staff; it runs generally all the way to the edges. Average distance of the lines is ca. 4.5 mm; height of the text line[17] varies slightly. The vertical lines are doubled on both sides. Pricking not preserved. — Early gothic semiquadrate script by, it seems, more than one person in the main text, certainly in the rubrics. Ampersand is used ca. 10 times more often than the (uncrossed) tironian sign;[18] "y" is undotted except in some of the rubrics near end of the book; "d" with straight ascender is about as frequent as the other kind. — Ink somewhat weak but durable black. — The rubrics, almost entirely limited to captions, are red. — Square notes with sides and joining lines at an inclination of 65 to 85 degrees; the staves are marked with either the *do* or *fa* clef; the *B flat* and *B natural* occur.[19] — Parchment of modest quality; some stains; some repairs; leaves 13–15 damaged by cut near center.

Collation: i^{8}(= ff. 1–4; $i_{1,2,6,7}$ wanting) ii^{8}(= ff. 5–10; $ii_{2.7}$ wanting) iii^{8}(= ff. 11–15; iii_{1-3} wanting) $[iv–vi]^{8?}$ wanting (= 24? leaves following f. 15) vii^{8}(= ff. 16–23) $viii^{8?}$(= ff. 24, 25; $viii_{2-7}$ wanting) $[ix]^{8?}$($[ix]_{1,2,4.5}$ wanting; $[ix]_{3.6}$ = ff. 26.27; $[ix]_{7,8}$ = ff. 28 and 29 pasted near gutter to f. 27) $[x]^{8}$ ($[x]_{5}$ = unnumbered f. [33bis]) $[xi–xvi]^{8}$(= ff. 37–84) $[xvii]^{8?}$ wanting (= 8? leaves following f. 84) $[xviii]^{8}$(= ff. 85–92) $[xix+]^{8?}$ wanting (= all after f. 92, twenty or more leaves) — Considerable (ca. 45%) loss of text/music with the 70 + missing leaves.

Decoration: limited to modest decorative elements added by the rubricist(?) in some of the *litterae notabiliores* (with often not much attention to their relative importance); decorative intent may also have led to the sporadic use of greenish blue ink instead of red for some of these letters (the *A* which begins Easter in 6th line of f. 25r but also initia of much lesser significance on preceding pages); this doesn't occur after f. 25. Some minimal flourishing appears chiefly in the last fifth of the book, here and there, sometimes done in black ink. In most of the book a favored decorative feature is dividing the stem of a letter by a curved line of void white; another, adding round protuberances in the red of the letter to its thin-line sections.

Binding: 20th–century quarter-leather covers (spine and corners very dark bluish green morocco, the rest marbled paper primarily greyish blue).[20] — On spine, in gilt: PROPRIUM//DE//TEMPORE//[line]//ANTIPHONARY. Paper label with the Music Division call number near tail of spine. — On verso of the 5th free paper leaf, pre–1936 notes concerning correct order of the leaves; also: 241486; "acc. 402240"; and the call no.: M 2147//XIV M1//case.

No ownership inscriptions on the preserved leaves. — The antiphonary was purchased in March 1917 from J. Martini.[21]

2° fo.: (present f. 2:) uatorem meum et prestolabor — (pre–1936 f. 2, now f. 14:) tur nature deus homo factus est

MS 10 Bibl.: J. Martini's catalogs 10 (1913), no. 7; 11 (1914), no. 11; 12 (1915), no. 2; 13 (1917), no. 1 (not seen) — De Ricci, *Census* (1935), v. 1, p. 244, no. 163 (suggests 14th-century origin).

Concluding comments: Other aspects aside, the antiphonary corresponds to the state of Cistercian celebrations immediately after 1175 (when Trinity Sunday became a rule); absence of Thomas à Becket suggests a time not much after 1185.[22] In view of other archaic features it may be of interest that some items of the music (the *O* antiphons; the antiphon *ad M Magnum hereditatis* of Circumcision Vespers; *O admirabile* in 1st Vespers of Purification; the *ad Ben* of Innocents; others) are set a fifth higher than the same pieces in the printed Cistercian antiphonary of latter day: are these remnants of Cistercian chant before the big chant reform of ca. 1180? Incompleteness prevents seeing if many more additions have been made for feasts introduced in 13th century besides those of f. 83r. — Northern Italy is given as probable area of origin in De Ricci's *Census*; I think the script (including the undotted *y* and the rare but uncrossed tironian *et*) bears this out, as does, perhaps, also the relatively large amount of attention given to St. Ambrose of Milan on f. 81r.

APPENDIX: TEXT CHOICES IN MS 10 FOUND TO BE AT VARIANCE WITH MODERN CISTERCIAN ANTIPHONARY

(Edition used for comparison: *Antiphonarii Cisterciensis pars altera horas diurnas . . . complectens* [Westmalle, Belgium: Typis Ordinis, 1954]. Differences owing to introduction of later feasts and various minor differences [especially in choice of versicles] not noted. — The liturgical abbreviations used here are explained on p. xv.)

In the seasonal part, ff. 1–57r:

Advent, 2nd Sunday: *ad B* Super solium V_2 *a* Dixit Dominus *ad M* Beata es Maria

Advent, 3rd Sunday: V_2 *ad M* Tu es qui — *Tuesday*: *L a* Ecce veniet Dominus princeps *T a* Ecce iam venit plenitudo *S a* Ecce Deus noster *N a* Egredietur Dominus — *Thursday*: *P a* Conuertere *T a* De Syon veniet *S a* Consolamini *N a* Dominus legifer — *Saturday*: *V R* Non auferetur/Pulchriores

Advent, 4th Sunday: *L a* Alleluia; *P, T, S, N* ditto.; V_2 *a* Dixit Dominus — Monday through Vigil of Christmas: *L a* Canite tuba

Christmas Vigil: *L a* (variant:) O Iuda et Iherusalem

Circumcision: V_1 *R* Verbum caro factum est

Lent, 3rd week, *Thursday: ad B* Pater diligit *ad M* Sicut pater suscitat — *Saturday:* $V_{(2)}$ *R* Stetit Moyses/Dominus Deus Hebreorum

Lent, 4th Sunday: (V_1 = Saturday V_2 above) V_2 *R* Educ de carcere/Periit fuga — *Thursday: ad B* Cum audissent *ad M* Quidam autem — *Saturday:* V_2 *R* Multiplicati sunt/Qui tribulant/Dederunt/Et in siti

Lent, 5th Sunday: (V_2 = *Saturday* V_2 above) *L R* Principes persecuti

After Easter, 4th Sunday: V_1 *R* Viderunt te aquae/Illuxerunt

Ascension: V_1 *a* Alleluia (9x) *L a* Alleluia alleluia *R* Ascendo ad/Deum meum et/Ascendit Deus in/Et Dominus in *P a* Alleluia *T a* Alleluia/Exaltare/Cantabimus *S a* Alleluia/A summo/Et occursus *N a* Alleluia/Non vos/Veniam ad vos V_2 *a* Alleluia alleluia

Within Ascension octave: ("privatis diebus," ff. 30v–31r has as *a* from Lauds to Vespers an "Alleluia" followed by varying *R/v*) *Friday: ad B* Vado parare *ad M* Non vos relinquam — *Saturday: ad B* Pacem meam *ad M* Pater manifestavi — (*Sunday:* rubric calls for mostly same office as on the feast, with *Cum venerit* and *Haec locutus* for commemoration [!] of Sunday in *L* and V_2) — *Monday: ad B* Non turbetur *ad M* Euntes — *Tuesday: ad B* Dominus quidem *ad M* Viri Galilei — *Wednesday: ad B* Sic veniet *ad M* Pater manifestavi — *Friday after octave ad B* Illi autem profecti *ad M* Rogabo — *Saturday after octave ad B* Nisi ego abiero

Pentecost: V_1*a* Alleluia (6x) *L a* Alleluia alleluia *P a* Alleluia *T a* Alleluia/*v*. Spiritus/*v*. Et hoc *S a* Alleluia/Repleti/Et ceperunt *N a* Alleluia/Spiritus paraclitus/Docebit — ("privatis diebus," ff. 34r–35v, not compared)

Trinity: V_2 *a* Gloria et honor Deo

Mid-September Saturdays *ad M*: (Ne reminiscaris) Memor esto fili (Adonay Domine) + *R ad Vesp.* Omni tempore benedic/*v*. Memor esto fili

October Saturdays *ad M*: (after *Adaperiat, Exaudiat, Ornaverunt* and) (Tu Domine universorum) + *Ad Vesp. R*: Exaudiat Dominus orationes/*v* Adaperiat

November Saturdays *ad M*: (after *Vidi, Aspice, Super muros, Muro tuo* and) (Qui celorum) + *R* Aspice Domine de sede/*v*. Non enim in iustificationibus

(The *ad B* and *ad M* antiphons from Gospels, ff. 48r–57r differ from the series as printed in the modern Cistercian book chiefly because the set of Gospel readings differs, cf. comment to those pages, and note 9)

In the sanctoral, ff. 57v sqq.:

Stephen: V_2 *aa* Iste sanctus Qui odit Iste cognovit Nisi granum

John the Evangelist: V_2 *aa* Iam non dicam Tollite iugum Iugum enim Tradent

Agnes: V_1 *R* Pulchra facie (*CAO,* no. 7452) (*aa* 0?) V_2 *aa* Discede Dextram Posuit Induit

Conv. of Paul: V_1 *R* Scio cui (*CAO,* no. 7628(F)) (*aa* 0 ?) V_2 *aa* Qui operatus + *v.* Qui me segregaverit Scio cui + *v.* De reliquo Mihi vivere + *v.* Per quem mihi Reposita + *v.* Cooperante *ad M* In regeneratione

Purification: V_1 *a4* Germinavit *ad M* Salve regina V_2 *aa* Benedicta tu Sicut mirra In (.?.) Sancta Dei genitrix

Agatha: V_1 *R* Beata (*CAO,* no. 6160; *v.* A, var.: dicens jube me) *ad M* Mentem sanctam spontaneam (*CAO,* no. 3746) V_2 *aa* Ingenua Summa ingenuitas Ancilla Agatha ingressa

Chair of Peter: V_1 *ad M* Quodcumque ligaveris (initium only)

Benedict: V_2 a_2 Ab ipso puericie sue tempore a_3 Deum in hac terra

Annunciation: V_1 *aa* when before Easter: Non auferetur Dominus veniet Ecce veniet Leva Iherusalem *ad M* Salve regina *L, a* Beatam me dicent *P a* Ecce virgo concipiet *S a* Ecce ancilla *N a* Gaude et laetare V_2 a_3 Benedicta tu a_4 Quomodo

Ambrose (when after Easter; N.B. initia only): $V_{1,2}$ *ad M* Beatus vir qui metuit *L ad B* Qui manet R_{xii} In diademate (= *CAO,* no. 6898?)

(N.B. The several commons interspersed on f. 81r et al. not checked)

Mark: V_1 *R* Quattuor animalia *ad M* Ecce ego johannes *L, hymn* Traduntur igni (initium only) *ad B* Qui manet V_2 *ad M* Beatus vir qui metuit

Philip & James: V_1 *R* Tanto tempore

Finding of True Cross: V_1 *R* O crux gloriosa *hymn* Hymnum dicamus (initium only; = *AH* IV, 18?)

Commem. of Paul: V_2 *aa* Qui operatus Scio cui Mihi vivere Reposita est *ad M* In regeneratione

Mary Magdalen: V_1 *R* Dum transisset V_2 *aa* Veni sponsa (! cf. *CAO,* no. 5328) Nigra sum (! cf. *CAO,* no. 3878) Pulchra es (cf. *ibid.* 4417,–8) Revertere (cf. *ibid.,* no. 4648)

Peter's Chains: V_2? *R* Cornelius centurio (incipit) *ad M* Quodcumque

Finding of Stephen: V_2? *R* Videbant omnes

Lawrence: V_1 *R* Levita Laurentius *ad M* Beatus Laurentius dum in craticula V_2 *aa* Quo progrederis Noli me Non ego Beatus Laurentius *ad M* Levita Laurentius

Assumption: V_1 *aa* Que est ista Beata Dei genitrix Paradisi portas Virgo prudentissima (ms. breaks off here)

NOTES

1. Foliator missed leaf after f. 33; cf. collation.
2. Only one antiphon "super psalmos" for Vespers appears throughout the seasonal part of this book except in the (1st) Vespers of Trinity (f. 38rv).
3. See *CAO* (*Corpus antiphonalium officii*) 6, p. 284; texts of nos. 5006, 2508, 2543 not preserved. — For antiphon choices differing from later Cistercian antiphonary, see the appendix at the end of this description.
4. The *H* is blue-green. Page includes writing by a later hand over erasures.
5. The days of Stephen, John, and Innocents (in Cistercian books kept in the sanctoral part) required, when falling on Sunday, the "commemoratio Dominicae." — N.B. This manuscript does not include Becket.
6. Not signaled (no inserted leaf).
7. [i.e., xxiv]! See further. — Was there a time or region in which the (Mass and?) office for "1st Sunday after Pentecost" was (were) assigned, following the introduction of Trinity, to the next Sunday?
8. A feast (stabilized eventually on the first Sunday after Pentecost) not fully accepted by Roman liturgy until 1334 but part of the Cistercian use since 1175. (Cf. Leroquais, *Brév.* 1, p. lxxxix).
9. No *Cum videritis abominationem*; for the 4th Sunday, the gospel is *Estote misericordes*. The series corresponds to the set or type coded ϵ by Hesbert in *PALÉOGRAPHIE MUSICALE* 14, p. 132 (without the *F* addition?).
10. Did the writer's exemplar predate the 1175 decision?
11. The antiphon is *Misereor super turbam* (Mk VIII,2.3), written on 3 lines; manner of ruling, notation, and script differ from the main text. Writer uses ampersand, two forms of *d,* "sevovae." Verso is blank.
12. Without "penitentis."
13. As usual, the sanctoral proceeds in the calendar order without giving dates. — Another book in which the sanctoral starts with Stephen (and not, as commonly, with Andrew) is the Cistercian Gradual, LC MS 11.
14. Post–1255 ("Petrus martyr," the Dominican of Milan, was canonized 1253 and introduced into Cistercian sanctoral in 1255; Robert was celebrated since 1224 but in our book the two additions were made at the same time). — Cf. B. Backaert, "L'évolution du calendrier cistercien," *COLLECTANEA O.C.R.* 12 (1950) and 13 (1951) (here, 12, p. 94).
15. We have called it f. [33 bis]. — F. 1 is preceded by altogether 6 (free) leaves of various sorts of paper, all modern; 6 leaves also at end.
16. Measured from the base of bottom text line to top line of the music staff (with which the page generally begins).
17. I.e., the distance from base line of the text to lowest line of the musical staff above it.
18. Ampersand occurs over 40 times on ff. 1–35, then (noticed) only on 75r in the variously irregular beginning of the office of St. Benedict. The tironian symbol appears in the black script on 15v, 49v, 61r; also in some red captions.
19. Gothic or German-type notation is used on the 3-line slip inserted between ff. 50 and 51, which differs from the rest also in other ways.

20. Incorrectly assembled when received in 1917, the manuscript was rebound, probably in new covers, in 1936. It was then that the blank paper sheets were inserted to represent missing parts.

21. *Sin fallor*, this was Giuseppe Martini, the collector and dealer in Lugano, Switzerland (*d.* 1944).

22. The absence could of course be due to simple absence of any chanted "proper" (antiphons special to the feast); same for Sylvester and Gregory. In modern Cistercian chant books, too, they have "omnia de communi."

MS 11

(Music Division: M2147 XII M1 Case)

CISTERCIAN GRADUAL

end of XIIth c.

Produced in Austria?[1] Parchment. (i), 143 leaves, ca. 200 × ca. 150 mm (bound volume: 210 × ca. 165 mm) 1 column. 8–9 lines (each consisting of a staff of music and a line of text)[2]

Prelim. leaf [i]rv: *A*ue p[re]clara maris stella in luce[m] ge[n]tiu[m] Maria . . . (ends imperfectly, at end of page:) . . . na[m] te fili[us] nichil ne

AH L, 241 (broken off in stanza 7a); not in Walther, *Initia.* A sequence[3] for the Mass of Assumption ascribed to Herimannus Contractus (d. 1054). Leaf apparently straying from another book (a sequencer?). In head margin of its recto, cursive (16th?-century) inscription: Das puech gehordt gen Sewsenstain (below it, what seems to be a later unskilled attempt to duplicate the inscription).

(1r, in head margin, cursive inscription [end of 16th century?]: Jacobus Wisser Von W[angen?; last part of the name obscured by repeated lining through])

1r–99v: (*A*)[3]*D TE LEVAUI*.//anima[m] meam . . . (98v:) . . . *d[o]m[ini]c[a] xxiii*[a]. (*D*)[1+] icit do min[us] ego cogito . . . (99v, 3rd–4th line:) . . . accipie tis et fi et uo bis (followed immediately by red caption signaling the feast of St. Stephen, see next item)

Choir parts for the Masses associated with the seasonal cycle ("temporal") of the liturgical year as celebrated in Cistercian monasteries towards the end of 12th century: ca. 80 formularies with words and music, beginning with that (marked by large initial but, unlike most, uncaptioned) for the first Sunday of Advent. — The first Mass of Christmas (11r) lacks caption. There is no mention of Circumcision.[4] — Three formularies for the Sundays between Epiphany and Septuagesima: i[a] post Epiphaniam (15v, *In excelso throno*), i[a] post octauas Epiphaniae (16v, *Omnis terra*), and "*scd̄a p[ost] theop[h]a[niam]*" (18r, *Adorate Deum omnes angeli eius*). Ash Wednesday is called (23v) "*In capite jejunii*"; each day of Lent has its entry. — The leaves containing the chants for the procession of Palm Sunday (ff. 57–58; and f. 59 with most of the Mass chants) are bypassed in the original red numbering-by-openings (60v–61r is numbered "*.lvii.*"); the same for leaves 65–66, with part of the Good Friday rites (incl. the *Hagios,*[5] *Ecce lignum*, most of the hymn *Crux fidelis*; 67v–68r is "*.lxii.*"). — Easter (with 4-line *R* for the introit *Resurrexi*) is on ff. 69v–70r,

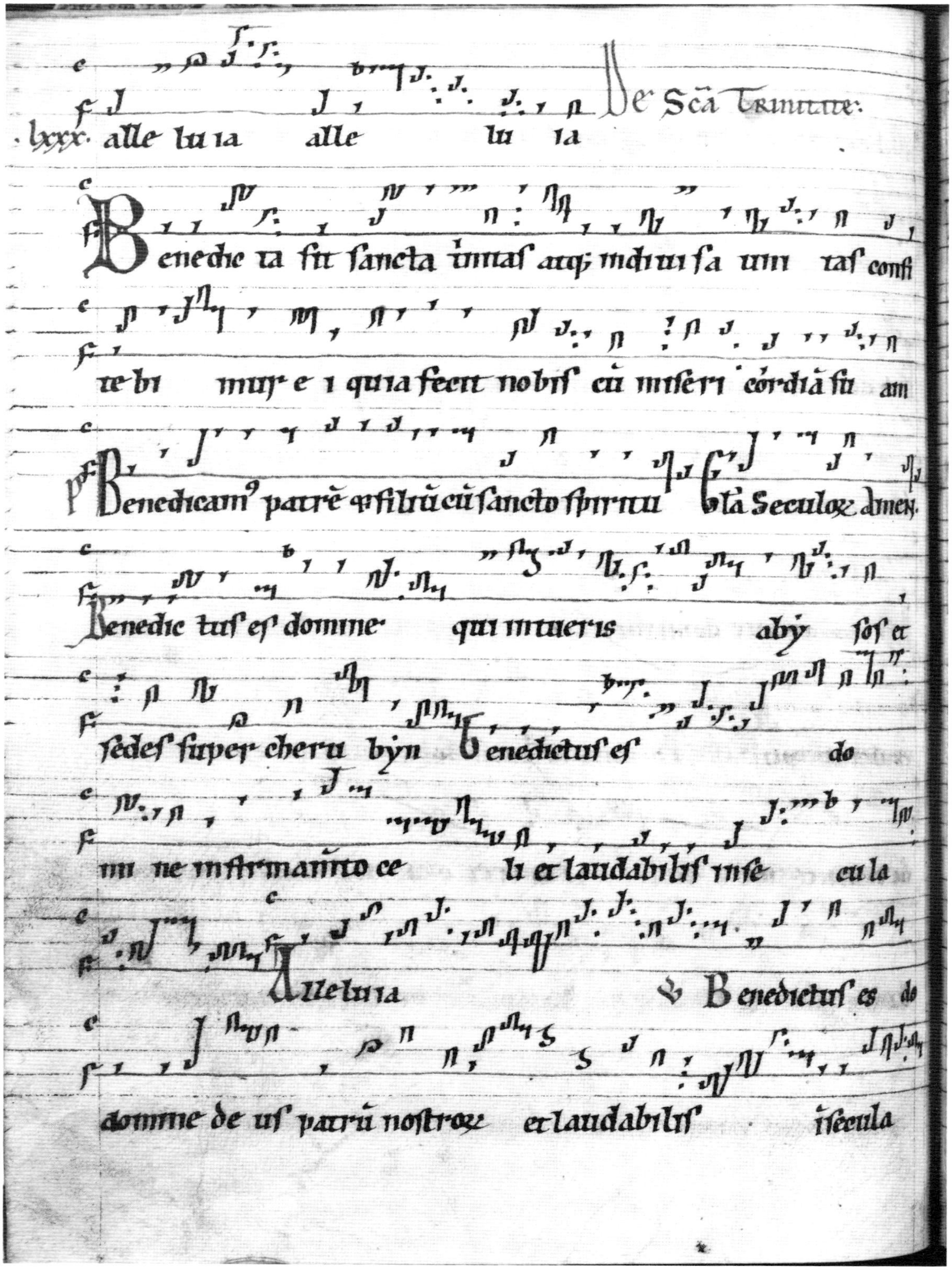

MS 11, f. 85v (actual size of the leaf: ca. 200 × 150 mm)

followed (70r–75r) by chants for each day of the Easter week; similarly provided is the week of Pentecost (82r–85v), followed by Trinity (85v, "Benedicta sit sancta t[ri]nitas . . .");*6* next (86r) is "*D[omi]nica .i^a^.*" (*Domine in tua misericordia*). This and the Sunday sets that follow are assigned the numbers (i^a^–xxiii^a^) which prior to the introduction of the Trinity Sunday marked their position after Pentecost.*7* The Ember days of September are placed (ff. 94v–96r) between the 17th and 18th Sundays. — A very disciplined hand using minuscule black *notula* has added in the margins of ff. 86–99 the information (by means of initia) concerning the collect, Epistle, and Gospel for each of the 23 Sundays (for the last one, two sets).*8*

99v–135v (beginning without major signal in 4th line of 99v:) *In DIE SCI Stephani p[ro]tom[arty]ris.* (*E*)[1]+t enim. Sederunt p'incipes . . . . . . (135v:) . . . *Thome apl'i* . . . *Co* Mitte m[anum] (followed immediately by next item)

The "sanctoral" of this chant book: the Mass propers for ca. 100 saints' days, in a calendar arrangement which, in this manuscript, begins with the first day after Christmas (the feast of Stephen) and ends with Thomas the Apostle (Dec. 21).*9* — The saints included are those honored in the Cistercian order by a Mass in mid-12th century;*10* the copy seems actually to have been made from an exemplar dating even further back, with some additions inserted immediately by the scribe or not much later by the rubricator-editor.*11* Absent are Thomas à Becket (Mass prescribed for his day in 1185), Peter, the Cistercian bishop of Tarentaise (1196), even the *Inventio S. Stephani protomartyris* (Aug. 3), a feast said to have been introduced before 1157; also the *Commemoratio fidelium defunctorum* (Nov. 2) which, however, may have been deemed covered by the Requiem Mass given (inadequately) further on in the book. — There are two sets of later ADDITIONS: (*a*) On 116r, in tail margin, close to *Vitalis m.*, a very careful hand added in a minuscule *notula*, in black ink, "Rudp[er]ti abb[at]is" and "Pet[ri] martyris,"*12* with initia of the texts to be used and references to where the chants were to be found; also on 117v, in 3rd line, "Pet[ri] epi̅ [et] [con]fessoris. sic[ut] d[e] sc̅o̅ amb[ro]sio." (*b*) Bernard of Clairvaux (Mass called for since ca. 1175) and the Eleven Thousand Virgins (1260) were found missing, it seems, at about same time (when the book was passed to the newly founded Säusenstein, ca. 1338?): added note on 129v (5th line) reads, "Officiu[m] de sc̅o̅ B[er]nhardo q[ue]re an[te] canonem"; on 133r, partly in margin, in same hand and ink: ".xi. m̅. v' q̅re a̅n canone̅."*13* — Other celebrations (Crown of Thorns, 1241; transfer of the relics of St. Benedict, 1291) remained neglected.

135v–138v: (beginning with 6th line of 135v:) (*T*)[1]+erribilis est loc[us] iste . . . (136r, beginning with 8th line:) (*R*)[1]+eqviem.Et[er]na[m]. . . . (beginning with 2nd line on 137r:) (*N*)[1]+os aute[m] gloriari o portet in cruce domini . . . (137v, 7th line:) *De sc̅a̅ maria* (*S*)[1]+alue sc̅a̅ parens . . . (138v, 2nd line:) *P[ro] familiarib[us]* (*E*)[1]+xavdi deus oratio nem . . .

(Choir parts for) votive Masses: *Dedicatio ecclesiae*; Mass for the dead (only initium is given for the introit antiphon *Requiem* and for its psalm verse, "Si ambulem in" [!]; the Tractus and Offertory in full; no *Dies irae*; of the uncaptioned Communion antiphon only the initium "Lux p.," running into the margin*14*); *De cruce* (lacking caption); the Mass honoring Mary; and another, for friends and relatives.*15* N.B. This book has no "Common of the saints."

138v–141v: (in 7th line of 138v:) . . . *Ad aqu[am]* Asperges me . . . (last words in last line of 138v:) *Prefatio Cotidiana.* (139r:) [P]er omnia scl'a seculor[um] . . . (last words on 139r:) *Prefatio In nat[ivitatis] d[omi]nice vigil[ia]* (139v:) [ornate, ca. 2-lines high standard symbol for the beginning of a Preface] Et[er]ne devs Quia p[er] incarnati u[er]bi mysteriu[m] . . . (line 6:) [the symbol, and:] . . . *IN epiphania dn̅i.* (last line:) *P[re]fatio d[e]*Sc̅a̅ MARIA. (140r:) . . . Et te in purificatione . . . (5th line:) . . . *IN Ieiun[i]o.* (7th line, rubric in margin:) *In pascali te[m]p[or]e* . . . (140v:) . . . *In Pentecoste.* . . . *In Ascensione.* . . . *De Apostolis* (141r:) . . . *De .S'. Cruce* . . . (squeezed between lines and written over faded musical staff:) *DE .S'. t[ri]nitate. p[re]fatio.* . . . (ends with 6th line of 141v:) cessant cottidie clamare dicentes *S'.S'.S'.*

N.B. Except for the several short responses which are given with the *Praefatio cottidiana*, all on 139r–141v is "presidential" (i.e., sung by the principal celebrant), not choir material = not strictly belonging in a gradual. The musical staves are largely faded; archaic features reappear.[16]

141v, continued: ADDITIONS in later hands: [i] Centum et 40 folia continet. [ii] De corpore Chr[ist]i Introitu[m] inuenies fol 77 (= our f. 82v which carries the red number ".*lxxvii.*" = *Cibavit eos*) Beata ge[n]s. Graduale 49. All[elui]a Caro mea . Offert[orium] in seq[ue]ntib[us] In q[ua]drages[ima] Introit[us] Du[m] sanctificat[us] fuero.48. Tract[us]. Sicut ceru[us] desid[erat[: 63 [iii] (hastily made short length of 4-line musical staff, with improved notation for:) cesant cottidie (cf. above, at end of preceding item)

(THE REMAINING 4 PAGES OF ADDITIONS ARE ON PAPER; they are obviously contemporary with the notice on 141v concerning Corpus Christi, and are, at least as far as the text is concerned, by the same writer; THE MUSIC IS ON 5-LINE STAVES, notation more or less *Hufnagel:*)

142r–143v: (A)$^{1+}$lleluia (C)$^{1+}$aro mea vere . . . (142v:) . . . Offertorium (S)$^{1+}$a cer do tes . . . Commun: (Q)$^{1+}$uoties cuncq[ue] . . . (143r, on 5th staff:) In festo visitationis B m[a]rie virg. Introit[us] Gaudeamus 27. Grad: Propter verit: 30 Vers: Audi filia 31 Allā cū versu Aue stillans melle. vt hic habetur. . . . (A)$^{1+}$ue stillans melle . . . (ends on 143v:) . . . receptaculum MAria. (A)$^{1+}$leluia. De sancta Anna m[at]ris [*sic*] M[a]r[i]ae officium Gaudeam[us] 27 Grad: Dilexisti . . . specie tua . . . Filiae regum . . . Cōm Diffusa e[st] gr[ati]a. 27. (last two staves and lines empty)

Corpus Christi was added to Cistercian list of feasts celebrated by a Mass in 1318; St. Anne, 1366 (more decisively, it seems, in 1454); *Visitatio B.M.V.* was permitted since 1476, prescribed 1533.[17] — The trope *Ave stillans mellis alvearium* (*AH* XLVIII, 395) is believed to be by Prague Archbishop Joannes à Jenstein who died in 1400.

* * *

Present foliation (in modern pencil) excludes the non-germane antiphonary leaf at the beginning and reaches (with the two paper leaves at end which contain text) the number 143.[18] — Early numbering of the openings, in red lowercase roman numerals, placed by the rubricator-editor near upper left corner of versos, begins on what is in the present pencil foliation f. 1v; it bypasses the present ff. 57–59 and 65–66 and goes from ".*lxxxvi.*" on 91v to ".*lxxxviii.*" on 92 v, reaching ".*xciiii.*" for the opening 98v--99r. It starts a new sequence on 99v,[19] with ".*i.*", and ends with ".*xxxix.*" on 137v.[20] The 7th, 8th, and 12th openings of this sequence do not have the numbers in their usual position; instead, remnants of cropped-off larger-size numerals can be seen in what remains of the head margins, placed on center of the page (105v, 106v, 110v).[21] — Preceding f. 1: free endleaf + 1 flyleaf (20th-century paper); 2 blank leaves (16th?-century paper); 1 nongermane vellum leaf from a sequencer (see contents). — Following the paper (16th?-century) leaves with text, 142– 143: 2 blank leaves (16th?-century paper),[22] 1 flyleaf + free endleaf (20th-century paper). — Written area (incl. music staves) ca. 170 × ca. 140 mm through f. 88; ca. 177 × ca. 130 mm in the last two-fifths of the book. — Only horizontal ruling, reaching to edges, through f. 88: 4-line music staves in faint black ink, the lines for text blind or not visible.[23] Clear margins and, for the most part, vertical ruling on ff. 89 through end; the vertical lines are, for the most part, doubled; horizontal lines for text go to the outer edge on some pages, the musical staves at most accidentally. — Pricking, near outer edges, preserved almost everywhere.[24] — The script is late Caroline to early gothic (or, *écriture cistercienne*), with changes occurring near f. 90: on leaves 1–86, the special sign used for *et* is an ampersand (of quite unusual shape, cf. illus.); on 87r–139v, uncrossed tironian note;[25] in ca. same area of change, curved-stem *d* begins to prevail over the straight-ascender kind.[26] — Ink varies from strong black to faded brown; no powdering. — Neumes (early gothic forms based on St.-Gall notation) on 4-line staves, with both the *fa* and *do* clefs shown at the beginning of each staff; throughout the book (with very few exceptions) the line with the *fa* key is retraced in red and that with the *do* in yellow. —

Rubrics (limited to captions and references) in red, probably done in two chronologically distinct stages.[27] — Parchment serviceable, fairly white, often stained; thickness ca. 24 mm per 100 leaves; numerous carefully made repairs done with yellowish green silk thread.

Collation: [i]–xvii^{8} [xviii]$^{6-1?}$(= ff. 137–141; sewing line between 139 and 140) (ff. 142–143 are a paper bifolio). — Black roman signature numbering, mostly cropped but partly visible in centers of tail margin on 72v (".viiii."), 80v, 120v, 128v, 136v.

Decoration: limited to calligraphic initials of which the first one, a ca. 65 × ca. 40 mm *A* on f. 1r, is the most ornate, done in red and brownish black inks. Their style varies: with the exception of a hint of scrollwork in *P* on 13r the decoration is mostly achieved by the use of a void-white division of stems.

Binding: Covers are (as of the time of this writing)[28] 20th-century half-leather (spine and corners in dark reddish brown long-grain morocco, rest marbled paper, shell pattern of gray and light brown tones); tight back, over 3 (false?) raised bands.[29] — On spine, in gilt: GRADUALE//TOTIUS//ANNI; on bottom panel, paper label with call no.: M//2147//.XII M1. — On verso of the 4th paper leaf in front, in pencil, LC order number: 372431//[19]28; also the call number; on verso of the parchment leaf preceding f. 1, in tail margin, penciled: acc[ession no.] 46226.

Former owners: (after 1338, the year of its founding) Cistercian abbey Säusenstein (*Vallis Dei*[30]) in Lower Austria, on the Danube (48° 12′ N, 15° 07′ E)[31] (ca. 1600?:) Jacobus Wisser von (Wangen? Vengingen?);[32] (17th?-century:) Abraham Shelhorn (name hastily inscribed, in modern Latin cursive, on 40v and 95v)[33] — Acquired by LC in 1928 from J. Rosenthal (Munich rare-book dealer).

2° fo.: (= f. 2r:) tum suum (under music staff) — (= f. 1r:) (*A*)^{3}*D TE LEVAUI*

Bibl.: *Bibliotheca Medii Aevi manuscripta, pars altera: einhundert Handschriften* . . . (München, [1928] = Jacques Rosenthal's *Katalog* 90), p. 44–46 (no. 141) (with facsim. of f. 14r[34]). — De Ricci, *Census* (1935), p. 244, no. 162; not (found) in the 1962 supplement by Faye and Bond.

Final comment: Cistercian version of the chant book known as "gradual" is the product of a revision of older books, made at Cîteaux in 1185–1189.[35] Early copies are not numerous. The present book was written close to the year 1200 but perhaps from an exemplar less than thoroughly updated: it lacked some celebrations introduced in 12th century. — Our speculation about Austrian origin of the book is based on its eventual presence and, it seems, use (there was some effort to maintain and update) at Säusenstein: although that abbey was founded only in 1338, a newly founded monastery is likely to have received its liturgical books from its mother outfit (which was, in this case, Wilhering) or perhaps from another not too distant Cistercian house; Zwettl, a nearby monastery (founded 1138 and still in existence), had a well-established scriptorium.

APPENDIX: THE SUNDAYS AFTER TRINITY IN MS 11

The 23 formularies found on ff. 86r–99v of the gradual are largely identical with those assigned to the 1st–23rd Sundays after Pentecost in the mid-13th century *Ordo Missalis secundum consuetudinem Romanae Curiae* printed in *SMRL* II, p. 261–270; from the program recorded there, the Cistercian book differs in what follows. (N.B. I have combined the information given in the late-13th century marginal notes, identifying the collects, Epistles, and Gospels, with that of the main text which dates from ca. 1200 and gives words and music for the introit with its psalm verse, the gradual, alleluiatic verse, offertory and communion antiphons; information from the two sources should be easy to separate.)

Dom. I^{a}: *Gos* Homo quidam erat dives
II^{a}: *AllV* Deus iudex
III^{a}: *Coll* Deprecationem nostram *AllV* Diligam *Comm* Ego clamavi
IV^{a}: *IntrPs* Unam petii *Coll* Protector *AllV* Domine in virtute *Gos* Estote misericordes

Vª: *Coll* Da nobis Domine ut et mundi *AllV* In te Domine speravi *Gos* Cum turbae irruerent
VIª: *Coll* Deus qui diligentibus *AllV* Eripe me de inimicis *Gos* Nisi abundaverit
VIIª: *IntrPs* Subiecit populos *Coll* Deus virtutum *AllV* Te decet hymnus *Gos* Cum turba multa
VIIIª: *Coll* Deus cuius providentia *AllV* Attendite *Gos* Attendite a falsis
IXª: *Coll* Largire nobis *AllV* (Quoniam elevata +) Propitius esto *Gos* Homo quidam erat dives qui habebat villicum *Comm* Primum quaerite
Xª: *Coll* Pateant aures *AllV* Exultate Deo *Gos* Cum appropinquaret Iesus Ierusalem
XIª: *Coll* Deus qui omnipotentiam *AllV* Domine Deus salutis meae *Gos* Dixit Iesus ad quosdam qui in se confidebant
XIIª: *Coll* Omnipotens sempiterne *AllV* (In Domino laudabitur +) Domine refugium *Gos* Exiens Iesus de finibus Tyri
XIIIª: *Coll* Omnipotens et misericors *AllV* Venite exultemus *Gos* Beati oculi
XIVª: *Coll* Omnipotens sempiterne Deus da nobis *AllV* Quoniam Deus magnus *Gos* Cum iret Iesus in Ierusalem *Comm* Panis quem ego
XVª: *IntrPs* Custodi animam meam *Coll* Custodi Domine *AllV* Timebunt gentes *Gos* Nemo potest duobus *Comm* Qui manducat
XVIª: *Coll* Ecclesiam tuam *AllV* Confitemini Domino et invocate *Gos* Ibat Iesus in civitatem quae vocatur Naim
XVIIª: *Coll* Tua nos quaesumus *AllV* Paratum cor meum *Gos* Cum intraret Iesus in domum

(Wednesday of the Ember days of September: *IntrPS* Buccinate in neomenia)

XVIIIª: *Coll* Da quaesumus Domine populo *AllV* Qui timent Dominum *Gos* Convenerunt pharisaei
XIXª: *Coll* Dirigat corda *AllV* Dextera Dei *Gos* Ascendens Iesus in naviculam
XXª: *Coll* Omnipotens (et) misericors *AllV* Qui confidunt *Gos* Loquebatur . . . homini regi qui fecit nuptias . . .
XXIª: *Coll* Largire quaesumus Domine *AllV* (Priusquam montes +) De profundis *Gos* Erat quidam regulus
XXIIª: *Coll* Familiam tuam *AllV* (Sicut unguentum +) Qui sanat contritos *Gos* Dixit . . . rationem ponere . . . *Comm* Dico vobis gaudium
XXIIIª: *Coll* Deus refugium nostrum *AllV* (In Deo laudabitur +) Qui posuit fines *Gos* Abeuntes pharisaei consilium inierunt

(The hand which added, probably at the end of the 13th century, the initia of the collects, Epistles, and Gospels, added one more set of these after the preceding: *Coll* Excita Domine *Ep* Ecce dies veniunt dicit Dominus (= Jer. XXIII,5?) *Gos* Cum sublevasset oculos Iesus et vidisset (= John VI,5 sqq.))

NOTES

1. Perhaps in the monastery Wilhering (near Linz) or (more likely?) at Zwettl in Lower Austria, with a known scriptorium; see final comment.

2. On leaves 1–50 mostly eight staves + lines, from there to the end mostly nine.

3. = hymn of the kind used in the Mass just before the Gospel.

4. No such mention was absolutely needed: the choir parts for Circumcision were identical with those for the third Mass of Christmas (in our ms., f. 13rv).

5. Spelled "Agyos." — N.B. Dotting of *y* is very inconsistent in this codex.

6. The Trinity Sunday was introduced among Cistercians in 1175.

7. = the series given in Hughes, *Medieval manuscripts* (1982), p. 141. — There is no rubric in our ms. to suggest transposition of the "1st Sunday" set to a weekday. — See appendix at end of this description for text choices which differ from the Roman model.

8. These sets differ from those in the Curia Missal (cf. *SMRL* II, p. 261–270) chiefly owing to a shift which associates the collects and Gospels with the "wrong" Epistles (see the appendix).

9. The book gives, as usual, no dates.

10. For the dates, etc., cf. B. Backaert, "L'évolution du calendrier cistercien," *COLLECTANEA O.C.R.* XII (1950):[81]–94, [302]–316; XIII (1951): [108]–127.

11. Confirming this impression (and perhaps reconstructing what was in the exemplar) would require much more detailed study. — The sanctoral as edited by the rubricator covers very exactly (minus the *Inventio Stephani* and the *Commemoratio defunctorum*) the feasts having a Mass in Backaert's calendar.

12. This is certainly post-1255 (cf. Backaert, *op. cit.*, end of April). It is the same hand which added in the margins of ff. 86–99 the information on the collects, Epistles, and Gospels of the Sundays after Pentecost (cf. Appendix).

13. Neither of the two propers is actually found anywhere in the book. — The canon is not expected in a gradual; were these notes mechanically repeated from the updating of a missal?

14. The full versions are nowhere in the book.

15. Communal remembrances of relatives are a feature of Cistercian books; cf. Backaert, *op. cit.*, Nov. 20.

16. Notably the ampersand, in the unusual shape used throughout on ff. 1–86 (cf. descriptive paragraph following the contents). The notation here gives the impression of primitiveness (and of diastematic unreliability?).

17. Reference to it ("... q[ue]re in fine"), in same hand, appears in outer margin of f. 124v.

18. Traces of a second modern-pencil numbering: "56a," "56b," "56c" and "61a," "61b" on versos of ff. 57–59 and 65–66 (as an effort to supplement the early numbering by openings).

19. The sanctoral begins on 99v in the 4th line, where the temporal cycle ends. Like us, the rubricator-editor-numerator must have chosen to heed the contents rather than the poor *ordinatio textus* of the copy. The irregularities in his numbering can be partly explained by its limited objective, i.e., to enable the editor to make references: the items found on the unnumbered openings were one-occasion chants, not usable for other purposes (so suggests the author of the Rosenthal catalog description [Ernst Schulz?], cf. bibl.).

20. Thus this early numbering does not cover the collection of prefaces which begins in last line of 138v. — N.B. On f. 138v, "*xlvii*" appears in the area used elsewhere for the numeration; as noted in pencil by a German-writing person, this is a reference to the opening so numbered.

21. The remnants (also red) show that the numbers matched the left-corner sequence.

22. Watermarks partly visible on the 3rd preliminary leaf (lower part of shield with half-portrait of a man) and on leaf following f. 143 (lower part of an eagle). Neither found in Briquet in exactly same form.

23. The pricking provides for them.

24. The pricking marks are in groups of five; they have been sometimes rather disregarded by the person who did the ruling in the last third of the book even though the ruling is quite regular.

25. In both parts the other sign occurs also; the proportion, however, is in both cases ca. 100 to 3.

26. If this means change of scribes, the fact has been obscured by updatings, erasures, and, perhaps, filling of blank areas (?).

27. The second rubricator acted as editor. He refers to both numbering sequences (without distinguishing them). The captions and references (also brief black additions?) added by him in the sanctoral do not go beyond the Cistercian calendar of ca. 1150, but his script is younger than that of the 1175 Trinity Mass on 85v sq. He uses the tironian *et* sign and the *d* with curved ascender.

28. It is likely that the present, quite unsuitable covers will be removed.

29. Prior to its purchase by LC the book was in 16th-century wooden boards covered with stamped pigskin, with two clasps (cf. the descriptions in the Rosenthal catalog and in De Ricci). The rebinding was a deplorable mistake owing perhaps to poor control of materials during World War II.

30. De Ricci says "Gottesthal" but I haven't found this German equivalent of "Vallis Dei" in reference to Säusenstein anywhere else; on an old engraving, it is "Seisenstain" (cf. *Festschrift zum 800-Jahrgedächtnis des Todes Bernhards von Clairvaux* [Vienna, c1954], p. 7 [also map] and pl. 1.) — The abbey was abolished in 1798.

31. Inscriptions: prelim. f. [i]r (see contents); 50r, in head margin: "Iste liber p[er]tinet ad mon[asteriu]^{m} Vallis Dei//Cistercien[sis] ordinis, alias Sewsenstain"; 81r, in tail margin: "Vallis dei mon^{m} e[st] d[omin]us [et] possessor meus." — All seem to be by same writer, and written in the 15th century.

32. Inscription in head margin of f. 1r, cf. contents.

33. De Ricci has, erroneously, "Schelhorns."

34. Contains the Introit and part of the Gradual for the Sunday within octave of Christmas. Facsimile does not show the yellow of the *c*-clef lines.

35. Cf. *New Grove* (1980), article Gradual.

MS 12

(Faye and Bond 127)

GOSPEL LECTIONARY ca. 1200?

Written in northern France or in the adjacent area of Belgium. Parchment. 173 leaves, ca. 320[1] × ca. 235 mm (bound volume: ca 338 × ca. 240 mm) 1 column. 21 lines.

ff. 1v–138r: (I)[21]n illo t[em]p[o]r[e]. *Scd'm Ioh'em.* Cum subleuasset oculos . . . [=John VI,5–14] (f. 3r = p. 3:) . . . *D[o]m[ini]c[a] .i. in aduentu d[omini]* . . . (f. 135r = p. 267:) . . . *Dm̄c. xxiiii* . . . (f. 136v = p. 270:) . . . *In dedicatione eccl[esi]e* . . . (ends in 2nd line of f. 138r = p. 273:) . . . cuncta se impetrasse letetur. P[er] dn̄m.

Gospel pericopes for the whole liturgical year, the seasonal part (the *temporale*). The collection is for monastic (Benedictine) use, and corresponds to the non-Roman "Frankish" series.[2] The starting point is set unconventionally (and without caption) on the last Sunday before Advent. —Throughout the year, special Gospels are given for Wednesdays and Fridays (in some cases also Saturdays); in Lent and in the Easter week, for every weekday. — The first Sunday of Advent (p. 3) has, oddly, the Palm Sunday Gospel *Cum appropinquassent Hierosolymis* (Matthew XXI,1–9); the scribe actually refers back to it when he reaches "Dominica in Palmis ad privatas Missas," p. 110. — Christmas has "ad nocturnos" (p. 14) the *Liber generationis* (Mt I,1–16), followed by the usual three Gospel pericopes for the three Christmas Masses. Stephen, John, and the Innocents are included here. "In octavis Domini," p. 22, has the Gospel *Pastores loquebantur* (Luke II,15–20) followed by the Circumcision text Luke II,21. — There is one Sunday "post Nat. Domini"; after Epiphany, "Dominica infra octavas" (p. 26) precedes the 1st through 5th Sunday "post Epiphaniam." — Ash Wednesday (p. 50) is called "feria iiii in capite ieiunij." — In the Holy Week, the parts of Jesus in the Passion reports according to Matthew (p. 110–124), Mark (p. 128–139), and Luke (p. 139–151) have added (not expertly) staffless, adiastematic musical notation;[3] there is none in the Passion according to John (p. 152–161). — Easter, p. 162, is remarkably unsignaled (no special initial). — After Easter, 5 Sundays, Rogations, and Ascension (p. 185). — The first Sunday after Pentecost is called (p. 199) "In octavis Penthecostes" (and assigned John III,1–15); the Sundays which follow are at first called correctly *i* and *ii* "post octavas Penth."; for the next one, however, the caption changes to "iii post Penth"; the rest, "quarta" (p. 210, with the Gospel

MS 12, p. 290, lines 10–21 (actual size of area shown: ca. 145 × 165 mm)

Estote misericordes, Lk VI,36 sqq.) through "xxiiii" (p. 267, with Mt IX,18 sqq.) have numbering without specification. — Three, apparently alternate Gospel pericopes are provided for the *Dedicatio ecclesiae*, p. 270–273 (Lk XIX,1–10; Lk VI,43–48; Jn X,22–29). — In addition to the Gospel readings, for certain occasions the book gives also the collect:[4] for Christmas (p. 15), Stephen (p. 20), John the Evangelist (p. 21), Innocents (p. 22), the Eighth Day of Christmas (p. 22), Epiphany (p. 26), its Octave Day (p. 28), Easter (p. 163), its Octave Day (p. 172), Ascension (p. 186), Pentecost (p. 190), the Octave Day of Pentecost (p. 200), dedication of a church (p. 272).

138r–151v: (f. 138r = p. 273:) ***In natalitijs sanctorum p[er] totum annum.*** (new line:) Siluestri pape (space) Vigilate. req[uire] conf. . . . (ends, f. 151v = p. 300:) . . . Thome apl'i (space) . . . require in dominica in octauis pasche.

The *sanctorale* part of the Gospel lectionary. Although completely silent about months and dates,[5] the listing follows the calendar order, beginning with the first saint's day occurring after Christmas and not included in the *temporale;*[6] this suggests that the compiler was thinking in terms of the "Nativity style" of the calendar, counting the year as beginning with Christmas.[7] — Listed are 163 festive occasions, each with either a full text or an identifying *initium* of the pertinent Gospel pericope. No graphic signals are used to distinguish occasions of greater importance. Special collect is included in 13 cases; a pericope in full, in 18.

The 163 occasions:[8]
(Gosp = the pericope text is written out in full; Coll = special collect is included)

[Dec.:] Silvestri

[Jan.:] Hylarii, Remigii, Felicis; Mauri abb.; Marcelli; Prisce; Fabiani et Sebastiani; Agnetis; Vincentii; Conversio Pauli; Preiecti; Policarpi; Agnetis

[Feb.:] Ignatii; Purificatio sc'e marie (Gosp, Coll); Agathe; Amandi et Vedasti; Scolastice; Valentini; Eleutherii epi. [of Tournai] (Coll); Cathedra Petri; Mathie.

[March:] Gregorii pape; Benedicti (Coll); Adnuntiatio dominica (Coll)

[Apr.:] Ambrosii (Paschali tempore/alio tempore); Tiburtii, Valeriani; Georgii, Felicis, Fortunati; Marci Ev.; Vitalis.

[May:] Philippi et Jacobi (Gosp); Athanasii; Alexandri, Eventii, Theodouli; Inventio s. Crucis; Johannis ante Portam Latinam; Gordiani et Epimaci; Nerei et Achillei; Victoris; Potentiane; Urbani.

[June:] Nicomedis et Rever[iani]; Marcellini et Petri; Honorate et Florine;[9] Medardi; Primi et Feliciani; Barnabe; Basilidis, Cirini, Naboris; Basilii; Landelini conf. [abbot of Lobbes]; Cirici et Julitte; Marci et Marcelliani; Gervasii et Protasii; Vigilia s. Johanis Bapt. (Gosp); [Joh. Bapt.] ad matutinalem missam (Gosp); post nocturnos et in die ad missam (Gosp, Coll); Johannis et Pauli; Leonis pape; Vigilia apostolorum Petri et Pauli (Gosp); [Petri et Pauli] ad nocturnos et in die ad missam (Gosp, Coll); Commemoratio Pauli; Martialis epi.

[July:] Oct. s. Johannis; Processi et Martiniani; Translatio Thome ap.; Dominica infra oct. apost. (i.e., Petri et Pauli, pericope indicated as "quod volueris de apostolis"); Translatio Martini (Coll); In octavis apostolorum (Gosp); Septem fratrum filiorum s. Felicitatis (Gosp); Transl. Benedicti; In octavis eiusdem; Margarete; Praxedis; Marie Magdalene; Apolinaris; Christofori et Cucufatis; Jacobi (Gosp); Nazarii, Celsi, Pantaleonis; Felicii, Simplicii, Fausti; Abdon et Sennes; Germani epi.

[Aug.:] Petri and Vincula; Stephani pape; Inventio Stephani; Syxti, Feliciani, Agapiti; Ciriaci sociorumque; Vigilia Laurentii; In die eiusdem; Tiburtii m.; Gaugerici epi.; Ipoliti sociorumque; Eusebii; Vig. s. Marie Virg. (Coll); In die eiusdem; Oct. s. Marie; Oct. s. Laurentii; Agapiti; Philiberti abbatis; Bartholomei ap.; Audoeni epi. [Rotomagensis]; Augustini; Hermetis et Juliani; Sabine; Decollatio Johannis Bapt.; Felicis et Adaucti.

[Sept.:] Egidii abb.; Prisci mar.; Bertini abb.; Humberti epi; Evurtii epi.; Adriani; Nativitas s. Marie (Coll); Dorothei et Gorgoni; Audomari; Cornelii et Cipriani; Exaltatio s. Crucis (Gosp); Octave s. Marie; Nicomedis et Valeriani; Eufemie [et] Lucie germanarum; Lamberti epi.; Vigilia s. Mathei (Gosp); In die [s. Mathei] (Gosp); Mauritii et soc.; Firmini epi.; Cosme et Damiani; Michaelis Archangeli (Gosp, Coll); Jeronimi.

[Oct.:] Remigii, Bavonis; Piati mart. (Coll); Leodegarii; Fidis virg.; Marci pape; Gisleni, Richarii; Dionisii et soc.; Calixti pape; Luce Ev.; Amati epi.; Undecim millium virginum (Coll); Crispini et Crispiniani; Amandi epi.; Vig. Simonis et Jude; Simonis et Jude; Quintini; Vig. Omnium Sanctorum.

[Nov.:] In die eorundem [i.e., Omnium SS.] (Coll); Cesarii, Eustachii, Benigni; Quatuor Coronatorum; Theodori[ni?] mart.; Vigilia Martini; In die eiusdem (Coll); Brictii epi.; Aniani et Gregorii; Cecilie; Clementis m.; Felicitatis m.; Crisogoni; Saturnini m.; Vig. s. Andree (Gosp); In die [s. Andree] (Gosp)

[Dec.:] Eligii epi.; Nicholai epi.; Eulalie; Gentiani, Victori[ci?]; Lucie; Auberti epi. [Cameracensis]; Nichasii et soc.; Thome apostoli.

152r–170r: In illo tempore. *De ap[osto]lis* . . . (f. 154v = p. 306:) *.i. m̄r* . . . (f. 157r = p. 311:) . . . *Plurimor[um] martiru[m]* . . . (f. 161v = p. 320:) . . . *In natale scōrum confess.* . . . (f. 165v = p. 328:) *De virginib[us]* . . . (f. 116v = p. 330:) . . . *De scā trinitate.* [John I,1–14] *Aliud.* [John XV,26–XVI,4] *De sp[irit]u scō* . . . (f. 167v = p. 332:) *De scā cruce* . . . (f. 168r = p. 333:) . . . *De scā maria uirgine* . . . (f. 169r = p. 335:) . . . *Pro pace.* . . . *P[ro?] p[er]secutione.* . . . (f. 169v = p. 336:) . . . *P[ro] quac[um]q[ue] t[ri]bulatione.* . . . *Ad serenitate[m] postuland[am]* . . . (f. 170r = p. 337:) . . . *Ad pluviam postulandam* . . . *Pro salute uiuorum* . . . *Pro infirmis* . . . (ends:) . . . in capite ieiunij.

The *Commune sanctorum* section of the evangeliar, followed by Gospel pericopes for votive Masses. Includes 8 choices for the Apostles, 7 for a martyr, 13 for groups of martyrs, 9 for confessors, 2 for virgins, 3 for the *De Cruce*, 4 for Masses in honor of the Virgin Mary. The whole section begins on a new page, with several lines blank at the end of the preceding page; blank lines also at end of ff. 165r (= p. 327) and 170r (= p. 337). Running titles in red in center of top margin duplicate some of the captions in the text.

170v–172r: *Pro fidelibus defunctis.* . . . (ends on f. 172r = p. 341, in lines 13–14:) . . . Om[ne]s enim ei uiuunt. (last 7 lines blank)

Six choices: John XI,21–27; V,21–24; VI,37–40; VI,51–55; V,25–29; Luke XX,27.34–38.

172v–173r: (ADDITIONS IN OTHER HANDS, FROM 14TH OR 15TH CENTURY:) *De sacramento altaris. Euangeliu[m]* (John VI,56–59) . . . (another hand:) *In visitatione b'te m[ari]e v'gis.* (Luke I,39–56) (ends on f. 173r = p. 343, with the 11th line:) [et] reversa [est] ī domū suā. (rest of the page blank; f. 173v = p. 344 and the pastedown numbered as p. 345 are blank)

INSERTED (sewn in) following f. 173, an undersize gathering of 6 paper leaves. It contains (beginning on verso of the first leaf) an updated listing, in longhand of ca. 1800, of the Gospel pericopes, with page references (using "fol." with the page numbers) to what precedes. The listing corrects or changes some of the medieval assignments: e.g., prescribes for the first Sunday of Advent the Gospel *Erunt signa* and for the "Dom. 24 post Pentec.," the *Cum videritis abominationem* (Matthew XXIV,15 sqq.). It adds *Trinitatis* and *Corpus Christi*; also, in the section captioned "Series Festorum Sanctorum" (ff. 2v–4r of the insert), a pericope for *In festo omnium Monachorum* (a Cistercian feast) and *Conceptio B.M.V.* In this list, the *Dedicatio Ecclesiae* is placed between May 3 (Finding of the Cross) and early June *(Florinae et Honoratae).* — Last three pages are ruled but blank.

* * *

Modern paging (p. 1–345) in black ink; it does not include f. 1 which has text (and decoration) on verso; p. 345 is the pastedown of lower cover. — Written area 243–245 × ca. 150 mm. — Fully ruled with stylus; verticals are single lines; they, and the two topmost as well as the two lowest horizontals reach to the edges. First line of text is above the top ruled line throughout. Pricking not preserved. — The script is a rather large, very regular, non-energetic *gothico-carolina* text hand, perhaps all by one scribe.[10] Ink (at least now) brown; the *litterae notabiliores* alternately red and green. Rubrics (mostly captions) red. — Additions on ff. 172v–173r (= p. 342–343) are by two different later hands using black ink and two varieties of textual gothic. — Parchment thickness ca. 26 mm per 100 leaves.

Collation: $1–22^8$ (1_8 = f. 8 = p. 13/14 is a cancel(?) attached to stub conjugate with 1_1; 22_2 = f. 170 = p. 337/338 is a cancel; 22_5 following f. 172 wanting, without text loss; $22_{7,8}$ are pasted to the inside of lower cover: 22_7 is blank, its recto is numbered as p. 345; only scraps remain of 22_8). — Three paper *bifolia* forming 6 leaves[11] are inserted between 22_6 (= f. 173) and 22_7 (i.e., between p. 344 and 345, at end); the chain-line marks are horizontal; watermark: fleur de lis.

Decoration: originally minimal, limited to red or green calligraphic initials: the largest of them mark the beginnings of the pericopes and are 5 to 7 lines high; the most frequent among them is the capital *I* of "In illo tempore," always set off into the margin and decorated by a simple void white vertical running through the center of the letter. The collects, when given, are signaled by 2-line red or green letters, often with some flourishing. (Rather artless flourishes, apparently done by brush, have also been added to some of the large initials.) Within a pericope, the first letter of the actual Gospel text is larger than other capitals, although basically in one line; it, too, is red or green.[12] Decorative extensions of some of the letters are marred rather than improved by repeatedly occurring short straight crosslines.[13] — Much showier decoration appears on f. 1v where the text begins: here, the original scribe had left the left-hand portion of the page blank, in anticipation of a very large initial; the one now occupying the area seems to have been supplied in 14th century. It consists of an illuminated rectangle representing the initial *I*, with branches extending into all margins; its central part includes a representation of Christ in Majesty in an interlaced vesica-shape frame on blue and gold checkerboard ground; around it, symbols of the four Evangelists and in the corners of the rectangle, their quasi-realistic representations. The prevailing colors are blue, muted red, and gold. — Possibly the same craftsman added also an illuminated initial *J* on f. 122v (= p. 342); it begins the 14th-century added text *De sacramento altaris.* (The initial *I* of the last reading, on same page but by another hand, was never executed.)

Bound in old oak boards ca. 20–22 mm thick,[14] with masterfully and elaborately carved deep compartments for ornamental plaques and/or jewels, none of which remains; numerous holes both on the face and on the edges of the covers show former location of fasteners. The boards are oversize for the text block in its present state[15] and may have been taken from another book, perhaps added at same time as the illuminated initials on ff. 1v and 122v. The book is rebacked with leather, gold-stamped in 18th-century manner and nailed to the edges of the boards. The leaves' edges are gilt.

Former owners: probably through the 18th century, an unidentified Benedictine nuns' establishment in northern France or southern Belgium, probably in the diocese of Cambrai. — Rev. Edwin A. Dalrymple of Baltimore (ownership label on inside of upper cover). — Nathaniel D. Sollers, Baltimore. — Acquired by LC in 1934 (Ms. Ac. 558564).

2° fo.: duos pisces. Sed hec quid sunt inter tan

Bibl.: De Ricci, *Census* (1935), p. 901, no. 2 (when owned by N. D. Sollers); Faye and Bond (1962), p. 121, no. 127 (Lectionarium Evangeliorum, 13th century, written in Germany). — *Illuminated books* . . . (1949), p. 51, no. 138 ("Germany (Rhineland), ca. 1300") and pl. LIII (reduced black-and-white reproduction of f. 1v). — *The History of bookbinding 525 —1950 A.D.: an exhibition* . . . (Baltimore: Walters Art Gallery, 1957), no. 12 (p. 9–10 and pl. VI).

The evangeliar (Gospel lectionary) was originally written for (quite probably in) a Benedictine nuns' establishment somewhere in the diocese of Cambrai, neither strictly Cluniac nor Cistercian but under some influence of Cluny traditions in its sanctoral and of Cistercian asceticism (then fashionable) in its style; perhaps under the control of the independently Benedictine monastery of Lobbes. — Earlier efforts to date the manuscript seem to have been overly influenced by the illuminated f. 1v which is not in style with the rest of the book and is no doubt a 14th-century addition. The script is that of French monastic scribes of the 12th century.[16] The text ignores the Transfiguration, promoted from Cluny since ca. 1130, and leaves unmentioned the founder of Cîteaux (Bernard, canonized 1174).

NOTES

1. Ca. 324 mm near the gutter, ca. 319 mm along the fore edge.

2. Lectionary variant B.2(b) as classified by A. Chavasse in *REVUE BÉNÉDICTINE,* 62 (1952) ("Les plus

anciens types du lectionnaire et de l'antiphonaire romains de la messe"), p. 10 and 13; however, for the 18th Sunday after the octave of Pentecost, our ms. gives Matthew XXII,34–46. — Cf. also the schemes given by Dom Hesbert in *PALÉOGRAPHIE MUSICALE* 14 (1931), p. 130, 132: our ms. doesn't correspond fully to any, having after the *Erat homo ex phariseis* (John III,1–15) assigned to the Pentecost octave the Hesbert numbers 1–24, type β but without any additions to the pericope no. 18.

3. The notation was not provided by the scribe; added by another hand above the pertinent text lines. It is primarily a rising or sinking series of neumes of the *virga* kind similar to form *B4* on p. 62 of Suñol's *Introduction à la paléographie musicale grégorienne* (1935); what seem to be the *torculus* (cf. *C3, op. cit.*, p. 66) also occur, as do *quilisma* or perhaps *scandicus liquescens (op. cit.*, p. [108], form 6).

4. "Collecta," also "oratio collecta": the formally worded official prayer used just before the readings in traditional Latin liturgy.

5. Lack of statement of month and date is common in the sanctoral parts of medieval liturgical books.

6. Thomas Becket (Dec. 29) is not included in either part. Becket was canonized in 1173 and his feast was incorporated in Cistercian books in 1185; in Benedictine (incl. Cluniac) sources only much later.

7. The Nativity style was used in French Hainaut but apparently not in Cambrai. Cf. Cappelli, *Cronologia*.

8. Inclusion of particular saints should indicate provenience; since my atttempts to determine local ties have failed, I give a complete listing (simplified by omission of epithets, etc.). — There are elements which bespeak the influence of Cluny (Cucuphat; Philibert; Hermetis et Juliani; Dorothei et Gorgoni; Nichomedis et Valeriani assigned, it seems from the sequence, to Sept. 16; Cesarii/Eustachii/Benigni; even the absence of Catherine and Barbara) but the most important Cluniac festivities are absent. "Landelinus" suggests the monastery Lobbes or, perhaps, as a number of other names, the area of Cambrai. The monastery Honnecourt is a candidate. — Cf. for the calendar of Cluny: G. de Valous, *Le monachisme clunisien* . . . 2nd ed. (1970), v. 1, p. [397] sqq.

9. The two not widely known female saints had each a Benedictine establishment (of nuns) named after her: Ste-Honorine de Bout-de-Bois (in the diocese of Nantes); Ste-Florine (diocese of St. Flour in Auvergne). (N.B. The much later listing of contents on the paper leaves inserted at end has them as "Florinae et Honoratae.")

10. The scribe uses an ampersand with disproportionately large lower loop; in the sanctoral, the "et" used to connect names of two saints celebrated together has an unusual shape (see illus.); "ergo" is frequently contracted as a *g* with a diminutive *o* directly over it.

11. The six leaves are undersize: ca. 293 × ca. 225 mm.

12. A very pleasing use of the red-green color scheme matching the brown of the text ink was made in the sanctoral, p. 273–300.

13. Perhaps actually marks of disapproval made by an ascetically minded corrector?

14. The upper cover is slightly thicker and carved more elaborately: altogether 17 compartments of various sizes, in elegantly curved shapes; the slightly less thick lower cover has provisions for one round center piece surrounded by a hollowed-out rectangular field reaching to ca. 20 mm from the edges. — See also the description and photograph of the binding in the 1957 exhibition catalog *The History of bookbinding* listed in the bibliography.

15. In 12th–13th century books, the size of covers did not normally exceed the size of the leaves.

16. A note (by Otto Pächt?) penciled in the margin in LC Rare Book Reading Room copy of De Ricci observes that the text was written in France ca. 1200 and the miniature added ca. 1350. — In the Walters Art Gallery publication *Illuminated manuscripts* . . . Dorothy Miner included a remark on the archaic character of the script.

MS 13

(Faye and Bond 52)

CARTHUSIAN HOMILIARY, summer part ca. 1200 (+ through ca. 1300)

Written in SE France. Parchment. 258[1] leaves, ca. 350 × ca. 240 mm (bound volume: ca 355 × ca. 240 mm) 1 column (except ff. 1–7 and 24–25 which have 2 columns) 27 lines (ff. 144–147 and 250v–266v: 22–23 lines)

ff. 1r–7v: *In exaltac[i]one scē crucis. Sermo beati augustini ep̄i de u[er]bo dn̄i: sicut moyses exaltauit* . . . Magnum sacramentum . . . (7v:) . . . ut renascamini in ueritate. Tu aute[m] d[omi]ne miserere nostri

An ADDITION codicologically different (2 columns, first line of text below top ruled line, decoration) from the rest of the book; procured perhaps shortly before the (late 13th-century?) binding; it corrects what may have been a confusion with the *Inventio s. Crucis* found on f. 146r sqq. The 12 readings for the *Exaltatio* (chiefly from Augustine's *Tractatus in Ioannem;* as in ms. 33 of the Bibliothèque de la ville de Grenoble[2]) were a part of the Carthusian office as early as 1170, those of the *Inventio* were included only in 1249;[3] but a deleted marginal note suggests the two sets found their way into our manuscript in reverse order.

8r–75v: *Dom̄c. i. post octabas pasche: Lc. scī eugl'ij. scd'm ioh'm* . . . (26r:) . . . *In die sc̄o Pentecost[es]* . . . (37v–41r:) . . . *In octab' Pentecostes* (1st, 2nd, and 3rd Sundays after the octave are omitted, without caesura, next item starting on the same page where the preceding concludes, 41r:) . . . *Dn̄c. iiii* . . . (followed by the 5th through 9th Sunday; the 10th is omitted, without caesura; on 49v, marginal rubric notes the omission, referring the user to the "quadragenarium;" 49v:) . . . *Dm̄c. xi* (the *i* added in black to the original rubricator's *x*) . . . (50v–64r, Sundays *xii–xvii;* on 64r, marginal note: hic desū[t] due ome[lie] . . . and reference to leaves ccxxiiii and ccxxvii where the wanting texts are, in fact, found; 64r–75v, Sundays *xx* through *xxv,* ending:) . . . in panis fractione cognouerunt.

The summer part of the *temporale* of Carthusian liturgical homiliary; the scribe apparently copied it from an incomplete exemplar[4] without realizing that some of the Sundays are not provided for. — The selections of patristic readings of which the text consists (from Gregory the Great, Augustine, Ambrose, *et al.*) agree almost completely with those found in the ms. Grenoble 32 (Étaix, nos. 30–69) but go sometimes farther, sometimes less far; in such cases, e.g., in the 12th reading of *In octavis Pentecostes* (f. 41r) a corrector's marginal note states "Remanet," sometimes referring to a later part of the book where the remaining portion of the homily has been added.

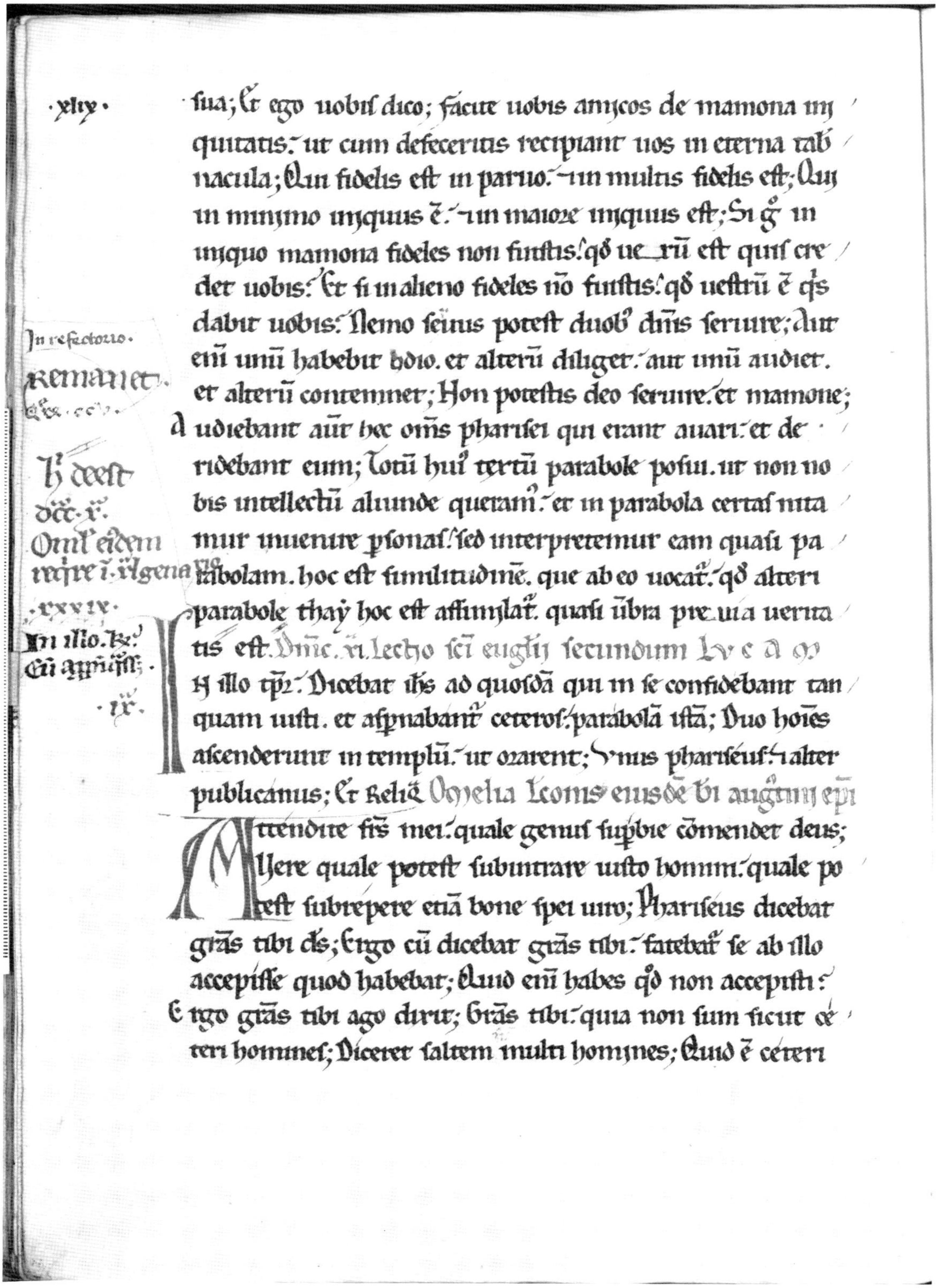

·xlix·

sua; Et ego uobis dico; facite uobis amicos de mamona ini
quitatis: ut cum defeceritis recipiant uos in eterna tab
nacula; Qui fidelis est in paruo: et in multis fidelis est; Qui
in minimo iniquus est: et in maiore iniquus est; Si ergo in
iniquo mamona fideles non fuistis: quod uestrum est quis cre
det uobis: Et si in alieno fideles non fuistis: quod uestrum est quis
dabit uobis: Nemo seruus potest duobus dominis seruire; Aut
enim unum habebit odio. et alterum diliget: aut unum audiet.
et alterum contemnet; Non potestis deo seruire. et mamone;
Audiebant autem hec omnes pharisei qui erant auari: et de
ridebant eum; Totum huius textum parabole posui. ut non no
bis intellectum aliunde queramus: et in parabola certas nita
mur inuenire personas: sed interpretemur eam quasi pa
rabolam. hoc est similitudinem. que ab eo uocatur: quod alteri
parabole thay hoc est assimilatur. quasi umbra preuia uerita
tis est. Dominica .xi. Lectio sancti euangelii secundum Lucam [illegible]
In illo tempore: Dicebat ihesus ad quosdam qui in se confidebant tan
quam iusti. et aspernabantur ceteros: parabolam istam; Duo homines
ascenderunt in templum: ut orarent; Unus phariseus: et alter
publicanus; Et reliqua. Omelia Leonis eiusdem beati augustini episcopi
Attendite fratres mei: quale genus superbie commendet deus;
Uidere quale potest subintrare iusto homini: quale po
test subrepere etiam bone spei uiro; Phariseus dicebat
gratias tibi deus; Ergo cum dicebat gratias tibi: fatebatur se ab illo
accepisse quod habebat; Quid enim habes quod non accepisti?
Ergo gratias tibi ago dixit; Gratias tibi: quia non sum sicut ce
teri homines; Diceret saltem multi homines; Quid est ceteri

In refectorio. Remanet.

MS 13, f. 49v (left-hand side of opening *xlix*)
(actual size of the leaf: ca. 350 × 240 mm)

An apparently later hand relegates final sections of some of the very long 12th readings to "in refectorio" (in the case of the 4th Sunday *post oct. Pent.,* on 42v, this is added to the earlier "remanet" note.) For the 1st Sunday after Ascension, the readings are *Sermo beati Ambrosii* (Cum Christus ascendit . . .), different from what the Grenoble ms. has (Étaix 35a); the corrector's note says: "hic debet dici . . . ," referring to f. 212 where the right selection (agreeing with Grenoble 32) is copied. The non-original leaves 24–25 (2 columns, same hand as the ff. 1–7) give as the 9th–12th readings for the octave day of Ascension, with Gospel quotation Luke XXIV,49, a homily by the Venerable Bede, "Ego inquit mitto . . . ,"[5] not included in the Grenoble ms. 32, which lacks a special homily for that occasion (cf. Étaix, no. 36b). — As in the Grenoble manuscript, Ascension, the Sunday in its octave, the octave day itself, Pentecost, and the Sunday *In octavis Pentecostes* have 12 patristic readings each; for the other Sundays, the homiliary gives only the pertinent Gospel quotation and a homily on it, marked as readings *viiii* through *xii*; the 1st–8th readings for those Sundays were from the Bible and are not included. Three (patristic) readings are given each weekday of the Pentecost week; there is no Trinity mentioned as such, and no Corpus Christi (introduced only 1318). — The readings are numbered in the outer margins by the rubricator, in red, sometimes duplicating earlier numbering done in black which was partly cropped in the (late 13th-century?) binding. — The Sundays after Pentecost are clearly counted, as in the Grenoble ms., not from the Pentecost itself but from its octave,[6] although the term "post octabas Pentecostes," found explicitly in that source (with the 1st of the Sundays, Étaix no. 45), does not occur in our copy where the 1st–3rd Sundays are wanting; in fact, in the section of "in refectorio" readings, i.e., continuations, ff. 184v–214v, the 4th (200^{bis}r) and 5th (201v) Sundays are called "iiii post pentecost[en]" and "v post pentecost[en]," while their readings continue those of the Sundays numbered "iiii" and "v" in the earlier section. The Gospels assigned these Sundays are the same as those in the Grenoble ms.; as there, their sequence seems to be quite out of step with the Roman program as recorded ca. 1244 by the Franciscans and eventually codified in official Roman liturgical books.[7]

75v–184v: . . . *In nat[a]li ap[osto]lor[um] philippi et Jacobi* . . . (79r:) . . . *joh'is baptiste* . . . (82v:) . . . *petri et pauli* . . . (86v:) . . . *In cōmemoratione scī pauli* . . . (91v:) . . . *marie magdalene* . . . (95v:) . . . *Jacobi* . . . (99v:) . . . *Laurentij* . . . (104v:) . . . *In assūptione beate marie* . . . (110r:) *D[omi]nica infra oct[a]b[a]s* . . . (119v:) . . . *Infra octabas (p[ri]ma die* . . . *Q[ui]nta die)* . . . (125v:) . . . *In octab' beate marie* . . . (130r:) . . . *bartholomei* . . . (133r:) . . . *In decollatio[n]e scī joh'is baptiste* . . . (138r:) . . . *In natiuitate beate marie* . . . (143v and 148r–152v:) . . . *cornelij et cypriani* . . . (144r, later addition:) . . . *In octab' natiuit' be' marie* . . . (146r–147v, later addition, ending imperfectly:) . . . *In inuent[i]o[n]e scē crucis* . . . (152v:) . . . mathei . . . (156r:) . . . *In sollemnitate scī michaelis archang[e]li* . . . (161v:) . . . *symonis et Jude* . . . (166v:) . . . *In sollemnitate omniu[m] s[an]c[t]or[um]* . . . (175r:) . . . *martini* . . . (180r:) . . . *In dedicatione eccl[es]ie* . . .

The summer part[8] of the *sanctorale* of the homiliary; limited, with the exception of the 1st–5th days in the octave of Mary's Assumption, to the feasts celebrated by 12 (generally patristic) readings. The feasts and the peculiarly Carthusian selection of texts agree with those in the ms. Grenoble 33 (Étaix, p. 86–92, nos. 20–38), the major difference being (aside from the additions ff. 144–147) the inclusion in our manuscript of the readings for Mary Magdalen and for the Beheading of John the Baptist in the original sequence;[9] in this respect, our ms. resembles a late 12th-century copy which combines, like ours, the seasonal and the sanctoral elements of the office for summer in one volume, the ms. 22(100) of the Grenoble municipal library (cf. Étaix, p. 100–101); that manuscript includes in its original text also the readings for St. Maurice which in our ms. are added near the end (ff. 243r sqq.) together with some other feasts datable in the period 1174–1259 (see further on in the contents). — The beginning of the readings for *Cornelii et Cypriani*[10] on 143v has been crossed through in red, probably at the time when the leaves 144–147 were being inserted into the center of the gathering (gathering 18, with twelve leaves). The two sets of readings which the insert contains (see above) were incorporated into the Carthusian office in 1249; the *Inventio Crucis* is, however, a festivity observed on May 3, not belonging anywhere near the September birthday of Our Lady; a late hand,[11] in fact, added in large red letters in the margin "In nat[a]li s. Alexa[n]dri et socior[um] ei[us]," to be understood as an indication of the time of year in which the readings should be used, not as a suggestion that the martyrs Alexander, Eventius, and Theodoulos, traditionally commemorated on May 3, should be celebrated by twelve liturgical readings.[12] The set of readings for the *Inventio* ends imperfectly in *lectio VI,* and f. 148 (conjugate with 143) continues instead the readings for Cornelius and Cyprian (through 152v); perhaps at that point the editor despaired.[13] — Marginal additions and references, by various hands, some in red, some in black include; (75v:) Marchi, quere infra circa finem libri .ccxiiii[14] (79r:) Barnabe, quere in quadrag[enario] .xxviij;[15] (82v:) Ioannis et Pauli, quere in quadrag.xxxv. homelia; (99v:) Petri ad Vincula, quere in fine libri .cclvii; (133r:) Quere lecciones beati Augustini in fine libri .ccl; (142r:) Dominica infra octab' natiuitatis b'e M'e facimus octo lecciones de hystoria et dicimus homeliam beati Hylarii . . .; (143v:) Lecciones de Exaltacione sce crucis quere in principio libri; (146v, in red, the note specifying the correct date of *Inventio Crucis,* "In natali s. Alexandri . . .," see above and note 12) (156r:) Mauricii (referring to "ccxlii," i.e., 243r); (161v:) Ieronimi (quere in quadragenario . . .) Dionisii (quere in quadragenario . . .) Firmini (quere in fine huius libri .cclii[16]) Luce (quere infra . . . ccxviii) Theodori[17] (quere in quadragenario . . .); (175r:) lectiones in dedicatione ecclesie quere post festum scī martini .clxxix; hic desunt lecciones et homel. in sollennitate reliquiarum, quere in fine . . . .ccxlv; (180r:) Hugonis, sicut scī martini . . . .clxxiiij; Clementis . . . in quadragenario; Catherine, in alio volumine in festo scē agate;[18] (184v:) in sollenitate reliquiarum quere ca. finem huius libri .ccxlv. — Some of the readings differ in length[19] from those in the ms. Grenoble 33; this may have happened by mistake or otherwise, presumably not all exemplars were in complete agreement; marginal notes in red or black signal in various places that the corrector/editor found the text to be incomplete, e.g., on 94r: "Remanet, quere in quadragenario .xxxiii" or, on 98r: "Remanet, quere .ccxi," to which another, probably later hand added: in refectorio.

184v–214v: *D[omi]nica ii post octb's pasche. in refectorio* Jam quippe resurrexerat . . . (185v:) . . . *Dn̄c. iiij p[ost] octb's pasche. in refectorio* . . . (188v:) . . . *feria iij. post pentecosten. in refectorio.* . . . (194 [written "clxliiii"]v:) *fr'a. iiij. post pentec'. in refectorio.* . . . (198v:) . . . *Sabbato p[ost] pentec'. in refectorio* . . . (200v:) *In octab'. pentec. in refectorio.* . . . (200bisr:) . . . *Dn̄ica iiij. post pentec[osten].*[20] *in refectorio.* . . . (201v:) . . . *D[omi]nica v. post pentec'. in refectorio.* . . . (202v, the 6th Sunday; 7th omitted; 204v, 8th; 206r, 9th; 10th omitted; 207v, 11th; 12th omitted; 208v, 13th; 14th omitted; 209r, 15th; all "*in refectorio*") (211v:) . . . *In nat[a]li scī jacobi apl'i. in refectorio.* . . . (212v:) . . . *Dm̄c. post ascensionem dn̄i. Sermo beati augustini epī.* Solle[m]nitate[m?] diei hui[us] . . . (= Étaix, p. 74, no. 35a; ends on 214v:) . . . diuisio accusata. (lower half of 214v blank, unruled)

The readings "in refectorio"[21] continued or were added to the biblical (not included in the homiliary) or patristic liturgical readings used in communal prayer. Some of those contained in this part complete the texts begun on ff. 8–75 by adding the remainder of what in the older manuscript Grenoble 32 is included in the basic set; e.g., the reading which starts on 184v continues Augustine's text from *Tractatus in Ioannem* cut short on ff. 9r–10v until all that the older source prescribed is available (cf. Étaix, p. 73, no. 31). — Omissions correspond in part to those noted earlier in the contents of ff. 8–75, suggesting that the exemplar had all the material together (as the Grenoble ms. does; not divided into readings in church and readings *in refectorio*) in the gathering or group of leaves which eventually (before copying) became lost. — The text for the 1st Sunday after Ascension (212v–214v) was meant to replace that found on ff. 16v–20v, as per corrector's note there added.

215r–222r: *In natali scī marci eu[an]g[e]liste* . . . (218v:) . . . *In natali beati luce eu[an]g[e]liste* . . . (ends on 222r:) . . . neq[ue] peram neq[ue] calciamenta (222v blank)

Homiliary readings for the feasts of the two Evangelists who were not from among the apostles; celebrated as "festa 12 lectionum" probably since before 1170.[22] Copied on a separate gathering (the 27th in our collation), by two hands (change of writer in 8th line of 217v). — The corresponding texts in the Grenoble ms. 33, there added in the 12th or 13th century, are slightly shorter (cf. Étaix, p. 94, no. 46ab; p. 95, no. 50ab).

223r–250: *Dn̄ica xxi.* . . . (9th–12th readings; duplicating texts already present on ff. 50v–52!) (224v:) . . . *Dm̄c. xviii* (9th–12th readings, signaled by marginal reference on 65r; text as in Grenoble ms. 32, Étaix, p. 78, no. 62) (227v:) . . . *Dm̄c. xviiii* (9th–12th readings, Étaix, *loc. cit.,* no. 63; also signaled on 65r) (229v:) . . . *In nat'li scī math[e]i* (9th–12th readings, as in Grenoble ms. 33, Étaix, p. 91, no. 34b; signaled in marginal note 156r) (241v:) . . . *[uncaptioned]* (9th–12th readings, Étaix, p. 95, no. 49b, i.e., for St. Maurice) (243r:) . . . *Mauricij et socior[um]* (1st–8th readings, Étaix, *loc. cit.,* no. 49a; at end, marginal note: Omelia e[st] an[te] sermone[m] (264r:) . . . *In festo reliq[ui]ar[um]* (12 readings, Étaix, *loc. cit.,* no. 51a,b; ending on 250r in line 21; rest of 250r blank)

ADDITIONS of uncertain, probably quite early date (not much after 1200). The readings for St. Luke (Oct. 18) added in the preceding gathering would properly belong after *Mauricii* (Sept. 12) and before the Relics (Nov. 8).

250v–266v: *In festo beati gregorij et beati ambrosij et beati augustini* . . . (cf. Étaix, p. 93, no. 42a,b) (258r, beginning a new gathering:) *In festo scī petri ad vinc[u]la. lectiones ex actibus Apostolorum. Lectio prima.* Factum est autem . . . (8 readings, Acts IX, 32–XII,24; on 263r, after the 8th lesson, words "Euangelium et homelia dicuntur sicut in Natali apostolorum Petri et Pauli" are crossed through in red) (263r:) . . . *In Conu[er]sio[n]e scī Pauli: Lecc[ion]es ex actibus apostolor[um]. Lc. i.* Saulus adhuc . . . (8 readings, Acts IX,1–31 and XII, 25–XIII, 52; on 266v, after the 8th lesson, words "Euāg[e]liū et homel[ia] dicit[ur] sic[ut] in [co]m̄em. s. pauli lxxxviii" are crossed through in red).

Codicologically different (22–23 lines) ADDITIONS, made perhaps in the 2nd half of the 13th century: the (Aug. 1) day of "Petri Ad Vincula" became a 12-readings celebration at some time before 1259. The *Conversio Pauli,* of the older date, doesn't properly belong into the homiliary for summer (its traditional date is January 25); may have been included for the biblical readings which tie in with the set for *Petri Ad Vincula.*

* * *

Thirteenth(?)-century foliation on versos, in roman numerals;[23] last leaf numbered 266 (cclxvi), due to misnumbering of the leaf which follows f. 229 as 240, this error carried to the end. Two smaller-size leaves (one following f. xxi, ca. 160 × ca. 230 mm, another following f. xxx, ca. 120 × ca. 240 mm) are not included in the numbering. One free endleaf at the beginning and one at end. — Written area ca. 265 × ca. 165 mm. First line of text above the top ruled line (except in the 2-column later additions). Ruled in plummet, with varying fullness and for the most part on the flesh side only. The vertical framing lines, when present, are always doubled. Pricking preserved in inner and outer margins. — Written by several hands, maintaining (except in late additions and marginal notes) much the same strong and clearly legible pre-gothic script; the 2-column additions (ff. 1–7, 24–25) are early gothic of ca. 1300. — Generous punctuation, using *punctus elevatus, flexus,* and colon. — Brownish black ink powdering off on some pages. Rubrics (mostly captions) and *litterae notabiliores* all in red, in some places noticeably thick and deep. — Modest quality parchment; thickness of text block ca. 60 mm (= ca. 23.3 mm per 100 leaves).

Collation: 1^{6+1}(f. v. is added singleton) 2^8 3^{8+4} (3_7 = f.xxiii is a cancel; unnumbered [xxi *bis*] and f. xxii are tipped to its recto, ff. xxiiii and xxv to its verso) 4^{8+1} (unnumbered [xxx *bis*] sewn in following 4_4) 5–17⁸ 18^{12} (= ff. cxxxx–cli) 19–28^8 29^{8+1} (f. ccxlvii is added singleton) 30^8 31^{8+1}(f. cclxvi is added singleton). — In gathering 11, f. xc is misnumbered xci, error continued through f. cc. where it is corrected by "cc" used also on [cc *bis*]. In gathering 28, leaf following f. ccxxix misnumbered ccxl, error continued through end of book. — Catchwords on versos of last leaves of all gatherings except 1 (gathering not original), 2 (last f.: xv), 7 (last f.: lviii), 11 (last f.: xci), 20 (last f.: clxvii), 26 (last f.: ccxiiii), 27 (last f.: ccxxii), 28 (last f.: ccxl), 29 (last f.: ccxlix)

Decoration: minimal, especially in the older parts which are the bulk of the volume; limited to calligraphic initials in red ink, the larger ones (up to 7 lines high when offset into margin) slightly embellished by use of void white and some simple black flourishes; they generally begin a set of readings (when a homily is preceded by a Gospel quote, the large letter begins the homily text). — On the non-original leaves 1–7, the initials are somewhat smaller but done alternately in red or green with pen flourishes in the other color (the initial *M* on f. 1r combines, by exception, both colors). Green decoration of a red letter appears also on verso of the added incomplete leaf 21*bis* (with an unusually formed *C*) and on 43r; on recto of the non-original 24r, homily is begun by an *E* in blue.

Binding: original wooden boards (rounded edges) with remnants of extremely deteriorated leather (pigskin?) covering. Sewn over 3 bands. Remnants of two leather clasps attached by metal fasteners.

Former owners: Carthusian monastery Valbonne in present dept. Gard, France: in 13th century, and quite possibly from its foundation in 1203 until 1901 (when its monks went into exile in Spain). — Obtained by LC in 1929 from Madrid (Ms. Ac. 4189(31), n. 1)

2° fo.: in eius nomine quē tāquā

Bibl.: De Ricci, *Census* (1935), p. 218, no. 77 ("Lectionarium . . . written in Italy"); Faye and Bond (1962), p. 119, no. 52.

The need for a set of homilies for saints Firminus and Ferreolus (marginal notes on ff. 161v and 252v, readings indicated on 252v–256r), with the two named together and with the celebration of Firmin noted (on 161v) after that of Denis but before that of Luke, hence identifying him, among the several saints by that name, as Firminus the former bishop of Uzès, and Ferreolus as the other former bishop and patron saint of that diocese, leads to the charterhouse Valbonne,[24] located in Uzès area. The book was probably begun elsewhere, perhaps at the original Grande Chartreuse itself, toward the end of the 12th century; judging from certain lacunae in its *temporale*, from an imperfect exemplar (cf. contents of ff. 8–75). Carthusian reserve regarding communication may account for other editorial imperfections. After the founding of Valbonne (1203), the book may have served as its communal homiliary (for the "summer" half of the year) for about a hundred years; it received during that time successive additions and underwent editing, reaching its present shape by ca. 1300; since it lacks any mention of feasts introduced in the 14th century (e.g., Corpus Christi), the ms. must have fallen into disuse shortly thereafter. It may of course have stayed in the monastery until its end and have been brought to Spain by the monks. — Both the obvious need for one and express reference in margin of f. 180r call for the existence of a corresponding volume for "winter," not unlikely rather uniform in format. Another book referred to in marginal notes (ff. 75–84) is the "Quadragenarium," i.e., Gregory the Great's *Homeliae quadraginta in Evangelia (PL* LXXVI).

NOTES

1. Last leaf numbered 266 (cclxvi); see description following contents.

2. Cf. R. Étaix, "L'Homiliaire Cartusien" (*SACRIS ERUDIRI* 13 [1962], p. [67]–112), p. 96–97. Étaix gives detailed lists of contents of two 12th-century

manuscripts from the Grande Chartreuse, now in the Grenoble municipal library: the ms. 32 which contains the seasonal part (the *temporale*) of Carthusian homiliary and the ms. 33 with readings for saints' days (the *sanctorale*); single items in each ms. are assigned numbers and the texts are identified; my description refers repeatedly to these numbers.

3. The most up-to-date source of information on these dates (correcting the earlier study in *Dict. d'archéologie chrétienne* 3,1 and the table in Leroquais, *Bréviaires manuscrits* 1, Introd.) is the article "Le calendrier (cartusien)" in *ÉTUDES GRÉGORIENNES* 2 (1957), p. 153–161, signed by fr. Benoît du Moustier, i.e., Benoît Lambres O.Cart. Some critical modifications have been suggested by Hansjakob Becker in his *Die Responsorien des Kartäuserbreviers* (1971, in the series Münchener theologische Studien, II, 39. Bd.), p. 42–49.

4. In that exemplar, presumably, leaves or gatherings with the missing Sundays had got lost; in the copy which is our manuscript, the lacunae do not correspond to any physically missing parts.

5. Bede, *Hom.*II, 15, lines 86–196 (*CCSL* 122, p. 282–285).

6. Corresponding to the numbering "post Trinitatem" sometimes used by others (Dominicans, also the Breviary of Lübeck, our MS 29) in later times.

7. The Gospel *Estote misericordes* (Luke VI, 36–37) assigned to "Dom. iiii" in the Carthusian homiliary goes to 1st Sunday after Pentecost in the *Breviarium Romanae Curiae*; the homiliary puts Luke V,1–3 on 5th Sunday after the octave of Pentecost, the Curia Breviary on 4th after Pentecost; this actual difference of two weeks is then maintained through the "Dom. xxiiii" of the homiliary, with Matthew IX,18 (Domine filia mea . . .) read in Rome two weeks earlier; while the pericope given and commented upon on the 25th Sunday (not numbered in Étaix, no. 69, but labeled "xxv" in our ms., f. 73v) in the homiliary, John VI,5 (Cum sublevasset . . .), seems to have had no place in the Roman order of pericopes of the time. On its side, the Carthusian source has nothing about the *abominatio desolationis,* Matthew XXIV,15, assigned to 24th Sunday after Pentecost by the use of the Curia. (Cf. for the Roman program: *Sources of the modern Roman liturgy,* ed. S. J. P. van Dijk [Leiden, 1963], v. 2, p. 104–109.)

8. From Phillip and James, celebrated on May 1 (the homiliary gives no dates) through St. Martin, whose day was Nov. 11; the *Dedicatio ecclesiae* appears to have come still later in the year in the charterhouse for which the manuscript was written (Valbonne?). — N.B. Our description separates the seasonal and the sanctoral parts but there is no caesura between them in the manuscript: the sanctoral begins with the 18th line of f. 75v.

9. In the ms. Grenoble 33 (the oldest preserved copy of the sanctoral, datable in its basic layer from first half of 12th century) both Mary Magdalen and the *Decollatio Joannis Baptiste* are later additions (Étaix, p. 94–95, nos. 47–48; cf. p. 81). There is some uncertainty about the point at which these two occasions became feasts "duodecim lectionum"; the calendar in the *ÉTUDES GRÉG.* says the upgrading dates from 1170 or at least before 1222; Étaix's study seems to support the earlier timing.

10. Originally, judging from the Grenoble ms. 33 and other indications, the day of Cornelius and Cyprian was celebrated by twelve readings; taken from the *Liber pontificalis* (cf. Étaix no. 33a) the first three are uncharacteristically (for the Carthusian homiliary) hagiographical. By the end of the 12th century, if not earlier, the main theme of the day (Sept. 14) shifted to "Exaltatio s. Crucis" with a quite different set of readings of its own (Étaix, p. 96–97, no. 60a–d); lack of these in the exemplar and/or confusion of the *Exaltatio* with the *Inventio* may have caused the situation we are describing.

11. Same as that which added "Hic deest Dominica x . . ." on 49v.

12. The readings given in our ms. for the *Inventio*, an incomplete set, are from Augustine's *De sermone Domini in monte,* 1. I,1,3 through 3,10 (*CCSL* 35, p. 3–7, "Beati pauperes . . ." through ". . . et haec postea,") ending imperfectly in the last line of f. 147v. A black marginal note (by Valbonne corrector-editor?) on f. 146r suggested that these readings could be used on the feast of the *Exaltatio;* that note was later crossed through, perhaps when the present ff. 1–7 were being added.

13. While the inserted section (ff. 144–147) is clearly later than the writing which precedes and follows, its texts for the octave day of *Nativitas B.M.V.* continue the Song of Solomon (ch. V,8–VIII,14) of which the readings for the feast itself cover only ch. I,1–V,7 (ff. 138r sqq.). In the Grenoble manuscripts 33 and 22, both from the 12th century, the whole Song is assigned to the main feast (Étaix, p. 90, no. 32a, and p. 100) and the octave day is not mentioned; it did not become a twelve-readings day until 1249. It may be that the main feast's reading pensum had by that time already been shortened.

14. In most cases, the roman numbering referring to a specific numbered two-page spread in the book itself is not by same hand as the rest of the note.

15. "Quadragenarium" = *XL homiliarum in Evangelia libro duo,* by Gregory the Great (*PL* LXXVI, 1075–1312).

16. The referral leads to another marginal note, on 252v: on 252v–256r, the long 8th reading for Gregory/Ambrose/Augustine is additionally marked to serve, split into sections, as 8 first readings for the two bishops and patrons of Uzès, Firminus and Ferreolus.

17. Theodoritus, patron of Uzès cathedral, celebrated Oct. 23 (information from R. Étaix).

18. Agathe = Feb. 5; the note confirms the existence of a corresponding volume for the winter season.

19. For the *Decollatio Joannis Baptiste*, our ms. (f. 136v sqq.) continues Jerome's homily well beyond what is included in the Grenoble 33 (in *CCSL* 27, it is *In Mattheum II,* 1115–1181 compared to 1115–1203); for *Michaelis,* the 8th reading (from

Gregory's *Hom. 34 in Ev.*) goes much further in the Grenoble ms. (ours is shorter by three sections) but the excerpt from Jerome in 1. IX–XII is longer in LC copy.

20. This should have been "post octavas Pentecostes," cf. our notes to section 8r–75v.

21. Carthusian rules limited communal use of the refectory to Sundays and certain feasts. Cf. *Consuetudines Cartusiae* (by Guigo I, *d.* 1136) in *PL* CLIII, 635–760 (ch. IV,32; VII,8; VIII,7; XXXIII)

22. Cf. the calendar in *ÉTUDES GRÉG., loc. cit.,* Apr. 25 and Oct. 18.

23. I have substituted corresponding arabic numerals except in the collation paragraph or where the original roman seems to help clarity. — N.B. There is considerable evidence (marginal notes on 75v, 156r, 175r, 180r referring to 215r as "ccxiiii," to 243r as "ccxlii," to 246r as "ccxlv," to 175r as "clxxiiij") that the Carthusian editor and/or foliator was thinking in terms of spreads or openings, counting always the two open pages before him as a unit; each of his numbers denotes the verso of one leaf and the recto of the next. For practical reasons, I have disregarded this in the contents and notes, using the foliator's numbers as if they had been meant to number leaves.

24. The monastery was suppressed in 1901. Since 1926, the place has been a leprosarium. Cf. A. Delord, *Valbonne* (Pont-St-Esprit, 1956).

MS 14

(Faye and Bond 9)

PSALTER XIIIth c., 1st half

Written in southern Germany. Parchment. 166 leaves, ca. 184 × ca. 140 mm (bound volume: ca. 190 × ca. 158 mm) 1 column. 18 lines.

p. 1–331: *ps̄ D̄D̄* (B)[16]eat[us] uir//*qui non*//abiit ī cō//*silio im*//pio[rum] et ī//*uia pec*//cato[rum] n̄ //*stetit et* . . . (p. 304, lines 11–12:) . . . om[n]is spiritus laudet dominum. (ibid. line 13:) (C)onfitebor tibi d[omi]ne quo[niam] iratus es michi . . . [= Is. XII,1–6] (p. 305:) . . . (E)go dixi ī dimidio . . . [= Is. XXXVIII,10–20] (p. 307:) . . . (E)xultauit cor meū ī dn̄o . . . [= 1 Sam. II,1–10] (p. 309:) . . . (C)antem[us] dn̄o gloriose enim . . . [= Ex. XV,1–19] (p. 312:). . . (D)nē audiui auditionē tuā . . . [= Hab. III,2–19] (p. 315:). . . (A)udite celi que loq[uo]r . . . [= Deut. XXXII,1–43] (p. 322:) . . . (B)enedicite omīa op[er]a . . . [= Dan. III,57–88.56] (p. 324:). . . (B)enedictus dn̄s d's isr[ae]l . . . [= Lk. I,68–79] (p. 325:). . . (T)e deū laudam[us] . . . (p. 327). . . (Q)uicumq[ue] uult . . . katholicā fidem . . . (ends on p. 331, line 15:) . . . esse non poterit.

The Psalms in straight biblical order, without titles,[1] numbering, or (originally) other additions. Liturgical (or traditional) divisions are marked by large illuminated initials (cf. Decoration); signaled in this manner are Pss. I, XXVII, XXXIX, [LII?], LXIX, LXXXI, [CII?], and CX.[2] — The text is a mixed one; in a number of places, readings originally present but found to be at variance with the Gallican Psalter (cf. Stegmüller 21) have been variously amended,[3] by additions, erasures and rewriting, or otherwise, in a rather unskilled hand more or less unsuccessfully imitating the original script.

The Psalms are followed, without interruption or (originally) caption, by the "canticles" (cf. Stegm. 21g sq.): from the Old Testament, the rather usual set of seven[4] but of the New Testament canticles only the *Benedictus*, followed by the non-biblical *Te Deum laudamus* and the Athanasian Creed.[5] None of these is captioned except by a later hand in the margin.[6] — The text of the canticles, too, differed originally from that of the Vulgate and was subjected to some very noticeable later corrections.[7]

p. 331–336: *Inuocatio ad sa[n]ctos.*[8] (K)yrieleyson. Xp̄eleyson. Xp̄e audi nos. Saluator mundi adiuua nos. (p. 332:) S[an]c[t]a Maria . . . Michahel . . . Raphahel . . . Tathee . . . Xixte . . . alexander . . . (p. 333:) . . . Emmeram[m]e . . . Lamp[er]te . . . Vite . . . Crisante . . . pantaleymon . . . Dyonisi cum sociis tuis . . . Gereon cū sociis tuis . . . Ciriace cū sociis tuis . . . hilari . . . Rv(o)p[er]te . . .

Wolfgange . . . Herharde . . . v(o)dalrice . . . valentine . . . Galle . . . Magne . . . (p. 334:) leonarde . . . Egidi . . . margareta . . . afra . . . Xp̄ina [= Christina] . . . walpurgis . . . Juliana . . . vrsula . . . kvnegvndis . . . katherina . . . (p. 335:) . . . Agne dei . . . (p. 336:) . . . (O)m[ni]p̄c sempit[er]ne deus respice[re] dignare sup[er] ap[osto]licam dignitate[m] . . . Omp̄c sempiterne d's q[ui] omnem homine[m] [con]fitente[m] tibi . . . peccata dimitte. p[er].[9]

The saints' invocations are arranged in double columns. — The litany names, after Mary, the angels, and apostles, 27 individual martyrs, 18 confessors, 15 women. The saints named in the quoted text above characterize South German calendars, corresponding perhaps best (in view of the absence of Oswald who was commemorated but not emphatically celebrated there) to that of Regensburg.[10] — Worthy of noting may be the omission of the third "eleison," and the "Saluator mundi . . ." invocation. — Added in later hands, under the first column on p. 332, "Scē Johannes baptista" (the "baptista" imperfectly deleted!); under first column on p. 334, "Scā Elisabeth." — Throughout, the phrase "ora pro nobis" is abridged or symbolized by a lowercase *o* followed by the sign usually representing "-rum."

MARGINAL ADDITIONS:

(p. 1, head margin:) (one or more lines cropped?) (est?) (b[ea]t[us]?) q[ui] n[on] cogitauit n[on] fecit n[on] docuit mala sic[ut] X[ristus] Meditac[i]o legis no[n] solu[m] est i[n] legendis sc[ri]pturis [sed] . . . o[mn]]ia facie[n]s meditat[ur] lege[m] die ac nocte

(p. 1, tail margin; probably another hand:) Materia h[uius] ps[almi] Est X[ristus] ad[am?] corp[us?] suo[rum?] ecia[m] fideliu[m] et Dyaboli [i.e.?] multitudo iniquoru[m] . . . Intenc[i]o ei[us] est a malis r[e]u[o]c(are?) et ad bona i[n]vita[r]e

Both items quoted date probably from the early 1400s, written in Southern Germany or perhaps in Austria; the script is the hasty cursive used at that time by students and teachers at the universities of Central Europe.[11] Marginal (or, occasionally, interlinear) notes and comments occur throughout the book but are much more numerous at the beginning. Of them, the commentary in the tail margin which starts on p. 1

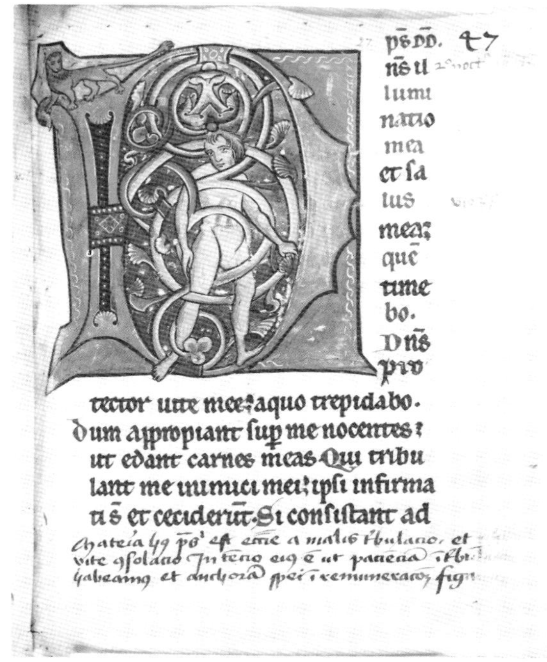

MS 14, p. 47 (beginning of Psalm XXVII) (actual size of area shown: ca. 170 × 135 mm)

is the most systematic: ca. 5 lines per psalm, always formulated according to the scheme "Materia . . . Intencio . . ."; it is provided to Pss. I through XX (p. 1–34) and again, after a gap, to XXVII and XXVIII (p. 47 and 49).[12] — Another hand, not very distant in time, added marginal notes of liturgical content, in particular antiphons. Some may have been erased or washed off; the preserved antiphonal material begins on p. 40 (at end of Ps. XXII) and runs through p. 235 (end of Ps. CIX).[13] — A verse count, in red cursive of ca. 1400 (always "v[er]s[us]" followed by the number in lowercase roman numerals) is given in the outer margin near the beginning of most psalms (incl. also the canticles, etc., through the *Quicunque*); it appears regularly beginning with the Ps. XXI (p. 35).[14] The count corresponds to the number of the red versals (plus the initial) and doesn't entirely agree — sometimes disagrees considerably[15] —

with the verse count which eventually became common in the Bibles. — Throughout the book, the margins bear signs of erasures or deletions by means of washing.[16]

* * *

Late medieval pagination in arabic numerals,[17] 1–336 (leaves containing p. 103–104 and 205–206 are lost) doesn't include free vellum endleaves, two in front and two at end, none original. — Written area ca. 133 × ca. 90 mm. — Fully ruled in bluish gray lead or crayon; except for the framing horizontals, the lines are drawn very lightly and do not go beyond the framing verticals; framing lines not doubled. Pricking not preserved. First line of text above top ruled horizontal throughout. — Large, regular early gothic script apparently by one scribe[18]; marginal additions (some commentary, corrections, etc.) by various hands and from various time periods. The main text was written in a brownish black ink which has kept extremely well; of the marginal additions, some are faded, some also erased or washed off. Parchment of good quality; thickness ca. 20.6 mm per 100 leaves; cropped especially in the upper margin, with loss of some marginal later-date material.

Collation[19]: [1–6]^{8} [7]$^{10?}$(= p. 97–116; [7]$_{4}$ = p. 103/4 wanting, text loss[20]) [8]^{4} [9]$^{1+10}$(singleton p. 125/6 attached to [9]$_{1}$) [10]^{6} [11]$^{1+8}$(singleton p. 159/60 attached to [11]$_{1}$) [12]$^{1+6}$(singleton p. 177/178 attached to [12]$_{1}$) [13]^{10}(= p. 191–210; [13]$_{8}$ = p. 205/6 wanting, text loss[21]) [14]^{6} [15]$^{1+8}$(singleton p. 223/224 attached to [15]$_{1}$) [16 – 18]^{8} [19]$^{8?\ (2+4+2?)}$ [20]^{8} [21]$^{8?\ (2+4+2?)}$

Decoration: Preserved[22] are six illuminated initials which mark, in a not entirely regular manner, the traditional liturgical divisions of the Psalter:

p. 1, with Ps. I (Beatus vir . . .): a 16-line *B*, ca. 123 × ca. 75 mm. The body of the letter is part of (not distinguished from) a vine-like scroll characterized by sharply angular bends, besides spirals and blossomy shapes. The scroll is chiefly light green, with some light blue, muted purplish red, and yellow; the whole is set in an irregularly rectangular unevenly mauve field with sharp triangular protuberances at the corners. All shapes are outlined in black; laid gold fills free spaces within the letter. The craftsmanship is mediocre. (See plate VII, p. xxii.)

p. 47, with Ps. XXVII (Dominus illuminatio mea): a 12–line square-letter *D*, light yellowish green, paneled in black. It is inhabited by a 68–mm blond-haired David in a loincloth[23] entwined in a vinelike scroll, on laid gold ground; on the outside of the letter, in the upper left corner, is a yellow lion. The whole is set in a mutedly mauve irregularly rectangular field ca. 90 × ca. 85 mm.

p. 76, with Ps. XXXIX (Dixi custodiam vias meas): 12–line uncial *D* in two shades of blue, upper terminal green; infilled with spiral scroll(s), green or muted mauve, gold ground; the whole in a mauve field ca. 100 × ca. 90 mm.

p. 133, with Ps. LXIX (Salvum me fac Deus): 13–line *S* styled as a scroll, light mauve with red, blue, and green areas. In the upper loop, a yellow lion, and in the lower, a horned lizard-like monster, light red; both animals on gold ground. The letter is set in a light blue rectangular field inside a pea-green rectangular frame, ca. 97 × ca. 75 mm.

p. 169, with Ps. LXXXI (Exultate Deo adiutori nostro): 11–line *E* in greyish mauve and light green, the latter (the center bar) painted over the gold ground and issuing in spiral scrolls. A lion standing on hind legs is attempting to penetrate the letter. The whole is set in a blue rectangle inside a red frame.

p. 235, with Ps. CX (Dixit Dominus): an 11–line uncial *D*; the only major initial in this ms. which does not begin a page (it is preceded by 7 lines of text). The letter is in two shades of green (upper terminal blue) and infilled with scroll. It appears smudged;

the metal (tin?) leaf used here instead of gold has deteriorated. (Basically rectangular frame, mauve, ca. 76 × 68 mm.)

In all these initials, some of the shoots of the vine-scrolls end in shell-like acanthus leaves. Two shades of hue, often used for the body of a letter, tend to meet without a marked dividing line. — In the presence of one of these letters, the beginning of a psalm is always split into short segments written in the remaining narrow column, with lines alternately red or black (cf. example in contents with the beginning of Ps. I).

Three-line calligraphic initials, mostly plain letters, alternately red or blue (occasionally bicolor) begin other psalms, also the segments into which the long Ps. CXIX was divided for liturgical purposes; they are omitted with the Pss. CXLIX (p. 303) and CL (p. 304) which were used as one unit in the Lauds of the office. The biblical canticles, the *Te Deum*, and the symbolum *Quicunque* which follow are signaled in the same manner. The three-line initials are accompanied by very modest flourishing in red, blue-black, or one of several tints of blue. — Ordinary versals are red throughout, with base slightly below the line; whenever a verse begins at the left margin, the versal is placed outside the text column.[24]

Bound in modern red velvet.[25] Gilt edges. — On the (vellum) pastedown of upper cover, an older and a more recent label of the Library of Congress;[26] penciled on one of them, "MS. 9" (its pre-accession number retained also by De Ricci and Bond). Other numbers penciled on the pastedown: "Temp. no. 15"; "(no. 13)"; "1306"; "202," crossed through in ink; in ink: "n° 15," crossed through in pencil; also penciled note: "Most beautiful very early MSS about the 11th or 12th century as shown by the style of the Capital Letters." — On p. 1, in outer margin, oval stamp: LIBRARY OF CONGRESS//[ ]81 //CITY OF WASHINGTON.

Former owners: none known.

2° fo. (= p. 3): a nobis iugum ipso[rum]. Qui habitat in

Bibl.: De Ricci, *Census*, v. 1 (1935), p. 182, no. 9; Faye and Bond (1962), p. 117, no. 9.

NOTES

1. "Psalmus David" (more or less abbreviated) is used (written in red) for the psalms signaled by major initials (except Ps. CX), and in 23 other cases, incl. two subdivisions of the long Ps. CXIX (not its beginning); this agrees only occasionally with the use of that title in the Bible. — N.B. A very recent hand has added the psalm numbers, in pencil, using arabic numerals and the now common numbering system, near the opening initials.

2. The beginnings of Pss. LII (Quid gloriaris in malitia; verses 1–5 wanting) and CII (Domine exaudi orationem meam; v. 1–3 wanting) are lost with the missing leaves [52] (= p. 103/104) and [103] (= p. 205/206). Since the psalms immediately preceding are in both cases complete, we assume that the pages 104 and 206 contained large initials, along with the missing text (it remains unclear why a whole leaf should have been needed in either case; the pages with large initials accommodate 3 to 5 verses). — Singling out the Pss. LII and CII for special treatment corresponds to a nonliturgical tripartite division of the Psalter said to be of Irish origin and not unknown in Germany (cf. Hughes, *Medieval manuscripts*, p. 225). — Liturgical purpose would have required further initials with Pss. LIII and XCVIII (Dixit insipiens, p. 105, and Cantate Domino, p. 200) but neither is marked in any special way; whether this should be interpreted as significant or merely a result of the scribe's or editor's carelessness, I do not know.

3. E.g., on p. 3, in Ps. II,9, "et" added after "ferrea"; p. 6, Ps. V,9 "tuo viam meam" changed to "meo viam tuam" (contrary to the Clementina and to the Breviary, but cf. the Stuttgart critical ed. of the Vulgate); p. 231, in Ps. CVIII, three interesting corrections made, in varying manner: in verse 8, "metibor" (itself not original?) corrected to "dimeciar"; in verse 10 (line 8), "Moab lebes" is a correction of what must have at first read "Moab olla"; in v. 12 (line 14), "exibis" replaced, probably, original "egredieris"; in this case and in some others the phrasing originally present was that of the Roman Psalter; in the Ps. XCV (Venite exultemus, p. 196 sq.), corrections leading to conformity with the Gallican (= Clementine Vulgate) version have been made even though common liturgical usage had retained the Roman text.

4. I think this set wasn't relegated (except for the *Benedicite omnia opera*) to penitential periods until modern times. (Disagreeing with Hughes, *op. cit.*, p. 365 sq.; cf. Haymo's *Ordo breviarii* in *SMRL* II, also *Lex. f. Theol. u. Kirche*, art. *Cantica*)

5. The Benedictus (Song of Zechariah) was part of the Lauds, the Te Deum of the Matins, the Athanasian Creed of the Prime. The absent Magnificat and Nunc dimittis belonged to the Vespers and Compline, respectively.

6. "Canticum feria 2ª" on p. 304, etc., only through "feria 5ª" on p. 309; all this written in red ink, over washed-off older marginalia.

7. In the text from Is. XXXVIII, in verse 14, "responde" corrected to "sponde"; in verse 15, "tibi" deleted after "Recogitabo." In Moses' song from Exodus XV, the word "magnificatus" in verse 1 is on a strip pasted over what probably had red "honorificatus," and "deiecit" over "proiecit"; both originally as in the *Vetus Latina* version? In the canticle from Deuteronomy XXXII, "vanitatibus" in verse 21 (p. 318, line 14) is a later substitution for another word, now illegible; the verse ends with "illos," poorly written over what must have originally been "eos" (etc.).

8. The rubric/caption begins in line 15, black text with 3-line initial *K* in the next line.

9. I.e., "per Dominum nostrum Jesum Christum . . . seculorum. Amen" (standard formula). — A later (14th? century) addition in faint ink at end: Deus cui p[ro]p[ri]um. p . . . ? dn̄e. Fideliu[m]. Om[ni]p[oten]s. (= further prayers used at end or after Litany, here indicated by initia) — N.B. In the Litany some names are rather clearly capitalized, some clearly are not, some are doubtful (so Maria, Michael, Magnus, with ornamental initial *m* with last stroke curving below the line).

10. Cf. Grotefend, *Zeitrechnung*, v. 2. — N.B. In addition to names not found in the Litany of the 13th-century "Regula" Breviary and Missal (cf. *OMRL*, p. 514 sqq.) I have quoted names spelled in a peculiar manner ("Tathee" for "Thadee," etc.).

11. In our book, this cursive (although by more than one hand!) lacks the upper loop in the letter *d* which is otherwise a characteristic feature of the style; this deviation marks some early 15th-century mss. from Lower Austria and Vienna. (Cf. *Kat. der datierten Hss. Österreich)*

12. Explicit of the last part, on p. 49: Inte[n]cio e[ius] e[st] nos ex[empl]o X[rist]i cor[r]obora[r]i i[n] afficcione. (Efforts at identification of this commentary have failed; possibly noted down from a live lecture? The quasi-analytical form seems to have been popular among lecturers of the time.) — Other marginal comments, involving one or more other hands, generally interpret one or another phrase (cf. the head margin on p. 1) of the biblical text.

13. Attempts to identify the use haven't been successful. A sample of the texts as assigned:
Dominus regit me . . . collocavit: jointly for the Pss. XXIII–XXIV (p. 40 and 42)
Oculi mei . . . ad Dominum: jointly for Pss. XXV–XXVI (p. 42 and 46)
Dominus defensor . . .: jointly for Pss. XXVII–XXVIII (p. 47 and 51)
Adorate Deum . . . sancta eius: jointly for Pss. XXIX–XXX (p. 51 and 53)
In tua justicia . . .: jointly for Pss. XXXI–XXXII (p. 53 and 58)
(Rectos decet collaudacio?): Pss. XXXIII–XXXIV (p. 58? and 63)
Expugna . . . impugnantes me: for Ps. XXXV (p. 63 and 66)
(Ps. XXXVI is marked [p. 66] "ad laudes feria secunda")
Spera in . . . bonitatem: for Ps. XXXVII (p. 68 and 72)
— As frequently done, generally only the initium is written before the Psalm and the (not always?) full text of the antiphon only at end. — The same writer also added with the beginning of the Psalm CX (used for Sunday Vespers): "domi[ni]c[is] dieb[us] n[on] d[i]citur D[i]x[it] dns," apparently also erasing the words from the old main text; they have been later rewritten in formal gothic style. — The script of the antiphon writer is a hybrid characterized by single-lobed *a* left open at the bottom; ink is weak.

14. A trace of what probably was part of this count is visible in the margin of p. 19, with Ps. XIII; perhaps also on p. 9, Ps. VII. — For unknown reasons, no count is given with the Ps. CXIX or any of its segments.

15. E.g., for the Ps. XXVII (p. 47) the count is "xx," agreeing with the verses as indicated by a period (dot placed ca. midway between the imagined lines) and a red versal. In later Bibles, the psalm is divided into 14 verses; in liturgical books, used for public singing or recitation, the count remained 20.

16. The notes now obscured could yield information on the history of the manuscript or on the uses to which it was put at various times. With suitable technical equipment some should be decipherable.

17. The "one" is sometimes dotted, often resembles a *j*; "2" z-form; "5" often as two short thick curves; a particularly distinctive "8" formed like an *s* with central axis inclined to 10–20° from the horizontal.

18. The *d* ascender is kept vertical; tironian "et" isn't used, ampersand is (rather rarely, e.g., on p. 26, 40, 53, 70, 80 . . .); most uprights are somewhat lozenged in a rounded manner. The writer tended to spell initial "ca . . ." with *k*: p. 1, line 10, "kathedra"; p. 84, line 6, "kataractarum." His punctuation was almost entirely limited to a *punctus* placed somewhat above the line, marking the end of a verse. A later hand added, in a different (weaker) ink, a number of intermediate interpunction marks, mostly variants of "*punctus versus*" (semicolon-like), with constitutive elements often round arches open downwards (same person as the supplier of antiphons? Cf. contents, marginalia.)

19. Doubtful, alas, in more cases than the question marks show; separations of conjugate leaves have occurred and repairs have obscured evidence.

There are certainly sewing-lines immediately following these pages: 8, 24, 40, 56, 72, 88, (106?), 120, 136, 152, 168, 184, 200, 216, 232, 248, 264, 280, 296, 312, and 328.

20. Certainly wanting Ps. LII,1–6a, probably with a large initial; also some other text?

21. Certainly wanting is the beginning (through most of v. 4) of Ps. CII (Domine exaudi orationem meam . . .); also another initial? rubrics?

22. Initials of similar kind (ornamental?) were almost certainly present on the two missing leaves ff. [52] and [103], completing the expected set of eight (cf. contents).

23. Unusually realistic; in its present shape, the figure may be a (not very good) product of 19th-century Bavarian romanticism.

24. The placement of these versals is therefore accidental and not associated with the meanings or uses of the texts. — Versals in the Psalter were of special importance because of group recitation or singing (see also our notes on the marginal verse count, at end of contents).

25. As of the time of this writing, upper cover and spine are detached from the text block.

26. The more recent one is that of the Library's Manuscript Division. Along with other ms. books, the Psalter passed into the custody of the Rare Book (now Rare Book and Special Collections) Division between 1935 and 1962.

MS 15

(Faye and Bond 75)

BREVIARY 126–[1]

Written in Paris. Parchment. 563 leaves, ca. 188 × ca. 123 mm (bound volume: 195 × ca. 130 mm) 2 columns. 32 lines (calendar, 34 lines)

(f.1 is free endleaf;[2] it contains on recto a LATER ADDITION, i.e., family notes in late 15th-century cursive:) Le xxiij[c] jour de may mil iiij[c] iiij[xx] et six [= 1486] Je fuz marie . . . (29 lines, ending:) . . . Du Roy/A paris.

Family name of the writer (he never identifies himself) seems to have been (Le) Picart (Jacques?); he married in 1486, and by the end of 1493 he had four children: Jacques, b. 1487; Bertrand, b. 1488; Katherine, b. 1490; and Marie, b. 1493; named as godmother to Marie is Madame Marie Chevalier, widow of Jean le Boulanger, premier président of the royal court of Parlement in Paris.[3] A nephew of the writer (named in line 27) is Dreux Budé; this is very likely the oldest brother (b. 1456, d. 1528) of the scholar Guillaume Budé; their mother was Catherine née le Picart.[4]

ff. 2r–3v: (KL)[5] Jam prima dies [et] septima fine timetur [*sic*][5]//*Januarius h*[*abe*]*t dies .xxxi.* . . .

Calendar reflecting the liturgical use of the French royal household as of ca. 1255; in blue and gold; imperfect: all after April 30 wanting. Available part (January–April) names 57 festive occasions.[6] — Written in gold are: (Jan.:) *Genovefe; Oct. scī thome /symeonis; Guillermi Bituricensis Archiepī; Felicis in pincis; Marcelli; Prisce; Fabiani et Sebastiani; Vincentii; Babile; Policarpi; Agnetis 2º; Batildis regine.* (N.B. Epiphany is in blue.) — (Feb.:) *Purificatio bē marie; Agathe;* (with Feb. 8:) *Obitus roberti comitis attrenbatensis* [sic; = Robert of Artois, brother of Louis IX; d. 1250]; *Eulalie; Honorine.* (N.B.: Blasii, Feb. 3, is rated "duplum," as is Mathie, Feb. 24; with Feb. 17, note in later hand in gutter margin: Obiit do[minus] J. Comes vindocinen[sis] [= Jean of Vendôme, d. 1362/3].) — (March:) *Gertrudis*; (March 27:) *Resurrectio dn̄i.* (N.B.: *Gregorii pape* is misspelled "Georgii pape"; *Annuntiatio dominica* is in red, the only day written in that color.) — (Apr.:) *Ambrosii; Eufemie; Georgii; Dedicatio scē capelle par*[*isiensis*] (= Sainte-Chapelle, dedicated 1248); *Petri martyris* (canonized 1253; most recent feast in this calendar). — Beyond a general Parisian character, the calendar bears no special relationship to the contents of the breviary it introduces.[7]

(Following f. 3, four leaves have been lost [cf. collation]. As may be seen from partial offset on f. 4r which shows in mirror image the month of December,[8] the leaves contained the missing months of the calendar. — ff. 4–5 are blank and unruled, although pricked in same manner as the calendar leaves.)

6r–15v: (J)[14]*N anno quo natiuitas domini die dominica euenerit . . . totum de uig[ilia] natalis domini . Sicut infra scriptum inuenies.*

Order of the office for Advent;[9] similar to but worded differently from the "Parisian tables" required since 1263 in Franciscan office books.[10] The text (written in black ink but throughout underscored in red) includes mentions of the *Festum Reliquiarum*, an event occurring in Advent at Notre-Dame.

(ff. 16r–17v blank, unruled but pricked in same manner as leaves 6–15)

18r–85r: *Hymnus.* Nocte surgentes. *Dominica in aduentu. a'* Ecce in nubib[us]. *a'.* Beat[us] uir. [et]c' *.a'.* Pro fidei meritis . . . (B)[6]eatus uir qui non abijt . . . (ends on 85r, 1st column, 13th line:) (sal)uus esse non poterit.

The Psalter, with much liturgical matter incorporated or added. The Psalms,[11] unnumbered, follow their biblical order but are accompanied (their sequence is interrupted) by antiphons, rubrics, and programs (using cues) for Lauds and for the minor hours. — The Old Testament canticles used in weekday Lauds are written out in full in their appropriate places, and captioned "ps(almus)." — The set of antiphons for Sunday Matins includes (ff. 19v, 21v, 22v, 23r, 23v, 24v, 25r, 25v, and 26r) the odd-sounding "rhythmical office" series *Pro fidei meritis.*[12] — Some *capitula* and hymns are included. — Following the Ps. CL on f. 82vb, the text continues with the Song of the Three (*Benedicite omnia opera*, Dn. III,57–88.56; captioned *"psalm[us]"*), the *Benedictus, Magnificat ("psalmus"), Nunc dimittis ("psalm[us]"), Te Deum laudamus* (*"ps."*), and the Athanasian Creed *(Quicumque . . .*; uncaptioned). — The Psalter has at some point lost 4 leaves, each of them containing the beginning of one of the eight liturgically important sections:[13]

lost with leaf following f. 27: Ps. XXVI,6–12, and Ps. XXVII *(Dominus illuminatio mea)*, verses 1–9a, with the beginning of Monday Matins and a major initial;

with leaf following f. 40: Ps. LIII *(Dixit insipiens)*, which opened the Matins of Wednesday (major initial expected); also Pss. LIV and LV,1–22a;

following f. 60, a leaf missing with the major initial for Saturday Matins: wanting Habakkuk III,8b–19 and Ps. XCVIII,1–8a *(Cantate Domino canticum novum)*;

another missing leaf followed the f. 68; lost with it, the Ps. CX (*Dixit Dominus Domino meo)* with a major initial to signal Sunday Vespers; also Pss. CXI, CXII, CXIII, CXIV, and the first word of Ps. CXV, *Non nobis.*[14]

Preserved are the initials of Pss. I (f. 18ra), XXXIX (*Dixi custodiam*, f. 34va), LXIX (*Salvum me fac*, f. 46rb), and LXXXI (*Exultate*, f. 54ra).[15] — The long Ps. CXIX (*Beati immaculati in via*, ff. 70v–74r) is broken into 21 of its 22 sections[16] (the decorator had missed the division at verse 9); the sections are, for the most part, individually captioned as *"ps(almus)."* — The semibiblical psalm titles ("In finem," etc.) are omitted, as usual. Less usual is the total absence of any signal that the doxology "Gloria Patri . . ." ought to be recited after each psalm.

85ra–87ra: (K)[2]yrieleyson . . . piis supplicat[i]onib[us] conseq[uan]tur. P[er]. (last 3 lines of 87ra, the whole column *b*, and f. 87v blank, ruled)

The Litany of Saints, beginning in the middle of a column and uncaptioned. — It names, after Mary, the apostles, etc., 32 individual martyrs (among them: Albane,

Alexander, Syxte . . . Corneli . . . Theodole . . . Eadmunde . . . Eustachi, Leodegari . . . Gorgoni, Saturnine, Quintine . . . Marcelline et Petre), 25 confessors (. . . Martialis . . . Turguale, Maudete, Ambrosi . . . Blasi . . . Remigi . . . Columbane, Bricci, Leonarde, Wandregisille, Maglori, Egidi), and 21 women (. . . Petronilla . . . Radegundis, Batildis, Genouefa . . .).

88r–327v: *Sabbato in aduentu domini* . . . *Capit.* (E)[4]cce dies ueniunt . . . (302vb, 27th line, immediately after the concluding "p[er . . .]" of the *oratio* for the 25th Sunday after Pentecost:) *In dedicat[i]one ecc[lesi]e* . . . (325vb, 5th line:) . . . *In nat[ali] dñi. Inuit.* . . . (327va:) . . . ut in diurnis actib[*us*]. *(327vb blank)*

The proper of the seasons (= the *temporale*) for the whole year; followed, without a break, by the commons (302v–325v) and some additional material. — The program for the regular weekly office, known in medieval times as the *psalmista,*[17] is included with the proper for the 1st Sunday after the octave of Epiphany, ff. 128v–136r; on ff. 292v–302v, a collection of homilies for the Sundays after Pentecost. — The responsories for Advent (cf. Leroquais, *Brév.* I, p. lxxviii sq.) are:

Dom. I: Aspiciens a longe / Aspiciebam in visu noctis / Missus est // Ave Maria / Salvatorem / Audite verbum // Ecce virgo / Obsecro / Letentur

Dom. II: Jerusalem cito / Ecce Dominus / Docebit nos // Civitas Jerusalem / Ecce veniet / Sicut mater // Jerusalem plantabis / Egredietur Dominus / Rex noster

Dom. III: Ecce apparebit / Bethleem / Qui venturus // Suscipe verbum / Egypte / Prope est // Descendet / Veni Domine / Ecce radix

Dom. IV: Canite tuba / Radix Jesse / Non auferetur // Me oportet / Ecce iam venit / Virgo Israel // Juravi / Non discedimus / Intuemini.

On 118rv, following the ninth responsory of Circumcision *In Patre manet eternitas*, the rubric reads: *vel sic*[*ut*] *in ecc*[*lesi*]*a p*[*ar*]*isien*[*si*] *R. Gaude maria* [*et*] *require in purificatione.*[18] — Responsories of the Holy Week (191r sqq.; cf. Leroquais, *op. cit.*, p. lxxx sq.): *Thurs.:* In monte / Tristis / Amicus // Unus ex / Eram quasi / Una hora // Seniores / Revelabunt / O Juda — *Fri.:* Omnes amici / Vinea mea / Tamquam // Barrabas / Tradiderunt / Jesum tradidit // Caligaverunt / Velum / Tenebrae — *Sat.:* Sepulto / Jerusalem luge / Plange // Recessit / O vos omnes / Ecce quomodo // Estimatus sum / Agnus Dei / Sicut ovis — *Easter Sunday* (197r sq.): Angelus Domini descendit / Angelus Domini locutus est / Et valde mane. — At the end of the Easter Matins, the breviary includes (197vb–198ra) a dramatization of the Easter discovery (short version of what is known as the Play of the Three Marys), with parts for "ang(e)li," "mulieres," "cantor," each of the three women individually, and the choir, as in the ms. lat. 13233 of the Bibliothèque nationale (Leroquais, *Brév.*, no. 614) but with the Latin rubrics preserved.[19] Also included are prayers and rubrics for an evening procession "ad fontes" performed every day during the Easter week (198vb–200va). — *De sancta Trinitate* is in its place (233r–235r; 1st antiphon: *Gloria tibi Trinitas*; 1st reading: *Credimus sanctam Trinitatem*); no mention of Corpus Christi. — Sunday Gospels, identified by short quotations in the section of Sunday homilies (292v sqq.[20]), have Luke VI,36 *(Estote misericordes)* with the 4th Sunday after Pentecost.[21] The Sundays which follow are each assigned a number higher by one than the general Roman nomenclature would call for; the sequence of the Gospel readings remains otherwise identical up to the 25th Sunday which is given the pericope *Cum sublevasset* (John VI,5). The choice of homilies to go with the Gospels is totally different from that in the Roman Curia breviary. — The commons, on f. 302v sqq., are the usual set, ending with *De non virginibus* on 325v. The next three pages contain a collection of Invitatories for various occasions; in it, the Psalm XCV (Venite exsultemus . . .) is repeated in full altogether four times. On 327ra–va, an oddly superfluous set of directives for Prime has the first stanza of the hymn *Iam lucis orto sidere* ca. 20 times. — The second column of f. 327v is blank, ruled.

328r–505v: *Nota quod in omnibus festis que fiunt infra aduentum* . . . (505v, in 1st column:) . . . magistri i[m]periu[m] sunt secuti. (rest of page blank; 506rv blank, recto frame-ruled)

The sanctoral (proper of the saints), from Andrew to Vigil of Andrew; copied from an exemplar quite obsolete; reflects, in a not quite up-to-date manner, the use of Notre-Dame of Paris in the first quarter of 13th century. — Among the ca. 200 feasts: (330v sqq.:) *In assumptione reliquiarum*, a celebration particular to the cathedral, held on December 4;**[22]** (380v sqq.:) *S. Germani* (Bp. of Paris, remembered in May), a feast expected in any Parisian book but here unusually emphasized by two illuminated initials; (391v sqq.:) *Eligii*, i.e., (as is clear from the readings) the celebration of the transfer of a relic of his arm to Notre-Dame in 1212, the most recent feast found in this section; (476v:) a highly decorated initial begins the readings for All Saints; (503v–505r:) a very curious set of readings for the Parisian November 26 celebration of certain miracles attributed to St. Geneviève.**[23]** — Not included: the Conception of Mary (although introduced in Paris before 1200); no *Honorinae* or *Gertrudis* (while both are entered in gold in the calendar); generally no festivity special to the Sainte-Chapelle. — On 450v, after the prayer of St. Nicomedes, a rubric: "*in ecc[lesi]a parisien[si] fiu[n]t .ix. l[ec]c[iones]* . . .

507r–559r: (section ADDED ca. 1300 to update the sanctoral:) *in susceptione reliquiarum* . . . (554rb:) . . . *incipit uita et officium sancti ludouici regis et confessoris* . . . (L)[4]udouicus decus regnanciu[m] . . . (1st reading, 555rb:) (G)[4]loriosissimi regis ludouici . . . (558va–559rb, the Mass proper:) (M)[2]agnificatus est rex pacificus . . . liberare digneris. p[er] dominum.

The section covers, with varying amounts of "proper" material, over forty events. It adds to the sanctoral the previously wanting *Conceptio* of Mary (*Hec est Regina*, ff. 510r–514r), Translation of St. Nicholas (took place in 1200), William of Bourges (Guillermus, canonized 1218), Translation of Thomas à Becket (an event that had taken place at Canterbury in 1220), St. Francis of Assisi (canonized 1228; here only a short instruction on f. 544va to use the 9 readings from the common of confessors), St. Elizabeth (canonized 1235; short directive on 551vb), the translation to Paris of the Crown of Thorns (in 1239; ff. 535v–539v), St. Peter Martyr (ca. 1253); also St. Anne (*Que est ista*, ff. 533r–534r); the Notre-Dame celebration of *Susceptio S. Crucis*, on 1st Sunday of August (534rb–535vb). — Updated from 3 to 9 readings are the offices of *Joannis et Pauli* (ff. 527r–530v, cf. earlier 392va–393rb) and *In die mortuorum* (= All Souls, ff. 550rb–vb); perhaps also the *In susceptione Reliquiarum* (differences between the text on 507r–510r and that on 330v–332v appear minimal). — On 529ra–530vb, an extraordinarily long reading for the octave of John the Baptist (Sollempnitates nobis . . . fidem ueritatis inquirit). — All of the preceding is generally in the order of the liturgical year; out of sequence are, beginning on 551v, the offices of Rigobert, Nichasius, and that of St. Louis (with the Mass); Louis IX was canonized in 1297 and his feast was celebrated in Paris since 1298.

559rb–562ra: (part of the material ADDED ca. 1300; begins in 27th line of f. 559rb:) *p[re]ces ad matutinas. in laudib[us]* (K)[3]yrieleyson .iij. . . . (559v:) . . . *p'ces ad primam* . . . (560v:) . . . *p'ces p[ro] mortuis* . . . *p'ces ad completoriū* (actually a short program for the Compline) (561r:) *Preces ad completorium.* Kyrie eleyson . . . *insipiunt* [sic] *b'nedicciones p[er] annū totum* . . . Benedictionem perpetuam tribuat nobis . . . (561v:) . . . *benedictiones de beata maria.* Alma virgo virginum . . . (ends 562ra:) . . . p[er]ducat nos regina angelorum. amen. (the rest of 1st column blank)

562r, 2nd column (perhaps yet another hand): *De s[an]c[t]a paula mat[r]ona. l[ec]c[io] i.* Si cuncta mei corporis membra uerterentur in linguam . . . (ends 562va:) . . . habitationis glorie tue. *Cetera sicut de beata batilda.* (562vb blank)

(Putative relics of the learned female acquaintance of St. Jerome were in the cathedral of Sens.)

On verso of the free endleaf numbered as f. 563, in (15th-century?) *notula,* a suffrage (antiphon, versicle, formal prayer) involving St. Gatian of Tours: O gl[or]iosu[m] p[re]sulam [*sic*] o su[m]me v[er]itat[is] p[re]conem . . . qui in turone[n]si requiescit eccle[si]a . . . muniam[u]r adu[er]sis (the hymn used as antiphon not in *AH?*)

On pastedown of lower cover, in (14th-century?) cursive, the Apostles' Creed (Credo in deum . . .; omits "et sepultus est"); also, in a different hand, a liturgical directive concerning use of the suffrage of all saints: Excepto t[em]p[or]e adue[n]tus [et] pascali . . ."

* * *

Foliated in modern pencil; the numbering includes both free endleaves, i.e., one in front and one at end. — Written area ca. 120 × ca. 80 mm. — Fully ruled, the older parts (calendar and ff. 18–505) in plummet, the later ff. 6–15 and 507–562 apparently blind (f. 6r, in red ink). Pricking preserved for the vertical lines, 4 per page (forming columns ca. 34 + 9 + 34 mm).[24] — Written professionally by at least two persons: the earlier scribe, working probably in the 3rd quarter of the 13th century, wrote the primary contents now forming ff. 18–505 and perhaps also the calendar pages; substantial amount of additional matter was added by another, closer to 1300, now on ff. 6–15[25] and 507–562. Both used script of two sizes: the larger kind (readings and prayers) is *textura quadrata*, very regular; the smaller (responsories, rubrical matter) is semiquadrate. — Black ink of excellent quality, rarely slightly browning in the older part; appearing somewhat fainter and perhaps with a bluish cast in the additions.[26] — Thin (ca. 9 mm per 100 leaves) parchment of high quality, (now) on the yellow side. — Rubrics partly in red, partly (especially the longer directives) small-size black script identified as rubrical matter by red underscoring (done sometimes without a ruler). — Numerous careful marginal corrections in the older part, perhaps by the original scribe; they are framed in red and positioned with an eye on the overall appearance of the page.

Collation: (f. 1 is free endleaf) 1^8(= ff. 2–5; 1_{3-6}wanting) 2^8(= ff. 6–13) 3^4(= ff. 14–17) 4^{14}(= ff. 18–30; 4_{11} following f. 27 wanting) 5–7^{16}(= ff. 31–75; 5_{11}, 6_{16}, and 7_9 following ff. 40, 60, and 68 wanting) 8–9^6(= ff. 76–87) 10–33^{16} (= ff. 88–471) $34^{16-1?}$ (= ff. 472–486) 35^{16} (= ff. 487–502) 36^4(= ff. 503–506) 37–39^{12}(= ff. 507–542) $40^{16?}$(= ff. 543–558) $41^{4?}$(= ff. 559–562) (f. 563 is free endleaf). — Catchwords (some cropped) on last versos of all gatherings except 1, 3, 5, 6–9, 12, 17, 18, 21–24, 34, 36, 40, and 41 (ff. 5, 17, 45, 60, 75, 81, 87, 135, 215, 231, 279, 295, 311, 327, 486, 506, 558, 562). Leaf signatures (mostly lowercase alphabet; in gatherings 11 and 12, roman numerals) in the first half of many gatherings (on rectos, in lower right corners); often cropped. — All leaves now wanting had text and decoration.

Preserved decoration consists of (*a*) 15 illuminated initials, present only in the older parts of the book (calendar, Psalter, the proper of the seasons, and the original sanctoral); (*b*) penwork initials, alternately red and blue (occasionally both) and flourished in the contrasting color,[27] used throughout the book to signal the beginnings of psalms, readings, etc.; (*c*) also in both the older and the "ca. 1300" parts, an alternately red and blue "*J*" motif, 2 to 3 lines in height, repeated along the entire left text margin of every column in which a 2-line penwork initial occurs.[28] —The illuminated initials, with vine-scroll infilling, and in some cases inhabited by charming zoomorphic creatures, extend into cusped-branch pendants;[29] the dominant color is a brilliant purplish blue, the letter itself being mostly pink and both colors patterned in white; a third color is brick red. The rectangular fields surrounding the letters are outlined in black ink, as are the pendants. Laid gold appears in the infilling, sparingly in the pendants, and the large initials (not the *KL*s of the calendar) are edged in gold. — Five large (6-line) initials of this kind serve to highlight the four preserved (out of eight) beginnings of liturgical divisions in the Psalter (on 18r, 34v, 46r, 54r), also the first reading of the feast of St. Germanus of Paris (on 381r) (see plate VIII, p. xxiii); somewhat smaller ones (4–5 line) signal the four preserved months of the calendar, the beginning of the proper of the seasons (88r), the feast of St. Germanus (380v) and also that of All Saints (476v). The 2–line illuminated letter on f. 503v introducing the commemoration of St. Saturninus was probably meant for the readings of Nov. 26 (see contents and n. 19); similar letters on 18v and 19r (with perching birds and a rabbit on the pendants) which introduce the Pss. III and V may indicate an original intention to decorate in like manner also other psalms.

Binding: 19th–century dark brown morocco[30] over what may be the original wooden boards (traces of indentations of 2 clasps). Sewn over 7 bands; gilt edges. — Endleaves (pastedowns and free endleaves, cf. above) are either original or at least were already used for notes in the 15th century (cf. contents). — More recent: on pastedown of upper cover: (*i*) red-wax seal with an unidentified coat of arms (*ii*) a pasted-on clipping from an English catalog of ca. 1880; it calls the book "Missale Romanum cum calendario" (*iii*) ownership label of Rev. Edwin A. Dalrymple, D.D., and, affixed to it, red-wax seal with monogram "E A D" (*iv*) tipped-in Library of Congress label. — On f. 1 (free endleaf) verso, in a handwriting of ca. 1600: De Bernage.

Former owners: Robert de France, Comte de Clermont (1256–1318; the ms. made for him?[31]); Catherine, Comtesse de Vendôme (d. 1412); ca. 1490, the family (Le) Picart in Paris (cf. f. 1r); (ca. 1600, De Bernage?, name written on verso of the endleaf); Rev. E. A. Dalrymple (Baltimore); acquired by LC in 1916 (ms. ac. 4560,3,6).

2° fo.: (KL)[5] Iam prima dies et septima fine timetur

Bibl.: De Ricci, *Census* (1935), p. 229, no. 103 ("early XVth c."); Faye and Bond (1962), p. 119, no. 75.

NOTES

1. The date applies to the main corpus of the breviary and to the calendar; some additions (noted as such in contents) were made ca. 1300. — For the dating and for much of what follows a debt is due to Prof. Rebecca A. Baltzer (University of Texas at Austin) who had made the essential discoveries and graciously shared them with the Library prior to publication. Prof. Baltzer is not responsible for any errors in my description.

2. The vellum of the endleaves is different from that of the text block. They may have been in another book in the 15th century but were probably with the breviary prior to its 19th-century rebinding: they share most (not all) wormholes with the adjacent text leaves.

3. Marie Chevalier died in 1521; her epitaph is transcribed in *Épitaphier du vieux Paris*, v. 1 (1890), p. 88. — Prof. Gabrielle M. Spiegel of the University of Maryland has very kindly helped with parts of this text.

4. Cf. C. Delaruelle, *Répertoire . . . de la correspondance de Guillaume Budé*, 1907 (repr. 1969), p. 159, n. 1. Concerning the family Le Picart, *ibid.*, p. 82–83, n. 4.

5. Correct would be: Jani prima dies et septima (a) fine timetur. Cf. Walther, *Initia*, 9771; Grotefend, *Zeitrechnung*, v. 1 (1891), p. 36. — Sayings for the three remaining months are the version given by Grotefend *l.c.* in 2nd column.

6. Not counting notices such as "Hic ponitur clauis .lxx.," "Equi noctium," etc., frequently in gold.

7. Prof. Baltzer has noted the rather extreme similarity between our calendar and the corresponding pages in MS. 300 of the Fitzwilliam Museum, Cambridge, the "Isabella Psalter."

8. The offset image is unfortunately limited to the decorative *KL* and the lines written in blue; the gold writing left practically no traces, making it impossible to tell, e.g., if the December 4 cathedral festivity (cf. contents, f. 330v) was noted in the calendar (more likely it was not).

9. Needed to solve inherent conflict between the fixed-date Christmas and the movable Sunday system.

10. Cf. *SMRL* II (p. [*399*]–*408*) for the text of the Parisian tables; comment on their history in *SMRL* I, p. 140–143.

11. The *Psalterium Gallicanum* version, with occasional variant readings (e.g., Ps. I,3b: ". . . semper prosperabuntur"; 4a: "Non sic non sic impii"; 5: "Ideo non resurgunt . . ."; only the "resurgunt" agrees with the *Romanum* version).

12. Cf. Walther, *Initia*, 14749; *Analecta Hymnica*, v. 17, p. [19] (full text). — The assignment of the series to 1st Sunday of Advent in *AH loc. cit.* seems to be a misunderstanding: in LC MS 15, too, the rubric "Dominica in aduentu" could be read that way while it is certainly meant to apply only to the antiphon *Ecce in nubibus* which precedes the *Pro fidei*; the scribe did not have a suitable rubric for

the latter. The proper of Advent in our manuscript prescribes of course the *Ecce in nubibus* (88va, 94ra, 98rb). — Other mss. in LC collection include the series: MS 22 (Breviary of Bruges) f. 107r ("a dominica Deus omnium usque ad Aduentum"); MS 18 (Breviary of Langres) v. I, f. 146v ("a festo s. Remigii usque ad aduentum").

13. The Sunday office with which the Psalter begins starts rather abruptly with the rubric "*Hymnus*," without any mention of the *Invitatorium*; the preserved opening sections of the Matins for Tuesday (34va), Thursday (46rb), and Friday (54ra) include the required invitatory in each case. The omission may mean a missing leaf before f. 18 but may also have been caused by a confusing arrangement in the scribe's exemplar.

14. In the Vulgate (as earlier in the Greek Septuagint) and in Latin Psalters, the Psalms CXIV and CXV were treated as one, numbered (when numbering was given) as CXIII.

15. See also the paragraph on decoration.

16. As required by the 22 Hebrew letters (in Hebrew, the psalm was alphabetical).

17. The "psalmista" filled the role of what eventually became *Ordinarium divini Officii* in the Roman breviary. Cf. *SMRL* I, p. 74; II, p. 46–61 (textually not identical with ours).

18. The rubric seems to imply that the text given first is *not* that used at Notre Dame (!?). — N.B. The Franciscan *Ordo Breviarii secundum consuetudinem Romane Curie* of 1244 called in this place for the responsory *Nesciens mater* (cf. *SMRL* II, p. 40).

19. In the Bib. nat. manuscript the Latin rubrics had been erased and replaced by French ones.

20. On f. 293r, the quote "Accesserunt ad Jesum publicani . . ." stands for Luke XV,1 which normally (i.e., in the Vulgate, also in the Curia breviary) reads: Erant (autem) appropinquantes . . .

21. In the 13th-century redaction by Franciscans of the Roman Curia liturgy (cf. *SMRL* II) the pericope Luke VI,36 (–42) was assigned (as later in the Tridentine books) to the 1st Sunday after Pentecost. — Cf. *PALÉOGRAPHIE MUSICALE*, v. 14, p. 60 sqq.

22. Cf. Perdrizet, *Calendrier parisien*, p. 271; also Leroquais, *Brév.* 1, p. cxii sq. — As usual, the sanctoral gives no calendar days: they must be deduced from the sequence of the celebrations.

23. Cf. Perdrizet, *op. cit.*, p. 263 sq. — The set is preceded by a prayer commemorating St. Saturninus, with mention of the Vigil of St. Andrew. Both would belong after the *Geneviève des Ardents* office, to Nov. 29; the readings for the vigil are actually there (505rb–va). Owing perhaps to the decorator's confusion (or for lack of space?) the Saturninus prayer is graced by an illuminated initial more likely intended for the Geneviève readings which begin a few lines lower (see also the paragraph on decoration).

24. The calendar leaves 2–5 are pricked and ruled for 6 verticals per page (9 + 3.5 + 9 + 4.5 + 51 mm); since recto and verso could not be made to match, there are 10 prick marks in each margin.

25. It isn't certain that the section ff. 6–15 is a later addition. All of it (rubrical matter throughout) is in the smaller script.

26. This could be merely an optical effect of the scribe's having cut his writing instrument to a narrower point.

27. The blue ink used in the flourishing of the red letters appears lighter and greenish, unlike the blue of the blue letters which is purplish. The blue used in the calendar entries comes closest to pure blue.

28. That is, almost every column in the book; a conspicuous exception is the two facing pages 529v–530r where (it is the long reading for the Octave of St. John) no 2-line initial was indicated.

29. As pointed out by Prof. Baltzer, the illumination bears a marked resemblance to that of the Isabella Psalter (Cambridge University's ms. Fitzwilliam 300) and other royal manuscripts. Cf. also Branner, *Manuscript painting in Paris*. (N.B. Branner, who died young in 1973, had apparently never seen our breviary.)

30. De Ricci, *Census* (1935), p. 229, no. 103, describes the covers as red velvet over original boards, by confusion with another codex. (N.B. The *Census* dated the manuscript as "early XVth c.")

31. Catherine de Vendôme married Robert Clermont's great-grandson (Prof. Baltzer). — If I have any doubts about the hypothesis they have to do with the breviary as a layman's book. Louis IX himself is, nevertheless, known to have had one, and Robert was his son. Unless the endleaves were taken from another book, the family chronicle in front seems to show possession by lay persons at the end of the 15th century.

MS 16

(Music Division: M2147 XIV M3 Case)

NOTED BREVIARY, summer part
ca. 1300?

Cologne (city?) Parchment. 305 leaves, ca. 193 × ca. 136 mm (bound volume: 220 × ca. 152 mm) 2 columns. 30 lines.

(ff. [1–4], on paper, a non-germane 17th-century ADDITION: instructional material in Latin concerning chant, captioned "DE TONIS." On 1v–4r, music of "octo toni psalmorum" and the *peregrinus:* 4-line staves with two clefs; the notes are unfilled diamonds with descenders; text in a utilitarian italic hand, long lines; black ink only. Theory includes, on 4v, the distinction "durus" and mollis"[1])

f. 5rv (vellum; the leaf is included in the medieval foliation as "*.cxx.*" but differs from the rest of the book, most notably by its 5-line staves; black ink only): Dicat nunc israhel . . . Dicant nunc qui . . . Dextera Domini . . . Benedictus qui venit . . . (5v:) . . . Lapidem quem . . . mirabile in oculis nostris (5vb:) Que est ista . . . (another hand:) Tu es pastor ouium . . . regni celo[rum]. e v o v a e.

Changing verses of the gradual *Haec dies* in Masses of the Easter week (cf. *SMRL* II, p. 252–253) followed by two office items; reasons for inclusion unclear.

ff. 6–126 (old foliation *.cxxj.–.ccxl.):*[2] *In vigilia pasche an[tiphona] s[upe]r p[salmu]m ad v[espera]s.* *A*[ll]e[l]via . . . . . . (125vb:) . . . *D[omini]c[a] p[ro]xi[m]a an[te] adue[n]tu[m]. [Secundum] Joh'em (J)*[4]N ill' Cu[m] s[u]bleuasset oc[u]los ihe[sus] [et] uidisset . . . (ends in 126rb with antiphon *Illi ergo homines:)* . . . *in hunc mundum Evovae. Coll[e]c[t]a vt s[up]r[a].*

The seasonal ("temporal") part of a breviary in which full musical notation accompanies all antiphons and responsories;[3] the summer half, extending in this case from Easter to the last Sunday before Advent. The old foliation notwithstanding, separation of this section from that which, presumably, went from Advent to Holy Saturday corresponds to the common practice of dividing bulky office books into manageable units and was no doubt intentional. — The responsories for Easter Sunday are: I *Angelus Domini descendit* II *Angelus Domini locutus* III *Dum transisset.* — Pentecost, marked at the beginning of its 1st Vespers by a large initial (extending over two music and two text lines, on f. 41vb; not otherwise captioned) is followed by captioned offices for Monday through Saturday; then (48vb:) "*i[n] oct[aua] pent[ecostes],*" a full office with the homily ("Iste nychodem[us] . . . ") divided into three readings, etc. The Trinity celebration, apparently not yet displacing this Sunday's office,[4] seems to

MS 16, f. 50r (beginning of the Trinity Office; see text) (actual size of the leaf: ca. 193 × 135 mm)

begin only with, or after, the afternoon Vespers of the octave (f. 50ra): two sets of antiphons *super psalmos* offered on these pages (ff. 49v–50r) seem to mean that Trinity Vespers were chanted after those of the octave; it also seems that the whole week that followed, rather than the Sunday, was given to Trinity celebration: after a set of Trinity responsories and antiphons (ff. 50vb–54ra) come the Trinity readings, all assigned to the weekdays;[5] culminating in a set captioned (perhaps inconsistently) "*in oct[ava]*" (Credimus sanctam . . . , 56ra–va). A modified version of this phase of post-Pentecost rearrangements is formulated in an obviously somewhat later note written carefully in a gloss-like *notula* in the tail margin of f. 50r: it prescribes splitting the three nocturns of Trinity among Monday through Wednesday, to be followed by Corpus Christi (an office found nowhere in the book!).[6] The note ends (while describing the octave of Corpus Christi): "Nisi sabato vesp[er]e et die d[omi]nica sole[m]pnit[er] cantet[ur] de sc̄a trinitate." — On 56vb–61ra, "hystoria" (with music throughout) to the readings from Samuel and Kings which follow; on 69ra–73rb, chants to the readings from sapiential books and on 77ra–81vb, to those from Job; in each case followed by the assigned biblical selections. The chants and textual segments of Tobias, Judith, Esther, Maccabees, and the prophets, ff. 84vb–109ra, are variously intermixed.[7] The highest-numbered Sunday after Pentecost is, in this section, the 24th (misnumbered *xiiii,* in 107vb). — On 109ra–126rb, assembled homilies for the Sundays after Pentecost;[8] here the numbering reaches 25 (f.125ra), then (f. 125vb) the "Dominica proxima ante Adventum." — The Gospel quotations which introduce the homilies are a series not represented among the ten non-Beneventan types recorded by Dom Hesbert in *PALÉOGRAPHIE MUSICALE* 14, p. 132: from the 1st[9] to the 24th Sunday, it is the rather standard non-Beneventan sequence beginning with Luke XVI,19 sqq., with the Gospel *Estote misericordes* assigned to the Sunday numbered as 4th, and with Matthew IX,18 sqq. to the 24th; but the "25th" Sunday has *Accesserunt ad Iesum pharisaei* (Hesbert's *A*), and the Sunday "closest to Advent," the *Cum sublevasset,* John VI,5 sqq.

126v (somewhat later ADDITIONS): *J*ustoru[m]) anime . . . *S*ancti tui domine florebu[n]t . . . *J*n feruentis olei doliu[m] . . . (another hand, lines 3–8 of 126vb:) Accepit autem omnes timor . . . plebem suam. magn.

Music on this page is on 5-line staves. — The first three items pertain to the sanctoral, the antiphon *Accepit autem* (from Luke VII,16) to the (in this book) 12th Sunday after Pentecost; it is referred to in the upper right corner of f. 120r by the hand which added it.[10]

127ra–264rb: *Georgii m[a]r[tyris]* *I*vstus germinabit sicut lilium . . . (259vb:) *De sc̄a Kat[er]ina ad v[espera]s.* *A*ve uirgo speciosa . . . (ending in the last lines of 264rb:) . . . pro quibus oras salus erit. E v o v a e. *Coll'ca vt s[upra].*

The sanctoral = assembled proper offices and commemorations celebrating saints, in calendar order (without dates); covering the "summer" part (Apr. 23 through Nov. 25) of the liturgical year.[11] — The roster of saints and related festivities, and the relative importance given them as reflected in the amount of music and number of readings, corresponds to the state of non-monastic liturgy in Cologne and vicinity at the end of the 13th century.[12] The most recent saint included is Dominic (canonized 1234), on f. 166r (collect only).[13] Apostles (with the exception of Peter and Paul) and evangelists (notably Matthew and Mark) are given little prominence. No Transfiguration, no Visitation. (Full listing of contents, with information on amount of textual and music material allotted each feast, is given as an appendix at the end of this description.)

264va–297va: *In dedicacione te[m]pli.* *G*loria tibi trinitas . . . (270ra:) . . . *Hystoria de apostolis (E)*$^{1+1}$cce ego mitto . . . (275ra:) . . . *De uno m^a^r[t]i[r]e.* . . . (280rb:) . . . *De m^a^[rti]ribus et confessoribus* . . . (286rb:) . . . *De confess[ore]* . . . (291ra:) *De confess[ore] et no[n] po[n]tifice*

MS 16 . . . (292vb:) . . . *Histo[ria] de v[ir]ginibus* . . . (297ra:) . . . *De plurib[us] v[ir]ginibus* . . . (ending in 297va:) . . . salte[m] per precem sequi . . . *Coll' ut sup[ra]*

The "commons" or *commune sanctorum;* as was often the case, not captioned and not marked off from the series of individual saints' offices which precede (nor from several which follow by way of additions). — These pages have a generally shoddier appearance than most of the book and contain more corrections; the red captions quoted above range from slightly ornate (the two beginning "Historia") to graphically very poor.

297va–305rb: *Ini[n]ue[n]tione sc̄ī Stephani Regem m[a]r[tyrum] d[omi]n[u]m . . . (299ra:) . . . de confess' Uigilate omnes . . . (299rb:) . . . De bt̄o pantaleo[n]e* (*A*)[1+1]dest beati pantaleonis festiua sollempnitas qui senatoris filius factus est senator curie celestis . . . (304va:) *In octa[ua] laure[n]cij* . . . (ending in 11th line of 305rb:) *R. Coll'. de sc̄o Laur[encio].* (rest of column and of page blank)

Supplementary to the sanctoral. — For the Finding of Stephen, ff. 165v–166r offer the collect, one reading, and (with music) the antiphon *Ostendit sanctus Gamaliel;* note on 297v refers to this, and added are ca. 5 columns of music.[14] — St. Pantaleon, whose feast on July 28 was red-lettered in 13th-century Cologne cathedral books,[15] was ignored by the original scribe of the sequence of feasts on f. 164r, but later a commemorative collect was added there in the lower margin; in these supplementary pages, his is a nine-readings office with almost 20 columns of music.[16] — The *Octava Laurentii* is signaled in red ink (with reference to leaf "clxxx retro"[17] in the margin of f. 179 (both recto and verso).

(On 305v, penmanship practice; includes several times the word "Ersamen" ["vnd" or "vnnd . . . "]; script of ca.1500?)

From MARGINAL ADDITIONS:

f. 50r, tail margin (in careful small 14th-century *notula*): Notandum quod de sancta trinitate servatur primus nocturnus feria secunda . . . Quarta feria vesperae sollemnes cantantur de corpore Christi . . . .

f. 104r, tail margin (perhaps by the writer of f. 1–4): *de S. Agilolpho Ad Mag 8* (under 4-line staff:) Iste est preciosus martyr, et Episcopus (The long-line text & music continues, with lacunae due to cropping, in head and tail margins through 107r; on 105v, captioned near head margin:) de S. Annone (for translation of his relics, celebrated in Cologne on April 29? N.B. These additions are in the seasonal part of the book, in the area of Sundays after Pentecost).

On inside of lower cover (on old vellum leaf pasted to modern pastedown; probably same writer as ff. 1–4): Anno 1629. 25 Aprilis hatte Herr K . . . (?) (altogether 12 lines of, it seems, accounting). — In different ink but same hand(?): Materia pro una amphora atramenti: Aquae pluuialis . . . Gallarum . . . Gummi arabici . . . Vitriolis . . . Aceti . . . (4 lines).

* * *

Modern foliation in pencil (the one followed in contents) includes the four 17th-century paper leaves at the beginning; they are preceded by two modern-paper flyleaves, blank; two such flyleaves also follow f. 305. Pasted to the inside of both covers are old vellum leaves with inscriptions from various periods (see further). — Medieval foliation using roman numerals written in ink in center of head margin has two sequences: the first one, *.cxx.–.ccxl.* in red, covers leaves 5–126; following f. 81 it omits through error the roman *cxcvii* and does not include leaves 83 and 84 (early substitutes for lost or faulty original). The second sequence, in black ink, begins with a *J*-form "I" on 127r, reaches *clxxx* on 305r; its *cxxxvij* = f. 263 is erroneously followed by *cxxxix* = f. 264 (nothing missing). — Written area (measured on the more regular all-text pages) ca. 147 × ca. 105 mm; space between columns ca. 10 mm wide. — Ruling inconspicuous, except for the music staves and some vertical framing lines rarely visible; the vertical and other framing lines are drawn for the most part in lead; in thinned-down ink on ff. 217–248, 268–305, and in the early addition on 126v. Where visible, the top horizontal line is doubled. All framing lines reach to edges. Only the two pricks for the central space between columns are preserved near tail edge of some leaves (66–90). — The script is *littera textualis* in several utilitarian variants, by several scribes: A (ff. 6–216 [except 83–84 and 126v] and 249–259r, perhaps also 259v–267?) B (217–248) C? (259v–267; see A) D (268r–299ra and, I think, 304va–305rb, i.e., end) E (299rb–304va, the Pantaleon office). The writer A, most formal of the group, uses a strongly black ink, two forms of *d,* a minuscule-type *a* with the upper lobe not completely closed, dotted *y,* and a crossed tironian *et* with up to 3-crested sharply wavy top line; beginning with f. 22, this scribe's ascenders are topped by slightly curved thin horizontal strokes (double *l* joined by one such stroke). Scribe B is characterized by a "con-" symbol of cursive appearance with a left-swung loop below line;[18] B's writing is uneven, his ink brown. "C" may be A writing under changed and more adverse conditions. D uses final *s* resembling mirror image of minuscule a; in D's *a,* the upper lobe is close to disappearing. The writer of the Pantaleon office uses a "two-floor" *a* and writes on fully and visibly ruled lines. The scripts deteriorate toward the end of the book, as does the ink. — *Punctus elevatus* is used for median pauses by all hands except E. — Yellowish parchment of fair quality (thickness ca. 14 mm per 100 leaves); some holes, some repairs. — Rubrics of two types: the captions are red, the liturgical directives black and marked by red underscoring.

Four-line staves with both the *do* and *fa* clefs; scribe A (incl. his "C" condition) with the *do* line yellow, *fa* line red, the remaining two in black (diluted?) ink. Scribe B used four black lines; D drew his red and yellow over black, sometimes next to the black line (creating on occasion a 5–line staff?). The scribe of the Pantaleon office (299rb–304va) uses a 5–line staff (this through 304vb). — The neumes are early *Hufnagelschrift* with minor differences following the several scribes.

Collation in full impracticable owing to tight modern binding; mostly twelves and tens. Folio 127 (beginning of the sanctoral and of the second sequence of medieval foliation) seems to be first leaf of a gathering; 126v hair side, 127r flesh side of vellum. Leaves 83–84 apparently a bifolio, 85 a singleton. A very unclear situation from f. 240 to f. 258, which has a catchword in tail margin verso.

Decoration modest, limited to calligraphic two-line or three-line initials in red, blue, or both, with flourishing in the other color or both. The two-color initials marking Easter and Pentecost (cf. contents) make a limited use of void white.

Binding: 20th century; sewn, apparently, over four bands; spine and corners in brownish orange leather, covers marbled paper with spiral patterns in light gray, orange, yellow, and white. On spine, in second panel from top, the imprecise identification "ANTIPHONARIUM" in gilt; in the lowest panel, label with LC Music Division call no.: M [horizontal line] // 2147// .XIV//M3. Leaves 270, 275, 280, 286, and 292 are provided with old (white pigskin?) tabs.[19]

On the inside of front cover, written on the old vellum leaf now pasted over modern-paper pastedown, two lines of what appears to be a 17th(?)–century ownership inscription heavily obliterated by ink scribbles and erasures. Under it, an 11–line penciled description of the manuscript in German, from the time of the Wolffheim sale in Berlin in 1929: the book, numbered "32," is identified as "Antifonale Romano-Coloniense." Near lower edge, numbers: 396561//30; Acc. 652126. — Tipped in, center, Library of Congress label printed: PRESENTED BY//THE FRIENDS OF MUSIC //IN THE//LIBRARY OF CONGRESS; also penciled call no.: M 2147.XIV M3. (For inscriptions on inside of lower cover, see at end of contents)

Former owners: (17th? century:) Johann . . . (mostly cropped name inscribed in head margin of f. 83r; perhaps identical to that obliterated on inside of upper cover); (early 20th century:) Dr. Werner (Joachim) Wolffheim (b. 1877, d. 1930); (Friends of Music in the Library of Congress)

2° fo.: Memento domine Dauid: et omnis mansuetudinis eius (under a 4-line staff with music)

Bibl.: *Versteigerung der Musikbibliothek des Herrn Dr. Werner Wolffheim . . . durch die Firmen Martin Breslauer . . . & Leo Liepmannssohn . . .* (Berlin, 1928–29) v. 2, n. 32 (pl. 3). — Leo Liepmannssohn (Berlin firm), *Katalog* 221 (1930), n. 20 (not seen). — *REPORT OF THE LIBRARIAN OF CONGRESS*, 1930, p. 190–191. — De Ricci, *Census* (1935), v. 1, p. 244, no. 165.

APPENDIX 1: THE SANCTORAL OF THE NOTED BREVIARY

(Key: saint's name in parentheses means there is text [often only the "collect"] but no music; SAINT'S NAME in capitals means 3 or more columns, with considerable amount of music; saint's name in regular type means there is some music. — N.B. The month and day indications shown here are not in the book)

(January through March and most of April are not included in the volume)

APRIL (f. 127r–128r)
23 Georgii 25 (Marci) 28 (Vitalis) (Quirini, collect ADDED in margin [Apr. 30])

MAY (ff. 128r–134r)
1 Philippi et Jacobi; Walburgis 3 INV. CRUCIS; (Alexandri) 6 (Johannis Ante Portam Lat.) 10 (Gordiani et "epymachy") 12 (Nerei Achilei et Pancracii) 13 Servacii 25 (Urbani) 29 (Maximini)

JUNE (ff. 134r–155v)
1 (Nychomedis) 2 Marcelline et Petri 3 (Herasmi, contemp.? ADDITION in margin [collect only]) 5 (Bonifacii) 9 (Primi et Feliciani) 10 (Maurini; incl. 6 readings) 11 (Barnabe ap.) 12 (Basilidis, Cyrini, Naboris, Nazarii) 15 (Viti, Modesti, Crescentie) 18 (Marci et Marcelliani) 19 (Gervasii et Protasii) 21 (Albani) 22 (Albini; incl. 6 readings) 23 Vigilia Johannis Bapt. 24 NATIVITAS JOHANNIS (18 columns) 26 JOHANNIS & PAULI (8 columns) 28 (Vigilia Petri et Pauli; Leonis) 29 PETRI ET PAULI (28 columns) 30 COMMEM. S. PAULI (19 columns)

JULY (ff. 155v–164r)
2 (Processi et Martiniani) 4 (Udalrici) 6 OCTAVA APOST. (7 columns) 7 (Willibaldi) 8 (Kyliani et sociorum) 9 (Agylolphi) 10 (Septem Fratrum) 11 ([Transl.] Benedicti) 12 (Felicis et Naboris, incl. 6 readings) 13 (Margarete) 15 In Divisione Apostolorum 21 (Praxedis) 22 MARIE MAGDALENE (13 columns) 23 (Apollinaris; Transl. Regum; for this latter, no music but an office of 9 readings) 25 (Jacobi, incl. 9 readings; Christophori) 28 (Pantaleonis [marginal ADDITION; but see also ff. 299r sqq., with music]) 29 (Felicis, Simplicii, Faustini, Beatricis) 30 (Abdon et Sennes) 31 (Germani)

AUGUST (ff. 164r–186r)
1 AD VINCULA PETRI; (Machabeorum) 2 (Stephani m. & pont.) 3 Inventio Stephani protom. (see also ff. 297v sqq., there with music); Nicodemi, Gamalielis, Abilon 5 (Dominici; Oswald ADDED in margin) 6 (Syxti, Felicissimi, Agapiti) 7 (Donati; Afre) 8 Cyriaci, incl. 6 readings 9 Vigilia Laurencii 10 LAURENCII (19 columns) 11 Tyburcii 13 (Hypoliti; incl. 6 readings) 14 (Eusebii) Vigilia Assumpt. 15 ASSUMPTIO (21 columns)[20] 17 (Oct. Laurencii signaled by note ADDED in margin, with a reference to 304v sq.) 18 (Helene; Agapiti, incl. 6 readings) 19 (Magni; Bernard noted in margin) 22 TYMOTHEI & SIMPHORIANI (6 columns) 23 (Bernardi abb' [mis?]placed (?)) 24 (Bartholomei; incl. 6 readings and homily) 25 (Genesii) 27 (Rufi) 28 (Hermetis) (Augustini) 29 DECOLLATIO JOHANNIS (11 columns) 30 (Felicis et Adaucti)

SEPTEMBER (ff. 186r–211v)
1 EGIDII (18 columns) 8 NATIV. MARIE (16 columns) 9 (Gorgonii) 11 (Proti et Jacincti) 14 CORNELII & CYPRIANI (12 cols.); EXALTACIO CRUCIS (3–4 cols.) 15 (Nychomedis) 16 (Eufemie; Lucie & Geminiani) 17 LAMBERTI (18 columns) 20 (Vigilia Matthei) 21 (Matthei) 22 MAURICII ET SOC. (5–6 columns) 26 or 27[21] (Cosme et Damiani) 29 MYCHAELIS (21 columns) 30 (Jheronimi)

OCTOBER (ff. 211v–244v)
1 REMIGII & soc. (23 columns) 7 (Marci pp.; Marcelli & s.) 9 DYONISII & soc. (22 columns) 10 GEREONIS & soc. (25 columns) 15 (Maurorum mm., incl. 9 readings) 16 (Elyphii, incl. 6 readings) 18 (Luce ev., incl. 9 readings) 21 XI MILLIUM VIRGINUM (19 columns) 23 SEVERINI (22 columns) 24 (Evergisli; with 6 readings) 27 (Vigil of Simon & Jude) 28 (Symonis & Jude; with 9 readings) 31 Vig. Omnium SS. (comm. Cesarii)

NOVEMBER (ff. 244v–264r)
1 OMNIUM SANCTORUM (15 columns) 8 (Quattuor coronatorum) 9 (Theodori) 11 MARTINI (19 columns) (Menne) 13 BRICCII (4 columns) 22 CECILIE (16 columns) 23 CLEMENTIS (5 columns) (Felicitatis) 24 (Crisogoni) 25 KATHERINE (20 columns)

(December not included; not expected in the summer part of the breviary)

APPENDIX 2: TEXTUAL VARIANTS IN ANTIPHONS CHOSEN BY THE *CAO*[22]

2647 Erat autem aspectus . . . vestimenta eius *sicut nix* [so corrected over illegible earlier text!] (f. 7vb)
2607 Ego veritatem . . . *nisi ego* . . . (29vb)
1490 Ascendit . . . *Et* Dominus in voce tube (35vb, 36rb, 38ra)
4920 Sic Deus . . . credit *in ipso* . . . (45vb)
4616 Reposita . . . in *illum diem* . . . (152va)
3892 *Noli me* derelinquere . . . (168va)
1640 Beatus Laurentius *orabat dicens* . . . *servi tui* (169ra)
5035 Strinxerunt . . . *insultat* . . . (170va, 171ra)
3381 Interrogatus te *Dominum* confessus sum . . . (170vb)
3216 In craticula . . . te *Christe* confessus sum . . . (172ra)
2088 Da mihi in disco . . . *iusiurandum* (185vb)
2016 Cum iocunditate . . . *beate* Marie . . . (194rb)
3852 Nativitas tua . . . *qui soluens* maledictionem . . . (191r)
3754 Michael *archangelus venit* . . . (268va)
2440 Dum committeret bellum . . . *audita est* . . . nostro. (210v–211r)
1872 Confido . . . *reddita sit* . . . (251ra)
4074 O quantus luctus . . . *quia pium est* . . . (252vb)
2437 Dum aurora . . . *beata* Cecilia . . . arma lucis (257v–258r)
3924 Non meis meritis . . . *sed* [!] *vestris coronis* . . . (259rb)
4124 Omnes gentes . . . *Christo Domino* (259va)
4546 Quis enim in omnibus . . . in regno *Dei* . . . (57ra)
4811 Sapientia clamitat . . . et eam *dum* invenerit . . . (69vb)
1980 Cum audisset Job . . . neque *stultum quid* . . . (77ra)
4426 Que mulier . . . *et* si perdiderit . . . (111ra)
2682 Estote ergo . . . *quia* et pater . . . *est.* (111va)
3894 Nolite judicare *ut* non . . . (111va)
4903 Si offers . . . *ante altare* . . . (113rb)
2202 Dicite invitatis . . . *dicit Dominus* (122va)
4873 Serve nequam . . . misertus sum *dicit Dominus* [corrector's addition? erasures after "sum"] (124ra)

NOTES

1. The theoretician erred in applying these categories (corresponding to English "major" and "minor") to the Gregorian chant.
2. Error in the old foliation is explained in the first paragraph after contents.
3. A "noted" breviary. Unlike antiphonaries, the "noted breviaries" include the many non-musical parts of the office, in particular the readings. In our book, ca. half of the used space is taken by music. See H. Hughes, *Medieval manuscripts* (1982), p. 123, for discussion of the purpose of this hybrid book type (to serve as master copies for selective copying?).
4. Celebration of the feast of Trinity on the Sunday following Pentecost dates, outside isolated circles, from 1334.
5. No nocturnal readings with suitable contents are provided between those for *In octava Pentecostes* on 49r and those for *feria ii* on 54v.
6. The feast of Corpus Christi was introduced in the Cologne area at the beginning of the 14th century: G. Zilliken, "Der Kölner Festkalender" in *BONNER JAHRBÜCHER* 119 (1910), p. 13–157, notes (p. 138, n. 3) that it was celebrated in the church of St. Gereon in Cologne since before 1279 but generally established in the diocese only ca. 50 years later.
7. Ending with Habakkuk II,4, at end of (poorly identified) selections from the Minor Prophets.
8. The first one, beginning in 1st column of f. 109r, with three lines of blank space where the caption/rubric should be. Book uses only "Dominica [number]," perhaps avoiding the "post Pentecosten" *vs.* "post Trinitatem."
9. Not counting the Nicodemus pericope for "In octava Pentecostes" (cf. above)!
10. N.B. Location of the antiphon is given as ".I. rct°": carelessness or confused vestige of the numbering-by-openings system?
11. The winter part, taking in a shorter section of the year, may have included the Psalter.
12. Resembling in this respect the memorial book of Stift Kaiserswerth of ca. 1300, excerpted by Zilliken, *op. cit.* (his *KW*). (The Kaiserswerth book lists, however, for the late-April through November season ca. 25 percent more celebrations, including two of its patron St. Suitbert, and does not include St. Helen, Eliphius, Evergislus, Bernard, or Dominic.)
13. No Francis of Assisi (canonized, 1228; also unknown to the Kaiserswerth book).
14. On 298r, 5 lines of text lack music (empty staves).
15. See Zilliken, *op. cit.*, p. 86.
16. But no reference to this on f. 164r.
17. The old numbering of the pertinent leaf is clxxix verso.
18. Somewhat like the capital *J* of the Palmer method longhand.

19. The Invitatory of a "common" is on the verso of the tab-marked leaf or on the recto facing it, in each case.

20. Invitatory: In honore beatissime Marie Virginis iubilemus Domino.

21. In Cologne, Cosmas and Damian were shifted to Sept. 26 because of the celebration on Sept. 27 of the dedication of the cathedral; our ms. makes no mention of this.

22. *Corpus antiphonalium officii*, v. 6 (1979), p. 283 sqq.

MS 17

(Faye and Bond 10)

PSALTER XIVth c.

Written in or near Metz. Parchment. 187 leaves, 160 × ca. 115 mm (bound volume: ca. 167 × ca. 125 mm) 1 column. 18 lines (in the calendar, mostly 17)

ff. 1r–12v: (KL)[3] *Januier .xxxj. iours.//La . lune .xxx.* . . . Sains . siluestre .pp.

Full calendar, in French. Written in yellowish brown and gold (captions red; left-hand column red, gold, red, blue), two pages per month, each month beginning on a new recto. — Among the feasts written in gold: "*la tn̄sl'.s̄. clement*" (May 2), "*dicaise s̄. saluotir*"[1] (June 19), "*la tn̄sl .s̄. mairtin*" (July 4), "*s. Remey euesque*" (Oct. 1), "*sains Mairtin euesq[ue]*" (Nov. 11), "*sains brice euesq[ue]*" (Nov. 13), "*sains climent euesq[ue]*" (Nov. 23), "*la concepciō nr̄e dame*" (Dec. 8), "*s̄te lucie. s̄.te. odelie*" (Dec. 13). — Among the days not emphasized: (*Jan.*:) (30:) Al[d]egonde, (31:) Vlfie; (*Feb.*:) (4:) Liefair, (7:) Agulien eu., (8:) Donis eu., (12:) Dedier eu. [= ?], (17:) Saluien eu., (18:) Legonce eu.; (*March*:) (1:) Aubin eu., (10:) Macidoine, (20:) Vrbice [eu.], (27:) Euroul (?), (31:) Vlfie (cf. Jan. 31!); (*Apr.*:) (1:) Walleri abb. [= Valericus], (17:) Libaire, (18:) Lutier [= Eleutherius], (30:) Eutrope [eu.]; (*May:*) (16:) tn̄sl' .s. Therente, (17:) Torpin et Rollans [= ?], (18:) Dioscore, (20:) Baudeire [= Baudelius], (23:) Desier eu.; (*June*:) (3:) Oside [= ?], (6:) Arthemien eu., (8:) Maidair eu., (12:) Av[oldus] et ses compagnons, (17:) Bouton [= ?], (27:) "la dicaice a la g[ra]nt esglixe"; (*July*:) (7:) Sebrone, (9:) Wibourc [= ?], (14:) Eracle, (18:) Transl. Arnoult, (24:) Seguelaine, (26:) Anne; (*Aug.*:) (16:) "arnoult euesq[ue] de mes"; (*Sept.*:) (3:) Mansuj eu., (15:) Cyure eu. [= Acardus of Clairvaux?], (28:) Exuperre; (*Oct.*:) (29:) "s̄ therente euesq[ue] de mes"; (*Nov.*:) (5:) Joious preste [= Laetus], (14:) Lorent eu. [of Dublin], (16:) Othenas [= Othmar of St. Gall?], (20:) Aymont rois [= Eadmund]; (*Dec.*:) (11:) sains Clo. euesque [= Clodulphus, bp. of Metz]. — The two dedication feasts as well as emphasis on Metz saints such as the bishops ("de mes" or "demes" = of Metz) identify the calendar as basically that of the diocese of Metz. It includes, however, many rather uncommon names;[2] among them, a more than usual proportion of saint bishops. —

The Marian feast of the Visitation, introduced fairly generally by 1390, is absent. Also not included: *Translatio Stephani*, May 7,[3] a celebration instituted in Metz probably to commemorate the arrival to the city of a major relic of the saint in 1376.[4]

13v–173r: (B)[7]EATUS UIR (14r:) qui non abiit . . . (Ps. CL ends on f. 173r, 6th line:) . . . omnis spiritus laudet d[o]m[inu]m.

Psalms,[5] in straight biblical order and without liturgical additions except the "Gloria" at the end of some (included or omitted quite randomly). Major initials marking, traditionally, liturgical divisions[6] with Pss. I (as shown above), XXVII (*Dominus illuminatio mea*, f. 38v), LIII (*Dixit insipiens*, f. 69r), LXIX (*Salvum me fac Deus*, f. 83v), LXXXI (*Exultate Deo adiutori nostro,* f. 102r), XCVI (*Cantate Domino canticum novum*, f. 117v), and CX (*Dixit Dominus*, f. 137r). Neglected, by the scribe's[7] or his exemplar's error, is Ps. XXXIX (*Dixi custodiam vias meas*, f. 54r). The Ps. XCVI has been singled out instead of the usual Ps. XCVIII, in all likelihood a confusion caused by identical initial words. The fore-edge margin of f. 117 has sewn into it a length of red thread forming a vertical line ca. 36 mm long near the Ps. XCVI initial but seen (in its present state?) mostly on the recto.[8] Similarly marked (but in the inner margin and clearly accompanying the large initial there, on 137r) is the beginning of Ps. CX, the first psalm of Sunday Vespers. The leaves which follow show evidence of considerable use, suggesting a lay person whose participation in the liturgical office would for the most part be limited to Vespers. — On ff. 143r–153r the 22 divisions of the long Ps. CXIX are all signaled by 2-line initials; many of them are also captioned "*psalmus dauid*" as if separate psalms. — The total absence of antiphons and of any liturgical rubrics, original or added, is rather exceptional for the period and certainly suggests a lay destinatary and user.

173r–185r: (beginning in the 7th line of the page, without special signal or caesura:) *psalmus dau[id]* [sic; actually Isaiah XII,1–6:] (C)[2]onfitebor tibi domine . . . (173v:) . . . *cantic.*[9] (E)[2]Go dixi in dimidio . . . [= Is. XXXVIII, 10–20] (174v:) . . . *cantica:* (E)[2]xultauit cor meum . . . [= 1 Sam. II, 1–10] (175v:) . . . *cantica:* (C)[2]Antemus (corrector's mark directing to insert from margin the missing word "domino") gloriose enim . . . [= Exodus XV,1–19] (177r:) . . . *[uncaptioned:]* (D)[2]Omine audiui . audic[i]onem tua[m] . . . [= Habakkuk III,2–19] (178v:) . . . *cantica:* (A)[2]Vdite celi que loquor . . . [= Deuteronomy XXXII,1–43] (182v:) . . . *psalmus* [sic; actually, the Athanasian Creed:] (Q)[2]Vicumq[ue] uult saluus esse . . . (ends on 185r, 4th line:) . . . saluus esse non poterit.

The "lesser canticles" used in the Lauds. Puzzling is the absence of the Song of the Three (from Daniel) needed on Sundays. — The famous doctrinal statement at the end was used in the Prime.

185r-187v: (beginning in 5th line of 185r:) (K)[4]yrie leyson . . . (ends on 187v, 17th line:) . . . Et clamor meus ed te ue[n]iat (last line blank)

The Litany of Saints. After Mary, the angels, the apostles, and the Innocents it names 7 individual martyrs (Stephane, Line, Syxte, Laurenti, Vincenti, Corneli, Cypriane), 11 confessors (last of them: Arnulphe), and 11 women (the last three are Fides, Spes, Caritas). — The one unusual name in the litany is Arnulphus; although there were several saints by that name (var. Arnoldus, Arnoult, etc.) this must be, in view of the calendar, St. Arnulphus of Metz, progenitor of the Carolingian dynasty and (after his wife's entry into a nunnery) bishop of Metz (d. 641). — The prayers which follow (and to some extent are a part of) the litany end somewhat imperfectly: a series of formal requests for the living and the dead would be expected.

* * *

Foliated in modern pencil; the numbering does not include endleaves, of 17th-century paper, four (free ones) in front and seven at end. — Written area ca. 108 × ca. 76 mm. — Fully ruled in (diluted) black[10] ink; framing lines run all the way to edges, the line horizontals sometimes overrun the framing (as does the script). Pricking not in evidence. — The primary text (ff. 14-187) probably all by one scribe; the script is a rather fully quadrate *littera textualis formata,*[11] the ink black to brownish black, prone to rub off in parts subjected to much use. The calendar (ff. 1-12) in *semiquadrata*, using for ink a grayish or brownish yellow (with important feasts well-handled thickly applied gold). — Good quality parchment, thickness ca. 16.8 mm for 100 leaves. — Rubrics (i.e., insignificant captions[12]) in red. — Marginal matter limited to minor corrections, mostly adding a missing word; they seem contemporary.[13]

Collation: 1^{12}(f. 13 a singleton) $2\text{-}3^{8}$(= ff. 14-29) $4^{6?}$ (= ff. 30-35) $5\text{-}16^{8}$ (= ff. 36-131) (ff. 132-133 a false bifolio made of two singletons) 17^{4-1} (= ff. 134-163; 17_4 removed, no text loss) $18\text{-}23^{8}$ (= ff. 137-184) (ff. 185-186 a bifolio?) (f. 187 a singleton?) — No trace of catchwords.

Decoration: Characterized throughout by generous use of glossy, slightly reddish burnished gold leaf over a noticeable thickness of gesso. — One large (ca. 90 × ca. 70 mm) illustration appears on f. 13v: Christ in Majesty, on blue-and-gold ground, in a diamond surrounded by (partly cropped) symbols of the Evangelists (not great art). The illustration appears to have been taken from another mid-14th-century manuscript;[14] it is certainly pasted by the edges to the blank recto of f. 13 from which a rectangle had been cut out; it does not completely match the original framing around the rectangle which issues from the large (ca. 40 × ca. 45 mm) initial *B* below. The initial itself is half blue, half faint magenta (both with white penwork) and infilled with blue and red (and magenta) leafy vines; the whole on an irregularly rectangular gold ground, with gold and blue and magenta branchwork extending from the corners to all margins except the top (where everything, incl. the illustration, is cropped). The letters *EATUS UIR* are gold on blue and magenta ground with white penwork. — Six large (mostly 5–line) illuminated initials mark the liturgical divisions of the Psalter (missing one): the letters are outlined in black and colored blue or magenta (with white penwork) on gold grounds outlined in black; they are inhabited:[15]

38v:	King David pointing to his eyes
69r:	fool with club and loaf of bread[16] (a 6–line *D*)
83v:	Christ above, David below (see plate IX, p. xxiv)
102r:	David playing carillon
117v:	two monks, one in white, one in gray, at lectern
137r:	Trinity

Partial frames formed by branches issuing from the initial include a straight bar running in each case along the left text margin (gold and part magenta, part blue). — The twelve *KL*s of the calendar, also the 4–line initial *K* of the litany (185r) are gold on blue and magenta grounds (with the usual white penwork in the non-gold areas). Individual psalms begin with 2–line initials of this type. — Versals, 1-line, are alternately blue or gold and surrounded by red pen flourishes for the blue letters, purple for the golden ones; where feasible, the rather skillfull penwork extends into the margins. — Line fillers in the litany consist of two or three repeated and connected lanceolate shapes half blue and half gold, with red and purple penwork added.

Binding: 17th-century French, light brown calf gilt "à l'éventail." Gilt edges. — On inside of upper cover,[17] ownership labels of the Duke of Sussex (see former owners) and of the Library of Congress; also various handwritten identification symbols and (erroneous) descriptive notes ("Breviarium," "ms. of 12th cent.," "Irish or Scotch"); of uncertain meaning: cum vita S^ti^ Stepha(n)i 10.19.0 (= purchasing price?).

Former owners: On f. 1r in head margin, in clear, modern-appearing cursive, black ink: Collegij Metēsis Soc. Jesu cat. inscriptus. The college was founded 1622 and

MS 17 closed in 1762, its library dispersed.[18] — In first half of 19th century in the collection of Augustus Frederick, Duke of Sussex (d. 1843; collection formed ca. 1815–43[19]); after his death, bought (in R. H. Evans sale) by T. Rodd (bookseller; d. 1849). Acquired by LC at end of 19th century?

2° fo.: (KL)[3] *feurier. ait. xxviij. iours.*

Bibl.: *Bibliotheca Sussexiana, a descriptive catalogue . . .* / by Thomas Joseph Pettigrew. London, Longman, 1827–39. v. I, pt. 1, p. civ, no. 29. — *Bibliotheca Sussexiana* [sale catalog of firm R. H. Evans]. London, 1844–45. v. 2, no. 389.[20] — De Ricci, *Census* (1935), p. 182, no. 10; Faye and Bond, p. 117, no. 10.

NOTES

Thanks are due to Mlle Marie-Claire Mangin of the Bibliothèque municipale of Nancy, France, for suggestions and kind assistance in matters pertaining to this codex.

1. The feast of the dedication of the collegiate church Saint-Sauveur in Metz. (Cf. H. Tribout de Morembert, *Le diocèse de Metz* [1970], p. 70–71; with city map on p. [305].)

2. Many of these are also found, with same dates, in the ms. Bib. nat. 823, a missal from the area of Trier; cf. *Catalogus codicum hagiographicorum Latinorum in Bibliotheca nationali Parisiensi*, t. 3 (Brussels, 1893), p. 587 and [606]–733. (N.B. Metz was a suffragan bishopric of the ecclesiastical province of Trier.)

3. Cf. the Metz calendar printed in Grotefend, *Zeitrechnung* 2, p. 125 sqq.

4. Cf. J. François, *Histoire de Metz* (1974 reprint ed. of 18th-century ed.), v. 2, p. 580.

5. The "Gallican" version used in most of Latin liturgy through ca. 1943. — The semi-biblical psalm titles ("In finem . . . " *et sim.*) are omitted, as is commonly the case in liturgical or quasi-liturgical books.

6. Cf. A. Hughes, *Medieval manuscripts for Mass and Office* (1982), par. 874 sqq. — N.B. We are using the psalm numbering of the Hebrew Bible (identical with that of the King James version), now commonly accepted; the numbers in Hughes' book are those of the Vulgate. The manuscript here discussed has no numbering.

7. The scribe had to leave appropriate space for the initialist.

8. It helps to find the much-needed invitatory psalm *Venite exultemus* (116v–117r) but that could hardly have been the original purpose. Alternately, the thread may have served to hold some further adornments, now lost, to the initial on f. 117v, so that what remains would be the wrong side.

9. As may be seen from the following, the scribe seems to have understood the word *cantica* as a feminine noun in nominative singular. — N.B. Where our transcription shows a colon (in this paragraph) the copyist used three dots arranged in a left-pointing triangle.

10. Except for the calendar, which is ruled in the ink of its script (see below).

11. Letter *y* dotted; *a* of two intermixed types (the form open to left more frequent); *i* distinguished by hairline sharp accent.

12. Except in the calendar (cf. contents), the recurring caption "*psalmus*" (with or without "*dauid*") is about all there is.

13. An unidentified 20th-century student of the manuscript (not the present writer) added various penciled marks in the calendar.

14. Alternately, the illustration may have been (prior to binding?) part of a leaf which preceded and formed a bifolio with the present f. 13. Stub is present.

15. For the themes of the initials and much other matter pertaining to medieval Psalters see the excellent treatment in: R. G. Calkins, *Illuminated books of the Middle Ages* (1983), ch. 6.

16. The club is green and the bread looks like the orb in Christ's hand in the 83v initial; did the initialist understand his theme?

17. At the time of this writing, the upper cover is detached. The book is in a recently made box covered in natural and grayish green linen.

18. Cf. Tribout de Morembert, *op. cit.*, p. 146–147.

19. Cf. S. De Ricci, *English collectors of books and manuscripts* (1960), p. 118.

20. Not seen.

MS 18

(Faye and Bond 2 and 3)

BREVIARY, summer part. ca. 1400?

Written in France in or near Langres. Parchment. 2 volumes, 163, 192 leaves, 195 × ca. 135 mm (bound volumes ca. 205 × ca. 150 mm) 2 columns. 27 lines.

Vol. I (Faye and Bond 2):

ff. 1r–92v: (preceding the present f. 1, a gathering of probably 8 leaves is wanting, with text loss) (1r, running title: *Dies d[omi]nica*; text begins imperfectly, in 2nd nocturn, Ps. XVIII:) et carbones ignis . . . . . . (ends imperfectly in first psalm of Saturday Vespers, Ps. CXLIV, on f. 92v:) . . . de aquis multis : et de manu

Liturgical Psalter, with the Psalms arranged according to their use in the Office; for use by secular (diocesan, not monastic) clergy. Lacunae at the beginning and the end and also following f. 88 (missing there, large part of Thursday Vespers). Various liturgical matter is integrated into the Psalter: antiphons, *capitula*, the Old Testament canticles for Lauds,[1] the Athanasian Creed, *preces*. The preserved basic antiphons of Sunday Matins are from the rhythmical set "Pro fidei meritis" (*AH* XVII, p. [19]).[2]

(following f. 92, one or more leaves wanting; see also collation)

93r–95va: (all running titles here consist of or begin with the word *Canticu(m)*; text begins abruptly in v. 9 of Ps. CXLVIII:) fructifera et o[mne]s cedri . . . (Ps. CXLVIII is followed by CXLIX and CL; f. 93va:) . . . *Laus ang[e]lo[rum] (T)*²e deu[m] laudam[us] . . . (94rb:) . . . *canticu[m] pu[er]o[rum]* (B)²enedicite o[mn]ia . . . (94vb:) . . . *Cant[icum] zacharie* (B)²en[e]dict[us] . . . (95rb:) . . . *Canticu[m] btē m[ari]e.* (M)²agnificat . . . (95va:) . . . *canticu[m] symeo[n]is* (N)²unc dimittis . . . (ends, line 21:) plebis tue israel.

The Pss. CXLIX and CL lack the usual caption "*p̄s̄*" employed throughout the preceding section; they do begin with 2-line capitals. — There is no suggestion of the "Gloria Patri . . . " doxology at end of any item in this group.

95va–98rb; (begins in line 22 of 95va:) *Letania* (K)²yrie//leyson . . . (ends in line 26 of f. 98rb:) domino. Deo gr[ati]as (last line empty; 98v blank, ruled)

The litany includes after Mary, the archangels, apostles, etc. (through the Innocents): 41 individual martyrs (. . . Benigne, Mammes, . . . Valeri, Gengulphe, . . . Florenti, . . . Leodegari, . . . Ferreole, Ferruci, . . . Quintine, . . . Desideri cum s., Speosippe, Eleosippe, Meleosippe . . .); 24 confessors (. . . Amator, . . . Vinebaude, . . . Theobalde, . . . Secane, . . .); 17 women (. . . Germana, . . . Columba, Barbara, Fides, . . . Martha, Iuliana). — 97rb: . . . Ut episcopos et abbates nostros . . .

99r–163v: (99ra, 99rb, and through 102va, running title: *De scā trinitate*; text, 99ra:) *De scā t[ri]nitate ad v[espera]s a[ntiphona]*. (*G*)[2]loria tibi t[ri]nitas . . . (102vb, running title: *feria scdā*; 104r(ab): *feria iiij fiu[n]t octabe scē t[ri]nitatis;* 104va, in text column:) . . . *Incipit officiu[m] corp[or]is xpī* . . . (*S*)[2]acerdos inet[er]nu[m] . . . (the temporal ends on 163va with reading from Zephaniah I:) . . . sup[er] iudam dicit dominus et sup[er] om[ne]s h[ab]itatores iherusalem.[3]

The temporal (proper of the seasons), from Trinity to Advent (through 25th Sunday after Pentecost or, rather, after octave of Trinity), i.e., covering the half of the liturgical year which the v. II (in caption on f. 1r) calls "tempus estiuale." — Leaves wanting, with loss of text, following ff. 108 (lost part of the Office of Corpus Christi and Friday of the octave), 114 (lost what followed 1 Sam. I,13a), 115[4] (wanting most of Tuesday after octave of Trinity), 119 (lost the Gospel quotation, etc., for 3rd Sunday after the octave), 125 (Bede's homily on Mark VIII,1–9, and part of the season's scriptural readings), and 157 (Gospel quote and homily for the 22nd Sunday). — Nine-lesson offices have generally nine responsories even when *Te Deum* follows. — Some of the biblical readings are presented in uninterrupted sections ("Legenda per ebdomadam") rather than divided into lessons. — The Office for Corpus Christi includes, at end of the Matins and before *Te Deum*, a "*prosa*" (108rb–va): Sospitati dat credentes . . . [5] The Sunday in the octave of the feast (= 1st Sunday after Trinity, 2nd after Pentecost, 109r–110r) has nine readings concerned with its justification, institution, and (*ll.* viii and ix) on indulgences associated with the celebration; no Gospel quotation, no homily; the next Sunday (2nd after Trinity, 3rd after Pentecost, 112v sq.) is called "*Dominica prima post octabam scē trinitatis*" and has the Gospel *Homo quidam erat dives* (Luke XVI, 19); next (117v sqq.) is "*Dominica ii^{a} post trinitatem*" (with *Homo quidam fecit coenam . . .)*, next (119v) "*tercia post trinitatem.*"[6] The "*Dn̄ca iiij*" (120v) is assigned the pericope *Estote misericordes* (Luke VI, 36); the Sundays numbered as 5th (122r) through 24th (159v) have Gospels and other features corresponding to the 4th through 23rd Sunday after Pentecost in Roman liturgical books;[7] the Sunday designated as 25th (161r) is given the Gospel *Cum sublevasset* (John VI,5).[8] The wording of the Gospel quotations is sometimes at variance with the Vulgata text. The homilies agree with the Curia breviary (as per *SMRL* II) in ca. one case out of three; Bede seems to have been the author most preferred.
(Text of v. I ends with 10 last lines of the temporal in first column of f. 193v; rest of the page blank except for an inscription of ca. 1500 in cursive: C'est a moy thomas (c?)olebeau pere. A cross drawn over the "pere"; signed, perhaps by the first inscriber's son: T Colebeau (fils ?))

Vol. II (Faye and Bond 3):

ff. 1r–168v: (1r, running title: *De scō desiderio*; text column 1ra:) *Sequu[n]tur festiuitates s[an]c[t]o[rum] t[em]p[o]ris estiualis* . . . (sanctoral ends in 168vb:) plorans omnibus uale dicebat. Tu a[utem Domine miserere nobis] (last three lines blank)

The sanctoral (proper of the saints), from *Desiderii epī Lingonensis* (Didier, Bp. of Langres, celebrated on May 23[9]) to *Eligii epī et confessoris* (Dec. 1); within this span, ca. 115 saints' days and similar occasions, among them:[10] (f. 4r:) Vinebaud(i); (7r:) Ferreoli et Ferrucii (in June; also their *inventio* in September, f. 91rv); (8r:) Achacii sociorumque; (after f. 8, missing leaf with the beginning of the office of John the Baptist; following f. 14, another leaf missing, with loss of end of the office of John's octave and of the beginning of Peter and Paul); (32r sqq.:) In solemnitate Marie Magdalene (with octave); (38v–41v:) Anne matris Virginis Marie (Inclita stirps Iesse . . .); (44r–46r, presumably on July 30:) Festum Reliquiarum;[11] (55r–59v:)

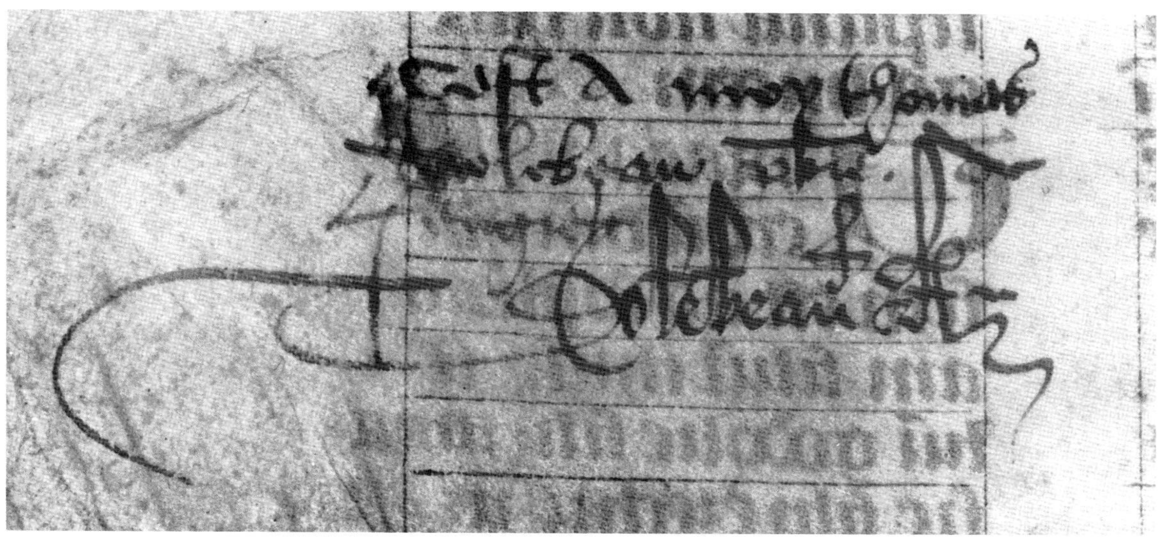

MS 18, volume I, f. 163v (inscription) (actual size of area shown: ca. 34 × 70 mm)

Transfiguracio Domini; (63v–67v:) In translacione scē Corone Domini; (75v–78r:) Mammetis (Aug. 17; also on 119v sqq., with octave, the feast of transfer of his relics, celebrated Oct. 10); (83r–86v, immediately after the Aug. 25 feast of Eusebius, Poncianus, Peregrinus, and Vincentius:) Dedicatio ecclesie[12] (this is followed by a lacuna: wanting are the octave readings of the *Dedicatio* and the beginning of *Decollatio Johannis Bapt.*); (103r–104r:) Inuencio sanctorum geminorum (= Speusippos, Eleusippos, and Meleusippos, Sept. 18; in the responsories, on 103v: "Lingones interea p[ro]ceres . . ."); (104r–105r:) Secani abbatis (on 104v, interesting, for the Champagne region, *lectio viii:* "Admoneo tibi . . . ut . . . modico vino vtaris . . ."); (115v:) Piati martyris; (116v–117v:) Francisci conf. (with readings apparently from Jacobus de Varagine[13]); on 122r, in the octave of *Transl. s. Mammetis*, a legendary account of how it came to be "quod ecclesia Lingonensis eius nomine tituletur"; (122v:) Bassoli; (123va, rubrical directions only for:) De sancto Berchario et Bolonia; (128v–130r; part of Matins lost with missing leaf between 128 and 129:) Valerii martyris (deacon, patron of Langres, celebrated Oct. 22); (another leaf wanting following f. 130, with end of *Symonis et Iude* and the beginning of:) Quintini (Oct. 31); (following f. 132, missing leaf with mid-section of Matins of All Saints; 135v–138v:) Benigni martyris (in Langres, Nov. 1); (following f. 138, lost part of octave of All Saints and the beginning of:) Translacio scī Gregorij epī Lingonensis (Langres, Nov. 6). — There is no mention of the *Visitatio B. M. V.* (promulgated 1389 but introduced only slowly); more interestingly, none of St. Dominic (Aug. 4), St. Louis (Aug. 25), St. Malachias (Nov. 5), all introduced into Langres liturgy in 1404 by Cardinal Louis de Bar (a number of older celebrations were at that time eliminated).[14]

169r–190r: (169r, running title: *De ap[osto]lis*; text column:) *Incipit com[m]une s[an]c[t]o[rum] et primo de ap[osto]lis* . . . (the commons end in lines 12–13 of 190ra:) et comparauit ea[m]. p̄ m[agnificat] *Or[aci]o ut s[upra]*.

The commons: apostles; one martyr, several martyrs; one confessor, several confessors (ending imperfectly: leaf wanting following f. 186; next item begins imperfectly:) one virgin.

MS 18, volume II, f. 104v and edge of 105r
(actual height of the columns: 132 mm)

190r–192v: (running title, 190r through end: *Officiu(m) defuncto(rum);* text begins in 14th line of column 190ra:) *Incipiunt vigilie defu[n]cto[rum]* . . . (P)[2]lacebo . . . (office ends imperfectly at the beginning of 3rd nocturn, in 192vb:) . . . ad adiuandum me respice $\bar{p}$ Expecta[n]s

The Office for the Dead, presumably according to the use of Langres. Invitatory *Regem cui omnia vivunt*; lessons and responsories, as far as preserved: L. I.: Parce R. I: Credo quod L. II: Tedet R. II: Qui Lazarum L. III: Responde R. III: Domine quando veneris — L. IV: Quis mihi R. IV: Requiem eternam L. V: Spiritus meus R. V: Heu mihi L. VI: Pelli meae R. VI: Ne recorderis (rest wanting).

* * *

Foliated in modern pencil; free endleaves (one per cover, paper) are not included in the numbering. — Written area ca. 127–130[15] × ca. 90 mm (ruled for 126–130 × 88 (39 + 10 + 39) mm). — Fully ruled: v. I in faint purple ink throughout, v. II partly in faint purple, partly in diluted brownish black. Pricking marks in most outer margins in v. I, often absent in v. II. — Most of the text in both volumes seems to have been written by one scribe; in v. II, ff. 177v to end (192v) by another. The script is a rather utilitarian, not very regular *littera textualis semiquadrata* of two purposefully differentiated sizes.[16] Good slightly brownish black ink. — Parchment of good quality and whiteness; thickness ca. 14.3 mm per 100 leaves. — Rubrics in red, including the running titles which are used throughout (some over individual columns even at the cost of repetition, some for whole pages). — At least 9 leaves are wanting in each of the two volumes, not counting what seems to have been a whole gathering (of 8?) preceding the present f. 1 of v. I (and possibly another at end of v. II). Text and possibly decoration have been lost with the wanting leaves.

Collation: Vol. I: $[1]^{8?}$(wanting) $2–12^8$ (= ff. 1–88) $13^{6?}$(= ff. 89–92; $13_{1.6}$ following ff. 88 and 92 wanting) $14^{6?}$ (= ff. 93–98) $15–23^8$(wanting 16_3 following f. 108, $17_{2,4}$ following ff. 114 and 115, $18_{1.8}$ following ff. 119 and 125, $23_{1.8}$ following ff. 157 and 163; the 23_8 probably blank)

Vol. II: $1–10^8$ (wanting $2_{1.8}$ following ff. 8 and 14) $11–12^{4?}$(= ff. 79–82, 83–86) (singleton or bifolio wanting following f. 86) $13–26^8$(wanting $18_{3.6}$ following ff. 128 and 130, $19_{1.8}$ following ff. 132 and 138, and $26_{1.8}$ following ff. 186 and 192). — Catchwords in *lettre bâtarde* at end of complete gatherings (mostly under the 2nd column, some closer to center of the tail margin).

Decoration is limited (in the present imperfect state of the work) to very simple red and/or blue *litterae notabiliores*, 2 lines (for the initial letter of most psalms and readings; red and blue alternate) or 4, occasionally 3 lines in height (tendency here to combine the two colors; used for the major liturgical divisions of the Psalter). Guide letters for the initialist, done in faint ink. Versals in the Psalter alternately red or blue. The logic of using initials of a particular size for a given level of text division is not consistently maintained.

Binding: 20th-century half leather, red (apparently replaced the "old brown calf" noted in De Ricci). Gilt edges. On inside of upper cover, labels of LC Division of Manuscripts (the book was in its custodial care for a time) and of the Rare Book Collection.

Former owners: (at least v. I) owned ca. 1500 by "Thomas Colebeau père."

2° fo.: v. I: (running title:) *Dies dn̄ica.* (text:) arum delebo eos. Eri — v. II: (running title:) *De sancto desiderio.* (text:) fendere cognoscebant.

Bibl.: De Ricci, *Census* (1935), p. 180, nos. 2 and 3; Faye and Bond, p. 117, nos. 2 and 3.

MS 18 Produced for use in the ancient diocese of Langres, France. A more detailed study may pinpoint the particular church or collegiate chapter in which the book was used. The almost total absence of decoration may be deceptive: many of the missing leaves included the opening words of important sections and may well have been removed for their initials.

NOTES

1. Except for Sunday, where only the cue is given (*Benedicite*, f. 4ra; full text in the section which follows). — N.B. With this exception, the canticles are those identified in Hughes, *Medieval manuscripts*, p. 365–366, as the set used during Lent [?!]

2. Rubric on f. 146r specifies that the set is to be used "a festo s. Remigii [= Oct. 1] usque ad Adventum." — See also our note 12 to the breviary LC MS 15.

3. The wording agrees with none of the variants offered in the Stuttgart critical edition of the Vulgate (2nd ed., 1975).

4. Folio 115r has running title "*antene de hystoria*"; the antiphons are from later parts of 1 Sam., from 2 Sam. and 1 Kings. On verso mostly rubrical matter, captioned "*Ordinariu*[*m*]."

5. Not in the *Analecta Hymnica?* — Full text: Sospitati dat credentes festum eucharistie Carnem Christi confitentes esse panem hostie In altari panis iste totum cibans hominem Tuum confert corpus Christe sic vinum et sanguinem Hic est panis angelorum hic calix inebrians Agnus legis azimorum pascha manna sacians O quam digne sacramenti tanti festum colitur In quo deus alme menti substancie iungitur.

6. It appears that the introduction of the feast of Corpus Christi (in 14th century) added further confusion to the system of Sundays after Pentecost, already disturbed by the earlier (as far as Langres is concerned) introduction of the feast of the Trinity, assigned to the first Sunday after Pentecost (cf. somewhat similar situation in the 13th-century LC MS 15, also our notes to its ff. 292v sqq.) — If abbé Marcel's wording in *Les livres liturgiques du diocèse de Langres* (1892; p. 127) is correct, the printed *Breviarium Lingonense* of 1505 counts the Sundays from Trinity; the "post octavam Trinitatis" used in LC MS 18 was a system followed by the Dominicans.

7. From the Curia breviary (cf. *SMRL* II, p. 105–109) to the *Breviarium Romanum* of 1570 (and up to the restructuring of Catholic liturgical calendar ca. 400 years later).

8. As in the Parisian breviary LC MS 15 and, it seems, other non-Roman sources.

9. None of the calendar days is in the manuscript; we are supplying them from reference sources (and from the sequence of celebrations in the text).

10. Selecting from the ca. 115 occasions those particular to Langres, also some which indicate the stage of development of the sanctoral; and those not fully accounted for, among these Vinebaudus, Achacius, Piatus . . . — For St. Vinebaud, cf. L. Marcel, *Les livres liturgiques du diocèse de Langres* (1892, p. 30; suppl. 1899, p. 46).

11. In Langres, the Feast of the Relics was celebrated on July 30, between Abdon and Germanus; this agrees with its position in our ms. Cf. Leroquais, *Brèv*. 1, p. 326 (his ms. no. 190).

12. Cf. Leroquais *loc. cit.* — The *Dedicatio* may be by another hand (?).

13. Cf. *ANALECTA FRANCISCANA* X, p. [681] sqq.

14. Cf. L. Marcel, *op. cit.* (1982), p. 69, n. (2). — In the case of the breviary there discussed (= Leroquais, *Brèv*., no. 190), a sumptuously decorated and illustrated book, liturgical obsoleteness may have been accepted more readily (rather as in the calendars of many books of hours); the present book seems to have been made (judging from what is preserved) for use rather than for visual appeal; it would have been, then, important to have an up-to-date text, wherein additions would have been freely made. At least one addition was made: on f. 37r (corresponding to July 24) a different, perhaps 15th-century hand has added in the outer margin: *Cristi[n]e u[ir]g[in]is q[ue]re i[n] fi[n]e lib[ri]*; the end of the volume is unfortunately lost.

15. Mostly 127 mm in v. I, mostly 130 in v. II, but varying somewhat in both.

16. The larger size for psalms, readings, formal prayers, also the (red) running titles; smaller script for responsories, versicles, invitatories, most rubrics. — Letter *y* not dotted; letter *i* often provided with sharp accent in faint ink.

MS 19

(Music Division: M2147 XIV M2 Case)

CHOIR MANUAL mid-XVth c.?

From the area of Lower Rhine? Parchment. 12 leaves,[2] ca. 285[3] × ca. 210 mm (bound volume: ca. 290 × ca. 215 mm) 23 long lines of text, or 8 or (5v, 6r, 11rv) 9 staves of music with text.

f. 1v (text without music): *K*yriel' (two words crossed through in red:) xp̄el' kyr' *P*ater n[oste]r Et ne nos *A* porta inferi *C*redo uidere . . . (ends in 18th line:) . . . cu[m] deo p[at]re. (ADDED in another hand on lines 21–22:) *B*eati petri apostoli q[uaesumu]s dn̄e intercessione nos p[ro]tege [et] a[n]i[m]as famulor[um] tuor[um] sac[er]dotum sanctor[um] tuor[um] iunge consortijs. P[er].

Liturgical commemorative prayers for the dead; the rite given here includes the formal *Partem beatae resurrectionis, Deus veniae largitor* ("ut nostre congregationis fratres et sorores . . ."), and *Fidelium Deus omnium.* — The prayer added at the bottom of the page, perhaps for deceased chaplains of the community, is marked for insertion before the *Deus veniae largitor.*[4]

2r–3r (with music): (*C*)$^{1+1}$Ircumdederunt me gemitus mortis dolores inferni circu[m]dederu[n]t me *p̄s* (*V*)$^{1+1}$enite exultemus . . . (ending in last line of 3r:) . . . et lux p[er]petua luceat eis (crossed through in red:) Circūded'; Dolor[es]

Introductory psalm of Matins (Ps. XCV) of the *Officium defunctorum,* with the gloomy Invitatory (*Circumdederunt*) peculiar, it seems, to the Lower Rhine.[5]

3v–12r: *Ordo ad officium kalendarum post festu[m] scī mychaelis* (with music:) (*S*)$^{1+1}$Vrge aquilo et ueni auster . . . (4v, in last line:) . . . (*A*)$^{1+1}$lma redemp(5r:)toris mater . . . (5v, in 8th line:) . . . *Inuit[atorium]* (*I*)$^{1+}$n honore beatissime marie virginis. Jubilemus domino . . . (10v:) . . . *Ad missam* (program by initia, without music) . . . (ibid., in 9th line:) *Sequitur ordo post festum pasche. Ad v[espera]s* (music resumes) . . . (*R*)$^{1+}$egina celi letare alleluia Quia . . . (11v ends:) . . . Quoniam pecca (continued on half-size f. 12r, by twelve densely written lines without any music:) toru[m] mole p[re]mim[ur] . . . (in 7th line) . . . *Ad c[ir]cuitu[m]* [!?] *R* B[e]n[e]d[i]c[t]a tu . . . *in c[ry?]pta* [!?] *y[m]n[us]*Aue mar[is] *In stac[i]o[n]e* [!?] Regina celi *In ascensu* [!?] xp̄i u[ir]go [paragraph mark] *Ad missa[m]* Salue scā *kyr' pasch'* . . . *Epl'a* Ego quasi vit[is] *P'mū all' H*[aec] est speciosior *ul'* Ma[r]ia dei *Scd'm all'* Surrexit pastor *Seqū* V'gīs ma[r]ie [cf. *AH* LIV,21] *Ewū* Staba[n]t iux[ta] *Credo off'* Recordare *p̄facō de dn̄a nr̄a Com* Bt̄a uiscera *.vj. [et] ix. secundu[m] modu[m] sup[ra]dictu[m]* . [*et*] *sufficit.* (5 blank lines; 12v blank, unruled)

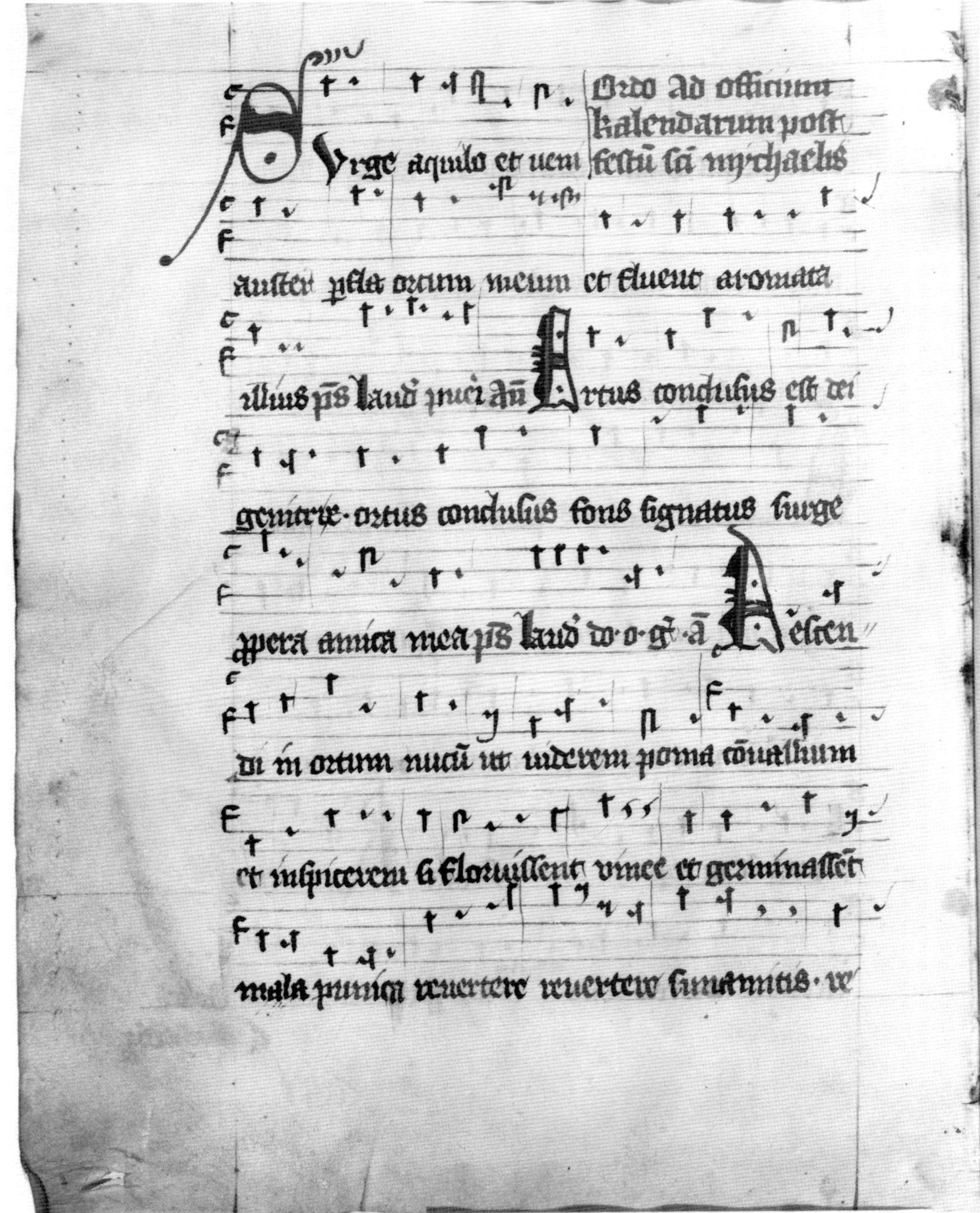

MS 19, f. 3v (actual size of the leaf: ca. 285 × 210 mm)

A full-scale (votive ?) office in honor of the Virgin, followed (10v-12r) by its Easter-season variant.[6] Both forms include programs (without music) for the corresponding Mass. Some unusual selections are included: besides the Rhenish[7] Invitatory *In honore,* most notably the *Alma Redemptoris mater* and *Regina celi* as antiphons to the Magnificat (see Appendix).

* * *

No foliation. — Written area varies, ca. 220 (incl. music staff) × ca. 140 mm.[8] — Ruled in faint black ink; the (not doubled) vertical lines reaching to the edges, as do two horizontal lines (embracing music staff and text) at head and two at the tail. Horizontal lines form, with few exceptions, eight groups of five on each page, guided by groups of five pricks made 8–16 mm from the fore edge (absent on ff. 1, 5–6, and 11). The wider (ca. 10 mm) space between the groups of five horizontals contains the text; the base of the text minims runs, without ruling, 1–2 mm above the ruled line, and the line is sometimes used in the notation. — The script is throughout *textualis* of rather utilitarian kind: larger, more formal, and quadrate (*fracta*) on the text-only f. 1v (except two lines added near tail), smaller and on the semiquadrate side in the texts with music; both are marked by a peculiar *a* in which the upper and right section of the letter has the shape of a tironian *et*; a thin stroke attached to the lower lobe more or less closes the upper area.[9] Letter *g* has lower loop closed by a thin line; the right half of *h* descends, *j*-like, below line; *u/v* beginning a word has randomly the "u" or "v" shape; in the second case, in the large script of f. 1v it resembles *y*. Both *i* and *y* ("hyemps", "ymber") are marked by very thin accent-like strokes (on 1v, mostly rounded or hooked) added, perhaps, after the text was completed. — The tironian *et* used 4 times in the condensed rubrics-and-initia section on f. 10v and once on 12r is clearly crossed there, whether red or black; in its three appearances elsewhere (1v, 2v, 3r) the stem is touched rather than crossed by one or two thin strokes; an odd uncrossed form resembling the barless median *r* is used in the final "*et sufficit*" on 12r. — The notation is *Hufnagel* or perhaps St.-Gall passing into Hufnagel, on five-line staves (cf. above) with two clefs at the beginning: *c* and (above it) *g* in the Office for the Dead (2r–3r), *c* and *f* in the rest of the book but with the *c* clef omitted when belonging to the highest line of the staff; the *f* comes in two different shapes used, it seems, randomly. The *b* symbol occurs several times. — Rubrics red;[10] the device of a red line drawn through a black-ink word ("Oremus"; "euor[um]"; for iterations of the Invitatory) is used somewhat like our parentheses. — Parchment of mediocre and varying quality, f. 11 poorer than most. Several repairs by sewing (ff. 1, 6, 7, 10); thread lost.

Collation: 1^{10+1}(following 1_8, inserted piece [f. 8bis] with stub following 1_2) $2^{2?}$(f. 11 and the now half-sized f. 12 may be conjugate; their gutter parts [or stubs] seem to end under the paper pastedown of upper cover)

Decoration: limited to decorative uses of the black and/or red ink in the larger capital letters, e.g., those which begin the individual verses of the invitatory psalm (ff. 2r–3r) or the second and further antiphons of the several "hours" in the office which follows: initials of the first antiphons and other major letters important to text arrangement are red-only and quite simple.[11] — Minor capitals touched with red; open spaces required within a text by its association with a melisma are filled with red *s*-curves or series of strokes.

Binding: Original (?) rounded wooden boards ca. 12 mm thick covered with whittawed (sheep)skin dyed purplish red; partly damaged; repaired, partly damaged in repair, and partly repainted red in recent decades. In the repair, the spine has been covered with orange morocco leather decorated or partly held in place by white-headed tacks. One doubtfully original back-to-front clasp consisting of brass hardware attached to leather strap (20th-century orange morocco leather).

On inside of upper cover, on paper pastedown, horizontally near gutter and head edge, in black-ink handwriting of ca. 1830 (?): GWUW. (?). — In outer corner, armored bookplate of ca. 1860[12] with motto: AUREA MEDIOCRITAS. — In center, armored bookplate of "George Richard Mackarness, D.D., Bishop of Argyll and the Isles. A.D. 1874"; below it, woodcut bookplate with calligraphically styled initials "WHC" (i.e., William Hayman Cummings); near top, LC bookplate. — On f. 1v, near end of lines 19/20, monogram which may perhaps be interpreted as standing for "W. CAYLEY." — Acquired by LC at the W. H. Cummings sale (London, 17 May 1917, n. 995) (accession no. 410765 penciled on f. 1v; also "243299//17"; also the call no. "M 2147//XIV M2//Case").

2° fo.: *C*Ircumdederunt me gemitus mortis [under music staff with clefs and notation]

Bibl.: De Ricci I (1935), p. 244, no. 164.

Place (Lower Rhine or, perhaps, on the Baltic?), time (especially if not from Lower Rhine), even the original character of the work (an adjunct to an antiphonary?) are uncertain. The obviously very local character of the rubrical directives on f. 12r may eventually provide an answer to some of these questions. Inserted slips mention the opinion that original users were Dominican nuns.

APPENDIX:
PROGRAM OF THE OFFICE, ff. 3v-12r[13]

I Vesp: *a* Surge aquilo *Ps.* CXIII *a* Hortus conclusus est Dei genitrix *Ps.* CXVII *a* Descendi in hortum nucum *Ps.* CXLVI *a* Anima mea liquefacta est *Ps.* CXLVII,1–11 *a* Tota pulchra *Ps.* CXLVII, 12–20 (*Hy* Ave maris stella) (*Cap* Ab initio) (*V* Post partum) *ad M* Alma Redemptoris mater [!] (*Coll* Concede nos famulos) *Suffr* Veni sancte Spiritus reple (ADDED in margin in cursive: "loco illius suff[ragii] Vltimo festiuitat[is] r[e]q[ui]re in oct[au]a scī sp̄s")[14] (*V* Emitte) (*Coll* Deus qui corda) *Suffr* Inter natos mulierum (*V* Fuit homo) (*Coll* Praesta quaesumus)

Compl: (*Hy* Fit porta) (*Cap* Multae filiae) (*V* Audi filia) "*Sup[er] nūc di[mittis]*": Ista est speciosa ("*p[re]ces solito* [sic] *cu[m] vno v* Digna[r]e") (*Coll* Concede misericors) (Salva nos)

Mat.: *Invit* In honore (*CAO* 1086) *Ps.* XCV *I Noct.*: *a* Benedicta tu in *Ps* VIII *a* Sicut myrrha *Ps* XIX *a* Ante thorum *Ps* XXIV (*V* Specie tua) (in margin, orig. hand: *l[e]c[ti]ones* Scā ma[r]i[a] *cu[m] rel[iquis]*) *1R* Sancta et immaculata (*V* Benedicta tu / Quia) *2R* Benedicta tu in mulieribus (*V* Ave Maria / Et) *3R* Felix namque (*V* Ora pro populo / Quia) *II Noct*: *a* Specie tua *Ps* XLV *a* Adiuvabit eam *Ps* XLVI *a* Sicut laetantium *Ps* LXXXVII (*V* Diffusa est) *4R* Beatam me dicent (*V* Et misericordia / Quia potens) *5R* Beata es . . . quae credidisti . . . (*CAO* 6165 version B,H,R) (*V* Ave [/ ?]) *6R* Ornatam in monilibus (*V* Astitit [/ ?]) *III Noct*: *a* Gaude Maria virgo *Ps* XCVI(?: "Cantate I") *a* Dignare me *Ps* XCVII *a* Post partum *Ps* XCVIII("Cantate II") (*V* Adiuvabit eam) (in margin, orig. hand: *Omelia* Extollens) *7R* Ista est speciosa (*V* Specie tua) *8R* (originally, on f. 8v, same as *5R* above but then crossed through; on insert 8bis recto, captioned "*Octauu[m] responsorium*":) Beata es . . . permanes virgo (*CAO* 6163) (*V* Aue Maria)[15] *9R* Super salutem et omnem pulchritudinem *V* Paradisi porta per Evam / Gaudent

Lauds: *a* Assumpta est *a* Maria virgo assumpta est *a* In odore unguentorum *a* Benedicta filia tu *a* Pulchra es et decora (*Cap* Ab initio) (*V* Audi filia) "*S[upe]r bn̄*": Quae est ista (*Coll* Concede nos famulos) *Suffr* Accipite spiritum sanctum quorum remiseritis (in margin, ADDED in cursive hand: "loco istius Suff[ragii] Nisi quis renatus fu[er?]it req[ui]re in oct[ava] p[ent]ecostes") (*V* Emitte) (*Coll* Deus qui corda) *Suffr* Elizabeth ("Elysabeth") Zachariae (*V* Fuit homo) (*Coll* Praesta quaesumus)

[WITHOUT MUSIC:] *Prime*: (*Hy* Ave maris stella) (*V* Sumens illud) (*V* Sit laus Deo Patri) (*a* Assumpta est, "*cu[m] rel[iquis] ad alias ho[ra]s*") (*Cap* Multae filiae) (*R* Christe fili) (*V* Qui natus es ex "ma"[ria?]) (*V* Audi filia) ("*p[re]ces sol[itae] cu[m]*" *V* Ora pro nobis) (*Coll* Concede misericors) ("*It[em]*" Domine sancte pater)

("*ad iij . vj . [et] ix R [et] V de vna v[ir]g[ine] y[m]nus ut sup[ra] Coll'* Concede nos")

(*Ad missam* Salue sancta parens *Coll* Concede nos "*It[em] de scō sp[irit]u [et] de scō Joh'e*" *Ep* Ab initio *Grad* Benedicta *All* Virga Jesse *Seq* Ave praeclara [!] *Ev* Extollens quaedam *Credo. Off'* Recordare Virgo *Co* Beata viscera)

(f. 10v, in 9th line, continuing without interruption:) "*Sequitur ordo post festum pasche. Ad v[espera]s an[tiphona] sup[er] om[n]ia laudate*" [MUSICAL NOTATION RESUMES] Alleluia (4 ×) (*Hy* Ave maris stella) (*Cap* Ego quasi vitis) (*V* Post partum "*cum all[eluia]*") *ad M* Regina celi [!] (*Coll* Prosit) (*Suffr* "*ut sup[ra] i[n] p[ri]mo ordi[n]e cu[m] all[eluia]*")

Compline: (*Hy* Fit porta [!] = *AH* LII,53 ?) (*Cap* Ego flos) (*V* Audi filia "*cu[m] All'*") "*s[uper] nu[n]c*" [i.e., to *Nunc dimittis*]: Alleluia sancta . . . intercede . . . alleluia (*Preces* "*solit' cu[m] v[ersu]* Dignare me *cū all'* ") (*Coll* Concede misericors) (Salva)

Matins (in Easter season): (*Invit* Ave Maria) *a* Ecce tu pulchra es . . . all' (*Ps.* VIII) *a* Sicut lilium ("lylium") . . . all' (*Ps.* XIX) *a* Favus distillans . . . all' (*Ps.* XXIV) (*V* Specie tua *cum all'a) (Omelia* Stabant *cu[m] expo[sicion]e augustini) 1R* Regali ex progenie . . . all'a *V* Corde et animo . . . sollemnitate . . . / Cuius *2R* Benedicta tu ("*q[ue]re sup[ra] i[n] p[ri]mo ordine* [= f. 6r!]") *3R* Christi virgo dilectissima . . . all'a *V* Quoniam peccatorum mole premimur . . . subveni domina

(ALL THAT FOLLOWS IS INDICATED BY INITIA; NO MUSIC:) (*Lauds:* Assumpta est "*cū rel' ut ī p'mo ordīe cū all'a.*" *Cap* Ego quasi vitis *V* Audi filia "*cū all'* " *ad B* Regina celi [!] *Suffr* Accipite; *also* Elizabeth ["Elyzab[et]"] *Coll* Prosit *Prime: Hy* Ave maris *V* Sumens *V* Sit laus *a* Assumpta *Cap* Ego flos *R* Christe fili "*cū all'* " Qui natus es *V* Audi fili[a] *preces V* Dignare *Coll* Concede misericors; *also* Domine sancte pater *Terce*: *Hy* Monstra te *V* Sit laus *a* Maria virgo *Cap* "*de epistola R de j^na v'g' cū all' ad om[ne]s h[or]as*" "*ad c[ir]cuitu[m]*" [!?] (FOR THE REST, SEE THE CONTENTS, to f. 12r)

NOTES

1. Possibly supplement to an antiphonary (less likely, a fragment?). De Ricci: "Responses and antiphons." Also known as the Cummings Antiphonal.
2. Eleven full-size leaves and a twelfth one which appears to be the upper half of a leaf originally of same dimensions; also a smaller insert following f. [8], added very soon after completion of the rest.
3. Both dimensions of the irregularly cut leaves vary: the height from 280 to 288 mm.
4. The insertion mark made before the prayer and repeated in its intended position is a cross within a circle, in red ink. — A monogram in black ink, undeciphered by me (includes *W*, two *E*'s, *A*, *L*[?]) is on lines 19/20, near gutter. (Perhaps = "W. Cayley"? Cf. the paragraph on inscriptions, etc., following that on binding.)
5. As Invitatory, the verse *Circumdederunt* appears also in LC MSS 30 (f. 156r) and 64 (among late additions following f. 62); in Netherlandish, in MSS 61 (f. 104r), 62 (f. 90r), 63 (f. 143r). This use of the verse (used in Roman books in other contexts) may be late: it does not occur as Invitatory in any of the twelve old antiphonaries analyzed in *CAO,* vols. I–III.
6. "Kalendae post festum s. Michaelis" = the time from Sept. 29 to Easter? The expression is not common in liturgical rubrics. (The Easter-time variant program refers repeatedly to the earlier pages, implying that only the two variants here given were needed.)
7. In use (in pre-Tridentine times) in the ecclesiastical province of Cologne (which included Utrecht); it would be desirable to know the full extent of its occurrence. Cf. *CAO* I, p. 284; II, p. 532.
8. Ruled area varies in height with extremes 217 mm (f. 6v) and 234 mm (f. 6r); width mostly 136 mm but on f. 11r it is 169 mm, on 11v: 171 mm; on the text-only f. 1v: 153 mm.
9. Within the smaller script, the "two-floor" *a* is used ca. half of the time.
10. A different *a* with rounded top (used in initial position) appears in the rubrics, alongside the peculiar shape described earlier.
11. The "*Ad Laudes*" in 6th line of f. 9r is written as a monogram (the stem of the *L* and the ascender of the *d* used as the two stems of *A*, etc.) with certainly some decorative intent.
12. The arms ("quarterly sable and [argent] on a bend of gules three mullets . . . " — De Ricci) belong to the ancient family Cayley, perhaps to its Wiltshire branch (lion in the crest is *argent*); the motto, not among those associated with the Cayley arms in reference sources seen, might help to still narrower identification. — Thanks are due to T. E. Wilgus, Research Services, Library of Congress, for kind help in this.
13. Spelling and captions mostly standardized, captions often supplied. — The manuscript identifies Psalms by initia (intelligently abridged, e.g., "laud. do. q. b."); I am using the now common Masoretic/AV numbering. Other items which the ms. doesn't give in full are enclosed in parentheses. (N.B. Some of these initia have music.)
14. This suggests that our "manual" is really a part of an antiphonary. It could, nevertheless, be a separately produced supplement.
15. The hand (writing style and letter forms, and also notation) of the insert is the same as that of the rest; the caption may have been added later.

MS 20

(Faye and Bond 150)

DIURNAL XIVth c.

Written in northern Italy. Parchment. 51 leaves, 114 × ca. 86 mm (bound volume: 117 × ca. 94 mm) 1 column. 15–17 lines.

ff. 1r–27v: senp[er] facio. *Or[aci]o ad uespū*. (O)²M-[ni]p[oten]s senpit[er]ne d[eu]s [et] q[ui]b[us] fiducia[m] sp[er]and[e] pietatis i[n]dulges . . . (27v:) . . . q[uia] tibi sine te place[re]

The *temporale* ("proper of the seasons"), diurnal (= daytime) parts; beginning and ending imperfectly and with lacunae in between. The preserved section begins with the end of the Magnificat antiphon for Monday of the 2nd week of Lent, and ends with the 19th Sunday after Pentecost (so numbered; cf. below). Judging from the preserved part of the sanctoral (ff. 28–51), the *temporale* in its original shape began with Advent,**[1]** i.e., covered the whole liturgical year; this means that ca. 16 leaves are wanting at the beginning and at least one at the end of the section, following f. 27. Also wanting: after f. 11, two leaves with most of the Holy Week and Easter; after f. 14, leaf with the 2nd and 3rd Sundays "post octavam Pasche"; and after f. 20, two leaves with the Pentecost and its octave. — Leaves 21 through 24 are misbound: their correct order would be 23, 24, 21, 22, with one leaf missing before f. 23 (the second of the two after f. 20), two between 24 and 21, and one following f. 22 (2nd through 5th Sunday after Pentecost). — The preserved parts suffer from a number of scribal or *exemplar* errors, beginning with the corrupt text of the prayer in first lines of f. 1r. — Sundays after Easter are counted as "post octavam Pasche." For the Vigil of Ascension, an odd *oratio* (15v–16r): Praesta quaesumus omnipotens Deus ut mentis intencio q° sollempnitatis uenture gloriosus auctor ingressus semper intendat et q° fide pergit conu[er]sacio perueniat. per . . . — A major variation from the Roman (Curia) program (as per *SMRL* II and also the Tridentine books) consists in a shift of texts (the *orationes*, and the somewhat variant antiphons to Magnificat) from what are the 5th–18th Sundays after Pentecost in the Roman books to the 6th–19th Sundays in our manuscript.**[2]** — Several hymns are included: *Vexilla regis* (7rv; = *AH* II, no. 42, without the 2nd stanza); *Iesu nostra redemptio* (16rv; = *AH* II, no. 49); *Veni creator spiritus* (19v–20r; = *AH* L, no. 144, without last stanza); *Adesto sancta Trinitas*

(23rv; = *AH* IV, no. 4, stanzas 1,2,6 = *AH* LI, no. 96, stanzas 1,2,5).

(following f. 27, two [?] leaves wanting)

28r: (begins imperfectly:) *doc̄. tu[n]c i[n]ferius int[er] mediis q̄ auacauerit faciendu[m] e[st] . . . siue in ip[s]is h'lli's [= homiliis?].*

End of what seems to be a corrupt text of rubrical directives on conflicts between Sundays and saints' feasts (or perhaps on ways of reconciling the standard set of Sunday propers with the varying position of moveable holidays). — The term "inchoare" (inchoanda, inchoari) occurs twice in the six preserved lines.

28r–51v: *In uig[ilia] s[an]c[ti] andree ap[osto]li . Ad uesp[er]um.* . . . (ends imperfectly in last lines of 51v:) . . . claritatis gl[ori]a (.?.) . ut uic[t]ores (ADDED in a much later hand, in red:) *L + amen + D* .

The *sanctorale* ("proper of saints"), diurnal parts of the offices from the Vigil of St. Andrew to the Vespers of All Saints, ending imperfectly. Only important festivals are included: after Andrew (with octave) comes St. Dalmatius (29r–30r; the saint whose bones rest in Borgo San Dalmazzo near Cuneo, Italy[3]); then: Nicholas, Lucy, Thomas the Apostle, Stephen, John the Evangelist. Two leaves are missing after f. 33, with feasts of the period from Dec. 28 through Jan. 20; follow: Agnes, *Conversio Pauli*, (36r–37v:) *"In anunciatione beate Marie"* (! presumably the rubricist's error: the office deals with the usual themes of Feb. 2);[4] further: Agatha, Cathedra Petri, Gregory, Benedict. Following f. 39, two leaves wanting; first seven lines on 40r contain end of the true (March 25) Annunciation office. 40rv: *"In natali quolibet festo pascali tempore"*; further: Mark, Philip, and James, *Inventio s. Crucis, Iohannis ante Portam Latinam,* (43v:) *"In sc̄o Vitale m'r : Omnia fiant sicut in uno martyre pascali* [sic] *temporis"* (= Vitalis of Ravenna? out of order?[5]) (same page:) *Iohannis Baptiste* (= June 24). Following f. 43, six(?) leaves

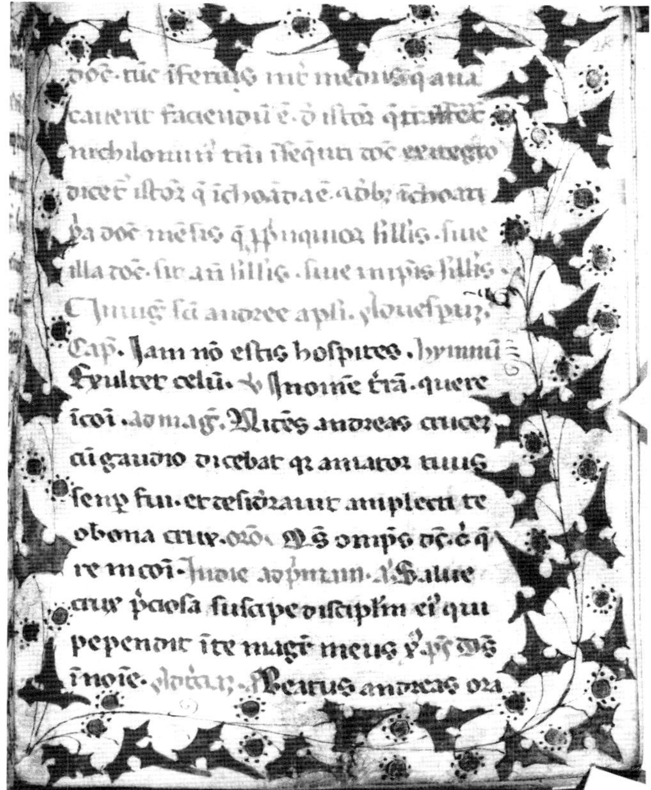

MS 20, f. 28r (actual size of the leaf: ca. 115 × 85 mm)

wanting, with loss of the end of June and all of July; on 44r, beginning imperfectly, part of the office of St. Peter in Chains; followed by: *Inventio s. Stephani, Laurentii,* (45r–47r:) *"In exaltacione sc̄e Marie"* (an unusual term for the Assumption); (47rv:) Bartholomew (ending imperfectly). Following f. 47, two leaves wanting, with saints of the period from Aug. 26 through Sept. 7; on 48r, beginning imperfectly in the middle of the Sext, the Nativity of Mary, through 48v. Follow: *In exaltatione s. Crucis,* (49r–50v:) *"In sc̄o Michaello"* [sic], *In vigilia Omnium Sanctorum* (with hymn *Iesu saluator saeculi* on 51rv and the office ending imperfectly with an unusual antiphon for Magnificat, *Beati estis sancti* . . .). Lost with wanting leaves at end: most of November (up to the Vigil of St. Andrew, Nov. 29).

* * *

Foliated in modern pencil. One free endleaf at end, none in front. — Written area ca. 85 × ca. 60 mm. — No traces of ruling. — Written probably by one person throughout, in a prehumanistic script similar to the *littera bononiensis,* of two sizes. Numerous uncorrected errors. — Brownish black ink of poor quality; some loss of legibility has occurred where ink had rubbed off. Rubrics in red. — Parchment of fair quality; thickness of the text block ca. 8 mm. — Rather tightly cropped, with some detriment to marginal added material. Ca. 40 or more leaves are wanting.

Collation: (two or more gatherings wanting at the beginning) 1^8 2^8($2_{4.5}$ following f. 11 wanting) 3^8 ($3_{1.8}$ following ff. 14 and 20 wanting) 4^8 (= ff. 21–24, misbound: correct order would be [4_1], ff. 23, 24, [$4_{4.5}$], ff. 21, 22, [4_8]; $4_{1.8}$ and $4_{4.5}$ are wanting) 5^8 ($5_{4.5}$ following f. 27 wanting) 6^8($6_{4.5}$ following f. 33 wanting) 7^8($7_{4.5}$ following f. 39 wanting) $8^{8?}$($8_{2-5?}$ following f. 43 wanting) 9^8($9_{4.5}$ following f. 47 wanting) f. 51, now a quasi-singleton, was formerly part of a gathering, the rest of it now wanting. — Considerable amount of text (and decoration) lost with the missing leaves.

Decoration may have been originally limited to the calligraphic *litterae notabiliores,* 2–3 lines in height, in velvety blue with simple, largely spiral red-ink flourishes or alternately in red ink with penwork in diluted, now much faded black; also one-line versals, red more often than blue, used in the hymns. Regular capitals touched with red. — A later hand added full borders to all pages now extant except 1rv, 2r, 12r, and 51v, apparently only after the cropping which affected some marginal material. These borders are unframed and consist of vines drawn in diluted black ink, with much conspicuous foliage (ivy?) painted green, yellowish green, or olive green; also gaudy brushed-gold bezants. The same brushed gold was also used to fill, rather artlessly, most of the large letters previously done in red, some (noticeably fewer) of the blue ones, and all versals. — Roundels, more or less successfully integrated with the vines, in tail margins of ff. 3v, 6v, and 10v: the first two contain, respectively, a coat of arms[6] and a cherub playing a stringed instrument with a bow; the third round shape is a spiked wheel.[7] — A miniature painting ca. 60 × 55 mm in size appears on f. 12r; it is enclosed, together with three lines of text, in a rather baroque-appearing, primarily gold (also magenta and some green) border, irregularly shaped. The miniature, in a rather poor quality version of Bolognese style, depicts a scene in which a standing man in knightly armour (on his golden breastplate, what seems to be a black eagle) speaks to a high ecclesiastic seated on a canopied throne; both men, and two of the three others present in the scene, have haloes around their heads; the action (a plea, a report, an argument?) seems to be taking place outdoors. A (red and white?) banner and a bishop's or abbot's staff are partly visible in the background. — A poorly executed painting in basically same (somewhat dirty) palette but without border, representing Mary holding the Child, 108 × 82 mm, is pasted to the inside of upper cover. — Borders of uncertain origin and date,[8] not skilled work, appear on the first three pages and on the last one. That on f. 1r, framed and entirely different in style from the rest of the manuscript, includes a seated saint with book, perhaps St. Mark; also, in center of the tail margin, another coat of arms: "gules a Saint Catherine's wheel argent (?), apparently accompanied in chief by a label of 3 points" (De Ricci, *Census* (1935), p. 490, no. 3; suggests comparing to Pecchi of Milan). The borders on 1v–2r, and the somewhat different one on 51v, are poor variations on the vine motif; they use gold bezants lavishly.

Bound in polished very dark purple calf or sheepskin; blind-stamped in center of upper cover, a medallion with a coat of arms now deteriorated beyond identifiability. The binding is of the fixed-spine type, sewn over 3 bands, apparently subsequent to the removal of unwanted parts (cf. final comment below).[9]

Former owners: John Davis Batchelder who acquired the book in Venice in 1924; came to LC as part of collection bearing his name in 1936.

2° fo.: p[er]petua[m] be[n]ignitate[m] largire po

Bibl.: De Ricci, *Census* (1935), p. 490, no. 3 ("Breviarium"); Faye and Bond, p. 123, no. 150.

Concluding comment: Written very probably in (or close to) the area of the present diocese of Cuneo in northern Italy, the sadly incomplete office book shows what may be traces of the Ambrosian (Milanese) rite. Some of the major peculiarities of that rite would appear in the parts which are now missing: the six-week Advent with the Annunciation ("De Incarnatione") Sunday, the beginning of Lent without an Ash Wednesday, the Milanese nomenclature for the Lenten Sundays; in the sanctoral, the *Christophoria* feast before Epiphany, etc. It is quite possible that the parts now missing had been removed precisely to do away with the Ambrosian (or otherwise irregular) character of the book: the Roman and non-Roman rites were at times in competition, and liturgical books found to be at variance with the practice canonically required in a particular area at a particular time were apt to be considered forbidden.

NOTES

1. Express references to Saturday and Sunday after the octave of Epiphany are on f. 21r.
2. "Dn̄ica p[ri]ma p[os]t pent[ecosten]" (24v) agrees with the Roman books; the Sundays presumably numbered as 2nd through 5th are lost, as is everything after the Sunday numbered "xviiij".
3. His day is Dec. 5. — N.B. The calendar dates used in this paragraph to indicate the extent of the lacunae do not appear in the manuscript.
4. Another oddity: on f. 36r, with cue for the hymn *Ave maris stella,* rubric: *quere in officio iste dominice.* Which Sunday is meant? (A Sunday "De Incarnatione" celebrating the Annunciation was included in the six-week Advent of the Ambrosian or Milanese rite prevalent in parts of northern Italy.)
5. The martyr by that name who is patron of Ravenna and whose name is (or was) in the Canon of Ambrosian-rite Mass (cf. *EEFL* 2127) is celebrated on April 28. There are, however, a number of saints sharing the name, and confusions were not unusual.
6. Per chevron Azure and Argent a Chevron Gules issuant from which a Mountain of three Coupeaux Vert, in base a Mullet of the third. — Not successfully identified but could be incorrectly drawn insignia of the Albani family. (Formula and suggestion provided by T. E. Wilgus, Library of Congress.) — Basic shape of the shield is Renaissance-style Italian.
7. The emblem of St. Catherine. — The roundels could be later additions.
8. Cf. statement in Faye and Bond, p. 123, no. 150: "possibly 18th or 19th cent."
9. The book is in a recently made box covered with natural and grayish red purple linen.

MS 21

(Faye and Bond 45)

FRANCISCAN BREVIARY, summer part ca. 1400

Written in Germany? Parchment. 323 leaves, 174 × ca. 130 mm (bound volume: 180 × ca. 147 mm) 2 columns. 24 lines (in the calendar, 32)

ff. 1r–6v: Calendar: 197 days have entries, 33 of them in red. Notable among the latter: *Agathe* (Feb. 5), *Dorothee* (Feb. 6), *Antonij* (A. of Padua, June 13), *Visitacio b. m.* (July 2), *Anne* (July 26), *Clare* (Aug. 12), *Ludeuici* (the Franciscan bishop of Toulouse, canonized 1317; Aug. 19), *Translacio s. Clare* (Oct. 2), *Co[n]cepcio b. vi. marie* (Dec. 8). — Among the days written in black (some surprisingly so): Translacio scī Francisci (in second place, with "Vrbani," May 25); festum niuis (Aug. 5); Ludevici regis Anglorum [!] (Aug. 25); Nativitas [added in red:] *sce m[arie] v'* (Sept. 7); Exaltacio s. crucis (Sept. 14); Translacio s. Ludewici epī (Nov. 7); Elisabeth vidue (Nov. 19)

A Franciscan calendar, with the black writing probably reflecting a model not updated; the red entries and the numerous rubrics added to black entries and specifying the rank of the celebration ("semi[duplex]," "min[us]," "mai[us]") correspond to the state of the office in the Franciscan order in ca. 1400.[1]

7r (All on this page believed to be LATER ADDITION): *yncipit pars scd'a in sabbato scō* . . . ( )[3]esp[er]e autē sabb'i . . . i[n] unit[ate] ei[us]. med *[sic]* (a line in more *formata* script:) *Meinsiacathobersisch* . . . (in capitals:) *FRICZ* (2nd column:) A A B C D . . . (3 incomplete alphabets of gothic capitals, lombards, and/or formal gothic minuscule; in this last style also:) (V)[3]Espe[re] aut[em] sabbati . . . all'a. (In same formal script but red:) *Eya gruss got katrusca teusca. fr̄ frideric[us] wecklein. d. d.* [= dono dedit] (7v blank, unruled)

Penmanship practice (in part perhaps model letters for a beginner's instruction?) added by a late (possibly 16th-century) hand. The fragmentary liturgical texts duplicate (or triplicate) the material originally written on f. 8r and still found there. The Slavic-sounding name Katruska may suggest a region with a Slavic (Wendic?) minority. The name at end may be genuine, i.e., that of a former owner.

8r–107ra: *Incipit pars scd'a jn sabbato scō* . . . (V)[3]esp[er]e autē sabbati . . . (Pentecost, 40rb sqq.; Trinity, 46rb sqq.; Corpus Christi with octave, 49va–61rb) . . . (section ends on f. 107r with the reading Nahum I,1–4, followed by rubric:) *Notādū qd' de festis q[ue] ueniūt . . . q[ue] celebrāt[ur] īt[er] pascha [et] pent[ecosten].*[2] (107rb blank)

The temporal, or "proper of the seasons" from Easter to the end of the liturgical year.[3] Rubrics and texts (here of course written out in full) generally as in the *Ordo Breviarii* compiled by the Franciscan general Haymo in ca. 1244[4] but with Trinity[5] and Corpus Christi (both of later date) incorporated. — Trinity has as the 1st antiphon to 1st Vespers *Gloria tibi Trinitas*; readings: I Credimus sanctam II Pater est plenus III Et idem Dominus IV In Patre manet V Teneamus ergo VI Quot nobis maxime VII (Ev.: *Si diligitis)* Spiritum sanctum VIII Ipse enim est de quo . . . — The office of Corpus Christi (introduced in the Franciscan order in 1319), beginning with the antiphon *Sacerdos in eternum,* has own readings for each day of its octave. — The series of Sundays after Pentecost begins on f. 61rb; at least some amount of confusion (caused, it would seem, by uncertainty whether the office of 1st Sunday after Pentecost was displaced or replaced by Trinity) is obvious from the captions: on 69ra, "*Dn̄ica secūda post oct[av]am pētecost'* " (with texts of Haymo's *2a post Pentecosten*); 69vb, "*dn̄ica ij*" has been corrected (in black ink) to read "iii"; from there on, the numbering has been corrected rather thoroughly (if not very neatly); what seems to be a cumulation of errors occurred nevertheless on ff. 76v–77r: after numbering corrections, notes made in the margins, a paragraph erased and rewritten on 76vb, and an addition written on 319v–320r, the texts for the 15th Sunday after Pentecost (Ev. *Ibat Iesus in civitatem*, hom. *De iuvene illo resuscitato*) remain wanting; added "*domīca xvi*" on ff. 319v–320r duplicates texts from 76v–77r.

107v–263v: *Incipiūt festiuitates s[an]c[t]o[rum] in tēpore estiuiali* [sic] . . . (section originally ended with 263va, 14th line:) honor [et] gl'a scla scl'o[rum] ame[n] (ADDED IN OTHER HANDS: (*a*) rubric:) *van fil* [!] *ap[osto]lo[rum] Jnvit.* (text:) Gaudete [et] exultate . . . [6] ((*b*) rubric:) *de sctō ludowico ā p'mo vesp* (text:) (T)[2]ecū fuit p[rin]cipiu[m] . . . (ends in 263vb, 19th line:) sol mūdo misit[7] (last 5 lines empty)

The sanctoral ("proper of the saints"): from *Tyburtii et Valeriani* (in the calendar, Apr. 14) through Katherina (written with a *K*; in the calendar, Nov. 25). — "*Bonifacij*," on ff. 120v–121r, is about the early martyr (in the calendar, May 13); the eponymous apostle of Germany (in the calendar, with June 5) is not mentioned at all.[8] — St. Anthony of Padua has an octave with altogether 27 readings, ff. 130r–138r.[9] — The Visitation, 155v sqq. (first antiphon *Candida plebs*), with 1st reading "Beatissimus in Xpo . . . Urbanus papa sextus . . . ," speaks about Urban as already dead (*l.* II, ". . . felicis recordacionis . . ."); Urban VI died 1389 and his office of the Visitation was incorporated into the Franciscan breviary in 1390.[10] — Nativity of the Virgin (213 sqq.) has an octave. — On 221v, a 15th(?)-century note, "Hic deficit stigmata scī frācisci"; that office, of much earlier date (1337), is added at end (ff. 320 sqq.). — The primary office of St. Francis, 230r–241r (including the octave), is the rhymed one by Julianus a Spira, with readings from Bonaventura's *Legenda maior*, beginning "Vir erat in ciuitate assisij . . ." (the prologue "Apparuit gratia . . ." is not included). — Louis d'Anjou, the Franciscan bishop of Toulouse given two days in the calendar, is absent from the sanctoral sequence as originally written; his office (Tecum fuit principium . . .), very incomplete, is added at the end of the section (263v). — The scribe or scribes seem to have been alert to very recent additions without realizing that the exemplar from which they were copying was quite out of date, lacking, besides Louis, also St. Martha (introduced 1319), the *Stigmata Francisci* (see above), and St. Yves (1350).

(f. [264] is a laid-in blank, ruled leaf of different provenience, different from the original leaves of the manuscript in size (171 mm), disposition of prick marks (central column is over 10 mm), and ruling (ruled for 25 lines prior to erasures))

265r–286v: *de ap[ostoli]s cap[itulum]* (F)[3]R[atr]es iam nō estis . . . (ends in the last line of 286vb:) . . . *y[mnus]* Angu[laris] *bn̄* Zachee.

MS 21 The "commons" (sets of texts used when an individualized office is not provided for an occasion): for apostles (265r–267r), evangelists (267r–268v), *In natali unius martyris* (268v sqq.), *plurimorum martyrum* (271r sqq.), etc., through the office commemorating the dedication of a church, 284v–286v. Choices of texts (here written out in full) generally as in Haymo's *Ordo breviarii* (*SMRL* II, p. 173–185).

287r–308r: ***In d[omi]n[i]cis dieb[us] a d[omi]n[ic]a t[erci]a post pe[n]tecostes usq[ue] ad kal[endas] octobris . ymn[us]*** **(N)^{2}Octe surge[n]tes . . .**

The Psalter; or, rather, only ca. 50 selected Psalms arranged, not very clearly (rubrics for the most part absent, except for repeated "*ps.*"[11]), for liturgical use, with added (some) antiphons, versicles, hymns, and canticles. Major items as follows:[12]

Nocte surgentes (*AH* LI, no. 24) Pss. I–XXI (ending on f. 294v), XCIX, C, LXIII, *Benedicite omnia opera* (Dan. III, 57–88 + 56), Pss. CXLVIII-CL (as one "*ps.*"; ending on 296vb) (chapter:) *Benedictio et claritas* (hymn:) *Eterne rerum conditor* (canticle:) *Benedictus* (= Song of Zechariah, Luke I,68–79) (hymn, 297ra:) *Ecce iam noctis* (*AH* LI, no. 31) (297r–308ra:) Pss. XXX, IV, V, XXIV, XXXIII, XXXIV, XLII, XLIII, XLV-XLVIII, LXI, LXIV, LXXXI, LXXXIV, LXXXVI, LXXXVII, XCVI-XCIX, XXIII, XXXII, LXVIII, CIII, CIV. — Notably absent is the Psalm CXIX, usually divided into segments assigned to the "minor hours" (Prime, Terce, Sext, None) of the office.

308r–318r: (rubric in last lines of 308ra:) ***de pasche [sic] de s[an]ct[i]s ymnus*** **(308rb:) (A)^{2}d cena[m] agni p[ro]uidi et stolis albis candidi, . . . (hymn collection ends in first line of f. 318rb:) (tra[n]s)lati i[n] req[ui]em. Gl[ori]a [et] honor**

Assembled hymns, for the most part introduced by rubrics indicating their use:[13]

(as quoted above)	Ad cenam Agni	*AH* II,44
	Rex eterne Domine	II,45
	Aurora lucis rutilat	II,46 (1–4)
(De apostolis)	Tristes erant apostoli	II,46 (5–11)

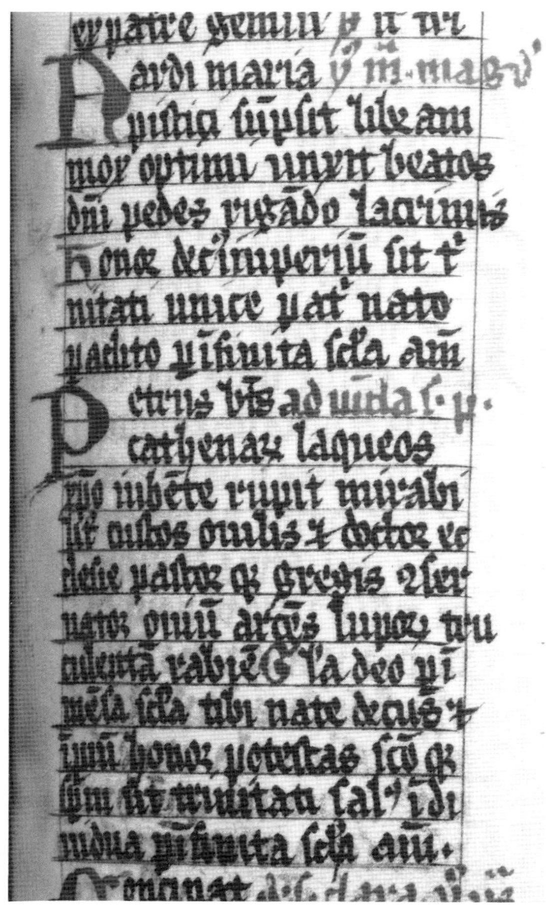

MS 21, f. 312ra (actual size of area shown: ca. 90 × 52 mm)

(De Ascensione)	Jesu nostra redemptio	II,49
	Aeterne rex altissime	II,47
(De Spiritu sancto)	Veni creator Spiritus	II,132
	Iam Christus astra ascenderat	II,50/LI,92
	Beata nobis gaudia	II,51
(De Trinitate)	Tu Trinitatis unitas	II,12
	Summae Deus clementiae	II,15
(De s. Antonio)	En gratulemur hodie[14]	IV,155
	Laus regi plena gaudio	IV,156
	Jesu lux vera mentium	IV,157
(De s. Joanne)	Ut queant laxis	II,52 (1–4)
	Antra deserti	II,52 (5–8)
	O nimis felix	II,53
(Petri et Pauli)	Aurea luce et decore roseo	II,58 (1–2,6)
(Comm. s. Pauli)	Iam bone pastor Petre	II,58 (3,6)
	Doctor egregie Paule[15]	II,58 (4,6)
(Marie Magdalene)	Nardi Maria pistici	?

(Ad vincula Petri)	Petrus beatus catenarum laqueos	?
(s. Clara)	Concinat plebs fidelium	LII,159 (1–6)
	Spretis nativo genere	LII,159 (7–9), 160 (1,7)
	Clarum lumen effunditur	LII,160 (2–7)

(312vb, de dn̄a nr̄a sc̄a maria: [initia only:] Ave maris stella, Quem terra pontus sidera, O gloriosa domina)

(De s. Francisco)	Proles de coelo prodiit	LII,195
	In coelesti collegio	LII,196
	Plaude turba paupercula	LII,197
	Decus morum dux minorum	LII,198
(De angelis)	Tibi Christe splendor Patris	L,156
	Christe sanctorum decus angelorum	L,146
(De omnibus sanctis)	Christe redemptor omnium[16]	II,81
	Jesu salvator saeculi	II,80 (3–8)
(De apostolis)	Exsultet coelum laudibus	II,94
	Aeterna Christi munera	II,95 (1–2,6–8)
(De sanctis)	Sanctorum meritis	L,153
	Aeterna Christi munera	L,17 (1,3–5)
	Rex gloriose martyrum	LI,112
	Deus tuorum militum	II,99
	Martyr Dei qui unicum	II,98
(De confessoribus)	Iste confessor	II,101
	Jesu redemptor omnium perpes	II,100
	Jesu corona celsior	LI,116 (1-6,8)
(De virginibus)	Jesu corona virginum	II,104
	Virginis proles	II,103
(Corpus Christi)	Sacris sollemniis	L,387
	Verbum supernum prodiens	L, 388
	Pange lingua gloriosi corporis	L, 386
(In dedicatione ecclesiae)	Urbs beata Ierusalem	LI,102 (1–4,9)
	Angulare fundamentum	LI,102 (5–9)

318–320r: (begins in 2nd line of 318rb:[17]) *ps̄. dauit* (C)²ofitebimur t' d's . . . (= Ps. LXXV) (318v:) . . . *ps̄. dauit* (D(²[omi]ne d's salutis mee . . . (= Ps. LXXXVIII) (319r:) . . . *y[mnus] ī ieme* (P)²[r]imo die[rum] o[mn]i[u]m quo mu[n]dus . . . (= *AH* LI,23) (319va:) . . . *domi[ni]ca xvj oracio de domīca* (T)²ua nos . . . (texts as per Haymo's *Ordo breviarii, SMRL* II, p. 108, ending with end of the 9th reading of Matins, 320rb, line 11:) . . . egritudo cordis.[18] (last 9 lines of 320rb blank)

320v–323v: (written by another, apparently unskilled scribe, using a script not basically different but poorly executed, and rather weak ink:) *D[iui?] F[rancisci] sticmata leccia* [sic] *prima* (M)²os erat ewangelii [?] a[n]gelico uiro frācisco . . . (9th lesson ends in 9th line of 323va:) (digito) dei uiuo

The readings are from Bonaventura's *Vita maior* XIII (cf. printed text in *ANALECTA FRANCISCANA X*), in a corrupt form. — Original absence from the book of this office (*Stigmata s. Francisci*, Sept. 17) which had been in Franciscan breviary since 1337 is noted in the margin of f. 221v; it is a later addition also in the calendar (f. 5r). — N.B. Rubrication ceases after 321r; spaces for 2-line initials on 321v–323v are unfilled.

323v: (beginning in 10th line of 323va; accompanied by caption in head margin; an ADDITION, IN 15TH-CENTURY CURSIVE:) (caption:) Visitacōnis marie cap[itu]l[um] (text:) Ecce ista venit saliens in mo[n]tibus . . . cancellos. (323vb:) Surge p[ro]pera amica mea . . . putacionis ad venit. Surge p[ro]pera amica mea . . . facies tua decora (ends in last line).[19]

* * *

Foliated chiefly in tens (1–8, 11, 21, 31, . . . 321, 323) in modern pencil. The count includes a blank, differently ruled vellum leaf laid in as f. [264];[20] not the paper endleaves (one free one in front, one at end; no watermarks). — Written area ca. 113 × ca. 90 mm. — Ruled in brownish black ink of varying strength, mostly fully, but some leaves (e.g., 33v–38) have the horizontals done in blind, and some appear to have been only frame-ruled (e.g., ff. 15–31). Pricking marks preserved on most leaves except in the calendar.[21] — Written by several non-professional scribes,[22] in a utilitarian book-hand reminiscent of early gothic; predominant is a script characterized by conspicuous lateral compression. — Ink varies: black, brownish gray, of varying intensity; very durable throughout. — Parchment of good quality, thickness ca. 17.8 mm per 100 leaves. — Rubrics red.[23]

Collation: [ ]^{6}(= ff. 1–6) i–xx^{8} xxi–xxiii^{10} (= ff. 167–196) xxiiii–xxv^{8} xxvi–xxviii^{10} (= ff. 213–242) xxviiii–xxx^{8} xxxi^{10} (laid-in f. [264], blank, follows xxxi$_{5}$) xxxii^{10} xxxiii$^{8-1}$ (= ff. 280–286; not clear which leaf lacks conjugate; no loss of text evident) [xxxiv]$^{8+2?}$ (= ff. 287–296; ff. 293–294 a bifolium inserted after [xxxiv]$_{6}$?) [xxxv]^{10} [xxxvi]^{8} [xxxvii]^{10} (= ff. 315–323; [xxxvii]$_{10}$ following f. 323

MS 21

wanting, probably blank). — Partially cropped signature numbering on center in lower margins of last versos of most gatherings, beginning with "i" on f. 14v and ending with "xxxiii" on 286v.

Decoration: limited to *litterae notabiliores*, alternatingly blue and red, most often 2 lines high (occasionally 3 or 1, without much consistency in the choice of size). Modest flourishing in red ink appears with the blue letters on ff. 8–39r.

Binding: dark brown calf leather over partly beveled wooden boards; executed in the (probably) second half of the 15th century in the Benedictine abbey of St. Stephen in Würzburg. The covers are blind-tooled with rosettes, fleur-de-lys in diamond, and scroll identifying the monastery bindery (Kyriss, plate 83,3; also rosettes, no. 2 or 4, *ibid.*; fleur-de-lys, no. 8, *ibid.*). Sewn over 5 bands. Remnants of two back-to-front clasps (apparently brass and leather), with two metal pins on the upper cover. — Rebacked, probably in 20th century. On spine in the 2nd panel, a dark brown leather label with gold-tooled: B(R)EVIARUM [sic] //ROMANUM.[24]

On pastedown of upper cover, ownership label of ca. 1700: Ad usum//JOSEPHI M. ZARINI//Civis Pratensis//Philos. ac Medicine//Doctoris.[25] Less well identified former owners are the "fr. Fridericus Wecklein," perhaps in early 16th century, and the beneficiary of his gift, a German lady referred to as Katrusca (cf. contents, to 7r). — Acquired by the Library of Congress in 1929 from Gonnelli, Florence (Ms. ac. 4189, 15).[26]

2° fo.: [blue:] (*KL*)³ [red:] *marci[us] h[abe]t dies xxxi d'luma* [sic] *xxx.*

Bibl.: De Ricci, *Census* (1935), p. 217, no. 70; Faye and Bond (1962), p. 118, no. 45.

NOTES

1. Cf. Leroquais, *Brév.* I, p. cviii; S. J. P. Van Dijk, *The origins of the modern Roman liturgy* (1960), p. 376. See also notes to the sanctoral (ff. 107v–263v). — N.B. The feast of St. Joseph (1399) is absent.

2. The rubric (written in black ink but marked by red underscoring) is that given in *SMRL* II (1963) (p. 132, 2nd item) as part of the sanctoral.

3. The "liturgical year" begins with the first Sunday of Advent and ends with the Saturday which precedes it.

4. Cf. *SMRL* II, p. 87–114.

5. The feast of the Trinity (eventually attached to the Sunday immediately following Pentecost) went through reverses among the Franciscans: cf. Leroquais, *Brév.* I, p. (lxxix,) cviii; also Van Dijk, *op. cit.*, p. 375, n. 2. — Our office is not that referred to as *In maiestatis solio* (Leroquais *loc. cit.*).

6. Cf. *SMRL* II, p. 173, line 5.

7. = 1st Vespers of the rhymed office of St. Louis of Toulouse (*AH* XXVI, no. 94, the first 5 antiphons; to Magnificat: Wisdom VIII,11; hymn: *AH* IV, no. 344, discontinued after first two verses). — The saint was a Franciscan.

8. One Low-German linguistic area ("van fil" for "von viel[en]") without an emphasized cult of Winfrid Boniface was Schleswig (cf. Grotefend, *Zeitrechnung*).

9. According to Leroquais' time clock (*Brév.* I, p. cviii) the octave would require dating the breviary after 1403; earlier Franciscan breviaries have, however, been reported which do include it: cf. C. Cenci, *Manoscritti francescani della Bib. nazionale di Napoli* (1971), codd. 180,h; 193,h.

10. Cf. Van Dijk, *Origins,* p. 376.

11. The sequence and intent correspond to Haymo's *Ordo breviarii* through f. 297r (= through the Song of Zechariah; as in *SMRL* II, p. 49–50, Matins and Lauds of Sunday of the "psalmista" section; cf. also *ibid.*, p. 105, first paragraph). I haven't found in the *Ordo* an equivalent of the selection of psalms on ff. 297ra–308ra.

12. The book gives no Psalm numbering; our numbers are those of the Hebrew Bible, now commonly preferred. Latin orthography of the several initia has been regularized.

13. Latin spelling in our listing is regularized. — Arabic numerals in my *AH* references represent the hymn numbers, not pages. — Attempt has been made to quote the version in the *Analecta* closest to the text found in the manuscript but further minor variants abound, as do obvious errors. Only a few peculiar readings have been brought out.

14. With "patrum celantes gloriam" (for correct "zelantes").

15. With "geminus" for correct "gerimus."

16. With "Mentem auferte perfidam" for "Gentem," in the 6th stanza.

17. The writing from 318rb, 2nd line through 318va, line 12 may be by a different scribe using the

same hand; or else, by the original scribe but working after an interruption and with a new quill. A rather clearly different copyist (still of the same time period) took over beginning with the 13th line of 318va; his writing deteriorates fast, through 320rb.

18. The texts for the 16th Sunday (after Pentecost) duplicate those found on ff. 76v–77r (cf. contents of 8r–107ra).

19. Apparently the same writer (same form of *g*, etc.) has added a puzzling entry or note on f. 6r, in the calendar, on the line separating Nov. 15 and 16: "oct[a]ba agathe." St. Agatha is celebrated (and entered in the calendar of this book, in red) on Feb. 5.

20. The leaf is now loose but seems to have been formerly attached by its corners.

21. Pricking done with gatherings already folded (sometimes from the first page, sometimes from the last). The rows of prick marks along the fore edge tend to be unusually far from the edge (as much as 12 mm) and not straight. — The verticals are dividing the space at approximately 41 + 9 + 39 mm (measured on recto).

22. It is not at all clear that the "frater Fridericus Wecklein" named on f. 7r was actually one of them (cf. contents).

23. Some of the rubrics are written in a particularly unskilled manner.

24. As of this writing (1984) the book is kept in a recently made box covered in natural and brown linen, with label "BREVIARIUM MINORUM (CA 1400)."

25. Cf. J. Gelli, *3500 ex libris italiani* (1908), p. 434. In LC MS 21 the inscription and the baroque cartouche which contains it are printed in red; size of the label is 70 × 68 mm. — The phrase "ad usum" suggests membership in the (Third) Order.

26. A slip mounted on recto of the free endpaper in front identifies the book as "Breviarium Romanum, pars secunda," with a short description in Italian which dates the book to 1390–1400 and places its origin in Germany. — Penciled numbers, etc.: "LC Ms. 45"; "g" (or "9"?) in a circle; "397998//30"; (at end:) "Br. 1344/88117."

Deus qui inui
sibiliter omnia
contines et tamen
pro salute generis hu
mani signa potencie
tue visibiliter osten
dis templum hoc
potencie tue inhabita
cione illustra: ut
omnes qui deprecaturi
huc veniunt ex quacum
que tribulacione ad
te clamauerint conso
lacionis tue benefi
cia consequantur:
Per dominum. ad complet.
ymnus. Hoc in templo
summe. ad magnificat. an.
Pax eterna ab eter
no patre huic domui
pax perhennis verbum
patris sit pax huic
domui pacem pius
consolator huic pres
tet domui. Se
quens an dicitur
infra octauas. an.
Domum tuam domine
alla decet sanctitudo
alla alla. v. Inter
ccs Non est hic ali
ud nisi domus dei.
Colleta. Deus qui sa
cratorum. quere ad .vi.
Inuit. Filie syon con
currite assumite cum
celebratione mentis vestre
sollempnia: Iubile
mus igitur deo nostro
vnanimiter qui sibi
eam gratuita ele
git clemencia. Ps.
Venite exul. Inuit.
Adoremus dominum in
aula sancta eius alla.
Et dicitur infra oct.
In p. n. a. Tollite
portas principes
vestras et eleuamini
porte eternales. Ps.
Do'e terra. a. Erexit
iacob dominus in dui
et lapis iste vocabitur
domus dei. Ps. Deus
in te sp. an. Edifica
uit moyses altare
domino deo. Ps. Magnus
dominus. v. Domus mea
Lc. leccio prima
Quociensumque
fratres karissimi
altaris vel templi

MS 22, f. 90r (actual size of written area: ca. 104 × 68 mm)

MS 22

(Faye and Bond 73)

BREVIARY (use of Bruges?), summer part XVth c.

Written in Bruges? Parchment. 405 leaves, ca. 150 × ca. 102 mm (bound volume: 157 × ca. 110 mm) 2 columns. 31–32 lines (calendar, 1 column, 33 lines)

(ff. 1r–3v ruled, blank except for modern penciled numbers, etc.[1])

4r–87r: (at head of f. 4r, a late, perhaps 17th-century inscription in ink: Collegij Societatis Jesu Brugis; at tail: M B) *De sc̄a trinitate. In p[ri]mis v[e]sp[eris] ant[iphona]* (G)[8]loria tibi trinitas . . .

Summer part of the *temporale* or "proper of the season" of breviary offices: from Trinity through 26th Sunday after Pentecost. — First reading of Trinity Matins begins: Legimus sanctum Moysen . . . — "*In solempnitate sa[ncti]ssimi sacrame[n]ti*" (= Corpus Christi) begins (8v) with the antiphon *Sacerdos in (a)eternum.*

87r–88v: *Nota. Ab octa[va] penthecostes vsq[ue] ad kalendas augusti leguntur libri regum* . . .

(Part of the) general rubrics (written in black but underscored in red). Their wording, at least, is quite different from that of the Roman Curia breviary (cf. *SMRL* II, p. 114 sqq.).

88v–97v: *In dedicatione ecc[lesi]e sup[eri]o[ri]s. i[n] p[rim]is v[e]sp[eris] ant[iphona]* (89r:) (S)[5]Anctificau[i]t dn̄s tabernaculu[m] suum . . . (90r, ant. of 2nd Vespers:) Pax eterna ab eterno p[a]r[c]e huic domui . . . (office ends on 97v:) . . . qui viderunt vel gustauerunt Tu aute[m] dne

Office for the anniversary of dedication of the cathedral church (of Bruges?). Some parts are rhymed.

(98r–99v blank, ruled)

100r–105v: Calendar with 195 entries, 54 of them in red; among these: *Amandi et Vedasti* (Feb. 6), *Georgii* (Apr. 23); *Basilii* (June 14, with octave on June 21); *Eligii* (June 25 and Dec. 1); *Egidii* (Sept. 1); *Remigii, Germani, Bavonis* (Oct. 1); *Dyonisii* (Oct. 9), *Donatiani* (Oct. 14), *Nichasii* (Dec. 14). — Among the entries written in black: *Translatio* of St. Donatus (Jan. 6, alongside the Epiphany which of course is red), *Dormitatio s. Paule* (Jan. 26), Crysolii (Feb. 7), Gudwali (June 6), Wulfrañi (Oct. 15), *Transl[atio] s. Amandi* (Oct. 26), Winnoci (Nov. 5), Livini (Nov. 12), Clementis (Nov. 23), Judoci (Dec., 13, alongside St. Lucy).

The calendar of Bruges.[2] Wanting (i.e., not included) is the *Festum reliquiarum* on July 18.

MS 22

107r–203r: *Inuitatoriu[m]* **Venite exultemus . . . (107ra, assembled ferial invitatories; 107rb:) (B)[4]Eatus vir qui no[n] abijt . . . (psalms of Matins, Sunday through Saturday = Pss. I-CIX, omitting XLIII, XLVI, LXVII and giving cues only for XC, XCII, XCIII; 165v–166r:)** ***Benedictiones*** **(166rv:)** ***laus angelorum*** **Te Deum laudamus . . . (ff. 167–176, psalms and canticles of Lauds; 177r–189v, the minor hours; 189v–202r, Vespers; 202r–203r, the canticles** ***Benedictus, Magnificat, Nunc dimittis)***

The ("Gallican" version) Psalter, arranged for liturgical purposes, with antiphons, hymns, and canticles (which the rubrics call "*ps[almus]*") incorporated. Rubrics seem occasionally faulty. The whole may reflect the liturgical use of Tournai (the diocese to which Bruges ecclesiastically belonged) or of Rheims (the ecclesiastical province). Some of the antiphons (the series "Pro fidei meritis . . ." as in *AH* XVII, p. [19][3]) are non-Roman (and have eventually disappeared from liturgical use).

203v–207v: ***P*****Arce dñe parce p[o]p[u]lo tuo . . .**

Litany of Saints, with non-standard (at least non-Roman) introductory words. It names, after the usual calls to Mary, John the Baptist, patriarchs, apostles, etc., 41 individual martyrs: among them Clement, Dennis, Gereon, Cornelius, Marcellin, Nicasius, Quintin, Piatus (patron of Tournai), Lambert; 37 confessors, among them Remigius, Paulinus, Germanus, Donatian, Amand, Eligius, Medard, Gildard, Audoenus, Audomar, Gaugericus, Bavo, Wandregisillus, Ansbert, Winnocus, Mauron, Trudo; and 42 women, including Geneviève, Juliana, Julitta, Christiana, Brigida (of Ireland?), Regina, Radegundis, Rictrudis, Walburgis, and the sisters Fides, Spes, and Karitas (so spelled).

207v–212r: ***Sequu[n]tur Vigilie mortuo[rum]. a'.*** **(P)[4]lacebo . . .**

The Office for the Dead, non-Roman. Non-Roman Invitatory: Circumdederunt me . . . Non-Roman readings and responsories:

	Lectio	Responsorium
I	Ne des alienis	Rogamus te
II	Melius est nomen	Domine qui creasti
III	Memento creatoris tui	Absolve Domine
IV	Vivent mortui tui	Ne tradas
V	Hec dicit Dominus de manu mortis	Ego sum resurrectio
VI	Multi qui dormiunt	Tuam Deus piissime
VII	Sicut in Adam	Qui Lazarum
VIII	Ecce mysterium	Requiem eternam
IX	In diebus illis audivi	Libera me Domine de morte

However, on ff. 210r–212r, following the Lauds (last part of the office), the manuscript gives also the Roman set of readings and responsories (readings *Parce, Taedet, Manus,* . . . through IX, *Quare de vulva;* responsories *Credo quod, Qui Lazarum, Domine quando, Heu mihi, Ne recorderis, Peccantem me, Ne abscondas, Memento, Libera me Domine de viis inferni).*[4]

212r–213v: ***Sequu[n]t[ur] co[m]me[n]dationes.*** **(S)[2]Ubuenite . . . Requiescant in pace Amen.**

Liturgical prayers used immediately after a person's death.

213v–215v: ***Seque[n]tes p[re]ces dicu[n]t[ur] i[n] xl'*** **[= in Quadragesima] . . .** ***ad mat. (E)***[3]**Go dixi . . . (214v:) Pro seniore n[ost]ro . . . pro co[n]gregac[i]o[n]e n[ost]ra . . . (215v, 1st column:)** ***lectio sexta*** **[i.e., quinta?] Homo natus . . . (215v, 2nd column blank)**

(ff. 216, 217, 218 blank, ruled)

219r–250r: ***Incipit co[mmun]e s[an]c[t]oru[m]*** **. . . (ends 250r:) . . . hu[m]ilibus salte[m] freque[n]temus obseq[ui]is. Per.**

The "commons," or offices to be used in absence of special ("proper") texts for a particular saint's day: one or more of each type (sometimes merely alternate sets of readings); suitable to celebrate apostles, martyrs, confessors, virgins, non-virgins.[5] Lacking is one for the dedication of a church (cf. 88v–97v; this may mean that the book was for the use of a cleric attached to the cathedral); there is also no common for the several feasts of Mary. The section includes blank spaces: most of second column on 223r and the whole first column of 223v.

251r–402v: ***Vrbani p[a]pe et m[arty]ris Coll[e]c[t]a*** **(D)[3]A q[uesum]us . . .**

The sanctoral ("proper of the saints"), from Urbanus (celebrated on May 27; the text gives no dates) through Maximus (Nov. 27), thus covering the "summer" half of the year. Contents do not entirely match those of the calendar on ff. 100–105: the Visitation,[6] a red-letter day in the calendar (July 2), is absent entirely. Other festivities, not mentioned in the calendar, are included: most notably the Transfiguration (301 sqq.);[7] also *Paulini* (265r), *Margarete* (290v), *Narcisci* (364r), *et al.* — In some cases (besides the placement of Transfiguration after Anne, also absence of *Translatio Donatiani* and of *Praesentatio* of the Virgin) the sanctoral approaches that of Cambrai more than that of Bruges;[8] elsewhere, it is the opposite: *Gudwali, Basilii* (258v–262v; cf. calendar), *Decem millium martyrum, Bernardi, Ludovici, Benedictae virg., Leonardi, Livini, Machuti, Maximi* are included; *Translatio Eligii* (270r–274v) has nine readings (it was six in Cambrai). — Absent from both the Bruges and the Cambrai calendars but represented in our sanctoral are the [Translatio] *Francisci* at end of May, *Clare* (316v–317r), *Anthonini martyris* (332v), *Fauste virg.* (344r), *Narcisci* (364r), *Germani ep. Capuani* (364v): these saints occur in the calendars of Utrecht (St. Fausta), Troyes (Narciscus), Senlis (Germanus). The attention given St. Clare and the additional festivity of St. Francis in May would be a mark of Franciscan influence; but neither the book as a whole nor the sanctoral in particular can be said to be Franciscan.

(ff. 403v–405v blank, ruled)

* * *

Foliated in modern pencil; free endleaves seem to be part of the original composition of the book and are included in the count (cf. contents and collation). — Written area ca. 104 × ca. 68 mm. Fully ruled in faint red ink; pricking marks preserved in several gatherings. — Written in *lettre bâtarde,* in slightly brownish black ink; main text appears to have been all done by one hand. The rubrics are red. — Parchment white, occasionally crinkled; thickness ca. 14.3 mm per 100 leaves.

Collation: 1^{4-1}(1_1 used as pastedown? 1_2 = f. 1) 2–6^8 7^{8-1}(7_5, following f. 47, absent; apparently no loss of text) 8–51^8 52^{4-1} (52_4 used as pastedown). — Of catchwords, probably lost by cropping, only that on 17_8 (= f. 130v) and upper part of one on 25_8 (= f. 194v) preserved. Some, apparently early signatures (in ink) are partly preserved in gathering 24 ("y") and 25 ("z").[9]

Decoration is limited to alternately blue or red initial letters; their size is 8 to 10 lines for the largest ones (not used with much logical consistency), mostly 3 lines for the intermediate type, 1 line for versals. Their shapes are simple and free of flourishes.

Bound in contemporary dark brown calf over rounded wooden boards. Sewn over 5 bands. — The covers are blind-stamped in the pre-1500 (images raised) manner. The stamping consists, on each cover, of a rectangle divided by a central horizontal ribbon of quatrefoils in two halves, each surrounded by a motto: "non nobis domine non nobis sed nomini tuo da gloriam" and "ab occultis meis munda me domine et ab alienis parce seruo tuo"; inside each, vinestems form eight medallions containing birds, hares, a scorpion (?), and a squirrel.[10] — Traces of five metal bosses on each cover; traces of two back-to-front clasps.

On pastedown of upper cover, ownership label of Rev. Edwin A. Dalrymple, D.D. (of Baltimore). On 1v, modern inscriptions: "No. 15012" (= number in the Van de Velde sale, cf. bibl.); "Ac. 4560 (3) no. 4" (= LC accession number); "DeR 101"; "MS. 73."

Former owners: (17th? century:) Jesuit college in Bruges; (early 19th century:) Jean-François van de Velde;[11] (ca. 1900:) Rev. Edwin A. Dalrymple. — Bought by LC in 1916 (Ms. Ac. 4560, 3, 4).

MS 22 2° fo.: (blank) (recto of second text leaf, i.e., of f. 5r, begins: est filius : deus vnus)

Bibl.: *Catalogue des livres rares et précieux. . . de la bibliothèque du feu monsieur Jean François Vande Velde* / par P. F. de Goesin-Verhaeghe (Gand, 1831–32), v. 2, p. 674, no. 15012. — De Ricci, *Census* (1935), p. 229, no. 101; Faye and Bond (1962), p. 119, no. 73.

NOTES

1. See at end, following the information on binding.
2. Cf. *Analecta liturgica* (W. H. Weale, ed.; *Insulis et Brugis,* 1889), p. [296] sqq.
3. See note 12 to the breviary LC MS 15.
4. Cf. Leroquais, *LH* I, introd., with the sets of responsories for several regional "uses," not including, alas, either Tournai or Rheims (or Utrecht).
5. One may observe the sociocultural phenomenon that the term "confessor" was reserved to men. Also, a certain resistance seems to have existed against the idea of a married non-widow woman saint other than a martyr.
6. Introduced in the area in mid-15th century (cf. Strubbe, *Chronologie*).
7. *Transfiguratio Domini* (referring to the event reported in Matthew XVII) was celebrated on August 6 in most places but on July 27 in Cambrai and July 26 in Bruges (cf. Strubbe, *op. cit.,* and the calendar of Bruges in Weale, *Analecta liturgica*). In our sanctoral, it follows Anne and precedes Panthaleon, which would point to July 27.
8. Judging from the 1495 calendar printed in the *Analecta liturgica,* p. [273] sqq. The calendar of Bruges printed *ibid.,* p. [296] sqq., is from a 1520 source. — The sanctoral of LC MS 22 does not have the Bruges *Festum reliquiarum* (July 18).
9. If the 25th gathering is *z,* either the signing began on present f. 4 (= our signature "2") or else the sequence included either *j* or *v.*
10. None of these stamps found in Kyriss.
11. "En son vivant docteur et professeur en théologie, dernier president du Grand collège et bibliothécaire de l'Université de Louvain" (*Catalogue des livres* . . . 1831).

MS 23

(Faye and Bond 53)

CARTHUSIAN HOMILIARY, sanctoral part XVth c.?

Spain. Parchment. 209 (actually 193)[1] leaves, ca. 478[2] × ca. 347 mm (bound volume: ca. 496 × ca. 360 mm) 2 columns. 29 or, in some gatherings, 28 lines.

ff. 1ra–209va: *Incipit s[an]c[t]urale in no[m]i[n]e dn̄i. In n[ata]li sctī andree apl'i. Sermo btī augustini epī* . . . (209va:) . . . non predia que nulla possidebat: set officia que propria dispensatione exequenda curaret.

Sanctoral cycle of the Carthusian homiliary, an original selection of (primarily) patristic readings peculiar to the Carthusian order and forming part of its liturgical office on certain feasts: each of these occasions is given a set of 12 readings, the last four of which are a homily on that day's Gospel pericope (identified by its opening words). In the present manuscript, the occasions represented and the readings assigned to them are as follows:[3]

(Nov. 30) 1r–6r Andrew: (*lectio I–IV:*) Mirum quibusdam . . . = Augustine, *Sermo 70* (*PL* XXXVIII, 443–444) — (*V-VIII:*) Audivimus in evangelio . . . = Augustine, *Sermo 69* (*PL* XXXVIII, 440–442) — (*IX-XII:*) (Mt IV, 18–19 and:) Audistis fratres karissimi quia . . . = Gregory, *XL hom. in Ev.,* hom. V (*PL* LXXVI, 1093–1095)

(Dec. 6) 6r–10r Nicholas / Hugo of Grenoble / Hugo Lincolniensis / Martin:[4] (*l. I-VIII:*) Dominus noster Iesus Christus et venit ad homines . . . = Augustine, *Sermo 108* (*PL* XXXVIII, 632–636) — (*IX-XII:*) (Mt XXV, 14 and:) Lectio sancti evangelii fratres karissimi . . . = Gregory, *XL hom. in Ev.,* hom. IX, 1–4 (*PL* LXXVI, 1105–1108)[5]

(Dec. 8) 10rb, last 3 lines: . . . *In [sanctificatione* corrected to:*] Conceptione btē virginis marie lectiones sicut in natiuitate ipsius [f.] clij.*[6]

(Dec. 21) 10v–16r Thomas Ap.: (*l. I-IV:*) Cum Dominus Iesus . . . = Augustine, *Tract. in Io.,* LXXXV, 1–3 (*PL* XXXV, 1848–1850) — (*V-VIII:*) Merito quaeritur . . . = Aug., *Tract. in Io.,* LXXXVI, 1–3 (*PL* XXXV, 1850–1852) — (*IX-XII:*) (Mt X, 5–6 and:) Cum constet . . . = Gregory, *XL hom. in Ev.*, hom. IV (*PL* LXXVI, 1089–1092)

(Dec. 26)[7] 16r–24r Stephen: (*l. I-IV:*) In diebus illis crescente numero . . . = (*Bible, N.T.) Acts* VI,l-VIII,4. — (*V-VIII:*) Hesterno die . . . = Fulgentius? *Sermo 3* (*PL* LXV, 729–732) — (*IX:*) (Mt XXIII,34 and:) Qui prophetas . . . = Hilary, *In Matthaeum,* c.

MS 23, f. 59r, lines 11–29 (note rubric in lines 14–15) (actual size of area shown: ca. 240 × 175 mm)

XXIV, 9–11 (*PL* IX, 1051–1052) — (*X-XII*:) Hoc quod antea . . . = Jerome, *In Matthaeum,* l. IV (*PL* XXVI, 172–175)

(Dec. 27) 24r–32r John Ev.: (*l. I-IV*:) Apocalipsis Iesu Christi . . . = *(Bible, N.T.) Rev.* I,l-III,22. — (*V-VIII*:) Duas vitas . . . = Augustine, *Tract. in Io.,* CXXIV, 5–8 (*PL* XXXV, 1974–1976) (imperfect: part of l. VII and whole l. VIII wanting due to lost ff. 28–29) — (*IX-XII*:) ([John XXI,19–20] and:) [Non parva questio . . .] = Augustine, *Tract. in Io.*, CXXIV, 1–5 (*PL* XXXV, 1969–1974) (imperfect: l. IX with Gospel quote, and part of l. X wanting)

(Dec. 28) 32r–38r Innocents: (*l. I-IV*:) Et vidi quod aperuisset . . . = *(Bible, N.T.) Rev.* VI,1-11; VI, 12–VII,8; VII,9–VIII,4; XIV, 1–13. — (*V-VIII*:) Semper quidem dilectissimi . . . = Leo, *Sermo 24* (*PL* LIV, 203–208) — (*IX-X*:) (Mt II, 13 and:) Parante Herode parvulis . . . = Hilary, *In Matthaeum*, c. I,6–II,l (*PL* IX, 923–924) — (XI-XII:) Quando Ioseph tollit puerum . . . = Jerome, *In Matthaeum*, l. I (*PL* XXVI, 27–29)

(Dec. 29) 38r–41r Thomas à Becket: (*l. I-VIII*:) Dicat ergo veritas, dicat: Si quis vult . . . humanum pudorem subdidit = Gregory, *XL hom. in Ev.*, hom. XXXII, 2–5 (*PL* LXXVI, 1234–1236) — (*IX-XII:*) (Lk IX, 23 and:) Quia Dominus ac redemptor noster novus homo . . . = Gregory, *op. cit.,* hom. XXXII, 1–2 (*PL* LXXVI, 1232–1234)

(Jan. 17) 41r–46v Anthony (the abbot): (*l. I-VIII:*) Omne quod agimus . . . = Gregory, *XL hom. in Ev.*, hom. XXXVII, 6–10 (*PL* LXXVI, 1277–1281) — (IX-XII:) (Lk XIV,26 and:) Si consideremus fratres karissimi = *ibid.* 1–6 (*PL* LXXVI, 1274–1277)

(Jan. 21) 46v–53v Agnes: (*l. I-VIII*:) Servus Christi Ambrosius . . . = Pseudo-Ambrose, *Ep. I,* 1–15 (*PL* XVII, 735–741) — (*IX-XII:*) (Mt XXV,1–2 and:) Saepe vos fratres karissimi admoneo . . . = Gregory, *XL hom. in Ev.,* hom. XII (*PL* LXXVI, 1118–1123)

(Jan. 22) 53v–59r Vincent (martyr): (*l. I-III*:) Magnum spectaculum . . . = Augustine, *Sermo 274* (*PL* XXVIII, 1252–1253) — (*IV-VI*:) In passione quae nobis hodie . . . = Augustine, *Sermo 276* (*PL* XXXVIII, 1255–1257) — (*VII-VIII*:) Magnum et multum mirandum . . . = Augustine, *Sermo 275* (*PL* XXXVIII, 1254–1255) — (*IX-XII*:) (Lk IX, 23 and:) Quia Dominus . . . = (as above with Thomas à Becket)

(Jan. 23) 59ra: *Sancti illefonsi* [sic; = Ildephonsus, Abp. of Toledo, d. 677] *sic[ut] sa[n]cti nicholai.*[8]

(Jan. 25) 59r–63v Conversion of Paul:[9] (*l. I-VIII*:) Saulus adhuc spirans . . . (*Bible. N.T.) Acts* IX,1–XIII,52. — (*IX-X*:) (Mt XIX,27 and:) Grandis fiducia . . . omnia possidentes. = Jerome, *In Matthaeum,* l. III (*PL* XXVI, 138–140) — (*XI-XII*:) Multa sunt quae non sinunt . . . efficiantur ex primis. = Hilary, *In Matthaeum*, c. XX, 2–4 (*PL* IX, 1028–1029)

(Feb. 2) 63v–69v Candlemas (*Purificatio B.M.V.*): (l. I-IV:) Primus homo quo cadente . . . viribus suis (= anon., text edited in Mai, *Nova patrum bib.* I, s. 116, p. 243–245) — (*V-VIII*:) Audi qui negas . . . = Quodvultdeus, *Tractatus adversus V haereses*, 5–7 (*PL* XLII, 1106–1107) — (*IX-X*) (Lk II, 22–23 and:) Non solum ab angelis . . . = Ambrose, *Exp. Ev. sec. Lucam*, l. II, 58–62 (*PL* XV, 1573–1575) — (*XI-XII*:) De illis beatissimi Symeonis . . . = Paulinus, *Ep. L*, 17–18 (*PL* LXI, 415–417)

(Feb. 5) 69v–74v Agatha: (*l. I-VIII*:) Inter parabolas . . . = Augustine, *De diversis quaestionibus lxxiii,* qu. 59 (*PL* XL, 44–48) — (*IX-XII*:) (Mt XIII, 44 and:) Coelorum regnum fratres karissimi . . . = Gregory, *XL hom. in Ev.,* hom. 11 (*PL* LXXVI, 1114–1118)

(Feb. 24) 74v–78v Mathias: (*l. I-VIII*:) Vos amici mei estis. O quanta . . . = Gregory, *XL hom. in Ev.*, hom. XXVII, 4–9 (*PL* LXXVI, 1206–1210) — (*IX-XII*:) (John XV, 12–13 and:) Cum cuncta sacra eloquia . . . = *ibid.*, 1–3 (*PL* LXXVI, 1205–1206)

(March 12) 78v–81v Gregory (the Great, Pope): (*l. I-VIII*:) Dominicus sermo quem debemus . . . dives in Christo = Fulgentius, *Sermo I,* 1–5 (*PL* LXV, 719–723) — (*IV-XII*:) (Mt XXV, 14 and:) Homo iste paterfamilias . . . purgatum septuplum =

Jerome, *In Matthaeum*, l. IV (*PL* XXVI, 186–188)

(March 21) 81v–87v Benedict: (*l. I-VIII:*) Fuit vir vitae venerabilis . . . = Gregory, *Dial.*, lib. II, prol., c. 1 and 35–37 (*PL* LXVI, 126–130 and 196–202) — (*IX-XII:*) (Lk XII, 35 and:) Sancti evangelii fratres karissimi aperta . . . durius dampnat = Gregory, *XL hom. in Ev.*, hom. XIII, 1–5 (*PL* LXXVI, 1123–1126)

(March 25) 87r–91v Annunciation: (*l. I-VIII:*) Morale est . . . = Ambrose, *Exp. Ev. sec. Lucam*, l. II, 19–29 (*PL* XV, 1559–1562) — (*IX-XII:*) (Lk I, 26–27 and:) Latent quidem divina mysteria . . . ad temporalis speciem sacerdotis = *ibid.*, 1–7 (*PL* XV, 1551–1555)

(Apr. 25) 91v–94r Mark ("Marchi"):[10] (*l. I-VIII:*) Sancta quatuor animalia . . . = Gregory, *Hom. in Ezechielem* lib. I, hom. III, 1–5 (*PL* LXXVI, 806–808) — (*IX-XII:*) (John XV, 1–2 and:) Iste locus evangelicus . . . = Augustine, *Tract. in Io.,* LXXX, 1–2 (*PL* XXXV, 1838–1840)

(May 1) 94r–97v Philip and James: (*l. I-VIII:*) Verba sancti evangelii . . . = Augustine, *Tract. in Io.,* LXX, 1–3 (*PL* XXXV, 1818–1820) — (*IX-XII:*) (John XIV, 1 and:) Erigenda est nobis . . . = *ibid.*, LXVII, 1–4 (*PL* XXXV, 1812–1813)

(June 24) 97v–101v John Bapt.: (*l. I-VIII:*) Solemnitates nobis diversorum . . . = Maximus of Turin, *Hom. LXV (PL* LVII, 383–388) — (*IX-XII:*) (Lk I, 57–58 and:) Habet sanctorum edicio . . . penam sermonis evasit = Ambrose, *Exp. Ev. sec. Lucam*, l. II, 30–35 (*PL* XV, 1563–1565)

(June 26) 101v–105r John and Paul:[11] (*l. I-VIII:*) Omnes electi quia summi capitis membra sunt . . . si pacienciam in animo veraciter custodimus = Gregory, *XL hom. in ev.,* hom. XXXV, 3–7 (*PL* LXXVI, 1261–1263) — (*IX-XII:*) (Lk XXI, 9 and:) Quia longius ab Urbe digressi sumus . . . = *ibid.*, 1–3 (*PL* LXXVI, 1259–1261)

(June 29) 105r–108v Peter and Paul: (*l. I-VIII:*) Omnium quidem sanctarum solemnitatum . . . = Leo, *Sermo 82* (*PL* LIV, 422–428) — (*IX-XII:*) (Mt XVI, 13 and:) Philippus iste est frater . . . edificabo ecclesiam meam = Jerome, *In Matthaeum*, l. III (*PL* XXVI, 113–117)

(June 30) 108v–111r Commemoration of Paul: (*l. I-VIII:*) Beatus Paulus qui tantam . . . ac providentie sue documenta prestabat = John Chrysostom, *De laudibus s. Pauli*, hom. 3 (*PG* L, 483–485, slightly variant Latin version) — "*Euangelium et homelia sicut in conversione eiusdem [f.] lxij*" (the number squeezed additionally into inadequate space)

(July 22) 111r–115r Mary Magdalen:[12] (*l. I-VIII:*) Quid fratres mei . . . = Gregory, *XL hom. in Ev.*, hom. XXXIII, 4–8 (*PL* LXXVI, 1241–1246) — (*IX-XII:*) (Lk VII, 36 and:) Cogitanti mihi . . . = *ibid.*, 1–4 (*PL* LXXVI, 1238-1241)

(July 25) 115r–119r James (the Greater): (*l. I-VI:*) Iste locus evangelicus . . . = Augustine, *Tract. in Io.,* LXXX, 1–3 (*PL* XXXV, 1839–1840) — (*VII-VIII:*) Vitem se dixit . . . in profunda submersionis = Augustine, *op. cit.*, LXXXI, 1–2 (*PL* XXXV, 1841) — (*IX-XII:*) (Mt XX, 20–21 and:) Unde opinionem habeat . . . = Jerome, *In Matthaeum*, l. III (*PL* XXVI, 142–145)

(Aug. 1) 119r–121r *Ad vincula Petri:*[13] Factum est autem . . . = (*Bible. N.T.) Acts* IX, 32–X,43. — "*Ev. et homelia sicut in natali eiusdem* [f.] *cvij*." (Rubric black, red-underscored; number red, squeezed in)

(Aug. 10) 121r–125r Lawrence: (*l. I-V:*) Cum omnium dilectissimi . . . = Leo, *Sermo 85* (*PL* LIV, 435–437) — (*VI-VIII:*) Beatissimi Laurentii martiris . . . = Maximus of Turin, *Sermo 70* (*PL* LVII, 675–678; cf. *PL* XXXIX, 2127–2128) — (*IX-XII*) (John XII, 24–25 and:) Se granum Dominus dicebat . . . et ipse ambulare = Augustine, *Tract. in Io.*, 9–12 (*PL* XXXV, 1766–1768)

(Aug. 15) 125r–130v Assumption of Mary: (*l. I-VIII:*) Cogitis me . . . = Pseudo-Jerome, *Ep. IX*, 1–4 (*PL* XXX, 122–126) — (*IX-XII:*) (Lk X, 38 and:) Sanctum evangelium cum legeretur . . . = Augustine, *Sermo 104* (*PL* XXXVIII, 616–618)

130–136v (3 readings for each of five weekdays of the octave of Assumption:) Talibus priores . . . Constat igitur . . . Haec idcirco . . . Hinc est karissimae . . .

Et ideo eam bene . . . = Pseudo-Jerome, *Ep. IX,* 11–16 (*PL* XXX, 133–139)

(Aug. 20) 136va *In festo scī bernardi abbatis*[14] *sicut in festo scī anthonij quere [f.] xlj . . .*

136v–140r Sunday in the octave of Assumption: (*l. I-VIII:*) Regina mundi hodie . . . ad iusticiam et salutem = Pseudo-Jerome, *Ep. IX*, 4–6 (*PL* XXX, 126–128) — (*IX-XII:*) (Lk X, 38 and:) Verba Domini nostri . . . sunt unum. = Augustine, *Sermo 103* (*PL* XXVIII, 613–616)

(Aug. 22) 140r–144v Eighth day of the octave: (*l. I-VIII:*) Nunc ergo dilectissimae . . . = Pseudo-Jerome, *Ep. IX*, 16–19 (*PL* XXX, 139–142) — (*IX-X:*) (Lk X, 38 and:) Subicitur hic Marthae exemplum . . . = Ambrose, *Exp. Ev. sec. Lucam*, l. VII, 85–86 (*PL* XV, 1720–1721) — (*XI:*) (without new caption:) Quod Martha excepit . . . = Augustine, *Quaest. evangeliorum*, l. II, qu. 20 (*PL* XXXV, 1341) — (*XII:*) Bene utrasque vitas . . . luce perficitur = Gregory, *Hom. in Ezechielem* lib. II, hom. II, 9 (*PL* LXXVI, 953–954)

(Aug. 24) 144v–146v Bartholomew: (*l. I-VIII:*) In lectione evangelica . . . = Augustine, *Tract. in Io.,* LXXXVII, 1–4 (*PL* XXXV, 1852–1854) — (*IX-XII:*) "*sicut in festo btī mathie lxxvij*" (folio number written in additionally, squeezed into inadequate space)

(Aug. 28) 146va, Augustine: "*sicut sancti Gregorii Pape* [f.] *lxxviij.*"

(Aug. 29) 146v–151v Beheading (*Decollatio*) of John the Baptist: (*l. I-IV:*) Cum sanctum evangelium . . . = Augustine, *Sermo 307 (PL* XXXVIII, 1406–1407) — (*V-VIII:*) Propter hunc locum . . . = *idem*, *S. 308 (PL* XXXVIII, 1408–1410) — (*IX-XII:*) (Mk VI, 17 and:) Vetus narrat hystoria . . . virum antea non habuerat = Jerome, *In Matthaeum*, l. II (*PL* XXVI, 97–99)

(Sept. 8) 151v–155v Nativity of Mary: (*l. I-VIII:*) Osculetur me . . . = (*Bible. O.T.) Cant.* I, 1–V,7. — (*IX-XII:*) (Mt I,1–2 and:) In Isaia legitur . . . = Jerome, *In Matthaeum*, l. I (*PL* XXVI, 21–24)

155v–157r Sunday within the octave: (*IX-XII:*) (Mt I,12 and:) Gradum quem Matthaeus . . . = Hilary, *In Matthaeum,* c. I, 1–4 (*PL* IX, 918–922)

(Sept. 15) 157r–159r Eighth day ("*In octabis natiuitatis btē marie*":[15] (*l. I-VIII:*) Adiuro vos filiae Ierusalem . . . = (*Bible. O.T.) Cant.* V, 8–VIII, 14. — "*Evangelium et homelia sicut in die nativitatis eiusdem cliiij.*"

(Sept. 14) 159r–166r Exaltation of the Cross:[16] (*l. I-II:*) Magnum sacramentum . . . = Augustine, *Tract. in Io.*, XII, 11 (*PL* XXXV, 1489–1490) — (*III-IV:*) Quid est hoc? Nihil enim . . . = Augustine, *op. cit.,* XL, 2–4 (*PL* XXXV, 1686–1687) — (*V-VIII:*) Haec est doctrina christiana . . . = Augustine, *Sermo 160,* 5–7 (*PL* XXXVIII, 876–877) — (*IX-XII:*) (John XII, 31 and:) Nunc iudicium est mundi . . . = Augustine, *Tract. in Io.*, LII, 6–13 (*PL* XXXV, 1771–1774)

(Sept. 21) 166r–(168v) Matthew: (*l. I-[VIII]*, broken off in *l. V* because of missing leaves:) Mystica vocatio publicani . . . = Ambrose, *Exp. Ev. sec. Lucam*, l. V, 16-[27] (*PL* XV, 1640–[1644]) — (readings *IX-XII* lost with the missing leaves 169–176)[17]

(Sept. 22) ? -177ra (Maurice and companions: because of the lost leaves, only 4 lines remain of the set, on 177r:) merita que premia . . . ipsorum est regnum coelorum = end of the homily on Mt V,1, Augustine, *Sermo 53* (ending in c. 6) (*PL* XXXVIII, 364–366)[18]

(Sept. 29) 177r- ? Michael (the Archangel): (*l. I-[VIII]*, broken off in l. *III* because of lost leaves 178–183:) Angelorum et hominum naturam . . . = Gregory, *XL hom. in Ev.*, hom. XXXIV, 6–[14?] (*PL* LXXVI, 1249–[1255?]) — (l. *IX-XII* lost with the missing leaves)

(Oct. 18) ? –187v (Luke:)[19] (*l. [I]-VIII*, beginning imperfectly in the middle of l. *IV:*) [Per sanctum prophetie spiritum . . .] demonstremus. Sed magna nobis de eisdem evangelistis . . . malis actibus superponimus = Gregory, *Hom. in Ezechielem* lib. I, hom. IV, 1–5 (*PL* LXXVI, 814–818) — (*IX-XII*) (Lk X,I and:) Ecce ego mitto vos . . . = Ambrose, *Exp. Ev. sec. Lucam*, l. VII, 44–53 (*PL* XV, 1710–1712)

(Oct. 21) 187vb: *Lectiones Vndecī miliu(m)//u[ir]ginū q̄re in festo sācte agathe. lxix// Homelia uero ī festo scē agnetis. lj* (Celebrated in whole order since 1352. Black, red-underscored rubric in the smaller script used also on ff. 136v, 159r, and elsewhere, probably original.)

(Oct. 28) 187v–192r Simon and Jude: (*l. I-III*:) Hoc est praeceptum meum . . . = Augustine, *Tract. in Io.*, LXXXIII, 2–3 (*PL* XXXV, 1845–1846) — (*IV-VIII*:) Plenitudinem dilectionis . . . = Aug., *op. cit.*, LXXXIV, 1–2 (*PL* XXXV, 1846–1848) — (*IX-XII*:) (Lk X, 1 and:) Dominus et Salvator noster fratres karissimi . . . = Gregory, *XL hom. in Ev.*, hom. XVII (*PL* LXXVI, 1138–1149)

(Nov. 1) 192r–197v All Saints (*l. I-VIII*:) Legimus in ecclesiasticis historis . . . per tormenta non cessaverunt = Pseudo-Bede, *Hom. LXXI* (abridged) (*PL* XCIV, 452–454) — (*IX-XII*:) (Mt V,1 and:) Praedicante dilectissimi Domino . . . = Leo, *Sermo 95* (*PL* LIV, 461–466)

(Nov. 8) 197v–[202]r Feast of Relics:[20] (*l. I-VIII*:) Beati qui lugent . . . = Chromatius of Aquileia, *Tract. in Matthaeum*, tract. 17, III-IX (*CCSL* IX A, p. 271–277) — (*IX-XII*:) (Mt V,1 and:) De terrenis et humilibus . . . = *ibid.*, I-II (*CCSL* IX A, p. [268]–270)

(Nov. 21) [202]ra: *Scī martini sicut scī nicholay. [f.] vj. Scī*

(Nov. 17) *hugonis linco[l]niensis epī. sicut scī nicholay. [f.] vj.* (continued on same line by: *Scī clementis . . .)*[21]

(Nov. 23) [202]r–[205]r Clement: (*l. I-VIII*:) Dicat ergo veritas dicat, Si quis vult . . . regnum citius adepturi sumus = Gregory, *XL hom. in Ev.*, hom. XXXII, 2–8 (*PL* LXXVI, 1234–1238) — *Euangelium et omelia sicut scī uincentij [f.] lvij.* (Black, red-underscored rubric probably by writer of [206]v–[208]v)

(Nov. 25) [205]ra: *Scē katherine sicut scē agathe [f.] lxix.*[22]

(?)[23] [205]r–[208]v *In dedicatione ecclesie*: (*l. I-VIII*:) Factum est autem cum exissent . . . = (*Bible. O.T.) 1 Kings* VIII, 10–66. — (*IX-XII*:) (Lk XIX, 1–3 and:) Zacheus statura pusillus . . . = Ambrose, *Exp. Ev. sec. Lucam*, l. VIII, 81–90 (*PL* XV, 1790–1792)

(?) [208]v–[209]v (ADDITION CONSPICUOUSLY DIFFERENT IN GENERAL APPEARANCE:)[24] *In festo compassionis d[omi]ne nostre: (l. IX-XII* only:) (John XIX, 25 and:) Haec nimirum illa est hora . . . = Augustine, *Tract. in Io.*, CXIX, 1–3 (*PL* XXXV, 1950–1951)

MARGINAL ADDITIONS:[25]

f.6r (outer margin; humanistic cursive): In co[n]cepcione btē m[ari]e sic[ut] in ei[us] nati[uitat]e. in fo. clij. (N.B. In same hand also note on *Praesentatio B.V.M.* in inner margin of [202]r; both notes are post-1470)

10r (outer margin; carefully hand-lettered humanistic roman): In conceptione Deipare virginis f° clij. (The note is close to the 3 last lines of 10rb which are original and include the significant correction from earlier terminology, cf. main contents)

38v (lower margin; a maltese-cross mark connects the note with 8th line of main text) Juxta fore legendum [et?] no[n] mixta // a Carthusia venit declaratu[m], ano 1557. (N.B. Similar note with same correction also on [202]r)

81v (lower margin; italics): In festo S. Ioseph, octo prime lectiones ex b. Bernardo . . . relique quatuor in dominicali // Fol. 9 ex ordinat. gener. cap. A. 1567.

101v (next to beginning of reading for *Joannis & Pauli*; in small humanistic hand): comune p[lurimorum] m[a]r[tyrum]

111r (lower margin; carefully hand-lettered prehumanistic script; referred to by a note in inner margin written in italics): In festo visitationis beate Marie prime octo lectiones vt in natiuitate eiusdem . . . Eua[n]g[e]l[i]um v[er]o cum sua hom[i]l[i]a hoc q[uo]d seq[uitu]r. *lectio . . . s[ecundu]m lucam.* (Lk I, 39 and:) Morale . . . (with reference to f. lxxxvij) // Dominica i[nfra] octa[ua]s . . . (I-VIII "ex lib. reg." and reference to f. 88 for homily "Et und hoc mihi . . .") "In Octavis . . ." (I-VIII as in oct. of Nativity B.V.M., hom. "sicut in die")[26]

119r (lower margin; large humanistic lettering:) In festo sancte Anne . . . (instructing to use for l. I-VIII same readings as for St. Agatha (fol. lxix) and for IX-XII "vt in festo natiuitatis beatissime Marie, folio cliiij")

151v (lower margin; in hybrid script of late 15th century (?); red): *In festo co[m]pasio[n]is dn̄e nr̄e . . . Omelia estabat iuxta cruc̄e que i[n] fine libri.* — (The initial "e" of "estabat" imperfectly deleted.)

154r (lower margin): In festo visitationis . . . (same instructions as in the lower margin of f. 111r, concerning the homily to be used after the eight readings which go from 151v to 154r)

[202]r (inner margin; referred to by a double-dagger mark placed after the rubric on Hugo Lincolniensis, before that on Clemens; brown ink): in prese[n]tatione bte̅ m[ari]e sic[ut] in ei[us] natiuitate in fo. clij. — (The feast was permitted 1470, made obligatory in 1474)

* * *

Contemporary foliation in red roman numerals, *i-cc*; 9 unnumbered leaves with text at end; 16 leaves of the numbered sequence are missing (cf. collation). The numbers are placed on rectos, in the outer margin and on the level of first text line (between two top ruled lines),[27] largely obscuring cursive guide numbers prewritten in lead. — Written area varies considerably, partly due to the presence of several gatherings (*b-f* = ff. 9–48) which use 28 lines per page while the rest (*a*, and *g* through end) has 29; it varies even within the same kind, from ca. 315 to 321 mm in height for the 28 lines, from ca. 326 (f. [203]r) to 338 (129r) mm for the 29. Height in the inner margin tends to differ from that near the fore edge by 2 or 3 mm.[28] The width (measured on ruling: the script exceeds or doesn't quite reach the right ruled vertical in about equal proportion) varies from 223 (103 + 17 + 103) mm (f. 77r) to 229 (106 + 18 + 105) mm (on f. 200r). — Ruling is done in several different ways and in several mediums: lead and blind ruling were used for the most part but faint black ink[29] (perhaps stylus occasionally stained?) occurs, and purple ink appears prominently[30] on ff. 1rv and 8rv–11rv. There are 4 vertical lines per page. In the 28-line gatherings (actually only through f_2 = f. 42) three top horizontals run from edge to edge, as does (not always) one at the bottom; in signatures *g* through end, the long lines are two at top and two at bottom (in the first gathering, such lines are 2 + 1 or, on $a_{4.5}$, 3 + 0?). In the addition on ff. [208]v–[209]v, a separate series of barely visible horizontals placed at ca. 1/4 of the distance between lines serves as the base of the script, leaving the main ruling, done in black ink, very conspicuous.[31] — Pricking is partly preserved, chiefly at the fore edge, some also in the head margin.[32] — The script is a *textualis formata* of the type used in liturgical books;[33] it is semiquadrate and the first two verticals of *m*, the first in *n*, the upper and lower extenders of *b, d* (used along with the more frequent uncial type), *p, g, h* (the upper extender), the upper end of *l* and the bottom ends of the tall *s* and of *f* are *praescissae*. The lower loop of *g* is closed by a diagonal hairline. The mark used to indicate the presence of an unwritten *n* or *m* following a vocal is diamond-shaped; that used over *q* in various contractions, a short vertical. The basic morphological features remain unchanged throughout, including the late (ca. 1490?) addition on ff. [208]v–[209]v. — A distinctive form of semicolon-like punctuation mark, with the upper part a horizontal zigzag (as a simple *w*) is used throughout (besides colon and simple *punctus*). A hairline mark is placed over *i*.[34] The tironian graph for "et" is rare or totally absent in some sections, quite frequent in others.[35] Use of the long (as *j*) form of *i* when next to an *m, n,* or *u* (for legibility) varies interestingly: it is frequent (with minor variations) at the beginning, through f. 77v where a change of scribes may have taken place (lines 12//13 of column *b?*); from there to the end, no instance found.[36] A mark indicating word division at the end of a line has been used throughout except on ff. 199–[201]; it is a straight hairline ca. 30° off horizontal (8 o'clock–2 o'clock) placed for the most part at the height of ca. middle of a minim but sometimes (chiefly on last 8 leaves) on the script base. From 1r through [206]r, accented syllables are marked by a red *accent aigu* (at 40–60° from horizontal).[37] — Red captions (written except for the color as part of the text columns) and lesson numbers (almost always within the column, and apparently planned for; occasionally spelled out). Some rubric-type statements (cf. contents) are written in black, in script smaller than the rest of the text, and underscored in red. — Black ink of generally good quality, changing abruptly to rather light (faded?) brown between columns *a* and *b* on f. 198v; becomes black again on [201]r. — Parchment of ca. 23 mm thickness per 100 leaves, with some holes and some repairs; now partly crinkled but with both sides almost equally smooth.

Collation: a-c^8 d^8($d_{4.5}$ = ff. 28.29 wanting, with text loss) e-s^8(= ff. 33–144) another (the final type) form of s^8(= ff. 145–152) t-u^8 $[v]^8$(= ff. 169–176) wanting, with text loss; x^8(= ff. 177.184; x_{2-7} = ff. 178–183 wanting, with text loss) y-z^8(= ff. 185–200) A^{12-3}(= ff. [201–209]; $A_{10,11}$ probably blank, absent except for stubs; A_{12} blank, used as pastedown. — There are 3 stubs before a_1, the last of them conjugate with the pastedown. — Catchwords on last versos of all signatures except *a, b, c, i,* and the final one. First four leaves of each gathering (first six, in the case of the last one) are signed (in lower right corner recto). The letters are in cursive minuscule, the numbers in lowercase roman; written in diluted brownish black ink.[38]

Decoration: Limited to the rather utilitarian *litterae notabiliores*, red or purple, 2 to 5 lines high, which mark each beginning of a reading set and also each individual lesson. The Gospel quote introducing the ninth lesson is generally given a separate 3-line letter. Consistency in assigning to a division of a certain type an initial of a particular size has not been achieved; a new set of readings (i.e., another festive occasion) sometimes starts with a 2-line red or purple letter. The colors begin to alternate (imprecisely) only on 21v where purple appears for the first time; on that page also stops the until then consistent use of the long-*J* form for initial *I*; it is thereafter replaced by the square-letter capital "I" (except in two instances: 22v, 72v). These initials are unadorned or at most decorated by use of void white; they fill spaces left for the purpose by the writer of the black text and correspond to guide letters found generally slightly to the left; they are very probably, at least in the signatures *d* -A_5, the work of one person. — The last set of readings, added after ca. 1490 ([208]v–[209]v), has the letters done in red or blue (the *I* on [208]v in both) with flourishes in purple or red. — Capitals of the black text are throughout the book touched with yellow.

Contemporary binding: Wooden boards (oak?), ca. 11 mm thick, originally covered with thick parchment (of which only ca. 60 percent remains); sewn over 6 raised double, alum-tawed thongs laced, together with 2 single-thong endbands, through holes located 2 and 5 cm from the edge of the board (8 holes at the 2-cm distance, 6 in the inner line, each endband sharing a diagonally placed hole with the top or bottom band). The boards are beveled on the side toward the text block except along the spine, where the beveling (or rounding) is on the outside; they are roughly flush with the text block at the fore edge, exceed it by ca. 0.5 cm at head and tail. — Holes and some minimal remnants of 2 (copper?) clasps, and of 4 corner pieces and a central round boss on each cover. On the spine, now accessible due to torn vellum, fragments of a choir book with red 5-line staff and black square notation.

Former owners: used in an unidentified charterhouse in Spain for at least a century;[39] not unlikely the monastery was one of several located in the Catalonian archdiocese of Tarragona (in view of the prominence given to St. Ildephonsus).[40] — Acquired by LC in 1929 from Madrid (LC accession no. 4189 (31) no. 2).[41]

2° fo.: que frigora, que p[er]icu[//la]

Bibl.: De Ricci, *Census* (1935), p. 218, no. 78 ("Lectionarium; . . . XIVth c. . . . Written in Italy . . . "); Faye and Bond, p. 119, no. 53 (same information)

NOTES

1. Preserved are 193 leaves: 16 are missing from the original sequence of 200 to which 9 have been added at the end of the 15th century.

2. The average measurement is 480.5 mm near the gutter, 475 mm near fore edge.

3. The English name forms, dates (the ms. gives none), and regularized (except for some peculiarities deemed worthy of notice) spellings of Latin words are ours. — Some interesting features of our ms. can be seen by comparison with the ms. 33 of the Bibliothèque de la Ville de Grenoble, probably the oldest extant codex with similar contents; cf. R. Étaix, "L'Homiliaire cartusien," in *SACRIS ERUDIRI* XIII (1962), p. [67]–112 (on the ms. Grenoble 33: p. 80–97). — An important source of information has been the summary "Le calendrier cartusien" (signed "fr. Benoît du Moustier," pseud. of B. Lambres O. Cart.) in *ÉTUDES GRÉGORIENNES* II (1957), p. 153–161.

4. Caption in the ms. names these four because the set of readings selected for St. Nicholas is to be used also for the other three; their days, however, are Apr. 1, Nov. 17, and Nov. 11 respectively. There are references to this leaf in appropriate places (f. 91v, [202]r).

5. Cf. Étaix, *op. cit.*, p. 92, no. 38b: in the 12th-century ms. Grenoble 33, the homily is read through to its end; it is reduced to ca. a half in our manuscript. Similar cuts can be seen throughout. (Cf. also the contents of LC MS 13, another Carthusian homiliary of early vintage.)

6. From 1341 to 1470, the term used in Carthusian liturgy was *Sanctificatio*; then changed to "Conceptio." The rubric (red-underscored black) as originally written dates from before 1470. The correction may be more recent than the marginal note listed (among other marginal additions) at the end of our contents.

7. In the ms. Grenoble 33 (and, it seems, in other early copies of the homiliary) the sanctoral part included also Christmas and Epiphany (elsewhere generally understood as belonging to the seasonal or "temporal" cycle).

8. The entry, written in red and apparently by same hand as the black text, is our primary reason for assigning the manuscript to Spain. — Note that Ildephonsus' name had not found its way into the listing of saints sharing the same readings given on f. 6r.

9. The occasion, celebrated by 12 readings since the end of the 12th century, does not appear in the Grenoble manuscript.

10. In the Grenoble manuscript, Mark is a later (close to 1300?) addition.

11. The festivity (Joannis et Pauli), given 12 readings before 1259, doesn't figure in the Grenoble manuscript.

12. In the Grenoble manuscript, Mary Magdalen is a 13th-century addition.

13. The occasion doesn't appear in the Grenoble ms.; in LC MS 13, "Petri ad Vincula" is a later addition.

14. Became a festivity requiring 12 readings in 1361 *(ÉT. GRÉG., loc. cit.)*. The black, red-underscored rubric (altogether 5 lines; continuation in column *b* concerns possible conflict between the feast and the ongoing octave) seems to have been written by same hand as the main text (though in appropriately smaller-size script).

15. No octave of Mary's birthday in the Grenoble manuscript. The 12 readings on the octave day were introduced in 1249. The (black, red-underscored) rubric is probably by same hand as the main text (although in smaller-size script); the red folio number was supplied later.

16. In the Grenoble ms., *Exaltatio Crucis* is an addition of ca. 1300. — N.B. There is no mention in our codex of the feast *Cornelii et Cypriani* which appeared in early copies of the homiliary, incl. the Grenoble 33 and LC MS 13.

17. For Matthew, the expected homily (cf. Étaix, *op. cit.*, p. 91, no. 34b) is: Chromatius of Aquileia, *Tract. XLV*, in Mt IX, 9–13 (*CCSL* IX *A* (1974), p. [417]–420).

18. Cf. Étaix, *op. cit.*, p. 95, no. 49(ab). In the Grenoble ms., the feast (*Mauricii et sociorum eius*) is a post-1174 addition.

19. Cf. Étaix, *loc. cit.*, no. 50(ab). In the Grenoble ms., an addition (late 12th or 13th century).

20. In the Grenoble ms., a 13th-century addition.

21. Cf. f. 6r: *In natali scī nicholai et btī hugonis gratianopolitani epī . et. scī hugonis li[n]co[l]niensis ep̄i. et btī martini ep̄i.* . . . — N.B. The two rubrics (both fully in red ink) were not written by same hand.

22. Catherine became an occasion with 12 readings "ante 1400" *(ÉT. GRÉG., loc. cit.)*. The rubric (or at least the black, red underscored "sicut scē agathe") seems to be by same hand as the text of ff. [206]v–[208]v.

23. The placement of this set after Nov. 25 (Catherine) and before (presumably) Nov. 30 (Andrew, with whom the book begins) could mean that the dedication of the monks' church in the particular charterhouse for which this was written was celebrated between the two dates; more likely it is accidental.

24. Solemn celebration of *Compassio B.V.M.* (= Our Lady of Sorrows) was optional since 1477, obligatory since 1486. It was a movable occasion, assigned to the Saturday immediately preceding Palm Sunday.

25. We wished to note items of relevance to the history of the codex and perhaps that of Carthusian liturgical ways. Omitted are especially most of the

more or less contemporary textual corrections (often in the same or similar script as the original text).

26. The Visitation of Mary was introduced into Carthusian liturgy between 1390 and 1468. For houses of the Avignon obedience (incl. the Spanish peninsula) the celebration was permitted since 1411. Cf. *ÉT. GRÉG., loc. cit.,* p. 157.

27. Exceptions: ff. 3, 102, 111, 139.

28. Crinkled material makes exact measurements problematic. The difference in height between the inner and outer margin is no doubt accidental: sometimes one and sometimes the other measurement is larger.

29. On some pages (43r, 44r, 58r, 147v) the ruling has a distinctly burnt-sienna color, due, I suppose, to chemical changes: parts of the line tend to appear blacker. Under a microscope, the hue can be seen inside the black parts of some letters.

30. The purple ruling may have been added after writing (over lead or blind-ruled lines), as a decorative element; the grid gives such impression especially on ff. 8–11.

31. A somewhat similar relationship between the script and the visible ruled line was caused on ff. 9–11 by, I believe, the person who added the purple (pseudo-)ruling a long time after the text had been written.

32. The tail margin was cropped at the time of binding (cropped sig. A_6).

33. For similar scripts used in Spain in the 2nd half of the 15th century, cf. A.G. Watson, *Cat. of dated & datable mss. . . . British Library* (1979): Add. 34663 (Missale Valentinense of 1477); Add. 30032 (Foundation deeds, Barcelona, 1489) (reprod. in v. II, *op. cit.*, nos. 798 and 862)

34. It is a semicircle open to the left on ff. 1-ca. 90; beginning a little earlier, a short straight diagonal (as an acute accent) appears instead with increasing frequency, then prevails completely through [201]r; it is omitted on [201]v and [202]r, reappears on [202]v as a semicircle open to the right; becomes acute accent through [206]r, then a vertical with a hook at top through [208]r; in the last addition, [208]v–[209], it is a short vertical.

35. Generally rare on ff. 1–199r, it appears in scattered bursts on 16v–17r, 22v–26v, 32r–33v, and perhaps in other limited portions of the text; its use may be associated in particular with Scripture passages.

36. The switch from one to another form of the mark over *i* (see note 34) occurs nearby.

37. There are several more or less clear changes of scribes in the last gathering. For the basic text, changes in the inclination of verticals together with other features suggest a different hand on ff. 7–11; a major change of scribe seems to have occurred on 77v. But I find it impossible to tell how many other relays have taken place, especially because codicological and other changes rarely coincide, and some changes of scribal practice occur progressively over several pages. In some of these, the copyist may have merely been following (perhaps with delays due to perception) the changing scribal practices which in his *exemplar* had been caused by changes of scribes.

38. Guide letters for the initialist, where visible, use same forms and may indeed be by same person.

39. A major revision of the homiliary was enacted in 1585, making our ms. unusable.

40. Montalegre near Barcelona? This establishment was founded in 1415, settled by monks from S. Jaime de Valle Paraiso, an older monastery (f. 1345) nearby which was being abolished. The move may have stimulated editorial improvement in the homiliary, which in this hypothesis would have originated in the older place. — R. Étaix, in a personal communication, suggests El Paular (Santa Maria del Paular), famous charterhouse near Segovia, founded 1390.

41. Together with the older homiliary from Valbonne (LC MS 13).

MS 24

(Faye and Bond 87)

PSALTER OF CISTERCIAN NUNS

XVth c.

Low Countries (South Holland?) Parchment. 155 leaves, 195 × ca. 129 mm (bound volume: 206 × ca. 139 mm) 1 column. 23–27 lines (in the calendar, 33 lines)

ff. 1r–6v: Calendar: 183 days have one or more entries, of which 67 are in red. Notable among the days in red: *Co[mmemoratio] ep[iscop]o[rum] [et] abb[atum]* (Jan. 11), *Rob[er]ti abb[atis]* (Apr. 29), *Co[mmemoratio] omn[ium] p[er]sona[rum] ord[in]is n[ost]ri* (May 20), *Dedicatio ecc[les]ie* (July 14), *Sancta anna xij l[ectionum]* (July 26), *Corone d[omi]ni* (Aug. 16), *Bernardi* (Aug. 20), *Missa de s[ancto] s[piritu] p[ro] g[e]n[er]ali cap[itulo]* (Sept. 12), *Co[mmemoratio] om[n]i[um] fr[atru]m et famil[iarium?]* (Sept. 18), *Dyonisij cu[m] s[ociis] suis* (Oct. 9), *Vndecim millia v[ir]g[inum]* (Oct. 21), *Malachie ep[isco]pi* (Nov. 4), *Ethmu[n]di epi[scopi]* (Nov. 16), *Co[mmemoratio] parentu[m] n[ost]ro[rum] xij l'* (Nov. 20), *Conceptio B' M[e] v'gis xij l'* (Dec. 8). — Among the days in black: "Rumoldi e' [et] mr̄." on July 1. — No entry for the octave of Purification (Jan. 9).

Many entries refer to the two series of alphanumerically coded collects given at the end of the book (ff. 150–153). — The calendar is Cistercian, while the Eleven Thousand Virgins in red indicate the ecclesiastical province of Cologne and the date given to St. Rumold, the diocese of Utrecht. — The rubric calling for a 12-lesson office on the day of St. Anne dates the calendar as post-1375 (when the 12-readings office was first permitted, "si conventus voluerit") or (more likely?) post-1454 (when it became obligatory). (Cf. B. Backaert, "L'évolution du calendrier cistercien," *COLLECTANEA O.C.R.* XII (1950), etc.)

7r–128v: *Feria ii ad primū [!] an[tiphona]* Seruite *Ps̄ da[uid]* (B)[9]Eatus vir qui . . .

Cistercian liturgical psalter; i.e., Psalms I-CL (the "gallican" version, commonly used in liturgy, without the inscriptions and numbers) with liturgical additions. Thanks to the old-fashioned character of Cistercian office, the writer was able to maintain the biblical order of the Psalms throughout while at the same time following its weekly course. The Old Testament text (often with indication of the traditional "Gloria Patri" at the end of the Psalm) is interrupted by rubrics indicating in which canonical "hour" the Psalms which follow are used, also antiphons, with music (mostly one line, plainsong notation), short readings (marked "Cap[itulum]" or Lectio)

and prayers ("Col[lecta]"). The Athanasian Creed and the Te Deum are relegated to next section (with the canticles, ff. 128v sqq.)

The Psalms are assigned as follows[1]:

Pss. I–VI	Prime, Monday	
Pss. VII–IX	Prime, Tuesday	
Pss. X–XII	Prime, Wednesday	
Pss. XIII–XV	Prime, Thursday	
Pss. XVI–XVIII,25	Prime, Friday	
Pss. XVIII,26–XX	Prime, Saturday	
Pss. XXI–XXXII	Matins ("ad noct[urnum]"), Sunday	
Pss. XXXIII–XXXVIII	1st nocturn	Monday
Pss. XXXIX–XLV	2nd nocturn	
Pss. XLVI–LII	1st nocturn	Tuesday
Pss. LIII–LIX	2nd nocturn	
Pss. LX–LXVIII	1st nocturn	Wednesday
Pss. LXIX–LXXIII	2nd nocturn	
Pss. LXXIV–LXXIX	1st nocturn	Thursday
Pss. LXXX–LXXXV	2nd nocturn	
Pss. LXXXVI–XCV[2]	1st nocturn	Friday
Pss. XCVI–CI	2nd nocturn	
Pss. CII–CV	1st nocturn	Saturday
Pss. CVI–CIX	2nd nocturn	
Pss. CX–CXIII	Vespers, Sunday	
Pss. CXIV–CXVIII	Vespers, Monday	
Ps. CXIX,1–32	Prime, Sunday	
Ps. CXIX, 33–56	Terce, Sunday	
Ps. CXIX, 57–80	Sext, Sunday	
Ps. CXIX, 81–104	None, Sunday	
Ps. CXIX, 105–128	Terce, Monday	
Ps. CXIX, 129–152	Sext, Monday	
Ps. CXIX, 153–176	None, Monday[3]	
Pss. CXX–CXXII	Terce, Tuesday	
Pss. CXXIII–CXXV	Sext, Tuesday	
Pss. CXXVI–CXXIX	None, Tuesday	
Pss. CXXX–CXXXIII	Vespers, Tuesday	
Ps. CXXXIV	"*Ad co[m]plet[orium] p[salmu]s*"[4]	
Pss. CXXXV–CXXXVIII	Vespers, Wednesday	
Pss. CXXXIX–CXLI	Vespers, Thursday	
Pss. CXLII–CXLV,1–9	Vespers, Friday	
Pss. CXLV,10–21–CXLVII	Vespers, Saturday	

Pss. CXLVIII, CXLIX, and CL are not statedly assigned; used (every day?) in the Lauds?

128v–140v: *f[eri]a ij in laud[ibus] c[anti]c[um]* Confitebor tibi . . . (= Isaiah XII) (129r:) *feria iij in laud' cca* Ego dixi ī dimidio . . . (= Isaiah XXXVIII, 10–20) (130r:) *fä iiij ī l' c̄c̄.* Exultauit cor meū in dn̄o . . . (= 1 Sam. II,1–10) (131r:) *(fä v ad laud' c̄c̄.* Cantemus dn̄o . . . (= Exodus XV, 1–19) (132r:) *fä vj in laudib[us]* Dn̄e audiui auditionē tuā . . . (= Habakkuk III, 2–19) (133v:) *Sabb' c̄c̄* Audite coeli . . . (= Deut. XXXII, 1–43) (136v:) *c̄c̄ triū puero[rum]* Benedicite omnia opera . . . (= Daniel III, 57–88.56) (137r:) *ymnus s[an]c[t]o[rum] ambrosij et augustini* Te deū laudamus . . . (138r:) *zacharie* Benedictus dn's d's israel . . . (= Luke I, 68–79) (138v:) *Cä btē marie virgis* Magnificat . . . (= Luke I, 46–55) (139r:) *c̄c̄ senex* [sic] *symeonis* Nunc dimittis . . . (= Luke II, 29–32) *simbolū athanasij* Quicunque . . . (= the Athanasian Creed, in Latin) (ends on 140v)

140v–141r: (versicle and prayer added to the Athanasian Creed)

141r–143r: *Letania.* Kyrieleyson . . .

The litany invokes, after the apostles, 5 individual martyrs, 10 confessors, and 8 women. Notable among the confessors: Edmonde, Malachia, Wilhelme . . . Roberte, Egidi; among the women: Scolastica.

143r–147v: *Incipiunt vigilie mortuo[rum] In primo noct' anthifo[nae]* (P)[3]lacebo . . .

Cistercian version of the *Officium defunctorum*; incomplete: preserved text ends in the middle of the 4th collect of the Lauds. — The office has no Invitatory; responsories: I Credo quod II Qui Lazarum III Memento mei IV Heu mihi V Ne recorderis VI Libera me Domine de vijs inferno[rum?] VII Peccante me VIII Domine secundum [actum] meum IX Libera me Domine de morte eterna

(following f. 147, one leaf wanting, with the end of the Office for the Dead and, presumably, part of the collection of invitatories, etc., which follows:)

148r: nite adorem[us] eū *Dc̄c̄ [= Dominica] ī passio[ne] īuit[atorium]* Hodie si vocē . . . *Dcc ii īuit'* Ipsi vero nō congnouerūt [sic] . . . *In die scē trinitat' īuit'* Deū verū vnū ī trinitate . . .

148r–149v: *Hy[m]n[us] . . . ad n[octurn]os . . .* (E)[5]Terne rerū conditor . . .

(148r–v: Eterne reru[m] conditor; 148v: Splendor p[ate]rne gl[ori]e; 148v–149r: IAm lucis orto sidere; 149r: Nunc s[an]c[t]e nobis sp[irit]us; also 149r: Rector potens verax deus; 149v: Reru[m] deus tenax vigor; also 149v: Deus creator omn[ium])

(following f. 149, two stubs; what follows may be the work of a different scribe, or written after a major interruption ?)

150r–151v: *Sanctorū qui proprias habent Collectas.* (a) (P)[3]Reces p[o]p[u]li tui . . . btī Marcelli . . .

Altogether 29 collects,[5] marked in the outer margin by letters of the alphabet, "a" through "x," then by lowercase roman numerals (i-viij). The collects are referred to (by their alphanumerical coding) in the calendar at the beginning of the book.

151v–153v: *Comemorationes s[an]c[t]o[rum] q[ui] p[ro]p[rias] n[on] h[abe]nt col[lectas]*

Twenty-five multiple-use formulas, marked *a-x* and *i-iiij* in outer margins; referred to from the calendar for offices of saints lacking an individualized "collect."

153v: *Hec no[m]i[n]a dicu[n]t[ur]* Tyburtij valeriani maximi Alexandri euentij & theodoli . . . Crispini [et] Crispiniani

The list gives the genitive forms of (counting "Quatuor coronatorum" as one) 34 names; presumably as an aid to good Latin.

153v–154v: *Ante psalteriū* Suscipe[r]e digneris scā trinitas hos p[salm]os . . . quos ego īdigna [et] peccatrix decantare cupio . . . debitrix extiti . . . (154r:) *Post psalteriū di[citur?]* Ne reminiscaris . . . mea vel parentū meo[rum] . . . *Coll'* Dona m[ihi] op̄s d's vt p[er] hec sacroscā psalterij celestis mella . . . *Coll'* Om[n]ip[oten]s sempiterne . . . (ends 154v:) p[er] xp̄m

This part, at least, is clearly intended for use by a woman. It seems to be intended for personal prayer, presumably before and after choir: the "decantatio" could hardly have been done privately.

154v–155r: *De s[an]c[t]a anna Inuitatoriū* Diem festū anne celebrans . . . iubilet eccl[es]ia *ymn[us]* (C)[3]lara diei gaudia modulizet ecclesia . . . ad celi ducat aditū. *Ad complet' y[m]n[us]* Chori plauda[n]t alacrit[er] . . . (155r:) . . . nos iungat celi ciuibus Amē *Ad iij y[m]n[us]* Omnis s[an]c[t]o[rum] contio . . . nos tua frui gl[ori]a Amē

Parts of a proper office of St. Anne. In the Cistercian Order, the festivity was either introduced or made a solemn one in 1454 (see note to the calendar); the special texts above were probably added to the ms. at that time. — For the hymn *Clara diei gaudia*, cf. P.-V. Charland, *Madame saincte Anne*, v. 2 (Paris, 1913), p. 631 sqq. and (incl. text) 687; *AH* LII, p. 98. Text and refs. for the hymn *Chori plaudant alacriter*: Charland, *Le culte de sainte Anne en Occident*, seconde période (Québec, 1921), p. 61; *AH* XXIII, 118.

155r: *Dit sijn die psalmē van den p[ro]fes In dē yersten die .vij. psalmē mettē letaniē* In exitu isrl' Dn̄s illumi Confitem[in]i p[ro?] B[ea]ti immaculati Quemadmodū Memēto dn̄e Ecce q[ua]m bonū Laudate dn̄m de celis Benedictus dn̄s d's isrl'

(155v blank, ruled)

* * *

Foliated in modern pencil; one paper endleaf precedes and one follows the 155 leaves of text. Following f. 6, an unnumbered (and uncounted) leaf, blank on recto, with full-page illustration on verso (see Decoration). — Written area ca. 144 × 84-89 mm. Fully ruled in light purplish ink; no pricking marks. — The script is a rather large, vertical *fere bastarda* in brownish black ink, with throughout the same peculiar combination of letter forms (including the calendar which, along with ff. 150r–155r and the rubrics, may have been written by another person).[6] The rubrics are red. — Parchment white and smooth on both sides, moderately thick (ca. 14.5 mm per 100 leaves).

Collation: 1^6; following 1_6, a singleton (conjugate stub follows 2_8; omitted in foliation) $2–12^8$ 13^4 $14–19^8$ 20^6(= ff. 147–149; 20_1, 20_2, 20_4 wanting; with 20_4, some text lost); ff. 150–151 = two singletons? (glued together in the gutter) 21^4.

Decoration: one large illustration (ca. 150 × 96 mm) on verso of the unnumbered leaf following f. 6: Crucifixion. The miniature is in a slightly arched frame made of simple bars done in (reddish) laid gold and grayish red. Three persons are depicted under the Cross: Mary, John, and

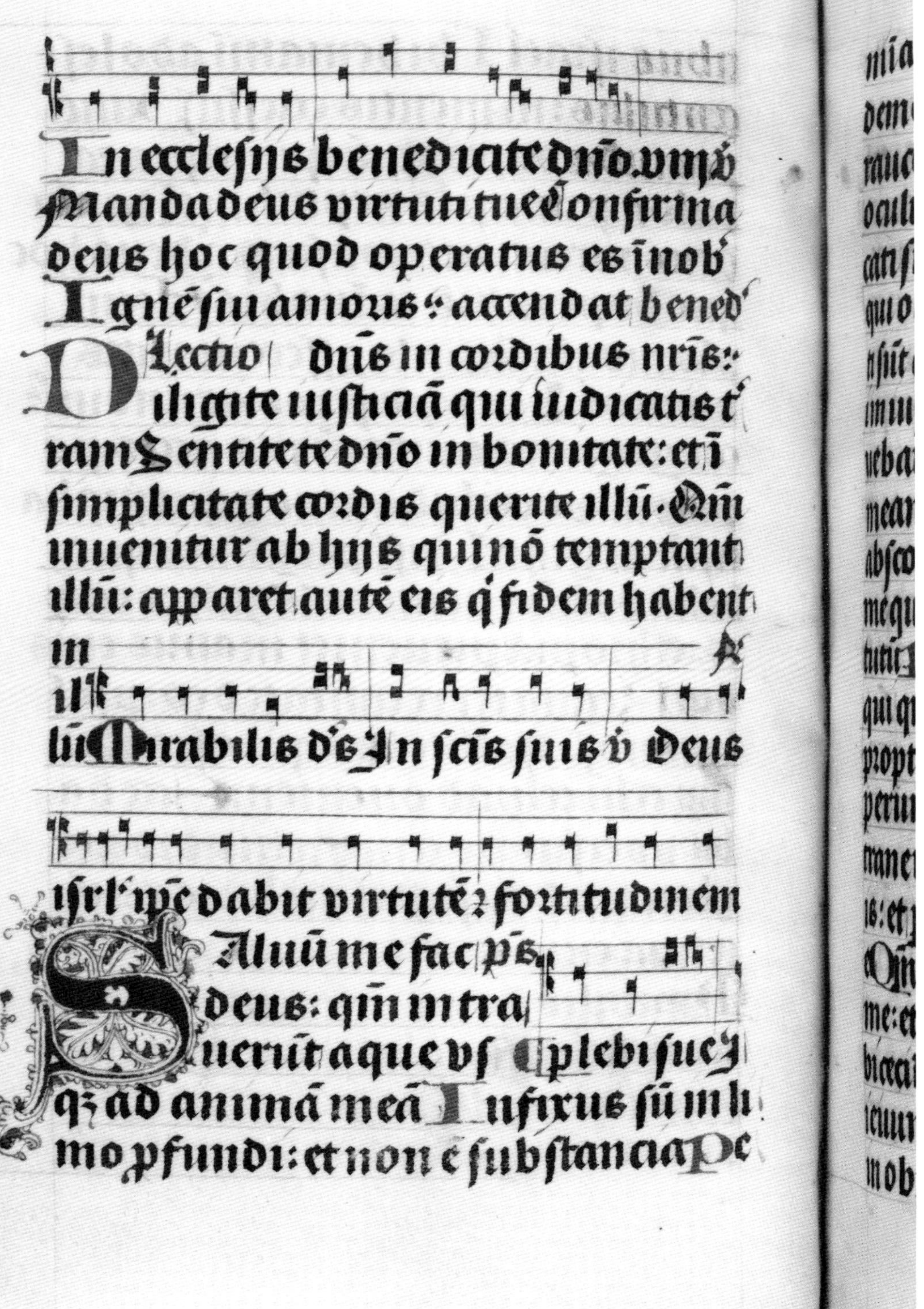

MS 24, f. 59v (actual size of written area: ca. 143 × 85 mm)

a kneeling nun in light brown tunic with darker-brown veil. — The second of the two miniatures noted in De Ricci is a historiated initial: King David with harp, in the initial *B* of the Psalter, on f. 7r. The 9-line letter is red with a gold-and-blue rim, with some additional red penwork on green ground. Neither this nor the large illustration facing the page could be called skilled work. — Other major (3–4 lines; on 77v, the capital *I/J* is 14 or 15 lines high) initials are bright red and blue combined to form the letter,[7] with red penwork botanical forms partly on green ground, both in the enclosed areas and surrounding the letters. — Two-line lombardic letters and one-line versals are alternately blue or red. Some black capitals are touched with yellow.

Bound in 18th-century vellum.

On pastedown of upper cover, in 19th- (or early 20th-) century handwriting, in red ink: "Mit 2 Miniaturen und schönen Initialen. 155 Blätter." Bookplate of Rev. Edwin A. Dalrymple, D.D. — On f. 1r in tail margin, in 19th-century Latin handwriting (blue ink): Barnheim. — At end, on recto of free endleaf, in pencil: Ac. 4560(3), n. 18/MS. 87.

Former owners: Geheim-Justizrat Barnheim (of Berlin; died 1873?); Rev. E. A. Dalrymple (Baltimore). — Acquired by LC in 1916 with the Dalrymple collection.

2° fo.: *KL Marcius habet dies . xxxj.*

Bibl.: *Bibliotheca typographica : Manuscripte, Incunabeln, Bücher . . . aus dem Nachlasse . . . Barnheim* (Berlin, 1873), no. 20 [not seen]. — De Ricci, *Census* (1935), p. 232, no. 115 (" . . . written in Germany"); Faye and Bond, p. 120, no. 87.

Netherlandish origin is at least probable, in view of the rubric on f. 155r and of the entry for July 1 in the calendar (Rumoldi; cf. Grotefend, v. 2, p. 163, also Strubbe, *Chronologie*, p. 176–177 and index). — The prayer on 153v and the kneeling nun in the Crucifixion scene facing 7r indicate an establishment of Cistercian nuns; of such, the Netherlands had several (cf. *Dict. mon. cisterc.* I(1976), map 25 sqq.). If occurrences of a similar not-very-frequent combination of script features (see note 6) in South Holland should be given weight, one Cistercian nuns' abbey to be considered is Loosduinen (f. ca. 1230; the location, with some preserved parts of the abbey church, is now part of The Hague). — The black text of the Psalter, etc., ff. 7r–149v, seems to be older than the calendar, the rubrics, and perhaps the ff. 150–155; perhaps the book was begun before mid-century and completed shortly after 1454.

NOTES

1. The Psalm numbers we are giving are those of the Hebrew (Masoretic) text, now generally preferred to those of the Vulgate (which, however, are those found in most liturgical publications until quite recently).

2. "Lectio" follows Ps. XCIV; rubric introducing the 2nd nocturn, Ps. XCV; one or the other is probably misplaced.

3. The expected rubric isn't there, presumably through inadvertence of the scribe.

4. Probably preceded by Pss. IV and XCI as generally in the Benedictine (and Cistercian) Compline but our ms. doesn't say so.

5. A "collect" (in Latin *collecta*) is a rather formal prayer standardly introduced by "Oremus" and concluded by a trinitarian "Per Dominum . . . in saecula saeculorum. Amen." For each occasion (such as feast of a particular saint) there tends to be just one, used both in the Mass and in the breviary office; in the latter, in each "hour."

6. One-lobed *a*; initial and median *s* modestly long-shaft (descending below base line); a peculiar final *s* shaped as an inverted two-lobed "a"; all stems kept nearly vertical and with endings between semiquadrate and *rotunda*; uncial *d* without upper loop; *g* with open lower curve ending in an almost straight horizontal; tironian *[et]* crossed, narrow, with lower half quadrated to balance the upper half. — A similar combination can be found in some manuscripts from South Holland (e.g., the *Horae* of ca. 1440 from Delft, ms. 74 G 35 of the Royal Library in 's-Gravenhage; see its *Schatten van de Koninklijke Bibliotheek* (1980), p. [180]).

7. But light blue by itself, well ornamented by white void, etc., occurs: 143r, (P)[3]lacebo; 150r, (P)[3]Reces.

MS 25

(Faye and Bond 91)

GRADUAL (winter portion of the seasonal part) XVth c.

Northern Italy? Parchment. 213 leaves, ca. 578 × ca. 420 mm (bound volume: ca. 620 × ca. 450 mm) 1 column. 6 lines (over each line of text, a 4-line musical staff)

ff. 1r–211v: (A)[2]D te leuaui . . .

Mass propers (words and music) for the seasonal celebrations from the first Sunday of Advent to the Monday of Holy Week;[1] beginning without caption. Folios 1r–28r cover the Advent season (4 Sundays plus the Vigil of Christmas), incl. the *Quattuor Tempora* (9v–24r, with a form of the *Song of the Three* from the deuterocanonical Daniel on 19v–22r); on 28r–37v, the three Masses of Christmas, followed (37v–53r) by what is actually the Christmastide part of the Sanctoral: the feasts of Stephen, John the Evangelist, the Innocents, Thomas à Becket, and Silvester. Circumcision is called (55v) "*In octava nativitatis Domini.*" — 56v–49r, Epiphany. — With "*Dominica iiii[a] post epyphaniam*" (69v), rubric directing that the same "officium" (in this case, = Mass) "*dicitur per omnes dominicas usque ad septuagesimam*" (Septuagesima: 69v–74r). — Ash Wednesday ("*Feria iii[a] Cinerum*", 82r sqq.) includes choir parts for the blessing and distribution of the ashes (82r–85r). — There is a special Mass for each day of Lent. — Palm Sunday (190r sqq.) includes the choir parts for the blessing of the palms and for the procession (*Pueri Hebraeorum*, 192v sqq.; *Gloria laus et honor,* 198v sqq.) — On 209r–211v, Monday of Holy Week. — Some of the carefully and handsomely written rubrics (e.g., the long one on f. 83r) read as if directed to the celebrant instead of to the choir: they may have been excerpted from an ordinal or similar book. — Rubrics which refer to a particular numbered folio indicate that the "folio" number, written always on verso, halfway down the page in the outer margin, was understood to stand for the opening (the two pages visible at one time) rather than for a leaf.[2]

211v–213v: Gloria Patri . . . (ends, 213v:) . . . seculorum. Amen.

(Not captioned; not signaled as new matter.) Series of 8 tunes for the *Gloria Patri*, with the text repeated in full each time.

* * *

Foliated on versos in large red roman numerals placed in the center of fore-edge margin, next to or partly obscuring identical numbers in smaller script written in faint black ink as guides. — The pastedowns are paper; no free endleaves. — Written area (including the musical notation) ca. 420 × ca. 297 mm. Blind-ruled for the text lines, originally perhaps also for the music staves; vertical framing lines in lead, simple, reaching to head and tail edges. No pricking preserved. Evidence of cropping in the tail margin. — Written apparently by one person throughout, with the possible exception of smaller-size (minims 5–6 mm) rubrics; prevailing script is an extremely large (minims ca. 16 mm) *littera Bononiensis*, done very skillfully, with some elegant embellishments.[3] — The (4-line) musical staves are red; the (square) notation is done with care.[4] — The "fa" clef is used more often than in modern editions, sometimes (e.g., 119r) in conjunction with the "do" clef. The "natural" sign (the sign canceling a *B* flat) is elaborate, decorative. — Some parchment repairs done after signature marking.

Collation: a-z^{8}(= ff. 1–184) [aa-cc]^{8} [dd]$^{6-1}$ (dd$_{6}$ absent without text loss). — Remnants of signatures written in ink in lower right corners, cropped in varying degree; the signer used (at least through *z*) cursive alphabet with cursive roman numerals.

Decoration: Four historiated initials: 1r, God speaking to David (ca. 145 × ca. 163 mm); 28v, Nativity (ca. 143 × 170 mm) (see plate X, p. xxv); 34v, Mary (kneeling) with the Child in a garden (ca. 129 × ca. 155 mm); 37v, St. Stephen (80 × 85 mm). — These, and three other illuminated initials which lack a representational element (on 41vr, 44r, 56v), share following characteristics: the body of the letter is purple and set in a roughly rectangular laid-gold field outlined in black; stemless foliate branches in various combinations of green, red, blue, orange, and/or purple, with some gold, issue from one or more corners of the field. In the largest initials, the purple letter is decorated with penwork in white ink or paint.[5] — The four paintings are multicolor, late medieval in style, moderately skillful work. Stephen's vestment (37v) is orange. The other three illuminated letters introduce the Mass propers of John the Evangelist, the Innocents, and Epiphany (56v, emphasized by the size of the initial); they are filled with foliate shapes in various colors, somewhat Renaissance-style, unimpressive. — Most Mass propers (provided they have an Introit of their own) are introduced by a ca. 65 mm high initial without gold: a large red (31 red ones) or blue (26 such) lombard, with stems or other wide sections divided by void white, with added penwork decoration often including musical staves, and some colors (red, pale yellow, blue, green) used to bring out foliate shapes in void white. — Versals are alternately red or blue. — With both the large and the smaller initials, the letter immediately following tends to be a capital, done in cadel style and decorated by subtly and skillfully drawn pen flourishes in diluted ink, subsequently touched up with pale yellow;[6] in some cases, the letter is filled with boxing-glove acanthus brought out by use of some amount of red ground.

Bound in contemporary covers sewn over 7 leather bands; rebacked in more recent period. The striking original covers are reddish brown goat over wooden boards heavily protected and decorated by sheet metal (brass?) around all edges, with added hexagonal spike-like projections, 19 per cover; on the surface of each cover, 5 hexagonal bosses protruding from octagonal rosettes; also trefoils and 4 eight-point stars. The metalwork is strong, somewhat crude; the overall impression being that of armor. — Two heavy leather straps, front-to-back, with metal reinforcements fitting over pins rising from triangular metal pieces on the

MS 25 lower cover. — The goatskin of the covers is also (blind-)stamped with fleurons forming a large rosette around the central metal ornaments, and tooled with a roll (not in Haebler) creating a large rectangular frame close to the scalloped protective metal; a row of fleurons of same type as those used for the central rosette further broadens the frame. — The leather of the spine, more recent, is dark brown. — A contemporary vellum label (ca. 25 × 64 mm) is nailed to the lower cover near tail edge; the partly damaged title inscription (in 15th-century script) reads: Gradu[a]le fe[ria]le ab aduētu//ad q[uartam] fe[riam] maio[ris hebdomade].

On pastedown of upper cover: (in pencil:) 3266; (in ink, on label:) A//I.//10; also other numbers in pencil. Pencil inscription: Graduale for Dominical Service from Advent to Palm Sunday. — On f. 1r, in upper right corner, embossed in a circle: MSS. Div. L.C.; penciled over it: Ac. 4560(6)//741. On 1v, in tail margin, penciled: 90115//ob.

Former owners: Samuel Whitaker Pennypacker (b. 1843, d. 1916); acquired by LC at his sale, April 1906 (see Bibl. below)

2° fo.: (under uppermost musical staff:) domine. *v. UI*

Bibl.: Stan. V. Henkel, *The extraordinary library of Hon. Samuel W. Pennypacker* . . . [Philadelphia, 1905-9], pt. 2 (sale Philadelphia, 25 Apr. 1906), no. 409 (with color facsims.) (not seen) — De Ricci, *Census* (1935), p. 235, no. 119; Faye and Bond, p. 120, no. 91.

NOTES

1. Or, part of the *temporale* of a Gradual.
2. E.g., rubric on 127v refers to a "fo. cxv"; the text and music referred to are on f. 116r (the number "cxv" is written on 115v). — N.B. In our description we have used these numbers as if they were meant to designate the leaves (recto and verso) on which they are written.
3. Such as a slightly broadened seven-o'clock end of the letter *x*. — The thin strokes are extremely thin and extend beyond the needed length (e.g., in the letter *e*).
4. Basic standard note is a square *punctum*; in a recitative, more often the *punctum inclinatum*. — A particularity is an engrailed-line grouping of identical two to four notes assembled together without free spaces in between, used at end of some phrases (where modern Solesmes books tend to use a punctum with added dot). — Extensive use is made of the *semibrevis* pause, written, as other pauses, in red.
5. The penwork is puzzlingly suggestive of a mixture of Greek and Latin alphabets or conventional signs. With imagination, one can read, e.g., on 28v, to the left of the Nativity scene: "Dixit ei ne timeas . . . " — ?
6. A frequently occurring shape is cusp; on 56v the flourisher produced a face in profile.

MS 26

(Faye and Bond 81)

MISSAL (use of Utrecht) 1451

Written in the Netherlands ("Hollandia"). Parchment. 295 leaves, ca. 370[1] × ca. 280[2] mm (bound volume: ca. 397 × ca. 310 mm) 2 columns. 33 lines (in the Canon, 22 lines; on music pages, 11 staves)

SUMMARY CONTENTS: ff. 3r–5v calendar; 6rv blessing of water, exorcism of salt; 7r–127v the *temporale* from beginning of Advent through Corpus Christi; 127v–142v votive and occasional Masses; 142v–143r two versions of Gloria, Credo; 143r–157v celebrant's *Kyriale* and prefaces with music; 158v Ordinary; 158v–160v prefaces without music; 161r–166r the Canon; 167r–200r the rest of the *temporale* from Corpus Christi to Advent; 201r–264v the *sanctorale*; 265r–278r the commons; 278r–292v a collection of liturgical *sequentiae*; 293r–295v blank.

CONTENTS IN DETAIL: (f. 1r: inscriptions; see in descriptive part at end)

1v–2r: LATE ADDITION (dated at end): 22 long staves of music (hastily drawn freehand, 4-line stave, individual notes roughly crescent-shape), i.e., the chant for the gospel of Nativity B.V.M. (not so or otherwise captioned),[3] Matthew I,1–16: D[omi]n[u]s Vobiscum . . . Liber g[e]n[er]ationis . . . qui vocatur x^{s}//1501. (2v blank, ruled only vertically)

3r–5v: Liturgical calendar of Utrecht, in black and red: 216 entries, of them 51 in red. Includes *Annorum Domini* for May 5, *Translacio Martini* July 4, *Victoris* (without "et Gereonis") Oct. 10; *Willibrordi epī*, Nov. 7, is in red (this doesn't seem standard for Utrecht);[4] no Visitation. — Cursive additions of uncertain date (but no doubt made before 1577) for May 9 (Macharii), 10 (Job), 15 (Digne uirg.), 16 (Theobaldi epī); also for June 3 (Erasmi).[5]

6r–v: *Ad aqua[m] b[e]n[e]dicenda[m]. versicl's.* Adiutoriu[m] n[ost]r[u]m . . . *Exorcism[us] salis* . . . (ends 6vb, line 14:) Amen. (6vb, lines 16–33, LATER ADDITIONS: In co[m]me[m]oracione sacramenti q[ua]n[do] no[n] cantat[ur] alleluya Int[ro]it[us] Salus p[o]p[u]li ego su[m] . . . [another hand? :] Vel sic[ut] i[n] lxx[ma] . . . Ego su[m] panis viuus . . . [another hand:] Tractus Laudate d[omi]n[u]m o[mn]es gentes . . . sup[er] nos m[isericord]ia eius)[6]

7r–127v: *D[omi]nica prima adue[n]t[us]. Int[ro]itus.* (A)^{10}D te leuaui . . . (Christmas, 14v sqq.; Epiphany, 20v sq.; 30va: . . . *In capite ieiunij* . . .; Palm Sunday, 69r sqq.; Easter Sunday, 103r sq.; Ascension, 115v sq.; Pentecost, 120v sq.; Trinity, 126v; Corpus Christi, called "*De sacramento*," 127r–v; ends in 127vb, lines 4–5:) percepcio prefigurat. Qui viuis.

The *temporale* (= "proper of the seasons") from Advent to Corpus Christi inclusive (see ff. 167r–200r for the remaining part

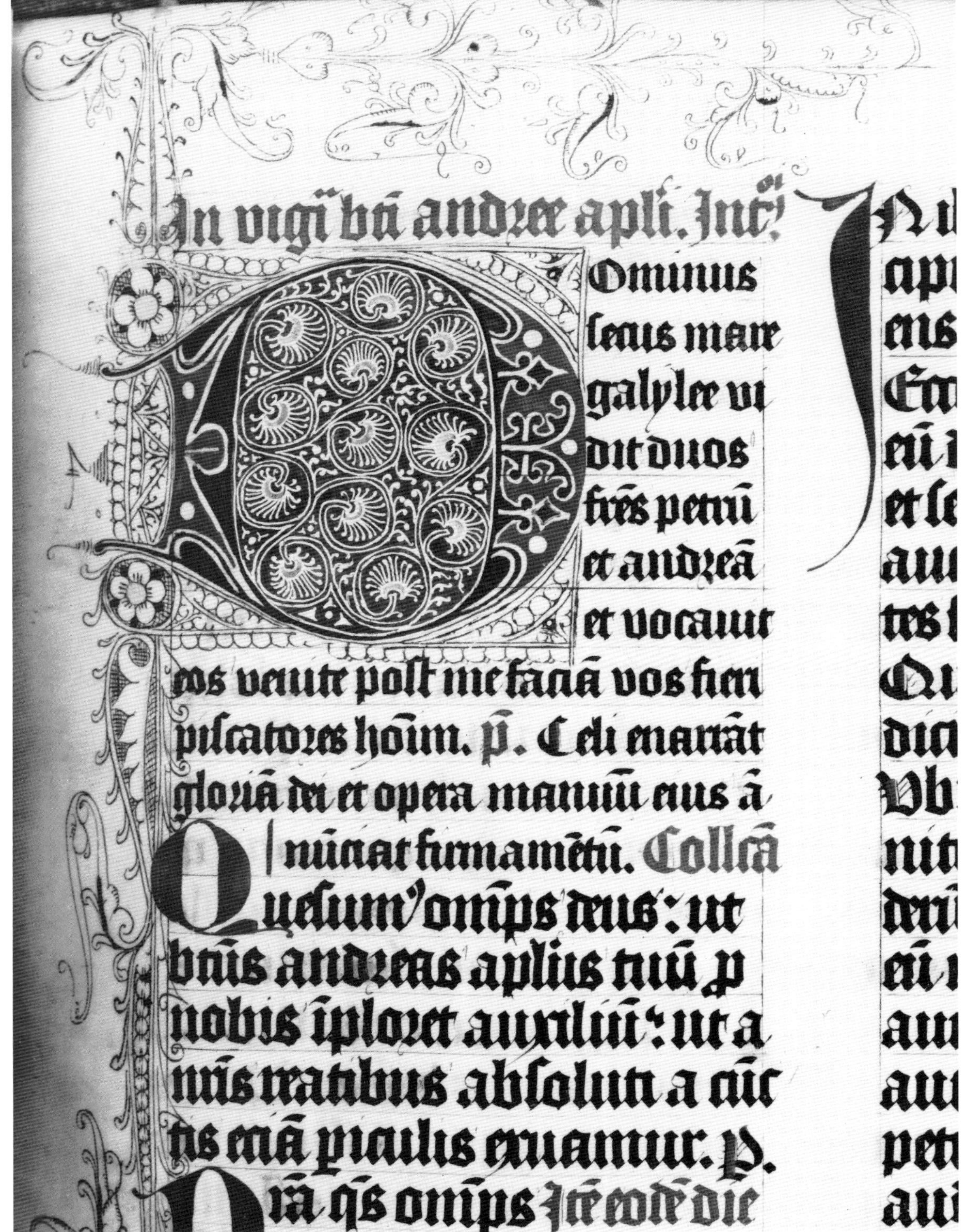

MS 26, f. 201r, upper left quadrant (beginning of the sanctoral) (actual size of area shown: ca. 175 × 125 mm)

of the year). As is the case with other major segments of this Missal, the section carries no title; it is, however, signaled by the large (and ornate) initial *A*. — The first Sunday of Advent is assigned the gospel pericope *Cum appropinquassent* (Matthew XXI,1–9). The three Christmas Masses have 3 readings each: the universally used epistle pericopes from Titus and Hebrews are preceded, in the Mass *In primo galli cantu,* by Isaiah IX,2–7, in that *In aurora* by Is. LXI, 1–3 + LXII,11–12; *Ad summam Missam* has Is. LII,6–10. — Stephen, John the Evangelist, and the Innocents are all included in this part, following Christmas.[7] — There are three Sundays "post octavam Epyphanie"; after them, "Dominica vacante" (25v), followed by *i[n] lxx[ma]* [= Septuagesima]. — With the blessing of the palms, an interesting preface, ff. 70vb–72ra (with music[8]). On 73ra, hymn *Magno salutis gaudio* (variant of *AH* LI, no. 74,[9] stanzas 1–5 and 13). — The Passion according to John on Good Friday (88r) is read "absque titulo." Holy Saturday ceremonies include (93v) hymn *Inventor rutuli* [i.e., rutili] (*AH* L, no. 31), stanzas 1–5, 7, and 12; after each, the first stanza is repeated, antiphon-style. — The Litany of Saints of Holy Saturday, 98vb–100ra, lists after Mary, angels, patriarchs, apostles, etc., 15 individual martyrs (last 2 are "Bonifati cu[m] so. t." and "Ponciane"), 13 confessors (after Nicolas: Willibrorde, Benedicte, Egidi, Lebuine, Odulphe, Wyro), 10 women (none unusual). — Music is included also with the *Popule meus*, etc., on Good Friday (91v,92r), with the *Exultet* (94r–96v), other Holy Saturday rites (100r–102v). — The last formal prayer of most Masses (the "Postcommunio" of Roman books) is throughout captioned as "*complenda*" (mostly abbreviated).

127v–142v: (beginning 127vb, 5th line:) *In co[m]me[m]oracio[n]e scī spi[ritu]s.* (S)[3]piritus dn̄i . . . (ending 142va, first 2 lines:) (par)ticipes. Qui viuis et regnas [et]c.

Not signaled by caption or major initial, a section of *commemorationes* (of Holy Spirit, the Cross, Our Lady, through 130v); followed by votive and occasional Masses: *De angelis, Pro quacumque tribulatione, Pro pace, Contra mortalitatem, Pro peccatis, Pro infirmo, "Generalis collecta de omnibus sanctis"* (what is provided for this and ca. 20 further themes is not a whole proper; rather, a set of the three prayers *collecta, secreta, complenda*, the last one equivalent to Roman *postcommunio*), . . . *Pro stabilitate loci*[10], *Pro concordia fratrum, . . . Item generalis collecta* (the set on 136vb–137va; the collect itself, beginning "Pietate tua quesumus Domine nostrorum solve omnium vincula delictorum," is extraordinarily long, occupying 37 lines). — On 138ra–142va, Masses for the dead, beginning with *In anniuersario et exequiis defunctorum*; signaled by a 4-line initial *R* (Requiem . . .). Altogether 19 variants; that captioned *In commemoracione defunctorum*, beginning on 138va, has introit *Si enim credimus* . . . and includes variant sets of readings for various days of the week. The collection includes (f. 141rv) *Pro in congregacione defunctis* and *Pro elemosinatoribus defunctis* (". . . quorum sustentamur elemosinis . . .")

142v–143r: (beginning without signal in 3rd line of 142va:) *De d[omi]na n[ost]ra.* Gloria in excelsis deo . . . (an interpolated version of the *Gloria* of the Mass, with Marian statements,[11] followed by the standard version; then, 142vb:) Credo in vnu[m] deu[m] . . . (ending 143ra, 10th line:) . . . (se)culi. Amen.

143r–157v: (beginning 143ra, after empty line 11:) *In summis festis.* Kyrie *fons bo[n]itatis* leyson . . . (143vb:) . . . (P)[4]Er om[n]ia secula seculo[rum] . . . (ends 157vb, last line:) (con)fessione dicentes.

Section of music. With the exception of *Kyrie eleison*[12] (for which the book offers 10 tunes) everything here is for the celebrant's use: 11 intonations of *Ite Missa est*, 7 of *Gloria,* 2 of *Credo*; followed by 34 *praefationes* (actually only 11 textually different "prefaces" with the various modes of singing them according to liturgical rules).

(158r blank, framed-ruled)

MS 26 158v–160v: (I)[8]N no[m]i[n]e patris . . . Quid retribua[m] dn̄o . . . Calice[m] salutaris . . . In sp[irit]u hu[m]ilitatis . . . Veni i[n]uisibilis s[an]c[t]ificator . . . Suscipe sca̅ trinitas . . . Orate pro me pecc[at]ore fratres et sorores . . . (P)[3]Er om[n]ia secula scl̅'o[rum] . . . VEre dignu[m] . . . (160va:) . . . Sanctus . . . Dn̄e ih'u xp̄e adiuua i[n]firmitate[m] mea[m] et conforta me in hac hora quia i[m]perfectu[m] meu[m] oculi mei uident.[13] Adoramus te xp̄e . . . Qui passus es pro nobis miserere nostri.[14] (160vb blank, ruled)

Part of the order of Mass (uncaptioned); what is included appears to cover the section between the readings and the Canon. On ff. 158vb–160r, 11 prefaces, same set as on 143v–157v but here without music. — Some of the texts differ considerably from those of the Curia missal and the Tridentine *Missale Romanum*; to a degree they resemble the Premonstratensian rite (cf. *EEFL* 3307, 3308).

(Following f. 160, an irregular stub suggesting that a leaf, perhaps one with the image of Crucifixion traditionally placed to face the beginning of the Canon, has been torn out)

161r–166r: (T)[7+]E igitur . . . (ending in penultimate line of 166rb with end of the prayer *Placeat*:) (seculo)rum. Amen.

The Canon (central part) of the Mass. The 11 pages are ruled for and written in large script (22 lines); on ff. 163v–164v, musical notation (chant) for the Lord's Prayer (in "nota solempnis" and "ferialis"). — Texts differing from the Roman canon begin after the *Agnus Dei* (165r): Fiat hec commixtio et consecracio . . . omnibus nobis sumentibus salus mentis et corporis in vitam eternam. . . . Pax tibi et ecclesie Dei. Habete vinculum pacis et caritatis ut apti sitis sacrosanctis mysteriis Christi. Amen. . . . (165v:) Corpus Domini nostri Iesu Christi custodiat animam meam et corpus meum in vitam eternam . . . (with the chalice, same request).

167r–200r: *D[omi]nica p[ri]ma p[ost] oct[avam] penthecostes* (D)[7]Omine in tua mi[sericordi]a speraui . . . (section ends 200rb, penultimate line:) (omni)bus dico: uigilate. (200v blank, ruled)

Second part of the *temporale*, for the time after Pentecost. Propers for 1st-22nd Sunday;[15] followed by (198v) "*Dominica vacante*", and (199v) "*Dominica xxiij*". — The series has, compared with that of the Curia missal[16] or the later *Missale Romanum*, interesting particularities. The series of Gospel pericopes is, as more or less expected, non-Roman (agreeing with that listed as variant *epsilon* of the sequence found in "non-Beneventan" manuscripts by Dom Hesbert in *PALÉOGRAPHIE MUSICALE XIV*, p. 132[17]); more interestingly, the combinations of texts in the individual propers are different: the Introit, Epistle, Gradual, Offertory, and the Communion antiphon are for each numbered Sunday those assigned to the Sunday of same number (albeit "after Pentecost") in the Curia missal; they are, however, combined with the *collecta, secreta*, "complenda" (= *postcommunio*) and, for Sundays numbered in our Missal as 5th though 22nd, also the Gospel of what is in the Curia missal the Sunday immediately preceding.[18] (The Gospel pericopes for the 1st-4th Sunday are Luke XVI, 19–31; Luke XIV, 16–24; Luke XV, 1–10; and Luke VI, 36–42, *Estote misericordes*.) — The "Dominica xxiij" (the last of the series here) has, with Introit *Dicit Dominus ego cogito*, a collect which is not included in either the Curia or Tridentine missals (199va): Excita Domine potentiam tuam et veni et quod Ecclesiae tuae promisisti usque in finem saeculi clementer operare. (Epistle Jeremiah XXIII, 5–8, Gospel John VI, 5–14, *Cum sublevasset;* the "complenda": Animae nostrae . . . velut clara lumina fulgeamus.) — Unlike either Roman book, the section includes also a set of readings (Epistle and Gospel) for every Wednesday and a Gospel pericope for every Friday of the season.

201r–264v: *In vigi[lia] bti̅ andree apl'i. Int[r]oi[tus]*. (D)[7]Ominus secus mare galylee . . . (264vb:) . . . ut perpetue uite sumentibus p[ro]curent substanciam: p[er]. (last 11 lines of 264vb empty)

The *sanctorale* ("proper of the saints"), from the Vigil of St. Andrew to *Lini pape et martyris,*[19] followed (263r sqq.) by *In dedicacione ecclesie* and *In dedicacionę altaris.* — The collection contains 166 primary (captioned) formularies ("propers"[20]) and over 40 commemorations; of the former, 13 are not in the calendar at the beginning of the book; of the saints given here a commemoration, the calendar names only 6. Among the saints not named in the calendar: *Marij et Marthe* (205v); *Severi ep[isco]pi* (208rv); Walburgis (comm., 217v sqq.); unidentified martyrs remembered on the day of St. Servacius (220v–221r); Mildrada, commemorated with Margaret (232v–233r); Plechelmus, Bp. (of Utrecht), with the Division of Apostles, 233rv; *Otgeri* (247v); *Mauricii et soc.* (250rv); St. Gereon ("*Gereonis, Victoris et al.*" while the calendar names only Victor); Felicitatis (comm., on the day of St. Clement, 261v–262r).[21] — The *In conceptione btē marie v̄gis*, 203rb, otherwise "sicut in Nativitate eius," has own collect: Deus qui beate Marie Virginis conceptionem angelico vaticinio parentibus eius predixisti . . .[22] — The *Purificatio*, 209r–211v, includes music for the blessing of candles. — Liturgical ranking of the various festivities is not specified (here or in the calendar), at most occasionally suggested by (unsystematically applied) decoration. — Marginal addition on f. 222r, corresponding to entry added in the calendar, observes: Tertia Junii celebratur festum (diui?) Erasmi; de hoc tenebitur missa . . . ut . . . in communi notatum est . . .

265r–278r: *In iugilia vnius ap[osto]li.* ***Introit[us].*** **(E)^{8}Go aut[em] sicut oliua fructificaui . . .** (265va:) ***In die sa[n]cto*** **(M)^{3}Ichi aute[m] nimis . . .** (278ra:) **. . . et celestibus nos semper instruant alimentis.//P[er].** (rest of line blank)

The "commons" (uncaptioned; standard Latin term is *Commune Sanctorum*). Some offer a choice of readings: that for an apostle, 5 alternate Epistles and 5 Gospels; *De uno martyre non pontifice,* 4 of each; "*De martiribus*" (*Sancti tui Domine* . . . , 269rb sqq.) includes 9 Epistles, 6 Gospels; etc.

278r–292v: **(beginning in penultimate line of** 278ra:) ***De natiuitate dn̄i nr̄i ihesu xpristi*** [sic]. ***In prima missa.*** (278rb:) **(C)^{7}Ongaude[n]t angeloru[m] chori . . .** (section ends 292vb, 16th line:) **(ipsum genuit puer)pera.**

A collection of 56 liturgical *sequentiae* (hymn-like prosodic creations used between readings on certain high feasts).[23] All have red captions indicating their use (almost always "*De* . . . " or "*In* . . . "). Texts only (no music). Included are:

OCCASION	INITIUM	*AH* vol., number
Christmas		
night	Congaudent angelorum chori	LIII, 104
daybreak	Eia recolamus laudibus piis	LIII, 16
in the day	Natus ante saecula Dei filius	LIII, 15
Stephen	Hanc concordi famulatu	LIII, 215
John Ev.	Iohannes Iesu Christo multum dilecte	LIII, 168
Innocents	Laus tibi Christe cui sapit quod	LIII, 156
Epiphany	Festa Christi omnis christianitas	LIII, 29
Agnes	Laus sit regi gloriae	LV, 51
Paul's Conversion	Dixit Dominus ex Basan	(Walther, *Initia* 4651)
Candlemas	Concentu parili	LIII, 99
Easter		
Sunday	Laudes Salvatori voce modulemur	LIII, 36
Mon.&Wed.	Laudes Christo redempti voce	LIII, 45
Other days	Victimae paschali	LIV, 7
Sunday before Ascension	Mane prima sabbati surgens	LIV, 143
De spinea corona Domini	Speciali gloria cunctis	XXXIV, 24
Johannis ante portam Latinam	Verbum Dei de Deo natum	LV, 188
Ascension	Summi triumphum regis	LIII, 67
Pentecost ("et in octava")	Sancti Spiritus adsit nobis gratia	LIII, 70
Mon., Wed., "et ceteris feriis"	Veni Sancte Spiritus	LIV, 153
Tues. after Pent.	Veni Spiritus eternorum alme	LIII, 71
In die sacramenti	Lauda Syon Saluatorem	L, 385
Trinity	Benedicta semper sancta	LIII, 81
John the Baptist	Sancti Baptistae Christi preconis	LIII, 163
Peter and Paul	Petre summe Christi pastor	LIII, 210
Visitation	Veni praecelsa domina Maria	LIV, 193
In translacione sc̄i Martini	Ave summa praesulum	LIII, 182
Division of Apostles	Celi enarrant gloriam Dei Filii	L, 267
Mary Magdalen	Laus tibi Christe qui es creator	L, 268

OCCASION	INITIUM	*AH* vol., number
James	Gaudeat Hispania totaque Germania	LV, 173
Anne	Testamento veteri Anna fuit genita	(VIII, 101?)
Lawrence	Laurenti Dauid magni martyr milesque	LIII, 173
Assumption	Congaudent angelorum ("Require ante, de Natiuitate Domini")	(LIII, 104)
Infra octavam	Ave Maria ("ut infra")	
In octava	Ave praeclara maris stella	L, 241
Bartholomew	Eya Christo cantica nostra	LV, 87
Augustine	Interni festi gaudia	LV, 74
Beheading of John	Psallite regi nostro psallite	L, 270
Nativity B.V.M.	Stirpe Maria regia procreata	LIII, 95
In exaltacione sc̄e crucis	Laudes crucis attollamus	LIV, 120
Michael	Summi regis archangele	LIII, 192
Undecim millium virginum	Virginalis turma sexus	LV, 333
All Saints	Omnes sancti seraphim	LIII, 112
Martin	Sacerdotem Christi Martinum cuncta	LIII, 181
Elizabeth	Laude [sic, for *Gaude*] Syon	LV, 120
Catherine	Katherine virginis vita felix	IX, p. 196
Andrew	Deus in tua virtute	LIII, 122
In dedicacione ecclesie	Psallat ecclesia mater illibata	LIII, 247
De apostolis	Clare sanctorum senatus apostolorum	LIII, 228
De ewangelistis	Iocundare plebs fidelis	LV, 7
De martiribus	Agone triumphali militum regis summi	LIII, 229
Item de martiribus	O beata beatorum martyrum sollemnia	LV, 14
De uno confessore	Ad laudes Salvatoris ut mens	LIV, 88
De una virgine	Virginis venerandae de numero	LIII, 246
De domina nostra feriis secundis et quintis	Ave Maria gratia plena Dominus	LIV, 216
In commemoratione de dn̄a nr̄a feriis tertiis et sextis	Inviolata intacta et casta	(Walther, *Initia* 9556)
De dn̄a nr̄a feriis iiij^{is} et sabb.	Verbum bonum et suave personemus	LIV, 218
De dn̄a nr̄a a pascha usque ad pent.	Virgini Marie laudes intonent	LIV, 18
De dn̄a nr̄a post Nativitatem Dni	Laetabundus exultet fidelis chorus	LIV, 2

(292vb, beginning in line 19, INSCRIPTION IN ANOTHER HAND, cursive:) Anno dni millesimo q[ua]dringentesi[m]o quinq[ua]gesimo p[ri]mo script[us] fuit iste liber a q[ua]dam moniali ([inserted, by same writer?:] in hollandia) [et] vendit[us] ecclesie ter mare pro decem [et] octo nobilib[us] aureis p[ro]curato[r]ib[us] fabrice ecclesie dn̄o Symone blieck (OR vlieck?) Curato et Johan[n]ne heynrici de Oesterlant vasallo comitis Qui curat[us] institut[us] erat p[ro]cu[r]ator p[er] an[n]u[m] ea de causa vt eme[re]t nouu[m] missale. (one line empty, then ADDED BY ANOTHER WRITER,[24] also in cursive:) Anno d[omi]nice incarnacionis 1503 Aprilis XV^{a} empta et co[m]parata fuit v[ene]r[a]bilissimi sacrame[n]ti siboria argentea quatuordecim libris decem solidis mo^{n}. flandrie, dn̄o Daniele corn[elio?] de Goes h[ui]us eccl[es]ie curato et fabrice p[ro]curatorib[us] Jacobo Joh[ann]is comiti et cornelio petro Joh[ann]is al[ia]s meerhouct(?).[25]

(293r–295r blank, fully ruled; following f. 293, irregular stub of a torn-out leaf conjugate with f. 294)

(295v, LATE ADDITION IN CURSIVE; probably by the writer who added the last note on 292v:) Missa de sancta Anna. Introit[us] Gaudeam[us] o[mn]es in dn̄o . . . (26 long lines, ending:) . . . filium tuu[m] (etc.?)[26]

On pastedown of lower cover (hybrid script, strong black ink[27]): In co[m]memoracione b[ea]te Anne . . . (Alleluiatic verse *Anna mater genitricis Dei*, Offertory antiphon *Felix namque es mater*, Communion antiphon *Ave regine celorum mater*; in a different hand, note referring to earlier section for the sequence *Testamento Veteri*).

* * *

Foliated in modern pencil (numbering includes everything except pastedowns). — Written area of the main text ca. 265[28] × ca. 180 mm. — Fully ruled in faint black ink; all verticals and, of the horizontals, two at top and two at bottom reach to edges.[29] Almost no pricking preserved (rarely some for the verticals, at tail edge). — Written in a fully quadrate liturgical *textura*, slightly (ca. 0.7 mm) above ruled line, primary text probably all by one person. In most of the text, two sizes of script are used: larger for the formal prayers and for readings, smaller for antiphonal matter; in the Canon (ff. 161–166), extra large script (minims ca. 8 mm). — Black, non-browning ink with tendency to rub off on the flesh-side pages. — Red used for captions; in the Canon and occasionally elsewhere also for rubrical directions which, far from copious, are generally written in black and signaled by red underscoring. On music pages, the staff is red. For the 2-line *litterae notabiliores* used for minor initia, red alternates with (ultramarine) blue.[30] — Parchment of fair quality, buckling, sometimes dirtied by the powdering ink, also stained. Thickness of text block at point of maximum compression near spine under 8 cm (ca. 28 mm per 100 leaves).

Collation: $1^{2?}$(= ff. 1–2) $2^{4?}$(= ff. 3–6) $4–20^{8}$ 21^{10}(= ff. 151–160; + poorly cut stub following f. 160 with conjugate straight-cut stub preceding f. 151 where no text is lost: singleton with illus. lost following f. 160?) 22^{6}(= ff. 161–166) $23–25^{8}$ 26^{10}(= ff. 191–200) $27–37^{8}$ 38^{4}(= ff. 289–292) 39^{4}(= ff. 293–295, blank; 39_{2} following f. 293 wanting, probably blank). — Catchwords or phrases, partly cropped, on last versos of most gatherings; some remnants of mostly cropped medieval signing in lower right corner of some first rectos (f. 119r, 127r, 135r, 143r, 233r, 249r, 281r).

Decoration may have originally included a full-page representation of the Crucifixion (following f. 160, facing the opening lines of the Canon); in the present state of the book it is limited to ornamental initials and several modest borders done chiefly by penwork. — The major initials (on ff. 7r, 16v, 103r, 115v, 120v, 169r, 201r, 265r, 278r), all with the letters in divided blue and red, have the enclosed areas infilled with reddish brown ground; on it, rather subtle and charming designs in painted white (phyllomorphic, and of several distinctive types); size varies from 5 to 10 lines. Atypical initial *T* of the Canon (f. 161ra; letter also divided red and blue) is large but undistinguished; void white plantlike shapes outlined in red ink on green ground. All are further adorned by flourishing (blue or purple and red) and borders, some entirely in penwork, some (7r, 16v, 103r, 120v) making use of one or two brownish red vertical bars and small foliate or bell-shape connectors done in brushed gold from which further flourishing issues; the borders always enter the head and tail margins but encircle the writing completely only on 7r and 161r. — Applied with less clear logic than the major ones, the 30-odd minor initials, 3-4 lines in height, come in two types: the more important ones (on 14v, 20v, 126v, 127r, 138r, 143v, 211r, 230r, 241v, 246v, 257v, 263r, 275v, 280v) are divided blue and red; the rest usually blue with void white shapes. Enclosed areas are infilled with penwork varying from small yellow-center blossoms (Epiphany, 20v) to rather run-of-the-mill red ink patterns. Conspicuous and felicitous is the use of a dense (blue) grid pattern as ground for the infilling in some of these initials (127r, 257v, 263r, 275v; it also appears as minor decorative element in the flourishing outside some major ones). — The 2-line,[31] alternately blue and red *litterae notabiliores* (the *KL* of the calendar pages, the beginnings of many propers and of their constitutive elements) have occasionally some flourishing added (18vb, the Innocents; 20rb, Circumcision). — One-line red or blue lombards often begin the antiphonal elements (written in smaller-size script). Limited use is made of (C-form) paragraph mark, blue or red. Capitals beginning a sentence inside a text are touched with red.

Binding: 16th-century (not before 1513, in view of the cropped inscription on f. 4v) covers: dark-brown calf over slightly beveled wooden boards, blind-stamped: rectangular central panels ca. 28 × 20 cm filled with a multiple-lozenge pattern (24 fields, incl. halves); inside each, a decorative stamp characterized by fanlike shapes. Remnants of two back-to-front brass buckles; four round, flat-top brass bosses on each cover, the one in upper right corner of upper cover missing. Fore-edge corners of the covers protected by metal strips; those at tail edge missing (several nails remain). Sewn over five apparently woven bands. Rebacked in 19th or 20th century in lighter brown morocco. — The volume weighs 18 lbs.

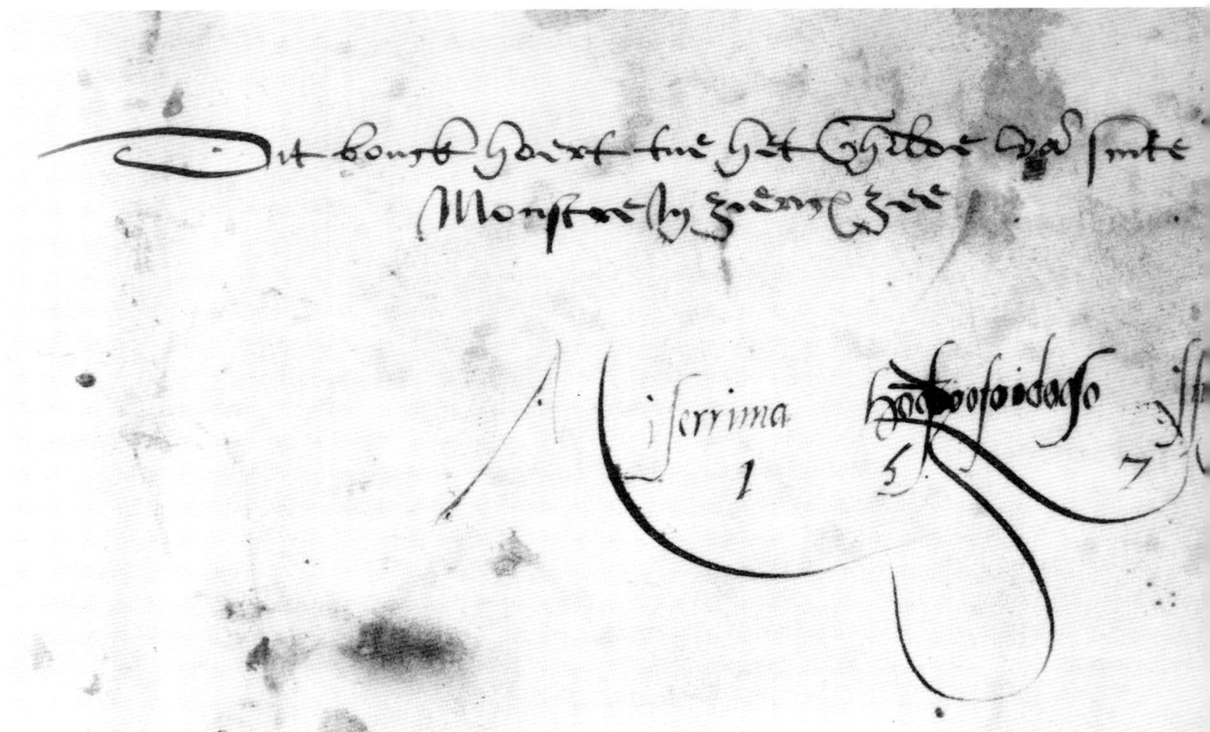

MS 26, f. 1r (inscriptions) (actual length of first line shown: 212 mm)

EARLY INSCRIPTIONS: on f. 1r, near top, in 16th-century cursive: Dit bouck hoert toe het Ghilde van sinte Vitus gilde(?) binnen Sinte Leuens Monster in Zierickzee.[32] — A little lower, a line of writing in italics, defaced and made illegible by nonsensical overwriting: Miserrima H(ispanica?) (invidia?) (S. . .?. . .)// 1577.

On pastedown of upper cover, ownership label of Rev. Edwin A. Dalrymple, D.D. (of Baltimore); on center of f. 1r, small label of B. Westermann & Co., New York. — In lower left corner of pastedown of lower cover, clipping from a French or Belgian sales catalog describing the book ("100 Missale Ecclesiae Romanae. In fol. 243 [sic] ff. . . . "). — At top of 1r, penciled LC accession no.: 4560 (3), n. 12.[33]

2° fo.: (music, with text:) autem genuit oziam . . .

Bibl.: De Ricci, *Census* (1935), p. 230, no. 109; Faye and Bond (1962), p. 119, no. 81; C. A. Goodrum, *Treasures of the Library of Congress* (1980), p. 48 (color reproductions of ff. 152v–153r [reduced size; the opening contains music and texts of several "prefaces"], of the initial *A* on f. 7r, and of the *T* on 161r)

NOTES

1. Near gutter, 370–373 mm; at outer edge, 366–370 mm.
2. Often more (up to ca. 285) at top edge, less (down to ca. 275) at bottom.
3. To be read (or sung) also in Christmas night, "post prosam noni responsorij": so rubric on f. 14vb. This seems to have been part of Utrecht use.
4. Cf. Grotefend, *Zeitrechnung* II.
5. In outer margin on f. 4v, next to July, a partly cropped obituary notice of [Josep?]hus de Gruninghe, Aurei Velleris Eques, curatus(?), who died July 8, 1513.
6. These additions do not continue or logically expand what immediately precedes or follows (the

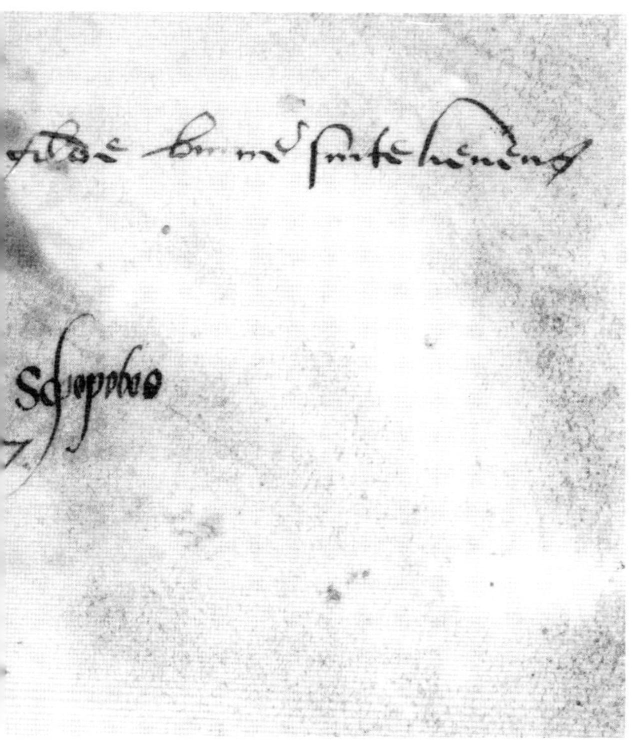

same is true of the Gospel on 1v–2r). They seem also quite incomplete as far as their special theme goes.

7. This was also the custom in (at least some) Carthusian books. In the use of Roman Curia, the three days were in the *sanctorale*.

8. The preface or, rather, preface-style part of the blessing, beginning (after the Vere dignum . . .) with the words "Te Domine inter cetera mirabilium tuorum precepta" = *Corpus praefationum* (1980), no. 1481 (text *CCSL*, v. CLXI, pt. C). — The music is on red 4-line staves, two columns, as in most other music pages (but on 72vb, a phrase of music, for "Ave rex noster," is on a 5-line staff).

9. *AH, loc. cit.*, has "Magnum salutis gaudium" but notes the variant.

10. Not, it seems, in the monastic sense (an individual's renouncement of change of scenery). The three prayers express concern for safety and continuation of the congregation and of the place ("et hunc locum"). — The next item suggests that although (judging from the colophon) not planned for a religious community, the Missal was nevertheless copied from a community book.

11. Text in *EEFL*, 3309, among selected texts from "ritus Praemonstratensis," i.e., peculiarities of the order founded by St. Norbert. Presence of the text in our Missal does not identify it as a Premonstratensian book: various elements of that order's liturgy had come from the tradition and use of the area of lower Rhine. Cf. note *op. cit.*, p. 1647.

12. Does this reflect a local use in which the celebrant would have intoned the *Kyrie*?

13. Prayer not in Pflieger, *Liturgicae orationis concordantia verbalia*, I; not in *EEFL*.

14. Added in cursive, 3 lines: Et famulos tuos N. Papam et N. Antistitem nostros . . . custodi. p[er] [deletion] d. n.

15. As seems to have often been the case in late Middle Ages, after the Trinity proper had occupied the place of the first Sunday after Pentecost (= the "octave" day of Pentecost), the nomenclature in our missal appears shaky: the term "post octavam Pentecostes" (that would really mean, second after Pentecost itself, the first after Trinity) is used only once, at the beginning; the rest of the Sundays are numbered without reference to a starting point. — N.B. A possibly significant erasure had occurred in the quoted caption.

16. Cf. *SMRL* II. — The *Missale Romanum* of 1570 (in use through 1969) counted the Sundays from Pentecost itself; the formulary (= "proper") for the First Sunday after Pentecost was to be used on next free weekday after the Trinity Sunday.

17. Without the additions coded "F" by Dom Hesbert with the 18th Sunday.

18. This means, most notably, that the Epistle-Gospel combinations are quite different. — The *Alleluia* verse after Gradual is more irregular. — Exceptions from the principle stated: the Communion antiphon for the 14th Sunday is (f. 185ra) *Panis quem ego dedero*, assigned to 15th Sunday in the Curia missal; for its 15th Sunday, our book has (186rb) *Qui manducat meam carnem . . .* , not represented in the Curia missal series.

19. The sanctoral covers the whole year: Vigil of St. Andrew = Nov. 29, St. Linus was celebrated in Utrecht on Nov. 26. As common in the Middle Ages, the dates are not given except in the calendar. — The two "dedications," i.e., anniversary celebrations of the consecration of the local church and (somewhat less commonly) of its main altar, are very probably put at the end because the date varied. Strictly speaking they are not a part of the sanctoral.

20. Some consist only of the three formal prayers *collecta, secreta*, and *complenda*, used in combination with a "common" suitable for the saint being honored. The "commemorations" are used when main attention is centered on another theme (e.g., Walburgis commemorated on the day of the apostles Philip and Jacob).

21. *Marii et Marthae* (Jan. 19) and *Walburgis* (commemorated on May 1) were in Premonstratensian calendars, not in that of Utrecht. St. Mildrada (Mildred), the 7th-century abbess of Thanet in Kent, whose relics were (still are?) in Deventer, was honored (commemorated) in Utrecht on July 13 but is not a Premonstratensian saint. Religious orders, of course, honored to a varying degree the various particular local cults.

22. Based, it seems, on apocryphal literature. In the *Missale Romanum*, the prayer is quite different. — There is also a *secreta* and *complenda*, of less interest.

23. Not a very usual ingredient of a missal. The number of these "sequences," grown rather high in later Middle Ages but greatly varying regionally, was sharply curtailed later; the *Missale Romanum* of the 16th century had only four (*Victimae Paschali, Veni Sancte Spiritus, Lauda Sion*, and *Dies irae*). — Premonstratensian use?

24. Same writer may have added the text with music on ff. 1v–2r; also the marginal note dated 1513 on 4v.

25. The "Mare" may well have been meant as Latin form. Two places in (Netherlandish) Limburg have, or in recent memory still had, the name Ter Maar (one now part of Klimmen, the other of Margraten). That area, however, belonged to the ecclesiastical jurisdiction of Liège, and the missal reflects the use of the pre-1559 diocese of Utrecht, not of Liège; to make it usable in Limburg, additions and changes would have been required. (It was certainly possible that the canonical requirement to follow the liturgical use of one's diocese would be neglected but local and regional devotional traditions could hardly be.) — Flemish currency was used, and the *ciborium* ("siboria" as singular is a corrupt form) purchased was of silver, apparently not goldplated, suggesting a small church. In 15th century, the diocese of Utrecht (which covered ca. two-thirds of today's Netherlands, incl. most of Zeeland but excluding North Brabant and Limburg) had some thousand parishes, some of them extremely small (cf. L. J. Rogier, *Hist. du catholicisme hollandais,* c1974, p. 12).

26. Further below, an odd line in cursive: Confessor credo[!?] no[n] vult [for "fuit"?] neque martir neque virgo.

27. Hand does not seem to be represented elsewhere in the book.

28. In column 230rb (with the beginning of Mass of *Visitatio*) the height of the written area changes somewhat suddenly to 258 mm (slightly smaller script on unchanged ruling); on the leaves which follow, deviations range from ca. 260 to ca. 268 mm. This could mean that the copying of the relatively recent proper was done from a different *exemplar,* or other merely psychological factors (rather than a different scribe).

29. On the music pages, only one horizontal at top and one at bottom; the top line is single also in the Order of Mass, ff. 158–168. — Distances of the vertical lines are ca. 81 + 16 + 81 mm; in the Canon (ff. 161–166) ca. 83 + 17 + 83.

30. N.B. Initial *I* or *J* ("In illo tempore," "In diebus illis," but also "Iustus . . . ") is sometimes J-like and entirely outside the text column, sometimes lombard-type wide *I* done, as other 2-line initials, in blank space reserved for it. — The whole phrase "Vere dignum et iustum est" in the prefaces is repeatedly reduced to a single combined quasi-letter (cf. ff. 159v–160r).

31. The *J* (when not in the lombard *I*-shape) is an exception: placed in the margin outside the written area, it runs past ca. 6 1/2 lines.

32. The church (which became Protestant with the change of political control of Zeeland, ca. 1580) was apparently not immune to threat of plundering during a temporary occupation of Zierikzee by Spanish troops in 1577: it is said that its valuable organ had to be kept from harm by a major payment. (Cf. Willem Lootens, *Beschrijving van het oude en nieuwe orgel in de Groote of St. Lievens Monsterkerk der stad Zierikzee* [Baarn, 1966].)

33. Library of Congress acquired the manuscript in 1916, together with a number of other items from the estate of Rev. Dalrymple.

MS 27

(Collitz breviary)

BREVIARY IN NETHERLANDISH

ca. 1455?

Written in (central) Netherlands. Parchment. 330 leaves, ca. 175 × ca. 115 mm (bound volume: ca. 178 × 127 [with clasps, 135] mm) 1 column. 27 lines (in the calendar, 31–32 lines)

ff. 1r–6v: Full calendar, in Dutch (with some Latin); in black and red.

The 52 red-letter days are the major feasts of (the diocese of) Utrecht, e.g., *Ponciaen, Pancraes, Seruaes, Odulf, Lebuijn* (both June 25 and Nov. 12), *Willibroert* (Nov. 7); they include also *Blasius* (Feb. 3) and *Agatha* (Feb. 5). *Visitatio Mariae,* which became a major feast throughout the Low Countries in 1440, is added in red after the (earlier) black entry "processi et martiniani"; Transfiguration, a feast spreading chiefly after 1457, does not appear at all. Several days are emphasized (additionally? or by a corrector?) merely by red underscoring: St. Gertrude (March 17), Benedict (March 21), *Resurrectio Domini* (added after "Guntrammi" on March 27), Margaret (July 13), "Die sceiding d'apl'n" [= *Divisio apostolorum*] (July 15), "Die elf dusent magheden" (Oct. 21). — Jan. 1 is called "Jaers dach"; scribal errors identify Sept. 8 as *"Ons' vrouwen hemeluaert"* and state that March "habet dies xxx." — Many of the names present do not seem to belong to the area at all: Dalmatius (Dec. 5); Ezechiel, the prophet (Apr. 10); Eustasius cum soc. (Sept. 19); Pelagia (Oct. 8); etc.**1**

7r: DIt voirscrue̅ kallengier beghint int iaer ons heren m.iii en̅ ii . . . Ite̅. xx. minute[n] sijn een vrr. *[sic]*

The scribe, or the text from which he/she was copying, is not unfailingly reliable when it comes to numbers (see the statement concerning the number of days in March, on 2r).

(7v blank, unruled)

8r–31v: *Hier beghint die ghetide vanden Aduent . . . Cap.* (L)[15]Aet ons soberlike[n] . . .

Proper of (= collection of proper offices for) the season of Advent: 8r–15r, 1st Advent Sunday; 15r–19v, 2nd; 19v–26v, 3rd (with the "O antiphons" on 26rv); 26v–31r, the 4th Sunday; and 31rv, antiphons to Magnificat for the weekdays of the last week before Christmas. — The Advent Sunday responsories are Netherlandish versions of the following:**2** *1st Sunday:* I Aspiciens a longe

II Aspiciebam in visu noctis III Missus est IV Ave Maria V Salvatorem VI Audite verbum VII Ecce virgo VIII Obsecro Domine IX Laetentur caeli *2nd Sunday:* I Jerusalem cito II Ecce Dominus veniet III Jerusalem sta in excelso IV Civitas Jerusalem V Ecce veniet Dominus protector VI Sicut mater VII Jerusalem plantatio VIII Egredietur Dominus de Samaria IX Rex noster *3rd Sunday:* I Ecce apparebit II Bethlehem civitas III Qui venturus est IV Suscipe verbum V Egypte noli VI Prope est VII Descendet Dominus VIII Veni Domine et noli tardare IX Ecce radix *4th Sunday:* I Canite tuba II Non auferetur III Me oportet IV Ecce iam venit plenitudo V Virgo Israel VI Iuravi VII Non discedimus VIII Intuemini IX Nascetur nobis

31v–34v: ***Hier beghint die ghetide van die vigelie des kersauont*** . . .

Office of Christmas Eve.

34v–49r: ***die ghetide va[n] kers auont*** (G)[7]Od wil dencke[n] in mij[n] hulpe . . .

Office of Christmas. In the Matins, the beginning of Matthew (the genealogy) is included just before the Te Deum, in addition to the usual nine readings.

49r–54r: ***Hier beghint die ghetide van ons heren ihesu cristi tott' eerst vesper*** . . .

Office of the Circumcision; here, as in the calendar, the translator (or a copyist) seems to have preferred to avoid that term; in the present context, failing to find a substitute.

54r–65r: ***die heilighe drie coninghen ghetide***

Office of the Epiphany, called the "thirteenth day" in the calendar but here, Cologne-style, the day of the Three Kings (putative relics of the Magi were held by the Cologne Church; the diocese of Utrecht was a suffragan of Cologne).

65r–71v: ***Hier beghint die ghetide vande[n] eerste[n] son[n]end[ach] inder vasten*** . . .

Office of the 1st Sunday of Lent; also (70v) "Die antif' binnē die weke"; but the 1st Sunday ends and the Palm Sunday begins on the same page; no explanation as to why the 2nd through 5th Sundays are omitted.

71v–79v: ***Hier beghint die ghetide vanden palmdaghe***

Office of Palm Sunday. — Nothing is given for the Holy Week between Palm Sunday and Easter; perhaps the Tenebrae, etc. (also the 2nd–5th Sundays of Lent) were to be found in a separate book.**[3]** — Stub between leaves 79 and 80 invites hypotheses: in a clearly liturgy-conscious milieu, this would have been the single place most suitable for an illustration.

80r–99r: [Beginning with a highly decorated page and large initial:] ***Hier beghinnet die ghetide vanden heilighe[n] paesche dach*** . . . (G)[11]Od wil dencken . . . (83r:) . . . ***D'mane[n]d.*** . . . (85r:) . . . ***des dinsdaghes*** . . . (86v:) . . . ***wonesd'*** . . . (88r–91v:) ***Ind' oct' van paschen*** (91v–93v:) ***die anderde sonnendag'*** (93v–95v:) ***die derde sōnend' va[n] pas'*** (95v–97r:) ***die vierde sonnend' va[n] [paschen]*** (97r–99r:) ***die vijfte sonnendach na [?] paesch***

Easter Sunday responsories (Netherlandish equivalents of those used in Cologne, cf. Leroquais, *Brév.* I, p. lxxxi): I Die enghel des heren daelde vande hemel II Die enghel des heren sprac III Als gheleden was die heilighe dage

99r–105v: (99r, last 2 lines:) ***Hier beghint die ghetide va[n] ons h'en hemeluaer[t]s dach*** . . . (104v–105v:) ***sonnend' twisschen octa'***

Office of Ascension Thursday (40 days after Easter) and of the Sunday which follows.

106r–115r: ***Hier beghint die ghetide vanden heilighen pi[n]xteren dach*** . . . (G)[9]Od wil dencke[n] in mij hulpe . . . (ends on f. 110r; 110r–115r:) ***des manēd.*** . . . [etc.]

Office of Pentecost and of the weekdays immediately following.

115r–125r: ***Hier beghint die ghetide van die heilige drieuoudicht*** . . .

Office of Trinity Sunday.

125r–131v: ***Die ghetide vande[n] eerwaerdighen sacrame[n]t*** . . .

Office of Corpus Christi Thursday.

132r–206r: [Beginning with highly decorated page] *Beatus vir qui no[n] abijt in consilio [symbol for "etc."].* I. (S)[14]Alich is die man die niet af ghegaen . . . (146v:) *Hier beghint die mane[n]daghes mette[n]* . . .

Psalms I-CIX in straight sequence, assigned to the Matins of Sunday (those for Sunday lack caption) through Saturday, each introduced by its Latin initium and number.[4] — The division is as follows: Sunday, Pss. I-XXVI; Mon., XXVII-XXXVIII; Tues., XXXIX-LII; Wed., LIII-LXVIII; Thurs., LXIX-LXXX; Fri., LXXXI-XCV; Sat., XCVI-CIX.

206r–219r: [Decorated borders of 206r indicate beginning of section] . . . *Hier beghint sonnendaechs vesp. Dixit dn̄s dn̄o meo* [symbol for *"etc."] C.ix* (D)[6]Ie heer segghede . . . (208r:) . . . *Manendach vesp.* . . . (216r:) . . . *Sat'dachs vesp.* . . . (ending, presumably, with the end of Ps. CXLIII on 219r)

The Psalms assigned to Vespers of Sunday through Saturday are: Sunday, Pss. CX-CXV; Mon., CXVI-CXVII and CXX-CXXI; Tues., CXXII-CXXVI; Wed., CXXVII-CXXXI; Thurs., CXXXII-CXXXVII; Fri., CXXXVIII-CXLII; Sat., CXLIV-CXLVII and CXLIII. — While some Psalms of the biblical sequence (CXVIII, CXIX) are bypassed in order to be used in the Prime, etc. (see below), the manuscript numbers all psalms consecutively in the order of appearance; this results in a numbering which is neither Vulgate nor Hebrew, beginning with the Ps. CXX (above, Monday) numbered as "Cxvij"; this idiosyncratic numbering is then continued on and on, through and including the canticles, so that the final number, assigned to the Song of Moses (Audite coeli) on ff. 237v–239v, is Clxxxv.

219r–222v [a group of canticles and other items supplementing the Psalter]: (219r:) . . . *Nu[n]c dimittis seruu[m]. Cxlvi* [!] Nu laet heer dine[n] knecht . . . (219v:) *Te deum. Cxlvij* [!] Wi loue[n] di god . . . di heer en̄ coninc der coninghen . . . *Magnificat a[n]i[m]a. Cxlviij* [!] Mijn siel maect groet . . . (220r:) . . . *Te deum laudamus te dum. Cxlix* [!] Di god louen wi di here belien wi . . . (220v:) . . . *Benedicite om[n]ia op[er]a d[omi]ni C.l.* [!] Benediet den heer alle werke[n] . . . (221r:) . . . *Laudate d[omin]um d' cel' Cli* [!] LOuet den h'e ghi vande[n] hemel . . . [= Ps. CXLVIII] (221v:) . . . *Cantate d[omi]no can[ticum] C.lij.* [= Ps. CIL] (222r:) . . . *Laudate dn̄m. Cliij.* [= Ps. CL] . . . *Benedictus d[omi]n[u]s deus isrl' Clv* [!] Ghebenedijt si di heer . . . [= Luke I, 68-79]

The Te Deum laudamus on 220rv is (translation of) the well-known text commonly used at the end of the Matins; that on 219v is a short entirely Christocentric statement; cf. printed version in Van Wijk, *Het Getijdenboek van Geert Grote* (1940), p. 120.

222v–239v: (222v:) . . . *Hier beghint die prime.* [symbol for *"etc."] D's i[n] ad[iutorium]* (G)[5]Od wilt dencken in mine hulpe . . .

Ordinary and Psalter for the minor hours: 222v–228v, for the Prime: with a Dutch rendering of *Iam lucis orto sidere,* Pss. CXXXVI and CXIX, 1–32, the Athanasian Creed (Soe wie behoude[n] will wesen, ff. 224v–226r), antiphons for various seasons, and *preces.* — 228v–230v, Terce: with Ps. CXIX, 33-80). — 230v–232v, Sext: with Ps. CXIX, 81-128. — 232v–234r, None: with Psalm CXIX, 129-176. — On 234r–239v, more biblical canticles: 234rv, the *Song of Isaiah,* Is. XII; 234v–235r, the *Song of Hezekiah,* Is. XXXVIII, 10-20; 235rv, the *Song of Hannah,* 1 Sam. II, 1-10; 235v–236v, the *Song of Moses* from Exodus XV, 1-19; 236v–237v, the *Song of Habakkuk,* Hab. III, 2-19; 237v–239v, the other *Song of Moses,* Deut. XXXII, 1-43.

239v–244v: *Die vij psalme[n]* Dn̄e ne i[n] furore. *vi.* Beati quoru[m]. *xxxi* . . .

Program for the Seven Penitential Psalms, by means of their Latin initia and numbers (using the idiosyncratic numbering developed on ff. 206-219: Ps. CXLIII is numbered Cxlv); followed, f. 239v sqq., by the Litany. After the usual introductory appeals (Heer ontferme di onser, etc.) and the usual group of Apostles and Disciples, the litany invokes 52 individual martyrs, 44 confessors, 46 women. Less than completely common among the martyrs are: Cornelijs, Dyonijs,

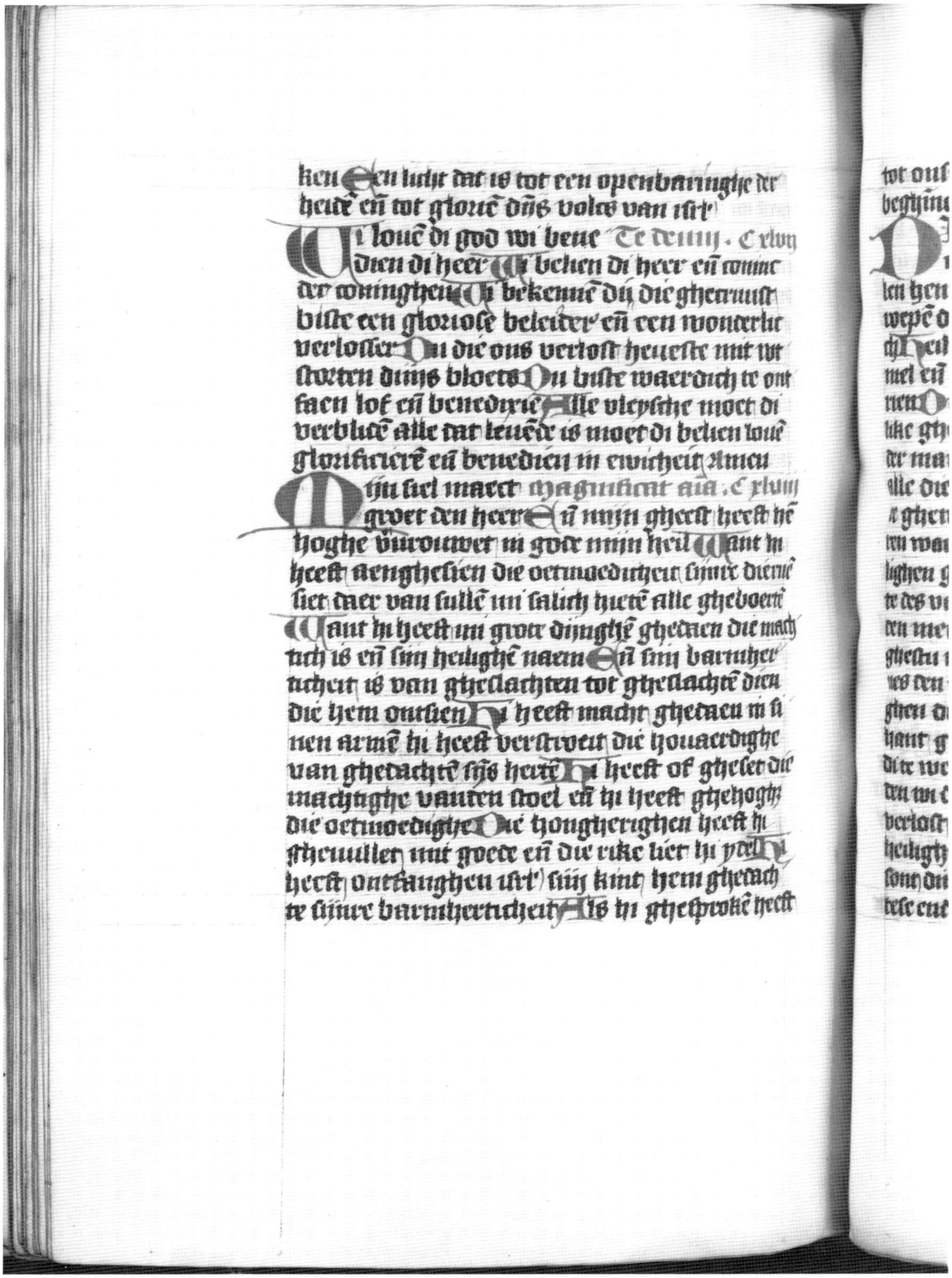
ken Een licht dat is tot een openbaringhe der
heiden ende tot glorien dijns volcs van israel
Wi louen di god wi bene Te deum . C xlvij
dien di heer Wi belien di heer ende coninc
der coninghen Wi bekennen dij die ghetruust
biste een gloriose beleider ende een wonderlic
verlosser Du die ons verlost heueste mit tie
stoeten dijns bloets Du biste waerdich te ont
faen lof ende benedixie Alle vleysche moet di
verbliden alle dat leuende is moet di belien louen
glorificieren ende benedien in ewicheit Amen
Mijn siel maect Magnificat anima . C xlviij
groet den heere Ende mijn gheest heeft hem
hoghe verurouwet in gode mijn heil Want hi
heeft aenghesien die oetmoedicheit sijnre dierne
siet daer van sullen mi salich hieten alle gheboerten
Want hi heeft mi grote dinghen ghedaen die mach
tich is ende sijn heilighen naem Ende sijn barmher
ticheit is van gheslachten tot gheslachten dien
die hem ontsien Hi heeft macht ghedaen in si
nen arme hi heeft verstroeit die houaerdighe
van ghedachten sijns herten Hi heeft of gheset die
machtighe vanden stoel ende hi heeft ghehoghet
die oetmoedighe Die hongherighen heeft hi
ghevullet mit goede ende die rike liet hi ydel Hi
heeft ontfanghen israel sijn kint hem ghedach
te sijnre barmherticheit Als hi ghesproken heeft

MS 27, f. 219v (actual height of the text column: 104 mm)

Maurijs, Victor, Gereon, Patrokel, Alexander, Tiburtius, Albaen, Brixius, Ponciaen, Yuo, Iorijs; among the confessors: R'migius, Germaen, Bau[o], Yelijs [= Eligius?], Vedast[us], Willibroert, Seuerin, Gall[us], Matern[us], Hubert, Cunibaert, Seuerus, Lebuijn, Ludger, Odolf, Adalbaert, Rabbat [= Radbodus?], Seruaes, Arnulph, Ansbert, Lodewich; among the women: Spes, Peternelle, Aechte, Eufemia, Columba, Benedicta, Walburch, Effrasina, Emerina, Cunera, Pignosa, Potenciana, Effra, Aldegont, Igne, Anna, Susana. — The prayers for liberation include some which are somewhat unusual, notably (242v): "Van onser groter onwetenheit ende onkundicheit ons selfs . . . "

244v–248r: *Die compleet tijde* (B)[3]Ekeer ons god . . .

The order of Compline, with psalms indicated by their Latin initia and by numbers. Includes, besides the (prose translation of) *Te lucis ante terminum,* also (in prose translation introduced by the Latin initia), alternate hymns for various seasons (*Ihesu saluator seculi, Criste qui lux, Corde natus, Summi largitor, O vere digna hostia*), a variety absent from postmedieval breviaries.

248r–297r: (248r has partially decorated border, perhaps as an afterthought, to indicate that a major section begins in the middle of the page:) *Hier beghint dat cōmune der heilighē. va[n] ene[n] apostel die I vesp[er]* (G)[5]Od wilt dencken in mijn hulpe . . . (250r–256v, *"van vele apostelen";* 256v–262v, *"vande[n] euangelisten";* 262v–269r, *"van ene[n] martelaer eñ gheen bisscop";* 269r–270r, *"van ene[n] martelaer eñ bisscop";* 270r–276v, *"vandē martelaren";* 276v–283v, *"van een confessoer eñ gheē bissc' ";* 283v–284v, *"van een confessoer eñ bisscop";* 284v–287v, *"van vele cōfessoren";* 287v–290v, *"vā eenir maghb[et]";* 290v–297r, *"van vele ioncfrouwen."*)

The "common of saints" (providing the variable parts of daily office for the feastday of any saint falling into a particular group). Since this breviary otherwise lacks a sanctoral ("proper of the saints"), with the exception of several items which follow, the "commons" may have been meant as a substitute.[5]

297r–299v: *Die ghetide van sinte vincentius . . . Altemael van enē martelaer [uit?] sonder die lessen die hier na volgē . . .* MS 27

Six lessons. The special attention given this particular saint suggests a local cult. Unfortunately, the saint's identity is uncertain: a St. Vincent, martyr and bishop, is named in the calendar with June 6, one of the many entries in black; the Litany (239v sqq.) includes only one saint by that name, named immediately after Lawrence; he must be the deacon celebrated (almost everywhere) on January 22.[6] The readings are uninformatively edifying and could be applied to either saint.

300r–307r: (on highly decorated 300r:) *onse vrouwē ghetide. Assu[m]p[tio] hoer v'heuīge* (G)[9]Od wilt dencken ī mijn hulpe . . .

Office for the day of Assumption. The text begins and ends on pages not containing any other matter. Includes prose translation of the hymn *O quam gloriosa luce coruscas* (O mit hoe gloriose lichte blenckestu, 300v).

307v–313v: (decorated page) *onse vrouwē ghetide, van hoer gheboerte* (G)[6]Od wilt denckē . . . (313v, line 14 sqq., rubric concerning:) *onse vrouwen ontfa[ngnis]* . . .

The office for Sept. 8, celebrated as Mary's birthday, and notes concerning the festivity of her conception, Dec. 8.

313v–321v: (313v, line 20:) *Hier beghint die ghetide van alle gods heilighen* . . .

Office for the day of All Saints (Nov. 1); with commemorations of St. C(a)esarius required by the church calendar throughout the Low Countries (cf. Strubbe, *Chronologie)*

321v–329v: (beginning 321v, 5th line:) *die ghetide vanden kermisse* . . . (ending on 329v, line 7-8) . . . Dat huus des heren is wel ghefundeert op enen vasten steen. [symbol for "etc."] (rest of 329v blank)

Office for the festival of dedication of the (local) church.

(f. [330]rv blank, ruled)

(On pastedown of lower cover, 27 lines of ms. text, not part of the breviary:) [H]ar ghedencke miinre na diinre ontfermherticheit . . . [D]ie onnosel eñ die ghe-rech (= Psalm XXV, 7b-21a, with blank spaces for versals; written in an extremely regular Windesheim-type script, not by the scribe of the breviary; perhaps a reject or fragment of an unfinished project)

* * *

Foliated (1-329) in modern pencil.[7] Two flyleaves precede f. 1: one is blank; the second, blank on recto, has on verso a full-page illustration (Crucifixion, with Mary and John). Following the blank f. [330], one free endleaf, blank; some ms. text on pastedown (cf. contents). — Written area ca. 104 × ca. 69 mm. — Fully ruled in faint brownish (diluted black) ink; pricking preserved in many outer margins. — The script is *textualis formata* of the Windesheim kind, in good black ink, slightly fading in parts (with an olive cast). — Captions are red; the rather rare liturgical directives tend to be written in black and underscored in red (e.g., on 13v, 30v, 69v, 297r). — Medium-quality parchment; thickness ca. 14.5 mm per 100 leaves. — Several strands of alternately red or green thread pulled through two holes and forming in tail margin on both sides of the leaf ca. 32 mm from the fore edge a vertical line ca. 15 mm long, ending (subsequent to cropping?) at the bottom edge, appear on leaves where important items begin: on ff. 34, 65, 80, 106, 125, 132, 143, 147, 156, 165, 175, 186, 196, 206, 222, 244, 248, 256(!), 276(!), 290(!), 300, 313, 321.

Collation: (preceding f. 1, singleton leaf with large illustration) [ ]^{6}(= ff. 1-6) [a]^{8}–[k]^{8} l$^{8-1?}$(= ff. 87-93; apparently no text loss) [m]^{8} n$^{8-1}$(= ff. 102-108; of n_5 which follows f. 105 only a stub but apparently no text loss) [o]^{8} p^{8} [q]$^{6+1}$(= ff. 125-131; f. 131 a singleton?) *a-x*^{8}(= ff. 132-299) *y*$^{8-1?}$(= ff. 300-306; y_1 absent, apparently no text loss) *z*^{8} *[?]*^{8} *[us]*^{8}(= f. 323-[330]; f. [330] is blank, ruled). — Early post-medieval leaf signatures (the first alphabet in black ink, the second in red) in most gatherings, usually partly cropped.[8]

Decoration: The Crucifixion on verso of the 2nd flyleaf (see above) is the only illustration in the book; it is an amateurish work, at least in its present heavily retouched state. The slightly arched area of the illustration (max. 112 × 71 mm) in a narrow black-gold-black frame is surrounded by a lightly framed floral border with blue-and-mauve acanthus leaves, also vine stems drawn in ink, with light green leaves, golden bezants, and a bird painted in several shades of brown; void spaces are overfilled with black (pen-drawn), unconnected curlicues.

Borders of somewhat different kind, probably chronologically closer to the production of the manuscript, are used to mark the beginnings of major sections of the work. They mostly issue from an initial and branch out into the head and tail margins; a bar, primarily gold and blue, may counterbalance or cover the main stem. They are not framed and are done skillfully by a competent if not very original artist. —All major sections are not treated with proportionate fairness: in particular, the common of the saints which begins halfway down the page (f. 48r), perhaps owing to the scribe's ignorance or inattention.

The very large initials (15-line on f. 8r, 11-line on f. 80r) are primarily blue and (burnished) gold,[9] with the enclosed area filled with acanthus leaves drawn in red or purplish red ink, with a three-dimensional effect, on light-green ground; other large initials are red and blue or blue with white, on rectangular, pen-drawn fields.

Beyond the cases mentioned, gold is little used. Many minor borders and border ornaments consist of flourishes skillfully done in faint red, brownish red, or purplish red ink, enlivened by touches of light-green to indicate leaves, or by a face-like shape, as on ff. 31v, 34v, 96r (the faces are drawn in profile and are often upside down). — Two-line initials and one-line versals are alternately blue or red.

Binding: 16th?-century covers, reddish brown calf over rounded boards. — On both covers an identical blind-stamped panel, ca. 95 × 58 mm (framed by double-ruled lines extending to edges) with base parallel to the spine (base near fore-edge on upper cover, on the spine side on lower cover); in it, as a central theme, round medallion (36 mm in diameter) with the Lamb of God (with cross banner), inside a vessica-shaped band with tête-bêche inscription SIET DAT LAM GOEDES/ DAT . . . DIE SOEND . . .; overlapping the band near panel corners, round medallions with the Four Beasts (Revelation IV,6, etc.). — Two back-to-front brass clasps. — Sewn over 7 raised bands; rebacked.

On verso of upper cover, two clippings from dealers' catalogs ("Beautifully illuminated manuscript: Sermons and homilies in Dutch . . . ," priced £ 12 12s; "Sermones et homiliae, cum Kalendario, Belgice . . . ,"), small diamond-shape label of "Downing, Chaucer's Head, Birmingham"; ownership label of Hermann Collitz; LC Rare Book Collection bookplate. — On recto of the free endleaf at end, in pencil: Bequest of Clara H. Collitz/Dec. 5, 1947 (also LC cataloger's record of headings and call number: "Catholic Church. Liturgy and ritual. Breviary. BX 2000.A5F5/1500z/Rare Bk Coll.")

2° fo.: KL Marcius habet dies .xxx. Luna xxx.

Bibl.: De Ricci, *Census*, v. 1 (1935), p. 857, no. 3 (when in the collection of Prof. Hermann Collitz of Baltimore). — LC printed card no. 62-55621.

The existence of a medieval Netherlandish translation of a more or less complete breviary[10] is a fact not entirely unrecorded[11] but, it would seem, not at all adequately appreciated: it is a very unusual phenomenon. The official and traditional Church Slavic office books of Dalmatia[12] seem to be the only other instance of a pre-1500 vernacular translation of the Latin Church's primary public prayer. Such translations remained very rare even later: a German version (possibly two) appeared in print in 1518 and 1535; but after the Council of Trent, in counterreaction to the Reformation, the translating activity within the Roman communion[13] ceased for something like two centuries, not to be really revived until our time.

NOTES

1. Altogether, the full calendar agrees with printed liturgical books of Utrecht of ca. 1500 approximately 75 percent; the ca. 90 disagreements are not easy to interpret. — N.B. St. Monica (May 4), a feast which one would expect in a book coming from the Windesheim (or Brethern-of-Common-Life) movement, is absent.

2. The responsories are important for identification of the liturgical "use." Cf. Leroquais, *Bréviaires,* I, p. lxxviii. — It seemed reasonable to give here the corresponding Latin initia (because those have to be used for comparisons), although the manuscript has only the Netherlandish translation.

3. This may have been so in the Latin original which the translator was using; that separate *Quadragesimale* (or similar) may of course never have been translated.

4. We are using the numbering of the Authorized Version; concerning the numbering used in the manuscript see notes to next item.

5. A "common of the saints" would, it should be observed, be included even if a *sanctorale* were present. There were always some saints for whom a full proper office had not been developed.

6. It is possible that the scribe, the translator, or the editor (of the translation or, more likely, of its model) wasn't aware of the difference.

7. Except for full hundreds, only the last two digits are written.

8. The first alphabet lacks signatures r-z: seven gatherings missing between Corpus Christi and the Psalter?

9. The blue has a textured quality, producing a peculiar velvety effect.

10. The statement that "Dutch manuscripts of canonical hours" are plentiful (P. W. Parshall in *Miscellanea F. Lyna* (1969), p. 333) must be understood to refer to the Hours of the Virgin; it certainly is not true of the canonical "hours" of the breviary.

11. Copies (all, I believe, partial) do not seem to be numerous: MS. 10 F 39 of the Rijksmuseum Meermanno-Westreenianum in The Hague (cf. its *Catalogus van de handschriften* . . . (1979)); MS. 3 of the R.C. Metropolitan See, Southwark, London (cf. Ker, *Med. mss. in Brit. libs.* I (1969), p. 322); H.S. 1039 of Utrecht University Library (its *Handschriften en Oude Drukken* . . . (1984), no. 44). (The MS. 207 of the Bib. de l'Univ. de Lille, Leroquais, *Brév.* II, no. 308 has rubrics in Netherlandish; also text?)

12. Cf. P. Salmon, *Les manuscrits liturgiques latins de la bib. vaticane,* v. 1 (1968), nos. 184 and 387 *(Breviarium Illyricum).* — I am told that Czech Utraquists, a group not quite separated from the Church of Rome, never went much beyond the *Pasionál* (ed. Z.V. Tobolka, Prague, 1926); Jan Hus himself, I believe, sang a breviary responsory in Latin when dying.

13. The Church of England included major elements of the old office in the Book of Common Prayer; other emerging churches showed little interest in retaining the old system.

MS 28

(Faye and Bond 47)

BREVIARY (DIURNAL) XVth c., 2nd half

Ferrara? (Italy) Parchment. x, 328 leaves, ca. 105 × ca. 74 mm (bound volume: 116 × ca. 83 mm) 1 column. 18 lines (in the calendar, 19)

Ir–Xv: *Januari[us] (KL)⁴ An̄[us] h[abe]t m[en]ses xij . . .*

Calendar: ca. 270 entries, of them 87 in red. In red are, among others, the January octaves of Stephen, John, the Innocents, also that of Epiphany (as are all days of the Christmas week in December). Notable among saints' days so emphasized: *Blasii* (Feb. 3), *Gregorii* (March 12), *Vitalis* (Apr. 28; abp. of Ravenna), *Maureli* (May 7; bp. and patron of Ferrara), *Leonis* (June 28); Visitation (July 2) and *Octava Visitationis* (July 9); *Malgarite* (July 13; = Margarite), *Marthe* (July 29); *"festu[m] niuis Et sci do[mini]ci"* (Aug. 5); *Romani* (Aug. 9); *"Jerol'i"* (Sept. 30; = Jerome); *Francisci* (Oct. 4; no octave); *Dedicatio basilice Salvatoris* and *basilice Petri et Pauli* (Nov. 9 and 18); *Ambrosii* (Dec. 7); *"Cōceptio btē. mᵉ.v'"* (Dec. 8), *Lucie* (Dec. 13). — Among the days in black, Ducentorum martyrum (March 1), Galli abbatis (Oct. 16), Triginta martyrum (Dec. 22). ADDED by later hand(s), in black: Joseph (March 19), Vincencii [con]fess. (Apr. 5; = Vincent Ferrer O.P., canonized 1455). — Written continuously, one month following another on the next line. — Except for the later-hand additions, the calendar reflects an earlier period than the *sanctorale* (the series of saints' offices, ff. 191r–248v): the Visitation, introduced ca. 1390, is the most recent innovation it includes. It seems to be ultimately based on the 13th-century Franciscan liturgical reform[1]; it is, however, neither Franciscan nor Augustinian. Its special celebrations (ignored in the sanctoral) point to northern or north-central Italy.

1r–110v: ***Incipit ordo officij diurni s[ecundu]m [con]suetudi[n]em roma[n]e curie Sab[bat]o p[rim]o de ad[ue]n[tu]*** **. . . (historiated initial *F*, with portrait representing St. Paul(?)) (F)⁶RATres sciētes . . . (ends on 110v with the antiphon *Super muros*)**

The temporal ("proper of the seasons"); rubrics (written with an extreme use of contractions, and numerous errors) and texts (spelled out) generally as contained or indicated by cues in the ordinal prepared

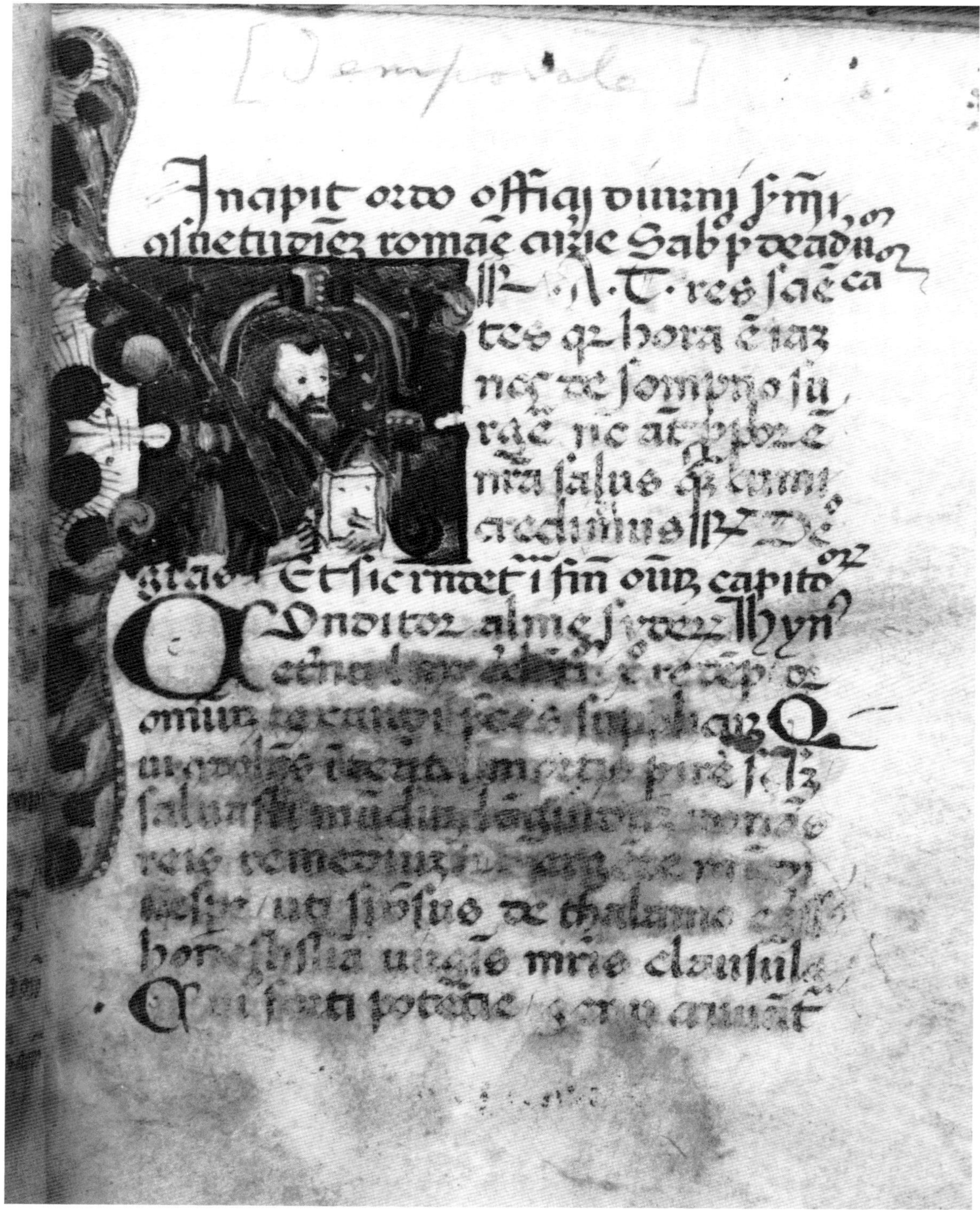

MS 28, f. 1r (actual size of written area: ca. 56 × 44 mm)

in the 13th century by Haymo, the fourth minister general of the Franciscan Order (printed ed. with title *Ordo breviarii* in *SMRL* II, p. [17]–114); however, everything pertaining to the Matins is omitted (hence "ordo officii diurni") and two major festivities introduced in the 14th century are incorporated in their proper places: the Trinity (92v–95v) and Corpus Christi (97v–100r)

111r–169v: (B)[2+]Eatus uir q[ui] n[on] abijt . . .

The Psalter; i.e., a selection of ca. 80 Psalms, organized, somewhat unclearly, for liturgical use. The order does not correspond to Haymo's Sunday and ferial cursus (cf. *SMRL* II, p. 48–60); psalms for festive Matins (cf., e.g, the Matins of St. Agatha, *op. cit.*, p. 129) are included even though corresponding directives in the sanctoral (ff. 191–248) are not. Canticles, hymns, chapters, versicles, other minor elements of the ordinary are (to some extent) incorporated. The order of the psalms and other major items is as follows[2]:

I–V, VIII, XI, XV, XVI, XIX, XXI; *Te Deum laudamus*, XCIII, C, LXIII, LXVII; *Song of the Three*, CXLVIII, CIL, CL; *Benedictio et claritas; Eterne rerum conditor; Ecce iam noctis; Song of Zachary;* XXXIII, XXXIV, XLV–XLVIII, LXI, LXIV, LXXV, LXXXIV, LXXXV, LXXXVII, LXXXVIII, XCVI–IC; *Iam lucis orto sidere*; XXII–XXVI, LIV, CXXXVI, CXIX,1–32; *Quicumque; Regi seculorum; Nunc sancte;* CXIX,33–80; *Rector potens;* CXIX, 81–128; *Rerum Deus;* CXIX, 129–176; CX–CXV; *Lucis creator optime; Magnificat*; CXVI, CXVII, CXX, CXXI; *Immense celi conditor;* CXXII–CXXVI; *Teluris igneus* [sic; *i.e. ingens?*] *conditor* (154v); CXXVII–CXXXI; *Celi deus sanctissime* (156v); CXXXII, CXXXIII, CXXXV–CXXXVII; *Magne Deus potencie;* CXXXVIII–CXLII; *Plasmator hominis* (163v); CXLIV–CXLVII; *O lux beata Trinitas*; XXXI,2–6, XCI, CXXXIV; *Te lucis; Nunc dimittis.*

The version is that of the Gallican Psalter, with a rare occasional slip into the "Roman" (e.g., in Ps. I,2).

170r–183r: *Incip[it] offi[cium] ĩ agēda def[u]ncto-[rum]* . . . Placebo . . .

The *Officium defunctorum*. Psalms written in full are those not included in the Psalter: VI, VII, XXVII, XL, XLI, XLII, LI, LXV; also the Song of Hezekiah (Is. XXXVIII, 10–20); other psalms are indicated by cues. Three nocturns, with lessons and responsories of the Roman use, as in Haymo's orders (*SMRL* II, p. 192–193) but with rubrics less numerous, shorter, and differently worded.

183r–190r: *psalmi p[e]ni[tenci]al[es]*

The Seven Penitential Psalms (VI, XXXII, XXXVIII, LI, CII, CXXX, CXLIII), with (186v sqq.) Litany; the last names, after the Innocents, 14 individual martyrs, 11 confessors, 9 women: the invocations not found in the (late 13th-century) revised Lenten litany printed in *OMRL*, p. 520–523 are: Georgij, Maurelij (the bp. of Ferrara!), Marceli, Clara, Dorothea, Anna.

190r–v: (In another, less skilled hand:) *Incepit* [sic] *no[c]tur[n]o[rum?] b'edictio* (E)[2]Exaudi d[omine] y[hes]u x[rist]e p[re]ces s[er]uo[rum] tuo[rum] . . .[3]

Short blessings for the readings of the Matins (added by a scribe apparently not conscious of the generally diurnal character of the book).

191r–248v: *Incip' festiuitates s[an]c[t]o[rum] p[er] ãni circul[u]m In sancti saturninj martiris or[ati]o* (D)[3]Eus q[ui] . . .

The sanctoral ("proper of the saints"); with rubrics and texts generally as contained or indicated by cues in Haymo's *Ordo breviarii* (*SMRL* II, p. 121–171) but omitting, in principle, the sections which pertain to the Matins (and no mention at all is made of celebrations for which Haymo's instructions concern only the nocturnal *lectiones*); one exception being the nine lessons of the common of martyrs, given in full on 205r–

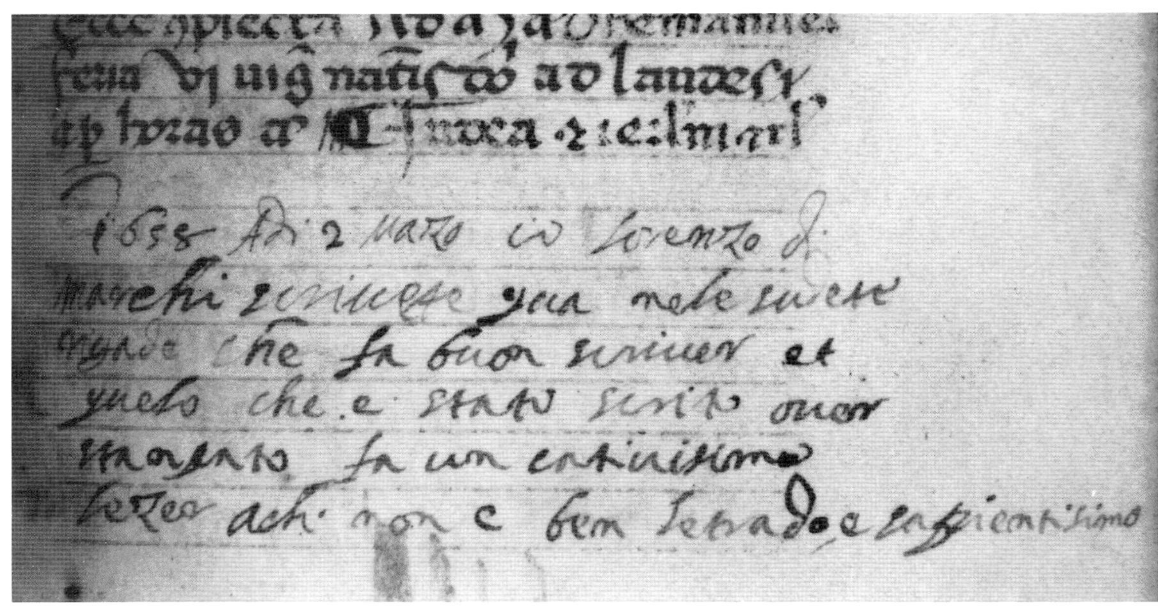

MS 28, f. 308r (lines 10–11 and inscription)
(actual size of area shown: ca. 35 × 65 mm)

207v (corresponding to *SMRL* II, p. 134–135). Added are the Marian feasts of the Conception (192v; "officium fit de Nativitate"), Visitation (220v–223v; "quod fuit approbatum per dominum Bonifatium Papam VIIIIum"; beginning with antiphon "Accedunt laudes Virginis admirande" and hymn "Iam vite viam"), apparently with an octave; also *Sanctae Mariae Virginis Ad Nives* (227r–228r), and the festivity of Transfiguration (228r–230v, "institutum de novo per sanctissimum dominum Calixtum, duplici celebratione festinandum [sic]"), this last one dating the ms. as written not before 1458. For all of these, too, the texts are limited to the diurnal parts. — Special Franciscan celebrations are given no prominence: both the day of St. Anthony of Padua (213r) and that of St. Francis himself (242r) rate only their proper *orationes*; no mention of *Stigmata scti. Francisci.*

249r–293v: ***Incip[it] comune s[an]c[t]o[rum] p[er] totum añum In natalitijs apl'o[rum] ad uesperas āt[iphona]*** Hoc e[st] p[re]ce[p]tu[m] m[eum] . . . (F)[3]Rs̄ iam n̄ . . .

The *Commune Sanctorum*, rather as[4] in Haymo's *Ordo breviarii* (*SMRL* II, p. 173–185), incl. the Matins. As can be seen, e.g., from the first few phrases quoted above, the agreement with Haymo's text is not perfect.

293v–302v: ***Incip[it] off[ici]um bt̄e m[ari]e v[irginis] s[ecundu]m [con]suetudi[n]e[m] ro[m]anem*** [sic]

Hours of Our Lady. Choice of texts (here, except for Psalms, generally written out) and most rubrics as in Haymo's *Ordo breviarii* (*SMRL* II, p. 185–191); however, the introductory rubric is omitted and the office starts with the Matins, with no mention of 1st Vespers; Vespers and Compline follow the None.

303r–308r: ***De sp[eci]alib[us] a[ntiphoni]s laud[um] q[ue] pon[u]nt[ur] a[nt]e nat[ivitat]em do[mini]*** . . .

"Tabula Parisiensis," as in *SMRL* II, p. 401–408. Mostly (rubrical material, hence) in red; rather extreme use made of contractions.

On f. 308r, in last 6 lines (originally blank), 17th-century non-calligraphic inscription in black ink: 1658 A di 2 marzo io Lorenzo di marchi . . .

308v–321v: *feria s[ecunda] ad la[udes] an[tiphone]* Misere[re] mei de[us] . . .

The diurnal parts of the "*psalmista*," or order of the weekly Psalter, inserted in Haymo's *Ordo breviarii* in the temporal after the octave of Epiphany (*SMRL* II, p. 53–61) and only incompletely copied on corresponding pages of the present manuscript (ff. 35v–39r)[5]; several rubrics on those pages refer to "p[salmist]a," suggesting that these additions (with occasional duplication) may have been made by the rubricator. As elsewhere, texts indicated in Haymo by cues are here written out, incl. several psalms, canticles, and hymns not found elsewhere in the codex: Pss. XLIII, XC, XCII, LXXII; songs of Isaiah (Is. XII, 1–6), of Hannah (1 Sam. II, 1–10), of Moses (Ex. XV,1–19), of Habakkuk (Hab. III,2–19), of Moses (Deut. XXXII, 1–43); hymns *Splendor paterne glorie, Ales diei nuntius, Nox et tenebrae et nubila, Lux ecce surgit aurea, Eterna celi gloria, Aurora iam spargit polum.* Incorporated are some additions not found in Haymo *l.c.,* notably alternate texts for use in Advent.

321v–323v: 321v–322r, commemoration or suffrage of the Apostles; 322r–v, diurnal proper of St. Jerome; 322v–323r, *Pro sancto Antonio* [abbate]; of St. Mary Magdalen, 323r; 323rv, *Pro omnibus sanctis;* 323v, *Pro pace.*

Original text ends on 323v with the prayer for peace; on 324r–328v, 17th-century ADDITIONS, i.e., indices, in black ink, non-calligraphic: 324r–326v, "Tabula psalmorum" (lists alphabetically, by cues, 118 Psalms and/or canticles, giving reference to the pages where their text is written out); 327r–328r, "Tabula hymnorum" (71 hymns); 328v, "Commune sanctorum" (page considerably faded or washed off). On 328v in lower part, inscription dated 1657 and signed: Carafa.

* * *

Foliated in ink in a 17th-century hand in the main sequence; roman numbering of the calendar (I–X) in modern pencil. One thick free endleaf of modern parchment precedes f. I, one follows f. 328.

Written area ca. 59 × ca. 45 mm. Ruling, in plummet or crayon, visible on some pages only; the vertical frame lines much more often than a full complement of horizontals (full, e.g., on 169v–180v). No pricking marks left. Written in a very neat, small prehumanistic gothic script, in brownish ink now much faded in some parts, and considerably rubbed or washed off especially in parts of the calendar. Main part written all by one hand, calendar doubtful. Rubrics red. — Italian parchment; thickness ca. 10.7 mm per 100 leaves.

Collation: $1–25^{10}$, 26^{8}(ff. 241–248) $27–34^{10}$. Vertical catchwords on last pages of most gatherings; not on 1_{10}(f. Xv), 12_{10}(f. 110v), 20_{10}(f. 190v), 26_{8}(f. 248v)

Decoration: One historiated initial (F) on f. 1r: St. Paul holding sword and book, in a roughly square field (ca. 21 × ca. 21 mm). Prevalent color is green; brushed gold has been used for the letter, for Paul's sword, and for the aureola. Acanthus leaves issue from the margin corners of the initial, one mauve, the other light blue; they are of the "boxing glove" type, and the round shapes are touched up in brushed gold. — Other initials, mostly two-line, also the one-line versals are all in alternating red and blue; the blue is on the Prussian blue side; the red, brick red. No flourishing.[6] Occasional paragraph marks are all in blue.

Bound in modern brown calf; covers blind-stamped with regularly arranged rows of x-shapes creating a pattern of star-like forms from the undepressed surface; all in a rectangular frame.

On pastedown of upper cover, in pencil: LC ms. 72; c[ensus] 72. On recto of front free endleaf, in pencil: Ac. 4189 (23); on its verso: 398006/30.

MS 28 Former owners: in the 17th century, a member of the family Carafa (Italian); perhaps Lorenzo di Marchi (the 1658 inscription on f. 308r seems not to be by an owner). Obtained by LC in 1929 from Gonnelli, Florence.

2° fo.: *xix* f *iij Scī Blasij ep̄i [et] m̄r'* L' j[a]

Bibl.: De Ricci, *Census* (1935), p. 217, no. 72; Faye and Bond (1962), p. 118, no. 47.

The work is primarily a diurnal. It was written in the 2nd half of the 15th century (cf. contents, 228r) for use of a (secular?) priest, probably of the diocese of Ferrara. In many parts, the book closely follows the *Ordo breviarii* formulated in the 13th century by Haymo of Faversham, minister general of the Franciscan order.[7]

NOTES

1. Cf. S. J. P. Van Dijk, *The origins of the modern Roman liturgy* (1960) (esp. p. 398–411).
2. Our numbering is that of the Hebrew Bible, now commonly preferred to that of the Vulgate; the ms. itself uses none.
3. The initial 2-line Lombardic *E* in red ink is followed by black majuscule *E*. — N.B. In this catalog, the presence and size of unilluminated initials is not indicated on a regular basis; some are shown, for various reasons, in this description.
4. Haymo's work, an ordinal, tells by means of cues and other devices which texts should be used; our ms., a breviary, gives the texts in full.
5. Later (17th-century?) hand has added in the margins of ff. 35v–39r appropriate references to ff. 309, etc.
6. A very insignificant exception is some doodle-like penwork in red around the blue *F* of the "Fratres iam non estis . . ." on 249r.
7. Text used for comparison was that edited by S. J. P. Van Dijk in v. II of his *Sources of the modern Roman liturgy* (Leiden, Brill, 1963; = *Studia et documenta Franciscana*, 1–2) (quoted as *SMRL* II).

MS 29

(Faye and Bond 74)

BREVIARY OF LÜBECK (Matins of the seasons) ca. 1477

Lübeck. Parchment. 280 leaves, ca. 131 × ca. 100 mm (bound volume: 143 × ca. 113 mm) 2 columns (except calendar) 32–38 lines.

ff. 1r–5v: Calendar; 203 days with entries, 43 in red; among these *Blasii et Anscharii* (Feb. 3), *Philippi et Jacobi/Walburgis* (May 1), *Visitacio Marie* (July 2). — Among the days in black: Florencii/Corona Domini, Festum patronorum, Cancii Canciani Cancianille (May 4, 16, 31) . . . Vigilia vigilie (Dec. 23).

The festivities are those of Lübeck; of the four sources used by Grotefend (*Zeitrechnung,* v. 2, p. 105) our calendar agrees best with the latest, a 1513 edition of the *Liber horarum canonicarum.* — The calendar is printed in one sequence, each month beginning wherever the preceding month ends.

6r–7v: *Sequit[ur] pasio dnī . . . secundū iohānem capl' xviij.* [unfilled space for 5-line initial *E*]Gressus [est] ih[es]us . . . posuerūt ih'm.

John XVIII,1–XIX,42. — In the earliest preserved printed edition (*Gesamtkat. d. Wiegendr.* 5374) the *Passio* is included at end of the Proper of the Saints of the Diurnale.

8r–238v: *Sequūt[ur] l[ec]ciones de ysaya capitula[r]iter disticte [et] no[n] ferialit[er] . . . ut legat vnusquisque iux[ta] libitū* . . . (238v:) . . . cōuertim[in]i ad me et salui eritis.

Bible readings and other variable parts of Matins for the seasonal offices (i.e., excluding, with some exceptions in the Christmastide, those in honor of saints) throughout the liturgical year[1]; with invitatories, responsories, versicles, and rubrics (mostly written in black and identified by red underscoring) in a very small script and grouped[2], as much as practical, near the biblical readings to which they relate; homily readings in the larger-size script, arranged by the day and numbered according to their place in the Matins; and the scriptural lessons (readings), also in the larger script, written and numbered, except as noted below, "capitulariter," i.e., whole segments of each book of the Bible used are kept together and numbered by chapters. They are assigned as follows:

Isaiah I–XI and XIII–XVI (ff. 8r–16r): for the season of Advent. "*Cap. xii habetur in psalterio,*" a rubric postulating the existence of a companion volume containing the Psalter. The "historia" and the homilies for Advent are on ff. 16r–31r; the responsories for Advent Sundays (cf. Leroquais, *Brév.* I, p. lxviii sq.) go as follows: I: Aspiciens, Aspiciebam, Missus est; Ave Maria, Salvatorem, Audite verbum; Ecce virgo, Obsecro, Letentur. II: Iherusalem cito, Ecce Dominus, Iherusalem surge; Ciuitas Iherusalem, Ecce veniet, Sicut mater; Iherusalem plantabis, Egredietur, Rex noster. III: Ecce apparebit, Bethleem, Qui venturus; Suscipe verbum, Egipte noli, Prope est; Descendet, Ecce radix, Docebit nos. IV: Canite, Vicesima quarta, Non auferetur; Me oportet, Ecce iam venit, Virgo Israel; Iuravi, Non discedimus, Intuemini.

(Beginning of the office for Christmas is missing, with the wanting leaf following f. 31; included for Christmas are parts of the Mass. Nine homily readings for each day of the Christmastide, through the octave of Epiphany (ff. 32r–86r))

Romans I–XV (ff. 87r–101v) and 1 Corinthians I–XV,44 (94v–101v): from the octave of Epiphany to the Septuagesima Sunday. The "historia" for the season is on ff. 86r–87r; the homily readings, on 101v–104v.

Genesis I–IX, XI–XIX, XXVII–XXXI, and XXXVII,2–XLI (ff. 105r–121v): from the Septuagesima to the end of the 3rd week of Lent. Some of the chapter numbering is in arabic numerals (of quite archaic forms). Homilies and the smaller-script items are variously intermixed on ff. 121v–135v; the story of Joseph and his brothers, left unfinished in the scriptural readings, is concluded by narrative responsories ("historia") on 133v sq.

Exodus I–IV (135v–137v): for the 4th week of Lent (introduced by the Laetare Sunday)

Jeremiah I–VII (142r–147r): from the Passion (Judica) Sunday through Tuesday of the Holy Week.

Lamentations I–V, 16 (and Hebrews IX,11–X,27) are arranged as in other breviaries, by lessons, included in the section for the last three days before Easter, ff. 154r–160v. The responsories (cf. Leroquais, *Brév.* I, p. lxxx sq.) are: Thurs.: I In monte II Tristis est III Ecce vidimus IV Unus ex discipulis V Ego quasi agnus VI Una hora VII Seniores VIII Revelabunt IX O Juda — Fri.: I Omnes amici II Velum templi III Vinea mea IV Tanquam V Barrabas VI Tenebre VII Tradiderunt VIII Ihesum tradidit IX Caligaverunt — Saturday: I Sepulto Domino II Ierusalem luge III Plange quasi IV Recessit pastor V O vos omnes VI Ecce quomodo VII Estimatus sum VIII Agnus Dei IX Sicut ovis — (Easter Sunday: I Angelus Domini descendit II Angelus Domini locutus est III Dum transisset Sabbatum)

(160v–168v, *historiae* and homily readings, three per day, for Easter Sunday and each day of Easter week, introduced and concluded by decorative borders)

Revelation I–VI (169r–171v): for weekdays of the first two weeks after Easter.

James I–IV (173v–175r), 1 Peter I–III (175r–176v), and 1 John I–II (176v–177v): weekdays from the 2nd Sunday after Easter to Ascension.

Acts I–VII,30 (ff. 182v–188r, interspersed by rubrics and captioned "ferialiter," not by the biblical chapters): for weekdays from Ascension to the eve of Pentecost.

1 Samuel I–IX (207v–213r) and 2 Samuel I–II (213r–214v): weekdays after Corpus Christi, through July 30.

Proverbs I–IV (215r–216v), Ecclesiastes I–III (216v–218r), Ecclesiasticus I–II (218r–219r), and Job I–V (220r–222r): from 1st Sunday after July 30 ("post Abdon") to 3rd Sunday of September

Tobit I–III (223r–224v), Judith I–III (224v–225v), Esther I–III (225v–227v): "usque ad kalendas Octobris"

MS 29, f. 160v (actual size of first column: 95 × ca. 36 mm)

1 Maccabees I–III (228r–232r), Ezekiel I–III (232r–234v), Daniel I–II (234v–236v), Hosea I–III (236v–237v), Joel I–II,20 (237v–238v), and Amos I (238v): to the end of the liturgical year.

The (partial) decorative borders indicate: on 8r, the beginning of the primary contents of the manuscript, or, perhaps, imperfect understanding on the part of the decorator of the structure of the book; on 16r, the beginning of the "historia" for Advent, probably through misunderstanding of the caption "Dominica prima in aduentu"; on 105r, beginning of the readings from Genesis; on 160v, Easter; on 168v, either conclusion of the Easter celebration or the passage to the book of Revelation.

238v–266v: *Incipiūt omelie estiuales . . .*

Seasonal homily readings from 1st Sunday after Trinity (homily on Luke XVI, 1–9 !) to end of the liturgical year (265r: *Do[minica] xxv et ulti[m]a*). On f. 264r, unusual (original, underscored) rubric: *No[t]a q[uod] seque[n]s omelia t[ri]bus d[omi]nicis sese sequentib[us] l[e]c[t]a fuit āno m cccc lxxv. propter temporis prolixitatem.* (In 1475, there were 28 Sundays after Pentecost[3] = 27 Sundays after Trinity, in the way the book, perhaps influenced by the Dominicans, counts them.)

266v–269r: *De dedicaci[on]e ecclesie . . .*

Program and texts for Matins, beginning with invitatory "Templum hoc . . ."; homily readings from Augustine and Bede.

269r–280v: *Sequit[ur] ordo vsualis quorūdā secūdū cōsuetudines eccl[esi]e maioris lubicens[is] quo[rum] no[n] meminit ordi[n]a[r]i[us]* . . . (ends 280v:) . . . *est regnum celo[rum] sagene Req[ui]re de vna virgīe in co[mmun]i [etc.]*

The part called "Officia annexa" in the *Gesamtkat. d. Wiegendrucke,* entry 5374 (*Breviarium Lubicense,* I, 5): 269r–v, rhymed "historia" of Imm. Conception (inc. Deus ante luciferum . . . cf. *AH* V, 51); office of St. Anthony, the abbot; (271r–276v:) special homily readings, 3 for each day, for Wednesdays, Fridays, and Saturdays of Lent; rhythmical office of St. Anne (Lucis huius festa . . .; cf. *AH* LII, 87); 279r–280v: *De scā Birgitta* (6 lessons in full, referring for the rest to the "Commune [sanctorum]," a section which is not in this volume, cf. *Gesamtkat. l.c.)*

* * *

Foliated in modern pencil. Written area ca. 96 × ca. 75 mm. Only vertical ruling, in faint brownish ink. Written in hybrid script of two basic sizes (small and very small) used systematically to distinguish the biblical or patristic readings for which the larger size is used from the "historiae" and red-underscored rubrics in very small script. Brownish black ink of uneven strength. Only some caption-type rubrics are completely in red. — Parchment white on both sides, feels thin although actual thickness is ca. 14 mm per 100 leaves.

Collation: 1^{8-1}(1_1[blank?] wanting; 1_8 = f. 7 a cancel?) $2–4^8$(4_5 = f. 28 a cancel?) 5^{8-1}(5_1 following f. 31 wanting) $6–15^8$(= ff. 39–118) (f. 119 a singleton) 16^{8-1}(16_8 following f. 126 wanting) 17^{10-1}(17_{10} following f. 135 wanting) 18^8 19^{10-1}(19_{10} following f. 152 wanting) 20^{8-1}(20_8 following f. 159 wanting) 21^{10-1}(21_{10} following f. 168 wanting) $22–35^8$ (followed by free endleaf). No loss of text in the incomplete gatherings except following f. 31.

The decoration consists primarily of ca. 30 illuminated 3–5 line initials, most of which extend by leafy branches into the margin; several (on 8r, 16r, 105r, 160v, 168v) are accompanied by partial borders. The borders on 8r and 16r are not fully connected with the initials and consist of vine stems of some width done in red, green, blue, and gold, accompanied by gold bezants; those on 105r, 160v, and 168v issue from the initials and their stems are, in the main, simple ink lines running, if necessary, between the columns and carrying in the margin red and purplish gray berries, also green quasi-realistic leaves. Most of the illuminated initials are in the second half of the book[4]; with few exceptions (on 16r, 87r, 168v, 218v) they are done in color on laid gold ground. In some of them, perhaps by a more skilled artist, two shades (one of which had added white) of the same hue are used for the letter: whitish red on dark red, whitish gray on gray, purplish white on purple; in other cases, the letter is rather plain blue (darker than the calligrapher's blue ink) only slightly relieved by void white hairlines. A very prominent color, however, is orange; orange is also the color most frequently used for the simple-line framing of the gold background (another is silvery gray). The leafy branches issuing from many of these initials are most often blue and/or orange, with some gold; added are curls and curlicues in faint ink. Often, a solitary gold bezant appears near the letter. — Two-line and 1-line capitals are alternately blue or red; in the Gospel homilies, the scriptural quote is introduced by a 2-line letter (an *I/J* tends to be shifted into the margin and extend past several lines), the homily itself by a 1-line capital of the contrasting color. Ordinary capitals are touched or filled with red.

Binding nearly contemporary (cropping some of the decoration), fixed-spine, dark brown calf over unrounded wooden boards, sewn over 3 bands. The covers are blind-stamped with identical centerpieces (oval, lanceolate at top and bottom) in rectangular fields (ca. 80 × 46 mm) outlined by triple fillets, with corners connected to those of a larger rectangle outlined near the edges. The oval centerpieces contain a palmetto (not in Kyriss). — Remnants of two back-to-front leather-and-metal clasps; traces of at least four metal bosses on each cover.

Former owners: Jean de Meyer (d. 1869 in Ghent); Fréd. Muller, bookseller in Amsterdam; Rev. Edwin A. Dalrymple, Baltimore; acquired by the Library of Congress in 1916 (MS. Ac. 4560, 3 (5)).

2° fo.: g a Adriani epī [et] mr̄is

Bibl.: *Catalogue des livres et manuscrits formant la bibliothèque de feu M. Jean de Meyer* (Gand : C. Vyt, 1869), no. 62; De Ricci, *Census* (1935), p. 229, no. 102; Faye and Bond (1962), p. 119, no. 74.

The primary contents of the manuscript are the seasonal night offices (Matins) of the *Liber horarum canonicarum Ecclesiae Lubicensis*, a breviary reflecting and perhaps revising the use of the diocese and cathedral of Lübeck, prepared by (or under the auspices of) the humanist bishop Albert II Krummedige (Krummendy(c)k, Crummedyckius; d. 1489).[5] Two early printed editions of the breviary are listed in the *Gesamtkatalog der Wiegendrucke* ("Breviarium Lubicense"), the earlier (GW 5374) printed in Lübeck in 1478; the contents of our ms. correspond to what the GW lists as Pars prior and Pars posterior of the *Proprium de tempore* of the Nocturnale of the breviary, incl. the "Officia annexa" listed with the *Pars posterior* (the 1478 printed edition seems to have no calendar; the Passion according to John which follows the calendar in our ms. is part of the Diurnale in the printed book). Written after 1475 (f. 264r), our ms. is very close to the first printed edition. The volume includes references to other parts of the breviary: to the Psalter (f. 14r), to the common of saints (f. 280v), and, repeatedly, to the Diurnal (the phrase "cetera habentur in diurnali," on ff. 141v, 142r, 149v . . .), quite conceivably surviving in another repository. — The most striking feature of this book is the arrangement of the scriptural readings[6] in uninterrupted segments, with all chapters actually used of each book of the Bible kept together in one sequence: an editorial feature befitting a humanist's outlook.

NOTES

1. Liturgical year begins with the 1st Sunday of Advent (Nov. 27–Dec. 3).
2. These parts are called "historia" throughout the book; e.g., "Incipiunt historie Geneseos," on 121v.
3. Cf. Cappelli, *Cronologia* (3rd. ed., 1969), p. 44–45.
4. (Near the beginning, on 6r, the 5-line space for the initial *E* remained unfilled.)
5. Cf. *Lex. f. Theol. u. Kirche,* art. Lübeck; *Dansk biografisk leks.,* 3. udg. (1981).
6. The *GW* says (col. 349) "Historien," but what is meant must be the Bible readings.

MS 30

(Faye and Bond 85)

BRIGITTINE BREVIARY mid-XVth c.

Written in North Brabant (Marienwater Abbey)[1] Parchment. 261 leaves, 195 × ca. 133 mm (bound volume: ca. 202 × ca. 146 mm) 1 column. 21 lines (in the calendar section, 30–33 lines)

(f. 1r blank except for penciled 20th-century inscriptions: Ac. 4560(3), no. 16; MS. 85)

2r–v: (I)[5]nden iaer ons heren .M.CC.eñ.lx. begã dese tafel h' ian van aswilte canonick eñ priest te colen . . . (ends on 2v, in 21st line:) lutien dach.

The two pages attempt to explain the tables which follow.

3r–v: (caption-like, blue:) *Numeri lune. Nume[r]i tabule.*

The table, which extends over two pages and covers the years 1260 through 1790, served to determine the date of Easter.

4r–9v: (KL)[2] *Januarius habet dies xxxi.* . . . (9v, last line, blue:) *Nox h[abe]t horas xviij . dies vi.*

Calendar, in Latin; in black[2] and red (with some blue notes). Altogether 226 entries, 42 of them in red. Among these: *Resurrectio Dñi nr̄i ih'u xp̄i* (March 27), *Seruacij* (May 13), *Visitacio marie* (July 2), *Lamb[er]ti* (Sept. 17), *Michaelis archangeli* (Sept. 29), *Canonizac[i]o b. birgitte patrona nr̄a* [sic] (Oct. 7), *Dyonisij* (Oct. 8), *Huberti* (Nov. 3), *Leonardi* (Nov. 6), *Martini* (Nov. 11), *Katherine* (Nov. 25), *Nycolai* (Dec. 6), *Concepcio bt̄e marie v'gīs* (Dec. 8). — The feast of St. Lambert has an "octave" day, on Sept. 17, as in Liège.

Among the days written in black: Hadelini (Feb. 3), Vrsmari (Apr. 18), Translacio Lamberti (Apr. 28), Transl. Birgitte (May 28), Natale Birgitte (July 23), Transfiguracio dñi [et commem.] Affre vg. (Aug. 5), Magdalberte (Sept. 7), Triumphus b. Lamberti (Oct. 13), Trudonis conf. (Nov. 24).

The entries suggest a Brigittine establishment in the area of the diocese of Liège, a description fitting the monastery Marienwater (*Ad Aquas Beate Marie*) near 's-Hertogenbosch. — The calendar includes several commemorative notes, some dated: with Apr. 18: Obiit . . . [con]fesso[r] n[oste]r Gherardus a[nn]o lxxxi;[3] with Dec. 5: Obijt dil[ec]ta m[ate]r mea mechteld' gielis a[nn]o d[omin]i mcccc.lxxx.

(f. 10rv blank, unruled)

11r–129v: (B)[14]//Eatus vir qui non abijt . . . (ends on 129v, lines 8–9:) . . . om[n]is spiritus laudet dn̄m.

The Psalms, in Latin, the "Gallican" version; not numbered. The regular sequence is interrupted once (on ff. 106v–108v): the Athanasian Creed ("*C' athanasij*") is placed between verses 32 and 33 of Ps. CXIX, corresponding to its use in the Prime of the liturgical office. Liturgical purpose, i.e., the division of the Psalter among the days of the week or assignment of its segments to various "hours" is also served by the placement of large (chiefly 9-line) initials at the beginning of Pss. XXVII (f. 28v), XXXIX (39v), LII (50r), LIII (50v), LXIX (61v), LXXXI (75r), XCVIII (87v), CII (89r), CX (101r); the initials are accompanied by decorative borders and, in the tail margins, charming miniatures representing:
28v, 50v, 101r: an angel holding a sign
39v: St. Gertrude of Nivelles (with spinning wheel)
61v: St. Catherina (with sword and wheel)
75r: St. Barbara (with tower and book)
87v: St. Apollonia (with pincers and tooth)
50r: a goat and a grotesque half-human figure
89r: a chase (deer, hare, part of another animal)

129v–139v: (in line 9 of 129v, blue "*C' N E*" [= ?]; lines 10 sqq.:) (C)[8]Onfitebor tibi dn̄e q[uonia]m iratus es michi . . . [= Isaiah XII] (130r:) . . . *C' Ezechiae* [= Is. XXXVIII,10–20] . . . (130v:) . . . *C' Anne* [= 1 Sam. II, 1–10] . . . (131v:) . . . *C' Moysi* [= Exodus XV, 1–19] . . . (132v:) . . . *C' Abacuc* [= Habakkuk III, 2–19] . . . (134r:) . . . *C' Deut[ero]nomij* [= Deut. XXXII, 1–43] . . . (136v:) . . . *Canticu[m] Ambrosij et Augustini* [= Te Deum laudamus] . . . (137v:) . . . *Triu[m] puer[or]u[m]* [= Daniel III, 57–88.56] . . . (138v:) . . . *C' Zacharie* [= Luke I, 68–79] . . . (139r: . . . *C' marie* [= Magnificat, Luke I, 46–55] . . . (139v:) . . . *Canticu[m] symeonis* [= Nunc dimittis, Luke II, 29–32] (ends 139v, 10th line:) . . . et gl[ori]am plebis tue isr[ae]l.

139v–144r: (in line 10 of 139v:) *versus.*//Ne reminiscaris . . . (line 13:) *letania.* (K)[3]yrieleyson . . . (143v:) (E)[3]xaudi . . . (J)[4]Neffabilem . . . (O)[2]m[ni]p[oten]s . . . (P)[2]Jetate tua . . . (ends on 144r, line 15:) concede. P[er] ih'm xp̄m dn̄m nr̄m Ame[n]

The Litany of Saints. It invokes, after Mary, the apostles, etc. (through Innocents), 33 individual martyrs, 26 confessors, and 31 women. — Among the martyrs: "Corneli," "Botwide," "Lamberte," "Dyonisi c. s. t.," "Mauriti c. s. t." — Among confessors: "Bricti," "Materne," "Egidi," "Leonarde," "Huberte," "Remigi," "Lodewice." — Among the women: "Birgitta," "Magdalberta," "Walburgis," "Appolonia," "Brigida," also "Sapiencia." — The selection shows a combination of Netherlandish, Scandinavian, and French influences natural in a North-Brabant house of a Swedish order in an area which (until 1482) was governed by the Duke of Burgundy.

144r–v: (144r, line 16:) *Iniciū scī euagelij scd'm ioh'em. Gl[ori]a t[ibi] do[min]e.* (I)[3]N principio . . . (144v, last lines:) . . . gracie [et] veritatis. Deo gracias. P[er] hec scā eua[n]gelica dicta. Deleant[ur] vniu[er]sa n[ost]ra delicta.

John I,1–14 (Vulgate version, with the Parisian "Quod factum est in ipso vita erat") presented as a liturgical reading (not as an element of a suffrage).

145r–146v: (C)[3]redo in deu[m] . . . (the Apostles' Creed) *Item voer elken psalm* . . . Xp̄s resurgens . . . *En[de] nae elken psalme dese* Cum rex gl[ori]e . . . (145v:) . . . *En[de] als dese psalters geeynt sij[n]* . . . Kyrieleyson . . . (P)[3]r[est]a quesum[us] . . . a morte anime resurgam[us] . . . (146r:) (D)[2]n̄e ih'u xp̄e . . . indulge a[n]i[m]e famule tue .N. . . . *Item desen psalter voerscreuen salmen op den paesdach beginne[n]* . . . (12 lines of rubrical matter) . . . *in den veghevuer.*

(146v:) (C)[2]onfiteor deo . . . marie et btē birgitte et btō augustino et om[n]ibus scīs dei . . . *Collecta pro peccatore.* (D)[2]eus qui iustificas . . . (last 4 lines:) (*A*)ue benignissime ih'u gr[aci]a plenus . . . et b[e]n[e]dict[us] sit p[re]ciosus sanguis o[mn]i[u]m vulne[rum] tuo[rum] A[men]

147r–v: *Lectrix in die d[omi]nica post matutinas.* (D)[3]Omine labia mea . . . *horista* Salua[m] fac . . . *chorus* Deus meus . . . *Ebdomadarie refector[ij?] dicentes* Bened[i]c[tu]s es dn̄e deus meus qui adiuuisti me et consolatus es me . . . (D)[2]Eus . . . quia p[er]acte ebdomade seruicia . . . compleuerunt . . . (the rite ends with another collect, 147v:) . . . (M)[2]isericors et mitissime deus . . . auge desideriu[m] ut recte sororib[us] suis impendant seruicia . . . Amen.

147v–154r: (beginning on 147v, lines 14–15:) *Hore de scō sp[irit]u. Ad matuti.* (J)[7]N vnitate sancti sp̄s benedicat nos p[ate]r et filius . . . (office ends on 154r, line 8:) P[er] eunde[m] ih'm xp̄m dn̄m nr̄m Amen.

The (longer) Hours of the Holy Spirit, based on the hymn *Veni Creator Spiritus*, with one psalm for each "hour"; cf. the printed version in T. Lundén's edition of the Brigittine breviary (*Officium parvum beate Marie Virginis / den heliga Birgitta och den helige Petrus av Skänninge*. Uppsala, 1976), v. II, p. 184–208.

154r–163v: (beginning 154r, line 10:) *Incipit* [sic] *vigilie defunctorum.//Anti.* Placebo. *Psalmus dauid* (D)[3]Jlexi . . . (156r, Invitatory:) Circu[m]dederu[n]t me gemitus mortis. Dolores inferni circu[m]dederu[n]t me . . . (office ends on 163v, line 20:) pijssime rex glorie Amen.

The Office of the Dead (Officium defunctorum); with responsories[4] as follows: I Credo quod II Qui Lazarum III Domine quando IV Heu mihi V Ne recorderis VI Domine secundum actum meum VII Peccantem me VIII Libera me Domine de viis inferni IX Libera me Domine de morte eterna. — The Invitatory[5] and, in part, the responsories differ from those in Lundén's edition (*op. cit.*, v. II, p. 210–238).

(f. 164rv blank, unruled)

165–244v: (On 165r, the *T*, largest initial letter in the book, is placed above 5 lines of text; the borders are highly decorated; in lower margin, half-portrait of St. Andrew (?)) (T)[16]Rinu[m] deum et vnu[m] pronis mentib[us] adoremus . . . (178r:) *Feria secunda Inuitato[rium]* (R)[8]Egem angelo[rum] de eius m[at]re exultanciu[m] Venite adorem[us] . . . (188r:) *Feria tercia . . . Inuitatoriu[m]* (F)[9]Jliu[m] dei quem p[ro]phete letantes . . . (199r:) . . . *Feria iiij* . . . (O)[9]Rtum virginis et m[at]ris marie celebrem[us] . . . (209r, with rubric on 208v:) *F[er]ia v.* (A)[9]Ve maria gr[aci]a plena . . . (220r:) . . . *F[er]ia vi* (R)[9]Egem v[ir]ginis filiu[m] pro nobis crucifixu[m] . . . (232v:) . . . *Sabb[at]o.* (J)[19]N honore virginis marie in celu[m] assu[m]pte . . . (the basic office ends in line 17 of 244v:) . . . O dulcis maria.

The Brigittine "cursus per hebdomadam," or office for each day of the week, with the order's own invitatories, hymns, antiphons, and, most importantly, readings: these comprise, divided into three lessons per day, the work known as *Sermo angelicus de excellentia Beatae Mariae Virginis,*[6] written in Swedish by St. Birgitta (d. 1373), the foundress of the order,[7] and translated into Latin by Petrus (Olavi, Olovsson; d. 1378) of Skänninge. — As in Lundén's edition, the elements of the rhymed office of St. Birgitta in our manuscript (173v, "Sponsa Regis doctrix legis . . ."; etc.) are limited to honoring her alone, without the extensions found in later mss. which include her daughter Katherina.[8]

244v–249v: (beginning in 18th line of 244v:) *In festo ma^e (= "marie"? "maiore"?)* (S)[2]Alue celi digna mitis et benigna . . . (245r:) . . . *In festo paschal[li]* (R)[3]Egina celi letare . . . *In aduentu dn̄i* (D)[2]e te virgo nascit[ur] . . . (245v:) *In natiuitate xp̄i.* (G)[3]Audendu[m] nobis est . . . *In annu*[n]ciacione . . . (246r:) . . . *In concepcione* . . . (246v:) . . . *In purificac[i]o[n]e* . . . (247r:) . . . *In compassione* . . . (247v:) . . . *In festa paschalia coll[ecta]* . . . (248r:) . . . *In visitacione* . . . (248v:) . . . *assu[m]pc[i]o[n]e* . . . (249r:) . . . *natiuitate* . . . (ends 249v, line 19:) Deus in adiutoriu[m] meu[m] intende. Dn̄e.

Alternate components of the office for special seasons or festivities. The section is similar (with differences) to that captioned "Laudes B.M.V." in Lundén's edition (v. II, p. 170–178); the rubrics in our manuscript are less fully explanatory.

250r–261v: (music; introduced by caption fitting the first item, in last line of f. 249v: *Dominica Inuitatoriu[m] ad matutinas.)* (T)[4]Rinu[m] deum . . . (the section ends, as does the book, on 261v:) . . . regine laudaueru[n]t eam.

Texts with music; four-line staff, square notes. The texts are initial words of various parts of the office: initia of the invitatories, hymns, antiphons, etc., in the sequence in which they would be used. The initial words of these items were commonly intoned by a single voice (by the abbess or by a sister entrusted with this task[9]). — At the end (261r–v), complete text and music of the Marian antiphon *Speciosa facta es.*

* * *

Foliated in modern pencil; f. 261 is followed by two free endleaves of rather thick parchment different from that of the text. — Written area ca. 110 × 73–78 mm. — Fully ruled in purple ink; two horizontal lines at top and two at the bottom extend all the way to the edges. Pricking marks ca. 5 mm from fore edge. — Regular, well executed text script, semiquadrate but very close to the Windesheim "*rotunda*,"[10] in very good black ink (except the ff. 1–9, cf. contents). Most of the text (ff. 11–249?) possibly by one scribe; the texts with music on ff. 250–261 probably by another; ff. 1–3 certainly and 4–9 possibly by a third one. — Rubrics in red; also blue in the preliminary section (tables, calendar). — Rather high quality, white, slightly translucent parchment; thickness ca. 15–16 mm per 100 leaves.

Collation: 1^{14-4}(= ff. 1–10; $1_{1,2,6,11}$ absent, no loss) $2–19^{8}$ 20^{12-2}(= ff. 155–164; $20_{1,2}$ absent, no loss) $21–23^{8}$ 24^{10-2+1}(= ff. 189–197; $24_{4,6}$ absent, no loss; f. 193 is paper cancel attached to stub of 24_{6}; added in 1824?[11]) $25–32^{8}$.

Decoration of the book consists of: (*a*) sophisticated calligraphic initials anchoring extensive flourishing; (*b*) images of saints or (in several cases) angels, in center of lower margin; sometimes associated with an all-around border; (*c*) also in tail margins but never on same page as the preceding, dadaistic grotesque creatures or chase scenes. — The first page of the Psalter, f. 11r, is decorated in a basically different style and will be described last.

(*a*) All initials are primarily red and/or blue; the larger ones, 8–9 lines or more in height, use both colors, combined with the white void of the vellum, to a felicitous effect reminiscent of ornaments on folk costumes. The red is that of the ink of the rubrics; the blue, on the ultramarine (slightly purplish) side, has a velvety character. Some use is made of sparingly applied green and yellow in the background areas, chiefly to make the omnipresent pen-drawn rosettes and acanthus leaves stand out. — Three-line and 2-line minor initials are alternately red and blue, sometimes with lace-like decorations made by use of the white void, always with pen-drawn acanthus and other botanical forms inside and around. — Rich, skillfully made sprays of penned flourishes in purple or red ink (as a rule, not combined) issue from the initials in size proportionate to their importance.

(*b*) Images of angels or saints appear in the center of lower margin on a number of pages throughout the book (ff. 28v, 39v, 50v, 61v, 75r, 87v, 101r, 165r, 209r, 220r). They are quite stereotyped, albeit charmingly drawn and colored, in flat hues of (striking) blue, red, yellow, purple, and green; a touch of gold, otherwise barely used at all, appears in the rather uniformly blond hair of the personalities portrayed. In all cases but one (the kneeling angel on 209r) only upper part of the body is shown. Only one man in included: St. Andrew (?), on 165r; his hair and beard are brownish or reddish. — Four-sided borders characterized by bold straight blue lines and red-ink penwork decorate the ff. 101r, 165r (see plate XI, p. xxvi), 209r, and 220r. The blue lines end at the top in tridents;[12] lower corners are covered by floreate medallions, and the saint's or angel's image is in the center of the lower horizontal.[13]

(*c*) Grotesque element: Curious half-human creatures appear in lower margins of some pages, particularly in the second half of the book (see plate XII, p. xxvii). They are pen-drawn and colored in the same lively palette as the images of saints but the coloring is sometimes limited to only some parts of the creature. Some of the oddly misshaped entities, with human faces, wear a bishop's mitre, always blue with red trim (166v, 251v). — Chase scenes involving quasi-realistic dogs, deer, and hares occur several times, e.g., on ff. 129v, 172v; a unicorn with gold-painted horn on 166v (here in combination with the mitred grotesque) and 199r.

MS 30 A technically ambitious but less interesting artist emulating the three-dimensional Franco-Flemish style produced the initial, with borders, for the *Beatus vir* on f. 11r: the four-sided border (full, outlined in faint ink) is inhabited by large, fat, chicken-shaped and giraffe-necked, buff-colored beasts (one with a man's face) variously entangled with blue-and-silver (now gray) foliage; strawberries, thistles, grapes, birds, faintly green strawberry and holly leaves, and golden bezants fill the spaces between. The large dim-blue initial *B* on a rectangular field of burnished gold contains in its enclosed area a fantastic (grayish orange) flower, and what was probably intended to represent the *lignum plantatum secus decursus aquarum* (Ps. I,3), with large apples, all originally silver, now blackened, on a ground which now appears gray. This page is, not unhappily, the only one in the book where silver and gold were used in any quantity.

Bound in contemporary light brown calf over rounded boards, sewn over 5 raised thongs; headbands stitched over with woven red and green strands; covers blind-stamped with a diamond-patterned rectangular center panel and rosettes. Remnants of two back-to-front metal (brass?) clasps; one of them, now lost, reportedly carried engraved inscription "S. Cristine."[14] — The book was thoroughly thumb-indexed by means of twenty miniature leather buttons (ca. 3 mm in diameter) attached to the fore edge of important leaves and arranged in two sloping lines; nine are preserved.[15]

On pastedown of upper cover, a 15th-century inscription in ink (careless cursive): sustor jutken//schomans (?) dit//boeck;[16] also 19th- and 20th-century notes in pencil ("Temp. no. 17"; "No. 4 (M.S.)"); also labels of B. Westermann & Co. (New York), Rev. Edwin A. Dalrymple D.D. (Baltimore), and the Library of Congress (with penciled: De R. 85). — On pastedown of the lower cover, penciled "in.-"; also mounted clipping from the 1859 Van Voorst sale catalog (cf. Bibl.) which describes the book as "Heures, de Pâques à l'Ascension."

Former owners: within the Marienwater community, in 15th century, the sister named on the pastedown (Jutke S . . . mans) and, later, Sister Cristine. In the first half of the 19th century, Rev. Dirk Cornelis van Voorst (d. 1835) and his son J.-J. van Voorst, both pastors in Amsterdam. Later, Rev. E. A. Dalrymple of Baltimore; acquired by the Library along with other items of his collection in 1916 (accession no. 4560/3, 16).

2° fo.: Inden iaer ons heren. M.CC.eñ.lx. begā

Bibl.: *Catalogue raisonné de la précieuse collection de manuscrits . . . de MM. D.-C. van Voorst et J.-J. van Voorst* . . . (Amsterdam, 1859) (no. 111; errors) — De Ricci, *Census* (1935), p. 232, no. 113 ("Psalterium cum canticis"; errors) — *Illuminated books* . . . (Walters Art Gallery, 1949), no. 148 ("psalter and abbreviated Hours, Germany (Rhineland)") — Faye and Bond (1962), p. 120, no. 85 ("Psalterium cum canticis," etc.) — Ulla Sander Olsen's (Copenhagen) communications (1977) filed in the Library's Rare Book and Special Collections Division stacks with the codex.

"En av de märkligaste litterära skapelserna från Sveriges medeltid" — Tryggve Lundén, *op. cit.*[17] Of literary interest are of course primarily the readings (cf. our comment to ff. 165–244) and the hymns (which are perhaps entirely the work of Petrus Olavi). — It should be observed for the benefit of readers unacquainted with Latin liturgy that the phenomenon of a prayer system created entirely anew for a nuns' order is very unusual, and that making a newly written set of meditations its main reading ingredient was an unheard of, bold (and perhaps not quite unexceptionable) idea.

NOTES

1. The place of origin was determined in 1977 by Ulla Sander Olsen, then a student in Copenhagen. Debt is due her also for a number of other points. — The Brigittine monastery Marienwater (also Coudewater) in Rosmalen, near 's-Hertogenbosch, Netherlands was founded ca. 1434–1440; it went out of existence (under outside pressures) in 1713. Cf. T. Nyberg, *Birgittinische Klostergründungen des Mittelalters* (1965); H. van Velthoven, *Noord-Brabant* (1949) (p. 238); H. de Werd, *Rosmalen in oude ansichten* (1972–1976) (v. 2, plate 31).

2. Or, rather, in a shade of light brown entirely different from the black ink of ff. 11 sqq. and the whole main text; only an addition in May ("Dympne") is black.

3. The necrology of Marienwater notes this death: "Heer Gherit (Gherik?) van Rossem die wel 20 jaer confessor was. Anno 1481." (Communicated by U. Olsen, cf. note 1. Cf. also Nyberg, *op. cit.*, p. 188, n.5)

4. Cf. Leroquais, *LH* I, p. xxxix.

5. The same cheerless Invitatory appears (in Netherlandish) in Geert Grote's 14th-century *Getijdenboek* (cf. Van Wijk's edition, Leiden, 1940, p. 156). Lundén's text of the Brigittine office (*op. cit.*, p. 218) has the Roman "Regem cui omnia vivunt / Venite adoremus."

6. Not so called in our manuscript. The Swedish original seems to be lost. The Latin text (along with a translation back into modern Swedish) in Lundén, *op. cit.* (v. I, p. 2–v. II, p. 166). — See also our concluding note.

7. Official name of the order (founded, or approved by Rome, in 1370) is Ordo Sanctissimi Salvatoris. Its establishments were formerly twin monasteries, with one house for women, one for men, and a church in between. — The foundress was a Swedish noblewoman and mother of eight children prior to her religious career (which began after the death of her husband). She is called Birgitta in her own country; in English sometimes Bridget, a form inevitably leading to confusions with the Irish saint of ca. 500 A.D.

8. Cf. C.A. Moberg, *Die liturgischen Hymnen in Schweden* I (1947), p. 145 sq.

9. The Sister Jutke S . . . mans named on the inside of upper cover? (Cf. below.)

10. I.e., to what the mid-15th-century calligrapher H. Strepel called "rotunda"; the script would now hardly be perceived as "round" (cf. *Nomenclature des écritures livresques*, fig. 27).

11. The paper leaf 193 contains on recto (verso is blank) 20 lines of handwriting dated 5 Apr. 1824. The text, in Netherlandish except for Latin quote at end, begins: "Door de afbeelding . . ." and ends "animi voluptatisque causa." The writer attempts to interpret some of the grotesque decorations found in some of the lower margins (cf. Decoration (*c*)), in particular the theme of a hare which he believes may represent the Devil. He refers to *ANTIQUITEITEN* (Groningen) II (1823), pt. 2, f. 139; also to Caesar's report on the taboo the Belgae had against eating hare. — The paragraph is not signed; it may be by the Rev. D. C. van Voorst (cf. former owners).

12. Trident was the emblem of St. Jutke (= Ivette), a Belgian recluse (d. 1228); perhaps the book was made for — or by — the "sustor Jutke(n) S . . .-mans" named in the inscription on the front pastedown. — A trident apears also in the hand of the angel on f. 209r.

13. The border on f. 220r (for the office of Friday) has no tridents; its four corner medallions show Christ's wounds; the initial contains the Cross and pierced heart; angel at bottom holds lance and sponge.

14. The information, repeated later in De Ricci's *Census*, had appeared in the 1859 Van Voorst catalog (see Bibl.). — N.B. Clipping of the pertinent notice (no. 111) from that catalog is mounted on pastedown of the lower cover of the manuscript.

15. The book is now protected by a solander-type (drop-back) box covered in grayish orange and purple cloth.

16. Correct reading of the name is not certain. It is possible that the sister is identical to one recorded in the Marienwater necrologue as having died in 1442, whose name has been transcribed as "Jutta Soermons" (cf. Nyberg, *op. cit.*, p. 181, n. 8).

17. (= "One of the most remarkable literary creations of medieval Sweden") — Full title of Lundén's work in our comment to ff. 147–154; it constitutes v. 27–28 of *Studia historico-ecclesiastica Upsalensia,* a subseries of the *Acta Universitatis Upsaliensis*. It includes an excellent bibliography of the Brigittine office, also an English summary of Lundén's findings. — A version with rubrics in English was published in 1969 by Henry Bradshaw Society (its v. 96), edited by A. Jeffries Collins, with title *The Bridgettine breviary of Syon Abbey*. — Music-oriented scholars have known the office (with or without its readings) for some time under the name *Cantus sororum Ordinis Sancti Salvatoris*; cf. Moberg, *op. cit.* (our note 8).

MS 31

(Faye and Bond 172)[1]

DOMINICAN HYMNARY AND VESPERAL PSALTER 148–?

Upper Rhine? Paper. 48 leaves, 169–171[2] × ca. 119 mm (bound volume: 176 × ca. 125 mm) 1 column. 17 lines.

ff. 1r–25r: *Ad laudes ympnus d[ie] eph'ie.* A p[at]re vnigenit[us] . . . (hymnal ends with the 5th line on f. 25r:) uite p[er]he[n]nis gr[aci]a Te nu[n]c rede[m]ptor (rest of the stanza was presumed known)

Dominican hymnary for feasts, primarily those introduced or given new prominence in that order's liturgy between ca. 1300 and 1480; texts only. Leaves 1r–4r contain the *temporale* (seasonal part); 4r (beginning, unsignaled, with the Innocents) through 24v, the sanctoral;[3] the arrangement in both groupings is by the calendar but nothing is expressly said about that. — The altogether 56 hymns (52 given in full) represent ca. one-third of the total required by the Dominican office of the period; the present collection is a supplement of what were more or less "officia nova." It contains:[4]

(Epiphany)
1r: A Patre unigenitus ad nos venit (*AH* II, 107 var.)
Summi largitor praemii (*AH* II, 35)
1v: Iam Christe sol iustitiae (*AH* LI, 59; our ms. lacks last stanza)

(Trinity)
2r: Adesto sancta Trinitas
2v: O Trinitas laudabilis et unitas mirabilis

(Corpus Christi)
3r: Sacris solemniis iuncta sint gaudia
3v: Verbum supernum prodiens nec Patris linquens dexteram

(Innocents)
4r: Caterva matrum personat (= stanza K of *A solis ortus cardine*)

(Translation of relics of Thomas Aquinas to Toulouse, in 1368)
4v: Superna mater inclyta novis exsulta gaudiis (*AH* LII, 355)
5r: Iubar coelorum prodiens (*AH* LII, 356)
Aurora pulchre rutilans (*AH* LII, 357)

(Cathedra Petri?)
5v: Iam bone pastor Petre clemens accipe
6r: Iesu redemptor omnium corona confitentium (cue only)

(Thomas Aquinas)
6r: Exsultet mentis iubilo (*AH* LII, 352)
6v: Thomas insignis genere (*AH* LII, 353)
7r: Lauda mater ecclesia Thomae felicem exitum (*AH* LII, 354)

(Vincent Ferrer, canonized in 1455)
7v: Mente iocunda iubilent fideles
8r: Lumen in terris populi fidelis
9r: Magne Vincenti nova lux olympi

(Peter Martyr O.P.)
9v: Magnae dies laetitiae nobis illuxit
10r: Adest triumphus nobilis (*AH* LII, 326)
10v: Exsultet claro sidere

(Catherine of Siena, canonized 1461)
10v: Haec tua virgo monumenta laudis (*AH* LII, 254 var.)
11v: Laudibus virgo nimis efferenda
12r: Iam ferox miles tibi saepe cessit

(Finding of the Cross)
12v: Salve crux sancta (*AH* L, 223, stanzas 1,2,5)
13r: Originale crimen necans (same, stanzas 3 and 4)

(Crown of Thorns)
13v: Aeternae regi gloriae (*AH* LII, 12)
14r: Lauda fidelis contio (*AH* LII, 13)

(Visitation B.V.M.)
14v: Magnae dies laetitiae (*AH* LII, 45)
15r: Lingua pangat et cor tangat
15v: Hymnum ("Ympnu[m]") festivae gloriae

(St. Praxedes [!])[5]
16r: Huius obtentu (cue only)

(Mary Magdalen)
16r: Lauda mater ecclesia lauda Christi clementiam
16v: Aeterni Patris unice nos pio vultu (*AH* LII, 284)

(St. Anne, a feast made "totum duplex" in 2nd half of 15th century)
17r: De stella sol oriturus (*AH* LII, 104; ms. has the fourth stanza written as a continuation of the third)
17v: Praeclari patris Abrahae (*AH* IV, 128)

(Transfiguration; added to Dominican calendar in 1456 or slightly later)
18r: O sator rerum reparator aevi (*AH* LI, 98, stanzas 1–4,9)
18v: Festiva haec sollemnitas (cf. *AH* IV, 16, *Festiva iam solemnia*; a variant)
18v: O nata lux de lumine (*AH* LI, 99)

(Elizabeth)[6]
19r: Hymnum ("Ympnu[m]") Deo vox iocunda (*AH* LII, 18, stanzas 1–4 and 10)
19v: Haec insignis haec beata pauperum nutritia (same, stanzas 5–9)

(Eleven Thousand Virgins)
20v: Gaude sancta Colonia (not found in *AH*)
21r: Hymnum ("Ympnu[m]") sanctis virginibus (*AH* LII, 371)

(Catherine of Alexandria)
21v: Catharinae ("Katherine") collaudemus virtutum insignia
21v: Pange lingua gloriosae virginis martyrium
22r: Praesens dies expendatur in eius praeconium

(Peter in Chains)
22v: Iam bone pastor (cue only)
Aeterna Christi munera/apostolorum (cue only)

(Remigius)
22v: Iste confessor Domini sacratus/sobrius castus (cf. *AH* LI, 118; manuscript combines verse 1 of first stanza with verses 2–4 of the second)

(Dominic)
22v: Gaude mater ecclesia laetam agens memoriam
23r: Novus athleta (ms.: "ad leta") Domini
23r: Hymnum ("Ympnu[m]") novae laetitiae/ dulci productum

(Augustine)
23v: Magne pater Augustine preces nostras suscipe
24r: Caeli cives applaudite

(*"De pluribus[us] martirib[us]"*)
24r: Aeterna Christi munera/et martyrum victorias

25r–46v: (on 25r, immediately following the end of the last hymn, 4-line music staff with notation for:) Alleluia, Euouae, Dix[it], Euouae (then:) Dixit d[omi]n[us] d[omi]no meo . . . (section ends on f. 46v with the *Magnificat*)[7]

Dominican weekly *cursus* of psalms (with texts in full) for the Vespers; as in Bonniwell, *History of the Dominican liturgy* (1944), p. 136.[8] — There are no captions or rubrics to identify the day of the week or even to suggest the beginning of another day's set. — The ordinary ferial antiphons are included, with music; also the basic intonation patterns for each psalm. — The distribution of the psalms is as follows:
[Sunday:] ff. 25r–28r (Pss. CX–CXV)
[Monday:] ff. 28r–30r (Pss. CXVI, CXVII, CXX, CXXI)
[Tuesday:] ff. 30v–32r (Pss. CXXII–CXXVI
[Wednesday:] ff. 32v–34r (Pss. CCXXVII–CXXXI)

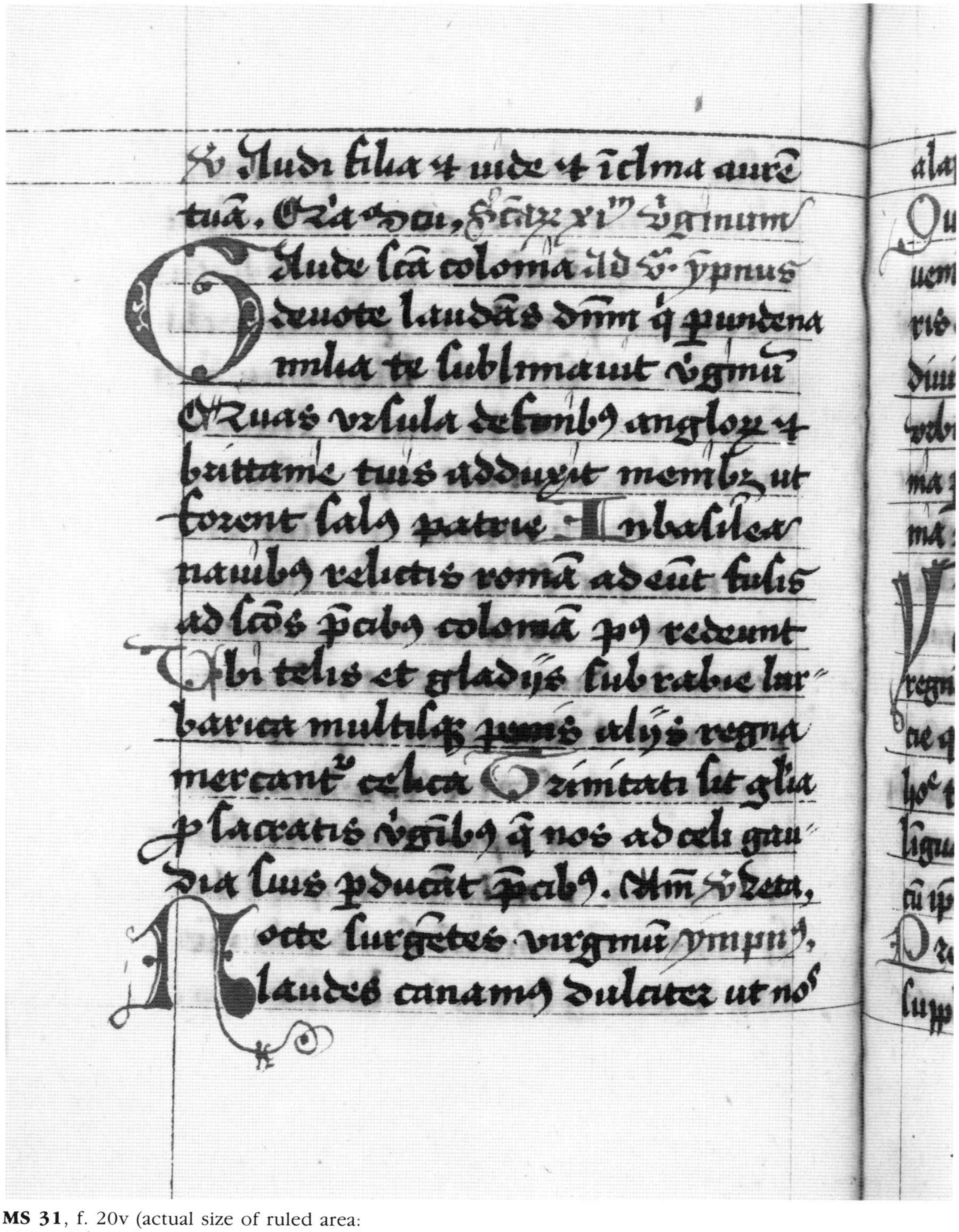

MS 31, f. 20v (actual size of ruled area: 110 × 74 mm)

[Thursday:] ff. 34v–37r (Pss. CXXXII, CXXXIII, CXXXV–CXXXVII)
[Friday:] ff. 38r–41v (Pss. CXXXVIII–CXLII)
[Saturday:] ff. 42r–46r (Pss. CXLIV–CXLVII)
(On 46v, the *Magnificat*, needed every day)

47r–48r: PAter n[oster] qui es in cel[is] . . . a malo Amen Aue ma[r]ia . . . fruct[us] ve[n]tris tui ih[esu]s Amen Credo i[n] deu[m] . . . descend[i]t ad inferna [!] . . . (47v:) . . . [et] uita[m] et'nam amen SAlue regina . . . o dulcis ma[r]ia. (the following WITH MUSIC:) Benedicamus domino (repeated five times, with five different tunes; ending on 48r)

(Lower one-third of f. 48r blank, ruled; 48v blank, ruled)

* * *

Foliated in modern pencil. Two modern free endleaves (paper) in front, two at end. — Written area ca. 108 × ca. 75–80 mm (ruled for ca. 110–115 × ca. 73–81 mm) — Fully ruled in black ink only slightly fainter than that of the script. Two ruled horizontal lines at top and two at the bottom run from edge to edge across the whole opening; other horizontal lines protrude variously beyond the framing verticals. Pricking not preserved. — Written in a hybrid script (*littera textualis currens*), perhaps by one person throughout. Good black ink. Captions red. — The paper is of two kinds: ff. 1–22 and 37–48 have watermarks of the type Piccard, *Ochsenkopf-Wasserzeichen, Abt.* X, 402; leaves 23–36 (= gatherings 4 and 5) have ox head of a different type: no. 271 of Piccard's *Abt.* IX.

Collation: 1^6 $2–4^8$ $5–6^6$ $7^{8?}$(= ff. 43–48, with $7_{7–8}$ wanting; no text loss). — Leaves 15.22 and 17.20 have vertical chain lines. — There is what seems to be an inside guard (strip sewn-in in central gutter of the gathering) between ff. 39 and 40. — No catchwords or other aids toward keeping the leaves and gatherings in sequence.

Decoration is limited to numerous calligraphic initials, 2 to 4 lines high (a 4-line *S*: on 12v, for *Salve crux sancta*) marking chiefly the beginning of a hymn.[9] The palette is mostly red or blue ink; also (only on ff. 1–13) light green, occurring only in letters which combine two or three colors; the combinations vary (on 1r, red, blue, and green; on 4v, green and red; on 7v, green and blue; on 23v and 25r, blue comes in two tones, one of which may be blue-green, within one letter). By far most of these *litterae notabiliores*, even the 3-line size, are monochrome, more or less alternately red or blue. Versals are red throughout.

Binding: Modern brown morocco. On spine, in gold: EXPOSITIO HYMNORUM.[10]

Former owners: William Hayman Cummings (sale, Sotheby, May 1917). — Bought by the Library of Congress on 21 Jan. 1946 (accession no. 0575E2).

2° fo.: suffert pietas Quiddāq[ue] p[e]n[itenc]ie da

Bibl.: *Catalogue of the famous musical library . . . of the late W. H. Cummings* (1917), 655. — Faye and Bond (1962), p. 116, no. 172.[11] — *A Bibliography of the Catholic Church* (1970), p. 242, NC 0218008. — LC printed card no. 51-45287 (rev. 1972).

The hymnal/vesperal was not written before 1461 (the year of canonization of Catherine of Siena) nor much after 1490 (no hymns for St. Denis, or, especially, for the Sanctification of the Virgin[12]). The watermarks on leaves 23–36 suggest date 1483; those on ff. 1–22 and 37–48, the years 1487–1488. Places where both watermarks have been attested are Frankfurt am Main and Freiburg im Breisgau; both places had Dominican and Dominican nuns' establishments. — Saint Praxedes (f. 16r, with a very inadequate hymn indication[13]) is the chief festive occasion not commonly emphasized in Dominican sources.[14]

MS 31 The book was very likely written by a woman. It is questionable whether a Dominican nun of the meditative "Second Order" would have had much use for it: the nuns had the obligation to recite the whole daily office. The up-to-date hymnary (or, rather, hymnary supplement) must have been produced at a (major) Dominican center but the intended user may have been a lay person, perhaps a Tertiary, whose attendance would be only occasional. The mistress of the choir, or of the novices, is another possibility. — It should be noted that no German phrase appears anywhere in the book; most liturgical manuscripts of Dominican nuns written in Germany toward the end of the 15th century do include such phrases.

NOTES

1. At one time numbered in LC as "Medieval ms. 11."

2. 169 mm near the gutter, 171 mm at the fore edge.

3. Neither term (*temporale, sanctorale*) appears in the book.

4. We have sacrificed the (red) captions of the manuscript in favor of English statements in this listing; and Latin spellings have been regularized. Reference to the *Analecta hymnica* is given only where deemed particularly useful. Folio numbers say only where a hymn begins, not necessarily that the page begins with it.

5. This seems to be local (not noted as an important feast in general Dominican sources). (See also concluding comment.)

6. Another case of what seems to be added importance of a saint's office in a particular locality.

7. N.B. The weekly *cursus* constitutes a "section" logically, and we treat it as such; in the manuscript itself the *ordinatio textus* doesn't go beyond the level of individual festivities in the hymnary, and individual Psalms in the part now under discussion.

8. Bonniwell uses, as the Roman Church did until recently, the Septuagint and Vulgate numbering for the Psalms. The manuscript uses none. (Our numbering is the now commonly accepted Hebrew Bible count which agrees with that of King James version.)

9. Some show (poverty of means notwithstanding) rather keen esthetic perception: so the 2-line *N* on 23r with one of the hymns to St. Dominic; or the 2-line *D* beginning the first psalm of Vespers (*Dixit Dominus*) on 25r.

10. The identification is erroneous; the rather popular (in its time) work with that title had a completely different character.

11. In Faye and Bond, the hymnary is listed among the manuscripts in custody of LC Music Division; in 1969 or 1970, the book was transferred to LC Rare Book Division and assigned no. "11" in the (now no more used) part of LC shelflist given to manuscript books.

12. Cf. Leroquais, *Bréviaires* I, p. ci; Bonniwell, *Hist. Dom. lit.*, p. 240–242.

13. The stanza (fourth in the hymn *Virginis proles*) tended to be used for holy women who were neither virgins nor martyrs (cf. *AH* LI, p. 138). (N.B. A set of proper hymns in honor of St. Praxedes existed and was in use on Majorca.)

14. The cult of St. Remigius (f. 22v) was well established locally or regionally in both areas concerned (cf. M. Zender, *Räume und Schichten* . . . (1973), p. 182 sqq. and map no. 11); same is true of St. Elizabeth. — For representative liturgical manuscripts of Dominican nuns (they did much copying and some are known by name) see in particular: *Kataloge der Universitätsbib. Freiburg im Breisgau*, Bd. 1, T. 2, *Die Musikhandschriften* . . . / beschr. von Clytus Gottwald (1979), p. 115, etc. — St. Praxedes is represented in the lectionary of the Dominican nuns' convent *Zum Heiligen Kreuz* in Regensburg, ms. Keble College, Oxford, no. 49 (f. 115; their sanctoral includes also St. Remigius, f. 221); cf. Parkes, *Med. mss. Keble College* (1979), p. 227.

MS 32

(Faye and Bond 126)

CARTHUSIAN MISSAL end of XVth c.

Charterhouse St. Alban near Trier. Parchment. 156 leaves, ca. 209 × ca. 139 mm (bound volume: ca. 220 × ca. 150 mm) 1 column. 33 lines.

ff. 1r–125r: *D[omi]nica p[ri]ma adue[n]tus d[omi]ni. Int[ro]itus.* (A)⁶D te leuaui . . . (ends, 125r:) . . . *Explicit de tempore.*

The *temporale*, or proper of the seasons, of a missal according to the use of the Carthusian order. — Included are, after Christmas, the days (9r–12r) of Stephen, John the Evangelist, the Innocents, and Circumcision; also, at end (ff. 124–125r), the *Dedicatio ecclesiae.* — Ash Wednesday is called (19r) "*In capite Ieiunii*," Palm Sunday (58r), "*In die palmaru[m]*," Holy Thursday (71v), "*In s[an]c[t]a cena Domini.*" — On Good Friday, among the *Orationes pro statu sancte ecclesie*, also (76r) "pro cristianissimo imperatore nostro." — Each weekday of the Easter week has its own proper. — Following the Mass of the fourth Sunday after Easter (89r:) "*Trib[us] dieb[us] cap[itu]li g[e]n[er]alis* . . .", a program of texts for Masses offered during the general chapter of the order. — Trinity Sunday is captioned (101v) "*De s. trinita[te]*" and has its specific Introit (Benedicta . . .) and Epistle (from Revelation IV) but the Gospel is "Erat homo ex phariseis nychodemus nomine . . ." (John III,1 sqq.).[1] — Corpus Christi (102v) is termed "*De vene[r]abili sacrame[n]to altaris*"; the Sunday immediately following, "*D[omi]nica p[ri]ma p[ost] oct[avas] pe[n]th[ecostes]*," and the Sundays thereafter are numbered as 2nd through 25th.[2] Their Gospel readings are same as those assigned to the corresponding Sundays (= Sundays with same sequential designation) in 12th-century Carthusian sources:[3] i.e., for the 1st Sunday after Trinity ("after the octave of Pentecost") the Gospel is Luke XVI,19 sqq.; for the 2nd, Luke XIV,16 sqq.; from the 5th through 24th Sunday, the scheduled Gospel pericope is two weeks behind that read in churches following the program of the Roman Curia;[4] to make things worse, the Introits (the entrance antiphons), with opening words often used to identify a particular Sunday, follow (for the Sundays after Trinity) a different pattern, staying generally only one week behind the missal of the Curia, resulting in different thematic associations. — The Holy Saturday litany (79v–80r) has in the margin of f. 80r an addition: s[anc]te albane (cf. our notes to his name in contents of the sanctoral part).

The *versus alleluiatici* for the Sundays after Pentecost run as follows:[5] (for Trinity, "Benedictus es Domine . . ."); Dom. I (post octavas Pentecostes!): Verba mea; II: Deus iudex; III: Diligam te; IV: In te Domine speravi; V: Omnes gentes; VI: Eripe me; VII: Te decet; VIII: Exultate; IX: Domine refugium; X: Dominus regnavit; XI: Venite exultemus; XII: Quoniam Deus; XIII: Dominus regnavit; XIV: Confitemini; XV: Paratum cor; XVI: Redemptionem misit; XVII: Laudate pueri; XVIII: Qui timent; XIX: Laetatus sum; XX: Lauda anima mea; XXI: Qui sanat; XXII: Lauda Iherusalem; XXIII: Qui posuit fines, XXIV: (same as XXIII? nothing between Epistle and Gospel); XXV: (statedly same [= as in XXIII?])

125r–153v: *De sacratissima virgine ac m[arty]re katherina*. Gaudeam[us] . . . (153v:) [re]dempcione capiam[us]. p[er . . .]

The *sanctorale*, or proper of the saints, containing Mass propers[6] (texts, no music) for saints' days and other fixed-date celebrations (but not for Christmas and several days after, cf. the temporal) for which the rather restrained Carthusian use permitted or prescribed a Mass.[7] — As is usual in medieval liturgical books, the sanctoral follows the sequence of the various occasions throughout the year (beginning with St. Catherine, celebrated Nov. 25) but does not expressly indicate any particular days. — Included are 75 occasions; among them, the characteristically Carthusian Hugo of Grenoble (135r), *Festum Reliquiarum* (152r), and Hugo of Lincoln (152v). — For the dating of the manuscript, most important are the Marian feasts of Conception (127v; called *Sanctificatio* among Carthusians prior to 1470), Visitation (142r; Mass permitted 1411, obligatory since 1468), and Presentation (153r; permitted 1470); also Barbara (126v; perm. 1397, oblig. 1463) and Anna (143v; 1412); not included by the original scribe but added at end of the book (*q. v.*) in other hands are St. Bruno (1515), *Compassio* B.M.V. (oblig. 1486), St. Joseph (ca. 1570). — Not commonly included in Carthusian calendars, hence helpful in placing the manuscript geographically, are "*De sancto Albano m[arti]re*" (126v, between Andrew and Barbara = Dec. 1);[8] Lubentius (133r, between Agatha and Cathedra Petri = Feb. 6); a rubric on f. 142v between octave of Peter and Paul and Margaret (= between July 6 and July 20) noting that *Dedicatio ecclesie* can be found on f. 124;[9] Arnulfus episcopus (146r, between Assumption and St. Bernard = Aug. 16); and Elizabeth (152v, between Hugo of Lincoln and Presentation B.V.M. = Nov. 19). All this points to the Carthusian monastery Sankt Alban at Trier.

153v–155r: (beginning without interruption:) . . . *De Apostolis in co[mmun]i . . . De vno martire* . . . (154v) . . . *De plurib[us] martirib[us]* . . . *vnius co[n]fessoris pontificis* . . . (155r:) . . . *vni[us] co[n]fessoris no[n] po[n]tific[is]* . . . *vni[us] abbatis . . . De vna virgine . . . Ite[m] de alia q[ue] non fuit martir* (the rubric ends the page and the series; the announced text remained unwritten)

The "common of the saints," sets of texts used in absence of an individualized "proper."

155v: Gloria in excelsis deo . . . propter gloria[m] tua[m] magna[m] . . . i[n] gl[ori]a d[e]i pa[tris]. Am[en] Credo in vnu[m] deu[m] . . . Et vita[m] fut[ur]i s[e]c[u]li. Amen.

The *Gloria* and *Credo* are the only parts of the "Ordinary of the Mass" represented in this missal. — Note slight variations from standard texts.

[156]r: (IN ANOTHER HAND:) *In festo Beati Brunonis . . . p[at]*ris *n[ost]ri . . . sic[ut] . . . de s. Anthonio . . . excepto Euangelio qd' est Sint lu[m]bi . . . et or[ati]o[n]ib[us] seque[n]tibus*. . . . (same page, last 6 lines, ANOTHER HAND, in cursive:) In festo [com]passionis btē m[ar]ie . . .

The Mass for the *Compassio B.M.V.* was introduced in 1486 but the information seems to have remained unrecorded in this missal until ca. 1515(?).

[156]v: (IN A VERY LATE CURSIVE:) *De S. Joseph.* . . .

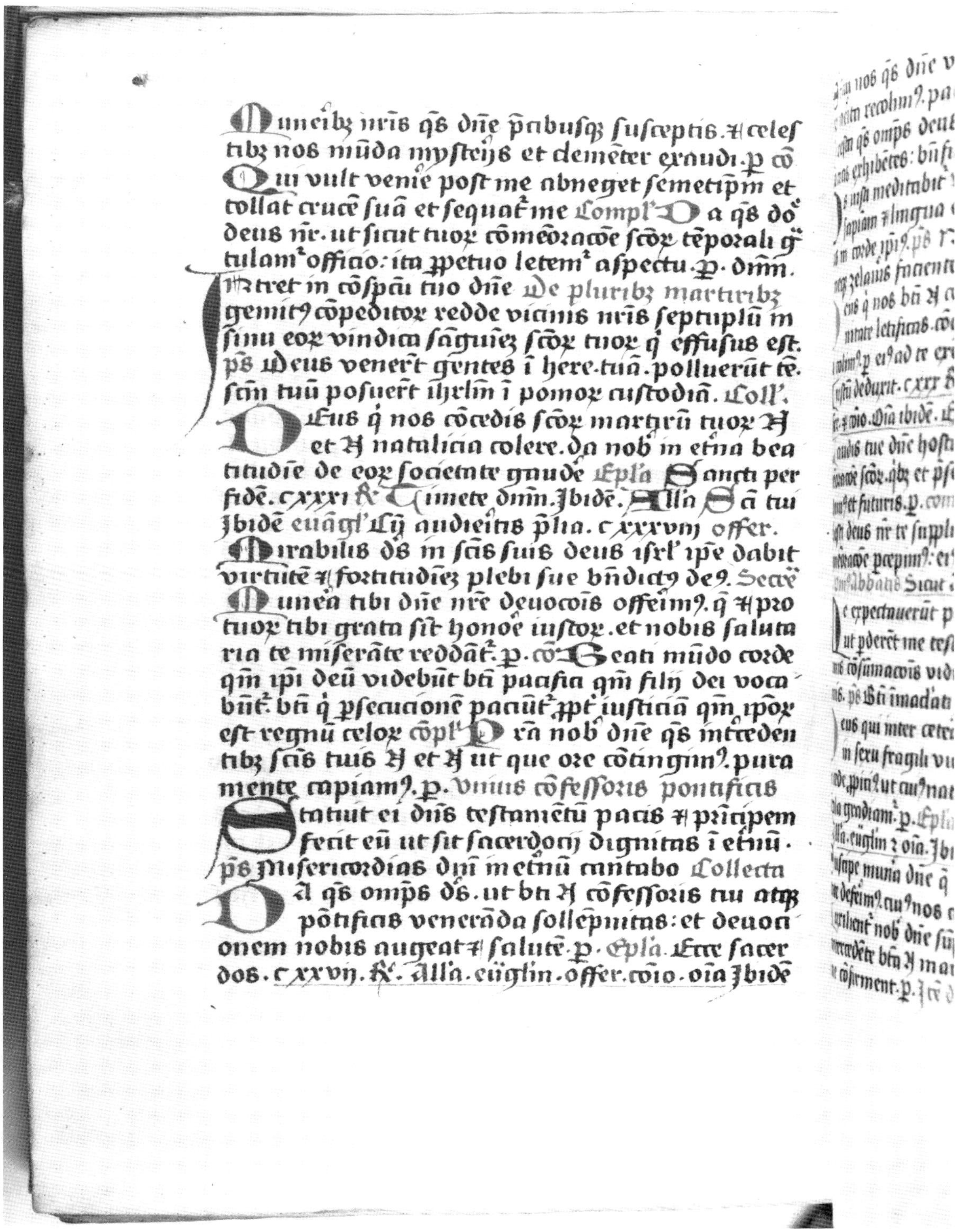

MS 32, f. 154v (actual size of the leaf: ca. 209 × 139 mm)

MS 32

(N.B. A blank leaf pricked on fore edge and ruled is pasted to the final free endleaf.)

* * *

Medieval foliation in black roman numerals in center of top margins recto (i–clv; leaf [156] unnumbered); one free endleaf in front and one at end. — Written area ca. 150 × ca. 96 mm. — Fully ruled in lead; pricking largely preserved (outer, top, tail margins). — Written, except for additions on f. [156], by one scribe, in a simple hybrid script which includes a peculiar form of the tironian "et" (a thin vertical to the right of the usual character).[10] — Captions in red; occasional notes of the kind considered "rubric" are written in black ink and underscored in red. — Good parchment, fairly white on both sides; thickness ca. 15–16 mm per 100 leaves. Leather index tabs attached to fore edge on ff. 23 (no obvious reason), 59, 64, 68, 73 (marking the four *Passio* readings), and 153 (beginning of the common of saints).

Collation: [a]^8 b–s^8 [t]^8 v^4 (signatures, more recent than the text, in faint ink in lower outer corners of rectos). — Catchwords (mostly not complete words) on verso of last leaf in each gathering except "i" where they were apparently cropped in binding.

Decoration: one illuminated initial, the 6-line letter *A* on f. 1r. The letter is primarily light green, foliate (acanthus) shapes standing out from ground darkened by red-dotting. The two areas framed by the letter contain silvery gray and light red leafy forms and two light pink three-petal blossoms on blue ground. The whole is in an irregular rectangle of laid gold. — All other initials are of the calligraphic red-or-blue kind, 3-, 2-, or 1-line in height; only the initial (J-shape) *I* of "In illo tempore" at the beginning of Gospel pericopes, set off into the margin, is made to run past 6 or more lines of the text. Some of the largest blue or red letters are modestly embellished by use of white void (often white *x* shapes). — Black capitals are touched with red.

Eighteenth(?)-century binding: covers yellowish brown mottled calf over paper boards. On spine, red leather label with gold-tooled title: MISSALE//CARTHUSIENSE.

Tipped to verso of upper cover, paper slips with handwritten opinions concerning the age, etc., of the manuscript: one, in French, suggesting the 14th century, the other, in English, attempting to prove that the missal must date from 1200 or earlier. Another paper slip, laid in, argues for much more recent origin (". . . after Clement VIII, 1602"). — Hidden under the tipped-in slips, ownership label of Rev. Edwin A. Dalrymple, D.D.

Former owners: Rev. E. A. Dalrymple; Nathaniel D. Sollers, Baltimore. — Acquired by LC, March 1, 1934.

2° fo.: existis i[n] desertu[m] vid'e. Aru[n]dine[m] . . .

Bibl.: De Ricci, *Census* (1935), p. 901, no. 1 (when owned by N. D. Sollers); Faye and Bond (1962), p. 121, no. 126.

It is a striking feature of this missal that it includes no *Ordo Missae*; also, less strikingly, no calendar; there is no evidence that either was ever present. A priest celebrating Mass was generally required to read the Canon (central part of the *Ordo*) even if he knew it by heart. Perhaps the book was written for other than altar use.

NOTES

1. The Gospel pericope was apparently retained from the time before the Trinity Sunday got its own proper.

2. Corresponding to the "after Trinity" method of counting the Sundays of what is now called "ordinary time." Rome counted them "after Pentecost," some areas "after Trinity," some "after the octave of Trinity"; practical differences such as described were probably due to misunderstanding rather than to intent.

3. Cf. The Gospel quotes, with homilies, in the Carthusian homiliary of ca. 1134 analyzed by R. Étaix in *SACRIS ERUDIRI* XIII (1962), p. 68–79 (nos. 45–

69); also the Carthusian homiliary for summer, LC MS 13.

4. Cf. *SMRL* II, p. 104–109 and 261–270; that program was eventually incorporated into the Tridentine *Missale Romanum* and remained in use until ca. 1970.

5. Cf. Leroquais, *Sacramentaires et missels* I, p. xxv.

6. Basically texts or indications of the *Introitus* (entrance antiphon), the *Collecta* (primary formal prayer of the day), the Epistle, the antiphonal texts between the Epistle and the Gospel, the Gospel, the Offertory antiphon, the *Secreta* (another formal prayer), the Communion antiphon, and the formal prayer generally known as *Postcommunio* but called "Complenda" in the present manuscript (except with the Conversion of Paul, on f. 132r: "*post communionem*"). N.B. Notice similarities in various details with LC MS 26.

7. Cf. the Carthusian calendar edited with historical notes in *ÉTUDES GRÉGORIENNES* II (1957; p. 153–161) by Benoît du Moustier (pseud. of B. Lambres O. Cart.); also some additional notes in: Hansjakob Becker, *Die Responsorien des Kartäuserbreviers* (1971), p. 42 sqq.

8. The only Albanus remembered on Dec. 1 was a mythical king of Hungary (cf. *Bibliotheca Sanctorum* [Roma, Istituto Giovanni XXIII] I, 661). The martyr honored by a Mass in this Carthusian ms. must be the saint generally celebrated on June 21, patron of Mainz and also of the charterhouse at Trier; it is puzzling that his feast should be here assigned to December.

9. At Sankt Alban at Trier, the *Dedicatio ecclesiae* was celebrated on the first Sunday occurring after July 9 ("post octavas Visitacionis"). Cf. Leroquais, *Psautiers* II, p. 266–267 (with no. 467, a book from St. Alban; note that it, too, has St. Elizabeth).

10. Perhaps by the same scribe as ms. 9 of the Bibliothèque municipale at Haguenau (Bas-Rhin, France) dated 1497 and written at the Carthusian monastery of St. Alban at Trier: cf. reproduction of its f. 1 in *MSS datés* V, plate CLXXVII and Leroquais, *Psautiers* I, p. 211 (no. 178).

MS 33

(Faye and Bond 84)

PRAYER BOOK end of XVth c.

Written in Germany (Württemberg?) Parchment. 121 leaves, 101 × ca. 73 mm (bound volume: 116 x ca. 85 mm) 1 column. 12–17 lines.

ff. 1r–10v: All in the cursive hand 2. At least one leaf missing at the beginning (another, the first one of the gathering, used as pastedown?); on 1r, text washed off and partly obscured by the 19th-century inscription (Liber precum . . . G. H. Schr.); it begins (imperfectly, with the word "lacrimosa") the sequence *Stabat Mater dolorosa*, here given in a rather corrupt version ending on 2v and followed by versicle and formal prayer (*Intercedat pro nobis quesumus* . . .). — On 3r–3v, morning grace (Gracias ago tibi . . .); on 3v–5r, evening prayer (Cum vadis dormitum . . . Confiteor tibi domine . . .); 5r–6r: "Post singulas horas oracio" (N.B. no "horae" are found in the book in its present shape); 6r–6v, "Ante accessum divinorum oracio sancti Bernhardi" (*Aperi Domine os meum* . . .); on ff. 6v through 10v, 9th line, suffrages addressed to: St. Bartholomew (O beatissime Bartholomee, 6v–8r), Andrew (Sancte Andrea apostole, 8r–9r), Christopher (Gloriose martir, 9r–10v).

10v–12r: All in hand 3 (also cursive): 10v (10th line)–11v, "Ad S. Ambrosium"; 11v, De S. Martino; 12r (first 9 lines), De. S. Nicolao. — The nine lines on 12r are written over washed-off or erased text which was in hand 1; on the blank rest of the page, remnants of three more lines done in black and three in red are discernible but could not be read.

ff. 12v–13v: *Pla[n]cta v[e]l co[m]passio btē marie v[ir]ginis* (S)[3]Tabat m[ate]r dolorosa . . . p[ar]adisi gl[ori]a ame[n]

Preserved hand-1 text begins with this item, here without versicle and formal prayer. (N.B. Duplication of the sequence by hand 2 in the first gathering suggests independent origin.)

14r–76v: *Nota* Propt[er] laudabilem plu[r]imoru[m]q[ue] [con]suetudi[n]e[m] . . .

The primary part of the prayer book as written by scribe 1 (at least as far as preserved); consisting (after an introduction, 14r–15r) of a series of prayers, mostly suffrage-type (antiphon,[1] versicle, and formal prayer) grouped by themes for single days of the week; a summarized program for this is given on f. 15r. — The red captions, the initia, etc., are as follows:[2]

(15v:) *Dominica die: De sancta trinitate: Ad patrem* . . . *Ad filium* . . . (16r:) . . . *Ad spiritum sanctum* . . . — *Oracio sancti Augustini ad sanctam trinitatem* (16v–17v:) O Tres coequales et coeterne persone . . . facias ut aquile canos meos. Amen

On f. 18r–v, in hand 2: Peccaui super numerum harene maris et multiplicata sunt peccata mea . . . (a penitential prayer using phrases from the *Oratio Manasse*, Psalm LI, and elsewhere)

(19r:) *Secunda feria: De angelis sanctis:* Michael victor draconis . . . Gabriel . . . Raphael . . . O vos omnes . . . precor ut me muniatis et ad celos perducatis. Amen. (19v:) *Rigmus* [sic] *Ad proprium angelum*: O Angele dulcissime . . . (cf. *AH* XV, no. 153) (21r:) *De omnibus angelis:* Omnes sancti angeli et archangeli throni et dominaciones . . .

(22v:) *Tercia feria: De sanctis patriarchis et prophetis sanctisque apostolis: De s. Johanne baptista:* Beatissime iohannes baptista precursor Xi et virgo . . . (23v:) *Ad omnes s. patriarchas et prophetas:* Omnes sancti patriarche . . . (24v:) *De sancto Petro* . . . (25v:) *De sancto Paulo* . . . (27r:) *De sancto Philippo* . . . (28r:) *De sancto Jacobo* . . . (29r:) *De sancto Johanne euangelista* . . . (29v:) *Ad omnes s. apostolos et discipulos Xi* (30r:) Omnes sancti apostoli dei . . . discipulis discipulabusque . . .

(31r:) *Quarta feria: De martiribus: De s. Steffano:* Sanctissime prothomartir et dignissime leuita . . . (32r:) *De sancto Laurencio:* Suffragator venerande laurenti . . . (32v:) *De sctō Vincencio* (33r:) O sancte Vincenti . . . (33v:) *De sctō Vito:* O preclare martir Christi . . . [metrical through 34r] (34v:) *De scō Ciriaco cum sociis suis* O sanctissime . . . (35r:) O Ciriace cum sociis tuis . . . [metrical] (35v:) *De X millibus martirum:* O decem mille martires gloriosi milites . . . (36r:) *De omnibus sanctis martiribus:* Ad vos omnes clarissimi . . .

(37v) *Quinta feria: De confessoribus: De sctō Gregorio* . . .

(38v:) *De sctō Augustino:* Doctor egregie . . . [not metrical]

(39r:) Salve gemma confessorum / scriba vite lux doctorum . . . (only 1st verse is as in the hymn to St. Sigfrid, *AH* VIII, no. 276)

(39v:) *De sctō Iheronymo:* O gloriose Iheronime / doctor sancte ecclesie . . . (not in *AH* XXVI, no. 33–40) (40v:) *De sctō Benedicto:* O Benedicte legifex . . . [metrical] (43r:) *De sctō Bernhardo . . . (44v:) . . . Antonio* . . . (45v:) *De sctō hinrico ymnus:* Hic est verus Christicola . . . (hymn = *AH* LII, no. 70) (46r:) *De sctō Francisco:* O odoriferum lilium . . . (47r:) *Ad omnes confessores:* O celestis firmamenti sidera rutilancia . . .

(48r:) *Sexta feria: De passione domini ut supra in oracionibus sctē Brigite* (N.B. The *Orationes sanctae Brigittae* are not included in the book in its present shape, suggesting unknown amount of material lost.)

(still 48r:) *Sabbato: De virginibus; Angelica salutacio devote extensa:* AVe fuit vera salus . . . (cf. *AH* XXX, .196 or 198 ?) (50v:) *Septem gaudia terrestria beate marie virginis:* Virgo templum sanctitatis . . . (through 54r:) . . . Et nos serves a peccatis et perducas cum beatis ad aterna gaudia Amen (54r–55v:) *Septem gaudia celestia beate marie virginis*: Gaude virgo mater christi / que sola meruisti . . . (N.B. only the initium and rhythm are as in *AH* XXXVI, p. 56 sqq.) (55v:) *De sctā Agatha:* Salue sancta agatha . . . (N.B. text imitates the *Salve Regina!*) (56r:) *De sancta Lucia:* (56v:) O Lucia virgo benedicta martir inclita . . . (57v:) *De sancta Agna* [i.e., *Agnete*]: Rubens rosa martirum . . . (58r:) *De sctā Cecilia* . . . (59r:) . . . *Scolastica* . . . (59v:) . . . *Katherina*: Ave virgo katherina . . . (hymn = *AH* XXXIII, no. 141, with some variants) (61v:) *De sctā Ursula cum sodalibus suis:* Virgo prudentissima ursula regalis . . . [metrical] (63r:) *De sctā Kunegunde*: O Kunegundis preclarissima stirpe procreata . . . [metrical] (63v:) *De sctā Barbara:* Ave martir gloriosa . . . (= *AH* LV, no. 79, + 2 additional stanzas) (65r:) *De sctā Margareta:* Ave virgo gloriosa margareta preciosa . . . (not *AH* XXXIII, no. 151) (65v:) . . . *Dorothea*: En iustissima Christi martir et virgo sctā dorothea . . . [more or less metrical] (66v:) . . . *Cristina:* O beata virgo et martir . . . (67v:) . . . *Aurea*: O sctā Aurea genere nobilissima / trecentarum puellarum Parisiis abbatissa . . . (68v:) . . . *Eufraxia*: O Eufraxia virgo sacrata summo Xpō sponso grata . . . (67r:) . . . recolo te expulisse demonem baculo abbatisse . . .

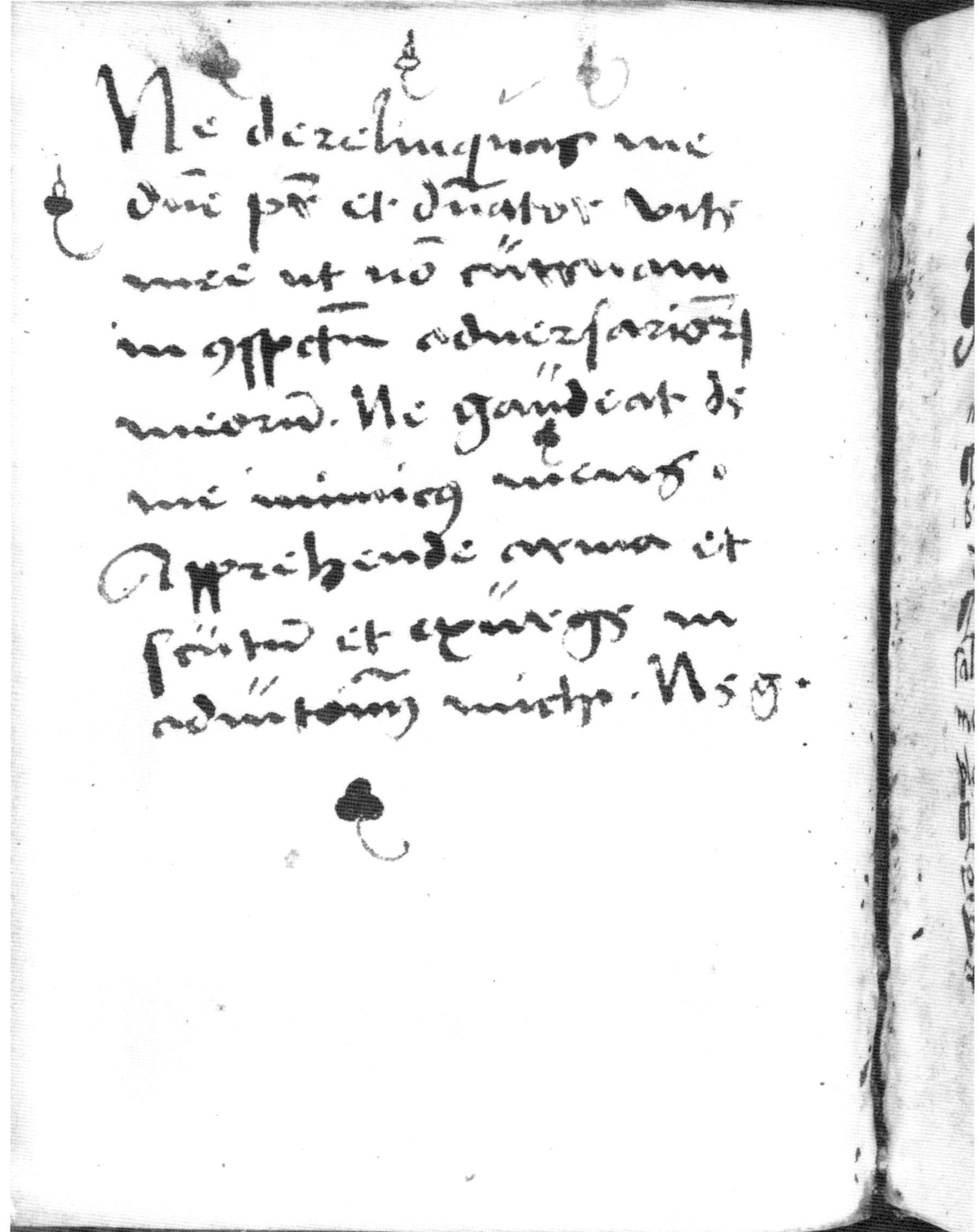

MS 33, f. 18v (scribe 2) (actual page height: 101 mm; the reproduction omits ca. half of the fore-edge margin)

MS 33, f. 19r (scribe 1) (actual page height: 101 mm; N.B. the reproduction omits ca. half of the fore-edge margin)

(70r:) *De omnibus virginibus*: O virgines sacre / angelis simillime . . . (N.B. the petitioner uses about himself masculine forms: . . . gravatus . . . suffultus . . .) (70v:) *De s. Maria Magdalena*: Ave plena magdalena que maria diceris . . . (= *AH* III, no. 70) (72r:) . . . *Elizabeth*: Iesu bone fac me dignum ut in caritatis signum . . . (74r:) . . . *Anna*: Gaude felix anna que concepisti prolem . . . (not *AH*, no. 188) (74v:) O rosa vernalis . . . (= *AH* XLII, no. 163, first 2 verses, + 4 more, unidentified) (75r: Ave Maria . . . et benedicta sit honestissima matrona mater tua . . .) (75v:) *De sctā Pelagia*: O sancta pelagia olim nigra et squalida . . . (rhymed part ends on 76v:) . . . deum meum videam. Amen. (versicle and formal prayer follow on same page, squeezed into inadequate space, with obvious intent not to carry the end to a new page and/or new gathering)

ff. 77r–82r: *Or[aci]o g[e]n[e]ralis ad btām v[ir]gine[m] Ma[r]iam aptabil[is] sing[u]lis festiuitatibus eiusde[m] v[ir]ginis gl[ori]ose* (S)[4]Alue o pia d[e]i m[ate]r . . . (77v:) . . . Succ[u]rre ergo miser[i]s iuua pusillanimes r[e]foue flebiles . . . (ends on 82r:) . . . Concede nos fa[m]ulas tuos [sic] . . . p[er] xm̄.

On 78r, the occasions enumerated: Purificacionem, Annunciationem, Visitacionem, Assumpcionem, Nativitatem, Presentacionem, Concepcionem, Commemoracionem. (N.B. The feast of Presentation of Our Lady was introduced to various areas at various times: to Paris at the end of the 14th century, to Saxony at the end of the 15th; cf. Leroquais, *Brév.* I, Introd. Also of interest for dating is the Visitation.)

82r–83v: . . . *Ad vnu[m] que[m]lib[et] s[an]ct[u]m cuiuscu[m]q[ue] stat[us] fuerit* O [superscript:] Beate [below it:] Beata [on line:] n. opem nobis po[r]rige . . . e[r]ige . . . et i[n] via[m] pacis nos di[ri]ge . . . (82v:) . . . *alia or[aci]o* O [superscript:] Scē .n. (Apostole, martir, cōfessor) [below it:] sctā .n. (virgo, dilect[ri]x) [on line:] dei effunde p[re]ces p[ro] me misero p[e]c[ca]tore . . .

83v–84r: . . . *Ad plu[r]es s[an]ctos cuiuscūq[ue]* [in margin, partly cropped, corrector's addition: *status*] *seu grad[us] exista[n]t* O vos sctī dei glo[rio]si N [et] N adiuuate me captiuu[m] et seruate semiuiuum . . . (84r:) . . . Oremus TVa nos q[uesumu]s d[omi]ne gr[aci]a s[em]p[er] p[re]ueniat et seq[ua]t[ur] . . .

84v–85v: . . . *Or[aci]o o[mn]em sollicitudi[n]em in deo statue[n]tis* D[omi]Ne maio[r] est sollicitudo p[ro] me[3] q[uam] o[mn]is cura q[uam] ego gerere possu[m] p[ro] me . . . (85r:) . . . Si vis me esse i[n] tenebris, sis b[e]n[e]dict[us] . . . volo bonu[m] et malu[m] de ma[n]u tua . . . (ends, 85v:) . . . vene[r]it sup[er] me Amen.

85v–86v: . . . *Qualit[er] insta[n]te t[ri]bulac[i]o[n]e d'[us] i[n]uoca[n]d[us] e[st] et b[e]n[e]dice[n]d[us]* Sit nome[n] tuu[m] d[omi]ne b[e]n[e]dictu[m] in secula q[ui] voluisti ha[n]c te[m]ptac[i]o[nem] venire . . . (ends, 86v:) . . . ta[n]to tibi facilior e[st] h[ec] mutatio dextere excelsi Ame[n] (last 8 lines of 86v blank; N.B., end of a gathering)

87r–96r: *De desiderio anime et siti eius in deum* (O)[3] Qua[m] gl[ori]osu[m] est r[e]gnu[m] . . . (ends, 96r:) . . . qui es i[n] sinu pa[tr]is sup[er] o[mn]ia b[e]n[e]dict[us] d[eus] in secula. Amen.

Long, meditative prayer (with tendency to oratory).

96r–v: . . . *Or[aci]o p[ro] sapie[n]cia* (O)[3] Sap[ienc]ia q[ue] ex ore altissimi p[ro]disti . . . (96v:) . . . cora[m] te o[mn]i t[em]p[or]e Amen. *v.* Emitte . . . Oremus INfu[n]de q[ues]u[mu]s dn̄e . . . Amen.

96v–103v: *Rosariu[m] b[ea]tissi[m]e d[e]i genit[ri]cis s[em]p[er]q[ue] v[ir]ginis ma[r]ie q[uo]d se[quitur]* co[m]positu[m] est p[er] que[n]dam deuotu[m] Cartusiensem in (97r:) domo Treuere[n]si . . .

A peculiar rosary consisting basically of 5 decades of Ave Marias, introduced respectively by the Magnificat, Pss. CXX, CXIX v. 17–24?, CXXVI, and CXXIII (all identified by initia in large display-type script, full texts not included); the meditation themes, more numerous and varied than in later standard rosary, include also events from Jesus' public life prior to the Passion; they are formulated as short rhymed clauses (e.g.: "quem concepisti de spiritu sancto non per carnis opera / ipse nos fecundet sancti timoris sui gracia"). Cf. similar (but apparently without rhymes) in Wilmart, *Aut. spir.*, p. [583].

104r–v: *DEcem p[ri]uilegia psalterij scīissi[m]e t[ri]nitatis et Marie v[ir]ginis . . .:* 1 P[e]c[ca]toribus p[re]stans pe[n]itencia[m] . . . 10 Mortuis mitte[n]s gra[cia]m ACcipia[n]t ergo hoc diuinissimu[m] psalteriu[m] . . .

The "psalterium" in question consists of the three "coronae" which follow. Cf. similar (at least in conception) in ms. 1 of the Bloxham School (Bloxham, Oxfordshire) ff. 116v–127v (cf. Ker, *Med. mss. in Brit. libs.*, II (1977), p. 147)

104v–110v: . . . *(P)*[3]*Rima ma[r]ie corona ex qui[n]q[ue] lilijs et q[ui]nq[ua]gi[n]ta flo[r]ib[us] albiss[im]is xpi̅ et marie conu[e]rsac[i]o[ne]m in t[er]ris indica[n]tibus.* (105r blank and presenting the appearance of having once had something [illus.?] pasted to it) (105v:) *Ave* maria aue b[ea]ta ave p[re]destinata . . . (106v:) . . . *(S)*[3]*Ecu[n]da marie corona ex qui[n]q[ue] rosis rubissimis* . . . (107r blank, with traces of erased or washed-off text; 107v:) SAlue maria *tecu[m]* . . . (108v:) . . . *(T)*[3]*Ercia marie corona ex qui[n]q[ue] solib[us] et qui[n]qu[a]ginta stellis* . . . (109r blank; 109v:) GAude maria *fruct[us]* . . .

The text of the first "corona" includes five Aves with, each time, a different word written in red; with each Ave, a two-part paragraph, the second part beginning with "O." — In the second "corona," each paragraph begins with "Salve"; in the third one, with "Gaude." The sequence of the red-written words inside the repeated Aves continues throughout (through "Christus") even though they appear free of context.

(Hand 1 ends with the preceding item. WHAT FOLLOWS IS ALL IN CURSIVE, BY THE SECOND OR FURTHER SCRIBES:)

111r–115r: *or[aci]o de b[ea]ta virgi[n]e i[n] o[mn]ibus eius festiuitatibus ora[n]da* Aue mu[n]di spes ma[r]ia aue mitis aue pia . . . (hymn ends on 114v:) . . . et cu[m] sorte ang[e]lorum p[er] infinita sec[u]la seculoru[m] amen kirie l'[i.e., eleison] xp̅e l' kirie l' p[ate]r n[oste]r . . . De[us] su[m]ma dulcedo concede nobis . . . (115r:) . . . p[er] eu[m] qui venturus e[st] iudica[re] viuos et mortuos et seculu[m] p[er] ignem. amen

Twenty-one stanzas of four verses each (*AH* XV,150 or XXXII,38?) followed by a prayer pattern much used in minor liturgical actions. — In hand 2.

115r–116r: De N[a]ti[ui]tate glo[rio]se virginis Marie Gaude glo[rio]sissi[m]a . . . (ends, 116r:) . . . gaudia lucis. O clemens O pia O dulcis Ma[r]ia. Amen

In hand 4, rather similar to hand 3 (cf. ff. 10v–12r).

116v–121v: [Additional saints' suffrages:] (116v, in hand 5:) De sctā Appollonia (Virgo Christi egregia . . . = *AH* XXV,108 ?) (117r–v, in hand 2(?):) De s. Valentino episcopo uno, et alio presbitero quorum festa una die concurrunt (Insignorum virorum miracula . . .) (118r, also hand 2(?):) De sctā Otilia virgine (O preclara Christi sponsa . . . = *AH* XXVIII, no. 36; followed, 118r–v, by "Alia": O beata Otilia sponsa Xi et filia . . .) (119r–120r, hand 2:) Aue Gerdrudis virgo grata . . . (the hymn, f. 119rv = *AH* VIII, no. 179) — (120r–v, two prayers with the Passion theme:) Domine Ihesu Christe fili dei vivi qui mortem in cruce pro nobis . . . in gloria tua gaudere. amen. (120–121v:) Alia oracio: Domine Ihesu Christe fili dei vivi qui manus tuas et pedes tuos et totum corpus tuum . . . intellectum et graciam sacram usque in finem vite nostre. amen.

* * *

Foliated in modern pencil. No free endleaves. — Written area ca. 60–70 × ca. 46–53 mm. — No visible ruling or pricking.[4] — Written by several scribes, none, it would seem, professional, over a period of time. In probable chronological order, scribe 1 (the only one using a bookish script) produced the ff. 12v (originally also 12r), 17v, and 19r–110v; the script he uses is a small *hybrida* generally more careful at the beginning of a section and deteriorating as the section progresses; has 17 lines to a page.[5] Reference made on 48r to *Oraciones scte. Brigite*, to be found "supra" but in fact missing, as well as the evidence of text and rubric on 12r later washed off and written over by hand 3, indicate loss of an unknown amount of text even though the items which remained are complete. Scribe 2, using a rather hasty, poorly framed cursive with 12 to 14 lines to a page, wrote most of the added first gathering, i.e., presumably some text on the lost leaves preceding f. 1, the 1r, now mostly washed-off, 1v–10v (through 9th line), also the 18rv (conjugate with f. 11), 111r–115r (except last 3 lines on 115r), and 117r–121v. The parchment of these leaves is whiter than that used by scribe 1. An unskilled third writer, using a conspicuously thinner ink, added the prayers to Ambrose, Martin, and Nicolas on 10v (10th line) through 12r (9th line). A scribe 4, similar to 3, wrote the additions on 115r–116r (concerning Nativity B.V.M.) and a fifth person, also unskilled, the 116v (about St. Apollonia). — In the parts written by scribe 1, red captions; red or (rarely) blue underscoring is used to signal new verses, stanzas, versicles, etc.; red underscoring also occurs in the matter written by scribe 2. — Parchment is of uneven quality; thickness ca. 16.5 mm per 100 leaves. Some leaves cut poorly; the (conjugate) ff. 59 and 64 are very much undersize. — Short vellum strips glued as index tabs on ff. 22, 31, 37, 47, 57, 74, 82, 96, 105 (some evidence of a lost one on f. 15).

Collation: 1^{12-2}(= ff. 1–10; 1_{1-2} wanting, with text loss) 2^{8} $3–4^{10}$ 5^{10-1} (= ff. 39–47; 5_{10} wanting, stub present; no text loss) 6^{10-1} (= ff. 48–56; 6_{10} wanting, stub present; no text loss) $7–12^{10}$ 13^{6-1} (= ff. 117–121; 13_{6} wanting or, rather, used for pastedown; no text loss). — No catchwords.

Decoration: Except for the representation of the rosary on the pastedown of upper cover (see below), there is no illustrative matter (but some may have been present at one time, cf. note in contents with f. 105r). — Calligraphic initials, in red or blue, vary in size from 2 to 4 lines; they as well as red (on ff. 64–65, also blue) paragraph marks, and versals touched up with red, are limited to the parts written by scribe 1.

Binding: Covers (early 16th century?) are brown calf over wooden boards with beveled edges; the leather is stamped to form on each cover a rectangular central panel with double-lanceolate/hourglass-like shapes formed by curved lines,[6] decorated with palmettes; a framing band done with a roll (not in Kyriss, Haebler). Sewn over 3 bands. Remnants of two clasps. Rebacked.

On pastedown of upper cover, a 16th-century or later colored representation of a rosary (5 blossoms, 50 other more-or-less botanical shapes; inside the oval formed by the rosary, inscription in 16th(?)-century hand: D Jesu mise//rere mei fi//li david. Above the picture, old numbers in light ink ("22") or pencil ("18"; "41"; meaning the year 1841?) — On f. 1r, above deleted old text, in pencil: Ac. 4560(3), no. 15; over the text, in ink: Liber precum.//Fol. 121. d. 25. April.//1835. Bibl. Bülov. Beyern-[aumburg]//G.H.Schr.[7] — On 121v, below last words of the text, in 17th?-century hand: O Herr iesu christe mein//etler trost. [signed:] Speigel; in another hand: ex libris Fratr[is] Ioan[n]is//Ihnemani(?) et . . . (partly illegible because covered with melted brown glue). — On pastedown of lower cover: + // LIBER S. PETRI//Apostoli (= perhaps, as often, Erfurt; but could be Sankt Peter im Einsiedel, an establishment of the Brethren of Common Life in Württemberg?).[8]

Former owners: St. Peter, Erfurt?; Speigel (17th century?); Friedrich Gottlieb Julius von Bülow (d. 1831); (early 20th century:) Rev. Edwin A. Dalrymple, Baltimore; purchased by LC in 1916 (Ms. Ac. 4560, 3, 15).

2° fo.: donec ego vixero. iuxta [N.B. very faded or washed off]

Bibl.: G.H. Schäffer, *Bibliotheca Büloviana* [sale catalog] (Sangerhausen, 1834–36 (v. 3? [not seen]). — De Ricci, *Census* (1935), p. 231, no. 112; Faye and Bond (1962), p. 120, no. 84.

NOTES

1. In place of antiphon, sometimes an address in rather pedestrian prose; at other times, a metrical *pium dictamen*, or part of a rhythmical office. Choices are very different from the books of hours of the period.

2. We have more or less normalized the Latin in this listing (through 76v).

3. Thus, without "tua."

4. Vestiges of vertical framing appear in last two gatherings.

5. The hybrid script of hand 1 has as a peculiar characteristic feature, a *c* without any curve at the lower end of the down-stroke (rather like our printed lowercase *r*). — Hand 2 uses for final *s* a letter resembling Greek lowercase *gamma*, or the capital

S of German current script. — A diligent person added the German "Überstrich" mark (used since ca. 16th century to distinguish *u* from *n*) over most short *u*'s in the hand-1 text; hands 2–5 have often the double-stroke (which today would be read as an *Umlaut*) over the short *u*.

6. Very much like the *Rautengerank* 9 in I. Schunke, *Die Schwenke-Sammlung gotischer Stempel- u. Einbanddurchreibungen* (1979), p. 231 (by the "Laubstab-Meister" in Frankfurt-an-der-Oder!?).

7. The (deplorably placed and executed) inscription refers to G. H. Schäffer's catalog of the Bülow library; see the bibliography paragraph.

8. This doubt is partly based on the script, that of the text and that of the inscription; also on the unimpressive intellectual level of the prayer book. The ancient and well-funded Benedictine monastery of St. Peter in Erfurt had a disciplined scriptorium, and its collections do not seem to have included material similar to our manuscript. Ownership inscriptions of the abbey tended to mention the place ("Liber sancti Petri in erfordia" was perhaps most common). — Cf. J. Theele, *Die Handschriften des Benediktinerklosters S. Petri zu Erfurt* (1920).

MS 34

(Faye and Bond 86)

PSALTER FOR BRIGITTINE NUNS

ca. 1500?

Near Utrecht? Parchment. 192 leaves, ca. 192 × ca. 133 mm (bound volume: ca. 205 × ca. 149 mm) 1 column. 20 lines.

ff. 1r–12v: *KL Januari[us] h[abet] dies xxxi* . . . Siluestri pape

Full calendar, in Latin; in black and red; one month per leaf. — Among the 56 days singled out in red: *Ponciani* (Jan. 14), *Resurectio dn̄i* (March 27), *Pancracij* (May 12), *Seruacij* (May 13), *Translacio sc̄e birgitte* (May 28), *Odulphi* (June 12), *Lebuini et radbodi* (June 25), *Translacio marti[ni]* (July 4), *Natalis btē birgitte* (July 23), *Jereonis m̄r* (Aug. 17), *Augustini epī* (Aug. 28), *Glorificacio ma[ri]e/ Decolla[ci]o io. bapte.* (Aug. 29), *Lamberti* (Sept. 17), *Canonisacio Birgitte* (Oct. 7), *Willibrordi epī* (Nov. 7), *Lebuini cō.* (Nov. 12). — Among the days written in black, Feb. 24 is noted as "loc[us] bisextil[is]"; attention is given, as not quite commonly in the Middle Ages, to St. Joseph: Joseph nutricij dn̄i (March 20, an Utrecht peculiarity).

The calendar was written for the use of a Brigittine establishment located in the diocese of Utrecht.[1] The Scandinavian saints invoked in the Swedish order's litany (cf. ff. 169r sqq.) are for the most part not named in the calendar.

13r: Two circular graphs, each ca. 68 mm in diameter; the upper one for finding of the "golden number," the one below to determine the "Sunday letter." Both have in the 12 o'clock position: *m ccccc* (in red). Directions for use are in Netherlandish.

(13v, 14r–v blank, frame-ruled)

15r–157r: (15r, 14-line historiated initial, Samson and the lion, over 6 lines of text:) (B)[14]Eatus vir qui nō abijt . . . (36r, at the beginning of Ps. XXVII:) *feria secūda ps̄[almus]* (D)[5]omin[us] illu[m]i[n]acio mea . . . (50v, with the beginning of Ps. XXXIX:) *feria 3a ps̄.* (D)[9]ixi custodia[m] vias meas . . . (63v, with the beginning of Ps. LIII:) *feria quarta* (D)[7]ixit insipie[n]s . . . (76v, with the beginning of Ps. LXIX:) *fe. v. ps̄.* (S)[8]aluu[m] me fac deus . . . (92v, Ps. LXXXI:) *feria sexta psalmus* (E)[8]xultate deo adiutori n[ost]ro . . . (107r, begins Ps. XCVIII:) *psalmus* (C)[8]a[n]tate d[omi]no ca[n]ticu[m] nouu[m] . . . (N.B. No initial, no special rubric on 109r where the Ps. CII, "D[omi]ne exaudi orationem meam . . ." begins) (122v, with the beginning of Ps. CX, rubric:) *Dominicis diebus* (130r–131v, the Athanasian Creed, interrupting the Ps. CXIX between verses 32 and 33)

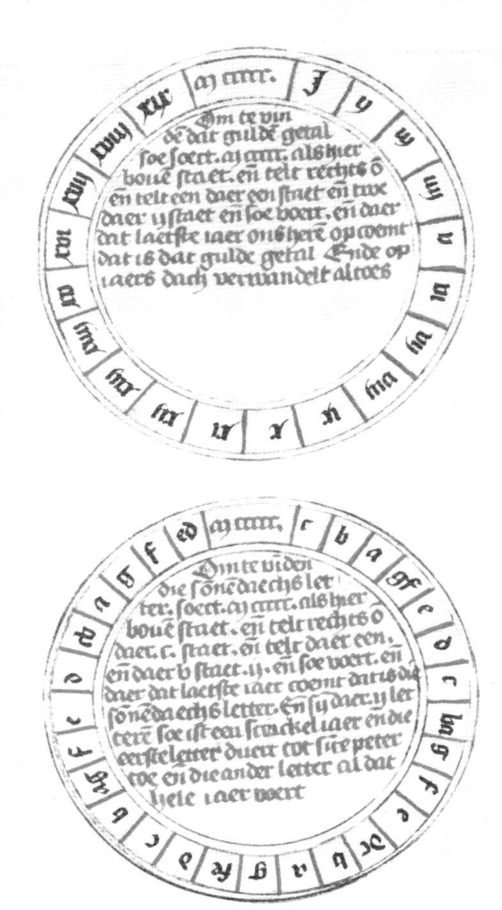

MS 34, f. 13r (actual diameter of outer circles: 68 mm)

The Psalms, in Latin, the "Gallican" version; not numbered. The rubrics assigning various segments of the Psalter to certain days of the week are a practical simplification; the actual distribution was more complicated: cf. T. Lundén (ed.) *Officium parvum* . . . (Uppsala, 1976), v. 1, p. xlii–xliv.[2] The insertion of the Athanasian Creed in the place indicated corresponds to its use in Sunday Prime (cf. Lundén, *op. cit.* v. 1, p. 28–32). — Many of the psalms (it seems to have been done when the thought occurred, and/or when space conveniently permitted) conclude with an indication, sometimes shorter, sometimes longer, of the traditional "Gloria Patri . . ."

157r–168v: The biblical (except for the last one) canticles commonly used in liturgical offices: 157r–v, *"ysaie"* (Isaiah XII); 157v–158v, *"echefielis"* [*sic;* i.e., Ezechiae] (Is. XXXVIII, 10–20); 158v–159r, *cātic̄u Anne"* (1 Sam. II,1–10); 159r–160v, *"canticu[m] moysi"* (Exodus XV, 1–19); 160v–162r, *"Canticu[m] abbacuc"* (Habakkuk III,2–19); 162r–165v *"Ca[n]ticu[m] deutronomij"* (Deut. XXXII, 1–43); 165v–166v, "Ca*[n]ticu[m] triu[m] puero[rum]"* (Daniel III,57–88.56); 166v–167r, *"Canticum zacharie"* (Luke I, 68–79); 167r–v, *"canticu]m] marie"* (= the Magnificat, Luke I,46–55); 167v, *"canticu[m] simeonis"* (= Nunc dimittis, Luke II,29–32); 167–168v, *"Canticu[m] Ambrosij et Augusti[ni]"* (= Te Deum laudamus)

168v–169r: *collecta* Protege q[uesumu]s dn̄e famulos tuos subsidijs pacis . . . redde securos. *collecta* (169r:) Deus a quo s[an]c[t]a desideria [et] r[e]c[t]a consilia . . . Amen

Traditional formal liturgical prayers for protection from enemies (Protege . . .) and for peace (Deus a quo . . .); used in the Brigittine office in Sunday Vespers (cf. Lundén, *op. cit.,* v. 1, p. 46, with full text). Reasons for their insertion on these pages are not clear.

169r–176v: *An[tiphona] cū Letania* (N)[6]E reminiscaris . . . p[e]c[ca]tis n[ost]ris *Ps̄* Dn̄e ne ī fu[rore tuo] . . . Kyrie e[leison] . . .

The antiphon is the one commonly used with the seven Penitential Psalms, here represented by only the first one (Ps. VI), indicated by its initium. The rather long litany thus introduced includes (selecting the less than usual invocations):

among the archangels: "S[anc]te vriel";

among the 38 individual martyrs: . . . olaue, erice, hinrice, eskille, botwide . . . kanute . . . answeri cū so[ciis] t[uis];

among the 26 confessors: . . . sigfride . . . iudoce . . . onofri . . . ;

among 36 individual female saints: . . . birgitta . . . walburgis, potenciana . . . beatrix . . . brigida, eugenia, eufrosina.

The liberation prayers include (173r) "a cecitate cordis." The *"Preces"* (175r–176v) which, as usual (with variants) follow or adjoin the litany, specify (176r): "et nos fa[m]ulos tuos et fa[m]ulas tuas . . . " " . . . iter fa[m]ulo[rum] et fa[m]ularu[m] tuaru[m] . . ." The Brigittine rule associated, in separate quarters but under one abbess, a house of nuns and a house of monks.

177r–185v: *Vigilie defūcto[rum]* (P)[6]Lacebo . . . *Inui.* Circūdederūt me gemitus mortis . dolores inferni circūdederūt me . . . (office ends on 185v:) . . . Requiescant in pace. A.M.E.N.

Officium defunctorum, with responsories (cf. Leroquais, *LH* I, p. xxxix) as follows: I Credo quod II Qui Lazarum III Domine quando IV Heu mihi V Ne recorderis VI Domine secundum VII Peccantem me VIII Libera me Domine de viis inferni IX Libera me Domine de morte eterna. — The Invitatory**[3]** and, in part, the responsories differ from those found in Lundén's edition of the Brigittine breviary (*op cit.,* v. II, p. 210–238); they are identical with those used in the Brigittine breviary from Marienwater Abbey, LC MS 30.

(185v, line 20: *Incipiūt hore de sancto spiritu)*

(186r [otherwise blank], line 20: *Ps̄ ad mat' ī horis de sc̄o spū.)*

186v–191v: (186v, last line: *Hore de sc̄o spū;* lines 1–17:) Beatus vir q[ui] . . . iter impiorum peribit (= Ps. I) (187r:) (I)[6]n vnitate scī sp̄s . . . (office ends on 191v:) . . . Ih's et maria sint s[em]p[e]r nobiscū in via Amen.

The (longer) Hours of the Holy Spirit; cf. printed version in Lundén, *op cit.,* v. II, p. 184–208 (Lundén adds a Swedish translation). Brigittine sisters were obliged to recite this office every day.

192r–v: *Lectrix me[n]se dicat:* Dn̄e labia. Salua[m] fac a[n]cilla[m] tua[m] . . . spiritu[m] elacionis. *Coquina[m] egredie[n]tib[us]* Bened[i]c[t]us es dn̄e d's m[eus] quia adiuuisti me et co[n]solatus es me Saluas fac ancillas tuas . . . *collecta* Deus cui hu[m]iliu[m] accepta sunt vota . . . vt quia p[er]acte ebdomade seruicia deuote . . . [com]pleueru[n]t . . . (192v:) *De i[n]gredie[n]tib[us]* Deus i[n] adiutor[ium] . . . vt r[e]c[t]e sororibus suis i[m]penda[n]t seruicia . . . Amen

Ceremony of the weekly kitchen detail.

* * *

Foliated in modern pencil. A ruled parchment flyleaf precedes f. 1; following f. 192, free endleaf of a character different from the rest; it and the conjugate pastedown are ruled with a 4-line staff now running vertically, without any musical notes. Pastedown of the upper cover is lower half of a leaf from an unidentified canon law commentary written ca. 1400. — Written area ca. 118 × 80–84 mm. Ruled in lead; visible are primarily the verticals and horizontals circumscribing the text area; other horizontal lines very faint. Some pricking marks (used to position the framing verticals) preserved in head and tail margins. — Written in a large, strong, not very regular *littera textualis,* in very good black ink. Rubrics red. — Parchment thickness: ca. 15.6 mm per 100 leaves.

Collation: 1^{8}(= ff. [i],1–7) f.8 singleton 2^{6} $3\text{–}16^{8}$ 17^{8+1} 18^{6} f.142 singleton $19\text{–}23^{8}$ 24^{10}.

Decoration consists of one half-page historiated initial (Samson overpowering the lion, f. 15r = the *B* of Beatus vir . . .; see plate XIII, p. xxviii) with a 3-side border, and eight 5–9 line initials of a quite different style. On 15r, the realistically painted man and beast stand out from void background inside the darkish blue letter in which the basic color is varied by irregular leaflike white and black shapes; the surrounding field is velvety purplish red decorated with botanical shapes partly done in the blue of the letter, partly created by areas left void, partly pen-drawn in yellow over the red. The border, without a visible frame, is made of botanical shapes with quasi-stems drawn in thick gold of a reddish cast carrying blue, orange, green, or white-with-red trifolia, and velvety purplish red fruit; golden bezants are placed in empty areas. Directly above the initial, the foliage is of a more French style, consisting of blue and pink acanthus leaves painted for three-dimensional effect. A burnished gold bar flanks the left margin alongside the 6 lines of text.

Other large initials (cf. contents) are light blue or combined blue and red, with enclosed areas and the roughly rectangular fields around the letters filled with pen-drawn acanthus leaves or other stylized botanical forms outlined and shaped in red; some light green is used as ground coloring. Flourishes done by pen in red ink issue from the large letters; they include much spiral element.

The *KL*'s of the calendar and other 2–3 line initials are alternately red (rather pale) or blue (rather light), as are the versals.

Bound in contemporary dark calf over unrounded wooden boards; sewn over 4 bands. Remnants of two brass back-to-front clasps. Covers blind-stamped: a field of diamond shapes (4 complete diamonds, 8 halves) within a rectangular frame made of 3 lines. The diamonds are filled with highly stylized anthemion-based stamps in which the leaves are decorated by numerous narrowly spaced cross lines (not in Kyriss).

On pastedown of upper cover, bookplate of Rev. Edwin A. Dalrymple, D.D.; in corner, small label of the firm B. Westermann & Co., New York; old LC bookplate with penciled "Temp. no. 35." — On recto of the flyleaf in front, penciled: Ac. 4560(3), no. 17; also: MS. 86. — On pastedown of lower cover, clipping from a French or Belgian sale catalog ("116 *Heures* communes, avec les Vigiles des défunts . . .").

2° fo.: *KL februari[us] h[abet] dies xviij* [sic]

Bibl.: De Ricci, *Census* (1935), p. 232, no. 114; Faye and Bond (1962), p. 120, no. 86.

NOTES

1. Of these, there were several: cf. T. Nyberg, *Birgittinische Klostergründungen des Mittelalters* (1965), p. 195 sqq. — The convent (abbey?) Marienburg in Soest near Amersfoort, with ties to Marienkron in Stralsund where the saints Eric, Olaf, Canute, Botwid named in the Litany were celebrated (cf. Roeskilde calendar in Grotefend, v. 2, p. 232 sqq.) is a good possibility.

2. Lundén uses the Psalm numbering of the Vulgate which makes our Pss. IX–X his Ps. 9, our Pss. CXIV–CXV his Ps. 113, our Ps. CXVI his Pss. 114–15, our CXLVII his 146–47; his Psalms 10 through 112 and 116 through 145 correspond to our Psalms XI–CXIII and CXVII–CXLVI; thus the Psalm used for Sunday day hours is what we call (following the Hebrew Bible's and King James version's count) Ps. CXIX.

3. The gloomy Invitatory may be characteristic of the northern parts of the Low Countries: it appears, in Netherlandish translation, in Geert Grote's *Getijdenboek* (cf. Van Wijk's 1940 ed., p. 156); Lundén's sources (*op cit.*, p. 218) use the "Regem cui omnia vivunt . . .". Cf. also H. Reifenberg, *Stundengebet und Breviere* . . . (1964), p. 95 (the "Circumdederunt . . ." does not seem to have come from Cologne).

MS 35

MS 35, p. 65 (actual size of written area: ca. 220 × 155 mm)

MS 35

(Faye and Bond 128)

GRADUAL / ANTIPHONARY (part)

XVIth c.?

Written in Italy. Parchment. 112 leaves, 340–345 × ca. 260 mm (bound volume: ca. 363 × ca. 270 mm) 1 column (p. 129–141, 2 columns) p. 1–148 mostly 6 lines; p. 149–224, 7 lines (each line of text has above it 4-line staff for musical notation)

p. 1–63: Mass propers (words and music of the choir parts) for the four older feasts of Mary (Annunciation, uncaptioned, p. 1–11; Assumption, p. 11–18; Nativity, p. 18–26; Purification, p. 26–35); also for the days of John the Baptist (p. 36–41), James (p. 41–47), and Michael (captioned *"in festivitatibus angelorum"* but only Michael is mentioned by name; p. 47–54); also *"In agenda mortuorum"* (p. 54–63). (p. 63, four last lines ruled for, blank)

Absence of caption in the first item suggests loss of some material which preceded; the Mass proper itself *(Vultum tuum)* is complete.

(p. 64 ruled, blank)

p. 65–101: Vespers (words and music of the antiphons; Psalms indicated by initia) for the same series of feasts; the last one is captioned (p. 96) *"in sancti Michaelis ad Vesperas";* nothing from the Office for the Dead. (p. 101, two last lines ruled for, blank)

Five antiphons (plus the one for the *Magnificat*) for each occasion, indicating nonmonastic use.

p. 102–122: A short *Kyriale* (not so or otherwise captioned; music with words for the *Kyrie, Gloria, Credo, Sanctus, Benedictus,* and *Agnus Dei*); limited to *"In solempnitatibus gloriose V. M[ariae]"* (p. 102–109) and *"In minoribus duplicibus"* (p. 109–122, with the *Credo* on p. 116–122).

Many erasures and redoings. In the first item, the *Gloria* (p. 103–107) had originally after "Domine Fili unigenite Iesu Christe" the phrase "Spiritus et alme orphanorum paraclite," and numerous Marian interpolations,[1] all later erased and amended in favor of the accepted text. — Changes were also made in the music: e.g., on p. 102, a melody for *Kyrie* resembling the later *Kyrie* IX *(Cum jubilo)* is replaced (though the old one remains to a large extent legible) by another which is closer to the later *Kyrie* II *(Kyrie fons bonitatis).*

p. 122–128: (DIFFERENT-HAND ADDITION; uncaptioned:) Mass proper (p. 122–123) and Vespers (p. 124–128) for St. Andrew.

p. 129–148: *In agenda mortuorum . . .* (p. 129–141, Matins of the Office for the Dead, with music where needed; p. 142–148, the sequence *Dies irae,* text and music)

MS 35 Pages 129–141 are written in two columns, unlike the rest of the book; however, the script and possibly the scribe are same as on p. 1–121. — Invitatory *Regem cui omnia vivunt;* only one nocturn, with full text of Psalms V–VII and full text of the three readings *Parce michi, Tedet animam, Manus tue.* Responsories (text and music): *Credo quod; Qui Laçarum; Libera me Domine de morte eterna.* — The *Dies irae* (again 1 column) is in another hand which doesn't seem to be represented elsewhere in the codex.

(ALL THAT FOLLOWS IS CODICOLOGICALLY DIFFERENT FROM ALL THAT PRECEDES: 7 lines, etc.; apparently written through p. 217 by one person)

p. 149–207: Matins and Lauds (words and music of sung parts only) of (p.149–161:) Christmas, (161–165:) Circumcision (Lauds only), (165–176:) Epiphany, (176–185:) Purification, (185–192:) Assumption, (193–199:) All Saints; on p. 200–207 what appears to be a common of several martyrs (no caption).

p. 208–215: (Introduced by rubric *"Ad missam . . ."* in two last lines of p. 207:) Mass propers (or, rather, commons[2]): *Protexisti* (for a martyr) and *Os iusti* (for a confessor).

p. 216–217: Five different intonations of "Benedicamus Domino" (for a *dup[lex] prime classis, dup. secunde classis, dup. minor, de Angelis, de Beata Virgine).*

(ALL THAT FOLLOWS HAS TEXTS IN HUMANISTIC SCRIPT:)

p. 217–220: *In fest[o] SS. Triadis Inuit[atorium:]* DEum uerū . . . (218:) *Ad Mat. hym[nus:]* SUmme parens clementie . . . (219:) . . . *Ad laudes* . . . (ends on p. 220, near bottom; whole of p. 221 is blank except for ruling)

Only one nocturn is provided for, although captioned *"In primo nocturno."* Chanted parts only.

p. 222–224: In Circumcisione Domini. Introitus. Puer natus est . . . (ends on p. 224:) . . . locutus est nobis in Filio suo. (last staff on p. 224 ruled, empty)

Mass proper for the day of Circumcision (= Jan. 1); ending imperfectly, at the end of the alleluiatic verse.[3] Chanted parts only. (N.B. The captions are here in black ink.)

* * *

Modern paging in ink, p. 1–224. One free paper endleaf in front (not conjugate with the pastedown), one at end.

Codicologically (though not as to contents) the book falls into two parts: p. 1–148 (with irregularities after p. 122) and p. 149–224 (some irregularities after 217):

In the first part, written area is ca. 225 × ca. 150–160 mm; basic layout is 6 lines of text with 6 staves of music. Ruling is reddish yellow for the text, the music staves are red. Through p. 124, the framing verticals are doubled, and some remnants of pricking are preserved near fore edge; on p. 125–128, the verticals are simple and pricking is right on them. — Pages 129–148 are ruled for double columns, although only p. 129–141 are so written. — Pages 1–122[4] and perhaps also 129–141 were written by the same scribe, in a regular *littera Bononiensis;* texts on p. 122–128 and 142–148 are two other hands not represented elsewhere in the volume.

In the second part (beginning with p. 149) the written area is ca. 260–265 × ca. 175 mm; blind-ruled for 7 lines of text accompanied by 7 staves of music, the staves in orange ink. The parchment is noticeably thicker than in the first part. — Pages 149–217 appear to have been written by one person (hand not represented in first part), in what seems to be a late occurrence of the Bologna script; the additions on p. 217–220 and 222–224 are in a poorly executed humanistic *rotunda.* — Musical (plainsong) notation in the second part shows preference for curved line (wavy neumes for the *porrectus* group; rounded top of many square notes). — Captions (there are no other rubrics) are red; some would be logically required but seem to have been neglected.

Collation: $1–3^{10}$ 4^{2}(= p. 61–64) $5–7^{10}$ 8^{2}(= p. 125–128) 9^{10} $10–13^{8}$(= p. 149–212) 14^{8-2}($14_{7,8}$ absent with possible loss of text/music, if ever written; the gathering consists entirely of single leaves pasted to

MS 35, p. 1 (tail margin) (actual distance between the vertical ruled lines: 147 mm)

stubs, with the sewing line between p. 220 and 221). — Catchwords in first part only: on p. 20, 40, 60, 84.

Two pages include miniatures: on p. 1, in tail margin, three medallions; the one in the center contains a representation of Mary with the Child, the other two, respectively, a rake-like instrument with two rows of spikes and a grill or roasting device.[5] — On p. 149 (beginning of the second part of the book), a historiated initial *C* (ca. 80 mm high) contains a Nativity scene. — The miniatures are multicolor; those on p. 1 done skillfully, that on p. 149 amateurish; all seem to be 16th-century work.

Initials in the first part (p. 1–148): the largest are ca. six times higher than the text minims; they are of the calligraphic kind; with one exception they are blue and somewhat decorated by use of white void; one, on p. 1, has added pen decoration in red ink consisting of acanthus-like patterns in and around the letter, the rest have no such additions: on p. 11, 26, 36, 47, 54, 57, 65, 69, 73(red), 76, 78, 90, 93, 96, 102, 109. Versals in this first part are alternately blue or red, ca. three times the height of average text minim. The blue is purplish in the additions on p. 123–128; on p. 142–148 the versals are red and somewhat larger. — In the second part, after the historiated *C* on p. 149, initials of same size occur on p. 161, 165, 176, 185, and 193; they are in various colors, rather amateurish, and contain varying amounts of Renaissance-style decoration.

Contemporary binding: covers brown goatskin over rounded wooden boards; sewn over 4 bands. Two front-to-back clasps of leather straps and metal. Large metal (brass?) boss in center of front cover; several metal buttons, and metal corner protectors (of which three are preserved, one lost) with filigree-style decoration.[6] — On paper pastedown of upper cover, small label with handwritten numbers . . . 36//2100 . . .; also penciled "3469" and LC accession number: Ac. 4984A(1). On verso of free

MS 35 endleaf in front, penciled: Gift of Dr. Ernest C. Richardson//Dec. 15, 1934.

Former owner: Dr. Ernest Cushing Richardson (former librarian of Princeton University; b. 1860, d. 1939).

2° fo.: dixit te deus in

Bibl.: De Ricci, *Census* (1935), p. 1187, no. 1; Faye and Bond (1962), p. 121, no. 128.

NOTES

1. Similar to those known from Premonstratensian sources (cf. *EEFL,* 3309); also in LC MSS 26 and 48.

2. Music (with words) for the changeable parts of the Mass tends to be called a "proper" by people who work principally with (choir) music; for liturgists, the term applies only to the sets assigned to any one specific festivity or occasion; sets which are used for various saints of any one category (apostles, martyrs, confessors, virgins . . .) are "commons."

3. "Alleluiatic verse" followed the "gradual" (not the book also so called) between the two readings of the Mass.

4. On p. 102–122, however, some of the original writing has been erased and parts have been rewritten, in a very amateurish way.

5. The rake-like tool is, I think, the double-row comb which is the symbol for St. Verena; the grill suggests St. Lawrence. These should be clues to the origin of the book but I haven't succeeded in interpreting them. Principal area of St. Verena's cult was the German-speaking part of Switzerland and southern Germany. A brotherhood named after her was approved early in the 16th century. See on the saint and her cult: A. Reinle, *Die heilige Verena von Zurzach* (Basel, 1948).

6. The book is now kept in a linen-covered box ca. 39 × 29 × 10 cm (grayish orange and brownish gray).

MS 36

(Music Division: M2147 XV M2 Case)

CHOIR MANUAL OF FRANCISCAN SISTERS ca. 1500

Written in France. Parchment. 114 leaves, 161 × ca. 110 mm (bound volume: 167 × ca. 125 mm) 1 column. 18 lines of text or 6 lines of text with 6 staves of music.

ff. 1r–7v: *(I)³N festo purificationis finita tercia . . . Deinde due sorores . . . cantantur.* (L)³umen ad reuelationem gentium . . . (1v:) . . . (E)³xsurge domine . . . (2r:) (A)³ue gratia plena . . . (2v:) . . . (A)³dorna thalamum tuu[m] . . . (3v:) . . . (R)³esponsum accepit symeon . . . (4v:) . . . (O)³btulerunt pro eo . . . (5v:) . . . (G)³aude maria virgo . . . (6v:) . . . (I)³nuiolata . . . (ends, 7v:) . . . permansisti.

The Candlemas (Feb. 2) procession, rubrics and chants (words and music). The rubrics include information about liturgical actions and words of the clergy only as far as needed by the choir. The texts sung are in black.

7v–21v[1]: *In die palmaru[m] completa tercia . . . a choro cantatur antiphona.* (8r:) (O)³sanna filio dauid . . . (C)³ollegerunt pontifices . . . (10r:) . . . (I)³n monte olueti oraui [*sic*, for "oravit"] . . . (11r:) . . . (P)³ueri hebreoru[m] portantes . . . (11v:) . . . (P)³ueri hebreorum vestimenta . . . (12r:) . . . (C)³um appropinquaret . . . (14r:) . . . (C)³um audisset populus . . . (15v:) . . . (A)³nte sex dies . . . (16v:) (O)³ccurrunt turbe . . . (17r:) (C)³um angelis et pueris . . . (17v:) . . . (G)³loria laus et honor . . . (20v:) . . . (I)³ngrediente domino . . . (ends on 21v:) . . . exierunt obuiam ei. Cu[m].

The Palm Sunday procession (rubrics, chants, etc., as in the preceding). The "Gloria, laus et honor . . ." begins with an ascending ligature (*podatus re-la*) for the first syllable.[2]

21v–34v: *Feria qui[n]ta in cena d[omi]ni post refectione[m]* . . . (M)³andatu[m] nouu[m] . . . (22r:) . . . (P)³ostq[uam] surrexit dominus a cena . . . (22v:) . . . (D)³ominus iesus postq[uam] cenauit . . . (24r:) . . . (M)³aria ergo vnxit . . . (24v:) . . . (V)³os vocatis me . . . (25v:) (D)³iligamus nos i[n]uicem . . . (26r:) . . . (U)³bi est caritas et dilectio ibi sanctoru[m] est congregatio . . . (27r:) . . . (C)³ongregauit nos christ[us] . . . (27v:) (M)³ulier que erat . . . (28r:) . . . (D)³omine tu michi lauas . . . (29r:) (S)³i ego dominus . . . (29v:) (I)³n hoc cognoscent . . . (ibid.:) (M)³aneant in vobis . . . (30r:) . . . (B)³enedicta sit sancta trinitas . . . (30v–34v:) . . . (U)³bi caritas et amor . . . secula per infinita seculoru[m]. Amen.

The *Mandatum*, or ceremonial washing of others' feet on Holy Thursday;[3] here, as a paraliturgical custom of a sisters' convent. — The rather numerous chants include, besides the antiphons marked by initials and listed above, also Psalm verses and other

MS 36, f. 30v (actual size of written area: ca. 110 × 70 mm)

minor items.[4] — The hymn *Ubi caritas et amor*, ff. 30v–34v, differs in various points from the version edited by Wilmart:[5] in the present manuscript it has nine stanzas, some with only three verses; it ends with the "Simul quoque cum beatis . . .", with "gloriantur" in the second verse, as in the 1570 *Missale Romanum*.[6]

34v–60r: (rubric = last 4 lines of 34v:) *Finita missa . . . ste[n]t i[n] circuitu feretri* . . . (35r:) (N)²on intres in iudiciu[m] cum ancilla tua domine . . . (ibid.:) (S)³ubuenite . . . (36v:) . . . (D)²eus cui omnia viuu[n]t . . . (ibid.:) Ne recorderis . . . (37r:) . . . (F)²ac quesumus dn̄e hanc cu[m] ancilla tua misericordiam . . . (ibid.:) Libera me domine . . . (37v:) . . . (A)²bsolue quesumus . . . (38r:) In paradisum . . . (38v:) . . . *psalm[us]* . . . (C)²onfitemini . . . (= Psalm CXVIII) (40r:) . . . Aperite michi portas iusticie . . . (40v:) . . . *psalmus.* (Q)²ue[m]-admodum desiderat . . . (= Ps. XLII) (41v:) . . . Ingrediar in locum . . . (42r:) (M)²emento dn̄e dauid . . . (= Ps. CXXXII) (43r:) *a.* Hec requies mea . . . (ibid.:) *ps.* (D)²omine probasti . . . (= Ps. CXXXIX) (45r:) . . . *an.* De terra formasti me . . . (ibid.:) *psalm[us]* (D)²n̄e exaudi . . . (= Ps. CXLIII) (46v:) . . . *an.* Non intres . . . (ibid.:) *p.* Laudat' do. (= Ps. CL, cue only) (47r:) *an.* Ego sum resurrectio . . . (ibid.:) *p'.*Bn̄dict[us] (= Song of Zachary, cue only) (ibid.:) *or'.* (O)²remus fratres carissimi pro spiritu sororis n[ost]re . . . (47v:) . . . *Or̄o.* (D)²eus cui o[mn]ia viuu[n]t . . . (48r:) . . . *or̄.* (T)²emeritatis quidem est . . . (49r:) . . . *Or̄o.* (O)² domine sancte pater . . . (49v:) . . . *Or̄o.* (D)²ebitum humani corporis sepeliendi . . . (50r:) . . . *Or̄o.* (O)²mnipotens sempiterne . . . (50v:) . . . *Or̄o.* (S)²atisfaciat tibi . . . (51r:) . . . *Resp'.* Memento mei deus . . . (ibid.:) *Or̄o.* (T)²ibi dn̄e co[m]mendamus . . . (51v:) . . . *R[esp.]* (C)²redo quod redemptor meus . . . (52r:) . . . *Resp'.* Qui lazarum . . . (53r:) . . . *Respons'.* Domine quando . . . (54r:) . . . *R[esp.]* Memento mei . . . (54v:) . . . *R[esp.]* Heu michi . . . (55v:) . . . *R[esp.]* Ne recorderis . . . (56r:) . . . *R* Peccantem . . . (57r:) . . . *R* Domine secundum actum meum . . . (58r:) . . . *R* (L)³ibera me domine de morte eterna . . . (59r:) . . . *R* Libera me domine de vijs inferni . . . (ending toward end of 60r:) . . . luceat eis. Qui p.

The *Ordo sepulturae*, funeral service (for a nun), corresponding closely if not exactly to the program edited in *SMRL* II, p. 394–397. The texts sung by the choir are given in full (and with music, except the Psalms), as are the prayers said by the priest (without music) which begin on f. 47r; rubrics are almost entirely omitted. — The responsories on ff. 51v–60r are those of the Office for the Dead *(Officium defunctorum)* which, as envisioned by the program printed *loc. cit.* should be performed before rather than after the rest of the funeral service.[7]

60r–65r: (rubric/caption at end of last line of 60r:) *prosa.* (60v:) (F)³regit victor virtualis hic franciscus triumphalis . . . (ends on 65r:) . . . tu nobis victor rex miserere. Ame[n].

AH LV,133 (p. 155); here with music.[8]

65v–70r: (on 65v, red caption centered in head margin:) *Pro defunctis p[ro]sa.* (text with music:) (M)³-iserere miserere miserere illi deus Tu iesu christe domine veniam eis concede. Creator deus omniu[m] te deprecamur domine huius defuncti anime regnu[m] celorum tribue. Tu iesu. . . . (ends, 70r:) . . . vobiscum est in requie. Miserere miserere.

The very folksy-sounding versified litany consists of 17 four-verse stanzas; the words "Tu Iesu Christe . . . concede" are repeated after each stanza except the last.[9] — With music throughout.

N.B. The ff. 65–70 constitute a gathering, one of six leaves while the rest of the book is in eights. The initial *M* differs conspicuously from other initials in the book. The text seems, however, to have been written by same person as the rest.

70r–v: (ANOTHER HAND, BOTH TEXT AND NOTATION; text is in an amateurish roman script:) CRuci coronae spineae sacro quae ferro [*sic*] lanceae . . . perpetua speramus, alleluia. (rest of 70v blank)

AH XXIV, p. 38?[10]

71r–73v: (K)³yrieleyson. Christeleyson . . . (ends on 73v:) . . . Christe exaudi nos. [followed by three requests added in another hand, in amateurish roman script: Ab ira et odio et omni mala voluntate. li[bera nos domine] A subitanea et improuisa morte . . . A fulgure et tempestate. lib.)

Litany of the Saints, of the short kind.[11] — After Mary, the archangels, and John the Baptist, the individually named saints are three apostles (Peter, Paul, John), three martyrs (Stephen, Lawrence, Vincent), four confessors (Gregory, Martin, Francis, Anthony), three women (Mary Magdalen, Agnes, Agatha).

ALL THAT FOLLOWS IS WITHOUT MUSIC:

74r–82r: *Ceste oraison se doit dire par lespace de trente iours . . . contre tout persecution tentation et tribulation . . .* (D)²ulcissime d[omi]ne iesu christe fili dei viui qui de sinu su[m]mi patris omnipotentis missus es in mundum laxare crimina redimere afflictos captiuos soluere . . . (79r, . . . "tribue michi peccatrici . . ."; 80v, . . . "michi ancille supplici tue . . ."; 81r, . . . "gl[or]iosi patris n[ost]ri francisci . . ."; prayer ends on 82r:) . . . peccatrici michi collatis tibi sincero corde laudes [et] gr[ati]as refero. Benedictio et claritas [et] sapientia et gratiarum actio . . . seculoru[m]. Amen.

A nonliturgical, artlessly verbose prayer, combining elements from more or less inspired sources.

82r–92v: *De sancto ludouico quonda[m] rege francoru[m]. Ad vesperas sup[er] psal[mos] anti[phonae].* (F)²rancoru[m] rex magnificus ludouicus vir celicus . . . (ends on 92v, with rubric:) . . . *require s[uperius] in primis vesp[er]is.* (rest of page blank)

(Without music.) Liturgical (for Franciscan use) rhymed office of St. Louis. To the rhymed office as in *AH* XIII, 73 (p. 192 sqq.) are added other necessary elements of the "proper": the chapters, hymns, the formal *oratio*, and the readings of the Matins. Psalms are indicated by initia. — The hymns are: *Gaude chorus fidelium* (*AH* XI, 323), *In celesti collegio* (*AH* XI, 324), *Beata nobis gaudia* (*AH* XI, 325). The readings: I: Beatus Ludouicus quondam rex Francorum II: Cuius profectui III: Demum providentia matris et procerum; IV: Quolibet enim sabbato V: Postmodum vero ardore fidei VI: Eductus autem velut alter Ioseph; VII: Sed in mari VIII: Nullus enim narrare sufficeret IX: Contigit enim quod in abbatia. — On 90rv, a ninth responsory not printed in *AH, loc. cit.*[12]

93r–101v: *In no[m]i[n]e d[omi]ni Amen. Sequitur ordinariu[m] a fratribus minoribus regularis obseruantie iuxta veritatem romane ecclesie obserua[n]du[m].* (A)³Duentus dni celebratur vbicunq[ue] dies d[omi]nica venerit . . . (101v:) . . . totiens fit de feria. *Additio capituli generalis.* Notandum q[uod] . . . in hymnis Que[m] terra [et] O gloriosa no[n] debet addi versus ille Maria m[ate]r g[ratia]e . . . or[ati]ones addite.

Rubricae generales of Franciscan breviary, considerably revised and added to since their first formulation by Haymo of Faversham in 13th century (cf. for his text *SMRL* II, p. 114–121). — The provision quoted from f. 101v seems to date from 1447 (cf. D. de Gubernatis, *Orbis Seraphicus*, v. 3[1684], p. 109); some other provisions in our text may be those of the chapter held at Toulouse in 1487 (cf. *op. cit.*, p. 131, 2nd column).

102r–111v: *Incipiu[n]t enodatio[n]es dubior[um] circa diuinu[m] officiu[m] per anni circulu[m] emergentiu[m]. [et] p[rim]o. De me[n]se ianuarij.* In s[e]c[un]dis vesperis circu[m]cisio[n]is no[n] fit aliqua com[memoratio] nisi . . . (107r:) . . . Item festum sc̄ti bonaue[n]ture celebretur a modo quartadecima iulij . . . (109r:) . . . Festu[m] presentationis beate marie fit duplex maius . . . (109v:) . . . in secundis vesp[er]is sancti ambrosij fit tantu[m] officium de conceptione cum co[m](110r:)memoratione sancti ambrosij . . . (the *Enodationes* end on 111v:) (historia) denominatur a responsorijs [et] no[n] a legenda vel lectionibus.

A collection of rule interpretations arranged by the months, with the most recent rulings dating from the end of the 15th century (cf. De Gubernatis, *op. cit.*, v. 3 [1684], p. 226).

111v–114r: *Incipiunt rubrice ordinarij spectantes ad officiu[m] nocturnu[m] et diurnu[m] psalmiste.* Notandu[m] q[uod] modo infrascripto antiphone laudu[m] prime tercie sexte [et] none in d[omi]nicis diebus . . . (113r:) . . . *Rubrica vigiliar[um].* Officiu[m] defunctorum secundum consuetudinem romane curie no[n] fit quandocunq[ue] fit de festo aliquo . . . (ends, 114r:) . . . vigilie feriarum . . . semper dicuntur post vesperas diei precedentis feriam. (ADDED LINE BY ANOTHER HAND, in amateurish roman script:) .IR.Realis amor nu[n]q[uam] desinit.AG.

(In tail margin of 114r, on center, a heart drawn in black ink, with letters *Z*(?) and *A* presented as first and last letter of name (?) hidden by the heart. Above the drawing, three erased cursive lines.)

* * *

Foliated in modern pencil. Eight paper endleaves in front, eight at end; the two closest to covers (and the pastedowns) are Van Gelder hand paper, the rest unidentified, vellum-like. — Written area ca. 112 × ca.

72 mm. — Frame-ruled in faint red ink; no pricking preserved. — With the exception of roman-script additions on ff. 70rv and 114r, written probably throughout (incl. rubrics) by one scribe, a careful and experienced person, using a very regular late gothic script *(littera textualis formata).*[13] — Rubrics in red, in longer passages a distinctly smaller size than the main script but of the same style. — Musical notation, occupying much of the pages 1r–71v, has 4-line staves in red, and black square notes.

Collation: $1–8^8$ 9^6(= ff. 65–70) $10–14^8$ 15^4. — Remainder of a mostly cropped catchword on 48v.

Decorated with numerous (ca. 80) initials, of two distinct sizes: (i) 15–19 mm high, used chiefly at the beginning of musical items; (ii) 12–13 mm (= 2 lines of text), found with texts without music. Most of either size are quite uniform in style: the letter is normally light blue, the blue further lightened by white penwork; it is placed in a more or less rectangular field of brick red lightened by penwork in gold. With some of the larger letters, the bars or stems would slightly protrude out of the red field into the margin and end in foliate terminals. The area enclosed by the letter contains, in each case, a flower or a berry-carrying plant with red, red-and-white, or white (8r, 17r) blossom or (red) berry and two or three simple green leaves, all on a simple-line red stem, on a smooth, slightly greenish painted-gold ground sprinkled with black or red dots. — Initials of same style but with the body of the letter white appear on 58r, 60v, 71r, 74r. On 24v, 29v, and 42r, the field is entirely painted-gold (no brick-red), outlined in black. On 65v, the *M* introducing the *prosa* "Miserere miserere miserere" is of a quite different style: a reddish painted-gold letter on an ultramarine blue field. — Neat one-line versals on 38v–46r and in the Litany (71r–73v) have letters in painted gold on alternately light blue or brick-red grounds; similarly done are the line fillers found chiefly in the Litany, and the paragraph marks used chiefly in the otherwise not much decorated regulatory texts, from 93r to end.

Binding (ca. 1900?): covers olive green calf. Edges gilt all around.[14] — On spine, leather label with gold-tooled title: OFFICIUM// CANTUS//GREGORIANUS; somewhat lower, gold-tooled: SAEC. XV. — Pasted to the inside of upper cover, armorial bookplate with name: Buckler. On the endleaf facing f. 1r, in pencil: Bequest Justine Bayard Ward, July 8, 1976. On pastedown of lower cover, LC cataloger's code, date (12/27/79), and main-entry heading: "Catholic Church. Liturgy and ritual"; also LC (Music Div.) call no.: M 2147//XV//.M2//-Case.

2° fo.: Aue gratia ple [with music above the words]

Not in De Ricci; not in *NUC* pre-56. — LC card no. 80-451082 (M).

On LC printed card, the date is given as "2nd half of 15th cent." The injunction on f. 107r to celebrate St. Bonaventura (canonized 1482) should have advanced the date to "end of" the century; further, the (involved) liturgical directives on 109v–110r concerning conflicting claims of the days of St. Ambrose (for the Franciscans, Dec. 7) and of Immaculate Conception seem to reflect the ruling made by the general chapter of the Ultramontane Observants held at Cologne in 1499 (cf. De Gubernatis, *Orbis Seraphicus*, v. 3 [1684], p. 226, 2nd column). The style of the script is one encountered in France in the early 16th century.[15]

The "Franciscan sisters" of our heading are not likely to have been the Poor Clares (Clarisses): the absence of St. Clare in the litany is too much against it. The Third Order Regular, perhaps the "Grey Sisters" whose foundations were, by 1500, numerous in Burgundy and elsewhere, are a more likely possibility.[16]

NOTES

1. The contents of leaves 1–21 could be termed a "processional."

2. Followed by *la la* for the remainder of the first word. This seems to be quite different from the *la sol sol-la* of the modern Solesmes books. (Other comparisons not made.)

3. Cf. Wilmart, *Auteurs spirituels* . . . (1932), p. [26] sqq.

4. Since the singing was meant primarily to fill the time required for the washing ceremony, this may mean that the book came from a large convent?

5. *Op. cit.,* p. 35–36.

6. Cf. Wilmart, *op. cit.*, p. 28, n. 1.

7. *SMRL* II, p. 393–394. For the program of the *Officium defunctorum* see ibidem, p. 192–194. — The office is not strictly a part of the funeral service. Here, as elsewhere, the manuscript seems to be poor at separating and captioning. (Passage to next item is equally unsatisfactory.)

8. Text in the *Analecta* is edited from 15th-century manuscripts and from early printed Franciscan missals (1520, 1535). The editor rightly questions occasional attribution of the rather low-quality poem to Thomas de Celano.

9. Apparently not in the *Analecta.* Sample stanzas (capitalization and verse division ours): (67r:) Precursor Christi Baptista / tu Enoc atque Helya / precibus iam subuenite / huius defuncti anime. Tu Iesu . . . (69rv:) Magdalena restituta / Katherina Margareta / animam huius defuncti / sponso vestro presentate. Tu Iesu . . .

10. Volume not available at the time of this writing.

11. Not identical with either that in *OMRL*, p. 514 sqq., or that in *SMRL* II, p. 390 sqq. — The absence of St. Clare (shocking in a Franciscan sisters' book) and presence of Mary Magdalen may suggest that the convent was one concentrating on the idea of penance, a theme which might befit the branch called Third Order Regular.

12. The responsory reads as follows (with spelling normalized): Regnum mundi supergressus et eius ornatum / regnum coeli iam ingressus sibi praeparatum / Nostros ad se regat gressus post hunc incolatum. *v.* Peregre Iacob egressus ad patris mandatum / Deum vidit sic professus vitae celibatum. Nostros . . . Gloria Patri . . . Post hunc . . . *Ps.*[!] Te Deum.

13. Marked by a tendency to concaveness in the upper right shoulders of *n* and *m*; rather resembling (though less exuberant than) the early 16th-century script of Paris Bib. nat. nouv. acq. lat. 1415 (*MSS datés* IV,1, plate CV); also similar to: Nancy, Bib. mun. 13 (of 1493; *MSS datés* V, pl. CLXXV); Verdun, Bib. mun. 90 (of 1514, *ibid.*, pl. CLXXXII) and 94 (of 1508–1514, pl. CLXXXI); Troyes, Bib. mun. 41 (of 1522, pl. CLXXXIII).

14. The covers described here were removed in 1986, in preparation for rebinding and other conservation measures not yet completed as of this writing.

15. The manuscript does not mention (it would be on f. 103v, *De mense martij*) among the new rulings, etc., the celebration of St. Joachim, made "duplex minus" in 1505 (cf. Leroquais, *Brév.* I, p. cix); this supports dating into "early" 16th century.

16. Cf. J. Moorman, *A history of the Franciscan Order* (1968), p. 567–568.

(N.B. Several bifolia and some individual leaves have been variously misbound; the correct order seems to be: ff. 1–28, [missing leaf], 29–44, 47, [missing leaf], 54, 55, [missing leaf], 56, 45, [missing leaf], 48–53, 59, 46v, 46r [missing six (?) leaves], 57, [missing two (?) leaves], [58], [missing three (?) leaves], 60–105, [missing two (?) leaves], 106–127. Our list of contents follows this corrected order.)

MS 37

(Faye and Bond 32)

ʼΑΡΧΙΕΡΑΤΙΚΟΝ (Greek Orthodox Archieraticon) ca. 1600?

Place of writing unknown.[1] Paper. [i], 127, [2] leaves, 227 × 184 mm (bound volume: 227 × ca. 190 mm) 1 column. 12 lines.

ff. 1r–3r: ΤΆΞΙΣ ΓΙΝΟΜΈΝΗ ʼΕΠῚ ΧΕΙΡΟΤΟΝΊΑ ʼΑΝΑΓΝΏΣΤΟΥ ΚΑῚ ΨΆΛΤΟΥ *Προσαγόμενος τῷ ἀρχιερεῖ ὁ τοιοῦτος . . . προκείμενον.*

The rite of instituting liturgical readers and cantors. Text as in Habert,[2] p. 305–306 (cf. also p. 37–38), with some variant readings.

3r–6r: ΤΆΞΙΣ ΓΙΝΟΜΈΝΗ ʼΕΠῚ ΧΕΙΡΟΤΟΝΊΑ ʽΥΠΟΔΙΑΚΌΝΟΥ *[Τ]οῦ ἀρχιερέως ἱσταμένου πρὸ τῆς ἁγι[ας] τραπέζης . . . ἔπεισιν εἰς τοὺς ὑποδιακόνους.∴* (last eight lines of f. 6r blank)

Instituting or ordaining a subdeacon. Cf. Habert, p. 306–307 (and/or p. 45–46); text of the prayer in our manuscript as printed in Habert, rubrics rather variant.

6v–16r: (on 6v, a 4-line headpiece; the caption and the text through end of 7v are in gold, in liturgical capitals:) ʽΗ ΘΕΊΑ ΛΕΙΤΟΥΡΓΊΑ ΤΟΥ͂ ʼΕΝ ʽΑΓΊΟΙΣ Π[ΑΤ]Ρ[Ὸ]Σ ʽΗΜ[Ω͂Ν] ʼΙΩ[ΆΝΝ]ΟΥ ΤΟΥ͂ ΧΡΥΣΟΣΤΌΜΟΥ // ΕΥ̓ΧῊ ΤΗ͂Σ ΠΡΟΘΈΣΕΩΣ // [ʽΟ]^3 Θ[ΕῸ]Σ ʽΟ Θ[ΕῸ]Σ ʽΗΜΩ͂Ν . . . (= *EEFL 2881*-a) . . . 7v, last line: . . . ΘΕΊΩΝ ΣΟΥ ΜΥΣΤΗΡΊΩΝ (continued on 8r in gold minuscule:) (ʽO)^{2}τι ἡγίασται . . . (8r, line 8:) (E)^{2}ὐλογημένη ἡ βασιλεία . . . (8v, in black ink except for the *litterae notabiliores* which are in gold and set off into the margin:) (ʼE)ν εἰρήνῃ . . . (10r:) . . . ΕΥ̓ΧΗ ʼΑΝΤΙΦΩ͂ΝΟΥ Α´ ου(13r:) . . . ΕΥ̓ΧῊ ΤΗ͂Σ ΕἸΣΌΔΟΥ //(Δ)^{3}έσποτα κ[υρι]ε . . . . . . (= *EEFL* 2883-a) (14r:) . . . ΕΥ̓ΧῊ ΤΟΥ͂ ΤΡΙΣΑΓΊΟΥ . . . (= *EEFL* 2884; through f. 16r, 8th line:) . . . τ[ῶν] αἰω[νῶν]

The initial portion, up to the readings, of the Liturgy of St. John Chrysostom.[3] Only the parts for the presiding ἀρχιερεύς are given in full; those of the deacon are abridged, and the texts sung by the choir (or by the assembled clergy and people) are more or less omitted. (This system holds throughout the book.)

MS 37

16r–23r: (on 16r, signaled by a headpiece, a gold caption begins in last line:) ΤΆΞΙΣ ΓΙΝΟΜΈΝΗ ʼΕΠῚ ΧΕΙΡΟΤΟΝΊΑ (16v:) ʼΕΠΙΣΚΌΠΟΥ // (red:) (Μ)[3] *ετὰ τὴν τοῦ Τρισαγ[ίου] συνπλήρωσιν . . . ἐν ᾧ γέγραπται ταῦτα* (17r, in gold:[4]) (Ψ)[4]*ήφῳ καὶ δοκιμασίᾳ [τῶν] ἱεροτατῶν μ[ετ]ροπολιτῶν . . . ἀρχιεπισκόπων* . . . (ʻΗ)[2] *Θεία χάρις* . . . (rite ends on 23r, with red rubric:) . . . *αὐτὸς καὶ τῷ χειροτονήσαντι μεταδίδωσιν.*

The consecration of a bishop; as in Habert p. 316–319, with very minor differences. — The alternative offered in Habert's text (p. 316) for the case when the *χειροτονῶν* is not a patriarch is not mentioned.

23v–31v: (on 23v, caption in red minuscule:) *ἄρξ[ο]ν τ[ῆ]ς λειτ[ουρ]γ[ίας]*[5] // *μ[ε]τ[ὰ] τ[ὲ] τὸν ἀπόστολον κ[α]ὶ τὸ εὐα[γγέλιον] ὁ // διάκονος.* // (black text:) (Ε)ʼ*ίπωμεν πάντες* . . . (24r:) . . . ΕΥ̓Χ[Ὴ] ΤΗ͂Σ ʼΕΚΤΕΝΟΥΣ ʻΙΚΕΣΊΑΣ[6] (Κ)[4][*ύ*]*ρ*[*ι*]*ε* . . . (Bri. p. 373b) (25r:) . . . ΕΥ̓Χ[Ὴ] ΚΑΤΙΧΟΥΜΈΝ[ΩΝ] ΠΡῸ ΤΗ͂Σ ʻΑΓΊΑΣ ʼΑΝΑΦΟΡΑ͂Σ (Κ)[4][*ύ*]*ρ*[*ι*]*ε* . . . (Bri. p. 374b–375) (26v:) . . . ΕΥ̓ΧῊ ΠΙΣΤΩ͂Ν Α'η ΜΕΤᾺ ΤῸ ʻΑΠΛΩΘΗ͂ΝΑΙ ΤῸ ΕἸΛΗΤῸΝ (Ε)[5]*ὐχαριστοῦμεν σοι* . . . (= *EEFL* 2886 = Bri. p. 375b–376) (28v:) (Π)[5]*άλιν καὶ πολλάκις* . . . (= Bri. p. 376b through line 24) . . . *Θυσιαστηρίου.* [wanting leaf with end of the prayer and the title and beginning of the *Εὐχὴ τοῦ χερουβικοῦ ἀδομένου*] (29r:) [*σαρ*]*κικαῖς ἐπιθυμίαις* . . . (= Bri. p. 377, line 11 sqq.; ending on f. 31v:) . . . *αἰῶνας τῶν αἰών*[*ων*] (Bri. p. 378, line 11)

Continuation of the Liturgy of John Chrysostom which had been interrupted by the rite of *χειροτονία ἐπισκόπου.* (As commonly in liturgically oriented Christian communities, the major orders are conferred during the eucharistic service.)

31v–38v: (on 31v, under end of the preceding, a decorative band and gold caption:) ΤΆΞΙΣ ΓΙΝΟΜΈΝΗ ʼΕΠῚ ΧΕΙΡΟΤΟΝΊΑ ΠΡΕΣΒΥΤΈΡΟΥ // (red, except for multicolor *M:*) (Μ)[2]*ετὰ τὸ εἰσενεχθῆναι . . . πληρωθῆναι* (32r:) *τε τὸν μυστικὸν ὕμνον* . . . (32v, in gold:) (ʻΗ) *θεία χάρις* . . . (this part of the rite ends on 38v:) . . . (red:) *κ[α]ὶ λειτουργεῖ καθεκάστην ἐπὶ ἡμέρας ἑπτά.*

First segment of the rite of ordaining a priest; closely interwoven into the eucharistic service, the rite will resume again (in the present manuscript, imperfectly) after the *ἀνάμνησις* of the regular liturgy (with the leaf numbered 54).

38v–44v, 47rv, 54r: (on 38v, lines 6–12, the Deacon's invitations to prayer, Bri. p. 380–381; on 39r, large caption in gold:) ΕΥ̓ΧῊ ΠΡΟΣΚΟΜΙΔ[Η͂Σ] ΜΕΤᾺ ΤΗ͂Ν ʼΕΝ ΤΗ͂ ʻΑΓΊΑ ΤΡΑΠΈΖΗ ΤΩ͂Ν ΘΕΊΩΝ ΔΏΡΩΝ ʼΑΠΌΘΕΣΙΝ // (Κ)[4][*ύρι*]*ε ὁ* Θ[*εὸ*]Σ *ὁ παντοκράτωρ* . . . (= *EEFL* 2889 = Bri. p. 380b–381b) . . . (42r:) . . . ʻΟ ʼΑΡΧΙΕΡΕΥ͂Σ ΚΛΙΝΌΜΕΝΟΣ ʼΕΠΕΎΧΕΤΑΙ // (ʼΆ)[5]*ξιον καὶ δίκαιον* . . . (= *EEFL* 2898 = Bri. p. 384–385, the beginning of the *ἀναφορά*) . . . (44v:) . . . *ἁγιάσας, κλάσας,* (47r:) *ἔδωκε τοῖς ἁγίοις* . . . (words of the Institution, 47rv, as Bri. p. 385–386 through line 16:) . . . *τριημέρου* [a leaf wanting, with loss of the text Bri. p. 386, line 16 through p. 387, line 11] (54r, in gold:) [*ποτη*]*ρίῳ τούτῳ τίμιον αἷμα* . . . (ends with the fifth line:) *ἀμήν. ἀμήν. ἀμήν.*

Continuation of the eucharistic service, including its central part; to be interrupted by further rites pertaining to the ordination of a priest:

54r, line 6–55r: (54r, red:) (see plate XIV, p. xxix) (ʻΌ)[2]*τε δὲ τελειωθῶσι* . . . λ[ε]γ[ῶ]*ν οὕτως* (black:) (Λ)*άβε τὴν παρακαταθήκην ταύτην* . . . (54v:) . . . *ἀπαιτεῖσθαι αὐτήν.* (beginning in the 4th line, red:) *ὁ δὲ λαβὼν* . . . (rubric ends on 55r, in 4th line:) . . . *τὴν ὀπισθάμβωνον εὐχ[ὴν]*

A historically important segment of the rite of ordination, with the handing over of the *παρακαταθήκη*; cf. Habert, p. 112, 315, 328, and 152–153.[7] — Our text is except for very minor linguistic details identical with that printed in Littledale, *Offices,*[8] p. 37 (line 21)–38 (line 8).

55rv, 56rv, 45rv: (on 55r, 5th line, gold caption:) ʻΟ ʼΑΡΧΙΕΡΕΥ͂Σ ʼΕΠΕΎΧΕΤΑΙ // (ʻΏ)[4]*στε γενέσθαι* . . . (= *EEFL* 2898e, last paragraph = Bri. p. 387, lines 25–28) (55v:) . . . *κατάκριμα.* ʼ΄*Ετι προσφέρωμεν* . . . (= *EEFL* 2898f = Bri. p. 387–389) . . . *εὐαγγελιστῶν* [missing leaf with: *μαρτύρων . . . ἐλπίδι ἀναστάσεως ζωῆς αἰωνίου*] (56rv:) *καὶ ἀνάπαυσον αὐτούς . . . εἰρηνικὸν τὸ βασίλειον • ἵνα* (45r:) *καὶ ἡμεῖς* . . . (45v:) . . . (Μ)[5]*νήσθητι . . . ὁδοιπορούντων, νοσούν*[*των*] [missing leaf with: *των, καμνόντων . . . καὶ ἔσται τὰ ἐλέη . . . ἡμῶν* (Bri. 390) and the beginning, with caption, of next item (ordination of a deacon, see below)]

The imperfectly preserved and partly misarranged section continues the eucharistic service which had been interrupted by the rite given on ff. 54r–55r.

48r–53v and 59rv: (48r begins abruptly in the middle of rubric:) *[Μετὰ] τὴν ἁγί[αν] ἀναφορὰν κ[α]ὶ τὰς θύρ[α]ς ἀνοιγέναι* . . . (48v:) . . . (gold:) (ʻΗ)[2] *Θεία* χάρις . . . (53v:) . . . ὁ ἐπὶ τοῦ ἄμβωνος δι (59r:) άκονος λ[ε]γ[εῖ]ν τὸ , πάντων τῶν ἁγίω[ν] . . . (section ends in 10th line of 59v:) . . . ὡς προεγράφη.

Ordination of a deacon. Wanting is, in particular, the initial caption, expected to have read: ΤΆΞΙΣ ΓΙΝΟΜΈΝΗ 'ΕΠῚ ΧΕΙΡΟΤΟΝΊΑ ΔΙΑΚΌΝΟΥ. Cf. Habert, p. 308–312 (prayers agreeing completely, rubrics not as to wording).

59v, 46v, 46r, 57rv: (on 59v in 11th line, gold caption:) ἄρξον τῆς λειτουργ[ίας] // (black text:) (Π)[2]άντων τῶν ἁγ[ίων] μνημονεύ(46v:)σαντες . . . (Bri. p. 390a–391) . . . πν[εύματο]ς δεηθῶμεν (46r:) ('Υ)πὲρ τοῦ ῥυσθῆναι ἡμᾶς ἀπὸ // (gold:) ὁ ἀρχιερε[ὺς] ἐπεύχεται // (black:) (Σ)[6]οὶ παρακατατιθέμεθα . . . (Bri. p. 390b but ending imperfectly:) . . . πν[ευματ]ικῆς τραπέζης • μ[ε]τὰ [6(?) leaves missing] (57r:) [ἀναπέ]μπομεν τῷ π[ατ]ρὶ καὶ . . . (Bri. p. 398, lines 7–8) (Τ)[6]ὸ πλήρωμα τοῦ νόμου . . . (ibid., lines 12–14) (ending on f. 57v:) . . . καὶ εἰς // τοὺς αἰῶνας // τῶν // αἰ // ώ // νω // ν // ἀμήν.

Last parts of the Liturgy of John Chrysostom. Among the texts lost with the missing leaves are, in particular, the prayers and/or rites of the Communion.

58rv and 60r–105v: [before f. 58, two (?) leaves missing] (58rv:) (gold:) 'Ο ΔΙΆΚΟΝΟΣ // (black:) ('Ε)[2]ν εἰρ ή[νη] τοῦ κ[υρίο]υ δε[ηθῶμε]ν // ('Υ)[2]πὲρ τῆς ἄνωθεν εἰρήνης . . . τῆς εἰρή[νης] τοῦ σύμπαντος κοσμοῦ . . . τοῦ ἁγίου οἴκου τούτου . . . τοῦ ἀρχιεπισκόπου ἡμῶν . . . (58v:) . . . τῶν εὐσεβεστάτων . . . βασι[λέων] . . . τοῦ συμπολεμῆσαι καὶ ὑποτάξαι . . . τῆς ἁγίας μονῆς ταύτης . . . εὐκρασίας ἀέρων . . . πλεόντων . . . τοῦ ῥυσθῆναι ἡμᾶς ἀπὸ πάσης θλίψεως ὀρ[γῆς] [3(?) leaves missing] (60r:) ὁ τρισαγίῳ [*sic*] φωνῇ . . . (= *EEFL* 2884, lines 8 sqq. = Bri. p. 313a) . . . (61v: . . . ΕΥ̓Χ[Ὴ] ΠΡῸ ΤΟΥ̃ ΕΥ̓ΑΓΓΕΛΙΌΥ) . . . (63v: . . . ΕΥ̓Χ[Ὴ] ΤΗ̃Σ 'ΕΚΤΕΝΟΥ̃Σ 'ΙΚΕΣΊΑΣ) . . . (68v: ΕΥ̓ΧΗ 'Η̃Ν ΠΟΙΕΙ̃ 'Ο 'ΑΡΧΙΕΡΕΥ̃Σ ΤΟΥ̃ ΧΕΡΟΥΒΙΚΟΥ̃ 'ΑΔΟΜΈΝΟΥ ΚΑΘΕΑΥΤῸΝ(?) . . . (71v: . . . ΕΥ̓Χ[Η] ΜΕΤᾺ ΤῊΝ 'ΕΝ ΤΗ̃ 'ΑΓΊΑ ΤΡΑΠΈΖΗ ΤΩ̃Ν ΘΕΊ[ΩΝ] ΔΏΡ[ΩΝ] 'ΑΠΌΘΕΣΙΝ . . . (the ἀναφορά begins in last line of 74v, Στῶμεν καλῶς; words of the Institution, ff. 84r–85r) . . . (103v: . . . ΕΥ̓ΧῊ 'ΟΠΙΣΘΆΜΒΩΝΟΣ; the liturgy ends on 105v with the end of the prayer "Ηνυσται καὶ τετέλεσται, Bri. p. 411:) . . . εἰς τοὺς αἰ//ῶ//ν//ας//τῶν//αἰώνων//ἀμήν.

The Liturgy of St. Basil, the second most important form of the eucharistic service in the Eastern Church;[9] beginning imperfectly in the ἔναρξις. — The deacon's invitations to prayer mention notably "ἀρχιεπίσκοπος" and "this holy μονή [= monastery]." — Beyond the large captions quoted above, three (on 78v, 86r, 97v) in a similar style (gold ink, liturgical-type capitals) read: 'Ο 'ΑΡΧΙΕΡΕΥ̃Σ 'ΕΠΕΎΧΕΤΑΙ (78v, " . . . ΜΥΣΤΙΚΩ̃Σ"); the phrase is also used several times as a gold-minuscule rubric. — The use of gold subsides to some extent in this section, especially in favor of blue. — The Cherubic hymn, the Creed, the Lord's Prayer are again omitted, the deacon's texts sometimes truncated.

106r–127v (two[?] leaves missing before f. 106): 'Υπὲρ τῶν εὐσεβεστάτων καὶ θεοφυλάκτων βασιλέων ἡ[μῶν] // 'Υπὲρ τῆς ἁγίας μονῆς ταύτης πάσης πόλεως χώρας καὶ // 'Υπὲρ εὐκρασίας ἀέρων . . . // . . . πλεόντων . . . // . . . τοῦ ρυσθῆναι ἡμᾶς ἀπὸ // 'Αντιλα [βοῦ] σῶσον . . . // Τῆς παναγίας ἀχράντου ὑπ[ερ]// εὐλογημένης δεσποίνης ἡ[μῶν] (106v:) ('Ο)[2]τι πρέπει σοι πᾶσα δό[ξα] . . . (blue:) Ε'ΥΧῊ 'ΑΝΤΙΦΩ̃ΝΟΥ Α΄[ου] . . . (108r:) . . . Ε'ΥΧῊ 'ΑΝΤΙΦΩ̃ΝΟΥ Β΄ . . . (109r:) . . . Ε'ΥΧΗ 'ΑΝΤΙΦΩ̃ΝΟΥ Γ΄ . . . (110r:) . . . εὐχὴ τῆς εἰσόδου . . . (111v:) Εὐχὴ τῆς ἐκτενοῦς ἱκεσίας . . . (112v:) . . . εὐχὴ ὑπὲρ τῶν κατηχουμένων μυστικῶς . . . (116v:) . . . εὐχ[ὴ] πιστῶν α΄ . . . (118r:) . . . Ε'ΥΧῊ ΠΙΣΤΩ̃Ν Β΄ . . . (119v:) . . . Ε'ΥΧῊ ΜΕΤᾺ ΤῊΝ 'ΑΠΌΘΕΣΙΝ ΤΩ̃Ν 'ΑΓΊΩΝ ΔΏΡΩΝ . . . (125v:) . . . εὐχὴ ὀπισθάμβωνος . . . (127r:) . . . Ε'ΥΧῊ 'ΕΝ ΤΩ̃ ΣΥΣΤΕΙ̃ΛΑΙ ΤᾺ 'ΑΓΙΑ . . . (concluding on 127v:) . . . κληρονόμους ἀνάδειξον τῆς // βασιλείας σου. νῦν καὶ ἀ//εἰ. καὶ εἰς τοὺς αἰῶ//νας τῶν // αἰώ // νων // ἀμήν.

The Liturgy of the Presanctified, also known as the Liturgy of Gregory the Great;[10] beginning imperfectly. No gold is used here: captions are mostly blue, occasionally red; the rubrics, red; *litterae notabiliores*, red or blue; large initials, red or blue.[11]

* * *

Foliated (1–127) in modern pencil. — Paper of Italian origin, cut and arranged (basically) in 4°. Watermarks: *(a)* capital *M* surmounted by six-point star, all in a shield;[12] *(b)* crown surmounted by star;[13] *(c)* chevron over dog, in a circle surmounted by crown(?).[14] — All leaves of the manuscript (including the endleaves) are thoroughly saturated with beeswax;

MS 37, f. 56r (see note 16) (actual size of written area: ca. 140 × 95 mm)

this is probably due to a quite late (19th century?) preservation effort; it gives the paper a yellowish-brownish cast, and a waxy odor. — Written area ca. 140 × ca. 95 mm. — Fully (as is evident chiefly from the blank f. [128]) blind-ruled; only some of the vertical lines remain visible. A column ca. 19 mm wide (and ca. 6 mm from the text frame) was provided for initials[15] in the outer margin only, placing major initials outside of the text column when on versos but forcing the scribe to leave space (sometimes inadequate) for any major initials occurring on a recto. — Written probably by (at least) two scribes, both using (except for the mostly gold display lettering) a similar stylized archaizing minuscule. Most of the black text is due to a scribe endowed with an outstanding esthetic sense and graphic creativity; most of the red rubrical material seems more subdued.[16] — The black ink is of excellent quality, the red on some pages on the pale side, the blue (used primarily in the last third of the book for captions, etc.) uneven; the gold, used extensively at the beginning of the Chrysostomus Liturgy, and elsewhere for captions, minor initials, and some rubrics, has suffered some rubbing-off, besides the diminished legibility caused by the overall yellow cast of the wax-saturated ground. — Occasional wormholes.

Collation: $1–2^{8}$ 3^{4+1}(= ff. 17–21; f. 18 a singleton) 4^{8}(= ff. 22 – 28; 4_{8} wanting, text loss) 5^{8} 6^{6+1} (= ff. 37–43; f. 38 a singleton) 7^{8}(= ff. 44, 47, 54.55, 56, 45; $7_{3.6}$ wanting, with text loss) 8^{8}(= ff. 48–53, 59; 8_{1} wanting, with text loss) $9^{8?}$(9_{1} = f. 46; 9_{8} = f. 57; rest wanting, with major text loss) $10^{6?}$(10_{3} = f. 58; f. 60 is last leaf of the gathering; rest wanting, with text losses) 11^{8+1}(= ff. 61–69; f. 62 a cancel, f. 67 a singleton) 12^{6+1}(= ff. 70–76; f. 73 a singleton) $13–15^{8}$ $16^{6?}$(= ff. 101–105; 16_{6} wanting, with text loss) 17^{8}(wants 17_{1}, text loss) $18–19^{8}$(wants 19_{8} immediately following f. 127; probably blank)

Decoration of the book, originally quite sumptuous,[17] has suffered from mistreatment (by beeswax and otherwise); some was probably lost with the missing leaves of the beginning of the Liturgy of St. Basil. Apart from the extensive use of (painted) gold and the liturgical display capitals (particularly at the beginning of the Chrysostomus Liturgy, ff. 6v–7v), preserved decoration consists of five headpieces and ca. 75 ornamental initials, mostly combining (painted) gold and a variety of colors. — The headpieces are rectangular frames (on 1r and 6v the outside line is red ink, elsewhere gold) containing stylized botanical forms in colors on gold ground; small palmettes extend outward from the four corners. Largest is the headpiece on f. 1r, followed by that on 6v (introducing the Chrysostomus Liturgy); on 3r, 16r, and 31v the frames are ca. 24 × 105 mm. — The initials vary in style; all use the void of the paper as ground and some are basically calligraphic, their decorative effect relying on contrast of gold letter and ink outline or vice versa (ff. 8v, 16v, 17r, etc., mostly medium-size; also the oriental-looking Epsilon on 26v, a major initial 105 mm high); many are built, with not undisputably happy result, of short varicolored segments (28v, 45v, 46r, etc.). In other cases, the shape of the letter is suggested by foliate forms and more or less filled with stylized flowers and leaves in various colors, outlined in gold (e.g., the Omicron on 68v). Average height of a major initial is ca. 55 mm for the letter; in many cases, unconnected leafy forms are added above and below. — On ff. 102r, 103v, and 104v, three major initials are drawn (or painted) in gold only, in three different styles. Gold is discontinued after f. 105.

Binding ("in Turkish style" — De Ricci): contemporary (ca. 1600) dark-brown calf or smooth goatskin over "waterleaf" pasteboard, with doublures of same material; decorated with deeply sunk compartments in center-and-corner-piece style, the center having a many-lobed vesica shape, with appendages above and below.

The compartments are filled with raised floral motifs on (painted?) gold ground.[18] — Heavily damaged by bookworm (ca. one-third of front covering eaten); gold mostly rubbed off; spine preserved only partly; both covers detached from the text block.[19]

On recto of the free endleaf in front, penciled: acc. 3831. — On f. 1v, in tail margin, penciled: 513645//Jy 11 39.

Former owners: Kirkor Minassian (book lent by him to LC in 1930 and sold in 1936).

2° fo.: (red ink:) *φαινολ·´. ἐνδιδύσκει*

Bibl.: De Ricci, *Census* I (1935), p. 209, no. 53 ("Liturgy of S. John Chrysostom, in Greek"); Faye and Bond (1962), p. 118, no. 32 (ditto.)

NOTES

1. Athos? Cyprus? Patmos? — There are other possibilities, including the mainly 17th-century school of Lucas Buzău (Wallachia, even Moscow). The watermarks, however, seem to point to the time before 1600. (For the Buzău writing group, see L. Politis, "Persistances byzantines dans l'écriture liturgique du XVIIe siècle," in *La Paléographie grecque et byzantine* [1977; Colloques internationaux du C.N.R.S. no.559]).

2. I.e., the *'APXIEPATIKON, Liber pontificalis Ecclesiae Graecae* / meditatione et labore Isaacii Haberti, Parisiis : 1643 (also 1970 reprint). — Habert was a Catholic and his work, published, presumably, as an ecumenical effort, includes considerable comment; it is, however, the only reasonably accessible source for these Orthodox texts. (Both U.S. libraries listed in the *NUC* pre-56 [No 0140167] as possessing copies of the Orthodox *'Αρχιερατικὸν* published in Athens in 1902 have recently reported their copies missing.)

3. Cf. Brightman *(Liturgies eastern and western,* I), p. 360–370. — The term *λειτουργία* or its cognates are used in Eastern churches for the eucharistic service (the "Mass" in the Roman rite terminology); the Liturgy of John Chrysostom, named after its supposed author, is the form of eucharistic service most frequently used in the Byzantine rite. Editions of its text vary in details, notably in the wording of rubrics, while the primary prayers remain quite uniform.

4. The page (f. 17r) includes corrections or rewritten words (perhaps the golden script had become too difficult to read) in black ink (non-calligraphic, careless). The words *μετροπολιτῶν* and *ἀρχιεπισκόπων* are, however, certainly original. They suggest that the exemplar from which our copy derived was a patriarch's book, or at least an imperfectly modified copy of a patriarchal book.

5. Meant must be "the Liturgy resumes." Cf. similar on f. 59v.

6. In gold, liturgical display capitals (this is true of all captions here transcribed in capitals, unless stated otherwise).

7. The friction-producing controversy concerning the nature of the "depositum" (*παρακαταθήκη*) and the placement of the pertinent rite within the eucharistic service; perhaps also the question whether or not the subject of the ordination participates in the consecration of the bread and wine. In our manuscript, the entrusting of the deposit to the newly ordained priest takes place after the consecration. (N.B. Leaves 54 and 55 are conjugate.)

8. I.e., *Offices from the service-books of the Holy Eastern Church : with translation, notes, and glossary* / by Richard Frederick Littledale (London, 1863; repr. New York, AMS Press, 1970).

9. Cf. Brightman, p. [400]–411, also [309]–344. Neither text is as complete as that found in R. Engdahl's *Beiträge zur Kenntnis der byzantinischen Liturgie* (1908, repr. 1973), p. [43]–77.

10. For the somewhat varying texts, cf. Brightman, p. [345]–352; C.A. Swainson, *Greek liturgies*, p. [173]–187; Dēmētrios N. Moraitēs, *'Η λειτουργία τῶν προηγιασμένων* (Thessalonikē, 1955).

11. All this perhaps because the rite is used primarily on penitential days. Some of the all-capital blue captions are, however, also done in a much less skilled manner than the highly stylized gold captions found in the earlier parts.

12. Gatherings 1, 2, 3, 7, 8, 12, 13, 17, and 18; also $6_{3.4}$(= ff.40.41), $11_{1.8}$(= ff. 61.69), and $14_{2.7}$(= ff. 86.91). The watermark resembles Briquet 8391.

13. It is clearly a star on $4_{4.5}$(= ff. 25.26), $5_{1.8}$(= ff. 29.36), $11_{3.6}$(= ff. 63.66), and in gatherings 15 and 16 (= ff. 93–105). A similar image with a star (if it is one) quite unclear (deformed [?] into an elongated diamond?), perhaps a true twin of the preceding, occurs in signatures 4_1(= f. 22 [conjugate leaf is wanting], $5_{3.6}$ (= ff. 31.34), and $6_{1.6}$(= ff. 37.43).

14. The last-named watermark, probably important for the dating of the manuscript, appears on signatures $9_{1.8}$(= ff. 46.57), $14_{4.5}$(= ff. 88.89), and throughout the gathering 19 (= ff. 122.127, 123.126, 124.125). It seems to be that listed by Briquet as a variation (crown rather than star) of his no. 1131; said to be attested in Ferrara from 1576 to 1597.

15. The column is also used for the frequently occurring directive "*ἐκφώνως*" (= "aloud") written as a *monokondyllion* similar to that which appears next to lines 12–15 on plate 55 in A.D. Komines, *Πίνακες χρονολογημένων Πατμιακῶν κωδίκων* (Athens, 1968).

N.B. The script of the ms. there reproduced (scroll 886 of the library of the monastery of St. John on Patmos), written in 1558 by a monk Ioasaph, is of the same type as that of our codex (but more restrained).

16. The black-text hand bears considerable resemblance to ms. Athos, Lavra H 152 written in 1405/06 by Ioasaph, monk of the Hodegon monastery in Constantinople, cf. (with reprod.) L. Politis, *Paléographie et littérature* . . . (London, 1975), VI; or to the ms. Dionysiou 545 done between 1554 and 1577 by Theokletos, cf. *idem* in his "Persistances byzantines . . . " referred to earlier (n. 1); the script of our Archieraticon is, nevertheless, freer. (Lines 1–12 of Theokletos' page reproduced *op. cit.*, p. 377, fig. 1 may be compared with identical text on f. 56r of our ms.) It averages 19 letters per line (the less exuberant red rubrics, ca. 21 or more). — N.B. To write no more than 12 lines per page was not at all common in the 16th century (the only other case of such generosity seen in reproduction is the Bodleian Library's ms. Oxon. Holkh. 6, a *Synodicon* written ca. 1050 [*Repertorium der griechischen Kopisten* 1, C no. 140]).

17. The book was made to be used by a high ecclesiastical dignitary (of the Orthodox communion) in performance of certain functions reserved to him and occurring infrequently. Archieraticon is analogous to the Pontifical of the Latin Church.

18. Minor center decoration (gilt, reticulate pattern) and simple gold line framing on the doublures.

19. This partial disassembly may be the work of recent decades; it seems, though, that the covers had been detached and the text block disassembled once before, prior to the beeswax treatment. The misplacing (and perhaps also the loss) of sundry leaves occurred probably at that time: it seems that the person who did the reassembling was no longer able to read the script and tried to find the correct order by guesswork, e.g., by matching black with black, as in the case of ff. 56 and 57. — N.B. As of the time of this writing, the book is kept in a plain brownish tan box of drop-back construction, labeled "De Ricci 32."

MS 38

(no previous listing; in Music Division)

ANTIPHONARY (part of the sanctoral of winter) early(?) 16th c.

Spain. Parchment. 117, [2] leaves,[1] ca. 763[2] × ca. 570 mm (bound volume: ca. 825 × ca. 600 mm) 6 long lines of music (5-line staff in red) and 6 of text to a page.

(On pastedown of upper cover, an upside-down leaf from the ordinary of the office or perhaps hymnary: first stanza of the Sunday matutinal hymn *Nocte surgentes*; 5 lines of text and music, ending imperfectly; not germane to the contents of the codex)

ff. 1r–117v: (1r, red caption in center of the page:) *In festo btī andree apl'i ad vesp[er]as sup[er] p[salmo]s an[tiphon]a.* (1v, in all-around border:) (*U*)$^{2+2}$Nus ex du//obus qui . . . (ending with last line of 117v:) [om]nibus exquisiui. *ca[nticum]* Magn̄t. (See plate XV, p. 62.)

The choir parts (primarily antiphons and responsories) of the liturgical celebrations known as the (Divine) Office, performed with chant by religious communities. The present codex covers only the segment of the liturgical year extending from the evening before Andrew (November 29/30 [no dates in the manuscript]) through Vespers at end of the feast of St. Vincent (Jan. 22), limited to those occasions dedicated to saints, i.e., leaving out Christmas and other events of the seasonal cycle.[3] This December–January part of the "sanctoral" is itself reduced to nine saints' days observed more solemnly than others (traditionally, by custom of the house, or by institutional directive):

1r–17r: Andrew
17r–32r: Nicholas
32r–35v: Lucy
35v–37r: Thomas the Apostle
37r–54r: Stephen
54r–69r: John the Evangelist
69v–82v: Holy Innocents
82v–97v: Agnes
97v–117v: Vincent (the deacon and martyr)

For each of these occasions (exceptions below), the antiphonary gives text and music of: one antiphon "super psalmos" and the antiphon to Magnificat for First Vespers; Invitatory; for each of three Nocturns, three antiphons to the Psalms (the Psalms identified by initia), a versicle/response (text only), and three responsories; five antiphons and "ad Benedictus" for the Lauds; and "ad Magnificat."[4] The textual choices in this non-monastic scheme are often those usually met in monastic sources (e.g., the rhythmical antiphon *Copiose caritatis*

Nicolae pontifex [f. 32r], or responsories *Sancte Dei preciose prothomartir Stephane* [50v], *Christi miles preciosus levita Vincentius* [107v]). — Reference to another book ("Responsoria VIII de communi unius virginis") is made in the office of St. Lucy; it seems to be implied in that of Thomas which offers only the antiphons to Magnificat and Benedictus; as Invitatory, a puzzling "Venite" (only that word) is given for the Innocents,[5] and nothing for Agnes (in an office otherwise rich in special material).

(The book as a meaningful unit ends with f. 117; the irregularly shaped two [end]leaves which follow, numbered in upper right corners "119" and "122," are from a Psalter. The text is without music, 22 or 21 lines to a page:) (*D*)³Eus iudicium tuum regi da . . . (= Ps. LXXII [Vulg. 71]; followed immediately by LXXVI [Vulg. 75, *Notus in Iudaea,* preserved through v. 6a]; on recto of the pastedown numbered "122," end of Ps. XCII [Vulg. 91: v. 10b-16] and beginning of CIII [Vulg. 102, *Benedic anima*])

* * *

Foliated in brownish black ink with 16th-century arabic numerals; the numbers are in fore-edge margin of recto, ca. two-thirds of the page down from top; written in a rather hasty manner. — Written area: ca. 565 (from top line of music to base of minims in last line) × ca. 400 mm. — Ruled in lead or crayon for the vertical boundaries (double, the two lines ca. 7 mm apart, from edge to edge) and for the text lines (ca. 18 mm wide). (The Psalter fragments at end which are used as endleaves are heavily ruled in purple ink.) — The script is the rather large *rotunda* of gothic inspiration common in the large choir books of Iberian origin. The feet of vertical strokes are either *praescissi* (*a, d, f,* the shaft of *h, i, m, n, p, q, r* [ca. half of the time: see below], long *s*) or (in this codex, frequently, and regularly with *l, t*) gently curving upward, never quadrate. Letter *a* has a residual upper lobe formed by inward curling of a very thin pen line; the short broad stroke which, attached to the right-hand vertical by two thin ones, forms the lower lobe, is here concave.[6] The usual two forms of *d* are used, it seems, randomly; the curved stroke of *h* ends sometimes in a thin line going down beyond the base, sometimes widens to stop on it. Traditional two forms of *r*; the one resembling ours often ending at the base in a curve similar to that of *c* or *e*. The medieval character for "-rum" is used, also superscript final *s*, melting adjoining curves (*oc,* et sim.), contractions (horizontally crossed *p* for "per," *q* with short vertical stroke over it for "qui"); macron convex to upward, done in one curving stroke thin at the start and wide at the downward end at right. An extremely thin vertical stroke appears over *i*; it seems to grow from the letter and gives it something of the appearance of a candle. Undotted *y*. No tironian "et" found. — Very good black ink used for both text and music. Captions (often at end of page preceding that where music/text begins) in red ink; that at the beginning (1r, for Andrew) and the one for Stephen (37r) are written in large letters the size of those used for the black text.

Music staves in red ink, 5-line, ca. 62 mm from first to fifth line (ca. 33 mm between staves). Black square notes ca. 10 × 10 mm *Do* or *fa* clefs; the latter is formed by an assembly of three closely juxtaposed black lozenges, very narrow. The *custos* signaling at the end of each music line the position of the first note on the next line has the form of a half-width *virga.*

Writing material is calfskin of the Segovian kind (hair side unevenly yellow and oily-looking, flesh side white),[7] of good quality. Hair side faces hair side throughout. Repairs, some by sewing, some by pasted patches (both methods combined: f. 52). Thickness of compressed text block between 40 and 50 mm. — Overall weight of the book ca. 57 lbs.

Collation: 1–14⁸(= ff. 1–112); f. 113 a singleton; 15⁴(= ff. 114–117). — No catchwords, no signature markings. — A number of the bifolia were created by joining together two leaf-size sheets.

MS 38 Decoration consists of one full border (1v) and numerous functional calligraphic initials. The largest of these (height two lines of music with two lines of text, ca. 180 mm) is used for the opening of the St. Andrew office on f. 1v, preceded only by the caption on recto; elsewhere throughout the antiphonary, the beginning of a saint's office is marked, as are major items within it, by a one-line (music plus text, ca. 100 mm high) initial letter. All of these are red and blue divided by void white (red to left, blue to right alternates with the reverse), filled with flourishing in purple or red (vines with comb-like edges or, in other letters, golf-club acanthus) and surrounded by more of same. The red of the letter body appears glossy on some pages. — At a lower level of distinction (introducing, e.g., the second and third psalm antiphon of each nocturn) are the *lettres cadeaux*;[8] normally black, these appear also in the red script of the two large-letter captions, for Andrew on 1r and for Stephen on 37r. The cadelled letters in this codex include as a peculiar element a ribbon wound around main parts of the letter. — The border on 1v consists of frets and flourishing; the interlaced, mostly straight-line bars of which the frets are built are blue in parts of the border, red in others. An emblem appears in the center of tail margin: in a circle (diameter ca. 32 mm), the black-and-white lily cross (in eight segments alternately black and white) used by Dominicans (especially, it seems, those in official positions with the Inquisition?[9]). It is surrounded by blue ornament which is original but the emblem itself may have been added at a later time.[10]

Binding: covers brown, diagonally cross-hatched tanned calf or cowhide over thick oak boards made (certainly the lower one) of three vertically joined pieces. — Sewn over 7 bands of double cords; headbands decorated (original oversewing preserved at head only) with combination of blue and natural string. Each of the seven bands is separately protected by a leather strip tacked to the boards. — One front-to-back, rather roughly made iron clasp; two leather straps attached to the upper board (with traces on the lower) remain from what may have been earlier closing devices. — Metal ornaments and protective devices, fully preserved on lower board only: four corner pieces (measuring ca. 80 mm at each edge) of thick brass decorated by cutouts; four flat-top bosses and, in center, a half-spherical one, on four-pointed bases, also brass; and two folded strips of iron sheet protecting head and tail edges.[11] (On upper cover, only one corner piece and the two iron strips remain.) — The lower cover is also blind-tooled with a ca. 35 mm wide roll; the tooling forms a quadrangle with corners covered by the four flat-top bosses.

Former owners: none known.

2° fo.: (*A*)[1+1]Mbula ns ihesus [under a 5-line red music staff with notes]

Bibl.: None known. Not in De Ricci; not in Faye and Bond.

NOTES

1. The two leaves at end noted in brackets are from another book (a Psalter) and have been used as free endleaf plus pastedown.

2. Height of the leaves is 761–765 mm at fore edge, 751–753 near gutter.

3. This is therefore but one of a number of volumes which would and probably did cover the whole liturgical year, both its "sanctoral" and its seasonal ("temporal") cycles. (The largest reported set of this kind, in Escorial, gives to the Office ca. 150 volumes.) — The very large format was used to make possible simultaneous reading of the text and music by the whole choir (or at least by one side of the choir).

4. The variously abbreviated caption is mostly written at a right angle to the text (base to the right).

5. The *CAO* notes (v. III, p. 18) under no. 1173 the use of the invitatory "Venite adoremus Dominum, qui in sanctis gloriosus est" for the day of the Innocents in one of its monastic sources. Perhaps this is what the uninformative initium in our manuscript means.

6. Cf. the forms of *a* described with MS 41.

7. Cf. V. Rabanal, *Los cantorales de El Escorial* (El Escorial, 1947), p. 22.

8. These letters are formed by imaginative multiplication of the calligrapher's pen strokes with decorative intent. The term *cadel* (pl. *cadels*), for either the letters so decorated or the decoration, has, I believe, a standing in English-language specialized literature but hasn't as yet been sanctioned by dictionaries. — Cf. J. J. G. Alexander, *The decorated letter* (1978), p. 27 (with reproductions).

9. Cf. B. B. Heim, *Wappengebrauch und Wappenrecht in der Kirche* (Olten, 1947), p. 95. — *Encic. univ. ilus. europeo-americana* (Espasa-Calpe), v. XVI, p. 628, 2nd column.

10. The obvious suggestion that the book may have been made for and used by a Dominican house could not be definitely confirmed or rejected.

11. Iron nails or tacks with pyramidal heads hold in place both the brass and the iron.

MS 39

("Stravinsky Antiphonal"; in Music Division)

ANTIPHONARY (diurnal). Proper of the saints, July–December XVIth c.?

Spain. Parchment. 151 leaves, cropped to ca. 420 × ca. 300 mm (bound volume: ca. 470 × ca. 350 mm) 6 long lines of music (5-line staves in red) and 6 of text to a page.

ff. 1r–151v: (1r blank except for 3-line red caption at bottom:) *(J)³n festo sancte marie magdalene . Ad vesperos. Re̅.* (on 1v, beginning imperfectly due to missing part of the leaf:) ctore // cero // dominum maria re//condēs unxit // purgantem. *p̓*.Ba//ptismi gurgite. . . . (151v, last lines, imperfect ending of office of St. Lucy:) . . . sira//cusana decora

Choir chant for the diurnal parts of (selected?) saints' offices from July through December (book gives no calendar dates): 1r–7r, Mary Magdalen (2r–4r, over erasures; 4v begins abruptly with end of the 4th antiphon of Lauds); 7r–14v, James (7r–9v, 1st Vespers, over erasures); 14v–20v, Anne; 21r–25v, Peter *ad vincula;* 25v–32r, B.V.M. "de nivibus" (29v–30r, captionless *Sancta Maria succurre miseris* substituted for *ad iii^m R;* 30v begins abruptly); 32r–38v, Transfiguration (32r sqq., 1st Vespers, over erasures); 38v–45r, Lawrence; 45r–56r, Assumption (with vigil); 56r–61r, Beheading of John; 61r–70r, Antoninus (of Apameia); 70r–76v, Nativity B.V.M. (with vigil); 77r–82v, Exaltation of the Cross; 82v–94r, Michael; 94r–101v, All Saints; 101v–109r, Martin; 109r–113v, Brice; 113v–119r, Presentation B.V.M.; 119v, Thomas the Apostle (in this place because of lack of space elsewhere? only the antiphon to Magnificat, 4 lines over erasures); 120r–123r, Cecilia (on 120v, first four lines erased); 123r–128r, Clement (126v over erasures? 127r begins abruptly); 128r–133v, also 148, Catherine; 134r–140v, Andrew (138, 139 torn out, fragments remain); 140v–146r, Nicholas; 146v, Conception B.V.M. (preserved is only the beginning of *super psalmos* of first Vespers); following f. 146, two stubs, with loss of material; 147rv and 149r–151v, Lucy (beginning and ending imperfectly; 149r continues from 147v, interrupted by 148 which contains part of the Catherine set; f. 149 is followed by three stubs, apparently without text loss).

A typical full entry for a celebration consists here of: for the 1st Vespers, one antiphon to the psalms, a responsory,[1] an indication of the hymn (most often by its text initium), and the antiphon to Magnificat; for Compline, mostly an indication, without music, of the antiphon to the psalms and of that to *Nunc dimittis;* from the Lauds, the five antiphons to psalms are included in full, captioned globally as antiphons to the hours of the day, "ad horas antiphone de laudibus" (and the antiphon to Benedictus is not given); follows, as an unexpected feature, *"ad iii^m^ R[esponsorium]";* for 2nd Vespers, chiefly the antiphon to Magnificat, sometimes preceded by notes such as "Antiphone laudum" or, more interestingly, "Alleluia et prosa ut in missa."[2] This general scheme is variously disturbed by irregularities caused in part by erasures and substitutions (those noted above and more), perhaps also by cropping; some leaves are mutilated, notably f. 1, with loss of the beginning of the office of Magdalen; some material lost and some apparently misplaced near end. — Spanish origin of the manuscript is textually confirmed by some rather patriotic texts given St. James (see appendix); further relevant to the question of provenience is the inclusion in this major-feast oriented book of St. Antoninus of Apameia, the patron (known locally as San Antolín[3]) of the diocese of Palencia in northwest Spain and of its cathedral. Less easy to interpret is the presence of St. Brice ("bricii"), the once scandalous, later penitent second bishop of Tours.[4] — On 94v, an added note in a different but no doubt contemporary[5] hand (calligraphic roman bookhand of smaller size): "todas las demas a[nte]ñas destas v[espera]s estan en otro libro sino esta de Magnifica [*sic*] q[ue] se sigue." — Transfiguration, St. Anne, Presentation of Mary are late medieval feasts, adopted sporadically; Anne's day and the Presentation were not universally celebrated until post-Tridentine times, by decrees of ca. 1585; the antiphons and responsories assigned to these occasions in this antiphonary are nevertheless not those prescribed in post-16th-century Roman books.[6] — All occasions represented here are found in an early 16th-century liturgical calendar of Toledo;[7] a number of other feasts of equal rank are, however, listed there and absent from our antiphonary, among them Dominic, Bernard, Bartholomew, Augustine, Matthew, Jerome, Francis, Luke, Elizabeth, Barbara.[8] — Liturgical directives are more numerous and ample than expected in choir books (e.g., on 54r, 9 lines concerning the Assumption octave), and they are, contrary to general custom, written in black ink (in slightly smaller script than the chant texts); only captions are red.

* * *

The leaves are unnumbered (result of cropping?). — One free endleaf of modern paper, marbled on recto, in front; one, marbled on verso, at end. — Written area ca. 400 × ca. 235–240 mm. — Lightly ruled (plummet?) for the (double) vertical boundaries and for the text lines. No pricking preserved. — Script is the Spanish kind of *rotunda* with feet of the vertical strokes *praescissi* (except *l, t*). The thick stroke of the lobe in the *a* is straight (more or less square); ascender of the *b* curves directly into its lobe, that of the non-uncial *d* does not. A *d* beginning a word is always of the uncial kind. Cedilled *e* occurs *(mulier quę erat).* Final stroke of *h* goes below the base line. One-stroke *i, praescissum* at both ends; *m* and *n* of two kinds, one with a hook at top of first stroke. Two *r*'s; foot of the modern one curves to right in imitation of *c* or *e*. Undotted *y*. Old characters for *-rum, -us;* uncrossed tironian *et* (except on 123r in caption for Clement).

Music on 5-line staves done in red; from 1st to 5th line, ca. 43.5 mm; between staves, ca. 24 mm. Black square notation includes some diamond-shaped notes; *do* or *fa* clefs (*fa* formed by juxtaposition of three lozenges). *Custos* shaped as a check mark.

Poor quality calfskin, with even the flesh side often yellow (perhaps in part due to erasures); many stains. Some leaves mutilated, mostly by removal of initials, sometimes by cutting with scissors from the edge of the leaf to reach the desired area. — Thickness of the text block ca. 65 mm.

Collation appears impracticable because of the tight rebacking. Some leaves are certainly missing and some misplaced (cf. contents).

MS 39, f. 38v (detail) (actual size of area shown: ca. 140 × 160 mm)

Decoration, as far as preserved, is limited to calligraphic initials of the common kind: the *super psalmos* of 1st Vespers or their responsory, if nothing precedes, is given the more elaborate initial letter in divided blue and red with flourishing in both colors; the responsory "*ad iii*^{m}," the antiphon to Magnificat, and the two antiphons for Compline begin with a red or blue letter with flourishing in the other color. In both cases, the flourishing forms a roughly rectangular field ca. 60–65 mm high (one line of music plus one of text). — Fourteen initials have been cut out, mostly those with the letter in two colors: from ff. 1 (torn off), 21, 23, 25, 26, 54, 57, 63, 65, 82, 116, 126, 129, 135; it is not likely that these were radically different except perhaps that on f. 116 which seems to have been two lines high (for the first antiphon of *per horas diei* of the office of St. Anne). — On the tampered-with leaves 2 and 3 and scattered elsewhere (it seems everywhere where existing material is a substitution over erasures), poorly drawn red letters without flourishing take the place of the traditional type described above. — Cadels mark the beginnings of minor items (e.g., the 2nd–5th antiphons *per horas diei*). — Victim of early revisors and of modern initial raiders, the manuscript has lost much of its modest beauty.

Binding: modern half-leather (spine very dark blue leather, covers black paper) over (hardly original) (wood?) boards ca. 14 mm thick. The boards are protected by brass ornaments probably original, of a style different (less rough and differently shaped) from that of other large-size choir books from Spain in LC collections; six pieces on upper cover, including a catch for a leather back-to-front fastening strap, five on lower cover; on lower cover, the strap is attached by means of a number of what seem to be tacks with white tops. — Originally sewn over 5 bands (after the reckless cropping, the 1st and 5th are where headbands should be). — On inside of both covers, pasted over marbled pastedowns, leaves from a 7-line choir book, probably a Gradual (the leaf on lower cover includes caption and beginning of a Requiem).

Former owners: Igor Stravinsky, who donated the book to the Library of Congress in 1963 (date penciled on inside of lower cover is March 7).

2° fo.: *hym L*Auda mater ec [partly under musical staff with notes; 5th line of the staff lost by cropping]

Bibl.: None known. Not in De Ricci or Faye and Bond.

APPENDIX: SELECTED LESS FAMILIAR MATERIAL IN MS 39

James:
***V*₁**, hymn (8v): Defensor alme hyspanie *ad M*(9v): Honorabilem eximii patroni nostri diei huius alumni domini iacobi solennitatem celebremus . . . liberari *"ad iii^m R"*(12v, 13r): O beatum apostolum qui inter primos . . . O gloriosum hyspanie regnum tali pignore ac patrono munitum . . .

Anne:
***V*₁**, *R* (15r): Gloriosa de te dicta radix iesse benedicta . . . *p*⁹ Qua preclara insignita . . . *v* Ex te consurgens virgula dei per virtutem per quam reflorent singula et habent salutem. *p* Qua. *v* Gloria . . . *p* Qua pre. — *ad M* (16r): Celeste patrocinium refloruit in anna . . . ut manna . . . damna . . . magna

Transfiguration:
***V*₁**, *ad M* (33v): Christus Jesus splendor patris . . . apparere dignatus est.

Antoninus (of Apameia):
***V*₁**, *ad pss* (61r): Peracto namque multis in locis . . . ad apamiam. *R* (61v): O fortis athleta et martyr egregie Antonine . . . hodie. *p* Pro nobis quesumus . . . *v* Gladio vitam temporalem . . . *p* Pro . . . *v* Gloria . . . *p* Pro . . . *ad M* (63r): Solemnitatem beatissimi martyris Antonini . . . devotus.
Comp, *ad pss* (64v): Beatus martyr et fortis agonista . . . *ad Nunc D* (65r): Angelus enim Domini per dies septem . . . *"ad iii^m R"* (67v): Agnoscens Festus . . . *p* Atque in eodem . . . *v* Eum enim . . .
***V*₂** "Antiphone laudum" . . . "All'a et prosa ut in missa" . . . *ad M* (69v): Hic est martyr Antoninus cuius corpus . . . divisum . . . in celestibus.

Nativity B. V. M.:
"ad iii^m R" (74v): Solem iustitiae regem paritura supremum *p* Stella maris hodie processit ad ortum *v* Cernere divinum lumen gaudete fideles *p* Stella . . . *v* Gloria . . . *R* Solem . . . (cf. *CAO* IV, no. 7677)

Brice *("scti bricij"):*
***V*₁**, *R* (109r): Sanctus bricius satisfaciens populis prunas ardentes ad urbe in birro suo deferens *p* Vestimentum eius . . . apparuit *v* Amplexatus quoque . . . (N.B. Same text [through *apparuit*] is given, with a different tune, as 5th antiphon to Lauds.)

Presentation B. V. M.:
***V*₁**, *ad pss* (114r): Rore celestis gratie in utero perfunditur . . . oritur *R* (114r): Ordo rectus servatus noscitur . . . conditur . . . perfruitur *p* Sic ad alta mens eius . . . *v* Cum in mente verbi lux oritur . . . *ad M* (115r): Nove laudis adest festivitas (rhymed)
L, a_1 (116r): Lauda felix ecclesia alme matris infantiam a_2 In templo Dei a_3 Omnis eius actio a_4 Quicquid egit penitus a_5 Quantum facultas sufficit *ad iii^m R* (117v): Nuptam sic ex indicio floris et sancti spiritus ***V*₂** "All'a et prosa ut in missa" *ad M* (118v): Oliva fructifera mater pietatis

All Saints:
***V*₁**, *ad M* (97r): Salvator mundi salva nos . . . perfrui mereamur. (N.B. This *ad M* seems to have been the one originally given; apparently replaced during a revision by *Angeli archangeli throni* . . . on 94v–95, over erasures)

NOTES

1. For 1st Vespers of Transfiguration, four antiphons to psalms, no responsory. The four antiphons indicate, normally, monastic use. For James, though, five antiphons (with initia of five psalms), no responsory; an earlier scheme which seems to have had four antiphons/psalms and a responsory has apparently been changed by erasures (on 8r).
2. A touch of the old rite of Toledo?

3. Cf. the Espasa *(Encic. univ. ilus. europeo-americana),* v. 5, p. 822. Identity of the saint confirmed op. cit., v. 5, p. 836 (there as Antonino, one of several homonymous martyrs) or, more importantly, by the texts of his office in our manuscript (see appendix for selected quotations).

4. His cult was widespread but I do not know how important it was in Spain. — N.B. The antiphons present him as unjustly accused and vindicated by miracles, with only perhaps the slightest hint at some need for his later penance.

5. Contemporary, I suppose, with the revision in which substitutions such as that of the antiphon to Magnificat *Angeli archangeli* on 94v sqq. for the *Salvator mundi* (preserved on 97r sqq.) in 1st Vespers of All Saints. Documented dating of these changes is at present hardly feasible but the last quarter of the 16th century is not unlikely.

6. Unless part of a non-Roman tradition retained beyond the "Tridentine" uniformity (only few very old divergent uses were permitted to survive), these texts seem to have been written down, and much used, at some earlier time. I wonder if the book doesn't date from before 1500.

7. Cf. *Analecta liturgica*, ed. W. H. J. Weale (Insulis et Brugis, 1889), p. [158] sqq. The source calendar dates from 1512; it ranks all occasions found in our antiphonary as *"vj. cap."* except Brictius (spelled "Bricii," as in our book; ranked *"ix lect."*).

8. The selection principle used by the people who fashioned MS 39 is a mystery. The book is not what is known as (a collection of) *Nova festa:* Lawrence, Martin, Catherine were anything but new.

9. In this manuscript, *p* with contraction mark over it alternates in responsories with the usual *v* (*versus* or *versiculus*). I am not sure of its correct interpretation.

MS 40

(Music Division: M2147 XVI M2 Folio; the "O'Hara Hymnary")

DOMINICAN HYMNARY (for Matins and Lauds) XVth c., last 3rd?[1]

Spain or Southern France? Parchment. 120 [i.e., 92] leaves,[2] ca. 508 × ca. 360 mm[3] (bound volume: ca. 538 × ca. 380 mm) 5 long staves of music with 5 lines of text, or 15 lines of text.

ff. 1r–50r: (*V*)1 + 1enite exultemus . . . seculorum. Amen.

Leaves 1, 2, 36, and 47 are replacements or cancels. — The section contains a set of nine different tones for the invitatory psalm (Ps. XCV); the beginnings are on ff. 1r, 6r, 11v, 17v, 23r, 28v, 34r, 39v, and 43r respectively; the psalm is always repeated in its entirety. The fourth tone is incomplete owing to missing f. 19.

50v–112v: (On 50r, rubric below what normally would be the last text line:) *Jn utroq[ue] festo sci̅ mich[a]el[is]. ad matutinas .hy̅.* (50v:) (*T*)1 + 1Jbi christe splendor patris . . . (53v:) . . . . . . *bt̅i d[omi]nici p[at]ris n[ost]ri* . . . . . . (97v:) *Jn festis sanctoru[m] : hymni matutinales. In purificatione* . . . . . . (112v:) . . . uotis uoce psallimus alter (ends imperfectly; N.B. 112v is crossed off)

A collection of Office hymns,[4] some of them distinctly proper to the Dominican order; limited to the hymns for Matins and Lauds.[5] At least in the present state of the book, the sanctoral cycle prevails (with ca. 28 hymns), interrupted by the large lacuna

MS 40, f. 6r (actual size of the leaf: ca. 508 × 360 mm)

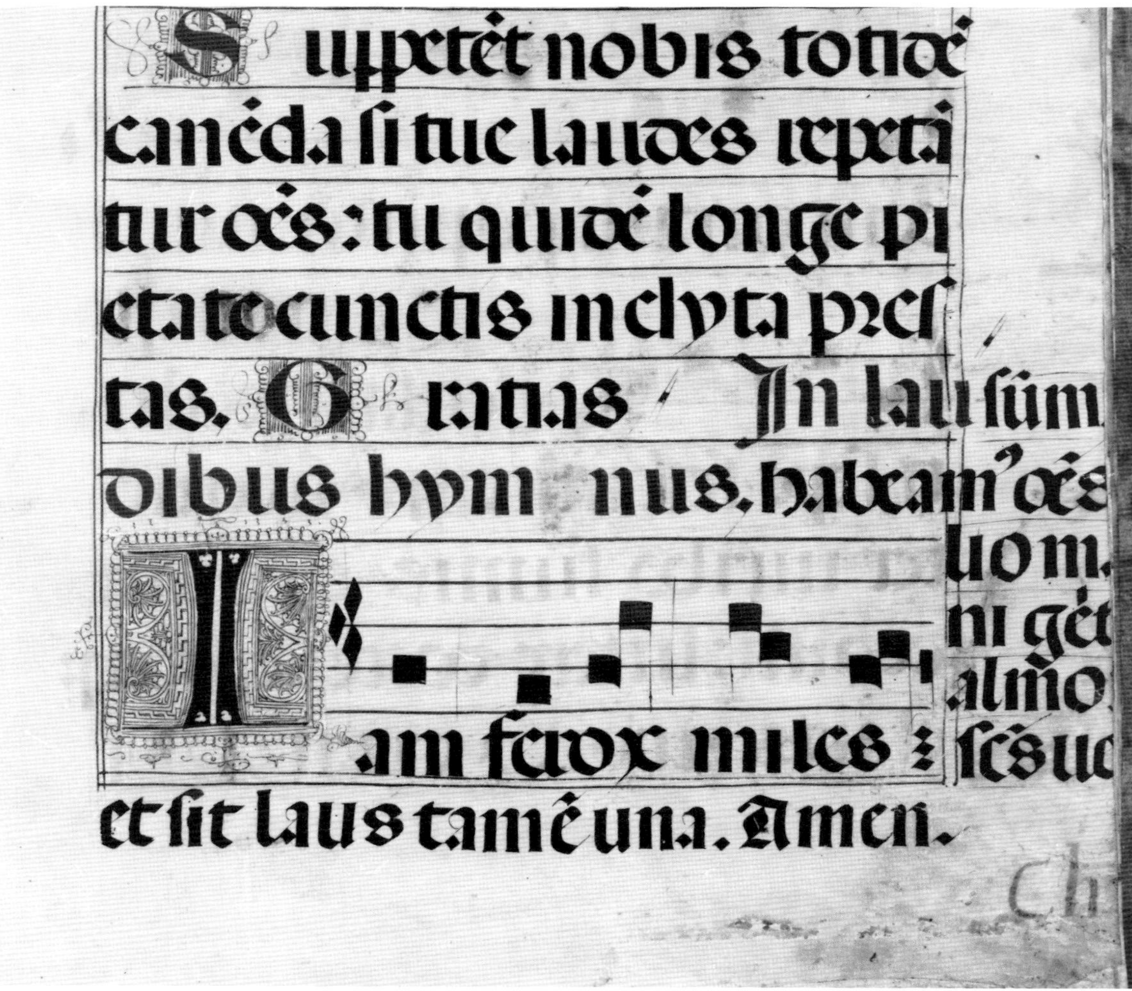

MS 40, f. 107r (lower half) (actual size of area shown: ca. 290 × 330 mm)

between ff. 66 and 88 and the group of seasonal (Ascension, Pentecost, Trinity, Corpus Christi, and Dedication) hymns on ff. 88–97r.[6] — Included are hymns in honor of the Dominican Vincent Ferrer, canonized 1455, and Catherine of Siena, canonized 1461; St. Dionysius, whose celebration was given a high rank in the Dominican order's liturgy in 1481, is absent.[7] — With only 18 different occasions (plus several sets doing double duty and several sets lost) in the sanctoral,[8] the hymnary seems to be a supplement to older Office books: it concentrates on newly introduced feasts and perhaps other changes introduced by 15th-century decisions of Dominican general chapters. The sanctoral covers selectively the whole year, returning at the end (on 112rv) to the set (subsequently crossed off) for the two feasts of Michael the Archangel.[9] — Numerous erasions/corrections; the most important of these extends from the lower third of 65v to upper part of 66v: the area originally contained the set for Eleven Thousand Virgins which has been replaced (in another, later and much less skilled hand) by Transfiguration.[10] — The text spells "ti" where most medieval sources had "ci" ("letitie," but also "dulti"!). — Music accompanies only the first stanza of each hymn. Marginal notes "Org." or "Ch." occur repeatedly.[11]

(What follows are 16th-century ADDITIONS, in a later hand, different in format from the preceding:)

113r–120v: (text beginning abruptly under one line of music:) letitie nobis illuxit celit[us] . . . (115r:) . . . *In S^{ti} Antonini . ad M . hy[m]n[us].* . . . (116v:) . . . *In festo Angeli Cust.* . . . (118v:) . . . *In fest^{o} Sācti Gabrielis.* . . . (ending on 120v:) . . . nos quoque gloriam per cuncta tibi secula. [Added in another hand:] *Adorate Deum.*

(For identification of the hymns, see appendix at end of the description.) The Anthony of f. 115rv is the 15th-century (*d.* 1459) archbishop of Florence, a Dominican, canonized 1523. The relatively uncommon feasts of the guardian angel(s) and of the Archangel Gabriel were known, notably, in parts of Spain (e.g., the archdiocese of Tarragona).

* * *

Present foliation, in black-ink arabic numerals, predated the loss of 28 leaves (see note 2); it was, nevertheless, done with some leaves missing already (see collation); these were missing even earlier when an earlier numbering, partly showing under the present one, was being done: this earlier numbering, also in arabic numerals but in fainter or now washed-off ink, began with the present f. 51 (disregarding the *Venite exsultemus* section); its values are then consistently the present number minus fifty, ending with "68" on present f. 118. — The present (unnumbered) f. 1 seems to have originally been an endleaf. — Written area in the first section ca. 360–365 × ca. 245 mm;[12] on f. 51–112, ca. 390–397 × ca. 240 mm; it varies considerably in the 16th-century additions at end. — Ruling: in the first section, in lead; double vertical head-to-tail bounding lines, top horizontal (slightly above the music staff) from edge to edge; some (barely visible) horizontals for the text lines. Very different is the ruling in the original hymnary proper (ff. 51–112): in slightly diluted black ink, forming a frame of double lines all around each text page (top omitted where it would conflict with music staff); and very visible horizontals inside the framing; the base line of the script is here ca. 5 mm above the ruled line. This decorative ruling has, however, been added over lead ruling of the same kind as on the fifty-leaf section which precedes.[13] — No pricking noticed. — Script in the older areas (ff. 3–112 except rewriting on ff. 65v–66v and substitutes 36 and 47) is large[14] "round gothic," very regular, combining very thick and very thin strokes with excellent esthetic sense; uncial *d,* two forms of *r, a* with upper lobe open; thin vertical strokes over *i*; tironian *[et]* uncrossed, *y* undotted;[15] the contraction marks (sc̄i, etc.) have the form of a diamond-shaped dot rather than that of a macron. On f. 1, roman letters, less skilled. On ff. 113–120, unoutstanding mixture. — Music on 5-line red staves (orange on f. 1rv), with noticeably thicker lines in the first section (through f. 50). *Fa* clef (consisting of three diamond-shape dots) or *do* clef. Square black notes. — Rubrics red. — Parchment of rather poor quality, fairly white on one side, quite yellow or dirty-yellow on the other. Some sewn repairs, some repairs by pasted patches; piece of f. 13 torn off, some leaves have cuts near gutter, f. 62 torn. The text block is now ca. 38 mm thick (= ca. 41 mm per 100 leaves).

Collation: 1^8(1_1 wanting, free endleaf serving as substitute) 2^8 3^8(= ff. 17–24; 3_3 = f. 19 wanting; text loss) 4^8 5^8(5_4 = f. 36 substitute or cancel?) 6^8(6_7 = f. 47 is a substitute or cancel) $7^{2?}$(= ff. 49–50) 8^{8-1}(8_1 absent; pertinent text [copied?] on 7_2) $9^{8-2?}$($9_{1,3,4,8}$ not in; 9_3 or 9_4 = wanting f. 59, with text loss; text loss also with unfoliated 9_8) $10^{6?}$(= ff. 63–66; $10_{1,2}$ following f. 62 and stub wanting, with text loss) ($11^{8?}$, $12^{8?}$, $13_{1-7?}$ = ff. 67–87 [and 2 unnumbered leaves?] wanting, with major text and music loss; 13_8 = f. 88) 14^8(14_{2-7} = ff. 90.95 and 14_8 = f. 96 wanting, with text losses) 15^8(= ff. 97–104) $16^{8-1?}$(16_1 absent, no text loss; $16_{3.6}$ = ff. 106.109 wanting; text loss) 17^8(= ff. 113–118; 17_1 following f. 112 wanting, text loss; 17_8 absent, replaced by bifolio ff. 119.120, no text loss) 18^2(= ff. 119.120). — Catchwords (or syllables) in script of the text on last verso of each gathering (unless lost); they are written at a downward slant of ca. 15°.

Decoration: at least in the present state of the book (and possibly from the start) limited to calligraphic initials: larger ones, the height of the music staff plus the text line, are blue or red lombards "divided" by void white, with red or purple flourishing filling a roughly square area, and are used at the beginning of each hymn, also of each *Venite exultemus* on ff. 3–50. Varied and skillfully done black cadels ca. 2 text-lines high begin sections of the Ps. XCV in the first section. In the hymnary proper (ff. 50v–112v), the one-line high red capitals beginning each stanza of a hymn are flourished in purple. In the section of additions at end, initials are often merely outlined in black or done poorly.[16]

Binding: Covers are old parchment, now rather worn and damaged at tail edge, over oak boards ca. 14 mm thick, slightly beveled on the outside of fore edge. Sewn over 4 bands. Two iron front-to-back clasps; two four-pointed copper rosettes (82 mm square) preserved on upper cover out of original three; one on lower cover. — The binding appears to date originally from the 15th century but has undergone changes later (perhaps when the 16th-century section was being added): the gatherings seem to have been resewn;[17] the lower cover was turned around, its notches used in attachment of the sewing-support bands and headbands now on the fore edge; new notches or perhaps tunnels were apparently made at same heights, causing the square (the part of the board reaching beyond the text block) not to match that of the upper cover. Leaves (three on inside of upper cover, four on lower) from a printed quarto Missal are used in lieu of pastedowns. (On inside of upper cover, an engraving of the Nativity, 290 × 180 mm, of uncertain date, is pasted over the Missal leaves.)

Former owners: Inscribed in pencil on verso of f. 1: Gift//Mrs. Eliot O'Hara//June 4, 1959.[18]

2° fo.: niā non repellet dominus (under a staff of music)

Bibl.: LC printed card no. M 59–1670 (reproduced in *A Bibliography of the Catholic Church* [1970], p. 243 [NC 0218010])

The hymnary is a choir book, made large to make it possible for several people to read the words and music together; to that purpose it remained useful and was maintained well into the 16th century and perhaps beyond. — Spanish origin is suggested by the festivities added at the end, and by various aspects of the format; the apparent hesitancy concerning the question when a year begins (cf. note 9) would suggest French influence. One may think of the ancient diocese of Elna, near the present French-Spanish border, subject in the 16th century to an ecclesiastical tug-of-war between the French province of Narbonne and the Spanish one of Tarragona (it was also for a time [1511–17] subject directly to the Holy See, which could explain the inclusion of the feast of Chair of Peter?).

APPENDIX: THE HYMNS INCLUDED IN MS 40[19]

(Michael, May 8 and September 29)
50v: Tibi Christe splendor Patris
51v: Christe sanctorum decus angelorum

(Dominic, May 23 or 24 [Transl.] and August 5)
53r: Novus athleta Domini
54r: Hymnum novae laetitiae

(John the Baptist, June 24)
55r: Antra deserti
56r: O nimis felix

(Peter and Paul, June 29)
57r: Aurea luce et decore roseo (*AH* II, 58; also LI, 188)
58r: Olivae binae pietatis unicae (= two last stanzas of the preceding; ending imperfectly) (f. 59 wanting)

(Visitation? [July 2])
60r: (beginning abruptly:) intulit in vatem dum se obtulit. Helisabeth hoc . . . (= ? Initium, with all music, wanting)

(Mary Magdalene, July 22)
60v: Lauda mater ecclesia
61v: Aeterni Patris unice

(Anne, July 26)
62r: In Annae puerperio (ends imperfectly) (*AH* XIX, 73) (between ff. 62 and 63, leaf or leaves missing)

(Augustine, August 28)
63r: Magne pater Augustine
64r: Coeli cives applaudite

(Transfiguration, August 6: IN ANOTHER HAND, over erased Eleven Thousand Virgins [October 21])
65v: Quicumque Christum quaeritis (not in *AH*?[20])

(All Saints, November 1)
66v: Iesu salvator saeculi (ff. 67–87 wanting)

(Ascension and its season, movable)
(*M*?) (preserved is only the concluding rubric)
88r: (*L*) Tu Christe nostrum gaudium

(Pentecost, movable)
89r: (*M*) Iam Christus astra ascenderat (f. 90 wanting)

(Trinity, the Sunday immediately following Pentecost)
91v: (*L*) O Trinitas laudabilis

(Corpus Christi, Thursday after Trinity)
92r: Sacris sollemniis
93v: Verbum supernum prodiens

(Dedication of church)
(lacuna after broken-off caption on f. 96)
97r: (beginning abruptly:) Omnis illa Deo grata (= last 4 stanzas of *Urbs beata Hierusalem, AH* LI, 102)

(Purification B.V.M., February 2)
97v: Quem terra pontus ethera
98v: O gloriosa domina

(Chair of Peter, February 22)
99v: Iam bone pastor
100v: (Jesu redemptor CUE ONLY)

(Thomas Aquinas, March 7)
100v: Thomas insignis genere
101v: Lauda mater ecclesia Thomae felicem exitum

(Vincent Ferrer O.P., April 5)
102r: Lumen in terris populi fidelis
103v: Magne Vincenti nova lux olympi

(Peter Martyr O.P., April 29)
105r: (*M*) Adest triumphus nobilis (f. 106 wanting)

(Catherine of Siena [canonized 1461], April 30 or 1st Sunday in May)
107r: (beginning abruptly in 5th stanza of:) Laudibus virgo nimis efferenda (music lost with the beginning of the hymn)
107r: Iam ferox miles

(Finding of the Cross, May 3)
108v: Salve crux sancta (*AH* L, 223; breaks off in 3rd verse) (f. 109 wanting)
110r: (hymn resumes in 3rd stanza, 2nd verse)

(Crown of Thorns, May 4)
110v: Aeterno regi gloriae
111v: Lauda fidelis contio spinae tropaeum inclytum

(Michael [see above !], "in utroque festo")
112v: Tibi Christe splendor Patris (but whole page crossed off by double diagonal lines)

HYMNS ADDED IN 16TH CENTURY, ff. 113–120: (unnumbered leaf wanting before f. 113)

(Peter Martyr O.P.: for his *Translatio*, May 7)
113r: (*V*!) Magnae dies laetitiae (first two words lost)
113v: (*M*) Adest triumphus nobilis
114v: (*L*) Exsultet claro sidere

(Anthony, Abp. of Florence [canonized 1523], May 10)
115r: Atrae noctis obscuritas (*AH* IV, 145)
116r: Cum sol ad cursum properat (*AH* IV, 146)

(Guardian Angel [March 14 in Compostella, July 13 in Tarragona])
116v: Custodes hominum
117v: Orbis patrator optime

MS 40 (Gabriel, the Archangel [March 18 in Compostella, Sevilla])

118v: Gabrielem veneremur (*AH* XVI, 219)

119v: O robur Domini lucide Gabriel (not in *AH*?[21])

NOTES

1. With 16th-century additions; cf. contents, ff. 113–120.

2. Missing are numbered leaves 19, 59, 67–87, 90, 95, 96, 106, and 109; several unnumbered leaves are wanting, some with text loss (see the collation paragraph).

3. The height of the leaves varies from ca. 506 to ca. 510 mm near the gutter, from ca. 495 to ca. 503 mm at the fore edge.

4. Full listing in appendix following the description.

5. Not included are those for the Vespers (cf. LC MS 31).

6. Order of the sections doesn't seem to have been tampered with: the end of the *Venite exultemus* section and the beginning of the sanctoral are on same leaf, as are the end of the Dedication hymns and the beginning of the second sanctoral sequence on 97v. The rubric on 97v (see quote above) is nevertheless puzzling.

7. Cf. Leroquais, *Brév*. I, p. CI.

8. The loss of ff. 67–87 (perhaps more prior to the numbering) makes it difficult to assess the seasonal part now limited to ff. 88r–97r.

9. The proper date for this set is May 8 (see sequence shown in the appendix). No liturgical year known to me begins in May; however, in France of that time (and up to ca. 1570) the calendar year began with Easter ("a Resurrectione," cf. Cappelli, *Cronologia*); the latest date on which Easter can occur is April 25.

10. Added to Dominican calendar in 1456 or slightly later. Cf. Bonniwell, *Hist. Dom. lit.*

11. *The New Grove dictionary of music and musicians* (1980) mentions in its article "Dominican friars" the practice of Dominican choirs ("from the later Middle Ages onwards"), frowned upon by church authorities, to alternate organ and choir.

12. Measured from the top line of musical staff to base of last-line minims.

13. In the last (16th-century) part (ff. 113–120), the ruling is again lead, and very simple (simple verticals).

14. Minims ca. 15 mm high in first section, ca. 14 mm on ff. 50v–112.

15. Only exception noticed: in the rubric on 112v, first line.

16. Quite nonrepresentative is the initial (simple orangish yellow letter) on the substitute f. 1.

17. The string of the primary sewing has the right-handed ("*S*") twist; some partly preserved string of what I think was the original kettle stitch is of the "*Z*" or left-handed kind.

18. Mrs. O'Hara was the daughter of Herbert Putnam, the Librarian of Congress from 1899 to 1939.

19. Initia in standardized orthography. *V* = Vespers, *M* = Matins, *L* = Lauds. In the complete sets of two, the first hymn is for Matins, the second for Lauds. — Calendar dates supplied (as usual, the source gives none). — In several instances I quote the *Analecta hymnica* but the texts, incl. some apparently not in *AH*, can be found in *The hymns of the Dominican Missal and Breviary* edited by A. Byrnes (St. Louis and London: Herder, 1943).

20. Text in Byrnes, *op. cit.*, p. 244, 246.

21. Text in Byrnes, *op. cit.*, p. 452, 454, 456.

MS 41

("Kelsch Gradual"; in Music Division)

GRADUAL. Proper of the saints.

(early?) XVIth c.

Spain. Parchment. 171 leaves (numbered *i-clxvii,* CLXVIII-CLXXVII, with *xlix-lviii* omitted, *cxxxvi-cxxxviii* repeated, last leaf unnumbered), ca. 725 × ca. 510 mm.[1] 6 long lines of music (5-line staves in red) and 6 of text to a page.

ff.[2] *i*ᵛ-*clxv*ᵛ: (*i*ʳ blank; *i*ᵛ, within all-around border, without caption:) (*D*)2 + 2Ominus secus mare galilee . . . (*iv*ʳ:) . . . *In .festo.s.andree apl'. Introit[us].* (*M*)2 + 2Jhi aute[m] nimis honorati sunt . . . (*lxxvi*ʳ:) . . . *In .f .S̄cti thome de Aquino* . . . (*lxxx*ʳ:) *In.f .S. Joseph co[n]f[essoris]* . . . (*cxiv*ʳ:) . . . *S̄acti silueri pape [et] martyris.* . . . (*cxxvi*ʳ:) . . . *In festo visitationis beate marie . virginis* . . . (*cxxx*ʳ:) . . . *Bonauenture* . . . (*cxxxv*ᵛ:) . . . *In festo transfigurationis dn̄i nostri Jesuchristi.* . . . (*clvii*ᵛ:) . . . *In festo sancti francisci confessoris.* . . . (*clxi*ᵛ:) . . . *Tryphonis Respicij et Nimphe* . . . (*clxv*ʳ:) . . . *Catherine* . . . (ending on *clxv* verso in area corresponding to 1st line of music/text,with the end of St. Catherine program:) . . . *Com.* Confunda[n]tur. *clxiiij.*

A *Graduale de Sanctis,* i.e., collected Mass propers (choir chant only) for saints' feasts arranged according to the liturgical year: beginning with the Vigil of Andrew, Nov. 29 and ending with St. Catherine (Nov. 25; N.B. the manuscript does not give dates). Of the 107 occasions named here, 13 are introduced by extra-large initials (2 lines of music + 2 of text in height): the Vigil of Andrew (1v, with full all-around border), Andrew (4r), Conversion of Paul (39v), the second celebration of St. Agnes (48v), Purification (67v, beginning of the Mass; the Candlemas procession chants begin on 66v), Agatha (71r), George (84r), Finding of the Cross (88v), John the Baptist (117r; with full border, as on 1v), Peter and Paul (123v), Transfiguration (135v), Lawrence (142r), Francis (155r).[3] — Of interest for placing or assigning the manuscript may be the *Cathedra Petri* (judging from the sequence, the less common January feast of Chair of Peter in Rome, not the universally celebrated February occasion); John Chrysostom (45v); Thomas Aquinas (76r); St. Joseph (80r); in June, Silverius (several Spanish dioceses honored him); the joint celebration of Tryphon, Respicius, and Nympha (in the calendars of several religious orders); and Gregorios *Thaumatourgos* (162v; rare in Western calendars.[4]). — Relevant to dating are in particular the feast of St. Joseph, in the Roman calendar since ca. 1480 (given higher rank ca. ten years later)[5] and that of St. Bonaventure who was canonized in 1482. — The proper (*Illuxerunt*) for Transfiguration (feast legislated in 1457 but finding its way into diocesan calendars rather

MS 41, f. 117r (actual size of the leaf: ca. 725 × 510 mm)

slowly) which begins in last two lines of f. 135v and ends on fifth line of 138v (there, last line empty) looks like an afterthought: the next leaf after 138 was originally numbered *cxxxvi*: this number has been torn out and it now carries none but the next leaf is "*cxxxvij*" and this numbering sequence is then continued. — For some of the occasions (specified in the appendix), the "proper" is completely or in part limited to a program, with references to the written-out items using leaf numbers.[6] — On 133v, in outer margin, ADDITION in black ink, unskilled hand: "In festo S. An[n]e Missa Gaudeamus . . . Off S[ancte] Agnetis."

*clxv*ᵛ-CLXXʳ: *C[ommuni]o.* (*S*)¹⁺Jmō ioannis diligis me . . . *gr[aduale].* (*B*)¹⁺Enedicite do (*clxvi*ʳ:)minum omnes angeli . . . (*clxvii*ʳ:) (*A*)¹⁺Lleluia. *v.* Senex puerum portabat . . . (*clxvii*ᵛ:) . . . *v.* Sancti tui domine florebunt . . . (*clxviii*ʳ:) . . . *Co.* (*M*)¹⁺Agna est gloria eius . . . (CLXIXʳ:) . . . *Int[roitus].* (*C*)¹⁺Lamauerunt ad te . . . (CLXIXᵛ:) . . . *Com.* (*I*)¹⁺Oseph fili dauid noli . . . (ending on CLXXʳ in 2nd//3rd music/text line:) . . . de spiritu sa[n]c//to est. (rest of CLXXʳ blank, ruled for text only, with spaces for music staves; verso blank)

Collection of chant items not written out earlier. E.g., the proper of St. Joseph, on f. 81, refers to this section for its Communion antiphon (using the leaf number, "*clxix*").

(following f. CLXX, four stubs)

CLXXIʳ-CLXXVᵛ: (LATER [16th-century?] ADDITIONS:) *In Festo Corone Dn̄i Ad missa[m] Jntroit[us].* (*G*)²⁺²Audeamus ōnes in Domino diem festum . . . (CLXXVᵛ:) . . . *Jn festo Angeli Custodis.* . . . (ends imperfectly at end of f. CLXXVIIᵛ, in the Offertory antiphon:) (*A*)Dorate dominū omnes Ange[li]

Neither addition (the first introduced by a three-color calligraphic initial indicating heterogeneous origin) was required by the general development of the Roman calendar; presence of both together may suggest Dominican influence. — An instruction to guide the rubricator, in rather modern longhand, is preserved under and near the *Angeli Custodis* rubric.

[clxxviii]ʳ (a later, perhaps 16th-century, ADDITION:) five columns or indexes written in roman minuscule, mostly in faint brown ink; in the first column, index of the feasts in red ink (text partly obscured); the rest are initia arranged by genre, with red captions in roman capitals: INTROITOS, PSALMOS, ALLELUAS, OFFERTORIOS, POSTCOMMUNIOS, GRADUALES (last caption, illegible, is for the Candlemas procession hymn). Within each genre, the arrangement is alphabetical.

* * *

Foliated in red lowercase roman numerals placed in the head margin of rectos, ca. 1/3 of page width from fore edge; on some leaves, the number has been obscured by pasted-on patch, perhaps while planning to correct the disturbed sequence (cf. opening paragraph).[7] On leaves CLXVIIII-CLXXVII the numbering is in roman capitals written in black ink. A partly redundant foliation in modern pencil and arabic numerals appears in tail margins beginning with f. 100 (= *c*); it reaches "142" for f. *cxxxix*ᵇⁱˢ, then ceases, to make a solitary reappearance on f. *clvii*, assigning it, quite incorrectly, arabic "157." — Written area (from top line of music staff to base of minims in the bottom line) ca. 575 × ca. 360 mm. — Ruled blind, from the flesh side, for vertical boundary lines (simple, reaching to edges) and for the text lines.[8] No pricking found. — Script of the liturgical texts is a large (minims ca. 16 mm high), precisely drawn, simple *praescissa* and *rotunda* gothic (or based on gothic), maintained throughout, including the leaves numbered in roman capitals (with minor difference in the form of the *a*[9]). Two forms of *d* (uncial and straight-shafted). Lowercase *g* is two-lobed with right-hand descender unsplit and end of the upper lobe extending beyond it to the right; lowercase *q* has an extremely simple form of arabic *9* with descender straight. Letter *h* doesn't extend beyond base line. The *i* has in place of our dot a narrow, slanting triangular stroke, with the pointed end aimed at the letter. Two forms of *r*; the one similar to the modern letter has the downstroke curving to the right rather like the lower third of a *c* or an *e*. Undotted *y*. Capital *O* (capitals are used as next letter after an initial) has an opening to the left, capital *E* is mirror image of arabic *3*. Uncrossed tironian *[et]*; the old characters for final *[rum]* and *-m*; superscript final *-s*. Adjoining curves of *o* and *c*, etc., melt. The mark for macron or tilde is a lozenge with the longer axis horizontal. Occasional cedilla on the final *e* for the feminine genitive singular. — (The unnumbered last leaf, with indices, is in humanistic roman; see contents.) — The smaller (minims ca. 9 mm), less disciplined red script of the rubrics (captions) is marked by (inconsistently used) capital letters with fancifully curved descenders (notably *P*).

Music on 5-line red staves (ca. 58 mm high),[10] black square notation, using *fa* or *do* clefs; the *fa* clef is represented by an assembly of three closely juxtaposed black lozenges of equal size. The *custos* at end of each line has the shape of a check mark.

The writing material (calfskin) has hair side smooth, unevenly yellow, oily-looking; flesh side, smooth and white, perhaps whitened with chalk. Page of one type generally faces another of same appearance except in the irregularly assembled group beginning with f. *cxxxv* (group numbered as gathering 17 in our collation below); there, e.g., the flesh side of f. 136bis faces the hair side of 137bis but the two seem to be joined together as one bifolio (!); a number of the very large double leaves required by the size of this codex seem, in fact, to have been originally made from two roughly leaf-size sheets. Quality of the skins is uneven; some seem to have been of inadequate size from the beginning; some repairs by sewing or by patching; also some unrepaired holes and other defects. Thickness of the text block when compressed is between 80 and 90 mm.

Collation: $1–6^{8}$(= ff. i-xlviii) (ff. xlix-lviii absent; binding structure shows loss of a gathering [10 leaves??] but text continues uninterrupted from xlviii^{v} to lix^{r}) $7–13^{8}$(= ff. lix-cxiv) $14^{2?}$(= ff. cxv and cxvi [conjugate?]) $15–16^{8}$(= ff. cxvii-cxxxii) $17^{?}$(= ff. cxxxiii-cxxxviii, $cxxxvi^{bis}$, $cxxxvii^{bis}$, $cxxxviii^{bis}$, cxxxix, cxl; sewing lines suggest conjugateness cxxxvii.cxxxviii and $cxxxvi^{bis}.cxxxvii^{bis}$) 18^{8}(= ff. cxxxxi-cxxxxviii) 19^{6}(= ff. cil-cliv) 20^{8}(= ff. clv-clxii) 21^{4}(= ff. clxiii-clxvi) 22^{4} 23^{8-4}(= 4 stubs and ff. clxxi through clxxiv) 24^{8-4}(= 4 stubs and ff. clxxv-clxxviii). — No catchwords; no signatures. — Some of the bifolia are made of two pieces (one leaf-size, one overlapping in the fold) joined by pasting or gluing; in some cases, apparently (in the 17th gathering of our numbering), not matched by the hair/flesh side.

Decoration: limited to calligraphic initials and borders conspicuous by hatched grounds, and cadels. — Initials are used only for occasions for which some music is given directly, whether an Introit or another part; not for feasts, it seems, of any rank which are covered only by a program and references. — The larger initials (in double frames 2 music/text lines high, ca. 190 × 190 mm) are used for thirteen (plus one added) feasts (the sometimes puzzling choices are listed in our comment in the contents section); smaller ones (in frames slightly over one music/text line, ca. 100 × 90 mm) for ca. eighty. Both consist of a blue or red (the two alternate) lombardic letter (accentuated by black outlining on one side) floating in front of a field filled with void-white simple botanical forms outlined by pen on a ground horizontally hatched (outlines and hatching black), set into a rectangular black and white frame which, in the case of the smaller initials, has a three-dimensional appearance. Combination of straight-line framing, botanical forms left void white, and black-hatched ground is also used for the all-around borders given the Vigil of Andrew (or rather, presumably, to the beginning of the book) and to John the Baptist (f. 117r). — In the additions, the initial *G* of the Crown of Thorns proper (CLXXIr) is in four colors (letter divided blue and red, ground patterns void white on green, frame includes yellow); other initials in this part are red on mild purple fields, with patterns on the inside and outside of the letters entirely independent. — Black cadels, some made with impressive skill, mark the beginnings of many subordinate items.

Binding: The text block is now completely separated from its boards. Sewn over 5 double cords; headbands undecorated. First five gatherings, and four gatherings at end, are side-stitched, in addition to the primary sewing. — The (separated) boards are contemporary oak ca. 10 mm thick; each board is made of two vertical halves, neatly joined; beveled from outside at spine edge; size of whole board ca. 775 × ca. 540 (upper board) or 530 (lower) mm. The lower board appears to have previously served another book, perhaps a Psalter: black offset image of 14 lines (no music) from Ps. CXXXVI (Vulg. 135) fills ca. 3/4 of its inner surface.[11] — Cords entered the board from the outside through round holes in the beveled edge, were imbedded on the inside in very short (ca. 40 mm) channels, and secured by round plugs in holes leading back to the outside. The entrance and the exit holes are aligned horizontally on the upper board, diagonally, and with one additional hole at the meeting point of each pair of diagonals; some wooden plugs preserved. — Original covers of deep-brown calf protected/decorated by brass bosses ca. 31 mm in diameter, in one piece with 8-petal whirly (clockwise) rosette base (diameter ca. 80 mm): three out of original four preserved on the upper board, two on the lower one. In center of both boards, traces of what might have been a different device. Corners protected by basically square-shape (base ca. 73 mm) flat pieces (thick brass) decorated by cut openwork; from the lower board, one is lost and another preserved on broken-off (sawed off?) piece of the wood. Catch of the lower of two brass front-to-back clasps still on the lower board; only traces of the clasps on the upper one. — Both covers are also blind-tooled with rolls. Boards and covers are in poor shape and variously damaged. — Before the separation, the spine was covered by a wide strip of leather tacked to the boards from the outside, ca. 80–100 mm from the spine edge.

Former owners: On f. 2v, in tail margin, inscribed in pencil: Gift//Effects of//Dr. Ernest Kelsch//Sept. 23, 1943.

2° fo.: (under staff of music:) catores hominum. *p̄s.*

Bibl.: None known.

The codex is a "choir book," made very large so that the words and music would be legible to all members of the performing choir or *schola.* Choir books of this sort are rarely dated, and their makers, probably mostly nuns, show little tendency to identify themselves or their house. In a world deficient in communication, a newly made book may have been less than up-to-date on liturgical developments. Scribal ways obsolete elsewhere may have been carefully imitated. For all this, the book almost certainly predates 1600, and on the face of it would seem to have come from not much after 1500.

APPENDIX: THE 110 OCCASIONS COVERED IN MS 41

1v:	Vigil of Andrew
4r:	Andrew
7r:	Nicholas
10v:	Ambrose
13r:	Conception B.V.M.
16r:	Damasus
19r:	Lucy
21v:	Thomas the Apostle
22v:	Paul the Hermit
26r:	Marcellus (*program*)
26r:	Chair of Peter (in Rome)
29v:	Marius & Martha
32v:	Fabian & Sebastian
36r:	Agnes
39v:	Timothy (*program*)
39v:	Conversion of Paul
44r:	Polycarp
45v:	John Chrysostom
48v:	Agnes "secundo"
53v:	Ignatius
66v:	Purification B.V.M.
71r:	Agatha

75r: Mathias
76r: Thomas Aquinas
77r: Forty martyrs
79r: Gregory (the pope)
80r: Joseph
81v: Annunciation
83v: Leo
84r: Tiburtius & Valerian ("*omnia de communi*")
84r: George
86v: Mark (*program*)
86v: Philip & James
88r: Athanasius
88v: Cross, Invention of
91v: Monica
93v: John *ante Portam Latinam (program)*
93v: Michael, Apparition of
97r: Gordian & Epimachus
98v: Nereus, Achilleus, & Pancras
100v: Urban
101r: Marcellinus & ? ("*Sanctorum martyrum .Marcellini.*")
103v: Primus & Felician
106v: Barnabas
107v: Basilides, Cyrinus
110v: Basil
111r: Vitus & Modestus
112v: Mark & Marcellian
113v: Gervase & Protasius
114r: Silverius (*program*)
114r: Paulinus (*program*)
114r: Vigil of John the Baptist
117r: John the Baptist
119v: John and Paul
122v: Vigil of Peter and Paul
123v: Peter and Paul
124v: Commemoration of Paul
126r: Visitation B.V.M. (*program*)
126v: Peter and Paul *infra octavam*
127r: Peter and Paul *in Octava*
128r: Seven brothers, Rufina, Secunda
130r: Bonaventura (*program*)
130r: Alexius
131v: Symphorosa and sons (*program*)
131v: Praxedes
132r: Mary Magdalen
133v: Apollinaris (*program*)
133v: James (*program*)
133v: Martha (*program*)
(133v: Anne [marginal ADDITION])
133v: Abdon & Sennen
135r: Stephen, pope & martyr
135v: Dominic (*program*)
135v: Transfiguration
136 bis r: Donatus
136 bis v: Cyriacus, Largus, Smaragdus
139r: Vigil of Lawrence
142r: Lawrence
145r: Vigil of Assumption (*program*)
145r: Assumption B.V.M.
147v: Octave of Lawrence
148v: Bartholomew
149r: Louis
149v: Augustine (*program*)
149v: Beheading of John the Baptist (*program*)
149v: Felix & Adauctus
150r: Nativity B.V.M. (*program*)
150r: Cross, Exaltation of
151v: Vigil of Matthew
152v: Matthew
154r: Cosmas & Damian (*program*)
154r: Michael, Dedication of church of (*program*)
154r: Jerome (*program*)
155r: Francis
156v: Mark, pope
157v: Dionysius, Rusticus, Eleutherius
158r: Callistus (*program*)
158r: Luke (*program*)
158r: Vigil of Simon & Jude (*program*)
158r: Simon & Jude
158v: Vigil of All Saints
159v: All Saints
161v: Tryphon, Respicius, Nympha
162r: Martin
162v: Gregory Thaumaturgus (*program*)
163r: Cecilia
164v: Clement
165r: Catherine (*program*)
171r: (LATER ADDITION) Crown of Thorns
175v: (LATER ADDITION) Guardian Angel

NOTES

1. At the time of this writing, the text block is unprotected; see the paragraph on binding for description of the separated original boards.

2. Folio numbers in the contents are those found or extrapolated from those found in the codex, retaining roman numerals in the quote paragraphs but using corresponding arabic numbering in the comment; the second occurrence of numbers 136–138 is identified by "bis."

3. Of the six feasts of the Virgin (Conception, Purification, Annunciation, Visitation, Assumption, Birth) only the second is decorated in this manner; the choice of the apostles' days so marked appears quite random. These apparent inconsistencies may or may not attest a particular liturgical tradition.

4. Grotefend, *Zeitrechnung* II, lists only "Kreuzherren" as honoring this Eastern saint. The term may denote any of several orders: in this case, perhaps, the Portuguese Canons Regular of the Cross of Coimbra? They flourished on the Iberian peninsula in the 16th century.

5. Joseph's day came earlier (before or ca. 1400) to the Franciscan and Dominican calendars and here and there to a diocesan cult before its official acceptance by Rome. A comprehensive study of both the liturgical legislation and the actual inclusion of the feast in reliably localized manuscripts (books often lagged behind legislation) would be much desired.

6. The number covers both recto and verso of a leaf; it does not refer to an opening (as it did in some Carthusian books).

7. The structural gap without text loss after f. *xlviii*, and other oddities of the numbering seem to suggest that this codex was, entirely contrary to customary procedure, sewn and foliated before the writing started (?).

8. As common in Spanish calfskin manuscripts, the flesh side is the white(r) one.

9. Letter *a* is basically that of our printed roman type; simplicity of its design is spoiled by inward curling of the upper end in the main text. The (lower) lobe consists of a short thick stroke at 7–8 o'clock, attached to the vertical at right by two thin straight lines. In the main text, the short thick stroke is convex; in the additions at end, straight (and at right angles to the attaching thin lines).

10. I.e., ca. 58 mm from first to fifth line. The distance between two staves (normally including text) is ca. 40 mm.

11. What is, I suppose, a secondary offset (from the board to vellum) shows on verso of the last leaf (f. 178v) of the gradual.

MS 42, f. 61r (actual size of the leaf: ca. 560 × 405 mm)

(On the inside of upper cover, upside-down offset of a page which may have originally been a part of the Kyriale; not identified [part of *Vidi aquam?* Cf. end of contents for offset on the lower cover])

MS 42

(Music Division: M2147 XVI M1 Folio; the "Wilson Kyriale")

KYRIALE and varia XVIth c.?

Italy. Parchment. 78 leaves, ca. 560 × ca. 405 mm (bound volume: ca. 570 × ca. 410 mm) 5 long lines of music (4-line staves in red) and 5 of text to a page.

(N.B. Leaves numbered 1–4 are bound at end, following f. 78.)

ff. 1r–4v: (*A*)1 + 1Lma rede[m]ptoris mater . . . (2r:) . . . *S*Alue regina misericordie . . . (3r:) . . . *R*Egina celi letare . . . (4r:) . . . *A*Ve regina celorum . . . (4v:) . . . nobis semp[er] xp̄m exora. (last 2 staves and text lines blank)

Plainchant and text of the four Marian antiphons, one of which would be sung at the end of a day's office by the community using this choir book. — The set is that found in the Roman breviary; text of the last item differs from it in several details (". . . salve radix sancta ex qua . . . gaude gloriosa . . . Vale valde decora . . ."). — It is uncertain where the leaves 1–4 belong: they are not included in the sequence of numbered gatherings *i-vii*; their script is closer to that of ff. 61–77 than to that of ff. 5–60. Their content may with about equal logic be placed at the beginning or at the end of this book.

5r–17v: (*T*)1 + 1Erribilis est lo (red caption begins between the two highest lines of the music staff and continues down, divided in small segments:) *In de//dica//tione//ecc[lesi]e. I[n]troit[us].* (2nd music/text line:) cus iste . . . (5v:) . . . *GR[aduale]. L*Ocus iste . . . (7v:) . . . *Off[ertorium]. D*Omine deus in simplicitate . . . (8r:) . . . *c[ommuni]o. D*Om[us] mea . . .

Choir portions of the Mass celebrating the anniversary of the dedication of the (local) church building.[1]

8v–17v: . . . *In agenda defu[n]ctorum. Introitus.* (*R*)1 + 1Equiem eterna[m] . . . (13r:) . . . *Sequentia. D*Ies ire dies illa . . . (17v:) . . . *P*Ie ihu dne dona eis requiem. Am[en].

Plainchant version of the familiar set of items constituting the choir parts of a Requiem Mass, without the Ordinary: *Requiem; Absolve;* the sequence *Dies irae,* here placed last; the offertory *Domine Iesu Christe rex gloriae,* the communion antiphon *Lux aeterna.* For the "ordinary" *(Kyrie, Sanctus, Agnus Dei),* a reference in margin of 9r (unskilled later hand, black ink over earlier badly scribbled note in burnt-siena crayon) sends the user (the choir) to f. 43. — Text of the *Dies irae* appears faulty: on 14r, "Mox stupebit et natura" may be a legitimate variant but "sedisti lapsus" (on 15v; with the *p* inadequately deleted) hardly so. On 17r, the "Oro supplex" stanza, omitted by the copyist, has been added in tail margin by a contemporary corrector, with appropriate marks of insertion (small red Maltese cross).

17v–48r: (beginning in 4th line of 17v:) . . . *In maiorib[us] duplicibus. K*Yrie *.iii.* leison. (18r:) *C*Riste *.iii.* leyson. *K*Irie *.iii.* leyson. *G*Loria . . . (ending in 1st line of 48r:) leyson.

This (uncaptioned and unseparated) section is the basic *Kyriale,* or collection of "ordinaries" (i.e., of various plainchant tunes, according to various occasions, for singing the *Kyrie, Gloria, Sanctus, Agnus Dei,* also *Ite missa est;* N.B. the *Credo,* also a normal ingredient of a Kyriale, is not included): 17v–21v, *In maioribus duplicibus;* 21v–25v, *In minoribus duplicibus;* 25v–29v, *In maioribus semiduplicibus;* 29v–33v, *In minoribus semiduplicibus;* 33v–37r, *In dominicis diebus;* 37r–38v, *In festis simplicibus sollemnioribus;* 38v–42r, *In festis simplicibus minoribus;* 42r–43r, *In ferialibus diebus et festorum trium lectionum;* 43r–44r, *In agenda mortuorum;* 44r–47v, *In missis beate virginis Marie et commemorationibus eiusdem;* 47v–48r, "*Kyrie regis.*" — Spellings vary as shown (although *y* prevails). The Greek ἐλέησον seems to have lost its initial vowel. Text of the *Gloria* as repeated for the various tunes includes some rare variations or corruptions, 19r: "Domine fili unigenite ihesu criste et sancte spiritus"; 27r: "Domine fili unigenite salus nostra ihesu xp̄e." The Gloria of the Marian ordinary, 44v–47r, was originally provided with the Marian interpolations known otherwise from the area of the lower Rhine and from the Praemonstratensian rite;[2] an apparently half-hearted effort was later made to erase them but several remained untouched and all are legible (both the music and the text). — ADDED in the tail margin of 47v through 49r, another *Sanctus* and *Agnus,* graphically quite different: two lines of music and two of text, all in black ink; text in italic script, the music notes are all black lozenges, joined in the melismata by winding connecting lines. — On 30r, near the beginning of Gloria (4th line), marginal note in Italian: *Gloria della Domenica.*

48r–60v: *Seque[n]tia in natiuitate dn̄i.* (*L*)$^{1+1}$Etabund[us] exultet . . . (50v:) *Seq[ue]ntia in resurrectione dn̄i. N*Atus passus dominus . . . (53r:) . . . *Seq[ue]ntia in annu[n]tiatio[n]e. M*Issus gabriel de celis uerbi baiulus fidelis . . . (57v:) . . . *Seq̄ntia beate marie. A*Ue maria gratia plena dn̄s tecum uirgo serena . . . (59v:) . . . *Sequentia de sc̄a maria. P*Ersonemus in hac die . . . (ending imperfectly at end of 60v:) Omni melle dulcior omni flore gratior p[er] qua[m] (catchword for the missing next gathering: salus)

More "sequentiae" may have followed. A considerable number of these (also called "prosae") were in use, recited or sung as part of the Mass celebration just before the Gospel reading, in the later Middle Ages and up to the introduction (in 1570) of the *Missale Romanum* (the "Tridentine" Missal), which did not accept any of those named here.[3]

(between ff. 60 and 61, missing leaf or leaves [a gathering of 8?], with loss of material)

61r–77v: *Incip[it] off[ici]um solle[m]pnitati sc̄e trinitatis. In primis uesperis. anth'.* (*S*)$^{2+2}$Edenti sup[er] solium co[n]gratula[n]s trisagium . . . (office ends imperfectly in the antiphon *ad Benedictus* at end of 77v:) . . . et q[uam] iocunda uisio lustrari trino (rest wanting)

Music and text of the rhythmical (and rhymed) office in honor of the Trinity believed to be (at least the text part) by the 13th-century Archbishop of Canterbury John Peckham (*AH* V, p. 19 sqq.;[4] cf. also L, no. 390). It was part of the Roman office (breviary) from the end of the 15th century to the *Breviarium Romanum* of 1570 in which it was replaced by non-rhythmical material.[5]

(following f. 77, leaf or leaves wanting, with loss of material)

f. 78rv: *Dominica de trinitate. Introitus.* (*B*)$^{1+1}$Enedicta sit sancta trinitas . . . suam. *Versus.* (78v:)

Benedicamus patre[m] et filium . . . *v.* Gloria patri et filio . . . (ending abruptly at end of 78v:) . . . *B*Enedictus es domine qui i[n]tueris abys (-sos, and rest wanting)

Beginning of the Mass proper for the feast of Trinity. The leaf is slightly smaller in size than the rest and may be from another book of similar format. — N.B. Continuing the Introit antiphon by a "versus" rather than by a Psalm verse was not a feature of Roman liturgical use.

(Following f. 78, four leaves numbered 1–4; see the beginning of the contents)

(On the inside of lower cover, offset of an upside-down page which may very well have originally been part of the intellectual content of the book: it contains a rubric and the beginning of *Asperges,* music and text in same format as the preceding; apparently [in view of the shape of *g*] by the scribe who wrote the ff. 61–77. The *Asperges* is usually included in a Kyriale. — The offset is partly obscured by pasted-on pieces of paper [see lower at end of the paragraph on binding].)

* * *

Old-style arabic numeral foliation in upper right corners of rectos; in the present state of the book, the leaves 1–4 are at end, following f. 78 (cf. comment to first item of contents). — Written area ca. 378 × ca. 280 mm on leaves 5–60, ca. 368 × ca. 280 mm on ff. 61–78 and 1–4. — Ruled in faint brownish black ink for the vertical boundaries (simple lines, head edge to tail edge) and for the text lines; no pricking visible. — Script is somewhere between semi-quadrate and *rotunda;* ascenders of *b,* of the (rare) straight-shaft *d,* of *h* and *l* are cut off straight, as are the descenders of *p* and *q;* the minims (ca. 12 mm high) are generally broken at top and hooked at the base. The *a* resembles our lowercase roman, with the lobe closed by a short and thick straight stroke; uncial *d* prevails in all positions; *g* on ff. 5–60 of the gothic type (on the right, an unbroken, mildly curved descending stroke); on ff. 61–77 and 1–4, resembling that of the *anglicana* (much like arabic *8* with added flag at top). The *h* doesn't go below base; *p* has a small hook at top of its descender; the lobe of *q* rounds smoothly downward into the descender; two forms of *r*; dotless *y* with the part below base a disappearing hairline. Groups *oc* and similar ones melt. Uncrossed tironian *et.* There seem to have been two or more[6] scribes sharing an almost identical tradition, the only clear difference being in their *g.* — The rubrics, mostly captions, are red, and written in smaller script than the text: minims ca. 7 mm high. — Music on 4-line red staves ca. 40 mm from bottom edge of first line to upper edge of the fourth; the lines are rather thick, ca. 1.5 mm on some pages, and very expertly drawn. Distance between staves ca. 37 mm. Black square notation includes lozenge forms where appropriate. *Do* or *fa* clefs, the latter made differently on ff. 5–60 (vertically positioned oblong rectangles, two close to each other in one line, the third in next line directly under the second) and on ff. 61 sqq. (more parallelograms than rectangles, one at mid-height to the left of the other two). The *custos* resembles a check mark (a very narrow rectangle made by an extremely short stroke of the *calamus* constituting the first stroke, the second stroke a thin line continuing a long side of the rectangle at ca. 60° from the base). Numerous red bar lines are a conspicuous feature here. — Black and red inks of good quality. — Writing material (calfskin?) of poor quality, not very white on either side, hair follicles very visible. Thickness of the text block (compressed) ca. 25 mm.

Collation (using the red lowercase roman numbering of the gatherings found, in i-vii only, on center in tail margins of first recto; in the book, the numbers have a dot at each side, at about mid-height): i-vii^{8}(= ff. 5–60) [a lacuna] [ix-x]^{8}(= ff. 61–76) [xi]? (f. 77 first leaf of a gathering with rest missing? f. 78 singleton brought in from another book? ff. 1–4?) — Catchwords at the end (center of tail margin of last verso) of gatherings *i* through *vii.*

Decoration: limited to basically calligraphic initials using blue and red, combined for the larger letters (in most of the book, one line of music plus one of text or somewhat less), one or the other for those of lesser importance, including versals; all have flourishings in one or both colors; the flourishing follows the overall shape of the letter). The letter *S* on 61r is larger (two lines of music/text), placed in a square-shaped field, and more ornate: the ground around the pen-drawn foliage of its flourishing is yellowish olive (poor-quality painted gold, or meant to imitate gold?); this was done also for the smaller initial *B* on 78r.

In wood boards (cypress?) ca. 15 mm thick, covered with dark brown leather attached to the inside of the boards by old (iron?) tacks with flat round heads ca. 9 mm in diameter. The covering is in poor shape, variously torn. Sewn over seven simple cords visible in rectangular channels (ca. 32 × 16 mm) on the inside of the boards, ca. 75 mm from spine edge. Remainder of headband seems to be of tawed hide, formerly decorated with, it seems, red string. The spine covering, a separate piece of leather reaching 120–140 mm onto the boards, is now for the most part torn off. — Worn-out sheets of thick paper laid in between the boards and the text block. — Originally eight simple bosses (iron or iron compound) on each board, evenly distributed in two vertical rows of four over the area beyond the spine cover; two preserved on the upper cover, five on the lower. Smaller bosses, partly preserved, protect(ed) the head and tail edges; traces of other metal protectors on fore edge. Traces of two back-to-front strap-and-pin fasteners. — Rectangular parchment tabs are attached to fore edge of leaves 28, 33, and 43.

Offsets on the inside of both covers (see contents). Over that of the upper cover, old LC ownership label with the call number: M 2147//XVI M1//case. On the lower cover, pasted over the offset, paper sheet (18th century?) with "Index rerum omnium que in hoc libro continentur," from "pag." 5 through 46; also fragments of a sheet with hand-drawn 5-line staves and unidentified music. — Leaf 35 is patched with fragment of a document dated *die xxvii Jan. MDCCX?* and signed: Cardinale Oliverio. — In tail margin of 5r, penciled: acc. no. 229302//[another hand:] 29537// 2708; on 5v: acc. 285750, M 2147//XVI M 1/ case.

Former owners: Thomas Wilson (1832–1902), curator of prehistoric anthropology at the Smithsonian Institution. — Purchased by the Library of Congress ca. 1925.

2° fo.: (leaf numbered "6"; under music:) est. *v.* *D*Eus cui — (leaf numbered "2," bound near end; under music:) se rere. Euouae.

Bibl.: *A Bibliography of the Catholic Church* (London, 1970), p. 192, no. NC 0216238 (reproducing LC Music Division's temporary cataloging entry 41 M 6948–2, which called the book a Gradual)

APPENDIX: THE RHYMED TRINITY OFFICE IN MS 42
(an overview)

1st Vespers:

a_1:	Sedenti super solium congratulans trisagium . . .	61r
a_2:	Sequemur per suspirium quod geritur per gaudium . . .	61v
a_3:	Si nosse ius haec gemina	62r
a_4:	Lux non decisa radium	62v
a_5:	Aeterno Patri gloria ex quo subsistunt omnia	63r
ad M:	O seraphim (ms.: "seraphyn") iocunditas	63v

Matins:

Invit.:	Regem trinum ac simplicem	64r
I Noct.:		
a_1:	Coelum terramque digitis qui tribus appendisti	64v
a_2:	De Deo Deus prodiens	65r
a_3:	Leventur cordis ostia (ms.: "hostia")	65r
R_1:	Confirmat hoc mysterium sacrarium Scripturae	65v
R_2:	Qui coeli fecit ambitum	66v
R_3:	Archam dat indaginem in opere finali	67r
II Noct.:		
a_4:	Excelso regi gloriae	68r
a_5:	O paucis quondam Trinitas Sion nota colonis	68v
a_6:	Descendit Dei filius ad pauperis honorem	68v

R_4:	Quid Abraham ad ostium (ms.: "hostium")	69r
R_5:	Aeterna mundi serie	70r
R_6:	Quis aquis vestem tribuit	71r
III Noct.:		
a_7:	A coeli terrae termino	72r
a_8:	Supernae lucis radius	72r
a_9:	Cor cantet vox et opera	72v
R_7:	Candor lucis per purum speculum	73r
R_8:	Sequamur testimonium	73v
R_9:	(no ninth responsory [replaced by *Te Deum?*])	

Lauds ("Ad Laudes et per horas"):

a_1:	Quam clara testimonia	75r
a_2:	Cum laudibus et iubilo	75v
a_3:	In te fons vitae sitiunt	76r
a_4:	Tres in fornacis medio	76v
a_5:	Laudet factura Dominum	77r
ad B:	Quam felix coeli civitas cui trina splendet claritas (the antiphon ends imperfectly, and the rest [antiphon to *Magnificat* of 2nd Vespers?] is wanting)	77v

NOTES

1. Musicians tend to refer to it as the "proper for the Dedication of the church." It is usually found, in Solesmes and other "graduals," among the commons.

2. Text in the *Enchiridion euchologicum fontium liturgicorum* (Rome, 1979), no. 3309. Occurs also in LC MSS 26, 35, 47.

3. Dominicans have retained the *Laetabundus*. N.B. Only this and the *Missus Gabriel de celis* are in the *Analecta hymnica*.

4. The volume is, unfortunately, missing from LC set and I haven't been able to compare the texts. — N.B. Major items of the office are indexed in our Index of Initia.

5. So Dreves in *AH* L, p. 594.

6. The leaves numbered 3 and 4 (at end) show some further peculiarities: e.g., an unflourished initial on 4r.

MS 43, f. 16r (actual size of the leaf: ca. 530 × 380 mm)

MS 43

("Biggers Gradual"; in Music Division)

DOMINICAN GRADUAL (part) preceded by Office of Thomas Aquinas

XVIth c.?

Spain. Parchment. 94 leaves (pastedown and leaves numbered 1 through 114 with gaps), ca. 530 × ca. 380 mm (bound volume: ca. 570 × ca. 400 mm) 6 long lines of music (5-line staves in red) with 6 text lines to a page.

(Music/text on the pastedown of upper cover: its recto not accessible; verso, partly obscured by ADDED pasted-on paper sheet with list of contents in Spanish, contains the beginning, with musical notation, of a rhythmical and rhymed antiphon to *Magnificat*:) . . . pago deitatis regie instar et ymago vi (interrupted by blank free endleaf)

ff. 1r–14r: (1r continues from the pastedown:) rtutis eximie culmen et indago . . . compago. *ca[nticum].* Magnificat. Secl'or[um] a[men]. (1v, large caption:) *In festo venerabilis co[n]fes//sor doctoris sa[n]cti th[om]e d' aq[ui]no // or. p[re]dicator[um]. ad v[espera]s.s[uper].p[salmo]s.an[tiphona]* [or *antiphonae?]. // (F)*1 + 1Elix tho//mas doctor ecclesie // lumen mundi splendor // ytalie cande[n]s virgo// flore mu[n]dicie bina (lacuna, ff. 2–5 wanting) (6r:) (*S*)1 + 1ydus de nube trahitur . . . *R.* (6v:) (*S*)1 + 1Colas thome paulus ingreditur . . . tande[m] per ra (lacuna, f. 7 wanting) (8r:) ti a mira fluxit et tumulo. . . . (8v:) Hic speciali gratia . . . *In laudibus antiphone.* (9r:) (*A*)1 + 1Dest dies leticie quo thomas doctor ynclitus . . . (9v:) . . . *a'.* Aurum sub terra tegitur . . . *ā.* (*A*)1 + 1lma (10r:) mater ecclesia . . . *āna.* (*P*)1 + 1ressus vi demo(10v:)nij cito liberatur . . . *a.* Tumor gule pellitur leprosus mu[n]datur . . . (11r:) . . . *hy[mnus].* (*L*)1 + 1Auda mater ecclesia thome felice[m] exitu[m] . . . (11v, 2nd stanza of the hymn, four lines of text without music:) *F*ossa noua tu[n]c suscipit . . . regni glorie.

(Further items, with music: 11v, *ad B:* Viror carnis flore mundicie . . . ; 12v, *ad M:* Militantis doctor ecclesie . . .; 13r, [*ad B of* the octave]: Collaudetur Christus rex glorie . . .; 13v, *ad B* [i.e., *ad M?,* of the octave]: O Thoma laus et gloria) — Full text of the (here unfortunately gutted) rhymed office is printed, with an English translation, in *The Hymns of the Dominican missal and breviary,* ed. A. Byrnes (St. Louis and London, Herder, 1943), p. 655–664 (the hymn *Lauda mater,* p. 594–596); it does not include the items which here precede f. 1v (from another office?) nor those on 13rv, for which see *AH* V, p. 232; in *AH* V, p. 230 sqq., also text of the whole rhymed office.[1]

14rv: . . . *Trac[tus].* (*Q*)1 + 1uasi stella matutina . . . *v.* Et quasi sol . . . (14v:) . . . *v.* Quasi archus refulge[n]s . . . quasi flos rosaru[m] in die (breaks off; f. 15 wanting)

For whatever reason, the last antiphon of Thomas' office is here followed by this item used, presumably, in the Mass on the saint's day (or on the eighth day?).

16r–114v: (16r, caption in head margin:) *Dn̄ica [erased: p̄ma] post trinitatem.* (*D*)2 + 2Omine in tua misericordia speraui . . . (19v:) . . . *Dn̄ica* [another hand, black ink, over erased *"ij"*:] infra oct' corporis christi, [orig.:]*post tr[i]nit[atem]. Off[icium].* (*F*)1 + 1Actus est domin[us] (breaks off owing to lost leaves) (23r): . . . *Dominica* [*"iij"* changed by erasure to:] *j. Off* (*R*)1 + 1Espice in me . . . . . . (series of Sundays after Trinity ends on 111v:) . . . *xxi* [achieved by erasures from *"xxiij"*] (*D*)1 + 1Jcit dominus . . . (this Sunday's proper ends imperfectly after the Offertory, with caption at end of last line of 114v:) *Com.*

A major section of Dominican *Graduale:* the "proper of the seasons" or "temporale" of summer. Counting Sundays from Trinity rather than from Pentecost was a Dominican tradition; however, in 1551, as part of a major revision of the order's liturgy ("revision of Salamanca"), a new system was introduced which spoke of Sundays "after the octave of Trinity";[2] this required reducing all numbers by one. In the present book, the number originally written is in each case reduced by two, suggesting that the count originally reflected the non-Dominican (i.e., Roman) system. — The proper of the first Sunday of the series (*Domine in tua misericordia,* 16r sqq.), here introduced by an extra large (and beautifully executed) initial, in reality lost its purpose by introduction (for the whole Roman rite, in 1334) of the feast of Trinity and was then used on a close weekday. — In the series which follows, rather much material is missing, including the openings of the Sundays which the corrector would have numbered *V (Omnes gentes), VII (Ecce Deus), IX (Deus in loco sancto),* and *X (Deus in adiutorium),* owing to loss of ff. 18, 20–22, 31, 48–49, 55, 57, 58, 61–63, 65, 90, 92, and of one or more leaves after 114. — An unnumbered leaf (it has on verso near gutter "102" but seems to have nothing to do with f. 102 of the regularly numbered sequence here), blank on recto, is inserted between ff. 42 and 43; on verso, following a fragment uniform with the rest of the book, an unskilled hand has entered four lines of *Te dece[t] hymnus;* another musical version of the alleluiatic verse is on the adjacent 42v and 43r. — For the Ember days of September, user of the gradual is told (on 90v): *"re[quire]* [over erasure, black:] in libro D. a' fol. 68." — On 100r, in fore-edge margin, a note by later hand: "no buelba" (meaning, not to go back to the *"R"* verse), confirming the Spanish past of the book. —Throughout, the introits are captioned *"Officium";* the term (here variously abbreviated) was part of liturgical terminology of the Order of Preachers until our time.

* * *

The foliation is in black ink, large, in upper right corners of rectos; the early modern arabic numerals tend to imitate printed forms, with serifs. — Written area ca. 437 (base of last line's minims to top line of first music staff) × ca. 285 mm. — Ruled in plummet (?) for vertical boundaries (double lines, head edge to tail edge) and for the text lines. — Script is the *rotunda* common in large-size Spanish choir books, with feet mostly *praescissi* (incl. that of the primary stroke of *a* and the vertical of one of the two types of *d*; not that of *l,* which has a hook, nor *r,* shaped at the base like a *c*); in this book, the tops of ascenders, also that of *i* have a very small left serif. Minims ca. 9 mm high. The hairline of upper quasi-lobe of *a* turns in (without, however, curling); in *b* and *q*, the vertical passes directly into the round lobe, not so in the straight *d* and in *p*. Letter *g* is of the gothic type (vertical stroke on right continuous, only moderately curved); the curved stroke of *h* becomes a hairline and goes below the base, ending below the vertical. Besides the standard (similar to ours) form of final *s,* occasionally a compressed form with the lower half reduced to a slightly curving hairline. Undotted *y* (except on the pastedown before f. 1, in "ymago," where it has a mark similar to sharp accent) with hairline section below the base often elegantly curved. A narrow triangular mark inclined as an *accent aigu* is placed over all *i*'s. The curves of *oc* and similar combinations melt. Old-style characters for "-rum," "-us"(elevated), final "-m"; no tironian *et.* — Music on red 5-line staves (ca. 47 mm from 1st to 5th line, between staves ca. 27 mm). Square notes ca. 9 × 9 mm; lozenges and notes connected to a slightly vaulted wide line with vertical ends occur. *Do* or *fa* clefs, the latter formed by three narrow lozenges; both clefs together on ff. 1–14 (in the Office of Thomas). *Custos* of the nearly vertical check mark kind, with the wide section slightly *U*-shaped. — Good black and red inks. — Writing material is calfskin, white on one side, yellow on the other; good quality. Thickness of text block (compressed) ca. 25 mm.

Collation: 1^8(= pastedown through missing f. [7]; $1_{3-6,8}$ = ff. 2–5 and 7 wanting) 2^8(2_8 = f. 15 wanting) 3^8($3_{3,5-7}$ = ff. 18 and 20–22 wanting) 4^8(4_8 = f. 31 wanting) 5^8 6^{8+1}(= ff. 40–47; unnumbered singleton between 6_3 and 6_4) 7^8 ($7_{1,2,8}$ = ff. 48, 49, and 55 wanting) 8^8($8_{2,3,6-8}$ = ff. 57, 58, and 61–63 wanting) 9^8(9_2 = f. 65 wanting) $10–11^8$(= ff. 72–87) 12^8($12_{3,5}$ = ff. 90,92 wanting) 13^8 $14^{4?}$(= ff. 104–107) $15^{8?}$(15_8 = f. [115] wanting). — Music/text losses with the missing leaves. Catchwords on all preserved last versos: on 23v, 39v, 47v, 71v, 79v, 87v, 95v, 103v, 107v; all except those on 23v and 107v are written vertically (base toward gutter).

Decoration consists of generally functional calligraphic initials, for the most part one line of music plus one of text in height; the largest, a *D* at the beginning of the Sunday series (16r) extends over two music/text lines, its flourishing forming a roughly square field 143 × 140 mm; the red and purplish blue (divided) letter is filled and surrounded by patterns expertly drawn in both colors of ink, and further (elegantly curving) flourishes extend up and down in the inner margin (slightly cropped at top). Other primary initials (those beginning the material for a Sunday) are smaller but mostly also two-color (red and purplish blue), in rectangular fields ca. 70 mm high formed by flourishings. Penwork inside the letter *O* on f. 98r differs in general style (a rather straight-line geometrical pattern) from the rest. (In the Aquinas Office on ff. 1–14, as far as preserved, only the *F* on 1v is in two colors.)

Sewn over 4 bands (at present not accessible). Unbeveled boards ca. 12 mm thick, covered with spottedly brown (distressed calf?) leather. — Brass studs (ca. 10 mm diameter) are arranged in a circle of ca. 130 mm diameter around one in center of each board, also in quarter circles in the corners. Lower edge is protected by strips of iron sheet. — Remains of two front-to-back clasps or straps (catches of non-iron metal on lower cover).

The pastedown of upper cover (a leaf which originally was part of the first gathering, cf. contents and collation) is attached to the board by a number of (old) tacks (also pasted?). It has pasted over its upper part a paper leaf 292 × 201 mm with a listing of contents of the book in Spanish, with "pagina" numbers mostly unfilled. Also on the pastedown, a marginal note in modern blue ink: *115 Hojas a ME//M G A E//L S S S//E S S S* [= ?]. (Pastedown of lower cover is blank parchment.) — On spine, remainders of a paper label, no text preserved.

Former owners: Willard B. Biggers, of Florida, who donated the codex to the Library in summer 1985.

2° fo. (numbered "6"!): *S*ydus de nube [under a red music staff]

Bibl.: none known.

The codex bears some similarities to LC MS 38 which probably, too, is Dominican.

NOTES

1. This couldn't be verified; volume missing.
2. Cf. Bonniwell, *Hist. Dom. lit.*, p. 268.

bsecro te dña sancta
maria mater dei pi

Books of Hours

(MSS 44–64)

The most common type of prayer book among lay Christians of Western Europe at the end of the Middle Ages was the book of hours. The case can be made for treating books of hours as liturgical material; it seemed more useful, however, to make the twenty-one manuscript *Horae* in the Library's collections a separate group.

The first sixteen books described (MSS 44–59) are principally in Latin; they are arranged by their "use," i.e., by the particular tradition which they follow in the text of the Hours of the Virgin and perhaps also in the Office of the Dead. Those which follow the use of Rome precede the rest. The MSS 60–63 are books of hours in Netherlandish, probably all based on the 14th-century translation made by the leading spirit of the *Devotio moderna*, Geert Grote. The multilayered MS 64 is placed last because of its irregular character and inserted printed matter.

Their similarities notwithstanding, books of hours vary in text and arrangement. As their worldwide census (done through catalogs such as this one) becomes more complete and the various pieces of information are more systematically sorted, the slowly emerging map and chronology of their evolution makes it possible to place and date the less standardized manuscripts; the books of hours become "yardsticks" for explorers of art and bookmaking history. Table C, which compares the Hours of the Virgin in the books of hours held by the Library of Congress, is meant as a contribution to this effort.

For persons unacquainted with the basic structure and contents of these books, probably the best introduction is that given by R. G. Calkins in his *Illuminated books of the Middle Ages* (1983), p. 243 sqq. and, importantly, Appendices 14 and 15 (p. 308–312; N.B. Psalm numbers given there are those of the Vulgate Bible). Fairly conveniently arranged texts of the Hours of the Virgin and of the Office for the Dead (in their eventually fixed Roman-use form, captioned "Officium parvum Beatae Mariae Virginis" and "Officium defunctorum") can be found in any copy of the pre-Vatican II *Breviarium Romanum* (for the old version of the Psalm texts, it should be an edition predating 1943).

As concerns their art content, the books in this group vary greatly; some have been over the centuries robbed of their illustrations, one (MS 50) is a work of art without containing any, some are good or very good workshop products (MSS 44, 45), and there are several gems: the MSS 46 and 52 in particular.

◀ XXV **MS 57, f. 18r** Thought to be from the workshop of Jehan Bourdichon. (Actual size of the leaf: 19.7 × 14 cm)

MS 44

(Faye and Bond 18)

BOOK OF HOURS (use of Rome)

XVth c., 2nd half

Written in Paris? Parchment. 139 leaves, ca. 147 × ca. 99 mm (bound volume: 151 × ca. 105 mm) 1 column. 20 lines (calendar, 33 lines)

(ff. 1r–6v, calendar; 7r–12r, Gospel readings; 12r–15v, *Obsecro te*; 15v–17v, *O Intemerata*; 18r–76r, Hours of Our Lady; 77r–90v, Penitential Psalms, with Litany; 91r–92v, Short Hours of the Cross; 93r–95v, Short Hours of the Holy Spirit; 96r–133v, Office for the Dead; 133v–139v, suffrages)

ff. 1r–6v: (KL)[2] *januier a xxxi iour* . . . saint siluestre.

Full calendar in French; primary feasts in gold, other days alternately red or blue; one month per page. — The saints, a somewhat curious collection, are those found in other books of hours commercially produced in 15th-century Paris; cf. Perdrizet, *Calendrier parisien* (1933), p. 16, etc. Different (from Perdrizet's Friedel Hours): May 25, *Saint eloy*, in gold; at end of July, no St. Anne but Panthaleon, Abdon, Germain, Firmin; Oct. 12, Cyprien; Nov. 11, Martin; Dec. 30, David.

7r–12r: (7r, large ill.: John the Evangelist) (I)[3]n principio erat . . . sequentib[us] signis Deo gratias.

The usual four passages from the Gospels: John I,1–14 (uncaptioned); Luke I,26b–38a; Matthew II,1–12; Mark XVI,14–20. Without the prayer sometimes included (in books of hours) after the reading from John. — Luke, Matthew, and Mark are each portrayed in a small illustration (not part of an initial).

12r–15v: (beginning in 6th line of 12r:) *Oratio deuota ad Virgine[m] maria[m]* (O)Bsecro te domina . . . mater dei et mi[sericordi]e : Amen.

Leroquais, *LH* II, p. 346 sq. In masculine form. — At the beginning, small illustration (not part of initial): Mary standing, with the Child on right arm (actually, hand) and in her left hand, an apple; Mary dressed in blue, Jesus in gold.

15v–17v: (beginning in 5th line of 15v:) *Ad Virginem maria[m] or[aci]o.* (O) intemerata et in eternum benedicta . . . (16r:) . . . O ioha[n]nes . . . (17v:) . . . in secula seculorum. Amen. (last 11 lines of 17v empty)

The variant addressing Mary and John; cf. Wilmart, *Aut. spir.*, p. 488–490. — Small illustration with the beginning: Pietà (Mary in blue).

18r–76r: (following f. 17, one leaf missing; text begins imperfectly in the Invitatory:) non repellet dominus plebem suam . . . (24v:) *Die martis et veneris dicuntur psalmi seque[n]tes* . . . (27v:) *Die mercurij et sabbati* . . . (following f. 32, leaf missing; the Lauds begin imperfectly, 33r:) laudabunt te. Sic benedicam te . . . (41v, large illustration: Nativity; with the beginning of the Prime) (46r, large illus.: the Shepherds; begins the Terce) (50r, large illus.: Magi; begins Sext) (54r, large illus.: Presentation in the Temple; begins the None) (58r, large illus.: Flight to Egypt; with the beginning of the Vespers) (65r, with the beginning of Compline, large illus.: Coronation of Mary[1]; see plate XVI, p. xxx) (69v:) *Incipit officium beate marie de aduentu* . . . (74v:) *Notandum est quod a prima die post oct. natiuitatis* . . . (75v:) . . . *Sciendum est quod ab octavis pasche usque ad ascensionem* . . . (76r:) . . . ora pro nobis deum alleluja. (76v blank, ruled)

The Hours (= Little Office) of Our Lady, use of Rome. The apportionment of the psalms of the Matins to various days of the week and the seasonal variations reflect a high state of development, quite similar to that fixed in the Roman Breviary of 1568. — The missing leaves almost certainly contained large illustrations: the Annunciation with the beginning of the Matins (the leaf missing between the present ff. 17 and 18) and the Visitation for the beginning of the Lauds (between the present ff. 32 and 33).

77r–90v: (77r, large illustration: David praying; with opening words:) (D)[4]Omine ne i[n] furore tuo . . . (90v:) . . . consequantur. Qui viuis et regnas deus. Per omnia secula seculorum. Amen. (last 8 lines empty)

The Penitential Psalms (Pss. VI, XXXII, XXXVIII, LI, CII, CXXX, CXLIII), followed (f. 87v sqq.) by the Litany of Saints. — The litany is conventional except for omission of St. Matthew (no doubt by error) and inclusion, among confessors, of St. Guillaume (Guillerme), patron of the university of Paris; and, among virgins, of St. Valérie (honored at Notre Dame) and St. Radegonde (once queen of France but not particularly honored in Paris).[2]

91r–92v: (following f. 90, a leaf missing; text begins imperfectly near the end of the Lauds:) animam meam nunc . . . (office ends on 92v:) . . . sis michi solatium in mortis agone. ā Adoramus te x̄p̄e. *Oratio*. Domine ihū xp̄e. (last 7 lines empty)

The rhythmical, psalmless Short Hours of the Cross, based on the hymn (or *pium dictamen*) *Patris sapienta veritas divina* (Walther, *Initia* 13840; text *AH* XXX, p. 32); the hymn is divided among the several "hours."[3] — The leaf missing between the present ff. 90 and 91 contained, very probably, a large illustration of the Crucifixion, along with the text, through the "inter iudicium tuum" in the formal prayer preceding the Prime.

93r–95v: (93r, large illustration: Pentecost) (D)[4]Omine labia mea . . . (95v:) . . . Vt viuamus iugit[er] celi regione. Amen. ā Ve[n]i//(O)mnipotens. (last 12 lines empty)

The rhythmical, psalmless Short Hours of the Holy Spirit, based on the hymn *Nobis Sancti Spiritus gratia sit data* (Walther, *Initia* 21189; text *AH* XXX, p. 15); as in the Short Hours of the Cross, the hymn is distributed among the several "hours" and complemented by quasi-liturgical openings, antiphons, and formal prayers.[4]

96r–133v: (96r, large illustration: Job and his friends) ā. Placebo *ps̄*. (D)[4]Ilexi quoniam exaudiet . . . (133v:) . . . saluator mundi. Qui viuis et regnas Deus. Per omnia.

The Office for the Dead.[5] Responsories same as those found in the 16th-century Roman Breviary.

133v–139v: (133v, 8th line:) *De sancto michaele. antȳ.* (S)ancte . . . . . . (139v:) . . . peruenire valeamus Per xp̄m.

Saints' suffrages, each accompanied by a small illustration (portrait, not part of an initial) of the saint invoked: ff. 133v–134r, Michael (Sancte Michael Christi Archangele defende . . .); 134r–v, John the Baptist (Inter natos mulierum . . .); 135r–v, John the Evangelist (Sancte Johannes Apostole et electe . . .); 136r–v, Peter and Paul (Gloriosi principes terrae . . .); 136v–137v, Sebastian (O quam mira refulsit gratia . . .); 138v–139r, Katharina (Virgo sancta Catherina Greciae gemma . . .); 139r–v, Barbara (O virgo cuius magna devotio . . .)

* * *

Foliated in modern pencil. Preceding f. 1, one free endleaf added in rebinding and one original blank leaf (with traces of ruling); at end, following f. 139, one original blank leaf (with traces of ruling) and one free endleaf added in rebinding. — Written area ca. 83 × 50 mm. Fully ruled in faint red ink. — Written in a not very regular *lettre bâtarde*, with some passages squeezed into inadequate space (e.g., the antiphon on 39v–40r). Weak, now rather faded ink of brownish cast. — The script of the calendar (red, blue, gold) is much smaller than that of the main text. Rubrics all blue. — Thin parchment of good quality, some leaves crinkled; thickness ca. 11.5 mm per 100 leaves.

Collation: impracticable owing to tight rebinding.

Decoration: Preserved are ten (out of thirteen? cf. contents) large (77–81 × 49–51 mm) illustrations, in windowlike arched frames decorated with an engrailed line[6] and, sometimes, with various architectural elements. Below each illustration, four to five lines of text with a 3–4 line initial, the whole surrounded by all-around framed borders[7] with mostly floral and foliate forms on grounds variously divided into golden and void fields; in three cases near the end of the book the ground is entirely (painted) gold. — Thirteen small (ca. 38 × 28 mm) rectangular miniatures are in the text: five of them (ff. 8v, St. Luke; 9v, Matthew; 112r, Mark; 12r, Mary with the Child; 15v, Pietà) are on pages with three-side borders (top, bottom, outer margin); the rest (133v, Michael; 134r, John the Baptist; 135r, John the Evangelist; 136r, Peter and Paul; 136v, Sebastian; 138r, Anthony [the Hermit]; 138v, Katharine; 139r, Barbara) are complemented only by vertical borders in the outer margins, 21–23 mm wide and as high as the written area; such borders are also on ca. half of all pages of the book. — With the exception of those associated with the large illustrations (see above) the borders use primarily void background and are composed of delicately drawn single-line vines with burnished-gold ivy leaves and bezants intermixed with foliage and vine stems done in blue and painted gold, berries and flowers in red, pink, blue, or white with very light green or painted gold leaves, also birds and little animals, mostly imaginary.[8] A favorite figure is a blue-bodied peacock (ff. 1r, 1v, 65r, 65v, 117v). Often the border on recto is repeated as a mirror image on verso.

The ten (mostly 4-line) initials found on the pages with large illustrations and initiating major text items are blue-with-white on laid gold grounds; the letters *KL* of the calendar headings and the 2-line lombards and 1-line versals throughout the book are alternately gold on void flourished with pen in blue or bluish-black ink, or blue on background flourished in red, with some of the flourishings projecting into the margins. Some important one-line initial letters are modeled gold on gold-flourished red or brownish black grounds. — Line fillers gold and blue, done free-hand by brush; many consist of a slanting gold line decorated by a comb-like set of short vertical blue strokes (same pattern in blue and red on some pages, e.g., 90v, 95v).

Binding: dark brown crushed levant, blind-tooled, by Rivière (& Son, [London]).[9] Gilt edges. On spine, impressed in gold: HORAE BEATAE MARIAE//VIRGINIS// SECUNDUM USUM//ROMANUM//SAEC. XV.[10]

On the inside of upper cover, LC label with penciled "MS. 18." — Purchased in 1911 from Dr. Vladimir G. Simkhovitch (LC order no. 175338; accession no. of LC Manuscript Division 1241/3).

2° fo.: (KL)[2] *Mars a xxxj iour*

De Ricci, *Census*, v. 1 (1935), p. 189, no. 31; Faye and Bond (1962), p. 117, no. 18.

The rather exquisite Horae were probably produced in a commercial workshop in Paris. The calendar, similar to that of books made in the second quarter of the (15th) century, was merely uncritically copied from an earlier *exemplar.*[11]

NOTES

1. Mary, in blue as always in this book, kneels in front of God the Father's throne.
2. The litany names altogether, after the usual series (Mary, angels, apostles, etc., through Innocents), 8 martyrs, 8 confessors (the last one is Fiacre), 9 women.
3. Text of basically the complete office is printed in the *Horae Eboracenses* (1920; The Publications of the Surtees Society, v. CXXXII) on p. 46, 49, 51, 54, 56, 58, and 61–62; as in some 15th-century manuscripts and 16th-century prints, the editor's text has the office intertwined with the Hours of the Virgin, hence without formal opening words of its own in each hour. We haven't met this arrangement in any of the LC books of hours (none of which is York or Sarum use).
4. The *Analecta hymnica* give the text of the hymn; I am not aware of any published text of the complete office.
5. = Officium defunctorum = "Vigiliae mortuorum."
6. Black outline gives this shape to the upper edge of framing gold band.
7. In the upper margin, the border is interrupted and reduced by the arched frame of the illustration. — The borders are outlined in thin penline, mostly black, or red similar to that of the ruling. — The border on f. 65r is of a different style, described further on in this paragraph.
8. The all-around border on 65r, with the Coronation of Mary, is done in this style.
9. The binding firm's name is stamped in gold (in very small type) on the lower edge of inside of upper cover.
10. The book is now kept in a protective case covered with charcoal-grey linen.
11. A book of hours, almost entirely independent of the liturgical year in general and of the sanctoral cycle in particular, didn't really require a calendar, even though by tradition it almost always had one; it didn't much matter if the calendar was out of date.

(ff. 1v–13r, calendar; 14–22, series of illustrations; 23r–120v, Hours of Our Lady; 121r–150v, Penitential Psalms, with Litany; 151r–163r, Short Hours of the Cross)

MS 45

(Hours Edith G. Rosenwald)

BOOK OF HOURS ca. 1340–1360

Written and decorated in Paris[1] Parchment. 163 leaves, 66 × ca. 48 mm (bound volume: ca. 69 × ca. 55 mm) 1 column. 10 lines (in the calendar, 17 lines)

ff. 1v–13r: (KL)[3] Januarius hī dies//xxxi . . .

Calendar, in Latin; in black and red; each month covers the verso of one leaf and the recto of the next (and thus can be surveyed at one glance). Of the altogether 139 entries, 58 are in red; among these: *Vincencii* (Jan. 22), *Amandi* (Feb. 6), "*Resurrectio D[omi]ni*" (March 27), *Basilii* (June 14), *Eligii* (June 25), *[Translatio] Thome Apostoli* (July 3), *Egidii abb.* (Sept. 1), *Remigii* ("et aliorum"; Oct 1), *Dyonisii* (Oct. 9), *Donatiani epī.* (Oct. 14), *Eligij epī.* (Dec. 1), *Nichasij ep.* (Dec. 14); N.B. no feast of Visitation on July 2. — Interesting among entries in black: Gudule (Jan. 8), Baltidis [i.e., Batildis] regine (Jan. 30), Milburge (Feb. 23), Dauid confessoris (March 1), Walrici epī. (Apr. 1), Brandani mr̄is (May 17), Bertini (Sept. 5), Lamberti (Sept. 17), Leonardi abb. (Nov. 6), Lazari mr̄s. (Dec. 17). — French, Flemish, and English or Welsh saints are represented. The red-letter days point to Tournai and/or to Bruges (Bruges was within the bounds of the diocese of Tournai). — In tail margins of the calendar, miniatures depict scenes of daily life and signs of the zodiac.[2]

(13v blank, not ruled)

14r–22v: (prefatory miniatures)[3]

A series of nine full-page illustrations, all on rectos (the versos are blank). They represent: 14r: Madonna enthroned, with Child in lap; 15r: John the Baptist; 16r: St. James the Great; 17r: Saint Christopher (see plate XVII, p. xxxi); 18r: St. Anthony (the Hermit); 19r: Saint Catherine; 20r: Saint Barbara; 21r: St. Geneviève; 22r: St. Margaret. — The appearance of St. Geneviève speaks in favor of Parisian manufacture of the book.

MS 45

23r–120v: (on 23r, large illustration: Mary's birth; with 2 lines of text:) (D)[2]Omine labia mea aperies : Et . . .

Hours of Our Lady, use of Rome.[4] — Each hour is introduced by a rubric written in the last line of page immediately preceding. The beginning of each hour (except the Lauds, 45r sqq. and the None, 91r sqq.) is signaled by a large illustration over two opening lines of the text: the Prime opens with the Annunciation (60v); Terce has the Visitation (77v); Sext, the Nativity (84r); Vespers, the Presentation in the Temple (97v); Compline, the Flight to Egypt (111v). — A gathering containing a large segment of the Lauds has been misbound into the Prime: the present leaves 63–70 would properly belong between the present ff. 46 and 47. — Leaf 91, which contains the beginning of the None, without illustration, appears to be a cancel, written by a person spelling *pulchra* where the original scribe would use *pulcra* (cf. 95r), also attempting to stretch very few words of text (a problem caused by the absence of illustration) over two pages.[5]

121r–150v: (On 121r, large illustration:[6] Christ sitting on the rainbow, displaying his wounds; three persons rising from their tombs in the lower part of the page, under the two lines of text:) (D)[2]Omine ne in furore tuo ar(121v:)guas me . . .

The Penitential Psalms,[7] with (145r sqq.) the Litany. The list of individual saints invoked in the litany comprises, after the apostles, etc., 11 martyrs, 8 confessors, and 11 women. — The only saint included here which was not found in standard Roman use is St. Cornelius (among the martyrs, after Sixtus and before Cyprian). A strong geographic concentration of the cult of this saint developed in the late Middle Ages in West Flanders.[8]

151r–163r: (On 151r, large illustration: the Kiss of Judas; with two lines of text:) (D)[2]Omine labia mea . . . (151v:) . . . (P)[2+]Atris sapiencia ueritas diuina . . . (ends on 163r:) . . . Deo gratias

The Short Hours of the Cross (psalmless and based on the hymn *Patris sapientia* which is divided among the several "hours").[9] — Each "hour" is introduced by a large illustration: 153v (Prime), Jesus before the High Priest; 155r (Terce), Flagellation; 156v (Sext), Crucifixion (i.e., Jesus on the Cross, with Mary and John standing by); 158r (None), Removal from the Cross; 159v (Vespers), the Entombment; 161r (Compline), the Resurrection.

(163v blank, ruled)

* * *

Foliated[10] in modern pencil. One free endleaf precedes f. 1, one follows f. 163. — Written area ca. 35 × 23.5 mm. — Fully ruled in faint red ink; no pricking preserved. — The script is a fully quadrate *littera textualis formata* in brownish black ink of very good quality. — Rubrics bright red. — Thin, high quality (but somewhat overly translucent) writing material.[11]

Collation appears impracticable.

Decoration: twenty-three (14 full-page and 9 three-quarter page) miniatures executed, as is other decoration, with great professional skill; cf. contents.[12] — Borders and initials combine laid gold and blue or magenta colors (enriched with white penlines); the 2-line letters are in color and on (laid) gold ground (outlined in black) and infilled with leafy vines; 1-line versals (used, e.g., for each verse of every psalm) are laid gold in a blue or magenta field, the letter infilled with the alternate color. Borders, which partly issue from the major initials, are in the mid-14th century Parisian style, with leafy vines on the void white of the page as primary element, enriched further by occasional realistic birds. — Of the calendar miniatures, the first one (on 1v, in tail margin) is probably not original;[13] the rest are in part charmingly humorous.

Binding: sewn over 3 raised bands. Early 19th- (or late 18th-) century bluish black morocco covers, sparingly gold-tooled with double framing lines, small 6-petal rosettes in corners, and a plant ornament in center; inside dentelles. Gilt edges. — On spine, in gilt: LIVRE D'HEURES.

On inside of upper cover, inscribed in black ink: No 23. On recto of free endpaper, in fainter and different ink: *Ce livre a appartenu à la Reine Jeanne de Naples.* On f. 1r, otherwise blank, in modern (19th-century) longhand, black ink: *Horarium// lat.//sec. XV.//Neapoli adlatum.*

The book is provided with a case (143 × ca. 70 × ca. 32 mm) covered in dark brown thinned calfskin and lined with brown velveteen; on the case, lettered in gold: *To EDITH From LESSING//August 9, 1951.*[14] The case contains, in one compartment, a brownish black leather-covered slipcase for the book, with gold-stamped: LIVRE D'HEURES//DE LA REINE //JEANNE DE NAPLES; in another compartment, a round magnifying glass ca. 40 mm in diameter, with gold rim and a folding golden handle. A pocket holds folded sheet titled "Descriptive label"; also a description in French.

Former owners: (perhaps:) Jeanne (Giovanna) II, Queen of Naples (b. 1371, d. 1435) — (prior to 1828:) Prince Mikhail Aleksandrovich Golitsyn (often "Galitzin"; b. 1804, d. 1860) — (prior to 1864:) Marie-Caroline de Bourbon-Sicile, duchesse de Berry, 1798–1870. — (prior to 1882:) E. M. Bancel. — Charles Isaac Elton, 1839–1900. — Baron Jean Vitta. — A. Besombes. (Bought from the Besombes collection by L. J. Rosenwald in 1951 through H. P. Kraus; donated by Edith G. Rosenwald to the Library in 1981)

2° fo.: (1st line empty except for red *A* [the Sunday letter]; 2nd line:) xviij b (kl) Marcelli pape

Bibl.: (In catalog of the 1864 Duchess de Berry sale, no. 17) — *Catalogue des livres précieux et des manuscrits avec miniatures composant la bibliothèque de M. E. M. Bancel* (Paris, A. Labitte, 1882), no. 8. — "A fourteenth century book of hours in the collection of Mrs. Lessing Rosenwald," by David S. Stevens Schaff: *MANUSCRIPTA* 21 (1977), p. 154–166. — *Library of Congress acquisitions: Rare Book and Special Collections Division, 1981–1982* (Washington, LC, 1984), p. 7 (with color reproductions of ff. 21r, 60v, 77v, 111v on p. 6). — *In retrospect : a catalogue of 100 outstanding manuscripts sold in the last four decades by H. P. Kraus* (New York, Kraus, 1978), no. 41 (with black-and-white reproductions of ff. 14r, 23r, 84r, 161r on p. 121)

Books of hours of this miniature size are rare. Ladies are said to have carried such attached to their belt in the second half of the 14th century; but few have been preserved.

NOTES

1. For use, it seems, in West Flanders or the British Isles.
2. The first leaf, including the page which contains the first half of January, is probably a later imitation (done before the ca. 1800 rebinding? Cf. also note 5 concerning leaf 91). — The name of St. Gudula is written oddly, as if "Gudisse."
3. The miniatures are discussed, along with the other fourteen found at key points of the book, in D. S. Stevens Schaff's article in *MANUSCRIPTA* 21 (1977), p. 154–166 (cf. Bibl.).
4. For textual details, standard and nonstandard, see table C.
5. The original leaf may be presumed to have contained the scene with the shepherds.
6. The scene may be interpreted as the Resurrection, as the "Harrowing of Hell," or as the Second Coming.
7. = Psalms VI, XXXII, XXXVIII, LI, CII, CXXX, CXLIII; in the traditional (liturgical) arrangement, they are followed by the Litany of Saints.
8. Cf. M. Zender, *Räume und Schichten mittelalterlicher Heiligenverehrung* (1973) (especially the map on p. 151).
9. See notes to ff. 91–92 in contents of MS 44.
10. Also paged (in modern pencil): page numbers on center in tail margins (through 325).
11. Thickness, measured by rather primitive methods, ca. 6.13 mm per 100 leaves (whole text block ca. 10 mm).

12. For discussion of the miniatures see D. S. Stevens Schaff's article cited in note 3. — The whole style of the decoration is "in the Jean Pucelle tradition, reminiscent of the first Master of the Breviary of Charles V" (H. P. Kraus in *In retrospect*, p. 120).

13. See note 2. It was the wonderment of an anonymous visitor to the Library concerning the almost modern dress of people depicted on f. 1v that first drew attention to this page.

14. The book was a birthday gift from Lessing J. Rosenwald to his wife.

(ff. 1v–13r, calendar; 15r, story of Creation; 17r–18v, *Salve sancta facies*; 20r–25v, Short Hours of the Cross; 27r–31v, Short Hours of the Holy Spirit; 33r–38v, Mass in honor of Mary; 38v–43v, Gospel readings; 45r–121r, Hours of Our Lady; 123r–143v, Penitential Psalms with Litany; 145r–186r, Office for the Dead; 188r–191v, *Obsecro te*; 192r–194v, *O Intemerata*; 195r–205v, suffrages; 206r–209v, Athanasian Creed)

MS 46

(Warburg Hours)

BOOK OF HOURS ca. 1500

Written/decorated in Flanders. Parchment. 213 leaves, 105 × ca. 78 mm (bound volume: 113 × ca. 80 mm) 1 column. 16 lines.

(1r blank) 1v–13r: (KL)[2] Januarius xxxi. . . . Silues-tri pape

Calendar, in black and red; 137 entries. — Among red-letter days: *Georgii; Translatio Thomae; Benedicti Abb.* (on July 11); *Jacobi et Xr[ist]ofori; Luce euang[e]liste; Nichasii.* — Among names in black: Pontiani (Jan. 15), Aldegundis, Amandi, Eleutherii (bp. of Tournai, Feb. 20), Petri Diaconi (Apr. 17), Syri (May 16), Desiderii (May 23), Willibaldi (July 7), Ludovici (regis, Aug. 25), Bertini, Huberti, Leonardi, Lacarii (so spelled; on Dec. 17, as in Tournai)

(14r blank; 14v, full-page illustration: Adam and Eve)

15r: *Prima die* (D)[2]iuisit deus lucem ad *[sic]* tenebras . . . ab o[mn]i op[er]e q[uo]d patra[ra]t.

Free summarization, by days, of the biblical Creation report.

(15v, 16r blank; 16v, full-page illustration: Salvator mundi[1]; see plate XVIII, p. xxxii)

17r–18v: *Salutatio ad s[an]c[t]am ueronica[m].* (S)[5]alue sancta facies . . . secula seculorum. Amen.

The suffrage (hymn, verse, formal prayer) is really centered on Jesus rather than on Veronica. (Hymn: Walther, *Initia* 17153; printed version Leroquais, *LH* II, p. 349 sq.)

(18v, 19r blank; 19v, full-page illustration: Crucifixion)

20r–25v: *Incipit officium s[an]c[t]e Crucis* (D)[5]omine labia . . . sic labori consonans consors sim corone Amen.

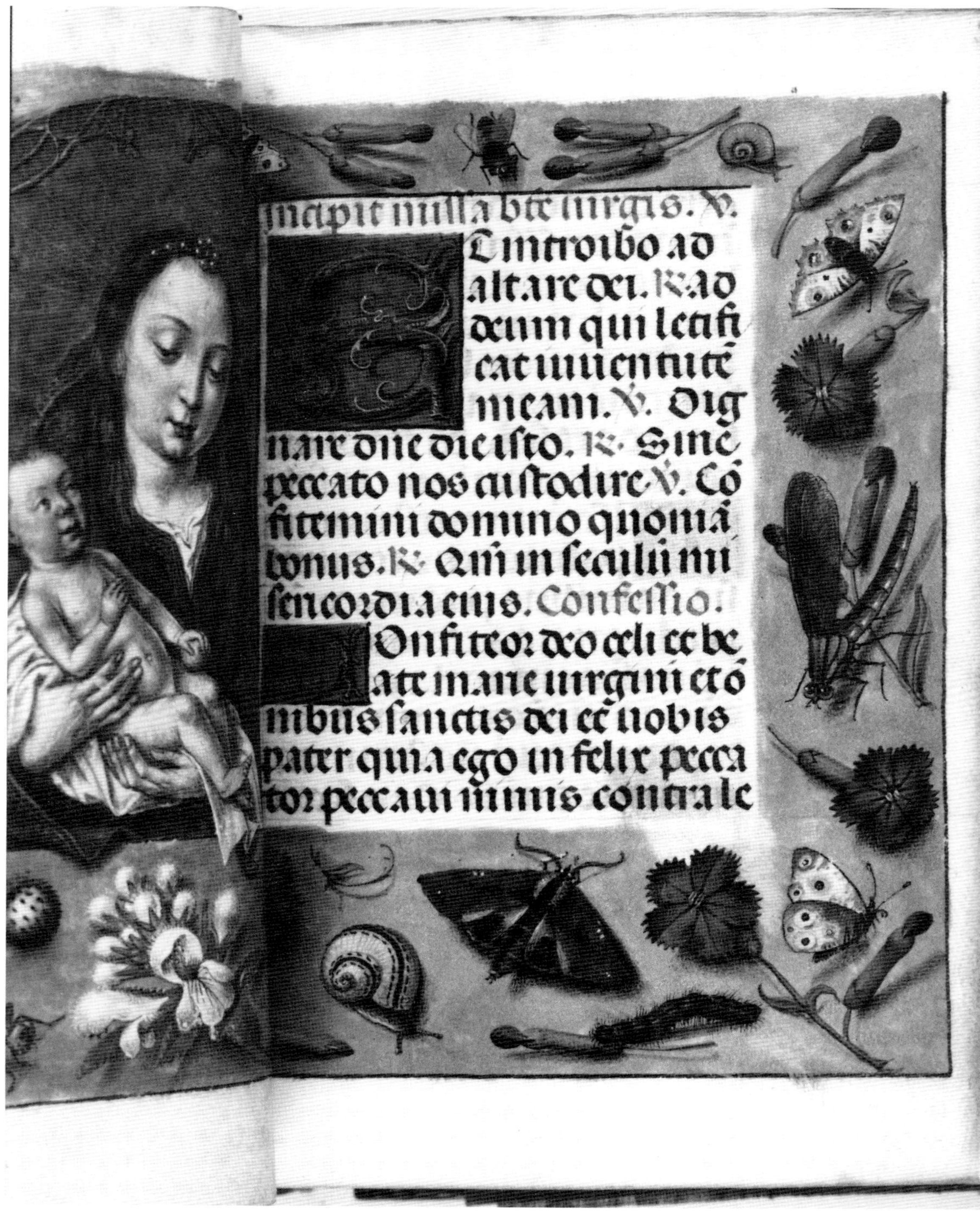

Incipit missa bte virgis. V.
Introibo ad
altare dei. R. Ad
deum qui letifi
cat iuventutē
meam. V. Dig
nare dne die isto. R. Sine
peccato nos custodire. V. Cō
fitemini domino quoniā
bonus. R. Qm̄ in seculū mi
sericordia eius. Confessio.
Onfiteor deo celi et be
ate marie virgini et ō
nibus sanctis dei et vobis
pater quia ego infelix pecca
tor peccavi nimis contra le

MS 46, f. 33r and part of f. 32v (actual size of written area: 57 × 40 mm)

The psalmless Short Hours of the Cross based on segments of the hymn *Patris sapientia veritas divina* (Walther, *Initia* 13840).

(26r blank; 26v, full-page illustration: Pentecost)

27r–31v: *Incipit officiu[m] sancti sp[irit]us.* (D)[5]omine labia . . . Sed uiuamus iugiter celi regione. Amen.

The short (psalmless) office based on the hymn *Nobis Sancti Spiritus gratia sit data* (Walther, *Initia* 21189).

(32r blank; 32v, full-page illustration: Mary and Child)

33r–38v: *Incipit missa b[ea]te uirg[in]is. V.* (S)[5]C introibo ad altare dei. *R.* Ad deum qui letificat iuuentute[m] meam. *V.* Dignare d[omi]ne die isto *R.* Sine peccato nos custodire *V.* Co[n]fitemini domino quonia[m] bonus *R.* Q[uonia]m in seculu[m] misericordia eius. *Confessio.* (C)[2]Onfiteor deo celi et beate marie uirgini et o[m]nibus sanctis dei et uobis pater quia ego infelix peccator peccaui nimis contra le(33v:)gem dei mei cogitatione locutione conse[n]su tactu uisu verbo ore et opere mea culpa mea culpa mea maxi[m]a culpa. Ideo precor beatissimam virgine[m] mariam et om[n]es sanctos et s[an]c[t]as dei et vos orare pro me peccatore. *Absolu[tio].* (M)[2]Isereatur uestri omnipotens deus et dimissis omnibus peccati v[est]ris perducat nos et vos ih[es]us xp'us sine macula cum gaudio ad uita[m] eternam. Ame[n]. . . . (34r:) *Introitus.* (S)[3]Alue sa[n]c[t]a parens . . .

The formula for opening of the Mass, and the confessional formula as given here are not commonly listed in sources.[2] — The rest of the Mass: (Introit verse *Sentiant omnes*) *Kyrie, Gloria,* collect *Concede nos*, epistle *Ab initio*[3], gradual *Benedicta et venerabilis,* verse *Virgo Dei genitrix,* alleluiatic verse *Post partum*; gospel *Loquente . . . extollens vocem quaedam mulier . . .*[4] *Credo*; offertory antiphon *Felix namque; Sanctus, Benedictus; Agnus Dei*; communion antiphon *Beata viscera;* postcommunion *("ōro.") Gratiam tuam*; excerpts end (on 38v) with "Benedicam[us] dn'o Deo gratias."

38v–43v: (38v, 2nd line:) *Initiu[m] s[an]c[t]i euangelij secundu[m] ioha[n]nem* . . . (39v, 9th line:) *Secundum lucam* . . . (41r, 4th line:) *Secundu[m] matheum* . . . (42v, 4th line:) *Secundu[m] marcum* . . . (ends 43v, 2nd line:) . . . [se]quentib[u]s signis. Deo gra[tia]s. (rest of 43v blank)

Gospel readings: John I,1–14 (without the suffrage-type versicle and prayer often added in books of hours); Luke I,26–38; Matthew II,1–12; Mark XVI,14–20.

(44r blank; 44v, full-page illustration: Annunciaton)

45r–121r: *Incipiunt hore beate marie uirginis secundum usum romanum. Ad matutinu[m]* . . . (113r:) *Incipit officiu[m] gloriosissime marie uirginis q[uo]d dicitur p[er] totu[m] aduentu[m].* . . . (120v–121r, rubrics for other seasons)

Hours (= Little Office) of the Virgin, use of Rome.[5] — Matins include the three alternate sets of psalms governed by day of the week. — ff. 62v, 63r, 75r, 80v, 81r, 86r, 91v, 96v, 97r, 105r, 111v, 112r blank; full-page illustrations on:
63v: Visitation
75v: Nativity
81v: Shepherds
86v: Magi
97v: Flight to Egypt
105v: Slaughter of the Innocents
112v: Coronation of the Virgin
(There is no illustration for the hour of None, 92r–96v; expected would be the Presentation in the Temple.)

(121v, 122r blank; on 122v, full-page illustration: David penitent)[6]

123r–143v: *Incipiunt septem psalmi* . . . misericors dominus. Ame[n]

The Penitential Psalms, with (f. 134r sqq.) the Litany of Saints. — The litany includes, after Mary, apostles, etc. (through Innocents) 11 individual martyrs, 14 confessors, and 11 women. Among the confessors, St. Francis (no Dominic), and also (136r) St. Elsiarius ("s. Elziari"), a monk whose cult was rather limited.[7] (N.B. His name doesn't appear in the calendar at the beginning of the book.)

(144r blank; 144v, full-page illustration: Exequies)

MS 46 145r–186r: *Incipiu[n]t uigilie mortuorum An̄.* Placebo. *ps̄.* (D)[5]ilexi . . . (186r:) Requiescant in pace. Amen.

The *Officium defunctorum*, with regular Roman-use responsories.

(186v, 187r blank; 187v, full-page illus.: Lamentation over Christ's body taken down from the Cross)

188r–191v: *Oratio deuotissima ad beatissimam virgine[m] mariam.* (O)[6]Bsecro te d[omi]na . . . (190r:) . . . f[a]c[t]urus locuturus aut cogitaturus . . . Et michi famulo tuo . . . (ends 191v:) . . . mater dei et misericordie Amen.

Note masculine forms (= apparently written for a man).

192r–194v: (O)[3] Intemerata et in eternu[m] benedicta . . . o ioh[ann]es . . . in secula seculorum Amen.

195r–205v: (Suffrages:)[8] (195r–v:) *H[i]storia de s[an]c[t]o ludouico* ((F)[7]idelis seruus . . .) (196r–v:) *De sancto Michaele* ((M)[7]ichael archangele . . .) (196v–197r:) *De s[an]c[t]o iohan[n]e baptista* ((I)[7]nter natos mulierum . . .) (197r–v:) *De sa[n]c[t]o petro et paulo* ((P)[7]etrus apostolus et paulus doctor gentium . . .) (197v–198v:) *De sa[n]c[t]o iacobo ap[osto]lo* ((O)[7] lux et decus hispanie . . .) (198v–199r:) *De sa[n]c[t]o antho[n]io de padua* ((S)[7]i queris miracula . . .[9]) (199v–200r:) *De sancto Francisco* ((S)[7]alve sancte pater . . .) (200r–v:) *De sa[n]c[t]o iheronimo* ((C)[7]onfessor deo iheronime . . .) (200v–201r:) *De sancto nicholao* ((B)[7]eatus nicholaus adhuc puerulus . . .) (201v–202r:) *De s[an]c[t]a maria magdal[ena]* ((M)[7]aria vnxit pedes ihesu . . .) (202r–v:) *De sancta Katherina* ((V)[7]irgo sancta Katherina gretie gemma . . .) (203r–v:) *De sancta Barbara* ((A)[7]ue eterna lucifera . . .) (204r–v:) *De sancta Susanna* ((O)[7] Beata Susanna . . .) (204v–205r:) *De s[an]c[t]a Margareta* ((E)[7]rat autem margareta . . .) (205r–v:) *De omnibus sanctis* ((O)[7]mnes electi dei nostri . . .)

The 7-line initials which begin the antiphons depict the saints invoked.

206r–209v: *Canticum athanasij ep[iscop]i.* (Q)[7]uicumq[ue] vult saluus esse . . . saluus esse non poterit. Gloria p[at]ri

The Athanasian Creed, in Latin. The initial *Q* contains a portrait of, presumably, Athanasius, in episcopal regalia.

(ff. [210–213] blank; ruled through 213r)

* * *

Foliated (1–209) in modern pencil. Preceding the first numbered leaf, two free endleaves of thicker parchment followed by a blank leaf of same material as the text leaves but unruled. Following the ruled blank leaves [210–213] at end, again two free endleaves of thicker parchment. — Written area ca. 57 × ca. 40 mm. Fully ruled in faint red ink. No pricking. — Written in a steady, simple *littera textualis formata* (semiquadrate and rather Italian in overall appearance), in good black ink. — Very thin high quality material (thickness ca. 9.4 mm per 100 leaves).

Collation impracticable owing to tight binding.

Richly illuminated. Sixteen full-page illustrations (cf. contents), each ca. 66 × 39 mm, multicolor, in windowlike openings within illuminated borders. Full four-side borders, richly decorated and illuminated, are found on 73 pages: i.e., those of the calendar, those with full-page illustrations, and pages where major sections of text begin; a conspicuous feature of the book, they are filled with realistic depictions of jewels, flowers, berries, insects (some in the *trompe-l'oeil* manner), birds, snails, also several burlesque creatures,[10] all on framed painted-gold, ultramarine, purple, or green grounds.

Minor illustrations comprise, besides the 16 portraits of saints in historiated initials (cf. contents with ff. 195r–206r), 12 folklife scenes and 12 representations of the zodiac in medallions centered on lower borders of the calendar pages (ff. 1v–13r).

Except for the historiated initials of the concluding sections (the suffrages and the Athanasian Creed), the major, mostly 5-line-high decorative letters which introduce larger sections are constructed from foliate shapes outlined in gold and filled with magenta, blue, or painted gold; the ground is always painted gold. — Numerous 3- or

2-line initials (also occasional filler bars) are done in basically the same manner although simpler; generally in two colors (magenta and blue) with bright golden accents on matte brushed-gold ground; the 1-line versals, otherwise similar, use only one color for each letter.

Bound in black shagreen with silver ornaments (filigree pattern borders, center medallions with relief antique-style bust in left-facing profile, and one front-to-back clasp).[11] — Gilt edges. — Protected by a folder covered in pink silk and by a bookshape slipcase done in bright red morocco leather. On the spine side of the case, tooled in gold: HORAE B.V.M./ FLEMISH, 15TH CENT./GIVEN TO THE/ LIBRARY OF CONGRESS/IN MEMORY OF/FELIX M. WARBURG/BY HIS WIFE AND CHILDREN/ON HIS SEVENTIETH BIRTHDAY/JANUARY 14, 1941.

Former owners: J. de Bure *l'aîné*; A. Firmin-Didot; Baron S. de La Roche-Lacarelle; Eugène Paillet; Robert Hoe; F. M. Warburg. (On inside of upper cover, inscription of 23 January 1826 by De Bure, also ownership labels of Firmin-Didot and E. Paillet)

2° fo.: xviii b/vii c Anthonij abb[at]is

Bibl.: *Catalogue des livres rares . . . J. J. de Bure* (1853), no. 67 (p. 12 sq.; description by G. Duplessis includes error: "168 feuillets") — *Catalogue illustré des livres précieux . . . Ambroise Firmin-Didot* (1879), no. 26 (p. 73 sqq.; "sa célebrité est déjà grande sous le nom de manuscrit de Bure"; mentions attribution of several of the illustrations to Hans Memling) — *Cat. des livres rares . . . M. le baron S. de La Roche Lacarelle* (1888), no. 19 (p. 7 sqq.) — *La bibliothèque de feu m. Eugène Paillet* (Paris, D. Morgand, 1902), no. 1? (not seen) — *Catalogue of the library of Robert Hoe*, v. 1(1911), no. 2138 (p. 363) — De Ricci, *Census*, v. 2 (1937), p. 1850 sq., no. 13; Faye and Bond, p. 122, no. 139 — *Illuminated books of the Middle Ages and Renaissance, an exhibition . . .* (Walters Art Gallery, Baltimore, 1949), p. 74, no. 203 (also reduced black-and-white reproductions of ff. 14v–15r, on plate LXXVIII) — C.A. Goodrum, *Treasures of the Library of Congress* (1980) (color reproductions and views of the book on p. 46, 47, and 74)

"A little Horae with miniatures of the greatest charm and delicacy, by more than one hand" — D. Miner in *Illuminated books . . .* (1949), p. 74. — The artwork is a product of the Ghent-Bruges school given much attention in recent time in connection with the Grimani breviary and other works of renown but it seems to have largely escaped the specialists' notice. The borders, in particular, are throughout in the style pioneered by the Master of Mary of Burgundy (Sanders Bening?) but seem to differ from most similar ones in including, besides the realistic-to-naturalistic flora and fauna, also burlesque, slightly malignant gargoyle-like imps; this is the case in ca. 50 percent of the decorated borders in the Warburg Hours (though no more than one imp per border). — The illustrations are not all of same quality; among those occupying a full page, the rather striking Salvator mundi (f. 16v) stands out, his peculiar physiognomy recurring also in the trinitarian Coronation of the Virgin (112v). The folklife scenes in the calendar seem, too, to be worthy of notice, both for their charm and for their relatively uncommon disposition in medallions.[12]

NOTES

1. I.e., half portrait, *en face*, of Christ holding the world-globe in his left hand, blessing with his right.
2. The closest read-alike may be that found in the use of Trondheim, cf. A.A. King, *Liturgies of the past* (1959), p. 439. — An almost identical text appears, nevertheless, in the ms. Hours S. P. 12 and S. P. II.185 of Biblioteca ambrosiana (cf. its *I libri d'ore* (1973), p. 13 and 118).
3. Sirach XXIV, 14–17.
4. Luke XI, 27–28.
5. See table C for more detail.
6. David is grey, bareheaded; harp is on the floor.
7. More or less to the monastery of Saint-Savin-de-Lavedan and the diocese of Tarbes in southern France. — Rarely found elsewhere, the name also appears in the Litany of the ms. Hours S.P. II.185

of Bib. ambrosiana noted earlier for similar confessional formula (cf. our note 2; for Elsiarius, Ambrosiana's *op. cit.*, p. 121). In that book of hours, too, the saint is absent from the calendar.

8. Each "suffrage" consists (at least in principle) of an (often poetical) antiphon, a versicle with response, and a formal prayer which tends to be identical with the *collecta* of the Mass for the day of the saint invoked.

9. Antiphon taken from the rhymed office of St. Anthony composed by Julianus à Spira (responsory VIII of the Matins). (Cf. *S. Francisci Assisiensis et s. Antonii Patavini officia rhythmica* . . . ed. H. Dausend [Munich, 1934])

10. On f. 145r also skulls, and dog eating a bone.

11. The date and place of production of the beautiful and unusual silverwork have been estimated variously; early 19th century? Paris?

12. For the Ghent-Bruges school, cf. A. W. Biermann's study "Die Miniaturhandschriften des Kardinals Albrechts von Brandenburg" in *AACHENER KUNSTBLÄTTER* XLVI (1975), p. 15–310.

MS 47

(Hours Mrs. Carley Dawson)

BOOK OF HOURS (fragments)

ca. 1400?

France. Parchment. 77 leaves, ca. 130 × ca. 79 mm (bound volume: 137 × ca. 87 mm) 1 column. 19–33 lines.

(ff. 2r–3v, Short Hours of the Cross (incomplete); 4r–20v, Penitential Psalms (incomplete) with Litany (incomplete); 21rv, Seven Prayers of St. Gregory; 22rv, unidentified French prayer (incomplete); 22v–23v, Legend of Canon Arnoul (in French, incomplete); 26r–29v, Canon Arnoul's Prayer (incomplete); 29v–32v, Mass of the Virgin; 32v–34v, suffrages (Stephen, Anthony, Sebastian); 39r–72v, Hours of B.V.M. (different hand, incomplete))

(f. 1rv blank, ruled [for 24 written lines on each page]) 2r–3v: meus ad te veniat . . . et auerte iram tuam a nobis

Fragment of the Short Hours of the Cross;[1] preserved text begins with the end of the Matins and ends at the beginning of the Compline.

4r–20v: rigabo Turbatus e[st] a furore oculus meus . . . Deus cui propriu[m] e[st] misereri semper et parcere suscipe deprecationem n[ost]ram vt quos

Penitential Psalms, with (14r sqq.) Litany. The beginning is wanting, through verse 7 of Ps. VI; wanting also part of the Litany, from "Sancte phelippe" (14v) to "Sancte egidi" (on 17r; only a stub remains of f. 15, ruled, with several line endings on verso; f. 16, blank, unruled is a later addition), and part of the formal prayers at the end of the devotion. — Names worth noticing in the preserved text of the Litany: Egidi; Iuliane; Maure; Leobine; Sulplici *[sic]*; Leonarde; Guillerme; Fides, Spes, Caritas.

21r–v: neratum felle et aceto potatum . . . O domine ih[es]u xp̄e te deprecor per illam amaritudinem . . . O . . . adoro te in sepulcro positum . . . ([etc]; ending imperfectly, last line of 21v:) . . . propicius est *[sic]* michi

The devotion ascribed to St. Gregory the Great and beginning either "Adoro te Domine Jesu Christe in cruce pendentem" (as in *Horae Eboracenses* (1920), p. 81) or "O Domine Ihesu Christe adoro te in cruce pendentem" as in Leroquais, *LH* II, p. 346; ours is probably the latter variant, with extant text beginning in the middle of the second appeal and breaking off just before the end of the last one.

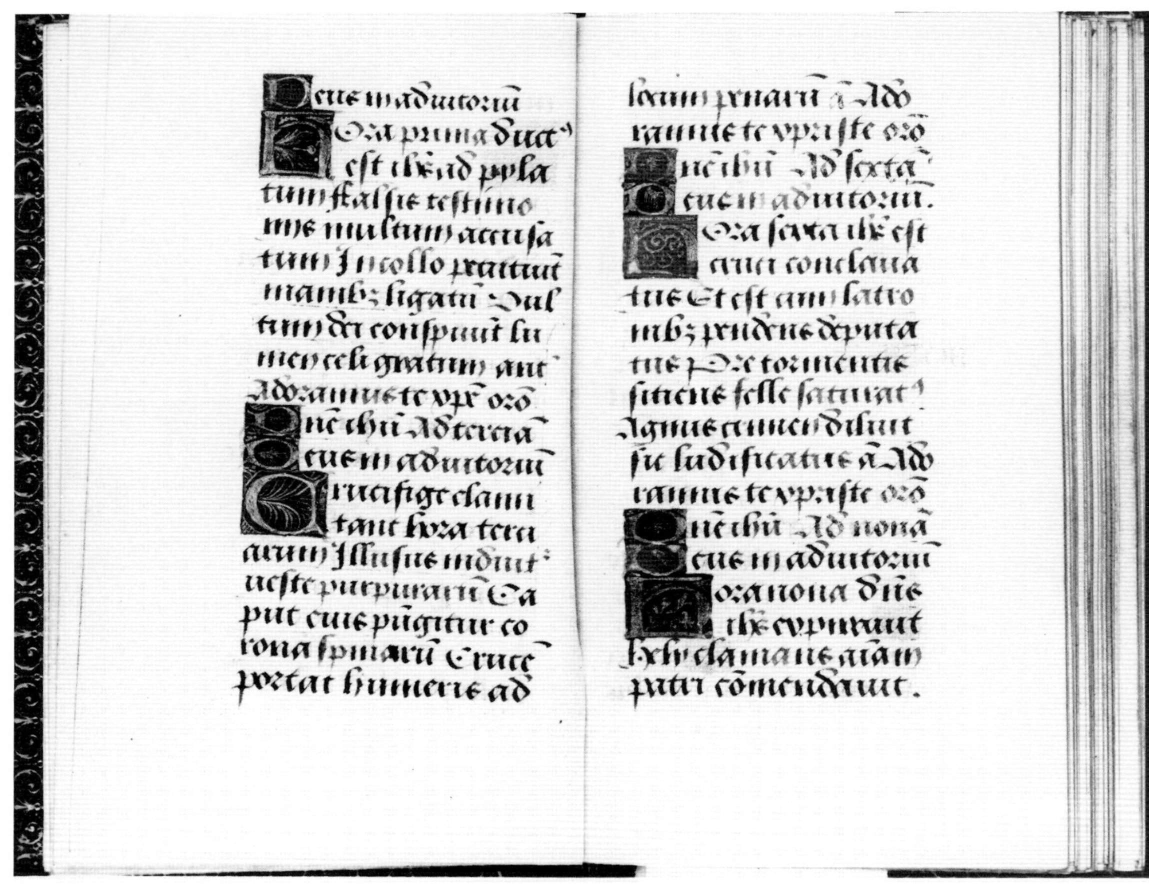

MS 47, ff. 2v–3r (actual height of the columns: 92 mm)

22r–v: gne de recōgnoissance vous par de ce petit tribut au matin et au soir . . . tous les saincts et sainctes de paradis Amen.

End fragment of an unidentified French prayer.

22v–23v: *Ceste oraiso[n] doit on dire chascu[n] samedi en l'ho[n]ner de n[ost]re dame. Ong ho[m]me* (23r:) *religieux et chanoine regulier estoit q' eut no[m] Arnoul* . . . (rubric ends on 23v:) . . . *co[mm]e emperier[e?] du ciel et de la terre* (remaining 4 lines blank)

The legend of Canon Arnoul, cf. Wilmart, *Aut. spir.*, p. 334; Leroquais, *LH* I, p. 95, 250; II, p. 89. Incorporated into the rubric, the legend serves as support for the longish prayer system which Canon Arnoul purportedly was encouraged to spread and which should follow; in the present state of the manuscript, the prayers, or the preserved part of them, are separated from the rubric by two blank leaves added (perhaps) in last binding:

(24r–25v blank, not ruled)

26r–29v: et mater que filium dei genuisti veru[m] deu[m] et ueru[m] hominem qui pro nobis in te natus est. d[omi]n[u]s tecu[m]. Vera virgo et mater que filiu[m] dei genuisti veru[m] . . . receptus est. Do[minus] tecum. Vera . . . (similar formula used 18 times) . . . (29r:) . . . viuos et mortuos et seculu[m] per ignem Amen *Oratio* Te deprecor ergo mitissimam . . . (29v:) . . . Pater noster. Aue maria.

The devotion introduced by the legend, or one version of it; cf. Wilmart *l.c.*, note 2; Leroquais, *LH*, as with the preceding item. Wanting is the beginning (= ca. one page); the normal incipit would be: Missus est angelus Gabriel.

29v–32v: (29v, last 2 lines:) *Incipit missa in honore beate marie virginis* (30r, text:) Salue sancta parens . . . (ends 32v:) . . . Ite missa est. Deo grat[ias]

The (votive) Mass of the Virgin (i.e., the proper, with some minor items from the ordinary, including [30rv] the *Gloria*). — (Introit *Salve sancta parens*; differs from the generally used text in preferring instead of the psalm verse *Eructavit* the antiphonal *Post partum* — Coll: *Concede nos famulos* — Ep: *Ab initio* — Grad: *Benedicta et venerabilis* . . . Virgo dei genitrix . . . Virga iesse floruit — Gos: *Loquente ih[es]u ad turbas* — Off: *Recordare uirgo mat[er]* dum steteris — Secr: *Tua domine propiciatione* — Comm [32r–v]: *Aue regina celo[rum]* mater regis angelorum o maria flos virginum velut rosa vel lilium funde preces ad filium pro salute fidelium. — Postcomm: *Sumptis domine*)

32v–34v: (32v–33r:) *De sancto stephano* . . . Stephanus plenus gr[ati]a . . . Just[us] germinabit . . . Omnipotens sempiterne deus q[ui] primitias martiru[m] . . . (33r–v:) *De sancto anthonio* . . . Anthoni pastor inclite qui cruciatos reficis . . . Ora pro nobis beate . . . Deus qui nos concedis obtentu beati anthonij confessoris tui morbidum igne[m] extingui . . . (33v–34v:) *De sancto sebastiano* O q[uam] mira refulsit gr[ati]a . . . Ora pro nobis . . . vt mereamur pestem epidimie illesi pertransire . . . Deus qui beatu[m] sebastianu[m] . . . solidasti . . . da nobis . . . co[n]tra peste[m] epidimie remediu[m] . . . ualeam[us] obtinere. P[er . . .]

Suffrages (antiphon + versicle + formal prayer): Stephen, Anthony, Sebastian. — Protection against the "Fire of St. Anthony," or ergot poisoning, may well have been one of the concerns of whoever selected these particular texts. Cf. similar emphasis in the 16th-century Hours LC MS 50 and literature quoted in connection with that ms.

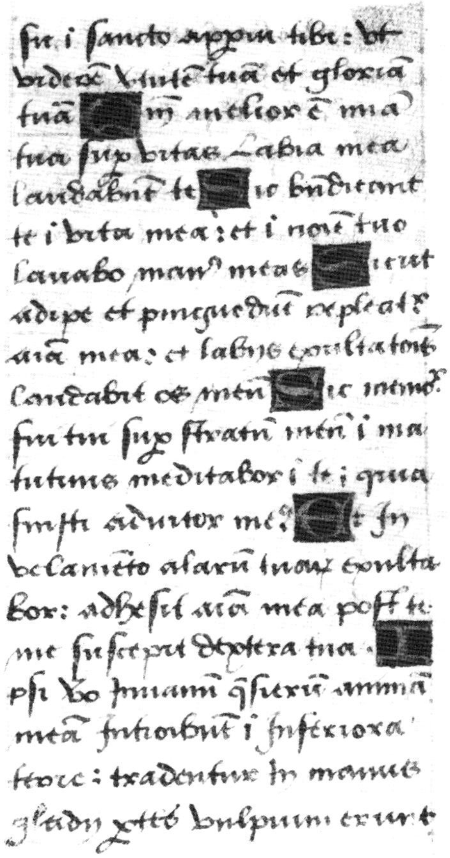

MS 47, f. 52r (actual height of the column: 89 mm)

(35–38 blank, of thicker material, not ruled)

ALL THAT FOLLOWS IS SIGNIFICANTLY DIFFERENT FROM THE PRECEDING; DIFFERENTLY RULED, WRITTEN BY A DIFFERENT PERSON (ONE OR MORE), IN A DIFFERENT SCRIPT:

39r–72v: pemus faciem eius in confessione et in spalmis *[sic]* jubilemus ei Aue maria . . . (text breaks off at end of 72v:) fu[n]da nos i[n] pace muta[n]s nome[n] eue

Hours of Our Lady, use of Rome (see tables); incomplete at the beginning (mid-first verse of the Invitatory) and at end (last part of the Vespers and all of the Compline wanting). Wanting are also the end of the Matins (last verses of the *Te Deum;* f. 50

which follows the truncated end is blank, unruled, perhaps added in binding) and the beginnings of all remaining hours, their places taken by blank leaves or pages: the rubric "*Ad primam*" is followed by blank, unruled leaf 58, perhaps added in binding; "*Ad tertiam*" by blank, ruled f. 61r; "*Ad sextam*," in last line of f. 64v, by blank, ruled 65r; the None should begin on 67v and the Vespers on 70r, both similarly blank and ruled.[2] The amount of text wanting would suggest in each case that a large illustration was being planned (the ruling notwithstanding?) to be accompanied by the several lines of text; it is less clear what happened where the non-original blank f. 58 replaces the opening, the hymn, and four verses of the Prime.

(ff. 73 and 74 are blank, fully ruled; "75," "76," and "77" are of thicker material presumably added in binding; they are followed by free endleaf)

* * *

Foliated in modern pencil. Preceding f. 1, free endleaf and 3 flyleaves of thicker material added, probably, with the modern binding, as are leaves 16, 24, 25, 35–38, 50, 58, 63, and 75–77, followed by a free endleaf; all these are blank and unruled. — Written area in the first part (ff. 2r–34v) 92 × 46–50 mm (exceeding the 44 mm width suggested by ruling); in the second part (39r–72v), 88–92 × ca. 48 mm. — Fully ruled in faint red ink; blank f. 1 is ruled for 24 text lines, ff. 2r–34v (except for the unruled blank leaves noted above) for 19 lines; the section which consists of leaves 39 through 74 is ruled quite irregularly, the number of text lines ruled for varying from 20 to 33. — The script of leaves 2–34 is a *littera cursiva formata* of good quality (characterized by the ascending line of the letter *d* swung at top to the right); the second section begins, 39r–40r, by a small-size semi-cursive hybrid and continues by a diminutive, not very skillful or pleasing *cursiva textualis* by another hand. — The ink is brownish black, weak but quite even in the first part; weak with an olive cast on 39r–40r; very uneven, constantly changing from stronger to fainter and back, in the last part. — Rubrics in the first part strong purplish red; in the second half, various shades of red.

Collation: appears impracticable; referring to the two main sections as fragments *A* and *B*, the summarized sequence of leaves is as follows: (free endleaf) (3 flyleaves, recent) f. 1(B) (stub of one of the recent blank leaves) (wanting 10 or more leaves (A)) ff. 2–3(A) (wanting leaf (A)) ff. 4–14(A) (remnant of f. 15(A)) (f. 16, recent; conjugate with one of the flyleaves?) ff. 17–20(A) (wanting leaf (A)) f. 21(A) (wanting leaf (A)) ff. 22–23(A) (ff. 24–25, recent) (wanting leaf (A)) ff. 26–34(A) (ff. 35–38, recent) (wanting leaf (B)) ff. 39–49(B) (wanting leaf (B)) (f. 50, recent) ff. 54–57(B) (wanting leaf (B)) (f. 58, recent) ff. 59–62(B) (f. 63, recent) ff. 64–72 (B) (wanting leaf or leaves (B)) ff. 73–74(B) (ff. 75–77, recent). — Sewing lines between ff. 8.9, 17.18, 24.25, 30.31, 36.37, 40.41, 47.48, 53.54, 56.57, 59.60, 62.63, 67.68, 73.74, 76.77.

Decorative elements are limited to initials, done with competent craftsmanship and pleasing result in the first part, in a very amateurish manner on leaves 41–72. — In the first part, the initials (2- or 1-line) are done in gold on light (opaque) blue or muted red backgrounds; the color of the background is relieved by minor decorative (floral) motifs also in painted gold. No outlines. Line fillers (in the Litany) follow same color scheme. — The initials of the second part: ff. 39r–51r, poorly shaped letters in painted gold with fuzzy edges, on dull red grounds unrelieved (except for 39r–41r) by further decoration; ff. 51v–72, 3-line letters done in blue on gold, both the letters and the ground outlined in red; esthetically a failure.

Twentieth-century dark brown morocco binding; both covers handsomely decorated by blind-tooling: a diaper of 15 squares with an identical floral motif repeated in each. — On the spine, impressed in gold: PSALTERIUM. Gilt edges. — Endpapers 19th-century, marbled (nonpareil style).

On verso of front free endleaf, in pencil: Fragment/manuscrit XVème siècle. On recto of next leaf, in center, red rectangular Oriental ownership seal; not well legible but the first character is *T'ao* (Giles 10,831 [p. 1343]; Matthews #6156 [p. 887]), probably beginning of the Chinese-character approximation of *Dawson.*[3]

Former owners: Mrs. Carley Dawson (of Washington, D.C.); presented by her to the Library of Congress as a gift, Aug. 28, 1967.

2° fo.: meus ad te veniat *orō*

(Not in De Ricci; not in Faye and Bond)

The two sections are complementary but their very different graphic style calls for an explanation. The first section was written in a workshop; it may have remained a surplus fragment when gatherings written by different scribes were being assembled to produce complete books; alternately, it may be a detached part of a vandalized book. In either case, at a later point an amateur decided to add the most important part which was missing, i.e., the Hours of Our Lady. This second, less skilled scribe (and a third one?) reserved nevertheless the right amount of space, i.e., blank pages, for illustrations and for the opening words of each hour, ruling them in the same manner as the text pages. When the book was being (re)bound, further blank leaves were added, not in each case in the right place.

NOTES

1. The devotion referred to as the Short Hours of the Cross was based on the hymn *Patris sapientia veritas divina* (Walther, *Initia* 13840), its stanzas distributed over the day; it didn't include any psalms. See also notes to ff. 91–92 of MS 44.

2. Blank, unruled f. 63, a modern addition, interrupts continuous text.

3. Although positive information could not be obtained, it seems likely that the book was at one time in China.

MS 48

(Faye and Bond 20)

BOOK OF HOURS early XVIth c.

Flanders? Parchment. 173 leaves, 126 × ca. 96 mm (bound volume: 135 × ca. 106 mm) 1 column. 17 lines.

(ff. 3r–14v, calendar; 15r–16r, *Salve sancta facies*; 16r–17r, *Oratio S. Bernardi*; 18r–23v, Short Hours of the Cross; 25r–29v, Short Hours of the Holy Spirit; 31r–36r, Mass of the Virgin; 36r–40v, Gospel readings; 42r–95v, Hours of B.V.M., Roman use; 95v–96v, *Salve Regina*; 97r–100r, *Obsecro te*; 100v–102v, *O intemerata;* 106r–124v, Penitential Psalms with Litany; 126r–164v, Office for the Dead; 164v–170v, *Orationes S. Brigidae* [later hand]; 170v–173r [varia, in later hand])

(ILLUSTRATIVE MATERIAL ON FF. 1–2 IS OF MUCH LATER DATE THAN THE ORIGINAL DECORATION OF THE BOOK: PROBABLY EARLY 17TH CENTURY)

(1r: illustration, standing St. Francis of Assisi, with legend "S. Franciscus. ora pro nobis"; all centered in a baroque shield forming, with cherubs and fruits, a four-side border)

(1v: coat of arms of Julius Echter von Mespelbrunn, Prince-Bishop of Würzburg (b. 1545, d. 1617?);[1] on multicolor bleeding-off ground)

(2r: illustration, Christ as the heavenly ruler, on skylike background, with globe beneath; within a four-side border formed of strewn flowers on brushed-gold ground)

2v: (LATE HAND, probably contemporary with the decorative material just described:) Oratio ad S. Franciscum. O sancte Francisce pater pie, imitator et signifer . . . (N.B. Six last lines of the prayer are written in tail margin of f. 3r)

3r–14v: (KL)[3] Januarius habet dies . . .

Calendar with 112 entries, in black and red. — Among the red-letter days: *Amandi* (Feb. 6), *Georgii* (Apr. 23), *Bonifacii (June 5), Basilii* (June 14), *Eligii* (June 25), *Translatio Thomae* (July 3), *Egidii* (Sept. 1), *Remigii et Bavonis* (Oct. 1), *Dionisii conf.* (Oct. 9), *Donatiani archiep.* (Oct. 14), *Eligii ep.* (Dec. 1), *Nichasii ep.* (Dec. 12). — Among the names in black: Juliane (Feb. 6), Babille [i.e., Balbine?] virg. (Mar. 31), Victoris (Apr. 20), Huberti (May 30), Bertini (Sept. 5), Leonardi (Nov. 6), Machuti (Nov. 15), Lazari (Dec. 17). — The set is very close to the calendar of Bruges.[2]

15r–16r: *Salutacio ad s[an]c[t]am faciem xp̄i.* (S)[4]alue sancta facies . . . amen.

Text of the hymn: Leroquais, *LH* II, p. 349.[3] — Sometimes presented as having to do with St. Veronica (cf. LC MS 46)

16r–17r: (LATE HAND:) Oratio Sancti Bernardi. O Bone Jesu, o dulcis Jesu . . . in te gloriari ac delectari in Saecula Saeculorum amen.

Cf. Leroquais, *LH* II, p. 200. (Also attributed to Bernardinus of Siena.)

(17v: full-page illustration, within four-side border: Crucifixion)

18r–23v: *Incipiunt hore sancte crucis.* (D)[4]omine labia mea . . . Patris sapientia veritas diuina . . . consors sim corone. amen.

The Short Hours of the Cross (psalmless, with segments of the hymn *Patris sapientia*[4] constituting the main contents of the individual "hours")

23v–24r: (LATE HAND:) Oratio Coram imagine crucifixi dicenda. Precor te amantissime Domine Jesu Christe propter illam eximiam charitatem . . . Amen.

Cf. Leroquais, *LH* I, p. xxxi and 336.

(24v: full-page illustration, within four-side border: Pentecost)

25r–29v: *Incipiunt hore sancti spiritus.* (D)[4]omine labia mea . . . Nobis sancti spiritus gracia sit data . . . Amen.

The Short Hours of the Holy Spirit (psalmless; main contents constituted by the hymn *Nobis sancti spiritus*[5] divided into segments)

29v–30r: (LATE HAND:) Oratio Pro inspiratione in dubijs Petenda a S. Sp[i]r[itu]. Veni Sancte Spiritus . . . Emitte quaesumus Domine Spiritum sanctum tuum . . . et da mihi seruo tuo illam . . . sapientiam . . .

The sequence *AH* LIV, 153, followed by prayer.

(30v: full-page illustration, within four-side border: Mary and Child)

MS 48, f. 17v (actual height of central illustration: 88 mm)

MS 48, f. 31r (actual size of area enclosed by the border: 84 × 58 mm)

31r–36r: *Incipit missa beate marie virg[inis]* (I)[4]ntroibo . . . Adiutorium . . . Confiteor deo celi et beate marie virgini et omnibus sanctis dei quia ego infelix peccator peccaui nimis contra legem dei mei cogitac[i]o[n]e locutione consensu visu verbo et opere . . . (31v:) . . . Misereatur vestri . . . perducat nos et uos ih[es]us xp̄us sine macula cum gaudio ad vitam eternam. amen. . . . *Introitus.* Salue sancta parens . . . (32r:) . . . Gloria in excelsis deo . . . (32v:) . . . Domine fili unigenite Iesu Christe. Spiritus et alme orphanorum paraclite Domine Deus agnus dei filius patris. Primogenitus Marie virginis matris. Qui tollis . . . suscipe deprecationem nostram. Ad Marie gloriam. Qui tollis . . . Quoniam tu solus sanctus. Mariam sanctificans. Tu solus dominus. Mariam gubernans. Tu solus altissimus. Mariam coronans. Iesu Christe cum . . . in gloria Dei Patris. Amen. . . .

Mass in honor of Mary (the proper,[6] and the more public parts of the ordinary). — The *Confiteor* formula is non-Roman, similar to that found in several other books of hours from Flanders.[7] — The *Gloria* with Marian interpolations, also non-Roman, can be found in Premonstratensian books.[8]

36r–40v: *Inicium s[an]c[t]i euangelii secundum iohannem.* (I)[3]n principio . . . sequentibus signis.

Readings from the four Gospels: John I,1–14; Luke I,26b–38a; Matthew II,1–12; Mark XVI,14–20. No liturgical additions beyond "In illo tempore . . ." and "Deo gracias."

41r: (LATE HAND:) Oratio ad Beatam V Mariam. O Maria dulcis mediatrix miserere mei . . . et gloria perennis. Amen.

(41v: full-page illustration, within four-side border: Annunciation)

42r–95v: *Incipiunt hore beate marie virginis secundum vsum romanum.* (D)[4]omine labia mea . . . (44r:) . . . *dieb[us] lune [et] Jouis* . . . (47v:) . . . *diebus martis et veneris* . . . (51r:) . . . *diebus mercurij et sabbati* . . .

Hours of Our Lady, use of Rome.[9] — Filling spaces left blank in the (natural) layout of the original text, ADDITIONS IN THE LATE HAND: (58v, at end of Matins:) Oratio Ad Beatam Virgine[m]. Salue o benignissima misericordiae mater . . . (68v, after Lauds:) Oratio Ad B. V. Mariam. Aue Maria gratia plena . . . miserere mei exulis pauperrimi. (72v, following the Prime:) Oratio . . . Laudo et saluto te . . . nobis succurras. Amen. (76v, after Terce:) Oratio . . . Recole o Mater pietatis . . . charitas tua copiosa. Amen. (80v, end of Sext:) Oratio . . . Aue immaculata Beatae Trinitatis amica . . . omni tempore. Amen. (84v, after None:) Oratio . . . Aue filia sion millies beata . . . conquiescat a[n]i[m]a mea. Amen. (91v, following the Vespers:) Oratio . . . Domina nostra mediatrix nostra aduocata nostra . . . benedictus in saecula. Amen.

95v–96v: *Salutacio beate marie virg[in]is.* (S)[2]alue regina mi[sericordi]e . . . Oremus . . . Ame[n]

Suffrage introduced by the familiar antiphon (*AH* L, 245).[10]

97r–100r: *Oratio beate marie virginis.* (O)[6]bsecro te domina . . . facturus locuturus aut cogitaturus . . . et michi famulo tuo .N. impetres . . . mater dei et misericordie amen. (Last 2 lines on f. 100r blank)

Leroquais, *LH* II, p. 346 sq. (text). — (Note masculine forms.)

100v–102v: *Alia oratio de beata maria.* (O)[2] intemerata . . . o iohannes beatissime . . . michi peccatori . . . amen.

Cf. Wilmart, *Aut. spir.,* p. 488–490.

103r–105r: (LATE HAND:) Oratio . . . Ad sanctitatis tuae pedes . . . Indignus sum . . . Memorare piissima non esse auditum a saeculo . . . Amen.

(N.B. The *Memorare* as incorporated here differs slightly from the form found in 19th- or 20th-century devotional sources)

(105v: full-page illustration, within four-side border: David penitent)

106r–124v: *Incipiunt septem psalmi peniten-[ciales]. Ant.* Ne reminiscaris. *Psalm[us]* (D)[4]omine ne in furore tuo . . . (115v, 13th line:) *Leta[ni]ae s[an]c[t]o[rum]* . . .

The Penitential Psalms (= Pss. VI, XXXII, XXXVIII, LI, CII, CXXX, CXLIII) followed, in accordance with custom, by the Litany of Saints. — The litany names three saints not included in the book's calendar: Blaise among martyrs, Louis (Ludovicus) and Julian among confessors; also, among monks, St. Egidius (in the calendar on September 1)[11]

125r: (LATE HAND:) Oratio Itinerantis. Fidelissime custos hominu[m] Jesu Christe, qui samaritani nomen . . . p[er omnia . . .][12]

(125v: full-page illustration, within four-side border: Exequies)

126r–164v: *Incipiunt vigilie mortuorum* . . . (D)[4]ilexi . . . (ending on f. 164v, in 14th line:) . . . Ame[n]

The *Officium defunctorum*, liturgical Office for the Dead; with the standard Roman responsories (and Roman Invitatory).

164v–170v: (LATE HAND:) ORATIONES S. BRIGIDAE. O Jesu Christe aeterna dulcedo . . . (166r:) Oratio 2a. O Jesu mundi fabricator . . . (170r:) Oratio 15a. O Jesu vitis uera . . . Conclusio. O Domine . . . sucipe *[sic]* hanc orationem . . . (ends, 170v:) da misericordiam gratiam et remissionem et vitam aeternam. Amen.

The "Fifteen Oes of St. Brigit" (cf. slightly variant text in *Horae Eboracenses*, ed. C. Wordsworth [1920], p. 76–80).

170v: (LATE HAND:) OCTO V[ERSUS] S. BERNARDI. Illumina oculos meos . . . uiuentium.

Cf. Leroquais, *LH* I, p. xxx.

171r–171v: (LATE HAND:) Commendatio ad Deum. DEUS PROPITI[US] ESTO MIHI PECCATORI et custos omnibus diebus . . . Sancte Michael Archangele . . . (171v:) . . . Ecce signum + crucis . . . Agios o theos . . . et Spiritus + Sancti. Amen. Qui habitat in adiutorio Altissimi . . . (= Psalm XCI; ends on f. 172v, 8th line)

172v: (LATE HAND:) Oratio Ad S. Franciscum. De[us] qui mira crucis mysteria . . . Per Domin[um] . . . (= the liturgical *collecta* of the Mass and Office of St. Francis of Assisi)

173r: (LATE HAND, erased or extremely faded:) V. Domine exaudi . . . R. Et clamor meus . . . Oratio. Omnipotens sempiterne . . . Regi Juda . . . Amen. (173v blank)

* * *

Foliated in modern pencil. One free endleaf (blank vellum) precedes f. 1, one follows f. 173. — Written area ca. 81 × ca. 55 mm. Fully ruled in faint red ink; no prickings preserved. — Two hands: the script of the original (estimated to be early 16th-century) is good *lettre bâtarde*; the numerous additions made, apparently, in the early 17th century are written in an amateurish-appearing calligraphic cursive of the style promoted by Jan van den Velde. — Texts in the earlier hand are rubricated. — Parchment of good, somewhat uneven quality, thickness ca. 11 mm per 100 leaves.

Collation: (ff. 1–2, 17th-century addition?) $1–2^{6}$(= ff. 3–14) 3^{8+1}(f. 17 singleton, with stub following f. 21) 4^{8+2}(ff. 24 and 30 are singletons, with stubs following ff. 33 and

27 respectively) 5^{8+1}(f. 41 singleton, stub follows f. 34) $6–11^{8}$ 12^{8+2}(ff. 94–95 are a bifolio sewn-in between ff. 93 and 96) $13^{4?}$ 14^{8+1}(= ff. 105–113; f. 105 is a singleton, with stub after f. 113) 15^{8} 16^{8+1}(f. 125 a singleton; stub follows f. 127) $17–20^{8}$ $21^{4?}$(= ff. 163–166) $22^{4(+4)}$(f. 167 probably conjugate with [174], 168 with 173; ff. 169–172 are smaller size, ca. 122 × 96 mm, of vellum of varying quality, inserted with use of glue)

Decoration: Six large (87–89 × 54 mm) illustrations (ff. 17v, 24v, 30v, 41v, 105v, 125v, cf. contents) are part of the original book; the rather mediocre artwork on ff. 1–2 is later (early 17th century?) addition. — Four-side borders in the style of the Ghent-Bruges school are found on altogether 13 pages pertaining to the older parts, and on f. 2r where the border may be a later imitation. The borders contain, on brushed-gold ground, multicolor realistic strewn or vased flowers, (straw)berries, butterflies, insects, caterpillars, birds, snails; also a childlike figure in soldierly armor (f. 17v) and a person protruding from a shell (41v). — Major initials are 4 lines in height when associated with a decorative border, 6 lines in other cases.[13] They are built of woodlike and foliate shapes painted in gold or whitish gray, made to stand out by means of shadows which they appear to throw on their ground fields; the fields are rectangular, framed, light green, magenta, or whitish gray. — The 3-line *KL*'s of the calendar months, the 2-line minor initials, the 1-line versals, and line fillers (used primarily in the litany) are gold on alternating blue or magenta.

Binding: early 17th-century black morocco, lightly blind-tooled with straight lines parallel to the edges; rebacked. — One of two back-to-front silver clasps preserved completely, the other partially; on the complete one, engraved "P.C. E.V.M.";[14] on the remnant, "5" (last digit of what once was "1625"?).

On verso of upper cover, pasted clipping (from a Tregaskis catalog?) misidentifying the book as "Missale Romanum." — On recto of the free endleaf in front, in pencil: Ac. 1270. De R 33; on its verso, other annotations, including, "159 11."

Former owners: At the beginning of 17th century, Julius Echter von Mespelbrunn, Prince-Bishop of Würzburg. — Acquired by LC in 1912 by purchase, through V. G. Simkhovitch.

2° fo.: [illustrative material: Christ in Heaven]

Bibl.: De Ricci, *Census,* v. 1 (1935), p. 189, no. 33; Faye and Bond (1962), p. 117, no. 20.

NOTES

1. Quarterly (1) Argent a Rake Gules (4) Azure a Racing Banner quarterly Gules and Argent with Staff Or and Peak Argent (2) and (3) Azure on a Bend Argent three Rings Azure. (Description kindly provided by Thomas E. Wilgus.)

2. Cf. Leroquais, *LH* II, p. 11; *Analecta liturgica* (W. H. J. Weale, ed.; 1889), p. [296] sqq.

3. = Walther, *Initia* 17153.

4. Walther, *Initia* 13840; text *AH* XXX, p. 32 (not seen).

5. = Walther, *Initia* 21189; text *AH* XXX, p. 15 (not seen).

6. With collect *Concede nos,* epistle *Ab initio,* gradual *Benedicta et venerabilis* (+ *Virgo Dei genitrix* + *Post partum*), gospel *Loquente Iesu . . . extollens vocem quaedam . . .,* offertory antiphon *Felix namque*, communion antiphon *Beata viscera*, postcomm. *Graciam tuam.*

7. Cf. note on similar (though not identical) text in the Warburg Hours, LC MS 46.

8. Cf. *EEFL* no. 3309, also note on p. 1647. — Occurs also in the missal LC MS 26 (f. 142v).

9. See table C for textual details.

10. N.B. The word *mater* is said to have been inserted into the opening words of the antiphon in the 16th century. Cf. *AH, loc. cit.*

11. After the usual names of apostles, etc., the litany invokes individually 12 martyrs, 14 confessors, 11 women.

12. A second suggestion in these (17th? century) additions of travel or exile; cf. f. 68v. Thirty-years War?

13. In the Hours of B.V.M. (ff. 42 sqq.) the opening initial is 4 lines high while in the Lauds and in the minor hours, also Vespers (85r) and Compline (92r), the initial *D* of the "Deus in adiutorium" is 6 lines high.

14. The "E.V.M." no doubt for *Echter von Mespelbrunn*; "P.C." for "Pax Christi"?

(ff. 1r–12v, calendar; 13r–16v, Short Hours of the Cross; 17r–19v, Short Hours of the Holy Spirit; 20r–26r, Mass of B.V.M.; 26r–31v, Gospel readings; 32r–71v, Hours of Our Lady; 72r–76r, *Obsecro te*; 76r–79r, *O intemerata*; 81r–98v, Penitential Psalms, with Litany; 99r–114v, Office for the Dead)

MS 49

(Faye and Bond 130)

BOOK OF HOURS XVth c., 1st half

Produced in Bruges? Parchment. 115 leaves, ca. 89 × ca. 62 mm (bound volume: 96 × ca. 80 mm) 1 column. 16 lines (in the calendar, 17 lines)

ff. 1r–12v: Calendar with 115 entries, 63 of them in red; among these: *Amandi episcopi* (Feb. 6), *Georgij mr̄is* (Apr. 23), *[Transl.] Basilij episcopi* (June 14), *[Transl.] Eligij epī.* (June 25), *[Transl.] Thome ap.* (July 3), *[Transl.] Benedicti abbīs* (July 11), *Jacobi et xp̄ofori* (July 25), *Egidij abbīs* (Sept. 1), *Remigij [et] Bauo[n]is* (Oct. 1), *Dyonisij mr̄is* (Oct. 9), *Donaciani archiep̄ī.* (Oct. 14), *Eligij episcopi* (Dec. 1), *Nychasij epī.* (Dec. 14). — Among the names in black: Aldegundis (Jan. 30), "Brigidi abbīs." *[sic]* (Feb. 1), Dauid confessoris (Mar. 1), Benedicti abbīs. (Mar. 21), Brandani epī. (May 17), Bertini abbīs (Sept. 5), Lamberti ep̄ī (Sept. 17), Brandani ep̄ī. (Nov. 21), Lazari mr̄is. (Dec. 17).

Some of the days singled out in red suggest Bruges, some Tournai. — The David named with March 1 is a Welsh saint. Overseas connections may have brought in the two Brandans.

(following f. 12, one or more leaves are wanting, with loss of the beginning of the next item and, very likely, a large illustration [Crucifixion?])

13r–16v: *v̄s[us]* Adoramus the xp̄e [et] benedicimus tibi . . . sim corone. Amen. (N.B. ends in first line of 16v, rest of page blank)

The Short Hours of the Cross;[1] beginning imperfectly near the end of the Matins.

(following f. 16, one or more leaves wanting, with loss of the beginning of the next item and, probably, a large illustration [Pentecost?])

17r–19v: sancte sp[irit]us reple tuor[um] . . . vt cum de[us]

The Short Hours of the Holy Spirit (psalmless, based on segments of the hymn *Nobis Sancti Spiritus gratia sit data*[2] divided over the day); incomplete, beginning near the end of the Matins and ending in the middle of the compline hymn.

(following f. 19, one or more leaves wanting, with loss of the end of the preceding item and of the beginning of the next; the large illustration expected but wanting would be Mary with the Child)

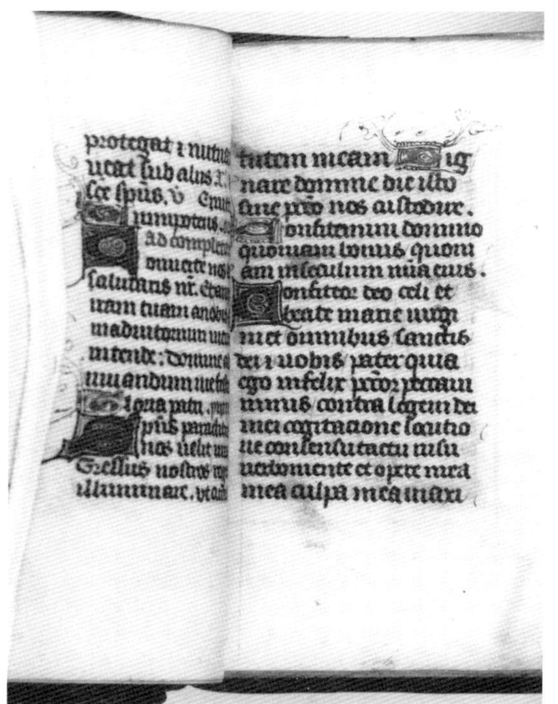

MS 49, ff. 19v–20r (actual height of written area: 49 mm)

20r–26r: tutem meam. Dignare domine die isto . . . Confiteor deo celi et beate marie uirgini et omnibus sanctis dei [et] uobis pater quia ego infelix p[e]cc[at]or peccaui nimis contra legem dei mei cogitacione locutione consensu tactu uisu uerbo mente et opere . . . (20v:) . . . Misereatur uestri . . . perducat nos [et] uos ihesus xp̄us sine macula cum gaudio ad uita[m] eternam. Amen. . . . (21r:) *Introit[us]* (S)^{2}alue sancta pare[n]s . . .

Mass of (in honor of) the Virgin Mary; i.e., parts of the ordinary and the proper, with collect *Concede nos,* epistle *Ab initio*, gradual *Benedicta et venerabilis,* offertory antiphon *Felix namque,* communion antiphon *Beata viscera,* post-Communion prayer *Gratiam tuam;* includes *Gloria* and *Credo.* — The text begins imperfectly, in the middle of the introductory prayers at the foot of the altar. — The formula of the *Confiteor* is very similar to that found in the Hours LC MS 46 and, it seems, other books of hours of Flemish origin.[3]

26r–31v; *scd'm iohannem* (I)^{2}n principio . . . (27v:) . . . *secundu[m] luca[m].* (I)^{2}n illo tempore. Missus est . . . (29r:) . . . *Secundum matheum.* (C)^{2}um natus esset . . . (30r:) . . . *s[e]c[un]d[u]m marcum.* (I)^{2}n illo tempore. Recumbentibus vndecim . . . (31v:) sequentibus signis. Deo gracias.

Gospel readings: John I,1–14; Luke I, 26b–38a; Matthew II,1–12; Mark XVI, 14–20. No major liturgical additions.

(following f. 31, one or more leaves wanting with loss, presumably, of a large illustration [Annunciation?] and of the opening phrases of next item)

32r–71v: mus faciem eius in confessione . . . (71r:) . . . (S)^{2}alue regina . . . (71v:) . . . (O)^{2}mnipotens sempiterne deus qui gloriose uirginis . . . sp[irit]u sancto

Hours of Our Lady, use of Rome. Beginning and ending imperfectly; also throughout the office the beginning of each "hour" and the ending of most are wanting. The lacunae follow ff. 42, 54, 56, 59, 61, 63, and 68; missing are in each case one or two leaves, including, very likely, large illustrations: Visitation, Nativity, Shepherds, Magi, Presentation, Flight to Egypt, Coronation of the Virgin. — The Roman use is not as fully developed as in later presentations: there is no mention of alternate sets of psalms for the Matins, and no seasonal variations are provided. (For specific information on the texts, see table C.)

(following f. 71, one or more leaves wanting, with loss of end of the preceding and of the beginning of what follows)

72r–76r: mi regis filia m[ate]r gloriosissima . . . (74r:) . . . f[a]c[t]urus locutur[us] aut cogitaturus . . . (74v:) . . . Et m[ihi] famulo tuo . . . (ends on 76r:) . . . dulcissima maria mater dei et mi[sericordi]e Ame[n].

The *Obsecro te* (cf. printed text in Leroquais, *LH* II, p. 346 sq.; *Horae Eboracenses* [1920], p. 66–67); preserved text begins in the tenth word ([sum]mi . . .) Masculine grammatical forms indicate, *ad minimum*, that the book was not consciously written for a woman. — The missing opening words would fit well under an illustration.[4]

76r–79r: *Ad uirginem mariam.* (O)[3] intemerata . . . O joha[n]nes beatissime . . . in secula seculorum A[men]

The second major prayer not fashioned after a liturgical pattern, among several such common in books of hours. This is the "Johannine" version developed, probably, in the 12th century; cf. Wilmart, *Aut. spir.*, p. [474] sqq. (printed text *ibid.*, p. 488–490; also in *Horae Eboracenses*, p. 67 sq.).

(79v and 80r blank, ruled; 80v ruled and blank except for LATE, perhaps 19th-century INSCRIPTION: "ce livre apartien a je ne sai qui celui qui le trouvera le rendra a la soeur magdelaine." — Following f. 80, one or more leaves wanting, presumably including large illustration [David penitent] and ca. 70 words of next item)

81r–98v: meo lauabo per singulas noctes . . .

The Penitential Psalms, beginning imperfectly in the middle of the first one (i.e., Ps. VI); with Litany (f. 92v sqq.) — After the (rarely varying) series of names of apostles, etc., the litany invokes individually 16 martyrs, 18 confessors, and 17 women. The only unusual names are s. Martha and s. Caritas (named here without her supposed sisters Fides and Spes).

(one or more leaves wanting after f. 98; lost is the beginning, ca. 50 words, of the office which follows; with it, most likely, a large illustration [a Funeral Service or possibly Job])

99r–114v: Conuertere anima mea in requiem mea[m] . . . (114v:) . . . De profundis clamaui

The *Officium defunctorum,* beginning imperfectly in the middle of the first psalm of the Vespers (Ps. CXVI) and ending imperfectly toward the end of the Lauds (with which the office normally concludes). — The Matins have only one nocturn. Lesson I: Parce michi; Responsory I: Credo quod; L. II: Tedet animam; R. II: Qui Lazarum; L. III: Manus tue; R. III: Libera me.

(after f. 114, one or more leaves wanting, with continuation of Ps. CXXX and perhaps further material. f. 115 blank, not ruled)

* * *

Foliated in 10s in modern pencil. Free paper endleaves precede f. 1 and follow f. 115. — Written area ca. 49 × ca. 32 mm. Fully ruled in faint red ink. No pricking marks (cropped?). — Script is an unassuming, small, occasionally tightly squeezed *littera textualis*. Brownish black ink; rubrics in red. — Parchment of good quality and except for the initial and final leaves, fairly white; thickness ca. 12.6 mm per 100 leaves; some leaves crinkled or stained.

Collation impracticable owing to tight rebinding. No catchwords. There seem to be (at least) 12 gatherings.

No illustrations; the number and location of text lacunae show either past presence or at least an intention to provide the usual set. — Surviving decoration is limited to rather numerous burnished-gold initials (3-line for the *KL*'s of the calendar and the *O* of the *O Intemerata*, f. 76r, 2-line elsewhere). Their background areas, outlined in more or less letterform shapes in black ink (as are the letters themselves) are throughout part dull pink and part blue, both colors decorated with white pen lines. One-line, blue versals with red pen flourishes alternate with gold ones flourished in black. Line fillers, used only in the Litany (92v sqq.), are simple ornamental lines or shapes done by brush in blue and pink.

Binding: covers are early 19th-century calf; sewn over 5 bands. More recently rebacked and otherwise repaired with use of brown morocco. The calf covers are blind-tooled with a simple rectangular frame and diagonal lines. Endpapers marbled. On verso of front free endleaf, penciled: R 3; Ac. 4984 A(3); "Gift Dr. Ernest C. Richardson, Dec. 15, 1934."

Former owners: "Soeur Magdelaine" (cf. f. 80v); Ernest C. Richardson (Princeton, N.J.).

MS 49 2° fo.: (KL)[3] Februari[us] h̄t̄ d'

Bibl.: De Ricci, *Census*, v. 2 (1937), p. [1187] no. 3; Faye and Bond, p. 121, no 130.

A workshop product of West Flemish origin (perhaps from Bruges in its beginning economic decline), the little book poses the question of whether it ever was complete. If so, it must have had something like the usual complement of about ten large illustrations, of the kind accompanied by a few lines of text. The surviving text begins quite often in the middle of a word (20r, 32r, 57r, 60r, 62r) but it is possible that the workshop scribe knew exactly where the text of the illustrated leaf would break off. Physical aspects of the book, rebound and rebacked and tightened, offer few clues: there are no stubs or other physical evidence of vandalization.[5]

NOTES

1. The psalmless devotion based on the hymn *Patris sapientia veritas divina*. See also notes to ff. 91–92 of MS 44.

2. Walther, *Initia* 21189.

3. Cf. note made with LC MS 46 (= the Warburg Hours), its ff. 33r–43v. — The formula as given here is one for use by a layman attending the Mass; it is not clear how similar was the formula used by the priest.

4. There is, however, no standard pattern to suggest its theme.

5. A possibly relevant fact is the ruled, blank f. 80 (see contents) with the very recent inscription on verso: wouldn't an inscription of this kind belong to the last page of a book?

MS 50

(Rosenwald 9/16)[1]

BOOK OF HOURS early XVIth c.

France (Touraine?) Parchment. 90 leaves, 138 × ca. 84 mm (bound volume: 145 × ca. 90 mm) 1 column. 25 lines.

(ff. 1r–8v, calendar; 9r–11r, Gospel readings; 11r–15v, Passion according to John; 15v–16v, *Stabat mater dolorosa*; 16v, *Devota commendatio ad B.V.M.*; 17r–47v, Hours of Our Lady; 47v–49v, Short Hours of the Cross; 49v–51r, Short Hours of the Holy Spirit; 51r–60v, Penitential Psalms, with Litany; 60v–80r, Office for the Dead; 80r–81r, prayers to Trinity; 81r–82v, *Obsecro te;* 82v–83v, *O Intemerata*; 83v–89v, suffrages; 89v–90r, prayers before and after Communion; 90r–v, Seven Prayers of St. Gregory)

ff. 1r–8v: Full calendar in Latin; in black and gold. — Notable among days singled out in gold: *Antonii abb.* (Jan. 17), *Sebastiani* (Jan. 20), *Marthae* (July 29), *Rochi* (Aug. 16), *Augustini* (Aug. 28), *Francisci* (Oct. 4), *Siluestri* (Dec. 31.) — Among days in black: Seueri & Erardi (Jan. 8), Martianae (Jan. 9), Transl. s. Marci (Jan. 30), Vgi [= Hugonis] (Mar. 10), Grondani [= Guntrammi] (Mar. 28), Zeni [= Zenonis] (Apr. 12), Maximi epi. (May 29), Pergentini & Lagentini (June 3), Ianuariae (June 21), Paulini epi. (June 22), Martialis (July 1), Ulderici epi. Augustae (July 4), Fortunati (July 12), Fantini (July 31), Candidi (Dec. 1), Antonillae (Dec. 18).

In emphasizing in gold the days noted above the scribe may have been under the influence of a Milanese and/or Franciscan model. "Sebastiani" instead of "Fabiani et Sebastiani" is Milanese; the emphasis on St. Martha, Franciscan; the attention to St. Roch, protector against epidemic disease (cf. f. 88r) may have to do with acute danger at the time of writing; major celebration of St. Silvester may be northern Italian or Franciscan. Some of the other names point to northeastern Italy; there is a considerable amount of agreement with the calendar of LC MS 52 (Rosenwald 10). — The calendar includes modern numbering of days of month; in addition, the Roman-style dating is spelled out for each day. — The introductory initial at the beginning of individual months is *K* rather than *KL*.

9r–11r: *Initium sancti euangelii secundum Ioannem. Gloria tibi domine* (I)[3]N PRINCIPIO erat verbum . . .

Gospel readings: John I,1–14; Luke I,26b–38a; Matthew II,1–12; Mark XVI,14–20. Except for the "rubrics" there are no liturgical additions.

MS 50

11r–15v: ***Passio domini Iesu christi secundum Ioannem.*** (E)[3]GRESSVS est . . . (Gospel text ends on 15r:) . . . posueru[n]t Iesum. *V* Qui passus es pro nobis. *R* Domine miserere nobis. *V* Domine exaudi. *oratio* (D)[2]EVS Qui manus tuas et pedes tuos . . . (ends 15v:) . . . seculum. *R* Amen.

John XVIII,1b-XIX,42 with suffrage-type additions. No amplifications in the mocking and torture scenes.

15v–16v: *Deuota contemplatio beatissimae Mariae virginis, iuxta crucem filii lachrymantis* (S)[3]TABAT mater dolorosa . . . (ends 16r, followed by versicle and response:) Tuam ipsius animam . . . Vt reuelentur . . . (16v:) (I)[2]Nteruenlat pro nobis quaesumus . . . doloris gladius pertransiuit . . . Amen.

The 13th-century hymn in a suffrage-type setting (the collect *Interveniat* was used in votive Masses in the pre-1970 *Missale Romanum*).

16v: *Deuota commendatio ad beatissimam virginem Mariam.* (D)[2]DOMINA *[sic]* mea sancta Maria me i[n] tuam benedictam fidem ac singularem custodiam . . . commendo . . . tuam voluntatem & meam necessitatem. AMEN

(Not in Leroquais, *LH* II, index)

17r–47v: *INCIPIT OFFICIUM DIVAE VIRGINIS MARIAE CHRISTIFERAE SECVNDVM VSVM ROMANVM//AD MATVTINVM* (D)[4]OMINE Labia mea . . .

Hours of Our Lady, use of Rome.**[2]**

47v–49v: *AD MATVINVM* [sic] *DE CRVCE* (D)[5]OMINE Labia mea . . . Patris sapientia veritas diuina . . . (ends, 49v:) . . . Sis mihi solatium in mortis agone. amen.

The psalmless devotion based on the hymn Walther, *Initia* 13840.

49v–51r: *DE SANCTO SPIRITV AD MATVTINVM* (D)[5]OMINE Labia mea . . . (N)[2]obis Sancti spiritus gratia sit data . . . (ends, 51r:) . . . Vt viuamus iugiter in coeli regione. Amen

The Short Hours of the Holy Spirit, psalmless, based on the hymn Walther, *Initia* 21189.

51r–60v: *Sequuntur septem psalmi poenitentiales. Antiphona.* Ne reminiscaris domine *psalmus* (D)[5]OMINE ne in furore tuo . . .

Penitential Psalms (cf. MS 44, f. 77r, comment); with Litany (56r sqq.). The litany is free of any saints of local character: only "sancte Blasi" among martyrs, and Anna, Martha, Clara, and Elizabeth ("Helisabeth") among women are not in the version eventually stabilized by the Roman Breviary (of the saints invoked there, Bernard among order founders and Anastasia among women are wanting in the present ms.)

60v–80r: *INCIPIT OFFICIVM PRO FIDELIBVS DEFVNCTIS AD VESPERAS An.* Placebo domino. *psalmus* (D)[5]ILEXI Quoniam exaudiet . . . (Matins begin on 64r; Lauds, 74v)

Office for the Dead, Roman use.**[3]** Three nocturns.

80r–81r; *Sequuntur suffragia plurium sanctoru[m] et sanctarum. Et primo de sanctissima Trinitate [!].* (A)[3]DORO te deum patrem & filium, & spiritum sanctum, vnam diuinitatem, aequalem gloriam . . . (80v:) . . . et omnibus sanctis. Amen. *A* Te inuocamus te adoramus . . . *V* Sit nomen domini . . . *R* Ex hoc nunc . . . *Oratio* (O)[2]MNIPOTENS sempiterne deus qui dedisti famulis tuis . . .

For the *Adoro te* . . . see Leroquais, *LH* II, p. 340 (a slightly longer variant). The antiphon "Te invocamus . . ." begins the suffrage proper; its formal prayer ("Omnipotens . . .") is the collect of Trinity Sunday in the 1570 *Missale Romanum*. — The apparent (and shocking) inclusion of the Trinity in "sancti et sanctae" occurs also in Hours LC MSS 52 and 53, all from first half of the 16th century and possibly all from the same workshop.

81r–82v: *Deuotissima oratio ad beatissimam virginem Mariam.* (O)[3]BSECRO te domina . . . (81v–82r:) facturus, locuturus aut cogitaturus . . . Et mihi famulo tuo . . . (ends, 82v:) . . . mater dei & misericordiae. Amen.

The standard prayer (Leroquais, *LH* II, p. 346 sq.), with grammatical forms suitable for use by a male.

82v–83v: *Alia oratio ad beatissimam virginem Mariam . et ad Sanctum Ioannem eua[n]gelista[m]*

(O)² INTEMERATA . . . (83r:) . . . ego miserrimus peccator . . . (ends, 83v:) . . . per infinita seculorum secula. Amen.

Cf. Wilmart, *Aut. spir.*, p. 488–490 (slightly variant)

83v–89v: (Saints' suffrages:)

83v *De sancto Michaele* (Michel [*sic*] archangele paradisi praeposite . . . (D)²EVS Qui miro ordine . . .)

83v–84r *De sancto Ioanne Baptista* (Inter natos mulierum . . . (P)²RAESTA Quaesumus omnipotens deus vt familia tua . . .)

84r *De sancto Ioanne euangelista* (Ioannes apostolus & euangelista virgo . . . (E)²CCLESIAM tuam . . .)

84r–v *De sanctis apostolis Petro & Paulo* (Petrus apostolus & Paulus doctor gentium . . . (D)²EVS cuius dextera . . .)

84v *De sancto Andrea apostolo* (Salue crux preciosa . . . (M)²AIESTATEM tuam . . .)

84v *De sancto Iacobo apostolo* (Lux et decus Hyspaniae . . . (E)²STO domine plebis tuae sanctificator . . .)

84v–85r *De pluribus apostolis* (Dum steteritis . . . (C)²ONCEDE Quaesumus . . .)

85r *De sancto Stephano prothomartyre* (Stephanus plenus gratia . . . (O)²MNIPOTENS sempiterne deus qui primitias martyrum . . .)

85r–86r *De sancto Christophoro* (Sancte Christophore martyr dei preciose . . . (D)²EVS Qui beatum Christophoru[m] martyrem tuum . . .) (N.B. The opening "antiphon" is really a rather prolix address to the saint)

86r *De sancto Laurentio* (Leuita Laurentius . . . (D)²A nobis quesumus . . .)

86r–v *De sancto Sebastiano* (O q[uam] mira refulsit gratia . . . (D)²EVS Qui beatum Sebastianu[m] . . . & in omni tempore contra pestem epydimiae remedium . . .)

86v *De sancto Dionysio* (O beate Dionysi magna est fides tua . . . (D)²EVS Qui beatum Dionysiu[m] martyrem tuum virtute constantiae . . .)

86v–87r *De .s. Antonio* (Anthoni pastor inclyte qui cruciatos reficis ignis calorem extinguis . . . (D)²EVS Qui concedis obtentu . . . morbidum igne[m] extingui, & membris refrigeria praestari . . .) (Possibly a reference to an actual epidemic, as may have also been the case with the suffrage of St. Sebastian (above) and that of St. Roch [cf. below, 88r])

87r *De sancto Nicolao episcopo* (Amicus dei Nicolaus . . . (D)²EVS qui beatum Nicolaum . . .)

87r–v *De sancto Martino* (O beatum pontificem qui totis visceribus diligebat . . . (D)²EVS qui conspicis quia ex nulla nostra virtute . . .)

87v–88r *De sancto Claudio* (O desolatorum consolator . . . (D)²EVS Qui beato Claudio . . .)

88r *De sancto Rocho* (Aue Roche sanctissime nobili natus sanguine . . . Vt mereamur praeseruari a peste epydimiae . . . (D)²EVS Qui beato Rocho per angelu[m] tuum . . .)

88r–v *De Sancta Anna* (Coeleste beneficium . . . (D)²EVS Qui beatae Annae . . .)

88v *De sancta Maria Magdalena* (Maria ergo vnxit . . . (L)²ARGIRE nobis clementissime pater . . .)

88v–89r *De sancta Caterina* (Virgo sancta Caterina Graeciae gemma . . . (D)²EVS Qui dedisti legem Moysi . . .)

89r *De sancta Margarita* (Virgo gloriosa christi Margarita . . . (D)²EVS Qui beatam Margaritam . . .)

89r–v *De sancta Barbara* (Gaude Barbara beata, summe pollens in doctrina . . . (I)²NTERCESSIO Quaesumus domine . . .)

89v–90r: *Oratio dicenda ante susceptionem corporis Christi.* (D)²OMINE non sum dignus . . . sed tu domine qui dixisti qui manducat . . . (ends, 90r:) . . . Qui cum patre.

90r: *Oratio dicenda post sancta[m] co[m]munionem* (V)²ERA perceptio . . . ad vitam praesentem et aeternam introductio. Per.

90r–v: *Septem deuote orationes beatissimi Gregorii Pontificis maximi.* (O)³ DOMINE Iesu christe adoro te in cruce pendentem . . . in cruce vulneratum . . . in sepulchro positum . . . (90v:) descendentem ad inferos . . . resurgentem a mortuis & ad coelos ascendentem . . . (O)² Domine Iesu christe pastor bone iustos conserua peccatores iustifica . . . (O)² Domine Iesu christe propter illa[m] amaritudinem . . . Deprecor te miserere animae meae in egressu suo. Pater noster. Aue Maria.

Known as "Seven Prayers of St. Gregory." Text (slightly variant) printed in Leroquais, *LH* II, p. 346.[4]

* * *

No foliation. Four vellum flyleaves precede f. [1] and four follow f. [90]; the first three at the beginning and the last three at the end are of thicker material than the text leaves. — Written area ca. 92 × ca. 50 mm. Ruled extremely lightly (to the point of invisibility) in very faint red ink; no pricking marks. — Written in an extremely even and well-formed italic script. Text black, rubrics in gold; captions in Roman capitals, some entirely in gold, some in combinations of gold, blue, and red. — Extremely high-quality writing material (thickness: ca. 8.3 mm per 100 leaves).

Collation impracticable.

No illustrations. Decoration is limited to initials, line-fillers, and paragraph marks. Of the initials 13 are major,[5] decorated with very delicate designs of birds, flowers, etc., in brilliant colors on framed fields of (brushed) gold. — Minor (2-line) initials and 1-line versals, also paragraph marks are all gold, with added tracery, on red or bright blue grounds. Line fillers are light blue or red (also combined) rectangles decorated with golden patterns.

Nineteenth-century red velvet covers. On spine, label with title (gilt on black ground): HORAE/B. M./VIRGINIS. Gilt and gauffered edges. The binding is worn at the hinges.

On pastedown of upper cover, penciled: 2259; (?); 5 7/16 × 3 6/16; "remarkable for the history & fineness of the make (?)"; 1320; 772; also ex libris of Cortlandt F. Bishop, the Rosenwald logo, and label: THE GIFT OF//LESSING J. ROSENWALD //TO THE LIBRARY OF CONGRESS. — Laid-in: ex libris of William Loring Andrews (made in 1894; engraving includes conspicuous date "1640" in no way associated with the book). — On recto of the last flyleaf (not conjugate with the pastedown), penciled by LC cataloger: "Catholic Church. Liturgy and ritual. Hours. (ca. 1540)"; "Rosenwald Coll. Ms. no. 9"; "MLS 1 D 49."[6] — On pastedown of lower cover, in pencil: Lot 1433. — Kept in a solander case covered in red morocco; on spine of the case: (label:) 16; (impressed in gilt:) OFFICIUM DIVAE//VIRGINIS MARIAE//MANUSCRIPT//1320// FRENCH//EARLY XVI CENT.

Former owners: W. L. Andrews; C. F. Bishop; L. J. Rosenwald.

2° fo.: e 16.14. cal. mar. Iulianae virginis

Bibl.: *The Cortlandt F. Bishop library* . . . (1938–39), v. 2, no. 1433. — (Library of Congress), *The Rosenwald collection* (1954), p. 3 (no. 11) — (Library of Congress), *The Lessing J. Rosenwald collection* (1977), p. 7 (no. 16).

Its lack of illustrations may have been the major reason why this thoroughly splendid product of calligraphic art never got much attention (see plate XIX, p. xxxiii). The style of its decoration as well as textual similarities (choice of text, calendar, formulation of captions) indicate a closeness of origin to the Hours LC MS 52 (Rosenwald 10/14). Working, no doubt, in France, the scribe copied a calendar influenced by the liturgical year of Milan and/or by the Franciscan use.[7] Was perhaps this book, too, planned as a royal-quality gift to somebody in northern Italy? — The epidemic on which several of the suffrages seem to focus may have been the "feu de saint Antoine" much feared throughout the Middle Ages and specifically noted also in 1530 (cf. A. Larcan, *Les intoxications par les dérivés de l'ergot de seigle* (1977), p. 67).

NOTES

1. No. 9 in old LC "Rosenwald shelflist"; no. 16 in 1977 second catalog of the LC Rosenwald Collection.
2. See table C for textual details.
3. As in the *Breviarium Romanum*, with Lauds in their pre-1911 form.
4. Another variant, beginning "Adoro te Domine Jesu Christe in cruce pendentem," in *Horae Eboracenses* (1920), p. 81.
5. Eleven *D*'s, one *C*, one *V*.
6. LC printed card 50-42680, reproduced in its older form in NUC pre-56 and (in a slightly revised format) in LC's MARC data base.
7. The list of saints is ca. 93 percent identical with that found in both LC MSS 52 and 53 (= Rosenwald 10/14 and 11/12); this includes many "odd," that is non-Roman and non-French choices (cf. notes to the two manuscripts). There is less agreement in the days singled out in gold.

MS 51

(Rosenwald 29/9)

BOOK OF HOURS beginning XVIth c.?

Flanders? Parchment. 136 leaves, 151 × ca. 100 mm (bound volume: 157 × ca. 110 mm) 1 column. 20 lines (in the calendar, 18 lines)

(ff. 1r–12v, calendar; 13v–19r, Gospel readings; 21r–23v, Short Hours of the Cross; 23v–26r, Short Hours of the Holy Spirit; 27r–60v, Hours of Our Lady; 63r–74v, Penitential Psalms, with Litany; 75r–85r, Office for the Dead; 87r–93v, daily prayers; 94r–96r, Seven Joys of Mary; 96r–125r, suffrages and various prayers; 125r–127r, Passion according to John; 127r–135r, various prayers and suffrages)

ff. 1r–12v: (KL)[3] Januarius habet . . .

Calendar, in black and red, with altogether 210 entries. Among the red-letter days: *Amandi ep.* (Feb. 6); *Translatio Thome; Egidii abb.; Remigii & Bavonis; Dyonisii cf.* (Oct. 9); *Donatiani* (Oct. 14); *Eligii ep.* (Dec. 1). — Among those written in black: Gudile, Macharii (Jan. 24), Jacincti (Jan. 31), Matrone, Pastoris, Claudiani, Olimpiadis, Paterni, Eutropi (Apr. 24), Papie, Huberti, Landoaldi (June 13), Aguardi (June 22), Nicostrasti [*sic*], Bertini, Evortii, Ferreoli (Sept. 18) Wulfranni (Oct. 15), Livini, Machuti, Gumberti (Nov. 16), Maximi (Nov. 27), Nichasii (Dec. 14), Mercurii (Dec. 20). — The saints are those of northern France or Belgium.

(13r blank)

13v–19r: (13v, large illustration: St. John the Evangelist on Patmos; with full border and five lines of text) *Inicium sancti euuangelij. Secundum iohanne[m]* (I)[4]N principio . . . (19r, first line:) sequentibus signis. Deo gra[cia]s. (rest of page blank)

Gospel readings: John I,1–14; Luke I,26b–38a; Matthew II,1–12; and Mark XVI, 14–20. — Each reading is introduced by a large pictorial representation of the pertinent evangelist, with full border and 5 or 6 lines of text (Luke: 15r; Matthew: 16v; Mark: 18r)

(19v–20v blank)

21r–23v: (D)[5]Omine labia mea . . . i[n] mortis agone. amen.

The Short Hours of the Cross (cf. notes to MS 44, ff. 91–92); introduced by large illustration: Crucifixion (within full border, with the initial lines of the text under the illustration).

23v–26r: (23v, last line, rubric:) *De sancto sp[irit]u.* (24r, under illustration:) (D)[5]omine labia mea . . . (ends on 26r:) . . . Quod uiuam[us] iugiter celi regione. amen. (26v blank, ruled)

The psalmless office based on the hymn *Nobis Sancti Spiritus gratia sit data* (cf. MS 44, notes to ff. 93–95). Introduced by large illustration: Pentecost (with full border, etc.)

27r–60v: (D)[5]Omine labia . . . omnes sancti tui.

Hours of Our Lady, use of Rome.[1] — Large illustrations, with full borders, introduce the Matins (f. 27r, Annunciation), Lauds (35r, Visitation), Prime (43v, Nativity), Terce (46v, Shepherds), Sext (49v, Magi), None (52r, Presentation), Vespers (54v, Flight to Egypt), and Compline (58v, Slaughter of the Innocents).

(61r–62v blank, ruled)

63r–74v: (D)[5]Omine ne in furore tuo . . . supplicationibus consequantur.

The Penitential Psalms,[2] introduced by a large illustration (63r, David penitent; within full border, etc.); followed by Litany of Saints, f. 71v sqq. — Notable invocations in the litany: s. mammes (not in the calendar; patron of Langres, celebrated also in Rheims), s. benigne; s. claudi, s. medarde, s. philiberte; s. maria magdalena, s. maria egypciaca, s. genouefa.[3]

74v–85r: (rubric on 74v in last 2 lines:) *Incipiunt uigilie mortuoru[m]. Et primo ad Vesperas.* (75r, beginning inside full border, under large illustration representing Jesus healing a leper:) *a[ntiphona].* Placebo. *P[salmu]s d[auid]* (D)[5]Ilexi . . . (ends in last line of 85r:) Fidelium Deus omn[ium][4]

The *Officium defunctorum*, with regular Roman readings and responsories.

(85v–86v blank, ruled)

87r–93v: *Quando surges de lecto* . . . (S)[4]urrexit dominus de sepulcro qui pro nobis . . . (ending on 93v, line 10:) [per]ducas ad uitam eternam. amen.

A collection of (not very familiar) daily prayers, introduced by large illustration on f. 87r: Kneeling man at prayer, next to an empty canopied bed.[5] The unidentified individual portrayed here appears also in the large illustration on f. 105r and in the smaller ones on 128v and 131r.

94r–96r: (G)[4]aude flore uirginali . . .

The hymn known as "Seven Joys of Mary," sometimes associated with Thomas of Canterbury;[6] with added two sets of versicles and formal prayers (the first one primarily for chastity); introduced by large illustration (94r, Mary nursing her child).

96r–100r: (first of two groups of saints' suffrages:)

96r (beginning in 11th line): (N)[2]Ouum sydus ecclesie . . . Ora pro nobis b[eat]e petre de lucemburgo . . . (D)[2]Eus qui beati petri lucemburgensis . . . (ends in 7th line of 96v:) . . . Per xp̄m̄ (rest of page empty, ruled)[7]

97r–99r: (introduced by large illustration: Mary Magdalen in the desert, with conspicuously bare breasts) (M)[5]ulier que riuulis lacrimarum uberrimis . . . (Suffrage aimed at Mary Magdalen; includes hymn *Gaude pie Magdalena.*)

99r–100r: (G)loriosissima virgo et martyr Katherina . . . ualeamus peruenire. per. (followed by 4 empty lines)

100r–101r: (Q)[2]uid est ihesus nisi saluator ergo bone ih[es]u per te ip[su]m redemptus sum. . . . secundum magna[m] misericordiam tuam. amen.

Cf. Leroquais, *LH* II, p. 345. — The 4 empty lines on f. 100r had been left blank, no doubt, for a rubric which remained unwritten.

101r–104r: (introduced by large illustration: Trinity) (A)[5]Doro te deum patrem, filium et spiritu[m] sanctum . . . (101v:) . . . propicius esto michi peccatrici . . . (102v:) . . . ut liberata de manibus inimicoru[m] meorum . . . (ends 104r:) . . . fidei firmitate ab omnibus semper muniamur aduersis. per dnm̄.

MS 51 A strongly penitential devotion; written for use by a woman. Ending by the liturgical prayer used on Trinity Sunday and addressed primarily to God as Trinity; includes, however, also invocations of Michael Archangel (!?).

104r–v: (beginning with rubric in 3rd line) *In eleuatione corporis xpisti:* (A)²Ve salue mundi uerbum . . . (A)²ue uerum corpus natū.de maria uirgine . . .[8] alia (A)²nima xp̄i sanctifica me . . .[9] (ends on 104v, 7th line:) . . . seculorum amen. (rest of page empty)

105r–106r: (on 105r, large illustration: church scene with a priest offering Mass[10]) (A)⁵Ve domine ihesu x[rist]e uerbum p[at]ris filius uirginis agnus dei . . . (106r, 8th line:) *In eleuatione sangui[ni]s x[rist]i.* (A)²ue sanguis xr[ist]i sacratissime. Aue sanguis mundissime . . . seculoru[m]. ame[n].

Private (non-liturgical) prayers for use by lay people attending Mass. — The first prayer is variously attested as the "V [i.e., Quinque] Ave" or "Quinque salutationes Jesu Christi" (cf. Wilmart, *Aut. spir.*, p. 377, note, and text *ibid.*, p. 412, no. iii).

106v–108v: (introduced by partial border and a 7-line square illustration: half portrait of Christ, *en face*, blessing) *de btā Veronica (S)²Alue s*[an]c[t]a facies . . . (ends, 107v:) . . . cu[m] b[ea]tis. A[men] (followed, 107v–, by Ps. LXVII:) Deus misereatur nostri . . . (108r:) . . . fines terrae. Gl[or]ia patri . . . (followed by versicles and formal prayer:) (D)²Eus qui nobis signatis lumine uultus tui . . . (ends, 108v:) . . . s[e]c[u]lorum. Amen.

Text of the *pium dictamen* (which has little to do with St. Veronica): Leroquais, *LH* II, p. 349. — A shorter form of the suffrage (without the psalm) is used in LC MS 46 (ff. 17–18v) (Cf. also Keble College ms. 45 in Parkes, *Med. mss. Keble College*, p. 207)

108v–121r: (Suffrages and prayers, most of them accompanied by small illustrations:) 108v–109r, *De sancto Lazaro* (Tremuit spiritu . . .); 109r–v, *Ad p[at]rem or[ati]o* (Domine Deus pater . . .); 109v–110r, *Ad filiu[m] or[ati]o* (Domine Ihesu Christe . . .); 110r, *Ad s[an]c[tu]m sp[iritu]m* (Domine sancte spiritus qui . . .); 110r–112r, *De sancta anna* (Gaude mater matris Christi . . ., with small illustration representing St. Anne on 110v); 112r, *De sancta genouefa* (O felix ancilla dei . . .); 112r–113r, *De sancta appolonia* (Ista est virgo sapiens . . .); 113r–v, *Ante receptionem corporis xp̄i* (Ne irascaris domine Ihesu . . . [in form suitable for a woman: . . . conscia . . .]); 113v–114r, *In receptione corporis xpisti* (Dulcissime Ihesu saluator mundi qui non ventris servientis . . .); 114r–v, *post receptionem corporis xpisti* (Sacrosancta receptio . . .); 114v–115r, *De concepcione beate marie uirg[inis]* (Conceptio tua Dei genitrix virgo gaudium annunciavit . . .); 115r–v, *Co[mm]em[oratio] de b[ea]ta mar[ia]* (Salve regina misericordiae . . .); 115v–116r, *De o[mn]ibus sanctis* (Sancti Dei omnes intercedere dignemini . . .); 116v–117r, *De sancto michaele* (Michael archangele veni . . .); 117r–v, *De sancto stephano* (Stephanus vidit . . .); 117v, *De sancto anthonio* (Vox de celo ad beatum Anthonium . . .; N.B. aimed at St. Anthony the Hermit); 118r, *De sancto huberto* (Laudemus Deum qui . . .); 118v–119r, *De sancto spiritu* (Veni creator spiritus [the hymn]); 119r–121r, *De sancto sebastiano* (Sancte Sebastiane semper vespere et mane . . .)[11]

121r–v: (121r, last line:) *Sequitur vers[us] s[an]c[t]i bernardi* (121v, with small illustration representing a monk in a white habit, perhaps St. Bernard?:) (I)²llumina oculos meos . . . (ending imperfectly? in last line of 121v:) uţ sciam quid desit michi.

See Leroquais, *LH* I, p. xxx, etc.

(A bifolio seems to be lost between ff. 121 and 122; cf. collation)

122r–v: (beginning imperfectly, on 122r, 1st line:) Aue tu plena gracia Elizabeth leticia . . . (ends on 122v:) . . . gaudere in celis. per x̄p̄m.

122v–125r: (introduced by small illustration: Mary with Child) *De b[ea]ta maria* (O)² regina quam divina preelegit gratia . . . (rhymed through 124v:) . . . deus unus secula. amen (followed by versicle and formal prayer)

The hymn = Walther, *Initia* 12945.

125r–127r: (begins in 14th line of 125r:) *Passio d[omi]ni n[ost]ri ih[es]u xp̄i . Secundum iohanne[m]* (I)²n illo tempore. Apprehendit pilatus . . . (126v:) . . . uerum est testimonium eius. Deo gr[atia]s. (I)²n passione d[omi]ni qua datur salus homini . . . (ends, 127r:) . . . per o[mni]a secula seculoru[m]. amen.

The *Passio*, used as (no doubt primary) part of a devotional exercise, is strongly abridged John XIX, 1–35a (but with addition taken, it seems, from Matthew XXVII, 30).

127r–128r: (begins in 14th line of 127r:) *Testamentum peregrini per modu[m] orationis.* (P)^{2}ater ecce ego peccatrix . . . qui dedit illum. (128r, 6th line:) (O)^2 Bone ih[es]u duo in me agnosco natura[m] qua[m] tu fecisti et peccatu[m] quod addidi . . .

128r–131r: (French rubric begins in 17th line of 128r:) *L'oraison qui sensuit a este trouue a romme* . . . (ends on 128v, 12th line:) *Et aue maria.* (Text begins on 13th line, accompanied by miniature: man praying in cemetery:) (A)^{2}uete omnes a[n]i[m]e fideles . . . (131r:) . . . in no[m]i[n]e d[omi]ni.

Cf. Leroquais, *LH* I, p. 140; also *I Libri d'ore della Bib. ambrosiana* (1973), p. 121 (its ms. S.P. II 185, f. 152)

131r–132r: (begins in 12th line of 131r; accompanied by small illustration: man praying outdoors on his knees to God represented as crowned apparition in the sky) *Cu[m] aliquis fu[er]it i[n] aliqua tribulatio[n]e seu adu[er]sitate dicat or[ati]one[m] seq[uen]t[em]* (A)^{2}me[n] ame[n] dico uob[is] quidquid ora[n]tes pecieritis . . . (131v:) . . . Deus qui sanctorum martyrum tuorum dionisi . eustachij . georgij . xp̄ofori blasij decem miliumq[ue] martyru[m] et sc̄orum confessorum nicolaij egidij [et] euperij et sc̄arum uirginu[m] ac martyrum tuarum katherine . margarete appolonie . barbare et marthe . memoriam agentibus . . . (ends 132r, 2nd line:) . . . Qui uiuis

132r–v: *Or[ati]o dicenda post deuotio[n]e[m] s[an]c[t]am.* Suscipe digneris domi[n]e . . . ego miserrima et i[n]digna peccatrix . . . seculorum. Amen.

132v–135r: (more suffrages; each accompanied by a small picture of the saint invoked:) 132v–133v, *De sancto xp̄oforo* (Sancte Christofore martyr Dei . . .); 133v–134r, *De sc̄a barbara* (O pulchra precipuum rosa dans odorem . . .); 134r–135r, *De sc̄o Claudio* (O desolatorum consolator . . .) . . . Q[ui] uiuis.

* * *

Foliated (1–135) in modern pencil. Leaves 20, 61–62, 86, and [136] are blank, ruled. Two free endleaves at the beginning and two at end. — Written area ca. 90 × 56 mm. Fully ruled in faint (except in calendar) purplish red ink; no pricking. — The script is *lettre bâtarde*; its quality suffered where inadequate space forced the scribe (or perhaps corrector) to write smaller (ff. 56r, 58r, 80v, 81r, 83v, 85r, 95v, 96r, etc.; limited to 4 or 5 lines). The ink has a tendency to powder, especially on what I take to be the flesh side of the parchment.

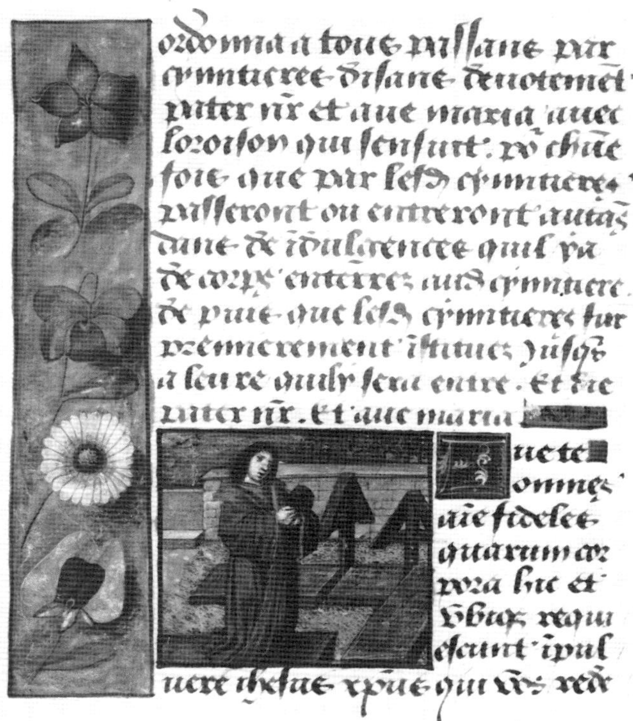

MS 51, f. 128v (actual height of written area: 90 mm; N.B. all text above the miniature is red rubric)

Collation: 1–2^6 3^8 4^6 5–8^8 9^4 10–16^8 17^8(= ff. 119–124; 17$_{4.5}$ following f. 121 wanting, with text loss) 18^8 19^4. — The signatures are numbered in modern pencil in lower right corner of first recto of each gathering.

Decoration: (*a*) twenty-one large (68–74 × 55–56 mm) miniatures in 3-side borders (no border in head margin); each is accompanied by a small portion of text, mostly 5 or 6 lines, with a 4–5 line initial: on ff. 13v, 15r, 16v, 18r, 21r, 24r, 27r, 35r, 43v, 46v, 49v, 52r, 54v, 58v, 63r, 75r (see plate

XX, p. xxxiv), 87r, 94r, 97r, 101r, 105r (cf. contents). — (*b*) twenty-four smaller illustrations (31–33 × 30–35 mm) accompany the suffrages (ff. 106v– 134r); those on rectos are complemented by a 3-side border (none in outer margin, the inner margin part a narrow vertical band), those on versos have only a vertical outer-margin border the height of the written space. — The borders are of the type favored by the Ghent-Bruges school, i.e., more or less realistic flowers, (straw)berries, birds on painted gold ground; they are moderately skilled work. — The illustrations, of decidedly greater excellence, have been attributed to the "Gebetbuchmeister um 1500."[12] — Initials (mostly foliate or imitating twisted tree branches) and line fillers (used throughout) have grounds magenta, very light green, or dark olive brown; the letters or filler decorations themselves are painted gold, pale blue divided by white, or silver. The grounds are mostly stippled or otherwise illuminated with painted gold or silver. — Except for those associated with the large illustrations, the initials are mostly 2 lines in size; versals, 1-line high.

Binding: 19th-century brown calf decorated with inlays; in dealer's letter of 1958[13] the binding is said to be "probably by Hagué." — Protected by a solander case covered in brown morocco, with title HORAE impressed on gold on the quasi-spine of the case.[14]

On the inside of upper cover, bookplate of A. Firmin-Didot, also label: "The gift of Lessing J. Rosenwald to the Library of Congress." On pastedown of lower cover, penciled heading "Catholic Church. Liturgy and ritual" and other markings by LC catalogers,[15] including the call no.: Rosenwald Coll. ms. no. 29.[16]

2° fo.: (KL)² Februarius h[abet] dies . . .

Bibl.: *Catalogue des livres . . . bibliothèque A. Firmin-Didot* (1883), p. 31–34 (with errors). — Faye and Bond (1962), p. 441 (Library of Lessing J. Rosenwald, no. 2). — (Library of Congress) *The Lessing J. Rosenwald collection* (1977), p. 5 (no. 9), also color reproduction of f. 13v.

The book was written for a woman (feminine grammatical forms are used in all prayers which allow such differentiation). The Firmin-Didot catalog of 1883 has drawn attention to the identity of the male donor pictured in this manuscript on ff. 87r, 105r, 128v, 131r with the man portrayed (as placing himself under the protection of John the Baptist) in another manuscript which had been on the market in 1882, the "Bancel Hours" (from its previous owner, E. M. Bancel): the woman depicted there in illus. 9, whose name was perhaps Margaret,[17] could be the person for whom the present book was intended. That it was meant to be used by a woman may also account for the anatomical frankness of the Mary Magdalen illustration. One may otherwise note the sharply penitential tone of the elective devotions in this book of hours.

The possible significance of the rather formal suffrage addressed to Pierre de Luxembourg (see contents, with f. 96), a personality infrequently mentioned in 15th-century books,[18] for placement (and dating?) of this manuscript has as yet remained unconsidered.

NOTES

1. See table C for details.
2. See LC MS 44, note to ff. 77r–90v.
3. The litany invokes, after Mary, the apostles, etc., through Innocents: 14 individual martyrs, 11 confessors, 10 women.
4. Rest of the prayer presumed known by heart?
5. Within a full border. All illustrations termed "large" in the description (cf. also the decoration paragraph at end) are accompanied by full borders and ca. 5 initial lines of text.
6. Cf. Wilmart, *Aut. spir.*, p. 329, note 1.
7. Suffrage centered around Pierre de Luxembourg whose cult as "blessed" was made official in 1527 (a more or less unauthorized cult prior to that date is well attested).
8. *AH* LIV, 167; Walther, *Initia* 1996.
9. The rather well-known prayer (also from musical settings); here without any controversial attribution.

10. The unidentified man previously portrayed on f. 87r is kneeling on the altar steps. — The theme of the illustration has been labeled (*Bib. Firmin-Didot*, 1883, p. 32) Mass of St. Gregory but that is not necessarily the case.

11. A very interesting litany-type prayer (119v–120v) is part of the suffrage.

12. The ascription is credited to Dr. Otto Pächt in dealer's communication to L. J. Rosenwald dated 1958. — For the artist (*Gebetbuchmeister um 1500*) see Winkler, *Flämische Buchmalerei* (1925), p. 128.

13. Arthur Rau, Paris, to L. J. Rosenwald.

14. As of this writing, a label above the title reads "9," the number assigned the book in the 1977 catalog of LC Rosenwald Collection.

15. The manuscript is represented by printed LC catalog card no. 65-58830.

16. The number "29" was assigned to the book in the old, now discontinued LC shelflist of manuscript books. LC Rare Book and Special Collections Division, custodian of the Rosenwald gift, changed the identification to "9" when the 1977 Rosenwald Collection catalog appeared.

17. Cf. *Catalogue . . . bibliothèque de M. E. M. Bancel* (1882), p. 11.

18. Or if invoked, then as "saint": cf. Leroquais, *LH* I, p. 34, 45, 349; II, p. 246. Ecclesiastical precision of the term *beatus* used in this book is odd. (N.B. He was in his time an Avignon man.)

MS 52

(Rosenwald 10/14)

BOOK OF HOURS 1524

Writtten and decorated in Touraine? Parchment. 113 leaves, 226 × ca. 141 mm (bound volume: 232 × ca. 150 mm) 1 column. 23 lines (calendar, 33 lines)

(ff. 1r–6v, calendar; 8r–11r, Gospel readings; 11r–16v, Passion according to John; 16v–17v, *Stabat mater dolorosa*, etc.; 17v–19r, *Obsecro te;* 20r–59v, Hours of Our Lady; 59v–62r, Short Hours of the Cross; 63r–64v, Short Hours of the Holy Spirit; 64v–75v, Penitential Psalms, with Litany; 75v–97v, Office for the Dead; 97v–98v, suffrage addressed to Trinity; 98v–99v, *O Intemerata* (Johannine); 99v–101v, *O Intemerata* (non-Johannine); 101v–111v, suffrages; 111v–113r, Seven Prayers of St. Gregory; 113r, prayers before and after Communion)

ff. 1r–6v: Full calendar, in Latin; in black and gold. Notable among the days singled out in gold: *Sebastiani* (Jan. 19!), *Ioseph* (Mar. 19), *Apparitio sancti Michaelis* (May 8), *Mariae ad Nives* (Aug. 5), *Ludovici* (*regis Francorum*, Aug. 25), *Augustini* (Aug. 28), *Francisci* (Oct. 4), *Ambrosii* (Dec. 7), *Siluestri* (Dec. 31). — Among days written in black: Seueri & Erardi (Jan. 8), Martianae (Jan. 9), Transl. s. Marci (Jan. 30), Vgi[= Hugonis] archiep. (Mar. 10), Grondani [= Guntrammi] regis (Mar. 28), Zeni [= Zenonis] epi. Veronensis (Apr. 12), Maximi epi. Paduani [i.e., Veronensis?] (May 29), Pergentini & Lagentini (June 3), Ianuariae virg. (June 21), Paulini epi. Nolani (June 22), Martialis (July 1), Vlderici epi. Augustae (July 3), Hermacore & Fortunati (July 12), Fantini (July 31), Candidi (Dec. 1), Antonillae [= ?] (Dec. 18)

Saints and celebrations of northern and northeastern Italy seem conspicuous; mixed with what may be a Franciscan element.[2] Owing to patronage by Louise of Savoy?

(7r blank; 7v, full-page illustration: John on Patmos)

8r–11r: *Initium sancti euangelii secundum Ioannem. Gloria tibi domine.* (I)²N principio . . . (8v:) . . . Deo gratias. *A.* Te inuocamus . . . trinitas. . . . *or[ati]o* (P)²ROTECTOR in te sperantium . . . Amen. (7-line illustration: Luke portraying Mary) *Sequentia* . . . *Lucam.* . . . (9v: 9-line illustration: St. Matthew) . . . *Sequentia* . . . *Mattheum* . . . (10v: 7-line illustration: St. Mark) *Sequentia* . . . *Marcum* . . . (ends, 11r:) . . . sequentibus signis.

Gospel readings (John I, 1–14; Luke I, 26b–38a; Matthew II, 1–12; Mark XVI, 14–20); with liturgical additions especially after the Johannine prologue (= the first reading).

11r–16v: (11r, large illustration: Jesus in the Garden of Gethsemane; and 7 lines of text, incl. blue rubric:) *Passio domini nostri Iesu Christi secund*[*um*] *Ioannem.* (E)[2]Gressus e[st] dominus Iesus cum discipulis . . . (ends 16r:) . . . posuerunt eum. (versicle, response, "*Oratio*":) (D)[2]Eus qui manus tuas et pedes tuos et totum corpus tuum . . . (ends 16v:) . . . et puram conscientiam vsque in fine[m] Per te iesu christe saluator mundi. Qui . . . Amen.

John XVIII, 1b–XIX, 42, with suffrage-type additions.

16v–17v: *Deuota contemplatio beatissimae Mariae virginis iuxta crucem filii lachrymantis.* (S)[2]TABAT mater dolorosa . . . (ends 17r:) . . . paradisi gloria. Amen. *V.* Tuam . . . *R.* Vt reuelentur . . . (17v:) . . . ("*Oratio*":) (I)[2]Ntereueniat pro nobis . . . doloris gladius pertransiuit . . . Amen.

The 13th-century hymn, followed by the liturgical collect (used in the pre-1970 *Missale Romanum* for votive Masses).

17v–19r: *Oratio multum deuota ad beatissimam virginem Mariam.* (O)[3]BSECRO te domina . . . (18v:) . . . facturus, locuturus, aut cogitaturus . . . mihi famulo tuo . . . (ends 19r:) . . . mater dei et misericordiae. AMEN.

The standard prayer (Leroquais, *LH* II, p. 346 sq.); masculine forms indicate the book was made to be used by a male.

(19v, full-page illustration: Annunciation)

20r–59v: (caption:) *INCIPIT OFFICIVM DIVE MARIE VIRGINIS SECVNDVM VSVM ROMANE ECCLESIAE* . . . (text:) (D)[5]OMINE Labia mea . . . (ends on 59v, 13th line:) . . . Ora pro nobis deum, alleluia.

Hours of Our Lady. As in Leroquais, *LH* I, p. xxxviii, use of Rome (text in *Breviarium Romanum*, Officium parvum B.M.V., "extra tempus paschale"); Matins have three sets of psalms to vary according to the day of the week; also provided are seasonal variations (for Advent, ff. 55v–58v, and for Christmastide, ff. 58v–59v).**3** — On 55v, "SALVE Regina," introduced by rubric: *Canticum filiorum Euae.* — Full-page illustrations: 30v, Augustus and the Sibyl of Tibur; 37v, Nativity (with 6 lines of text); 40v, Shepherds; 43v, Magi; 46v, Presentation; 49r, Flight to Egypt (with 4 lines of text); 53r, Death of Mary (with 5 lines)

MS 52, f. 30v (Sibyl of Tibur, detail) (actual size of area shown: ca. 70 × 40 mm)

59v–62r: (caption begins on 59v, 15th line:) *SEQVITVR OFFICIVM DE CRV//CE DOMINI NOS//TRI IESV C//HRIS//TI* . . . (text:) (D)[3]OMINE Labia mea . . . (60r, large illustration: Jesus carrying the cross meets Veronica [see plate XXI, p. xxxv]; with 5 lines of the text) . . . (ends, 62r:) . . . Sis mihi solatium in mortis agone//AMEN.

The Short Hours of the Cross (based on the hymn *Patris sapientia*).**4**

(62v, full-page illustration: Pentecost)

63r–64v: *SEQVITVR OFFICIVM DE SAN//CTO SPIRITU.* . . . (D)[3]OMINE Labia mea . . . (63r:) (N)[2]OBIS sancti spiritus gratia sit data . . . (ends 64v:) . . . Vt viuamus iugiter coeli regione. AMEN.

MS 52 The Short Hours of the Holy Spirit, based on the hymn *Nobis sancti Spiritus.*[5]

64v–75v: (64v, beginning with 16th line:) *INCIPIVNT SEPTEM P//SALMI PENIT//ENTIALES. Anti.* Ne reminiscaris *psal[mus]* (D)[3]OMINE Ne in furore tuo . . . (on 65r, full-page illustration: Bath-sheba, nude, emerging from bath; with 4 lines of text)

Penitential Psalms, with Litany (71r sqq.) The litany is without any saints of local character; only "sancte Blasi" among martyrs, and "Clara" and "Helisabeth" among women are not in the litany as printed in the *Breviarium Romanum*; of the saints invoked there, Bernard among order founders and Anastasia among women are not included here.

75v–97v: (caption:) *SEQVITVR OFFICIVM PRO FIDE//LIBVS DEFVNCTIS.* (rubric:) *Ad Vesperas Antiphona* (text:) Placebo domino. $\overline{ps}$ (D)[3]ILEXI Quoniam . . . (76r, large illustration: Raising of Lazarus; with 5 lines of text) . . . (79v, full-page illustration: Job and his visitors) . . . (office ends, 97v:) . . . Requiescant in pace. *R* Amen.

All as in the *Breviarium Romanum* prior to the reform of 1911. Three nocturns.

97v–98v: *Sequuntur suffragia plurimorum sanctorum: Et primo de sanctissima trinitate [!] Deuota oratio ad sanctissima[m] trinitatem.* (A)[3]DORO Te deum patrem, et filium, et spiritum sanctum: vnam diuinitatem: aequalem gloriam . . . (ends 98v:) . . . et omnibus sanctis.

Cf. Leroquais, *LH* II, p. 340 (text, slightly variant).

98v–99v: *Oratio ad beata[m] v[ir]gine[m] & ad sanctum Iohannem euangelistam.* (7-line illustration: Mary, crowned, with the Child) (O)[2] INTEMERATA . . . O Ioannes . . .

Wilmart, *Aut. spir.,* p. 488 sqq. (text). — Masculine forms ("mihi miserrimo peccatori," "ego peccator")

99v–101v: *Item alia oratio ad beatissimam virginem Mariam dei genitricem.* (O)[2] INTEMERATA . . . De te enim dei filius . . . (ends 101v:) . . . et requiem conferat sempiternam. Amen.

The 14th-century (non-Johannine) prayer noted by Wilmart, *Aut. spir.,* p. 493 sq. (with text, p. 494 sq.; cf. similar in Leroquais *LH* II, p. 336 sq.; both differ from the present variant in minor details)

101v–102r: *Deuota commendatio ad eandem.* (S)[2]PES Animae meae post deum virgo Maria: in illam co[m]mendationem . . . (102r:) . . . Amen. *A[ntiphona]* Sub tuum presidium confugimus . . . *Oratio* (P)[2]ROTEGE Domine famulos tuos . . . Amen.

102r–102v: *De sancto Michaele archangelo. an[tiphona]* (M)ichael archangele paradisi praeposite veni in adiutorium . . . (102v, 7-line illustration: Michael fighting the Dragon) . . . (D)[2]EVS Qui miro ordine . . . Per.

102v–103r: *Oratio ad proprium angelu[m] custode[m].* (6–line illustration: Angel with trumpet) (C)[2]VSTOS mi angele gloriose . . . Per christum dominu[m] n.

103r–103v: *Item alia oratio ad eundem* (O)[2]BSECRO te angelice spiritus . . . cum christo in secula seculorum. Ame[n].

Pseudo-Anselmian "Oratio LXII" (*PL* 158, col. 967–968)

103v–111v: Suffrages (for each saint an antiphon, versicle, and formal prayer; in all cases except the "de omnibus apostolis" also a small, mostly 6-line illustration portraying the subject); they concern:

103v–104r John the Baptist (Inter natos mulierum . . .)
104r John the Evangelist (Ioannes apostolus et euangelista virgo . . .)
104r–v Peter and Paul (Petrus apostolus et Paulus doctor gentium . . .)
104v–105r St. James the Greater (Lux et decus hyspaniae . . .)
105r St. Andrew (Cum peruenisset . . .)
105r–v De omnibus apostolis (Dvm steteritis . . .)
105v St. Stephen (Stephanus plenus gratia . . .)
105v–106v St. Christopher (Sancte Christofore martyr preciose . . .)
106v–107r St. Lawrence (Leuita Laurentius . . .)
107r–107v St. Sebastian (O quam mira refulsit gratia . . .)

107v–108r St. Dionysius (O beate Dionysi magna est fides tua . . .)
108r St. Anthony [the Hermit] (Anthoni pastor inclyte qui cruciatos reficis . . .)
108r–v St. Martin (O beatum pontificem . . .)
108v–109r St. Nicholas (Amicus dei Nicolaus . . .)
109r–v St. Claud (O desolatorum consolator . . .)
109v–110r St. Roch (Ave Roche sanctissime nobili natus sanguine . . .)
110r St. Anne (Coeleste beneficium . . .)
110r–v Mary Magdalen (Maria ergo unxit . . .)
110v–111r St. Katherine (Virgo sancta Caterina Graeciae gemma . . .)
111r St. Margaret (Virgo gloriosa Christi Margareta . . .)
111r–v St. Barbara (Gaude Barbara beata . . .)

111v–113r: (111v, last 2 lines, golden rubric:) *Sequuntur Septem orationes beati Gregorii Papae.* (112r, large illustration: Mass of St. Gregory; with 5 lines of text:) (O)[3] DOMINE Iesu christe adoro te in cruce pendentem . . . (112v:) (O)[2] Domine Iesu christe adoro te i[n] cruce vulneratum . . . . . . in sepulchro positum . . . . . . descendentem ad inferos . . . . . . resurgentem a mortuis . . . . . . pastor bone . . . (O)[2] Domine Iesu christe propter illam amaritudinem . . . (ends, 113r:) . . . Pater noster: Aue Maria.

Known as the *Seven Prayers of St. Gregory*. (Text, slightly variant, printed in Leroquais, *LH* II, p. 346.)

113r: *Oratio dicenda ante sanctam communionem.* (D)[2]Omine non sum dignus vt intres . . . Qui cum patre et spiritu sancto. *Oratio post sanctam communionem.* (V)[2]ERA perceptio corporis et sanguinis tui omnipotens deus . . . per omnia secula seculorum. Amen.

* * *

Foliated (b–e, 1–113, v–z; "z" is free endleaf) in modern pencil ("[a]–c" are 18th-century paper, "d–e" vellum, probably original; "v–w" original vellum, blank, extremely lightly ruled, including "w" verso; "x–z" again 18th-century paper). — Written area ca. 128 × ca. 66 mm. Fully ruled in very faint red ink. Pricking marks along the fore edge of many leaves. — Roman script, extremely neat and precise, resembling Jenson roman type. — Very black ink. Rubrics gold or blue; major captions written in capitals in iterated sequences or symmetrical arrangements of gold, blue, and red. — Excellent white material; thickness ca. 8.8 mm per 100 leaves.

(Collation impracticable)

Sixteen large illustrations: full-page 7v, 19v, 30v, 40v, 43v, 46v, 62v, 65r, 79v;[6] occupying large portion of the page and with several lines of text: 11r, 37v, 49r, 53r, 60r, 76r, 112r (for themes, see contents). Each of these is surrounded by a rich architectural border, drawn in realistic (or *trompe l'oeil*) perspective, in painted gold monochrome. — Twenty-six small (height 30–44 mm, width 33–42 mm) portraits of saints (see contents).

Illuminated borders are found on pages facing the large illustrations; six of them (8r, 31r, 44r, 48v, 63r, 75v) are in the Ghent-Bruges style (strewn flowers, insects, etc. on painted gold ground; not outstanding), the remaining ten use Italian, often architectural decorative motifs (columns, vases, masks, shells) arranged into systems, done in gold monochrome on ground of reddish purple, metallic blue, blue, or bluish green; also (64v) in white-over-metallic-blue on painted gold ground.

Many small initials, impressively beautiful primarily thanks to excellent taste in choice of color and precision of the work. Of 1- or 2-line size, they are painted in gold over blue or red grounds,with delicate gold tracery; the numerous paragraph marks and ca. half of the line-fillers are executed in same manner. Relatively few large initials (3-line or 4-line), in white-on-color over painted gold grounds. About half of the line-fillers are styled as cut twigs, done in gold with green, red, or black.

MS 52 N.B. The illustrations are discussed in some detail and put into the context of other art of the period in M. Orth's thesis listed in the bibliography, esp. in its ch. V, "The 1520's Hours Workshop." They are the work of more than one artist; none has been quite identified. — It is somewhat irregular that there is no Crucifixion; the scene from the Way of the Cross (60r) takes its place.

Eighteenth-century French binding in red morocco, decorated in gilt *à la dentelle*, in the manner of Derôme. Gilt edges. — On spine, impressed in gold: HEURES// SUR//VELIN. Kept in a solander case done in dark greenish blue morocco; on spine of the case: PRECES//PIX//MS. VELIN// GEOF. TORY//1524.

On the inside of upper cover, Rosenwald logo, ex libris of C. F. Bishop, and LC book label identifying the book as a Rosenwald gift. On verso of first free endleaf, W. Beckford's inscription in pencil: Les heures de Préfond. The endleaves are drawn marbled paper.

Former owners:[7] Prior to 1757, P. Girardot de Préfond (*Cat. des livres*, 1757, no. 42);[8] from 1757 to 1768, L.-J. Gaignat (sale 1769; v. 1, 194); 1768?–1769?, De Bure le Jeune (G. F. Debure); 1769?–1780, Duc de La Vallière (Louis César);[9] sold in 1784 (cf. L. C. La Vallière, *Cat. des livres*, 1783, v. 1, 303) to Née de la Rochelle for William Beckford; 1784–1844, W. Beckford; 1844–1889, in the W. Beckford collection in Hamilton Palace (cf. A. Hamilton-Douglas, 10th Duke of Hamilton, *The Hamilton palace libraries*, 1882, 463; Hamilton sale 1889, 58); 1889?–ca. 1900, F. G. A. Guyot De Villeneuve (*Cat. des livres*, 1900, I, 7; sold to the bookseller Th. Belin); 190-?–1911?, Robert Hoe (*Cat. of mss.*, 1909, p. 115 sqq.); 1911?–1938, Cortlandt F. Bishop (*The Cortlandt F. Bishop library . . .*, 1938–39, v. 2, no. 1432); bought in 1938 by L. J. Rosenwald through Rosenbach.

2° fo.: (KL)[2] *Martius habet dies.xxxi.*

Bibl.: Robert Hoe, *Catalogue of manuscripts* (1909), p. 115 sqq., with black-and-white reproduction of f. 65r. — S. De Ricci, *Census*, v. 2 (1937), p. 1656, no. 9. — *LC QUARTERLY JOURNAL*, v. 3 (1945), no. 1, p. 9. — *Illuminated books . . .* (1949), no. 221 (erroneously called "Offices of the Virgin for the use of Bourges") and plate LXXVI [a] (black-and-white reproduction of f. 40v). — LC card no. 50-41712. — Library of Congress, *The Rosenwald collection* (1954), no. 10. — Faye and Bond (1962), p. 124, no. 157. — D. Diringer, *The illuminated book* (2nd ed., 1967). — *A Bibliography of the Catholic Church* (1970), p. 228, NC 0217224. — M. D. Orth, *Progressive tendencies in French manuscript illumination, 1515–1530* (1976 doctoral thesis; University Microfilms, DCJ 76–19530), ch. 5 (p. 344 sqq.) passim and p. 444 (with bibl.) — Library of Congress, *The Lessing J. Rosenwald collection* (1977), no. 14 (also color reproduction of f. 40v on p. [112]). — See also J. Plummer, *The Last Flowering* (1982), p. 102–103.

A next-to-perfect art product of striking beauty and technical perfection, the manuscript did not get the attention it deserved until our time, perhaps owing to its late origin. In 1976, Myra D. Orth in her doctoral thesis (cf. Bibl.) presented considerable evidence that the book was produced in an anonymous, probably royally sponsored (by Louise de Savoy, mother of Francis I of France) workshop operating, in Prof. Orth's opinion, in Touraine; other products of the workshop being, e.g., the Walters Art Gallery ms. 449, the 1527 Hours for the use of Rome in the Estelle H. Doheny Collection in Camarillo, Calif., the undated hours for the use of Paris, ms. 452 of the Pierpont Morgan Library, etc. (more listed in Orth, *op. cit.*, p. 338). In these works the Flemish, French, and Italian traditions mix with enjoyable results. — The thesis does away with the hypothesis of Geofroy Tory's (the Parisian printer-publisher's) part in production of the present manuscript. It does repeat, somewhat unfortunately, the appellation "Hours for the use of Bourges," an error corrected already by Marion Schild in the 1954 LC Rosenwald catalog; both the Hours of the Virgin and the Office for the Dead are, indeed, pure Roman use. Further attention should, perhaps, be given to the non-Roman, non-Parisian, non-Bourges, non-Tours selection of saints and festivities in the calendar; to the present writer, the extreme northeastern Italy seems over-represented; and a Franciscan influence to be present in the prominence given to Francis of Assisi, to B.V.M. *Ad Nives*, and perhaps also in noting in gold the day of St. Joseph; perhaps also in inclusion of St. Clare in the Litany (a saintly 15th-century namesake of Louise de Savoy died as a sister of St. Clare). The 15th-century archbishop of Florence Antoninus, not in favor with the Medicis, canonized 1523 (feast May 2), is ignored, as is Francis of Paula, canonized 1519. — It seems to the present writer that the face of Louise of Savoy herself appears two or three times in the book: as that of Sibyl in the *Visio Augusti* (f. 30v), the unidentified female in forefront of the Presentation picture (holding basket) (46v), and possibly also as Veronica, in the Way-of-the-Cross scene, f. 60r. In 1524, Louise had good reasons for sending royal-quality presents to influential men of Italy: her son was engaged in a war there. The book certainly seems to have been prepared for a man (the masculine grammatical forms) of not much asceticism (the Bathsheba), not a Frenchman (no French prayers) but inhabiting north Italy (the calendar).

NOTES

1. No. 10 in old LC "Rosenwald shelflist"; no. 14 in the second catalog (1977) of LC Rosenwald Collection.
2. Some of the least usual names (Pergentini and Lagentini; Ianuariae; Antonillae) appear, however, also in the hours printed or published by G. Tory in Paris in 1525 (information from letter of M. Harrsen to L. J. Rosenwald of May 7, 1941).
3. See also table C.
4. See note to contents of MS 44, ff. 91r–92v. — Text of the office is printed in *Horae Eboracenses* (Surtees Soc., 132), p. 46 sqq.
5. See description of MS 44, note to ff. 93r–95v.
6. The date "1524" appears, in gold and blue, in the illustrative matter on f. 79v: in the shield surmounting the scene of Job and his visitors.
7. Based in part on research done by Anthony Hobson of Sotheby & Co. (his communication to L. J. Rosenwald dated Jan. 22, 1958). It corrects De Ricci's error concerning the Galitzin collection (the book was never a part of it).
8. Hence called "Heures de Préfond" by W. Beckford.
9. It was probably La Vallière who had the book re-bound; in the Préfond sale catalog of 1757 it is described as bound in blue morocco.

MS 53

(Rosenwald 11/12,[1] the Lallemant Hours)

BOOK OF HOURS (use of Bourges)
152–?

Written/decorated in France (Touraine?) Parchment. 148 leaves, 133 × ca. 70 mm (bound volume: 136 × ca. 80 mm) 1 column. 22 lines.

(ff. 1rv, computistic text; 2r–13v, calendar; 15r–19r, Gospel readings; 19r–25v, Passion according to John; 26rv, *Deus qui manus tuas;* 26v–69v, Hours of Our Lady; 69v–83r, Penitential Psalms, with Litany; 83r–115v, Office for the Dead; 115v–116v, *Avete omnes animae fideles;* 116v–118v, prayers to Trinity; 118v–119v, *Salve sancta facies;* 119v–122r, *Obsecro te;* 122r–124r, Marian antiphons; 124r–133r, suffrages; 133r–137v, "louanges, petitions, oraisons"; 137v–138r, suffrage St. Martin; 138r–139v, *Stabat mater dolorosa;* 139v–140r, Five joys of Mary; 140v–144r, Short Hours of the Sacrament; 146r–147r, Psalm XCI; 147r–148r, Seven verses of St. Bernard)

1r–v: *Tabula huius calendarii.* Modus inueniendi coniunctionem . . . post nonam incipit dies Lunae. & c.

Computistic text (partly edited from this manuscript by M. D. Orth in her study "Two books of hours for Jean Lallemant le Jeune," *JOURNAL OF THE WALTERS ART GALLERY*, v. 38 (1980), p. 90, n. 32)

2r–13v: Full calendar (in Latin), in black and gold. — Notable among days singled out in gold: *Antonii abbatis* (Jan. 17), *Sebastiani* (Jan. 20), *Thomae de Aquino* (Mar. 6 [!]), *Ioseph* (Mar. 19), *Petri m. O.P.* (Apr. 29), *Bernardini* (May 20), *Antonii* (of Padua, June 13), *Viti et Modesti* (June 15), *Apparitio s. Marci* (June 25), *Rochi* (Aug. 16), *Augustini* (Aug. 28), *Nicolai de Tolentino* (Sept. 10), *Hieronymi* (Sept. 30), *Francisci* (Oct. 4), *Ambrosii* (Dec. 7), *Siluestri* (Dec. 31.)[2]

The calendar is not, as might be expected in view of the Lallemant destination and the form of the Little Office used further on, that of Bourges: characteristic Berrichon saints (Guillaume, 10 or 11 January; Ursinus, 30 December) are absent. With few exceptions the black-ink entries agree with those found in LC MS 52 (Hours Rosenwald 10/14) intended, probably, for northern Italy; the choice of feasts emphasized in gold differs: singled out in this manner are Dominican and Franciscan saints (also Venetian June 25 and Milanese December 7).

(14r blank; 14v, full-page miniature: red lion holding in front paws seven-seal book with motto "DELEAR PRIVS"; in rear paws, coat of arms of Jean Lallemant)[3]

15r–19r: Gospel passages: John I,1–14, with liturgical additions (prayer *Protector in te sperantium*); Luke I,26b–38a; Matthew II,1–12; Mark XVI,14–20.

(At the beginning of each pericope, one of two alternating cryptic miniatures [cf. the paragraph on decoration]: on 15r and 17r, seven-seal book with the motto; on 16r and 18r, hair shirt)

19r–25v: (seven-seal-book miniature) *PASSIO DOMINI NOSTRI IESV CHRISTI SECUNDUM IOANNEM.* EGress[us] est dominus . . . (ends 25v:) . . . posuerunt Iesum. Deo gratias.

John XVIII–XIX; without the amplifications added from elsewhere in some books of hours.

26r–v: DEus qui manus tuas et pedes tuos . . . O Beatissime domine Iesu christe respicere digneris super me . . . (ends 26v:) . . . et cum latrone in secula seculorum te videam. Amen.

26v–69v: *Sequitur officium beatae Mariae virginis secundum vsum Bituricensis ecclesie.* (hair-shirt miniature) DOmine labia mea . . .

Hours of Our Lady, use of Bourges;[4] with the Short Hours of the Cross (those based on the hymn *Patris sapientia*) and the Short Hours of the Holy Spirit (based on hymn *Nobis Sancti Spiritus*) inserted in appropriate places. — The alternating miniatures appear at the beginning of individual "hours": on ff. 26v, 47v, 49r, 56r, 61r the hair shirt; on 39r, 48r, 52r, 58v, and 65v the seven-seal book with the motto "DELEAR PRIVS."

69v–83r: *Incipiunt septem psalmi penite[n]tiales. An.* (hair-shirt miniature) Ne reminiscaris . . .

The Penitential Psalms (= Pss. VI, XXXII, XXXVIII, LI, CII, CXXX, CXLIII), with (ff. 77v sqq.) Litany. — The litany has,[5] among martyrs: Line, Clete, Clemens, Corneli, Ypolite cum sociis, Dionysi cum sociis, Maurici sum sociis, Eustachi cum sociis, Satire cum sociis . . . Christofore, Private . . . Panthaleon, Lauriane, Adriane, Georgi, Blasi; among confessors: Hilari . . . Ludovice, Ursine, Guillerme, Austregille, Sulpici, Maure, Leonarde, Eligi, Egidi, Bonite, Martialis, Germane, Marcelle . . . [N.B. neither Dominice nor Francisce]; among women: Anna, Maria Aegyptiaca, Margareta, Barbara, Eustadiola . . . Genouefa, Clara, Valeria, Berthoaria, Scholastica, Radegundis, Avia, Apolonia, Gertrudis, Fides, Spes, Charitas.

83r–115v: *Sequuntur vigiliae mortuorum. Ad Vesperas Antiphona.* (miniature with the seven-seal book and DELEAR PRIVS; the scattered letters in the background are, this time, an alphabet beginning with *A*) Placebo . . .

The Office for the Dead, presumably according to the use of Bourges. Order of responsories: I Credo quod II Qui Lazarum III Requiem aeternam IV Induta est caro V Memento mei VI Peccantem me VII Ne recorderis VIII Heu mihi IX Libera. (Invitatory: *Regem cui omnia vivunt;* ad Ben. ant.: *Ego sum resurrectio*) — Prayers of the (1st) Vespers (but not those of Lauds) include, appended to the usual series concerned with various groups of those who died, a prayer for the reigning monarch ("famulus tuus rex noster," f. 89rv). — At the beginning of the Matins (89v), the hair-shirt miniature.

115v–116v: *Oratio pro defunctis in cimiterio inhumatis.* AVete omnes animae fideles . . . (116r:) . . . Non intres in iudicium . . . ("Oratio":) DOmine Iesu christe salus et liberatio . . .

Cf. Leroquais, *LH* I, p. 140.

116v–118v: *Sequuntur suffragia sanctorum et sanctarum. Et primo de sanctissima trinitate.* [!] Sancta trinitas vnus deus: miserere nobis. *Antiphona* Te inuocamus . . . (117r:) . . . Omnipotens sempiterne . . . (= collect of the Trinity Sunday) (miniature: seven-seal book) *Oratio ad deum patrem.* Pater de coelis deus: miserere nobis. *Oratio* Domine sancte pater omnipotens aeterne Deus, qui coaequalem . . . (117v:) . . . *Oratio ad filium.* Fili redemptor mundi deus miserere nobis. Domine Iesu christe fili dei viui qui es verus . . . (cf. *PL* CI,1399; also Wilmart, *Aut. spir.*, p. 497) (118r:) . . . *Oratio ad spiritum sanctum* Spiritus sancte deus: miserere nobis. Domine spiritus sancte deus qui coaequalis . . .

It may be hoped that the introductory rubric originally (in the scribe's *exemplar* or earlier) preceded the material here found on ff. 124r–133r.

118v–119v: *De sancta facie.* SAlue sancta facies . . .[6] (119r:) . . . Deus qui nobis famulis tuis lumine vult[us] tui signatis . . .

Cf. Leroquais, *LH* II, p. 349–350 (printed text). — (On 118v, miniature: hair shirt)

119v–122r: ***Oratio deuotissima ad beatissimam virginem Mariam dei genitricem.*** (miniature: the seven-seal book) OBsecro te domina sancta Maria . . . (121r:) . . . facturus locuturus aut cogitaturus . . . mihi famulo tuo . . . (ends on 122r:) virgo Maria mater dei et misericordiae. Amen.

The standard prayer (Leroquais, *LH* II, p. 346 sq.); masculine grammatical forms.

122r–124r: ***Sequuntur salutationes ad beatissimam virginem Maria[m] per totum annum. Et primo*** . . . (124r:) . . . pertransiuit, et in resurrectione tua nouus amor accendit. Qui viuis . . .

The primary texts here (*Ave regina coelorum; Salve regina misericordiae; Alma redemptoris mater; Regina coeli laetare*) are those eventually stabilized in Roman Breviary as the "Antiphonae finales B.M.V."; with versicles and formal prayers, including seasonal variations, partly at variance from the later official arrangement.

124r–133r: (Suffrages, as follows:)[7]

124r *De sancto Michaele* (Michael archangele paradisi praeposite . . .)
124v *De sancto Ioanne baptista* (Inter natos mulierum . . .)
124v *De sancto Ioanne euangelista* (Ioannes apostolus et euangelista virgo . . .)
125r *De omnibus apostolis* (Dum steteritis ante reges . . .)
125v *De sancto Stephano* (Stephanus plenus gratia . . .)
126r *De sancto Laurentio* (Leuita Laurentius . . .)
126r *De s. Christophoro* (O sancte Christofore martyr Dei preciose . . .)
127r *De sancto Sebastiano* (O q[uam] mira refulsit gratia . . .)
128r *De pluribus martyribus* (Isti sunt sancti qui pro Dei amore minas hominum contempserunt . . .)
128r *De sancto Claudio* (Desolatorum consolator . . .)
129r *De S. Fiacrio* (Beate Christi confessor Fiacri . . .)
129v *De sancto Rocho* (Ave Roche sanctissime nobili natus sanguine . . .)
130r *De sancta Anna* (Coeleste beneficium . . .)
130v *De sancta Maria Magdalena* (Maria ergo unxit pedes Iesu . . .)
131r *De sancta Catherina* (Virgo sancta Catherina Graeciae gemma . . .)
131v *De sancta Barbara* (Gaude Barbara beata summe pollens in doctrina . . .)
132r *De sancta Apolonia* (Beata Apolonia grave tormentum . . .)
132v *De sancta Genouefa* (Nunc Genouefa virgo clemens . . .)

The antiphons (or what serves as such), sometimes unusually long, are in each case followed by versicle, its response, and formal prayer. — Miniatures: hair shirt on 124r (with the Michael suffrage), also on 124v, 126r, 127r, 129v, 130r, 130v, 131v, 133r; seven-seal book on 124v (with John the Baptist), 125v, 126r, 128v, 129v, 131r, 132r.

133r–137v: *Sensuyuent plusieurs de uotes louanges, petitions requestes et oraisons. Premierement diras au matin quant tu te leueras* (133v:) In matutinis domine meditabor in te . . . *Quant tu ystras hors de ta maison.* Vias tuas domine demonstra . . . *Quant tu prendras de* (134r:) *leaue benoite.* Asperges me domine . . . *Quant tu seras deuant le crucifix.* Salua nos christe saluator . . . CRucem tuam adoramus . . . Per dominum [*sic*]. (134v:) *Quant le prestre se retourne* Spiritus sancti gratia illustret . . . *A lesleuation du corps nostre seigneur.* Anima christi . . . (135r:) *Quant on lieue le calice dy.* AVe vere sanguis domini . . . Amen. Salue sancta caro dei: per quam salui fiunt rei . . . (135v:) . . . Frange meos inimicos, fac eos mihi amicos . . . Amen. *Quant on prent la paix.* Da pacem domine in dieb[us] nostris . . . *Quant on veult receuoir le corps de n[ost]re seigneur.* Domine non sum dignus . . . sed tu domine qui dixisti . . . (136r:) . . . *Quant on la receu.* VEra perceptio corporis et sanguinis tui . . . *Contre la tempeste.* A Domo tua quaesumus domine . . . (136v:) . . . *Pour le Roy* DEus regnorum . . . *Contre la te[n]tatio[n] de la chair* VRe igne sancti spirit[us] . . . *Contre les mauluaises pensees.* OMnipotens mitissime deus respice propicius . . . (137r:) . . . *Pour quelque tribulation.* INeffabilem misericordiam tuam . . . *Pour lamy viuant en tribulation* DEus qui iustificas impium . . . *Pour ceulx qui vont en voyage.* ADesto domine supplicationibus nostris (137v:) viam . . . *Pour nos bien sfaicteurs.* PRaetende domine famulis et famulabus . . . dexteram . . .

137v–138r: *De s. Martino. an[tiphona]* (miniature: the seven-seal book) O beatum pontificem . . . (138r:) . . . DEus qui conspicis quia ex nulla nostra . . . Per

138r–139v: *Deuota contemplatio .b. virginis, iuxta crucem filii lachryma[n]tis.* (miniature: hair shirt) Stabat mater dolorosa . . . (139r:) . . . paradisi gloria. Amen *V* Tua[m] ipsius animam . . . *R* Vt reuelentur . . . *Orat[i]o* INteruenlat pro nobis . . . (139v:) . . . pertransiuit. Per te Iesu christe . . . Amen.

The familiar 13th-century hymn, followed by liturgical additions.[8]

139v–140r: *De quinque festiuitatibus beatissimae virginis Mariae.* AVe cuius conceptio solemni plena gaudio . . . (followed by 4 other "Ave . . . ") (140r:) . . . DEus qui nos conceptionis, natiuitatis, . . . gaudia recolendo laetificas . . . (ends 140r, last line:) Qui cum . . . v. [. . .]

140v–144r: *Incipit officium sacrame[n]ti* (miniature: seven-seal book) Domine labia mea . . . (ends 144r:) . . . Taleam[i.e., Valeam] te sumere cum deuotione. AMEN

An infrequently encountered short office based on the hymn *Corporis mysterium pange gloriosi.*[9] Cf. Wilmart, *Aut. spir.*, p. 369.

(In tail margin of f. 144r, INSCRIPTION in 18th-century cursive: ce Livre a apartenu au venerable Serviteur de dieu piere Fourier de Matincourt: il vient de Mgr Hanry de Thiard Bissy eveque comte de Toul en 1720—)

(144v–145v blank, ruled in same manner as all preceding leaves)

146r–147r: *Psalmus contra inimicos et diuersas ac varias tribulationes* QVi habitat in adiutorio altissimi . . . Acuto [*sic*; for "scuto"] circundabit te veritas eius . . . (ends 147r:) . . . et ostendam illi salutare meum. Gloria . . . seculorum Amen.

Psalm XCI.

147r–148r: *Sequuntur septem versus beati Bernardi* O bone IESV // ILLVMINA oculos meos . . . O ADONAY // In manus tuas . . . O MESSIAS // Locutus sum in lingua mea (147v:) . . . O REX FILI DAVID // Fac mecum signum in bonum . . . O ELOY // Dirupisti domine . . . O EMANVEL // Periit fuga a me . . . O CHRISTE // Confiteantur tibi domine (148r:) omnia opera tua . . . Gloria patri et filio . . . Amen.

The devotion discussed in Leroquais, *LH* I, p. xxx, with an unusual set of addresses added (and without concluding prayer).

(148v blank, not ruled)

* * *

Foliated (in tens) in modern pencil. Both preceding f. 1 and following f. 148, two flyleaves of thicker vellum, not ruled. — Written area ca. 83 × ca. 39 mm. Fully ruled in very faint red ink; no pricking marks. — Roman script, extremely neat and precise, resembling Jenson roman type. Black ink; rubrics in blue or gold. — Excellent, very thin parchment.

Collation appears impracticable owing to tight binding.

Decoration: One full-page miniature on f. 14v (cf. contents) and 40 small ones, 5- to 6-lines high (height 17–26 mm, width 19–22 mm, including frame).[10] Except for serving the *ordinatio textus* by indicating the beginning of various items of the text, the small miniatures seem to have no relation to the book's contents: they repeat what are essentially only two alternating designs (see plate XXII, p. xxxvi), one representing what is believed to be the seven-seal book of the Apocalypse (Revelation V, 1 sqq.), in bright blue binding, always with the same golden inscription not found in the New Testament source: DELEAR PRIVS;[11] the other design, also occurring twenty times, pictures what has been identified as a hair shirt. Both designs display in the background a number of variously arranged capital letters, very much suggestive of a code. — Each of the miniatures is placed in a three-dimensionally conceived golden frame.

MS 53 Initials, including the *KL*'s of the calendar, are 2-line; versals and paragraph marks, 1-line; all are in (burnished) gold on dark brown ground with gold tracery. — Line fillers of two types: one has golden patterns on rectangular dark brown ground, the other is styled as a twig. — All decorative work is done with extreme neatness and graphic precision.

Binding: reportedly by Charles Lewis, ca. 1825; covers are white vellum, fully gold-tooled (mosaic style).[12] — Rebacked, and provided with brown morocco doublures in the 20th century by St. James, London (label on inside of upper cover). — On spine: OFFICIUM//B.M.//VIRGINIS. — Two metal (silver?) clasps are thought to be replacements of original brass ones. — Kept in a brown morocco book-shaped case; on spine of the case: ORIGINAL MS.//BY// GEOFFREY TORY//1319[13]//1506 [dating now believed to be too early].

On the inside of upper cover (besides the English binder's label noted above), label with the Rosenwald logo (LJR). On first flyleaf recto, penciled: 1319; on recto of the first flyleaf, penciled in LC cataloger's hand: Catholic Church. Liturgy and ritual. Hours (initialed/dated: MLS 29N49); in another hand: Rosenwald Coll. Ms. no. 11; in lower outer corner, in another hand: # 7803.

Former owners: Jean Lallemant Le Jeune (d. 1548) for whom the book was made; (St.) Pierre Fourier (of Mattaincourt, founder of the Congrégation de Notre Dame, lived 1565–1640); Henry-Pons de Thiard de Bissy, cardinal, bishop of Meaux (prior to that, of Toul; lived 1657–1737); Lord Vernon (George Charles, 4th baron, lived 1779–1835); (sale, Payne & Foss, 1838); Robert S. Holford; Sir George Holford (sale Sotheby, 1927, II, no. 393); E. P. Goldschmidt; L. J. Rosenwald.

2º fo.: (KL)² Ianuarius h[abet] dies. 31. Lu-

Bibl.: E. P. Goldschmidt, *Les heures de Jean Lallemant written by Geoffroy Tory in 1506* (London, 1928; with black-and-white reproductions of ff. 14v and 49v) — *Illuminated books* . . . (1949), no. 219 — De Ricci, *Census*, v. 1 (1935), p. 665, no. 1; Faye and Bond, p. 123, no. 156. — *LC QUARTERLY JOURNAL*, v. 3 (1945), p. 1. — *A Bibliography of the Catholic Church* (London, 1970): NC 0217055, reproducing LC card 50–41711. — Library of Congress, *The Lessing J. Rosenwald collection* (1977), no. 12. — M. D. Orth, "Two books of hours for Jean Lallemant le Jeune," in *JOURNAL OF THE WALTERS ART GALLERY*, v. 38 (c1980), p. 70–[93] (with enlarged black-and-white reproductions of, or from, ff. 14v, 15r, 49r, 124v).

The probably erroneous dating (1506) based on the first date of the calendar table (f. 1r) survived from Goldschmidt's 1928 publication through the 2nd edition (1977) of the Rosenwald collection catalog, the private doubts of Library of Congress catalogers notwithstanding. Both the dating and the hero-worshipping ascription to G. Tory can now be abandoned thanks to Orth's studies. The book seems to come from the same "workshop" as LC MS 52 (Rosenwald Collection 10/14) with which it shares the script style (although details suggest another scribe) and much (ca. 92 percent) of the calendar, also the unsparing attention to graphic detail and perfection of craftsmanship.[14] It differs from the MS 52 in many other respects: the offices follow the variants ("use") of Bourges (Jean Lallemant was a prominent citizen of that city);[15] its rubrics slip into French; most significantly (and intriguingly), its decorative content is entirely unconventional. Its only close cousin in this respect is another Lallemant book of hours, ms. W. 446 of the Walters Art Gallery in Baltimore (Plummer, *Last flowering,* no. 129), with the same or very similar miniatures. Perhaps decoding of the presumed cryptograms, or study of uses of the motto "Delear prius," would bring more insight. The idea of a secret brotherhood comes easily to mind. — A hundred years later, the book was in the hands of a man revered by the Roman Church as a saint;[16] was he, too, privy to the code?

NOTES

1. As with other manuscript books in the Library's Rosenwald Collection, the book has undergone renumberings. At the time of this writing (1984) it is shelved in the Rosenwald Collection as item no. 12.

2. N.B. Days of the month are numbered in arabic numerals in the first column.

3. Quarterly 1st and 4th Gules a Chevron Or between three Roses Argent, 2nd and 3rd Azure a Cross Anchory Argent between three Cairns Or, over all an Inescutcheon Or charged with two Leopards passant Gules. (Heraldic description by Thomas E. Wilgus, Library of Congress)

4. See table C for textual details.

5. I am noting names not included in the Litany of the pre-Vatican II *Breviarium Romanum.* — Most of the less usual names are saints of Bourges (cf. Grotefend, *Zeitrechnung* II).

6. Cf. H. Walther, *Initia* (1959) 17153.

7. The folio numbers given here locate only the beginning of each suffrage.

8. The whole is also found (with identical rubric) in LC MS 52 which is dated 1524 and was produced (perhaps) in the same workshop.

9. Not identical with the *Pange lingua gloriosi.*

10. The pictorial aspects of the manuscript were analyzed in 1980 in M. D. Orth's article in the *Journal of the Walters Art Gallery* quoted in the contents (with f. 1) and in the bibliography; the article includes black-and-white reproductions of the designs. Orth's conclusions are generally accepted in our description; see also positive but critical comment by John Plummer in *The last flowering* (1982), p. 101 sq. (the Rosenwald Coll. Ms. 11 noted there is the one now being discussed).

11. Not in the index of mottoes in Henkel-Schöne, *Emblemata* (1967). — In Orth's article (cf. note 10), the first word is repeatedly misprinted as "Deliar."

12. In Orth's article (cf. note 10), the book is mistakenly said to be bound in red morocco (an unfortunate result of numbering changes in the Rosenwald Collection catalogs).

13. This was the old number of the book in Lessing J. Rosenwald's library.

14. The "workshop" must have been operating in the twenties of the 16th century; very likely it was associated with or sponsored by the French court (cf. M. D. Orth, "A French illuminated treaty of 1527," *Burlington Magazine*, v. 122, no. 923 [Feb. 1980], p. 125 sq.). Its products are anything but ordinary. — (See also J. Plummer, *The last flowering* (1982), p. 102 sq.)

15. By an unfortunate error introduced, perhaps, in the 1949 exhibition catalog *Illuminated books* . . . (in it, no. 221) it has been sometimes assumed that the Rosenwald 10/14 (LC MS 52), too, reflects the use of Bourges. Its offices (both that of the Virgin and that for the dead) are pure Roman.

16. In his biography (*Un missionnaire de la Contre-Réforme,* Paris, c1965) by H. Derréal mention is made (p. 107) of a pocket book of hours carried by a Charles-Henry de Livron, marquis de Ville, who frequently visited Pierre Fourier at Mattaincourt in the years, apparently, ca. 1621–1631. (The mention is quoted from the 2nd ed. of *La vie du très R.P. Fourier,* 1656, repr. 1869, p. 298 and/or 304 which could not be consulted directly.)

MS 54

(Rosenwald 33/15, the Collins Hours)[1]

BOOK OF HOURS XVIth c., 1st half

Central France. Parchment. 181 leaves, 143 × ca. 93 mm (bound volume: 148 × ca. 100 mm) 1 column. 18 lines (calendar, 17 lines)

(ff. 1r–12r, calendar; 13r–17v, Gospel readings; 17v–26r, *Passio secundum Ioannem*; 26v, *Deus qui manus tuas;* 26v–30r, *Obsecro te*; 30r–32r, *O Intemerata;* 32r–100v, Hours of Our Lady; 100v–116v, Penitential Psalms, with Litany; 116v–157v, Office for the Dead and related prayers; 157v–172v, suffrages; 173r–174v, Eucharist-related prayers in French)

ff. 1r–12r: Calendar (254 entries) in Latin; in black and red. — Notable among the 51 entries singled out in red: *guillermi archiep̄i by* (Jan. 10; with the octave, Jan 16, noted in black), *Dyonisi cum so.* (Feb. 8), *Patrici* (March 16), *luciani ep̄i. et marty.* (July 5!), *Francisci* (Oct. 4), *vrsini archiep̄i. bituriē.* (Dec. 30, but should probably be 29; octave is noted on Jan. 5)

Prominent saints of Bourges (Guillermus, Ursinus) are well represented; the calendar is, nevertheless, not simply that of Bourges: St. Patrick shouldn't be in red. The days in black, in their turn, include saints Richard (Apr. 3), Guthlacius (Apr. 11), Alphegus (Apr. 19), all more at home in the British Isles than in Bourges. — N.B. In this calendar, a month does not begin on a new page except accidentally (January, February, November).

(f. 12v: full-page illustration: John on Patmos)

13r–17v: Gospel passages (John I, 1–14 with the liturgical prayer *Protector in te sperantium*; Luke I, 26v–38a; Matthew II, 1–12; Mark XVI, 14–20)

On 14v, small (6–line) rectangular picture of St. Luke; on 15v, Matthew (7–line); on 17r, Mark (7–line).

17v–26r: (rubric on 17v:) *Passio domini nostri iesu xp̄i secundum iohannem.* . . . (18v, large illustration: Jesus in Gethsemane; with 3 lines of text, beginning:) (E)[3]Gressus est . . . (ends, 26r:) . . . posuerunt iesum. Deo gratias.

John XVIII–XIX (without amplifications)

26v: *Or[ati]o* (D)[2]Eus qui manus tuas & pedes tuos . . . Iesu christe saluator mundi. Qui viuis . . . A//ME//N.

(Shorter form of the prayer; cf. longer variant in LC MS 53, f. 26r–v)

26v–30r: (26v:) ***Oratio deuotissima ad beatissimam virginem mariam.*** (27r, large illustration: Mary with the Child, sitting in front of a tent; two angels with musical instruments at each side; and 3 lines of text, beginning:) (O)[3]Bsecro te domina . . . (29r:) . . . facturus locuturus aut cogitaturus . . . mihi famulo tuo . . . (ends, 30r:) . . . mater dei et misericordie. Amen.

The standard prayer (Leroquais, *LH* II, p. 346 sq.); grammatical forms masculine.

30r-32r: *Alia oratio ad beatam virgi* [without any mark of abbreviation] (O)[2] Intemerata . . . (30v:) . . . O ioha[n]nes beatissime . . . (ends, 32r:) . . . Qui cum patre coeterno et consustantiali viuit et regnat . . . Ame[n]

Cf. Wilmart, *Aut. spir.*, p. 488–490 (slightly variant)

32r–100v: (32r, rubric:) *Hore beate marie virginis secundum vsum ecclesie bituri[c]e[nsi]u[m].* (32v, large illustration: Annunciation; and 3 lines of text, beginning:) (D)[3]Omine labia mea . . .

Hours of Our Lady, use of Bourges. Identical disposition (alternate sets of Psalms for the Matins; corresponding segments of the Short Hours of the Cross and of the Short Hours of the Holy Spirit inserted after each "hour" of the Marian office) and texts as in the MS 53 except for absence of the suffrages *De omnibus sanctis* and *De pace* at the end of the Lauds.

Large illustrations on:
(32v, Annunciation, see above)
49r (Visitation, with the beginning of Lauds)
59r (Crucifixion, with the beginning of Matins of the Holy Cross)
60v (Pentecost, with the beginning of the Hours of the Holy Spirit)
62r (Nativity, with the opening words of the Prime)
69r (Shepherds; begins Terce)
74v (Magi; begins the Sext)
80r (Presentation in the Temple, for the None)
86r (Flight to Egypt, with the beginning of the Vespers)
94r (Coronation of the Virgin, with the Compline)

100v–116v: (100v, rubric:) *Sequuntur septem psalmi penitentiales.* (101r, large illustration: David penitent, with the beginning of Psalm VI:) (D)[3]Omine ne in furore tuo . . .

The Penitential Psalms, with (111v sqq.) the Litany; the litany has, at the end of the list of apostles and evangelists, St. Martialis;[2] among the martyrs: Dyonisi cum soc., Fiacri, Quintine; among confessors: Remigi, Marcelle, Germane, Medarde, Ludovice, Claudi; among women: Genovefa, Brigida, Radegundis, Scolastica, Fides, Spes, Charitas. The "libera nos" series includes unusual "Ab appetitu inanis glorie . . ."

116v–156r: (116v, rubric:) *Sequuntur vigilie mortuorum* . . . (117r, large illustration: the Rich Man in hell, beholding Abraham with the Poor Man in his arms; with 3 lines of text, beginning:) (D)[3]Ilexi . . .

Office for the Dead, presumably according to the use of Bourges (order of responsories same as in MS 53).

156r–157v: (156r, rubric:) *or[ati]o pro fidelibus defunctis.* (156v, 9-line rectangular miniature: Exequies, and beginning of the text:) (A)[2]vete o[m]nes anim[ae] fideles . . . Non intres in (157r:) iudicium . . . (D)[2]Omine iesu christe sal[us] et liberatio . . . (ends, 157v:) . . . collocare inter agmina sanctorum digneris . . . iubeas. Qui viuis . . . A//ME//N.

Cf. Leroquais, *LH* I, p. 140.

157v–172v: (157v, rubric:) ***Sequuntur suffragia plurimor[um] sanctorum et sanctarum. De sanctissima trinitate.*** [!] *An̄.*

(158r, large illustration: Trinity; and 3 lines of text, beginning:) (S)[3]Ancta trinitas vnus deus miserere nobis ("*An̄*":) Te inuocamus te (158v:) adoramus . . . (O)[2]Mnipotens sempiterne de[us] qui dedisti famulis tuis . . . (Cf. *Missale Romanum* [Tridentine], Trinity Sunday, collect)

158v–159v: *Oratio ad deum patrem.* Pater de celis deus miserere nob' (D)[2]Omine sancte pater omnipotens eterne de[us] qui coequalem . . . (with 8-line miniature, God the Father, on 159r)

tum tuum. Qui viuis
Oratio ad filium. Filii redem
ptor mundi deus miserere no
bis. Oratio.

O
mine
iesu chri
ste fili dei
qui es ve
rus et om
nipotens
deus splē
dor et ymago patris et vita eter
na cui est vna cum eterno patre
et spiritu sancto equalis honor
eadem gloria coeterna maies
tas vna substantia tibi gratias
ago te adoro te laudo te bene

MS 54, f. 159v (robe of the Son is silvery grey with golden accents; the throne, bright blue) (actual size of written area: ca. 90 × 50 mm)

159v–160r: *Oratio ad filium.* Filii [sic] redemptor mundi deus miserere nobis. *Oratio.* . . . (D)^{2}Omi[n]e iesu christe fili dei qui es verus . . . (Cf. *PL* CI, 1399; Wilmart, *Aut. spir.*, p. 497) . . . adiuua me propter nomen sa[n]ctum tuum. Qui viuis. (with 8–line miniature on 159v: God the Son; unconventional: a seated youngish person; identifying attributes limited to golden cross attached to golden globe held in left hand)

160r–160v: *Oratio ad spiritum sanctum.* Spiritus sancte deus miserere nobis. *Oratio.* (D)^{2}Omine spiritus sancte de[us] qui coeq[ua]lis . . . (with 8-line miniature on 160r: Holy Spirit; unconventional: standing youngish person with white habit, blue wings) (ends on 160r, lines 9–10:) . . . et ignem sanctissimi amoris tui. Qui viuis et reg.

160v–161v: *De sancta facie domini.* (S)^{2}Alue sancta facies . . . (161v:) . . . (D)^{2}Eus qui nobis famulis tuis lu[m]i[n]e vultus tui signatis . . . (= Leroquais, *LH* II, p. 349–350; here with a 7-line miniature on 160v: Veronica displaying the veil)

161v–163v: *Oratio sancti bernardini confessoris. ordi. minorum.* (O)^2 Bone iesu. O dulcis iesu . . . gloriari ac delectari in secula seculorum. Amen. (Cf. Leroquais, *LH* I, p. 258, etc.) (On 162r, 9–line miniature: Bernardine of Siena; on blue wall in the background, repeated combinations of capital letters: VORVQ[or &]VR VRVRURV)

163v–165r: *Les sept oraiso[n]s sai[n]ct grego[i]re.* (O)^2 Domi[n]e iesu xp̄e adoro te in cruce pe[n]dentem . . . et propicius esto mihi peccatori. Amen. Pater noster. Aue maria (= Leroquais, *LH* II, p. 346) (with 8-line miniature on 163v: Mass of St. Gregory)

165r–v: *De sancto michale* [sic] *An̄.* Michael archangele paradisi preposite . . . (165v:) . . . (D)^{2}Eus qui miro ordine . . . muniatur. (On 165r, 8-line miniature: Michael stepping on the defeated Enemy)

165v–166r: *De sancto iohanne baptista. An̄.* Helizabeth zacharie . . . (P)^{2}Resta qu[esumu]s . . . (with 8–line miniature on 165v: John the Baptist)

166r–v: *De sancto iohanne euangelista. An̄.* Iohannes apostol[us] et euangelista virgo . . . (E)^{2}Cclesiam tua[m] . . . (On 166r, 8–line miniature: John with chalice)

166v–167r: *De sancto petro et paulo. An̄.* Petrus apostolus et paulus doctor gentium . . . (167r:) . . . (D)^{2}Eus cuius dextera beatum petrum . . . (With 8–line miniature on 166v: Peter and Paul)

167r–v: *De sancto iacobo. An̄.* Lux et decus hyspanie . . . (167v:) . . . (E)[2]Sto domine plebi tue . . . (With 8–line miniature: St. James the Greater)

168r–v: *De sancto laurentio. An̄.* Leuita laurentius . . . (D)[2]A nobis quesumus . . . (With 8–line miniature on 168r: Lawrence on the grill)

168v–169r: *De sancto nicolao. An̄.* Copiose caritatis nicolae pontifex . . . (D)[2]Eus qui beatum Nicolaum . . . (With 8–line miniature on 168v: St. Nicholas facing three naked children in tub)

169r–v: *De sancto anthonio. A* Anthoni pastor inclite qui cruciatos reficis . . . (D)[2] Eus qui nos concedis . . . (With 8–line miniature on 169r: St. Anthony the Hermit bothered by devils)

169v–170r: *De sancta maria magdalena. ā.* Maria ergo vnxit pedes iesu . . . (L)[2]Argire nobis clementissime pater . . . (With 8–line miniature on 169v: Mary Magdalen reclining, presumably penitent)

170r–v: *De sancta katherina. An̄.* virgo sancta katherina grecie gemma . . . (D)[2]Eus qui dedisti legem moysi . . . (With 9–line miniature on 170v: Catherine being beheaded)

170v–171v: *De sancta margareta. An̄.* (171r:) vi[r]go gloriosa christi margareta . . . (D)[2]Eus qui beatam margaretam virginem tua[m] . . . (With 9–line miniature on 171r: St. Margaret with dragon)

171v–172r: *De sancta barbara. An̄.* virgo fide sana de stirpe creata prophana . . . (I)[2]Ntercessio quesumus domine beate barbare . . . (With 9–line miniature on 171v: St. Barbara with book and palm branch, in front of a tower)

172r–v: *De omnibus sanctis. An̄.* omnes sancti et electi dei memoramini . . . [I]N firmitatem [*sic*] nostra[m] . . . (With 8–line miniature on 172v: Seven human figures representing various classes of saints)[3]

ALL THAT FOLLOWS IS IN BASTARDA (FRENCH, 16TH CENTURY; AN EDUCATED WOMAN'S HAND):

173r–174v: *Oraisons fort deuotes pour dire auant la reception du tres digne sainct sacrema[n]t de lautel.* Iesus vous estes mon rede[m]pteur mo[n] vray et souuerain . . . (173r, last line, rubric:) *La seconde oraison* (173v, text:) Iesus aussi est mon Intencio[n] de vous vouloir receuuoir . . . (ends, 174v:) . . . et Royaulme celeste des cieulx. Ame[n]

174v–175v: (174v, rubric:) *Oraison a la sacree V[ie]rge marie aua[n]t q[u'] aller co[mmun]ier* (text begins 175r:) O vierge glorieuse hu[m]ble et misericordieuse plaise vo[us] p[rese]nter a v[ost]re doulx enfa[n]t le sain et sacree mamelles desquelles lavez allecte . . . (ends, 175v:) . . . qui rien ne vo[us] desnye

175v–176r: *Aultre oraison a la glorieuse v[ier]ge marie* Maintena[nt] a vo[us] dame qui estes sur toutes les femmes benoiste . . . a v[ost]re pouure mandiente et ulcereuse . . . affin q̄ ie soye faicte digne di celuy pain . . . Amen

176r–177v: *Aultre oraison* O mon dieu mon pere mon createur ie viens a vous . . . toute difformee par peche . . . co[m]me la pouure fille . . . co[m]me la pauure expouze desloyalle . . . (177v:) . . . q̄ ie ne suis q̄ vne pouure pecherresse . . . Amen

177v–178v: *Oraison po[u]r adorer le sainct sacrema[n]t quant le p[re]stre la porte et tient pour le donner a Recepuoir* (text begins 178r:) IE vous adore mon dieu et createur naturel . . . (ends 178v:) . . . mon createur mon dieu et mo[n] seigneur: Amen:

178v–179v: *Pour rendre graces a dieu ap[re]s la co[mmun]ion* mon dieu ie vous remer (179r:) cie de tout mon cuer . . . (ends, 179v:) . . . et au salut de tous mes bienffaicteurs vifs et deffunds. Amen.

179v–180r: *Aultre oraison a Jesus n[ost]re benoist redempte[u]r* O Mon doulx seigneur createur et rede[m]pteur ie vous remercie . . . en ce sainct sacremant Amen

180v–181r: *Oraison a la benoiste vierge marie.* O benoiste et glorieuse dame qui auez porte en v[ost]re sainct et sacre ve[n]tre . . . il luy plaise me pardo[nn]er toute l'irreuerance . . . ne ceste reception . . . Ame[n]

(f. 181v blank)

* * *

Foliated in modern pencil. Preceding f. 1, four paper flyleaves; same at end. — Written area ca. 92 × ca. 52 mm. Extremely light, often no more visible ruling in very faint red ink. No pricking marks. — Roman script rather resembling that of LC MS 52 (and Jenson roman type) but not as extremely precise. French additions, i.e., everything after f. 172v, are in a semicursive *lettre bâtarde* by another (probably a woman's) hand. — Ink throughout of uneven blackness, slightly brownish; rubrics in red. — Excellent-quality white parchment (thickness ca. 8.3 mm per 100 leaves).

Collation appears impracticable.

The 16 large (12v, 18v, 27r, 32v, 49r, 59r, 60v, 62r, 69r, 74v, 80r, 86r, 94r, 101r, 117r, 158r) and 24 small illustrations (cf. contents) are by two or more artists, none exceeding ordinary workshop quality. The small miniatures in particular are very naive (and perhaps retouched?). The large illustrations are set in architectural borders rather uniform in shape, done primarily in gold; the small ones (30–40 mm high, 30–50 mm wide) are in simple rectangular gilt frames.

Initials 2- or 1-line, all in gold on red or bright blue ground; the ground is decorated with simple leaf motives and other tracery in gold. — Line fillers have simple gold decorations on rectangular red or blue grounds.

Bound in (19th-century?) dark blue or bluish black goatskin; on spine, in gilt: L OFFICE//DE//L EGLISE. Doublures of brownish red morocco, gold-tooled à la dentelle. Gilt edges. On 1st (paper) flyleaf recto, in pencil: "16 large/24 small Miniatures"; "1460/10"; "HRcx"; also mounted label of the Library of Congress, with typed information: ROSENWALD COLLECTION/ Gift of//James S. Collins//1967. On 2nd flyleaf verso, in pencil: HOURS OF THE B.V. MARY according to the Use of BOURGES: early 16th cent. F.C.E. — At end of the book, on verso of 3rd flyleaf, in pencil: "LRc/HRcx"; "Gift//For the Rosenwald Collection//James S. Collins/May 26, 1964." On recto of penultimate flyleaf, in pencil, by LC cataloger: Catholic Church. Liturgy and ritual.//[Hours. (MS. Library of Congress. Rosenwald ms. 33)]; by another hand: Rosenwald MS. 33; LC cataloger's initials: RT 14je68.

Kept in a solander case done in bluish green morocco; on spine of the case: HORAE B.V.M.//BOURGES, 16TH CENT.// PRESENTED BY//JAMES S. COLLINS//1967 // ROSENWALD/COLLECTION.

Former owners: Mrs. Philip S. Collins; James S. Collins.

2° fo.: $(KL)^2$ *februarius habet dies*

Bibl.: LC printed card no. 74-206953. — Library of Congress, *The Lessing J. Rosenwald collection* (1977), no. 15 (same information as on the printed card)

Without being in the same class, the book has similarities with LC MSS 52 and 53 (Hours Rosenwald 10 and 11). The script resembles that of MS 52 although less good ink was used and less attention given to perfection. A common source for choice of the texts and to some extent for their ordering seems to have served in producing both these *Horae* and the MS 53. The artwork is, however, decidedly inferior. Was it a question of budget or was the book produced before the arrival of Italian master artists?

NOTES

1. No. 33 in old LC "Rosenwald shelflist"; no. 15 in the second catalog (1977) of LC Rosenwald Collection.
2. St. Martialis is patron of Limoges, a suffragan diocese of Bourges. Neither he nor other special patrons of Limoges (cf. *Catholic encycl.*, 1913) are, however, mentioned in the calendar.
3. The *I* of "Infirmitatem" (actually written, although hardly understood, as two words) left out, it seems, by miscalculation.

MS 55

(Faye and Bond 34)

BOOK OF HOURS early XVth c.

Paris? Parchment. 172 leaves, ca. 177 × ca. 126 mm (bound volume: ca. 182 × ca. 135 mm) 1 column. 14 lines (calendar, 17 lines)

(ff. 2r–13v, calendar; 14r–19r, Gospel readings; 19r–24r, *Obsecro te;* 24r–26v, *O intemerata;* 28r–88r, Hours of Our Lady (incomplete); 89r–106v, Penitential Psalms (incomplete) with Litany; 107r–110v, Short Hours of the Cross (incomplete); 111r–114v, Short Hours of the Holy Spirit (incomplete); 115r–162v, Office for the Dead (incomplete); 162v–167v, *Les 15 joies de Notre Dame;* 167v–170v, *Sept requêtes à Notre Seigneur.* ADDITIONS: 171rv, *Cinque Ave;* 171v–172r, *Cinque joies de la Vierge;* 172r, suffrage Mary Magdalen)

(f. 1rv, actually a free endleaf,[1] blank except for inscriptions, including an illegible remnant of an erased early one on 1v close to the mutilated top)

2r–13v: (KL)² januier . . .

Full calendar in French; major feasts (52 such) in gold, other days alternately red or blue; each month occupies one leaf. — The names written in gold are the saints particularly celebrated or popular in Paris (Maur, Vincent, George, Yves, Louis IX, *Leu* and *Gilles,* Denis, Elois . . .); not so emphasized, however, are Geneviève (Jan. 3), Sebastian (Jan. 20), Anne (July 28), Marcel (Nov. 3).[2] — Notable among the names in red or blue: Blanchart (Jan. 31), Osenne (Feb. 26; cf. Perdrizet, *Calendrier parisien* [1933], p. 101 and 240 sqq.; ms. also has s. Osanne, Aug. 4), Oportune (Apr. 21), Ysfemine (Apr. 29), Ierosine (May 17), Ruffin (July 12), Columbain (Dec. 30; i.e., Columba?)[3]

14r–19r: *Secundum iohannem.* (I)³N principio . . . (15r:) . . . *Scd' . lucā.* (M)²issus est . . . (16v:) . . . *Secundū matheū* (I)³n illo tempore. Cum natus . . . (18r:) . . . *Secund' . marchū.* (I)²N illo tempore. Recumbentib[us] . . . (ends, 194:) . . . seque[n]tibus signis

Gospel readings: John I,1–14; Luke I,26b–38a; Matthew II,1–12; Mark XVI,14–20. — No liturgical additions beyond the "In illo tempore" and, after the Johannine Prologue, the "Deo gracias."

19r–24r: (beginning in line 12 of 19r:) *Oracio de beata maria.* (O)²Bsecro te d[omi]na . . . facturus locuturus et cogitaturus . . . (ends in 12th line of 24r:) . . . maria mater dei m[isericord]ie. Amen.

MS 55 Leroquais, *LH* II, p. 346 sq. In masculine form (= written for use by a man)

24r–26v: *Oracio marie u[ir]g[inis].* (O)[2] intemerata . . . o iohannes . . . (26v:) cum eis uiuit et regnat deus per omnia secula seculorum Amen. (26v, lines 4–14 blank; 27rv blank)

Cf. Wilmart, *Aut. spir.*, p. 488–490.

(following blank, ruled [but not decorated] f. 27, one leaf missing)

28r–88r: [iubi]lemus ei. Aue maria gratia plena dominus tecum . . .

Hours of Our Lady according to the use of Paris;[4] incomplete, beginning in the middle of the first verse of the Invitatory; also wanting, the beginning of Lauds (leaf following f. 50), of Prime (following leaf 61), of the Sext (leaf after f. 70), None (after 73), Vespers (missing leaf following f. 76), and Compline (after 82).

Large illustration (the Shepherds; see plate XXIII, p. xxxvii) on f. 67r, with the beginning of the Terce, suggests that the book had originally the whole traditional series of miniatures (Annunciation, Visitation, etc.; cf. Leroquais, *LH* I, p. xlvi).[5] — Wanting (excised) is also lower half of f. 73 (with rubric announcing the beginning of the None?). — The text of the office agrees, as far as preserved, with the Parisian variant as identified by the table in Leroquais, *op. cit.*, p. xxxviii; the Matins, however, have three nocturns; the readings given by Leroquais, *loc. cit.*, are in the first nocturn.

(88v blank, ruled, decorated; following it, one leaf missing, presumably with an illustration of David penitent [and the beginning of next item])

89r–106v: meum lacrimis meis . . .

The Penitential Psalms;[6] incomplete, beginning in the middle of Psalm VI. — Follows (101v–106v), as traditionally, the Litany. After Mary, (arch)angels, and the apostles, the litany turns to St. Martialis before the appeal to "omnes sancti discipuli Domini"; this honor given to the first bishop of Limoges is characteristic of the litany as found in Parisian breviaries.[7] It also invokes, among martyrs, St. Dennis with companions, Nicasius with companions, Cornelius, Leodegarius; among confessors, St. Louis and St. Yvo; among women, Genovefa, Brigida, also Fides, Spes, Caritas, Sapiencia [!], Castitas [!].[8] — The prayers after the litany end in last line of 106v with last phrases of the prayer *Fidelium*.

(following f. 106, one leaf missing, presumably with illustration [Crucifixion])

107r–110v: (D)[2]omine ih[es]u xp̄e fili dei uiui pone passionem crucem et mortem tuam . . . (110v, last words at end of page:) . . . et uera[m] concordia[m] a nobis

The Short Hours of the Cross;[9] beginning imperfectly, with the end of the Lauds, and ending imperfectly, close to the end of Compline.

(following f. 110, one leaf missing; probably with illustration [Pentecost])

111r–114v: Et renouabis faciem terre. Domine exaudi or[aci]one[m] mea[m] . . . *Ad primam.* . . .

Short Hours of the Holy Spirit;[10] incomplete, beginning with the end of Lauds and ending just after the beginning of Compline.

(following f. 114, one leaf missing, probably with illustration representing Exequies)

115r–162v: Quia inclinauit aurem suam michi : et in di[e]b[us] meis inuocabo . . .

The *Officium defunctorum* (office for the deceased), presumably according to Paris use. Begins imperfectly, with the second verse of the first psalm of the Vespers. — The responsories are: I Qui Lazarum II Credo quod III Heu michi IV Ne recorderis V Domine quando VI Peccantem me VII Domine secundum VIII Memento mei IX Libera me . . .

162v–167v: (162v, lines 12–13:) *Cy commencent les xv. ioies de nostre dame.* (one leaf missing; 163r:) Aue maria (E)^{2}tresdouce dame pour ycelle grant ioie . . .

In (Middle) French. — Sonet, *Répertoire* 458; cf. Wilmart, *Aut. spir.*, p. 326 sqq.; Leroquais, *LH* II, p. 310 sq. (gives whole text; N.B. in its present despoiled state the manuscript does not have the prologue)

167v–170v: (167v, lines 7–8:) *Cy commencent les v. plaises n[ost]re seigneur ih[es]u crist.* (lines 9–14 of 167v empty; one leaf missing; 168r:) [envo]iastes u[ost]r[e] saint angle gabr[iel] . . . (ends on 170v with prayer:) (S)^{2}ainte uraye croys aouree . . . fes mourir. Amen. Pater n[oste]r

Known as *Sept requêtes à Notre Seigneur* (with 7 prayers beginning each with "Biau sire Dieu . . ."). — Sonet, *Répertoire* 504; text Leroquais *LH* II, p. 309 sq. For the prayer *Saincte vraye croys aourée*, cf. Leroquais, *op. cit.*, index (p. 447), and Sonet 1876. (In the present manuscript the prayer seems to be intended as a conclusion to the *Sept requêtes*.)

THE REMAINING PAGES ARE ADDITIONS IN ANOTHER HAND.[11] The leaves are mutilated: upper fore-edge corners missing, with partial loss of text.

171r–v: Je te salue Jhesu cri[st] . . .

French version of the *V Ave* or *Quinque salutationes Iesu Christi*; the first and second salutation here affected by the damage to the leaves; the third begins: Je te salue Jhesu Xpist resplendiseur du pere. Cf. Wilmart, *Aut. spir.*, p. 377, note, also text, *ibid.*, on p. 24 (another variant).

171v–172r: [Gaude . . .] (first words of several lines wanting; loss of text affects first three paragraphs) (171v, 11th line:) Oremus . . . (suffrage ends in 5th line of 172r)

The *Cinque joies de la Vierge* (one of several known versions); cf. Wilmart, *op. cit.*, p. 329, note (N.B. in the present case the probable *initium* is "Gaude Virgo mater Christi")

172r: (6th line:) De marie magdalene (7th line:) Maria ergo vnxit pedes Jhu . . . (ends on same page with formal prayer:) Sacratissimam nobis . . . Amen.

(172v blank except for ownership inscription: Donon, 1613; Dumet)

* * *

Modern pencil foliation in fives; (mutilated) free endleaf at the beginning is counted as f. 1. There are two free endleaves at the end, making the leaf count in De Ricci (I, p. 210, no. 56) "174 ff." — Written area ca. 95 × ca. 57 mm. Fully ruled in faint red ink. — *Littera textualis formata* of two (or three, if calendar is taken into the count) sizes, probably both by same scribe; in the smaller size are written, e.g., the antiphons of the minor hours in the Hours B.M.V. — Leaves 171–172 contain additions in (15th-century) cursive (*cursiva formata*) by another hand.

Collation: 1^{12}(= ff. 2–13) 2^8 3^6 4^8 (wants 4_1) 5–6^8 7^8 (wants 7_1) 8^8 (wants 8_5) 9^8 (wants 9_7) 10^8 (wants 10_3 and 10_7) 11^8 (wants 11_6) 12^8 (wants 12_5) 13–$14^{6?}$ 15^8 (wants 15_4) 16^6 (wants 16_1 and 16_6) 17–18^8 19^{10} 20^8 21^{12} 22^{10} (wants 22_3 and 22_9) 23^4 (wants 23_3) 24^2 (wants 24_2) (f. "173" is free endleaf conjugate with the former pastedown marked "174"). — Catchwords, partly cropped, at end of some gatherings. Partial loss of text (cf. contents) and probably of illustrative material originally present on the leaves now wanting.

The only illustration preserved (67r) from what very probably was the full traditional series (suggested by location and by the amount of text gaps) is 10 lines in height (68 × 57 mm);[12] together with the 4 lines of text (the beginning of Terce) it is separated from the border by a wide baguette decorated in blue, red, and gold. Bar border in gold and color (blue and pink) on outer margin, extending also partly to the head and tail areas, is present on all text pages and on some blank ones; often complemented, when on recto, by similar elements issuing from a major initial. The borders consist of vine-stem

MS 55 scrolls mounted with ivy leaves outlined in black ink and filled in gold or colored red, blue, or purple lightened by white lines. The stems of the golden leaves are drawn as single lines in black ink. On f. 81v the vine-stem ends in a gargoyle (colored red and blue).

The larger (2–3 line) initials are blue or pink divided in white, on gold grounds, infilled with finely drawn foliage colored blue, red, or pink. One-line initials and versals are gold on blue or pink-red grounds lightened by white-line ornament. Line fillers use similar palette and include segments in (laid) gold. Several large initials are smudged.

Binding: of ca. 1580, French brown calf over pasteboard, stamped in center and corners. In a more recent restoration effort the spine has been replaced by dark brown morocco. — The lower cover and leaves 76–172 are mutilated in upper fore-edge corners by mice. The destruction has affected progressively larger areas and resulted in increasing losses of text from f. 167 on. — Exposed parts of the pasteboard (inside of upper cover, inside and part of outside of lower cover) are lined with fragments of an early print of Terence's *Heuatontimorumenos* with commentary.

Owned in 1613 by Donon and ca. 1810 by Dumet (inscriptions on final endleaves; persons otherwise not identified). Given to Library of Congress in 1930 by Rev. Thomas J. Shahan (ms. ac. 4022)

2° fo.: (KL)[2] *januier*[13]

De Ricci, *Census*, v. 1 (1935), p. 210, no. 56; Faye and Bond (1962), p. 118, no. 34.

NOTES

1. Or, rather, a "freed" former pastedown.
2. Cf. Perdrizet, *Calendrier parisien* (1933).
3. Cf. Leroquais, *LH* II, p. 53.
4. See table C for a number of details on the text.
5. List given also in Calkins, *Illuminated books of Middle Ages* (1983) (p. 246).
6. = Pss. VI, XXXII, XXXVIII, LI, CII, CXXX, CXLIII.
7. Chronologically confused legend claimed for Martialis a place among the first seventy or seventy-two disciples of Jesus: cf. Perdrizet, *Calendrier parisien* (1933), p. 165.
8. After Martialis, the disciples, and the Innocents, the litany continues with 22 individually named martyrs, 12 confessors, 16 women.
9. See note with contents of ff. 91r–92v of MS 44.
10. See note with contents of ff. 93r–95v of MS 44.
11. Expertly executed *lettre bâtarde* or, perhaps, *cursiva formata*. The three pages (171r–172r) are unruled; the layout is, nevertheless, well planned.
12. Shepherds (two) in red and strikingly blue garments; angel appears from a background area done in blue, gold, and light magenta diaper pattern.
13. With "januier" in gold.

MS 56

(Faye and Bond 92)

BOOK OF HOURS AND PRAYER BOOK (Latin; calendar and most rubrics in French) ca. 1420

Written and decorated in Paris. Parchment. 221 leaves, ca. 132 × ca. 95 mm (bound volume: ca. 138 × ca. 110 mm) 1 column. 14 lines (calendar, 17 lines)

(ff. 1r–12v, calendar; 13r–18r, Gospel readings; 18v–20v, Passion according to John; 21r–73r, Hours of Our Lady; 74r–93v, Penitential Psalms, with Litany; 94r–112r, Office for the Dead; 113r–118v, Short Hours of the Cross; 119r–124v, Short Hours of the Holy Spirit; 124v–200r, various prayers; 200r–201v, *Obsecro te* [variant form]; 201v–208v, Marian prayers; 209r–212v, prayers to guardian angel; 213r–217r, *Obsecro te* [usual form]; 217r–221v, *O Intemerata* [non-Johannine])

ff. 1r–12v: Full calendar, in French; in (brushed) gold and alternating blue or red; one month to a leaf. — Notable among days singled out in gold: *Geneviève* (Jan. 3), *Maur ("S aint mor s. bon[et],"* Jan. 15), *Yves* (May 19), *Eloy* ([Transl.], June 25), *Louis* (Aug. 25), *s. Leu s. Gille* (Sept. 1), *Rémy* (Oct. 2), *Denis* (Oct. 9), *Eloy* (Dec. 1), *Lucie* (Dec. 13). — Among the days not emphasized: Emille (? Mar. 30), Guinofle (= ? Apr. 22), Règle (= ? Apr. 28), Nerin (= ? May 11), Ieroisine (? May 17), Cancian (May; = Cantius), Anne (July 26(!)), Osenne (Aug. 4), Regnault (Sept. 13), Agolin (? Oct. 15), Columbain (Dec. 30)

Probably meant to be the calendar of Paris (cf. Perdrizet, *Calendrier parisien* (1933)), although the date of the day of St. Anne, celebrated in Paris on July 28, and the emphasis given to St. Lucy pose problems. Some of the names (Guinofle, Règle, Nerin . . .) may be a product of workshop dictation, cf. Perdrizet, *op. cit.,* p. 46.

13r–18r: *Initium sancti euua[n]gelij secund'.iohannē.* (I)[4]N principio . . . (14r:) . . . veritatis.deo gratias *Secundum lucam.* (I)[4]N illo tempore . . . (15v:) . . . *Secundum matheū* (C)[2]Um natus esset . . . Deo grās. (17r:) . . . *secund' marcū.* (17v:) (I)[3]N illo tempore . . . (ends, 18r:) . . . signis. Deo grās

Gospel readings (John I, 1–14; Luke I, 26b–38a; Matthew II, 1–12; Mark XVI, 14–20) — No liturgical additions other than the introductory phrase and the "Deo gratias" at end.

18v–20v: *Passio d[omi]ni n[ost]ri ih[es]u xpī secundum iohanne[m]* (I)[4]N illo tempore: Apprehendit . . .

John XIX, 1–35a, strongly abridged but with addition taken from Matthew XXVII, 30.

21r–73r: (21r: full-page illustration [Annunciation] and the opening words:) (D)[3]omine labia mea . . .

Hours of Our Lady according to the use of Paris; as in Leroquais, *LH* I, p. xxxviii. There are no seasonal variations and no variations in the choice of psalms for the Matins. — *Te Deum* is captioned by rubric *"Canticum angloru[m]."*

Full-page illustrations also on 33r (Visitation, with the beginning of Lauds) and 45v (Nativity, with the beginning of Prime). All remaining hours begin—and Terce, Sext, and None also end—imperfectly, owing to missing leaves following ff. 51, 54, 58, 61, and 68. — It is highly probable that the missing leaves contained full-page illustrations of the traditional series (the Shepherds, the Magi, Presentation in the Temple, Flight to Egypt, Coronation of the Virgin); cf. Leroquais, *op. cit.,* p. xlvi.

(73v blank, unruled)

(following f. 73, one leaf missing; very likely with full-page illustration, David penitent)

74r–93v: Penitential Psalms, beginning imperfectly, in the middle of the first psalm (i.e., Ps. VI, 6b: lectum meum lacrimis meis . . .); with Litany, ff. 87r sqq. — The litany has, among the archangels, Uriel;[1] among martyrs: Dyonisi cum sociis, Maurici cum sociis; among confessors: Lamberte, Guillerme, Urbane, Egidi, Remigi, Maure, Yvo; among women: Oportuna, Elysabeth, Genovefa, Apolinea, Clara, Spes, Fides.[2]

94r–112r: (93v, lines 10–11, surrounded by blank space, rubric:) *Ci commencent les uigiles des mors alusaige de paris* (94r, full-page illustration: dead man and the struggle for his soul; with the opening lines:) Placebo Domino. *p̄s.* (D)[3]Ilexi quoniam . . . (office ends on 112r with the prayer *Fidelium* and:) . . . Deo gratias. (last 3 lines empty)

Office for the Dead, presumably Paris use. No invitatory; only one nocturn. — Responsories: I Qui Lazarum II Credo quod III Libera me. Antiphon for Benedictus: Credo Domine Deus meus Ih[es]u xp̄e carnis resurrectionem . . .

(112v blank, unruled)

(following f. 112, leaf or leaves missing; very likely with full-page illustration: Crucifixion)

113r–118v: The (Short) Hours of the Cross;[3] beginning imperfectly, near the end of Matins (tus afflictus. *ant.* Adoramus te . . .); ending imperfectly, near the end of Compline (118v, last line: mortis agone. *ant.*)

(following f. 118, one leaf (or 2 leaves?) missing; very likely with full-page illustration: Pentecost)

119r–124v: Short Hours of the Holy Spirit (based on the hymn *Nobis Sancti Spiritus gratia sit data);*[4] beginning imperfectly (119r: Deus in adiutorium . . . Nobis sancti spiritus . . .)

124v–134r: (beginning with the 5th line on 124v:) *Ci commence tres excellente oroison de n[ost]re seigneur.* (D)[3]omine ih[es]u xp̄e qui in hunc mu[n]dum inter nos peccatores de sinu patris aduenisti ut de ade peccato nos redimeres . . . exaudi me . . . peccatorem . . . indignum . . .

A primarily penitential nonliturgical prayer, very eloquent; in masculine form. On 133r, after "negligens sum de opere dei," added in different ink: & de ordi[n]e meo. — A prominent feature of the prayer are cumulated requests (126rv) beginning with the phrase "Deus omnipotens libera me de . . ." (10 such, with minor variations). — Possibly same as the prayer ascribed to Augustine in Bib. nat. ms. lat. 1063? (Cf. Leroquais, *LH* I, p. 48, etc. — Cf. also the ms. Keble College 40, ff. 207v–211v, where it says "ut peccatores de sinu patris adam redimeres"[5])

134r–142v: (134r, lines 10–11, rubric:) *Oroison de nostre seigneur ihū crist.* (text:) (D)[3]omine deus omnipotens qui es trinus et vnus qui es semper in omnibus . . . (142r:) . . . me famulum tuum philipum . . . (ends, 142r–v:) in seculorum secula amen.

With minor variants, the text is that printed by Migne in *PL* XL as ch. XL of the pseudo-Augustinian *Meditationes.* Some of the variants may suggest avoidance of any mention of monks (138r "anachoritarum" instead of *PL*'s "monachorum," etc.)

142v (beginning in 2nd line:) (A)[2]nima xpisti[6] . . . in secula seculorum amen.

Cf. Wilmart, *Aut. spir.*, p. 367, note 6. (Text in Leroquais, *LH* II, p. 340.)[7]

143r–v: (D)^{2}eus qui uoluisti pro redemptione mundi a iudeis reprobari . . . amen.

Cf. Leroquais, *LH* I, p. 153.

143v–144r: (D)^{2}omine ih[es]u xpiste q[ui] hanc sacratissimam carnem de gloriose uirginis marie utero assumpsisti . . . corpus tuum quod modo in altari tractatur . . . amen.

Cf. Leroquais, *LH* I, p. 36, etc.; Wilmart, *Aut. spir.*, p. 377, n. 1, no. 10; text in *Horae Eboracenses* (1920), p. 72.

144v–146v: (D)^{2}eus inestimabilis misericordie deus imme[n]se pietatis deus conditor et reparator humani generis . . . et miserere miseri huius.

Prayer formerly attributed to Anselm of Canterbury. Cf. Wilmart, *Aut. spir.*, p. 147 sqq. and passim; text in *PL* CLVIII, col. 876 (*Orationes,* VIII)

146r–154r: (X)^{2}riste domine uerbum p[at]ris qui venisti . . .

Another prayer ascribed in the past to Anselm; *PL* CLVIII, col. 891 sq. (*Or.* XVI)

154v–157r: (D)^{2}omine sancte pater omnipotens deus per benedictum filium tuum . . . intende a me hodie et dirige . . .

A morning prayer. Cf. Leroquais, *LH* I, p. 340.

157r–158v: (A)^{2}ltissime deus creator omnis creature . . . deus lux uera . . . (157v:) . . . confugio ad te. Pater noster. (O)^2 beata trinitas te laudamus . . . auge in nobis fidem auge spem auge caritatem . . . (158r:) . . . in seculum. (158r, 6th line and following:) (S)^{2}cio domine scio et fateor . . . (158v:) . . . ut in pace dormiam et requiescam in te . . . amen.

Night prayers. For the *Scio Domine*, cf. *PL* CLVIII, col. 905–906 (no. XXI in the mostly pseudo-Anselmian *Orationes*)

158v–159v: (D)^{2}Eus qui es sanctoru[m] tuorum splendor mirabilis atq[ue] lapsor[um] subleuator . . . a[m]e[n].

Cf. Leroquais, *LH* I, p. 312.

159v–160r: (A)^{2}doro te domine ihesu xpiste in cruce[m?] ascende[n]te[m?] deprecor te ut ipsa crux . . . sed ante dimittas quam iudices amen.

160r: (rubric, beginning in 12th line:) *Ci comme[n]cent tre^s excellentes oroisons de n[ost]re seigneur ihū crist.*

160v–163r: (beginning with a 4-line initial:) (A)^{4}d te domine lacrimabiliter ingemisco . . . concedas michi . . . timorem et amorem et intellectu[m] et desiderium tui . . . amen.

163r–164v: (D)^{2}Eus bone qui merentium non despicis gemitum . . . exaudi me . . . pro seruis tuis humiliter implorantem . . . a[m]e[n]

164v–168r: (C)^{2}onfiteor tibi domine ih[es]u xp̄e omnia mala mea . . . cecidi ego peccator per alios et multi per me ceciderunt . . . indulgentiam tam pro me quam pro illis postulo . . . amen.

168r–v: (B)^{2}enignus et misericors deus qui reuocas errantes . . . amen.

168v–171r: (A)^{2}D mensam dulcissimi conuiuii tui . . . accessurus uereor . . . Qui uiuis et regnas et cetera *[sic]*

Cf. Leroquais, *LH* I, p. 258, etc.; Wilmart, *Aut. spir.,* p. 381, note 2.

171r–173r: (D)^{2}Eus qui ab initio humane creature misertus es . . . amen.

173r–v: (S)^{2}alua me domine saluator rex eterne glorie qui potes saluare . . . Da michi scire, posse, uelle . . . amen.

A very slightly variant version of the prayer included in the Merovingian *Libellus precum, PL* CI, col. 1383 sqq. (this item, attributed to Augustine, in col. 1398).

173v–174v: (F)$^{2+}$iat michi queso domine precibus et meritis beate . . . uirginis marie . . . firma fides in corde . . . in pectore uoluntas bona . . . amen.

174v–176r: *les huit vers saint bernart.* (I)llumina oculos meos . . . (175v:) . . . (F)ac mecum signum in bonum . . . consolatus es me. Oremus. (O)^{2}mnipotens . . . (ends, 176r:) . . . uiuit et regnat.

For the alleged diabolical origin of this devotion, cf. Leroquais, *LH* I, p. xxx.

MS 56

176r–187v: (176r, last 7 lines, rubric:) *Incipiunt orationes breues et proprie ad sanctissimam trinitatem et ad beatissimam uirginem mariam. Et primo . . . Oratio ad deum patre[m] in mane dicenda . . .* (176v, full-page illustration: God the Father; with opening lines of the following:) (A)[3]Peri domine os meum ad laudandum et benedicendum . . . (177r, 8th line:) (exau)di *[sic]* merear. amen. (D)[2]omine sancte pat[er] omnipotens eterne deus qui me creare et hactenus custodire dignatus es Tibi gratias ago . . . michi . . . (178r:) . . . famulo tuo.N. . . . (178v, 10th line:) amen. (line 11:) (P)ater de celis deus misere[re] nobis. (D)[2]omine sancte pater . . . (179v:) . . . (F)ili redemptor mundi deus miserere nobis. (180r:) (D)[3]omine ihesu xpe . . . (180v, last line:) (S)piritus sancte deus mi(181r:)serere nobis. (D)[2]omine sancte spirit[us] . . . (182r:) . . . (S)ancta trinitas unus deus miserere nobis. (D)[2]omine deus omnipotens eterne et ineffabilis sine fine atq[ue] inicio q[uem] unum in trinitate et trinum in unitate confitemur . . . (187r:) . . . amen. (B)enedicamus patrem et filium . . . (B)enedicat me deus pater . . . (C)ustodiat me dei filius . . . (187v:) . . . (I)lluminet me spiritus sanctus . . . (C)onseruet me in omni opere bono sanctissima trinitas . . . amen (P)ater noster. (A)ue maria gratia (S)ancta maria ora pro nobis.

The texts 176v–187v are a not unintelligently arranged[8] set of prayers mixing theological points with elements from both liturgical and nonliturgical devotion; traditional introductory invocations of the Litany (''Pater de celis Deus,'' etc.) serve as the connective element. — In the last lines of 187v, attention is turning to Mary, in a set connected (at least through 193v) by further litany addresses:

188r–200r: (A)[2]ue regina celorum aue domina angelorum. Aue salus miserorum et leuamen orphanorum. aue . . . (altogether 11 ''Ave . . .'', with some rhetorical interruptions) . . . (189r:) (S)ancta dei genitrix ora pro nobis. (O)[2] gloriosa mundi domina maria . . . (193v:) . . . amen. . . .(S)ancta uirgo uirginum ora pro nobis. (O)[3] Excellentissima et gloriosissima . . . (196v:) . . . seculorum a[m]e[n] (B)eata uiscera . . . (A)lma uirgo . . . amen. (O)[2] domina glorie et regina leticie . . .[9] (197v:) . . . (S)[2]ancta maria mater domini nostri ihu xpisti in manus eiu[s]dem . . . (199v:) . . . (A)[2]nime omnium fidelium deffunctorum . . . (200r:) (P)ater nr̄ qui es (A)ue maria

200r–201v: (O)[3]bsecro te sanctissima et gloriosissima uirgo maria mater summe benignitatis per illam ineffabilem leticiam . . . (200v:) . . . ut michi . . . famulo tuo philippo . . . (ends on 201v:) . . . Exaudi exaudi exaudi me dulcis maria mater mi[sericordi]e per ihesum xpistum filium tuum amen.

A variant of the prayer more frequently encountered in the form printed by Leroquais in *LH* II, p. 346 sq. (Cf. ff. 213r–217r)

201v–202r: (O) gloria mulierum gemma uirginum stella confessorum rosa martirum . . . amen.

202v–207r: (O)[2] sanctissima et gloriosissima et piissima dei genitrix maria unica spes mea . . . (203v:) . . . (G)aude gaudio sanctorum piissima domina . . . (ends on 207r:) . . . amen.

Prayer(s) for Christian death.

207r–208r: (O)[2] Beatissima et piissima uirgo uirginum dei genitrix maria fac mecum mi[sericordi]am tuam . . . amen.

208r–v: Aue maria . . . fructus uentris tui.

The usual form of the *Salutatio angelica* (or the first half of it).

208v–209r: (G)loria fine carens sit tibi uirgo parens amen. (A)ngele dei qui meus es custos pietate superna . . . guberna . . . scandere regna. amen.

(The passage from Marian prayers to a collection of addresses to the guardian angel; signaled inadequately)

209r–212v: (O)[2]bsecro te angele spiritus cui ego indignus . . . (211r:) . . . prestante domino . . . a[m]e[n]. (O)[2] sancte angele dei minister celestis imperii . . . (212r:) . . . in presentia omnipotentis . . . amen. (Q)[2]ueso te et obsequenter rogo sancte angele dei . . . (ending imperfectly, in last line of 212v: . . . ut adiuuante domino n[ost]ro)

Prayers addressed to the speaker's guardian angel; for the first one, formerly attributed to St. Anselm, see *PL* CLVIII, col. 967–968 (''Oratio LXII'')

(following f. 212, leaf or leaves missing)

213r–217r: (beginning imperfectly:) regis filia mater gloriosissima mater orphanorum consolatio desolatorum . . . per illam sanctam inestimabilem leticiam . . . Et per . . . Et per . . . (215v:) . . . Et michi famulo tuo . . . (217r:) . . . mater dei et m[isericord]ie amen.

The more usual variant of the prayer "Obsecro te" (cf. note with ff. 200r–201v); wanting are ten initial words (probably written under an illustration!)

217r–221v: *Or[ati]o de n[ost]ra d[omi]na.* (O)[3] intemerata et in eternum benedicta . . . ame[n]. Pater noster qui es in celis. Aue maria gratia plena. (in ANOTHER HAND:) —:1311:—[10]

Not the more often encountered prayer addressed to Mary and to John; rather, the oratorical address to Mary only, noted by Wilmart, *Aut. spir.*, p. 493 sq. (with text, p. 494 sq.)

* * *

Foliated in modern pencil. One free vellum endleaf at the beginning and one at end, not counted. Wanting, with loss of text and illustrations, are single or double leaves following those numbered 51, 54, 58, 61, 68, 73, 112, 118, and 212. — Written area ca. 75 × ca. 47 mm. Fully ruled in very faint red ink; the framing lines generally do not reach the edges. No pricking preserved. — Written in a regular fully quadrate *littera textualis* of two sizes (not counting the rather small script of the calendar): the smaller, more laterally compressed and less dark-appearing script marks the responsories of the Matins, also antiphons, versicles, etc. — Ink (at least now) varying from grayish brown to brownish black, but free of powdering tendencies. Rubrics red. — Parchment good to excellent, occasionally crinkled; thickness ca. 10 mm per 100 leaves.

Collation in detail is at present impracticable; the twelve leaves of the calendar are a gathering; the rest of the book seems to be (primarily?) in eights.

The 5 large miniatures preserved on leaves 21r, 33r, 45v, 94r (see plate XXIV, p. xxxviii), 176v (cf. contents) and attributed to the workshop or (that on f. 94) to a follower of the genius-type artist known as the Boucicaut Master (fl. ca. 1400–1420 in Paris)[11] are in arched compartments ca. 73–75 mm high and are accompanied, in each case, by 4 lines of text and full borders richly ornamented with colored (blue, light green, red, purplish pink; partly shaded) flowers, acanthus leaves, and small gold bezants and ivy leaves; sometimes they include an angel and/or a more or less human figure or grotesque. The border of f. 21r is smudged and may have been partly done over. Some of the illustrations have retouched faces. Some of the decorative elements in the head margin are slightly cropped.

Every text page has panel borders on both the inner and outer margins; they consist of vine scrolls with single black line stems carrying colored (blue, light green, orange red, pink) flowers and gold ivy leaves and bezants; in the left margins, the scrolls frequently issue from initials; in right margins, from line fillers.

One-line initials in burnished gold on red or blue grounds with white tracery; 2-line initials magenta or blue with white tracery and foliate infilling in blue or red on burnished gold ground; of same description are the occasionally occurring 4-line (on 18v, 160v), 5-line ("P" or 61r and also on 61v), and 6-line ("P" on 102v) initials. The 3-line initials, mostly associated with the full-page illustrations, are in magenta or blue with white divisions, have foliate infilling as above and backgrounds partly in contrasting color (magenta or blue). The 3-line initial on f. 21r differs from the rest, being shaped from a foliate wreath in blue, red, and green and infilled with a realistic, perspectival representation of a stone (off-white) vase with plants (lilies?) on a smudgy red field: probably a later work. Line fillers are bars with mostly foliate ornaments in red and blue with white tracery on burnished gold grounds. — The initials are done with care, skill, and more-than-usual attention to the divisions of the text.

Binding: French gold-tooled red morocco covers and full-gilt spine, of ca. 1630, used in 20th-century rebacking. Two leather straps (material is recent) attached to fore-edge of upper cover have holes fitting over metal pins attached to lower cover. Gilt edges.

On inside of upper cover, old LC bookplate (with penciled: MS. 92). — On recto of free endleaf, early 19th-century inscription: "An Old Roman Breviary splendidly illuminated, supposed to have been written in the Fourteenth century. Purchased at Charleston, South Carolina in the year 1807 by Robert Gilmor Jr." — On verso of the flyleaf, penciled: 307772//.22.

Former owners: Written for an otherwise unidentified Philippus (ff. 142r, 200v). — Robert Gilmor Jun., of Baltimore. — Acquired by LC in 1922 from J. M. Winkler, Baltimore (ms. accession no. 4560 (7)).

2° fo.: (KL)² *feurier ha .xxviij*

De Ricci, *Census*, v. 1(1935), p. 235, no. 120; Faye and Bond (1962), p. 120, no. 92. — *Illuminated books . . .* (1949), p. 35, no. 92. — M. Meiss, *French painting in the time of Jean de Berry : the Boucicaut Master* (1968), p. 137 and figs. 165, 296–298 (black-and-white reproductions)

The rather idiosyncratic collection of private devotional texts beginning on f. 124v shows it was written for a man by name of Philippus; either he or the scribe may have had reservations about religious orders: see note with ff. 134–142; on f. 139r, in a place corresponding to *PL* XL, col. 939, par. [3], where *PL* has "pro religiosis et saecularibus," the ms. has: "omnibus rectoribus et prelatis"; to "Deo dicatis," it adds: "sive devotis"; other instances of avoidance of any mention of "monks" can be found in the pseudo-Anselmian *Christe Domine* (ff. 146–154). In the address to guardian angel (ff. 209–211), the ms. adds to the situations mentioned in the pseudo-Anselmian text also: ". . . legentem, in divinis servitiis seu in temporalibus occupatum . . ."

Quite apart from the Boucicaut Master connection, the book is a very happy result of intelligent selection of texts and of attention given by a skillful master to the esthetics of the script, initial, border, and page.

NOTES

1. Known to both Jewish and Christian traditions as an archangel but not named in the Bible; Western Church frowned on his cult because of this. His name does not appear in the quasi typical Parisian book of hours analyzed by Perdrizet (his *Calendrier parisien*, p. 28).

2. After the Innocents, the litany invokes 19 individual martyrs, 17 confessors, 16 women.

3. See note to ff. 91–92 in description of MS 44.

4. See note to ff. 93–95 in description of MS 44.

5. Parkes, *Med. mss. Keble College* (1979), p. 181.

6. So written: as many times (though by no means consistently) in this manuscript, the otherwise excellent scribe hasn't used a mark of abbreviation.

7. The prayer is well-known to Roman Catholics of the older school; prayer books sometimes attributed it (quite mistakenly) to St. Ignatius.

8. Vastly superior compared to what one finds, e.g., in LC MSS 52 (f. 97v) or 53 (116v).

9. Cf. Leroquais, *LH* I, p. 143.

10. This cannot possibly be the true date of writing or decorating of the book. Fraud (e.g., on the part of an early 19th-century seller) seems the most plausible explanation.

11. Cf. Millard Meiss, *French painting in the time of Jean de Berry : the Boucicaut master* (1968), esp. p. 137 (LC "ms. acc. 4560(7)" = our MS 56); with black-and-white reproductions of the illustrations on ff. 21, 33, 45, and 94 (not 93).

MS 57

(Faye and Bond 93)

BOOK OF HOURS ca. 1470–1480?

Tours? Parchment. 145 leaves, ca. 197 × ca. 140 mm (bound volume: ca. 207 × ca. 145 mm) 1 column. 13 lines (calendar, 16 lines)

(ff. 1r–5r, Athanasian Creed; 6r–17v, calendar; 18r–22v, *Obsecro te*; 23r–25r, Johannine prologue; 25rv, *O Virgo virginum*; 26r–78r, Hours of Our Lady; 78v–81v, Short Hours of the Cross; 82r–85v, Short Hours of the Holy Spirit; 86r–89v, *O Intemerata*; 90r–112r, Penitential Psalms, with Litany; 114r–145v, Office for the Dead)

ff. 1r–5r: (Q)²Vicumq[ue] uult saluus esse . . . (5r:) . . . saluus esse non poterit. Gloria patri et filio . . . seculorum. Amen. (last 8 lines empty; 5v blank, ruled)

The Athanasian Creed, in (the original) Latin.[1]

6r–17v: (KL)² *Januarius* . . .

Calendar in black and red. — Altogether 150 entries, based on the calendar of Tours. Among the days written in red: *Gaciani episcopi Turonensis* (May 2), *Translatio s. Martini* (July 4), *Martini episcopi Turonensis* (Nov. 11).

18r–22v: (18r, large illustration: Mary with the child Jesus, in a perspectival portico; within full border, and accompanied by two lines of text:) (O)²bsecro te dn̄a sancta maria mater dei pi(1v:)etate plenissima . . . (ends on 22v:) . . . mater dei et misericordie. Amen. (last 2 lines empty)

Leroquais, *LH* II, p. 346 sq. — In masculine form (. . . facturus loquturus aut cogitaturus . . . Et michi famulo tuo . . .)

23r–25r: Inicium sancti euuangelii secundum Joannem. Gloria tibi domine. Qui natus es de virgine . . . secula. a[men]. (I)²N principio . . . (24v:) . . . et ueritatis. Deo gratias. Per euuangelica dicta . . . Te inuocam[us] Te adoramus Te laudamus O beata . . . trinitas . . . Oremus. (P)²rotector in te sperantium . . . vt non amittamus eterna. Per xp̄m . . . amen.

John I, 1–14 in a liturgy-like setting. — The collect *Protector in te sperantium* was used in the Tridentine *Missale Romanum* on 3rd Sunday after Pentecost.

25r–v: O Virgo uirginum O pia domina fac mecum misericordiam in illa hora . . . ame[n]

Cf. Leroquais, *LH* I, p. 315 (same or similar text in Bib. nat. ms. lat. 10526, of 13th century). — A rubric which had preceded the prayer has been erased.

26r–78r: (introduced by a large illustration on 26r: Annunciation; with full border and two lines of text:) (A)^{2}ue maria . . . in mulierib[us] (26v:) (D)^{4}Omine labia mea aperies . . .

Hours of Our Lady according to the use of Tours.[2] Major illuminated initials also with Prime (50v: (D)^{4}Eus in adiutorium . . .), Terce (56v, (D)^{3}Eus . . .), Sext (60r, (D)^{5}Eus . . .), None (63r, (D)^{4}Eus . . .), Vespers (66v, (D)^{4}Eus . . .), Compline (73r, (C)^{4}Onuerte nos . . .)

78v–81v: *Hore de cruce* (D)^{4}Omine labia . . .

The psalmless Short Hours of the Cross, built around the rhymed "pium dictamen" *Patris sapientia veritas divina* (Walther, *Initia* 13840).[3]

82r–85v: (rubric begins on 81v:) *Sequuntur Hore De* (82r:) *Sancto sp[irit]u.* (D)^{4}omine labia . . .

The psalmless Short Hours of the Holy Spirit, built around the rhymed hymn (or *pium dictamen*) *Nobis sancti Spiritus gratia sit data* (Walther, *Initia* 21189).[4]

86r–89v: O intemerata . . . O ioh[ann]es . . . (89r–v:) Oremus. Domine ih[es]u xpiste rex eterne . . . Amen. (last 4 lines empty)

Cf. Wilmart, *Aut. spir.*, p. 488–490.[5]

90r–112r: (90r, large illustration: David and Goliath; with full border and two lines of text:) *an̄.* Ne reminiscaris. (D)^{2}Omine ne in furore . . .

The Penitential Psalms, with (104v sqq.) the Litany of Saints. — The litany has, among martyrs: Dionisi . . . Extaci [= ?] . . . Maurici . . . Nichasi . . . Quintine; among confessors: Egidi . . . Eligi . . . Graciane . . . Huberte . . . Amate . . . Mauronte . . . Vedaste . . . Amande . . . Drogo . . . Aycadre . . . Sanson; among women: . . . Fides, Spes, Caritas.[6]

(112v, 113rv blank, ruled)

114r–145v: (114r, large illustration: Death riding a bull and threatening with spear a group of armed humans; with full border and 2 lines of text:) *an̄.* Placebo. (D)^{2}Ilexi quoniam exaudiet do(minus) . . .

Officium defunctorum: use of Tours? Antiphon to *Magnificat*: Qui Lazarum . . .; only one nocturn. Readings and responsories:

	lesson		*responsory*
I	Parce mihi . . .	I	Qui Lazarum
II	Taedet anima mea	II	Credo quod
III	Manus tuae	III	Heu michi

Antiphon to *Benedictus*: Credo Domine Deus meus Ihesu Christe carnis resurrectionem . . .

* * *

Foliated in modern pencil. The numbering does not include free endleaves (parchment), one at beginning and one at end. — Written area ca. 100 × ca. 69 mm (in the calendar, the vertical measurement reaches ca. 110 mm on some pages). Fully ruled in faint red ink. — The script is *littera textualis*, of two sizes (same scribe?): the slightly smaller and more compressed script (ca. 30 letter widths per line vs. ca. 26) is used for antiphons, versicles, etc. — Brownish black ink; rubrics red. — Parchment of somewhat uneven thickness,[7] rather white (with some non-original stains), the flesh and hair sides well distinguishable on touch.

Collation: 1^{6} (1_{1} [blank?] wanting) 2^{12} 3–18^{8}. — Vertically written catchwords on versos of 4_{6}, 5_{2}, 6_{2}, 8_{6}, 9_{6}, 10_{6}, 11_{6}, 12_{6}, 13_{2}, 14_{6}, 15_{6}, $16_{2.6}$, 17_{2}.

The four illustrations (on ff. 18r [see plate XXV, p. 276], 26r, 90r, 114r; cf. contents), in arched compartments, are high art; done, apparently, by a follower of Jean Fouquet (brushwork strokes of gold applied to robes, etc.); perhaps from the workshop of Jehan Bourdichon.[8] — The accompanying borders are conventional work, panels outlined by thin red penline, containing on void white ground blue and goldish yellow acanthus, with several kinds of inconspicuous blossoms or berries (no laid gold). Partial borders (panels as high as the written area) of similar style appear on pages with major initials. — Several of the major initials are of the conventional French 15th-century style (blue letter, with some white, on gold ground and infilled with red and blue vine; gemlike): on 18r, 26v (the 4-line *D*), 90r, 114r; most of those of large size and unassociated with an illustration are of a less usual kind: the basically blue or dark red letter is decorated with winding brushed-gold, finely drawn branches, placed on a field of the alternate (dark slightly purplish red or rather light blue) color and infilled with, mostly, finely drawn brushed-gold branches; in the 4-line *D* on 63r, at the beginning of None, the infilling consists, instead, of a field of heraldic-appearing golden fleur-de-lys. — The rest of the important letters, including the *KL* in the calendar and also all versals, is alternately gold or blue, with flourishing in bluish black for the golden letters and red for the blue ones; the flourishing is done with attention to detail and good esthetic sense.[9]

Binding: probably 17th-century. Sewn over 5 bands; covers black morocco.[10] Two clasps (of pewter?). — Pastedown on verso of upper cover bears penciled numberings, etc.: 102; M. O. Huff; Temp. no. 14; 145 ff.; Tours; P.I 102; also small label with number in ink: 6587, and LC ownership label, blank. Free endleaf in front has on its recto in pencil: Ac. 4560(8); MS. 93.

Former owners: M. O. Huff (?); (Miss) Susan Minns (of Boston; *b*. 1839?). (Acquired by LC in 1922 at American Art Association sale, from Miss Minns' collection.)

2° fo.: creatus et vn[us] i[m]me[n]sus

Bibl.: De Ricci, *Census* I (1935), p. 235, no. 121; Faye and Bond (1962), p. 120, no. 93. — *Illuminated books* . . . (Walters Art Gallery) (1949), p. 44 sq., no. 116a.

NOTES

1. Misplaced in binding? It is unusual for the *symbolum* to precede the calendar.
2. See table C for textual details.
3. See in description of MS 44 the notes with its ff. 91-92.
4. See in description of MS 44 the notes with its ff. 93-95.
5. N.B. The initial *O* is calligraphic, 2 lines high.
6. After "Omnes sancti apostoli [et] ewangeliste dei" (N.B. no Innocents), individually named 15 martyrs, 19 confessors, 14 women.
7. Overall ca. 15 mm for 100 leaves (text block ca. 22 mm).
8. This suggested in a penciled note in LC Rare Book Room copy of De Ricci; the note is signed "O.P." (= Otto Pächt).
9. I am, however, not sure if the book as a whole could be considered a work of beauty. Perhaps the fading of the ink has produced an impression of paleness.
10. The spine is broken, splitting the book between ff. 25 and 26. — Book is kept in a box covered with green linen.

MS 58

(Faye and Bond 174)

BOOK OF HOURS XVth c.

Northern or northwest France. Parchment. 118 leaves, ca. 181 × ca. 123 mm (bound volume: ca. 190 × ca. 130 mm) 1 column. 15 lines (calendar, 17 lines)

(ff. 3r–14v, calendar; 15r–57v, Hours of Our Lady; 58r–73v, Penitential Psalms, with Litany; 74r–75v, Short Hours of the Cross (incomplete); 76r–78v, Short Hours of the Holy Spirit; 79r–82r, *Obsecro te;* 82v–86r, *O Intemerata* (non-Johannine); 86r–91r, Gospel readings; 93r–116v, Office for the Dead; 116v–118r, *Avete omnes animae fideles)*

f. 1 (= first flyleaf) recto, in LATE HAND, i.e., 17th?-century cursive: officium beatae mariae manuscriptum (1v blank)

(f. 2 = 2nd flyleaf: blank)

3r–14v: (KL)[2] Januier// . . .

Calendar, in French: 143 entries; of them, 52 in gold, the rest in alternating blue and red. — Among the days written in gold: *Vincent* (Jan. 22), *Geruais* (June 19), *Martial* (July 3), *Anne* (July 26), *"Saint Sauueur"* (= Transfiguration; Aug. 6), *Taurin* (Sept. 5), *Denis* (Oct. 9), *Romain* (Oct. 23); for Jan. 20, "Sebastien" seems to have originally been included (in gold) but subsequently erased. — Among days in red or blue: Gaud (= Galdus, Bp. of Évreux; Jan. 31), Sever (Feb. 1), Aubert (Feb. 9), Aquilin (Feb. 15), Yldeuert (= Hildevertus, May 27), Lyeffroy (= Leufredus, June 21), Taurin (Aug. 11, as "Faurin," and Aug. 18; see also above), Lubin (Sept. 15), Nigaise (Oct. 11), Mellon (Oct. 22), Eamond (Nov. 20), Eloy (Dec. 1)

The calendar points to Évreux and to its metropolitan see, Rouen. — The feast of Transfiguration (Aug. 6) did not become a major celebration in the area until 1468. (Cf. Leroquais, *LH* I, p. 87.)[1]

15r–57v: (15r, full-page illustration: Annunciation; with 3 lines of text:) (D)[3]Omine labia . . . (48r, full-page illustration: Flight to Egypt; with 3 lines of text, i.e., the beginning of Vespers)

Hours of Our Lady, use of Évreux (?). (See table C for information on choice of texts, etc.)

58r–73v: (58r, full-page illustration: David penitent; with 3 lines of text:) (D)[3]Omine ne in furore . . .

Penitential Psalms, with (69 sqq.) Litany. — The litany has, among martyrs: . . . Dyonisii . . . Mauricii . . .; among confessors: . . . Remigij . . . Maure . . . Leonarde . . .; among women: . . . Fides . . . Spes . . . Caritas . . . Chri[sti]ana . . .[2]

73v (last 6 lines, ADDED IN another, presumably LATER hand imitating the script of the primary hand): O passio magna. O profu[n]da vulnera . . . (altogether 5 "O . . .") . . . da michi vitam eternam. Amen.

(Following f. 73, two(?) leaves missing with the beginning of the next item and, probably, full-page illustration [Crucifixion?])

74r–75v: meam nunc et in hora mortis mee . . .

The Short Hours of the Cross,[3] beginning imperfectly, near the end of Matins.

76r–78v: (76r, full-page illustration: Pentecost; with three lines of text:) (D)³Omine labia . . .

Hours of the Holy Spirit (based on the hymn *Nobis Sancti Spiritus gratia sit data*)[4]

79r–82r: (78v, last line, rubric:) *Oracio beate marie* (79r:) (O)⁴Bsecro te domina . . . (81r:) . . . facturus locuturus aut cogitaturus . . . (ibid. in 7th line, possibly by another hand:) . . . Et michi famula tua *[sic]* .N. . . .

Leroquais, *LH* II, p. 346 sq. — The ungrammatical feminine form in the 7th line of 81r was added either as a correction or perhaps to fill a space left blank in the workshop, once it was clear that the book was to be used by a woman; through ignorance or oversight, the masculine forms found a little higher on the same page were left unchanged.

82v–86r: (82r, last line, rubric:) *Alia or[aci]o beate marie* (82v:) (O)² Intemerata . . . de te enim dei filius . . . et requiem sempiternam. A[men].

Wilmart, *Aut. spir.*, p. 494 sq. (= the "rédaction prolixe de la prière," not the 12th-century address to Mary and St. John)

86r–91r: *Inicium sancti euangelij secu[n]dum iohannem. gloria tibi do*ᵉ. (I)²N principio . . . (87r:) . . . et ueritatis. *an̄.* Te i[n]uocam[us] te adoramus . . . trinitas . . . Orem[us] . . . (P)²rotector in te spera[n]ciu[m] . . . (87v:) . . . *Secundum luca[m]* (I)²n illo . . . (89r:) . . . *se[cun]d[u]m math[eum]* (I)² illo tempore recumbentib[us] . . . (89v:) . . . sequentibus signis. *Secundum marcum.* (I)²N illo . . . cu[m] nat[us] esset . . . (91r:) . . . in regionem suam. Deo gracias. (last 3 lines empty)

The frequently occurring collection of Gospel readings (John I, 1–14; Luke I, 26v–38a; Matthew II, 1–12; Mark XVI, 14–20), here with a startling misidentification (and transposition) of the Matthew and Mark selections. — The acclamation of Trinity and the collect *Protector in te sperantium* (3rd Sunday after Pentecost in *Missale Romanum*) associated with the Johannine prologue have been noted in several other books of hours, cf. index.

93r–116v: (93r, full-page illustration: Exequies;[5] with 3 lines of text:) *an̄.* Placebo. *p[salmus]* (D)³Ilexi . . .

Officium defunctorum (use of Évreux?). (Antiphon to Magnificat *Audivi vocem*;[6] no Invitatory in the Matins; only one nocturn. Lessons: Parce mihi . . . Taedet anima mea . . . Manus tuae . . .; responsories: Credo quod . . . Qui Lazarum . . . Libera . . . Antiphon to *Benedictus*: Ego sum . . .)

116v–118r: (beginning in 5th line:) *an̄.* Auete omnes a[n]i[m]e fideles . . . (117r:) . . . Oremus . . . Domine ihesu xpiste salus et liberatio . . . (117v:) . . . et paradisi amenitate confoueri ualeas. Q[ui] viuis . . . (118r:) omnia secula seculorum Amen. (rest of page blank except for later inscription [see reproduction])

Cf. Leroquais, *LH* I, p. 153, etc.

* * *

Foliated (every 4th–5th leaf) in modern pencil; 2 vellum flyleaves in front are included in the numbering. — Written area ca. 94 × ca. 64 mm. Fully ruled in faint red ink. — *Littera textualis* (modestly "formata") of two sizes; the slightly smaller and more condensed script (ca. 28 widths per

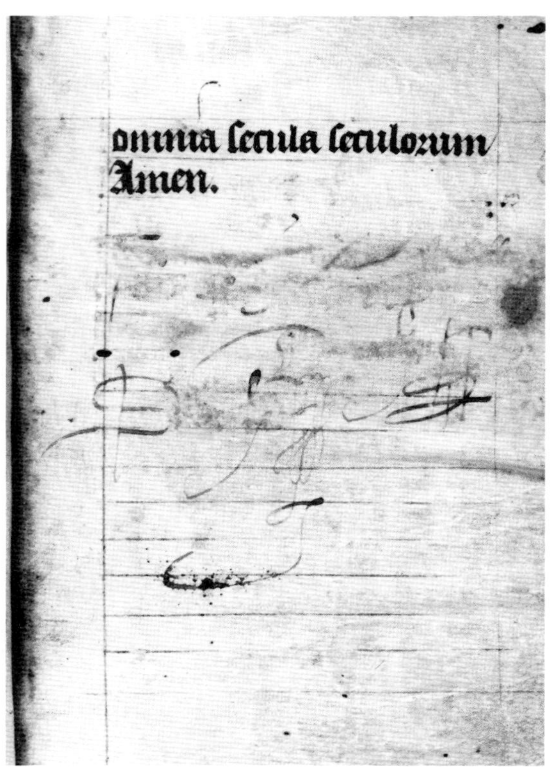
omnia secula seculorum
Amen.

MS 58, f. 118r (inscriptions) (actual size of area shown: ca. 130 × 90 mm)

line vs. ca. 26) is used for (some) antiphons, versicles, etc. Possibly more than one scribe. (Certainly a different hand added the text "O passio magna . . ." on f. 73v.) — Dark brown ink; rubrics in red. — Parchment yellowish, of uneven thickness and quality (thickness 19 mm for the whole textblock = ca. 16 mm per 100 leaves).

Collation: 1–2^6(= ff. 3–14) 3–4^8 5^{10}($5_{5.6}$ = two leaves after f. 34 wanting; text loss?) 6^6(= ff. 39–44) f. 45 a singleton? $7^{8?}$(= ff. 46–53) 8–$9^{2?}$ 10–11^8(= ff. 58–73) [$12^{2?}$(= wanting bifolium following f. 73)] 13^6(= ff. 74–79) $14^{10-1?}$(= ff. 80–88) 15^{10+2}(a *quinio* with a bifolium (ff. 91.92) inserted following 15_2) 16–17^8(= ff. 101–116) f. 117 a singleton? (f. "118" is free endleaf conjugate with pastedown). — Catchwords, variously faded or, it seems, erased at end of gatherings 3(= on f. 22v), 4(= on f. 30v; vertical); on f. 45v; at end of gatherings 10(= on 65v), 14(88v), 15(100v), 16(108v).

Five full-page (within full borders) illustrations: on ff. 15r, 48r, 58r, 76r, 93r (cf. contents). At least two more were probably present originally: one (Nativity?) following f. 34, another (Crucifixion?) after f. 73. — The illustrations, accompanied in each case by 3 lines of text, are within arched compartments, separated from the decorative borders by baguettes (red and blue floral patterns on burnished gold ground) on two sides (toward fore edge and tail), by a gilt bar toward the gutter. — In the illustrations which include Mary (15r, 48r,76r), the Virgin's face has been severely damaged, apparently by scratching; same has been done to the face of the Child in the Flight to Egypt scene (48r); the surrounding areas of the illustration, including faces of other individuals have, in each case, been left intact. — Borders which accompany the illustrations are conventional non-outlined panel borders with blue and goldish foliage on void ground. On some text pages, partial borders in fore-edge margin, consisting of a vine stem formed by a black penline, with foliage chiefly gold ivy, also some green leaves, a blue flower at top and a red (straw)berry at bottom end.

Illuminated initials in conventional French (early?) 15th-century style (letter in blue with white penwork, ground gold outlined in black, infilling red and blue vine), competently executed. Two-line letters gold in a field of blue or red, infilled with the other color; white penwork in the color areas. Versals gold with black flourishing or blue flourished in red. Line fillers (in litany) gold with blue comb-like topping.

Bound in red velvet, considerably worn, over wooden boards; sewn over 4 raised bands. — Kept in a 20th-century solander case (by Rivière & Son) done in bright red morocco leather; impressed in gold in the spine area of the case: MANUSCRIPT// BOOK//OF HOURS//CIRCA 1450.

MS 58, f. 48r (actual height of the illustration: ca. 95 mm)

On 1st free endleaf, inscription in 17th(?)-century cursive: officium beatae mariae manuscriptum. On pastedown of lower cover, in pencil: Gift Mr. & Mrs. Leonard Kebler, Jan. 27, 1959.

Former owners: Mr. and Mrs. Leonard Kebler.

2° fo.: (KL)^2 Feurier[8]

Bibl: De Ricci, *Census,* v. 2 (1937), p. 1192, no. 1; Faye and Bond (1962), p. 126, no. 174.

The style of decoration used for the initials and borders suggests an earlier dating than the calendar: before 1450 rather than after.[9] The presence of the Aug. 6 entry in the calendar (cf. contents) could perhaps be explained without setting the date as "after 1468."[10] — The defacing of some of the illustrations noted above is not a common occurrence; one may ask how much it may have had to do with the religious history of northern France; other possibilities are insanity or, perhaps, magical intent.

NOTES

1. But see (for the question of dating) the concluding paragraph.
2. The litany names individually, after Mary, the apostles, etc., through the Innocents: 11 martyrs, 9 confessors, 16 women.
3. See notes with ff. 91–92 of MS 44.
4. See notes with ff. 93–95 of MS 44.
5. The dead body is in a white garment with a black cross on the chest (the cross is of an unusual shape, more or less Maltese-like).
6. As the cue to the antiphon, before the text of the canticle, the ms. has "Qui [Lazarum . . .]"; but at its end, where the antiphon is spelled out in full, it is "Audivi . . ."
7. Lost is the beginning of Prime of the Hours of Our Lady, probably with full-page illustration (Nativity).
8. The month name is in the rather dark greyish red used (alternating with blue) in the calendar for the non-emphasized days.
9. Cf., e.g., the decoration of the Waddesdon MS 6, an Amiens book of hours of ca. 1430–40 (Delaissé, *Illuminated manuscripts,* p. 112–113, esp. also fig. 15 with the comb-like pattern on line fillers).
10. A day of "Saint Sauveur" may have existed in August (though not on Aug. 6?) at an earlier date in the area involved (cf. Strubbe, *Chronologie*). — It is otherwise known that the calendar was often the part added last.

MS 59

(Wilson Hours)

BOOK OF HOURS (ca. 1430?) AND FRANCISCAN PRAYER BOOK (ca. 1500?) XVth c.

Northern France. Parchment. 132 leaves, ca. 164 × ca. 114 mm (bound volume: ca. 173 × ca. 130 mm) 1 column. 16 lines (calendar, 16 or 17 lines)

([Book of hours, 1st half of 15th century:] ff. 1r–12v, calendar; 13r–49r, Hours of Our Lady; 49v–50v, *Seven Joys of Mary*; 51r–65v, Penitential Psalms, with Litany; 65v–68r, Short Hours of the Cross; 68r–70v, Short Hours of the Holy Spirit; 70v–82v, Office for the Dead; [lacuna] 83r–86v, *Quinze joies de Notre Dame*; 87r–90r, *Sept requêtes à Notre Seigneur*; 90r–91r, Johannine prologue; 91v, *Ave verum corpus*; 91v–92r, *Anima Christi*; 92r–94v, saints' suffrages; 94v–96r, *Obsecro te*; 96v–97r, prayer(s). — [Franciscan prayer book:] 98r–v, *Jesus qui es témoin certain*; 98v–100r, prayers; 100r–103v, Athanasian Creed; 103v–104v, prayers; 104v–105v, Luke I, 26–38; 105v–107v, suffrages; 108r–v, *V Ave*; 108v–111r, prayers; 111r–121v, rhymed office honoring St. Francis of Assisi; 121v–123v, saints' suffrages; 123v–125r, *Veni Creator Spiritus*; 125r–128v, various prayers; 128v–130r, *Sept vers s. Bernard*)

ff. 1r–12v: Calendar (163 entries) in French; in black and red; one month per leaf.

(See full listing in appendix at end of the description.) The saints emphasized belong to the area of Amiens, Arras, Thérouanne.[1] — N.B. There is no hint of any Franciscan bias; no mention even of St. Francis in October.

13r–49r: (13r, large illustration [Annunciation] and 6 lines of text:) (D)[4]omine labia mea . . . (office ends in last line of 49r:) . . . deo gr[aci]as.

Hours of Our Lady (use not determined).[2] — Captions mostly French: "*laudes*" but "*Prime*," "*Tierce*," "*midi*" (! 36v), "*Nonne*," "*Vespres*," "*complie*."

49v–50v: *Septem gaudia b[eat]e marie uirgi[ni]s* (G)[2]aude flore uirginali . . . (50v:) . . . [et] florescent P[er] et[er]na s[e]c[u]la. Amen. *V*. Exaltata es . . . *R*. sup[er] choros . . . *or*. Dulcissime d[omi]ne ih[es]u xpe qui beatissimam . . . tue b[eat]itudinis et eius eterna p[er]ueniamus. Qui . . . seculorum. amen.

The "Seven Joys of Mary" hymn (Leroquais, *LH* II, p. 343 sq.) sometimes associated with Thomas of Canterbury (cf. Wilmart, *Aut. spir.*, p. 329, n. 1) with added versicle and formal prayer (cf. Leroquais, *LH* I, p. 282).

51r–65v: (51r, large illustration [Second Coming][3] with 6 lines of text, beginning:) (D)[4]omine ne in furore . . .

Penitential Psalms and the Litany ("*letania*", 61r sqq.). — The litany has among martyrs: . . . Dyonisi cum sociis tuis, Maurici cum sociis tuis, Leodegarij . . . Quintine, Firmine; among confessors: . . . Ludouice (= Louis IX); among monks and hermits again: . . . Ludouice (the Franciscan bishop of Toulouse); women expressly named are, apart from the mother of Jesus, limited to: Mary Magdalen, Agnes, Lucia, Cecilia, Agatha, Catherine, Clara, Elizabeth.[4]

65v–68r: (beginning with rubric in line 12 of 65v:) *De cruce* (D)[4]Omine labia . . . (66r:) . . . (P)[2]atris sapi[enti]a u[er]itas diuina . . . (ends, 68r:) . . . in mortis agone. amen.

The Short Hours of the Cross (based on the *pium dictamen* "Patris sapientia"[5] and making no use of Psalms).

68r–70v: (68r, last line, rubric:) *De sancto spiritu. ad matut'.* (68v:) (D)[4]Omine labia . . . (N)[2]obis sancti spiritus gratia sit data . . . (ends, 70v:) . . . ut uiuamus iugiter celi regione. amen.

The Short Hours of the Holy Spirit, also psalmless and based on a versified meditation (Walther, *Initia* 21189).[6]

70v–82v: (70v, last lines:) *Pro deffunctis. antipho[na]* Placebo *ps̄* (71r, large illustration: Exequies; with first 6 lines of Psalm CXVI:) (D)[4]ilexi . . . (office ends on 82v, in last line:) (I)nclina dn̄e (F)idelium.[et]c̄.

The liturgical set of prayers for the dead (*Officium defunctorum*); a non-Roman variant, use undetermined. *Ad Magn.*: Absolue Domine animas eorum . . . *Inv.*: Regem cui omnia vivunt . . . (One nocturn only;) lessons: I. Parce michi . . . II. Tedet animam . . . III. Manus tuae . . . Responsories: I. Credo quod . . . II. Qui Lazarum . . . III. Libera . . .[7] *Ad Ben.*: Tuam Deus deposcimus pietatem . . . — Some psalms, and some other texts, indicated only by initia.

(Following f. 82, one or more leaves are missing)

83r–86v: vous luy prieurs. Et ie me a genoilleray . . . (E)[2] tresdoulce dame pour ycelle grant ioye . . . (ends, 86v:) et a la fin sa benoitte glo[i]re de p[ar]adis. (A)ue m[aria].

"XV Joyes Nostre Dame" (beginning imperfectly, in the middle of the prologue) = Sonet 458 (Doulce dame de misericorde, mère de pitié . . .) Cf. Leroquais, *LH* II, p. 310 sq. (slightly variant). — In the present ms., one of the "joys," the Presentation in the Temple, is omitted, probably through oversight, leaving only fourteen; among them, in connection with Jesus' death, the "ioie et amère compassion" of Leroquais's text is replaced by "grant doulour" (85v, 3rd line).

87r–90r: (86v, end of last line, rubric:) *les .vij. requestes.* (87r:) (Q)[4]uiconq[ues] vueult estre bien [con]seillies de la chose dont il a mestier . . . (87v, 3rd line:) (D)[2]oulx dieu doulx p[e]r[e] . . . biaulx sire dieu . . . (89v:) . . . me regardes en pitie [et] a mon salut . . . (line 11:) (S)[2]aincte uraye crois aouree . . . (ends, 90r:) . . . puisse mourir. amen.

The "Sept requêtes à Notre Seigneur" (Sonet 504; with the prologue Sonet 1760) followed by the "Sainte vraie Croix aourée," Sonet 1876.

90r–91r: *Inicium s[an]c[t]i euangelij secundum iohanne[m]. Gloria tibi domine.* (I)[2]N principio . . . (91r:) . . . gr[atia]e et ueritatis . . . (P)[2]rotector in te spe[er]anciu[m] deus . . . ut no[n] amittamus et[er]na. P[er] xp̄m.

John I, 1–14 (the Johannine Prologue) as a liturgical reading, and followed by the collect *Protector* . . . (Cf. ff. 23r–25r in LC hours MS 57, for use of Tours; also ff. 86r–87v in MS 58, hours for Évreux.)

91v: *Quant on lieue le corps i[es]ux[ri]s[t]* (A)[2]ue uerum corpus . . . fili marie. amen.

The (13th-century?) anonymous rhymed prayer known also from modern music settings (Mozart K.618, et al.)

91v–92r: *Quant on lieue le sanc i[es]ux[ri]s[t]* (A)[2]nima xp̄i sanctifica me . . . ut cum anglis laudem te. in s[e]c[u]la s[e]c[u]lorum. amen.

MS 59 The well-known, much translated prayer, later at times erroneously attributed to St. Ignatius. (Cf. *Lex. f. Theol. u. Kirche*, v. 1, col. 563 sq., with bibl.)

92r–94v: (beginning in line 5 of 92r:) *De saint iohan baptiste. a'*. . . .

Suffrages, introduced in each case by a French rubric beginning "De . . .": John the Baptist (Inter natos mulierum . . .), St. Nicholas (Beatus Nicholaus adhuc puerulus . . .), St. Christopher (Sancte Christophore . . .), All Saints (Sancti Dei omnes . . .), Mary Magdalen (Mulier que erat . . .), St. Catherine (Virgo sancta Katherina Grecie gemma . . .), St. Margaret (Erat autem Margareta . . .).

(94v, line 12 through last line of 97r are in a DIFFERENT HAND, a non-calligraphic 15th-century French cursive script; black ink only; spaces are left for initials on 95r and 96v)

94v–96r: (beginning in 12th line of 94v:) Chy sensieut Vne orison de nostre dame et qui tous les iours le dira . . . (95r:) [O]bsecro te s[anc]ta m[ari]a m[ate]r dei pietate ple[n]issi[m]a . . . (ends 96r, last line:) . . . dei at[que] mi[se]r[icordie]. Amen.

The standard prayer (Leroquais, *LH* II, p. 346 sq.); an attempt seems to have been made to avoid a distinctly masculine or feminine wording: ". . . ego *[sic]* indigno faciendo loquendo cogitando . . ."

96v–97r: (in head margin:) Qui dira ceste orison . . . (1st line of text area:) [D]Eus p[ro]pici[us] esto m[ichi] p[e]c[ca]tori et custos o[mn]ib[us] dieb[us] vite mee . . . (97r:) . . . Agios Agios Agios . . . Amen. pat[e]r [ave] m[a]r[ia]

(97v blank, ruled)

(ff. 98–130 are EITHER A LATER ADDITION or A PART OF ANOTHER BOOK, or perhaps quires originally intended for another book [a Franciscan-oriented prayer-book]. The ruling and layout are, nevertheless, unchanged; the script remains, after the cursive interruption on 94v–97r, a *littera textualis* basically similar to that of the older part but the scribe is less skillful and the script more rounded. Some of the contents point to the end of the 15th century.)

98r–98v: *Deuote orison a ih[es]uc[r]ist.* (I)[3]h[esu]s qui es tiesmoing certain . . . Que ie voeul morir en ta foy

(A variant of Sonet 975, Jhesus qui es souverain bien ?)

98v–99v: (lines 7–10, rubric:) *C Est che que vng bo[n] crestien doibt dire vne fois le iour* . . . (text:) Sire ie ay pechiet co[n]tre vo volente . . . (99r:) . . . Sire ie ay bon pourpos . . . Sire i ay bonne volente de moy confesser . . . (ends, 99v:) . . . et q'en la fin me ottroies le gloire de paradis. Amen.

The cerebral tone and theological terms suggest late origin. Cf. Sonet 1943 (Syre Dieu j'ay pechié ainsy et ainsy . . . [16th century])

99v–100r: (begins on 99v, line 13, with rubric: *respons*) Tua est potentia tuu[m] [imperium] domine tu es super omnes gentes. Da pace[m] . . . (100r:) . . . *v.* Creator omnium . . . misericors.

100r–103v: *le psalme de la foy* QVicumq[ue] vult saluus esse . . . saluus esse no[n] poterit. Gloria . . . Amen.

The Athanasian Creed, in Latin.

103v–104v: (begins on 103v, lines 7–8) *Reco[m]mendation pour deuant matines* Me tibi commendo . . . petendo ut me pausantem conserues et uigilantem. *Reco[m]mendation a le* [sic] *vierge marie* Me tibi virgo pia semp[er] commendo maria . . . (104r:) *Reco[m]mendation a son bon angle* Angele qui meus es custos . . . Ame[n]

104r–105v: *Sequentia sancti euuangelij secundum lucam.* Gloria tibi domine. IN illo tempore. Missus est . . . (ends 105v:) . . . secundum verbum tuum.

Luke I, 26–38a.

105v–107v: Suffrages ("*Memoire de* . . .") aimed at St. Martha (Gloriosa iam p[er] orbem rutillat sollempnitas . . .), St. Jerome (O iherosnime inclite . . .), St. Barbara (Ave luna lucifera . . .)

108r–108v: *Deuote orison a ih[es]ucrist* AVe domine ih[es]u xp̄e uerbum patris . . . requies nostra vita p[er]hennis.

The "V Ave" or "Quinque salutationes Jesu Christi"; cf. Wilmart, *Aut. spir.*, p. 377, note, and text, *ibid.*, p. 412, no. iii.

108v–110: *Orison tres deuote du non [i.e., nom] de ihesus* O bone ihesu. O dulcissime ihesu. O . . . qui inuocant hoc nomen sanctum tuu[m] quod est ihesus. Amen.

Cf. Parkes, *Med. mss. Keble Coll.,* 19:13,ii.

110v–111r: *quant on lieue le corps de ihesucrist* Ave uerum corpus . . . filij s[an]c[t]e marie miserere mei (111r:) qui passus es pro nobis. O panis viue . . . crimina dele.

See our note to the same prayer as found on f. 91v. — The repetition couldn't have been deliberate; was it due to careless perusal of pages written earlier?

111r: *Orison du sanc de ihesuscrist.* SAlue sacer sanguis xp̄i . . . Amen.

111r–121v: (11r, last 4 lines, rubric:) *Ches heures sont faites sus vij apparitions de la croix . . . au glorieux saint fran(111v:)chois . . . A matines.* (text:) (D)[4]Omine labia mea . . . (112r, "*hymne*":) Crucis arma fulge[n]tia . . . offert nobis celestia. Amen. *A laudes* Deus in adiutorium . . . (112v, "*hymne*":) Crucis ut ad supplicia . . . (118r:) *A complie.* Conuerte nos deus . . . (118v, "*hymne*":) Signum crucis thau littera . . . (basic office ends on 119v:) . . . Deo gratias. (then:) *Antene de sant franchois* O stupor et gaudium . . . gemitus ouuium tuarum. *v.* Ora . . . Ut digni . . . (120r, "*oriso[n]*":) Deus qui ecclesiam tuam . . . Amen. *Ant.* O martir desiderio . . . (120v:) . . . carius pretendisti. *A deuzimes vespres. Antene.* O virum mirabilem . . . consortes ciuium quib[us] es co[n]iunct[us] *pour les octaues A. benedictus Antene* Sancte francisce pro(121r:)pe ueni . . . extincto vicio. *A laudes A'* Plange turba paupera . . . tanti patris vicarium. *v.* Celorum candor . . . (121v:) . . . et opere.

A Franciscan rhymed office. Each "hour" appears to consist primarily of a stanza of the hymn and of the formal prayer "Deus qui mira crucis mysteria" (used in the Tridentine *Missale Romanum* as Postcommunion on Sept. 17); there is no suggestion of psalms.[8]

121v–123v: (suffrages, largely Franciscan: St. Bernardin of Siena:) *de saint franchois et de saint bernardin. An̄t.* Gaudeat ordo minorum . . . ad regna polorum. *orison* Deus qui ecclesiam tuam . . . beati bernardini . . . Amen. (St. Anthony of Padua: only "orison": Ecclesiam tuam . . .) St. Louis of Toulouse, O.F.M:) *de saint lois de marcelle. An̄t.* O flos germen florum ludouicus spretor honorum flos prelatorum . . . (St. Elizabeth of Hungary:) Veni sponsa Christi . . . (St. Clara:) Post clare vite terminum . . .

Must be presumed not to have been written prior to 1450, the year of canonization of Bernardin of Siena.

123v–125r: (123v, last line, rubric:) *hymne du benoit saint esprit.* (124r, text:) Veni creator spiritus . . . (hymn ends on 124v:) . . . nobisque mittat filius carisma sancti spiritus. Amen. . . . ("*Orison*":) Deus qui corda fidelium . . . (125r:) . . . Amen.

The 9th-century hymn (cf. Wilmart, *Aut. spir.,* p. [37] sqq.; also Szövérffy, *Annalen,* v. 1(1964), p. 220sqq.); with added versicle and the Pentecost collect.

125r–126v: *Pappe Jehan. xij[e]. a donne a toutes personnes qui . . . diront . . . en passant par vne cymetiere* . . . AVete omnes a[n]i[m]e fideles . . . (125v:) . . . DOmine ihesu xpiste salus et liberatio fidelium . . . (ends 126v:) . . . et paradisi amenitate confoueri iubeas. Qui . . . Ame[n] Pater noster, Aue maria.

Cf. Leroquais, *LH* I, p. 140.

126–127v: (126v, 3 last lines, rubric:) *Sensieult une deuote orison . . . le corps de ihesucrist.* (127r, text:) DOmine ihesu xpiste qui hanc sacratissimam carnem . . . (127v:) . . . periculis presentib[us] et futuris. Amen. O passio magna. O profundissima vulnera. O effusio sanguinis . . . da michi vitam eterna[m].

For the *Domine ihesu* . . . cf. Wilmart, *Aut. spir.,* p. 378, footnote no. 10; *Horae Eboracenses* (Surtees Soc. CXXXII), p. 72. — There are altogether five invocations beginning "O . . . " in the second item.

127v–128r: (beginning with a red 2-line Lombardic letter in line 9 of 127v:) AVe domina sancta maria mater [Dei?] regina celi porta paradisi . . . libera me ab omnibus malis et opera *[sic]* peccatis meis. Amen.

Cf. Leroquais, *LH* I, p. 249 (Rouen); II, p. 7 (Rennes), p. 167 (Rouen) (all are manuscripts from the 2nd half of the 15th century)

Post clare vite terminum clara
cum turba virginum ad celos evo
lavit suum complexa dominum
regno luminum quo dominus
regnavit. V. Ora pro nobis bea
ta clara. Ut digni efficiamur pro
missione xpi. Oremus. orison.
Famulos tuos quesumus
domine beate virginis
tue clare votiva suffragia re
censentes celestium gaudio
rum sua facias interventione
participes et unigeniti tui co
heredes. Per xpm dnm nrm
Amen. hymne du benoit
saint esprit.

128r–128v: *Orison a le vierge marie.* Ave Maria porta paradisi Stella mundi. destructio inferni. Gratia plena. perfecte caritatis. Virginitatis. Castitatis . . .

Interpolated first half of *Ave Maria*.

128v–130r: *les.vii.vers saint bernard. O bone ihesu.* Illumina oculos meos . . . aduersus eum. *O Adonay* In manus tuas . . . *O messias.* Loquut[us] sum in lingua mea . . . [etc.; altogether 9 rubrics beginning "O . . . ," and 9 psalm verses] (129v, "*orison*":) Omnipotens sempiterne deus qui ezechie regi iude . . . Concede michi indigno famulo tuo tantum spacium saltim . . . (ends on 130r:) . . . Amen. (last 12 lines empty; 130v blank, ruled)

Cf. Leroquais, *LH* I, p. xxx, etc. (N.B. None of the mss. listed in Leroquais' index seems to have the "O . . . " rubrics as above)

(ff. [131 – 132] (numbered "133" and "134") are blank; ruled through [132]r)

* * *

Foliated in modern pencil. The two blank, ruled leaves which follow f. 130 are numbered "133" and "134" respectively, suggesting loss of two (blank?) leaves. Three free endleaves (paper, no visible watermark) in front, three at end, not included in the foliation. — Written area ca. 96 × ca. 62 mm. Fully ruled in faint red or purplish ink; no ruling visible on ff. 95–97; on ff. 98–132, the horizontal lines cross the vertical border lines. — *Littera textualis* (modestly "formata") of two sizes, the slightly smaller and more condensed script used for (some) antiphons, versicles, etc.; by two main scribes: one (a professional) through f. 94v, a second one (no doubt much later, and probably an amateur) on ff. 98r–130v; yet another hand wrote the last lines of 94v and all of 95r–97r in French cursive. — Black ink, rubbed off or powdering with loss of legibility in some places, especially in what seem to be the older sections. Rubrics red. — Parchment of no more than fair quality (original spotted areas, etc.); thickness ca. 14.5 mm per 100 leaves.

Collation: $1\text{–}2^{6}$(= ff. 1–12) $3\text{–}6^{8}$ 7^{6}(= ff. 45–50) $8\text{–}11^{8}$ [$12^{?}$(= missing gathering following f. 82; unknown amount of text lost)] $13\text{–}14^{8}$ 15^{6}(= ff. 99–104) 16^{8} 17^{10} (= ff. 113–122) 18^{6} $19^{6?}$(= ff. 129–[132]; $19_{3.4}$, probably blank, seem to have been lost in our century)

Decoration: The earlier part (ff. 1 – 94) includes three large illustrations, on ff. 13r (see plate XXVI, p. xxxix), 51r, and 71r (Annunciation, Second Coming, Exequies; cf. contents). They are placed, in accordance with French custom, over several (six, in this book) lines of text, i.e., initial words of major items. The miniatures are inside rounded-arch windows and are surrounded, together with the text, by all-around borders consisting of hairline vine designs with gold ivy leaves, and colored flowers, fruit, and foliage more or less issuing from the major initial which begins the text. — No illustrations and no borders after f. 94. — Initials are all ornamental, and illuminated, Parisian-style, in the earlier part; calligraphic and quite simple on ff. 98–130. — Major (mostly 4-line) illuminated initials are on 13r, 21v, 29v, 34r, 36v, 38v, 41r, 46r, 51r, 65v, 68v, 71r, 87r; all are accompanied by borders, partial except for the three noted above. The letters are white-decorated magenta or blue in a field of the other color (outlined in black-gold-black), and are infilled with blue, green, and red foliage, with white accents, on ribbon-like vine on gold ground. The vine sometimes forms a straight-line cross or *X*. The numerous 2-line and 1-line initials or versals consist of gold letters on blue or magenta ground. — In the second main part (ff. 98–130) only one initial letter (a 3-line *I* on 98r) is in gold, on void ground. All other letters in this part, including a relatively ornate 4-line *D* at the beginning of the Stigmata office (f. 111v), are of the calligraphic type, blue or red (the *D* on f. 111

◄ **MS 59**, f. 123v (from the Franciscan part of the codex) (actual size of written area: ca. 95 × 60 mm)

MS 59 combines both colors and is further decorated by void white), and free of flourishes or other adornments; some black capitals are touched in yellow.

Binding: rebound (before 1902)[9] by Zaehnsdorf (London; the identification is on lower edge inside of upper cover); red morocco covers, inside dentelles in gold, marbled endpapers (peacock-feather pattern), gilt edges.

On inside of upper cover, armorial bookplate of Henry White.

Former owners: Henry White (d. ca. 1902); Woodrow Wilson. Acquired by LC with President Wilson's personal library in 1946.

2° fo.: (KL)[2] *feurier*

Bibl.: *Catalogue of the valuable and extensive library of . . . the late Henry White, Esq. . . .* (London, 1902), no. 1126. — Faye and Bond (1962), p. 125, no. 169.

The structure of the manuscript poses problems. Leaves 1–94 (through line 11) are probably the oldest part, written (perhaps in and) for use in a location presumably in the area of Amiens; the rest, in particular the contents of ff. 98–130, is a later addition, incorporating some distinctly Franciscan items (esp. ff. 111r–123v), hence perhaps made for a member of the Third Order of St. Francis. Was this later part really written with the earlier book already in hand? It repeats at least one item from the earlier section (the *Ave verum corpus,* ff. 110v–111r, and 91v).

NOTES

1. According to N. J. Rogers (personal communication), this is undoubtedly an Amiens calendar. — Some of its odd features are, I think, scribal or editorial error: e.g., John the Baptist placed on June 25 instead of 24.

2. See table C for text details. — From the localization key worked out years ago by F. Madan (*BODLEIAN QUARTERLY RECORD*, v. 3, no. 26 [2nd quarter 1920], p. 41–44) the Hours of Our Lady in this book would reflect the use of Thérouanne. That key seems, however, to have been oversimplified. The texts differ in a number of points from the *Heures pour l'usage de Thérouanne* printed in 1498 in Paris (Goff H 426). — The office agrees with Bodleian MS. Rawl. liturg.e.32, of the 1410s, and Glasgow Univ. Lib. MS. Euing 4, of ca. 1460, neither quite localized. (Information from N. J. Rogers, who also notes the common practice in northeast France of mixing various uses.)

3. Or, perhaps, "Harrowing of Hell"?

4. Individually named are (after Mary, angels, apostles, etc., through the Innocents): 12 martyrs, 13 confessors (with 5 "monks and hermits" brought up separately from the rest), 8 women.

5. Walther, *Initia* 13840. — See notes in description of MS 44 (with its ff. 91–92).

6. See notes with ff. 93–95 of MS 44.

7. A very long responsory; using the codes given in the *CAO* (*Corpus antiphonalium Officii*), v. IV with no. 7091, the string is: G–T(with "reprise" *Dum*)–X–N-*Quos mortui* (not in *CAO*)–D.

8. = the "Officium de stigmatibus S. Francisci" attributed to Geraldus Odonis? (cf. *Cath. encycl.*, v. 6 [1913], art. Gerardus Odonis; also Szövérffy, *Annalen,* v. 2[1965], p. 323 sq.)

9. The 1902 sale catalog (see Bibl.) describes the Zaehnsdorf covers.

APPENDIX: CALENDAR OF THE WILSON HOURS (MS 59)

(omitting, with few exceptions, the "saint," "saincte," "la," "les")

JANUARY	FEBRUARY	MARCH	APRIL	MAY	JUNE
1 *circoncision*	1 ignace	1 aubin	1 ualeri	1 *jaque & phelippe*	1 nichomede
2 oct. estienne	2 *Nostre dame*	2	2	2 quentin	2
3 oct. iehan	3 blaise	3	3	3 *sainte croys*	3
4 oct. innocens	4	4 adrian	4 ambroise	4	4
5 vigile	5	5	5	5	5 boniface
6 *iour des roys*	6 vaast	6	6	6 iehan	6
7	7	7 perpetue	7	7	7
8 iulian	8	8	8	8 augustin	8 medart
9	9	9	9 pierre	9 *nicholay*	9
10	10 scolace	10	10 lion	10 gordian	10
11 saueur	11	11	11	11	11 *barnabe*
12	12	12 gregoire	12	12	12
13 *fremin*	13	13	13	13	13
14	14 ualentin	14	14	14 victor	14 ruffin
15 mor	15	15 longin	15	15 *honnore*	15
16	16	16	16 calixte	16	16
17 anthoine	17	17 gertrur	17	17	17
18	18 symeon	18	18	18	18
19	19	19	19 ruffin	19 potencianne	19 geruais & pro-
20 sebastian	20 eleuthere	20	20	20	20 thais
21 agnes	21	21 benest	21	21	21
22 *uincent*	22 *pierre*	22	22	22 saturne	22
23	23 uictor	23	23 george	23	23
24	24 *mathias*	24	24	24	24 vigile
25 *pol*	25	25 *Nostre dame*	25 *marc*	25 urbain	25 *iohan baptiste*
26 pollicarpe	26 alixandre	26	26	26	26 *eloy*
27 iulian	27	27	27	27	27
28 agnes ii^e	28 romain	28	28 uital	28 germain	28 vigile
29		29	29	29	29 *pierre & pol*
30 audegout		30	30	30	30
31				31 perronelle	

JULY	AUGUST	SEPTEMBER	OCTOBER	NOVEMBER	DECEMBER
1 oct. saint iohan.	1 *pierre*	1 *fremin, leu, gile*	1 remi	1 *L atoussains*	*1 eloy*
2	2 estienne pape	2	2 ligier	2 *L es mors*	2
3	3 *estienne*	3	3	3 hubert	3
4 martin [transl.?]	4	4 Marcel	4	4	4 benest
5	5	5	5	5	5
6	6	6	6 foy	6	6 *nicholay*
7	7 donat	7	7	7	7 oct.'.s. andrieu
8	8	8 *Nostre dame*	8	8 .iiij. couronnes	8 *Nostre dame*
9	9 vigile	9 gregore	9 guillam	9	9
10 .vij. freres	10 *laurens*	10	10	10	10
11	11	11 iacien	11 uenant	11 *martin*	11 *fuscien*
12 felix	12	12	12	12 henin (?)	12
13	13 ypolite	13	13	13 brice	13 luce
14	14 vigile	14 *saincte croys*	14 calixte	14	14 nichaise
15	15 *Nostre dame*	15 oct' nre dame	15	15 machuth	15
16 alexis	16	16	16 seuerin	16	16
17	17 oct. laurens	17	17	17	17
18	18	18	18 *luc*	18 oct's. martin	18 gabriel
19	19	19	19 auie	19	19
20	20 bernard	29 vigile	20	20	20
21 margarite	21	21 *mahiue* [*sic*]	21 .xi.mille uirges	21	21 *thomas*
22 *la magdalene*	22 oct' nostre dame	22 maurice	22	22 cecille	22 uictor
23	23 vigile	23	23	23 *clement*	23
24 cristine	24 *berthelemieu*	24	24 maglore	24	24 vigile
25 *iaque, xpofle*	25 *louys*	25 *firmin*	25	25 *kath'ine*	25 *L eiour de nouel*
26 *anne*	26	26	26	26 lin	26 *estienne*
27 .vij. dormans	27	27	27 vigile	27	27 *iohan*
28	28	28	28 *symon, iude*	28	28 *L es innocens*
29	29 *iohan decollace*	29 *michiel*	29	29 vigile	29 *thomas*
30	30 fiacre	30 ieronisme	30	30 *andrieu*	30
31 germain	31		31 quentin. vigile.		31 seuestre

MS 60

(Faye and Bond 79)

BOOK OF HOURS IN NETHERLANDISH XVth c.

Netherlands. Parchment and paper. 170 + 15 leaves, ca. 138 × ca. 101 mm (bound volume: 146 × ca. 110 mm) 1 column. 15 lines (calendar, 16 lines)

(ff. 1v–13r, calendar; 13v–14v, Johannine prologue; 17r–72r, Hours of Our Lady; 74r–83r, Short Hours of the Cross; 83r–87v, Mass of the Cross; 88r–101v, Hours of the Holy Spirit; 102r–120r, Penitential Psalms, with Litany; 121r–150v, Office for the Dead; 150v–153r, *Psalmi Graduales* (program); 154v–157r, Prayer of the Seven Words; 158r–169v, various prayers, including *Anima Christi* and *Ave praeclarum vas*; [171r–185v], Hours of the Eternal Wisdom)[1]

(Flyleaf preceding f. 1, not a planned or added part of the book of hours, contains what appears to be a fragment of an office of the Passion in Netherlandish:[2] [blank space for initial *D*]Oe ihesus cristus die pijn des dodes leet ī dē cruce synt gewordē duyst'nissē eñ tegē die noentijt riep ihesus . . . des soens gaeds . . . [3] (verso:) . . . [blank space for initial *O*] here ihū xpē konÿck eñ bisscop die di seluē ter noen tijt geoffert heues . . . ī een loen [N.B. continued on f. 170r *q.v.*])

(On f. 1r, 19th-century inscriptions; see in the part following contents)

ff. 1v–13r: Calendar, in Netherlandish; 312 entries, 42 of them in red. The names of the months are given as: *Hardmaēt, Sporkel, Merte, April, Meye, Bramaent, Heumaent, Oest, Garstmaent, Ruselmaent, Alreheilgē maent, Duyst'maent.* — Among the days in red; *Sūte Agneta* (Jan. 21), *Georgen ridder* (Apr. 23), *S'pantaleon* (July 28), *S' gereoen eñ victoer* (Oct. 10), *Cecilia* (Nov. 20). Notable among days in black: Lucian[us] eñ maximian[us] (Jan. 7!), Vedast[us] eñ amandus (Feb. 6), Allexand' merteler (Feb. 9), Focus (Mar. 4!), Pigmenius (Mar. 24!), Regulus (Mar. 30), Olimpiadis (Apr. 15), Corona ioncfrou (May 14), Brandanus abdt (May 16), Arthemius (June 6), Ediltruda (June 23), Adalbert[us] (June 25), Agilolfus (July 9), Caprasius (Oct. 20), Evergislus (Oct. 24), Perpetuus bisc. (Dec. 30).

The days in red, including those not quoted, agree with the calendar of Cologne[4] but missing among them (written in black) is the major Cologne festivity of Translation of the Three Kings (July 23). The names noted in black, a curious mixture, point variously to Utrecht, Cologne, Liège, Trier, Münster, even Aberdeen (Regulus, Brandanus) and Copenhagen (Feb. 9).

13v–14v: *Hier begynt sūte Johīs ierste ewāgeliū of s'Johīs gheles* (J)[4]N den begīne was dat wort . . . ghenaden eñ wairheit ("Amen" deleted by red line) Bij den wordē . . . Gade segghen wi danck.

John I,1–14 in a (Middle) Netherlandish translation (the concluding formulas come from liturgical custom)

(15rv ruled, blank; 16r blank, unruled; on 16v, full-page illustration: St. Barbara, with branch, next to a tower)

17r–72r: (H)[7]Ere du salt opdoen mijn lippen . . .

Hours of Our Lady; basically Geert Grote's 14th-century version. None of the text choices (antiphons, readings, etc.[5]) differs from Van Wijk's edition (*Het Getijdenboek van Geert Grote,* Leiden, 1940); phrasing, grammar, and orthography differ in various degrees.

(72v blank, ruled; 73r blank; on 73v, full-page illustration: St. Catherine, with wheel, sword, and, puzzlingly, also a head of a [crowned?] man under her feet)

74r–83r: ***Hier begynt des heilighen cruys ghetide*** (H)[6][ere du salt opdoen][6] . . . Des vaders wijsheit . . . (ending in 1st line of 83r:) . . . eynde Amen

The Short Hours of the Cross (= those built around the hymn *Patris sapientia*), basically Grote's Netherlandish version, with linguistic variants (cf. text as printed in Van Wijk, *op. cit.*, p. [87]–91).[7] — Most of the pages in this part suffered damage at one time (not much after 1500) and have then been rewritten or retouched, by more than one hand, with some obvious errors but apparently without any intent to alter the text.

83r–87v: ***Hier begynt die mysse van den heilighē cruyce*** (O)[4]Ns ghebuert myt groter hogher eren verclaren . . . (84r–v:) Glorie si gode in dē ouersten trone . . . vrede den guettwillighen menschen . . . (85r:) (B)[2]roeders cristus is om onsē willē . . . (86r:) (I)[4]N der tijt . . . (87v:) (G)[2]od want du woldes hebgē . . . rusten in vrede   Amen.

Proper of the votive Mass *De sancta Cruce* (as in the Tridentine Missal, "extra tempus paschale"), in Netherlandish translation; included is also a Dutch version of the *Gloria.* The biblical readings are Philippians II,8–11 and Matthew XX,17–19. Wants the Communion antiphon: rubric "*Comū*" in last line of 87r is without text; on 87v is the *Postcommunio.*

88r–101v: (rubric in two last lines of 87v:) ***Hier begynt des heilighen geest ghetijde*** (88r:) (H)[6]Ere du salt mijne lippen op doen . . . (C)[2]Oem scepper geest vande dijnre dienre īwendicheit [= Veni Creator Spiritus mentes tuorum visita] . . . (89r:) . . . (S)[2]alich is die man die nyet af en genc . . . (office ends on 101v:) . . . Alle ghelouighe zielen moetē rusten in vrede   amen.

The (longer) Hours of the Holy Spirit, with the (here, translated) hymn *Veni Creator Spiritus* repeated at each "hour," and one psalm per "hour":[8] as in Van Wijk, *op. cit.,* p. [71]–86, with some linguistic differences.

102r–120r: ***Hier begynnen die seuen psalmen*** (H)[6]Ere in dynre u'b[ol?]genheit en straef my nyet . . . (103r:) (S)[2]alich syn die ghene . . . (104v:) (H)[2]Ere yn verbolgentheit . . . (107r:) (G)[2]Od ontferme di mijnre . . . (109v:) (H)[2]Ere uerhoer myn ghebet . . . (112v:) (H)[2]Ere van den diepen . . . (113v:) (H)[2]Ere verhore . . . (115r, rubric:) ***letania:*** (among martyrs, 116v:) . . . Sunte pantaleon . . . lambert . . . corneli . . . (117r:) Sūte dyonys eñ dyñ gesellen . . . Sū gereon myt dynen ghesellen . . . (among confessors:) . . . Seueryn . . . bricti . . . (117v:) . . . remigi . . . (among women:) . . . maria vā egipten . . . (118r:) . . . Brigida . . . [walbu?]rch . . . Cristina . . . Theodosia . . . Elizabeth . . . (Devotion ends on f. 120r with the collect:) (W)[2]ij bidden di here verhoer di bede [= ***Fidelium preces***] . . . onsen heren ihesū cristū   Amen.

The Penitential Psalms, rather as in Van Wijk, *op. cit.*, p. [139]–145, with a litany much shorter than that printed there (p. 145–154) but adding St. Theodosia, venerated in Utrecht (not mentioned in the calendar of our manuscript). — N.B. All black script in this section is retraced, text of the lower halves of 108r, 108v, 111r, 113r, 114v rewritten by another hand; apparently without textual changes. There is evidence that this was done to repair damage (caused by water?) which can also be seen on the blank f. 120v.

(120v blank, frame-ruled)

MS 60

121r–150v: *Hier begynt die vigilie in duytschen: Dilexi q[uonia]m exau* (I)[10]C mȳne wāt die here sal verhoren . . .

The *Officium defunctorum* in Netherlandish. Text differs from the version (from the use?) edited in Van Wijk, *op. cit.*, p. 156–195 in having no Invitatory[9] and only one nocturn. — Lessons: I Spaer my here . . . (= Parce mihi Domine) II Mijnre zielen verdriet . . . (= Taedet animam meam) III Dyne hande hebben . . . (= Manus tuae fecerunt). — Responsories: I Here die dyne dynre gescapen heuest ontferme hoerre . . . (= Domine qui creasti [cf. MS 22]) II Dyne hande . . . (= Manus tuae) III Ic bidde ghedencke here . . . (= Memento mei)

150v–153r: (150v, last 2 lines:) *Hier begynnen die XV grad[us?]* (151r:) (T)[3]Otten heren riep ic . . . (ends on 153r:) . . . in onser vrouwen cōpleten[10]

A program, by cues only, of the *Psalmi graduales* in Netherlandish. Of each, one or two initial verses are spelled out, followed by a reference to its location in the Hours of the Virgin. — The first and the fourth of the fifteen psalms lack the introductory rubric ("*die ander, die dirde, die viefte, die seste, die seue[n]de, viij,* die *neghe[n]de, die tiende, xj, xij, xiij, xiiij, die vieftie[n]de*").[11]

(153v and 154r blank, ruled)

154v–157r: (O)[2] Here ihū criste du sprekest seuen woerde doe du hengest aen den cruce . . . dactu my verghues wat ic gheso[n]dighet heb teghen die seuen doetsu[n]den . . . (155r, "Oratio":) O lieue he' alsoe du sprekest vader vergif . . . En alsoe du sprekest . . . En alsoe du sprekest . . . (ends on 157r:) . . . in mijnen rick ewelick sond' eynde Amen.

The prayer of the Seven Words, ascribed in some manuscripts to the Venerable Bede; here, in a Netherlandish rendering.

(157v blank, ruled)

158r–163r: *Hier begint een guet gebet van onser lieuer vrouwen* O edel conyngynne der hemelen eñ der eerdē reyne maget eñ moeder . . . om dē bitterē rouwe . . . Eñ om dat grote medelijden . . . Eñ doe hi di sunte Johannes beual . . . Eñ om dat lijden . . . (ends, 163r:) . . . bi dines kindes side myt hē te regnieren ewelick sonder eynde Amen

Cf. Meertens, *Godsvrucht* VI, ms. 33, 27 (p. 193). — Reminiscent of the prayer *Obsecro te domina.* (Cf. also the chapter "Prières de compassion" in Wilmart, *Aut. spir.*, p. [505].) — The item which follows may have been intended as a continuation.

163r–v: *Oracio bona* (O)[2] Maria moeder eñ reine maghet om alle dese vermanīghe die ic nu vermaent . . . (163v:) . . . eñ mijnre hoegster salicheit Amen *Hier les iij Aue maria eñ bid om die sake die du begheerste . . .*

164r–v: *Als men dat heilighe sacrament up buert soe sprect . . . vij Jaer aflaits* Ghegruet sijstu wair lijcham ons h'en . . . u onser armen menschen Amen

164v–165r: *Dit ghebet sal men oick lesen . . . dusent daghe aflaitz* O wair lijcham ihū xp̄i wes ghegruet o duerbar . . . op dat wi di behaghen moghen ewelick Amen

Rhythmical, and in part rhymed.

165r–166r: *Dit ghebet sal men oick* (165v:) *spreken ter seluer tijt . . . dusent dage aflaitz* O heilighe ziele ihū xp̄i maick my heilich . . . (ends, 166r:) . . . eñ beschouwen i[n] ewiger ewicheit amen.

A (Middle) Dutch rendering of *Anima Christi.*

166r–v: Ghegruet sijstu wair heil alle der weerldt een waert des vaders een heilige offerhande . . . vrolicheit en sueticheit der ewiger ewigheit amen.

A (Netherlandish) version of *Ave salus mundi Verbum Patris*? (Cf. Wilmart, *Aut. Spir.*, p. 377, no. 5, footnote)

166v–167r: Dat heilihe licham eñ bloit ons h'n ih'u xp̄i make mij heilich . . . vrouden des ewighen leuens. Amen

167r: *Eyn ander ghebet* Ghegruet sistu guetertierende h'e ihū xp̄e voil ghenaden . . . in ewicheit Amen Vley. swich eñ ruste hoer. sie eñ swych [= ?]

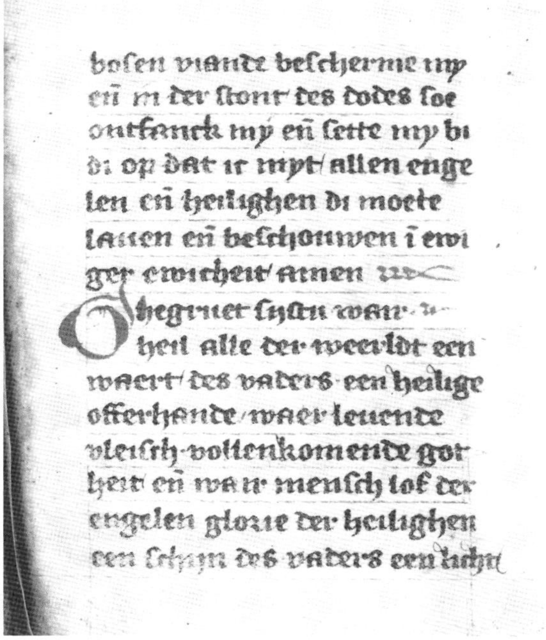

MS 60, f. 166r (actual size of written area: 88 × 64 mm)

(ALL THAT FOLLOWS IS IN OTHER HANDS and presumably by other scribes:)

167v (in a *notula* or *cursiva currens:*) O maria gegruet sistu yndes heilliger demolditheit Got gruet u . . . (10 salutations, each beginning "Got gruet u") . . . O maria west mij bij yn al my[n]re noet Amen[12]

168r–v (in same script as the preceding): Dit is dat doerluchtende vat der uytverskyespruch[?] des heillige[n] geest Dees ys dye gloriose stat gades Dees een . . . Dees ys . . . O here ihesu criste . . . dye regnires eñ loeues got . . . Amen

Prayer known as *Ave praeclarum vas,* often rubricated as a prayer for time of pestilence. Cf. Meertens, *Godsvrucht* VI, mss. 26bis (its item 22c) and 36 (item 25).

169r–v (in another hand, aiming at flamboyance; possibly 16th century): [I]N den name des Vaders [space] des soens [space] ende des heiligen geest [space] Segene ic my huden myt onses heren macht Myt onses heren craft Myt onses heren namen . . . Dat my gheen wapen steken noch snyden en moet nothmensche en moet haten . . .

A version of *Lorica Sancti Patricii*?

170r (continues the text from verso of flyleaf which precedes f. 1; in same *littera textualis formata*, by same writer): onser verlosȳge vyt gestort heues . . . tot dy die daer bist een wairachtich paradijs moge[n] kome[n]. die daer leues [et]c. Pat[er] n[oste]r Aue maria.

(f. 170v blank; it is followed by 15 paper leaves [1^{8-1}, 1_3 absent without text loss; 2^8] with text in a Netherlandish *bastarda*):

([171]r–[185]v:) (M)^{7}Jn siel heeft dij begeert in der nacht . . . ([172]r:) (H)^{4}Ere du salst op doen mijne lippen . . . ([175]v, Responsory I:) Ende utsendet heer die wijsheit . . . ([178]rv, following rubric *te deum laudamus*, text reads instead:) Dij cristum lauen wij dij ihesu[m] benedien wij die connijnck der koningen . . . ([179]r, hymn of the Lauds begins:) O Jhesu wonderlike coninck . . . ([183]v, in the hymn of the Terce:) . . . veruullende sonder verdriet . . . (preserved text ends on [185]v:) . . . want hy is ons helpen

The Hours of the Eternal Wisdom (= Heinrich Suso's *Cursus de Aeterna Sapientia*) in Netherlandish, basically the Geert Grote version (cf. Van Wijk, *op. cit.*, p. [92]–112), with some differences as partly shown above,[13] of which the Christocentric reformulation of the *Te Deum* is the most startling one. The prologue "Min(e) siel(e) . . . " (not necessarily part of the *Cursus*) is often present in Netherlandish manuscripts. — The office is incomplete, ending in the middle of the Sext (probably one entire gathering is missing at end).[14]

* * *

Leaves 1–170 are foliated in red ink,[15] the 15 paper leaves in pencil. Many leaves carry also penciled pagination. — Written area of the main text ca. 88 × ca. 64 mm. Fully ruled in faint brownish black ink. — *Littera textualis*; additions in *notula* or (the paper leaves at end) in a Netherlandish *bastarda*. — Black ink, in many places rubbed off; some passages rewritten (retraced or written over) by other hands, without text alteration. Rubrics in red or, on leaves 164 sqq., identified by red underscoring. — Parchment of poor quality; the two leaves with large illustrations are of thicker material than the rest. No watermarks discernible on the paper leaves.

Collation: (flyleaf, attached to stub conjugate with pastedown) 1^{8-1} (1_1 wanting, no text loss; 1_2 = f. 1) 2^8 3^{8-1}(3_8 wanting, no text loss) $4–9^8$ 10^{10-1}(10_8 wanting, no text loss) $11–12^8$ 13^6 $14–21^8$ $22^{6-2?}$(= ff. 166–169; $22_{1.6}$ absent, no text loss; stubs preserved) f. 170 a singleton, attached to stub of 22_6; (paper:) 23^{8-1}(23_3 wanting, no loss of text) 24^8 [25^8 wanting, text corresponding to ca. one gathering of 8 leaves lost][16]

Decoration:[17] The two full-page illustrations (on f. 16v: 72 × 48 mm; on 73v: 74 × 46 mm; cf. contents), both by the same rather primitive artist, share a palette of orange and dark blue for clothing, yellow with orange pen lines for hair, green for ground, with red spots for flowers on 16v. On both, the background is checkerboard in gold, red, and blue; both have simple straight-line frames without bottom horizontals; the frames are opaque grayish blue-green on 73v, part that color and part pinkish red on 16v. In each case the whole is surrounded by an unframed border consisting of a rather straight vine drawn in black ink, with blue-green and orange leaves, and nodes on the stem in gold. — Face features and a few other details are sketched in by pen. — The limitation of subject to the two saints (Barbara on 16v, Catherine on 73v) is not normal for a book of hours (no representation at all of Mary, and only a historiated initial on 74r shows Jesus, on the Cross); there is no clear evidence that more pictures were ever present.

Six large (6 to 10 lines) initials: on 17r, 74r, 88r, 102r, 121r, 171r (cf. contents); they are mostly blue (that on 88r, brownish purple), with some white penline decoration, on gold grounds. That on 17r is filled with gold, magenta, and light green checkerboard; that on 74r, historiated with a crucifix; the blue *H* on 102r, now rather dirty, contains two thistle blossoms. The 7-line *M* on the (paper) f. 171r, presumably by a different hand, is done rather simply in blue on the white void of the paper, surrounded by red flourishes and as-if architectural patterns done in pen.

The 2-line *KL*s of the calendar, of an unusual design (resembling *BP* as much as *KL*) are in gold on blue or purplish red. — Other minor (3-line or 2-line) initials are sometimes color (blue or magenta) on gold, sometimes gold on one of the two colors; the color areas are mostly decorated by white penlines. — Gold is not used at all in the paper portion of the book or in the additions on ff. 167 sqq.; most initials there are red. — Throughout the book the versals are red or blue. — Line fillers, used chiefly in the litany but occasionally elsewhere, consist of iterated squiggles done by the scribe, in red.

Besides the two illustration pages many other pages have borders; some of these are based on long vine stems in the margins but in many cases short stems appear as if from behind the frame-ruled written area; drawn in blackish brown ink, they carry leaves, flowers, and seed heads in gold, blue, magenta, or green. Some are done with good feeling for the general appearance of the page, some betray a less perceptive artist.

Animals, birds, and humans or humanoid beings appear in some of the borders: fox watching a rooster on 17r, dog and hare on 57v and 121r; dog and deer on 74r; dog, fox, and birds on 79r; a mother hen with her chicks on 93v; fox at top, a human (unclear except for face) in outer margin, also bird: 102r; birds also on 17r, 28v, 57v.

A shield with a simple red cross on white ground (arms of Genoa?) is centered in tail margin of 80v.

Two of the minor initials contain human faces drawn in ink and colored: the (G)[3] on 53r, at the beginning of the None of

B.V.M., and the (G)[3] at the beginning of Vespers of the Holy Spirit, 98v (a right profile).

Some of the decorations have been inexpertly freshened up or redone, with poor result, perhaps simultaneously (ca. 1500?) with the rewriting of portions of the text.[18]

Binding: probably Flemish, of ca. 1500: dark brown calf over wooden boards; blind-tooled with double fillets to form three vertical areas on each cover, these then filled with a now barely perceptible roll. — Sewn over 3 large single bands and 2 smaller bands near head and tail. No headbands. — Remnants of a single back-to-front clasp (brass and leather). — On the spine, gold-tooled horizontal lines, probably recent (19th century?), as is the spine title in *fractura*: Bed bok.

Pastedowns are vellum fragments of other manuscripts, in Latin, written in very small prehumanistic script: that attached to the upper cover contains part of the legend of St. Agatha; both are parts of a liturgical office lectionary or perhaps a breviary. — That in front has tipped to it the ownership label of Rev. E. A. Dalrymple. — Flyleaf attached to stub of the pastedown (cf. contents) has on its recto ownership, etc. notes: (penciled:) ac. 4560(3) no. 10; (purplish red ink, German current script:) *Vorstück*; (in tail margin, mixed script:) *Catalog der v. Minutoli . . . Auction. Leipzig 31 Mai 1868 . . . 89. no. 1566* [signed:] *Barnheim.* — On f. 1r, in identical ink and German current script: *Deutsches Gebet-Buch//aus der zweiten Hälfte//des 15ten Jahrhunderts//in der Cölner Mundart.* Somewhat lower, Barnheim's signature in black ink and Latin-type longhand.

Former owners: Julius, *Freiherr* von Minutoli (b. 1804, d. 1860); *Geheim-Justizrat* Barnheim (d. ca. 1870); Rev. Edwin A. Dalrymple; bought by LC in 1916 with other items from the Dalrymple collection (Ms. Ac. 4560,3,10).

2° fo.: xviii b *xvij* (kl) Marcellus pauwes

Bibl.: De Ricci, *Census* (1935), p. 230, no. 107; Faye and Bond (1962), p. 119, no. 79.[19]

NOTES

1. All of these texts are (Middle) Netherlandish translations or versions. Prussian *Geheim-Justizrat* Barnheim (or his informant) identified the language as (German) dialect of Cologne; in the 15th century the difference was, I believe, not considerable.
2. Or perhaps a devotion for use on Fridays, or similar. — Written in *littera textualis formata*, fully quadrate, by a skilled scribe.
3. On recto also modern inscriptions, see in the part following contents.
4. It should be kept in mind that prior to a reorganization in mid-16th century both Brabant (the diocese of Liège) and Holland (the diocese of Utrecht) belonged ecclesiastically to the province of Cologne. — Cf. *Atlas zur Kirchengeschichte* (Herder, c1970), map 80AB; Strubbe, *Chronologie* (1960), p. 232.
5. See table C for some of the details.
6. Words not fully legible owing to damaged leaf.
7. Concerning the Short Hours of the Cross and their Netherlandish translations or versions, see also Meertens, *Godsvrucht* I, p. 15, n. 63.
8. The psalms included are Pss. I, XV, LIV, LXX, LXXXVII, CXXVIII, and CXXIX. Also included are the canticles, some by reference to their text in the Hours of the Virgin: the *Benedictus* ("Ghebenedijt si die here god van israhel"), *Magnificat* ("Myne ziele grote maket den heren"), *Nunc dimittis* ("Nu laet h'e dynē knecht").
9. In Van Wijk's edition and, it seems, in many Dutch books of hours, the Invitatory (with the psalm *Venite exsultemus*) is placed before the "first" Vespers of the vigil (rather than at the beginning of the Matins!). Is ours an earlier or later form of the unusual "use"?
10. Clearly a rubric; the rubricator failed to underscore.
11. In the Bible, these are Psalms CXX through CXXXIV.
12. This is written, as far as I can see, as: " . . . west my by yn al mȳre noet Amen."
13. Van Wijk's text: Sent ut here die wijsheit . . . ; normal *Te Deum*; O ihesu mynnentlike coninc . . . ; . . . sonder moyenisse . . .
14. Cf. *Heinrich Seuses Horologium Sapientiae*, ed. P. Kunzle (Fribourg, 1977), p. 262 sq. on the translation; Latin text of the *Cursus, ibid.*, p. [606]–618.
15. Red ink of a purplish cast; modern numerals, ca. 1800?

16. Binder has, however, attached the present last leaf (24_8) to stub conjugate with pastedown.

17. Lest this description be misinterpreted: The book is, as a whole, neither high art nor even visually charming. Even apart from the water, dirt, and other damage it seems to have suffered, its decoration is amateurish and/or, perhaps, rather poor naive folk art.

18. But conceivably much later.

19. Both entries say "Hours (German)"; it is of course true that some forms of medieval Low German and some forms of Middle Netherlandish are barely distinguishable (if at all). The tendency to translate the liturgical or paraliturgical texts was, however, I believe, rather more common among the *Devotio moderna* people centered in the Netherlands than anywhere else.

(ff. 1r–12v, calendar; 14r–45v, Hours of Our Lady; 47r–60v, Hours of the Holy Spirit; 62r–80r, Hours of Eternal Wisdom; 82r–87v, Short Hours of the Cross; 89r–102v, Penitential Psalms, with Litany; 104r–123r, Office for the Dead)

MS 61

(Faye and Bond 8)

BOOK OF HOURS IN NETHERLANDISH ca. 1470?

Netherlands. Parchment. 123 leaves, 169 × ca. 123 mm (bound volume: 172 × ca. 130 mm) 1 column. 20 lines (in the calendar, 15–18 lines)

ff. 1r–12v: *(KL) Loumaent heuet xxxi dagen* . . .

Full calendar in Middle Dutch, written in black and red. Emphasized in red are the primary feasts of Utrecht; also St. Ieroen (=Jeron, Aug. 17). — Each month begins in first line and occupies two pages; their names are mixed: *Loumaent, Selle, Maert, April, Mey, Junius, Julius, Oestmaent, September, October, Nouember, December.* The verb vacillates: "heuet" (8 times); "heeft" (4 times).

(13r blank, unruled; on 13v, full-page illustration: Annunciation)

14r–45v: *Hier beghint onser vrouwen ghetide. Aue* g[*ra*]*t*[*ia plena?*] (H)[8]Ere du selste opdoen . . . voor ons allen.

Hours of Our Lady in Middle Dutch.[1] — The text differs from that of Geert Grote's translation[2] in numerous points of grammar, vocabulary, and phrasing (e.g., in the *Magnificat*, f. 40v, a version also found elsewhere in this manuscript: ff. 57v, 77r, 107v[3]). — Many uncorrected scribal errors.

45v: (begins in line 5:) *O florens* *O* bloyende rose . . . (ends on line 9:) . . . bidt voor ons allen.

45v: (10th line:) *Hier beghint een suete dancbaerheyt. G*hebenedijt moet sun den sueten naem . . . (line 17:) eñ voort an. Amen. (18th, i.e., last line, on center:) Leert steruen[!]

(46r blank, unruled; 46v, full-page illustration: Pentecost)

47r–60v: *Hier beghint die heilige gheests getide* (H)[8]Ere du selste . . . in vreden. Amen.

Hours of the Holy Spirit (the "longer" office, with psalms); text similar to that edited by Van Wijk, *Getijdenboek*, p. [71]–86, but with considerable differences in vocabulary and phrasing.

MS 61, ff. 88v–89r (actual size of the leaves: ca. 170 × 125 mm)

(61r blank, unruled; 61v, full-page illustration: Trinity)

62r–80r: *Hier beghint die ewige wijsh[eit] getide* (H)[8]Ere mn̄ ziel heuet di begheert in der nachte . . . (80r:) . . . Die ewige wijsh[ei]t moet benedien en̄ bewaren onse herte[n] en̄ onse lichamen. Amen.

The "Hours of Eternal Wisdom" = *Cursus de Aeterna Sapientia* of Heinrich Suso, in a Middle Dutch version.[4] The text is very similar to that printed by Van Wijk (*op. cit.*, p. [92]–112), with minor differences of accidence and orthography (*Magnificat*, 77r, quite different; cf. above).

80r–v: (beginning in 18th line of 80r:) *Dit is onser vrouwen hoochsten lof.* O Alrehoochste moed[er] des verlossers du bli(80v:)ueste ēē oepē poort des hemels . . . Amen.

In the form of a suffrage (the initial poetical antiphon is followed by versicle and the formal *"Collecte. Deus qui"*).

(81r blank, unruled; on 81v, full-page illustration: Crucifixion)

82r–87v: *Hier beghint die cruus getide* . . . (H)[8]Ere du selste . . . moeten rusten in vredē. A[me]n

The psalmless "Short Hours of the Cross" based on the hymn *Patris sapientia veritas divina* (82r, "Des vaders wijsheyt . . . "), in what seems to be basically the Geert Grote (prose) translation.[5]

(88r blank, unruled; 88v, full-page illustration: Harrowing of Hell[6]

89r–102v: *Hier beghint die seuen psalme* (H)[8]Ere in dijnre verbolghentheyt . . .

Liturgically arranged (= *Septem Psalmi Poenitentiales cum Litaniis*) Psalms VI, XXXII, XXXVIII, LI, CII, CXXX, and CXLIII, followed by the Litany of Saints, ff. 96v sqq. — The litany differs in its selection of saints[7] from that printed in Van Wijk's edition; notable is the inclusion of St. Erasmus ("Herasmus") and (among confessors) of St. "Eivout" (i.e., Evrout?).

102v: (beginning with 11th line:) *Een danckbaer lof.* Gebenedeyt moet sijn den sueten name ons heren ihesu . . . (ends in last line:) ewicheyt ende voort an. Amen.

(103r blank, unruled; 103v, full-page illustration: Exequies)

104r–123r: *Hier beghint die vigheli der doder* (M)[8]I hebben ombeua[n]gen die suchten des doots . . . moete[n] rusten in vreden. Amen.

The *Officium defunctorum* in what is apparently Grote's translation. Text differs from Van Wijk's edition (p. 156–195) chiefly in orthography. — The oddly chosen[8] Invitatory antiphon (each of its repetitions written in full) with its psalm (Ps. XCV) precedes, as in Van Wijk's text, the (first) Vespers, not the Matins. (!)

123r: (beginning in 9th line:) *Sinte bernaert seyt.* O Heer dij[ne] passie is onse . . . (line 16:) *Xristus* heuet inden cruce bewijst . . . (ends in last line:) vaert die vier hoeken des cruces

(123v blank, unruled)

* * *

Foliated in modern pencil. Preceding f. 1, parchment flyleaf; following f. 123, free endleaf of poor quality paper (no chain-lines, no watermark). — Written area ca. 95 × 73 mm. — Vertical ruled lines (diluted black ink?) mostly visible; the horizontals (blind?) only on a few pages (e.g., 29r, 54v). — Written in Netherlandish "rotunda," in what now appears as weak brownish ink. Rubrics (generally = captions) red. — Parchment of fair-to-good quality (thickness ca. 18.7 mm per 100 leaves) and whiteness, some leaves somewhat crinkled, some spotted or stained.

Collation: $1–2^{6}$ singleton f. 13 $3–6^{8}$ singleton f. 46 7^{8} 8^{6} singleton f. 61 9^{8} 10^{10} singletons ff. 80 and 81 11^{6} singleton f. 88 12^{8} 13^{6} singleton f. 103 $14–15^{8}$ 16^{4}. — The singletons are, with the exception of f. 80, of thicker material, with blank rectos and full-page illustrations on versos.

Decoration: The six large (ca. 90 × 60 mm) illustrations (cf. contents) are multicolor, in arched compartments with gold-and-color frames, within illuminated all-around framed borders (bar and foliage, also flowers, berries, animals). — Major (8-line) initials extend to three-side, unframed borders on ff. 14r, 47r, 62r, 82r, 89r, 104r. The letter is always blue, with some white penwork, and is placed in an irregularly rectangular field of burnished gold; area enclosed by the letter is brushed gold with red penwork. — Foliage of the framed borders surrounding the illustrations combines a blue of two or more shades and muted brushed gold of a strong olive cast; brown is used to suggest shaded areas. The unframed borders associated with major initials vary in style and content, mostly repeating in a mechanical manner an identical motif (chiefly blossoms;[9] also a series of some rather ineptly conceived peacocks, on 104r). — Minor initials are blue or red, many (the 4-line *G*'s of "GOd wilt dencken in mijn help/hulpe," always velvety light blue embellished with void white roundels) decorated with red penwork flourishes extending over whole margin (often smudged). Versals alternately blue or red.

Bound in contemporary brown calf over rounded oak boards.[10] Covers blind-tooled: floral panel and round stamps with rosettes, one (appearing on both covers) with a lute player(?). Original sewing onto 5 bands. Traces of clasps. — Small Library of Congress seal impressed in gold on lower cover and at the foot of the spine; on spine, at head, U.S. eagle impressed in gold; also, of earlier date, a red morocco label with title impressed in gold: GHETIDENBOEC//(line)//DUTCH MS.// 15TH CENT.

On verso of upper cover, pasted-on clipping from a 19th-century British sales catalog, describing the manuscript; also, penciled, "MS. 8"; pasted-on LC labels (one with "no. 12"). — On recto of the preliminary flyleaf, penciled: 905; on verso, penciled table of contents in a modern English or American hand; the same hand appears in occasional marginal notes, question marks, etc., made in pencil on several pages of the manuscript.

2º fo.: *KL Selle heuet xxxviii* [corrected to *xxviii*] *dagen.*

De Ricci, *Census* (1935), p. 181, no. 8; Faye and Bond (1962), p. 117, no. 8.

NOTES

1. See table C for selected textual details. — N.B. The question of precisely which liturgical "use" the translation reflects seems difficult to answer: basically it should be that of the diocese of Utrecht which couldn't have been very different from that of the metropolitan area of Cologne, but this may not at all explain all details.

2. Cf. critical edition of the 14th-century version in *Het Getijdenboek van Geert Grote*, ed. N. van Wijk (Leiden, 1940), p. [36]-70.

3. Begins: Mine siele maect groot den heer; cf. "Mijn siele grotet den heren" in Van Wijk's text (*op. cit.*, p. 66; N.B. Van Wijk notes the variant "maect groet").

4. See notes to leaves [171]-[185] of LC MS 60.

5. Cf. Meertens, *Godsvrucht* I, p. 15, n. 63. — Printed text: Van Wijk, *op. cit.*, p. 87-91.

6. With the breakthrough of the resurrected Christ into their green meadow-like world, the just of the Old Dispensation appear to be rising in their bodies. — The illustration seems to be of special iconographic interest: cf. G. Schiller, *Ikonographie der christlichen Kunst*, v. 3 (1971), p. 41 sqq.

7. After Mary, the apostles, the Innocents and disciples of the Lord, the litany invokes individually 33 martyrs, 19 confessors, and 20 women.

8. Dutch translation of "Circumdederunt me gemitus mortis / dolores inferni circumdederunt me"; readers unacquainted with the Invitatory rite may appreciate that the text is several times repeated inside the psalm which in the *AV* begins "O come let us sing unto the Lord: let us make a joyful noise . . . " — Was this Utrecht or Cologne use?

9. Best of these are probably the pansies on 62r.

10. Upper cover detached.

MS 62

(Faye and Bond 7)

BOOK OF HOURS IN NETHERLANDISH ca. 1477

Netherlands. Parchment. 166 leaves, 174 × ca. 123 mm (bound volume: 183 × ca. 130 mm) 1 column. 18 or 19 lines.

(f. lr, computus aids; 2r–12v, calendar; 13r–59r, Hours of Our Lady; 60r–67v, Short Hours of the Cross; 68r–85v, Penitential Psalms, with Litany; 86r–129r, Office for the Dead; 130r–142r, various prayers; 142r–148r, *O Intemerata* and other Marian prayers; 148r–156v, suffrages; 156v–166v, Eucharist-oriented prayers)

f. 1r: *Dat gulden ghetal. Die sonnedaechse letter.*

Two circular graphs, captioned in red as above. Both include the date "M.cccc.lxxvij."

(1v blank)

2r–12v: *KL Januarius heuet xxxi daech* . . .

Full calendar in Netherlandish; in black and red. The feasts in red are the primary feasts of Utrecht; written in red is also S. Jeroen (Aug. 17). No *Translatio Barbarae* on July 8, an occasion celebrated only in the city itself. — The calendar is written in one piece, i.e., the months do not begin each on a new page.

13r–59r: *Hier beghint o[n]ser vrouwe[n] getide* (H)[9]ere du sel[s]te op doen mijn lippe[n] . . .

Hours of Our Lady in (Middle) Netherlandish, basically Geert Grote's 14th-century version. Phrasing, grammar, and orthography differ occasionally from the text given by Van Wijk in *Het Getijdenboek van Geert Grote* (Leiden, 1940).[1]

(59v blank)

60r–67v: *Die corte cruys ghetide* . . . (H)[7]Eer du selste . . . *D*es vaders wijsheit . . .

The Short Hours of the Cross (psalmless, based on the hymn *Patris sapientia veritas divina*) in Grote's translation. The text varies somewhat from the version printed by Van Wijk.[2] — Cf. Meertens, *Godsvrucht* I, p. 15, n. 63.[3]

68r–85v: *Hier beghint die seuen psalme* (H)[7]Eer in dijnre verbolghentheit . . .

MS 62, f. 1r (actual diameter of outer circles: 42 mm)

Grote's version of *Septem psalmi poenitentiales cum Litaniis.* Cf. Van Wijk, *op. cit.*, p. [139]–154. The Litany (ff. 78r sqq.) differs variously from the printed version (*op. cit.*, p. 145 sqq.); among additional saints included are Gillys and Cunera.[4] — 83v, last line, through 85v, "*Die corte preces*," beginning "Ic sprack here ontferm di mijns . . . " (= Ps. XLI,4 sqq.) and ending with several formal collect-type prayers.

86r–129r: *Die vighelie van neghen lesse[n].* (I)^{8}C minde want die here sel verhoren . . . Si moeten rusten in vreden. Amen. Deo gratias.

Grote's version of the *Officium defunctorum.* Cf. Van Wijk, *op. cit.*, p. 156–195. (Arrangement of the initial parts differs: the Invitatory, "Mi hebben ombeua[n]ghen die suchten des doots . . . ," is at the beginning of Matins, 90r).[5]

(129v blank)

130r–132r: *Een suuerlick ghebet tot o[n]sen he[ren] om v'ghiffenisse der sonde[n] te v'crigen.* (V)^{5}Oer die voeten dijnre hoecheit . . . eñ lieuen enghe in der ewichheit. Amen.

Cf. D. van Heel, *Middeleeuwse handschriften op godsdienstig gebied in het bezit van de Bibliotheek der Gemeente Rotterdam* (Rotterdam, 1948), p. 182, no. 19 (same?)

132r–v: *Van onsen here ihesu xp̄o* (O)^{2} ontfermh[er]tighe lieue vader ick bidde . . . tijt mijn sonden te biechten eñ te beteren. Amen.

132v–136v: *Van die wonde[n] xp̄i. (M)^{2}En vint ghescreũen* . . . (19 lines of exhortatory rubric; 133r, 6th line:) (O)^{3} Here ihesu criste almechtighe god.lof glorie eñ eer eñ wairdicht . . . (136v:) . . . meer doen sel die wilt mi o mynlike here vergheuen doir v grote ontfermherticheit. Amen.

136v–139v: *Dit sijn seuen woirden die onse lieue here sprack an den cruce* . . . (137r:) (H)^{3}Ere Ihesu Criste leue[n]de goods sone die in der lester tijt uwes leuens . . . (139v:) . . . Eñ daer te bliuen ewelick en ӯmermeer sonder eynde Amen.

Cf. Meertens, *Godsvrucht* VI, ms. 26bis(12).

139v: *Een gruete tot onsen here ihesum cristum:* Weest ghegruet guedertiere[n] heer . . . bluet dijnre wonden ihesus cristus Amen.

139v–141v: (rubric in last 2 lines of 139v:) *Een deuoet ghebet tot onsen here ihesu[m] cristu[m]:* O alre guedertierenste ende alre lijdsaemste . . . dat ick di behaghe moghe inder ewicheit Amen.

141v–142r: *Van onsen guede[n] enghel.gebet:* (I)$^{5+}$C bidde di heilighe enghel goods dien ick te bewaren beuolen bin . . . (142r:) . . . God die hebste . . . die biste een onsterflick god. Die leues . . . sonder eynde. Amen.

Cf. Meertens, *op. cit.* VI, ms. 3(12).

142r–145v: ***Een ynnich ghebet an Marien*** . . . (142r:) (O)[5] Onbesmette ende inder ewicheit ghebenedijt . . . O alre salichste iohannes . . . in ewicheit de ewichede[n]. Amen.

Translation of *O Intemerata.* Cf. Meertens, *op. cit.* VI, ms. 6(6) (on the prayer itself, see Wilmart, *Aut. spir.,* p. [474], etc.)

145v–147v: ***Een ghebet van die vijff grueten tot marien:*** God gruet v guedertieren maria en blenckende dagheraert . . . bidt voir ons te gode. Amen.

Van Heel, *op. cit.,* p. 64, item 5; Meertens, *op. cit.* VI, ms. 12(sub 17)

147v–148r: ***Een ghebet van onser vrouwen maria:*** God gruet v maria dochter des ewighen vredes . . . alle mijn sonden sijn gedaghet Amen.

148r—156v: (Suffrages, i.e., for each saint, an antiphon, versicle/response, and formal prayer, invoking:)

(148r–v) St. Peter ((O)[4] heilighe Pieter apostel ons heren ihesu cristi ontbinde . . .)

(148v–149r) St. Andrew (Doe die heilighe apostel andreas quam dair hem dat cruys bereit was . . .) (Cf. Meertens, *op. cit.* VI, ms. 2[ter](5b))

(149r–v) St. John Evangelist (Here ontfanck mi op dat ick mit mine brueders mach sijn . . .)

(149v–150r) St. Lawrence ((O)[3]pten roester en heb ick di god . . .)

(150r) St. Sebastian (O heilighe Sebastiaen groot is dijn gheloue . . .)

(150v–151v) St. Jeron ("Yorijs") (Weest ghegruet ghewairdighe ridder . . .)

(151v–152r) St. Augustine ((V)[4]erblide di onse moeder iherusalem . . .)

(152r–v) St. Nicolas (O guedertierenheit goods . . .)

(152v–153r) St. Catherine ((G)[3]od gruet v gemme der clairheit . . .) (Cf. Meertens, *op. cit.* VI, ms. 21(20c))

(153v–154r) St. Apollonia (Die heilighe maghet ende martelairster . . .)

(154r–156r) St. Barbara (God gruet v gloriose heilighe maget . . .) (Cf. Meertens, *op. cit.* VI, ms. 26[bis](13b))

(156r–v) All Saints (Salich si di alle heilighen goods*)*

156v–157r: ***Alsmen onse h[er]e op buert i[n]der misse[n] so selmen dit ghebedekijn lesen:*** Ghegruet bistu salicheit der werelt . . . (157r) . . . ***Alsmen die kelck op heffet*** . . . . . . mijn siel in dat ewighe leuen. Amen.

Prayers suitable for a lay person attending mass, at the Elevation rite.

157v–163r: ***So wie dit ghebet liest een iair voir een ziele*** . . . (H)[6]ere om dine heilige pijnen ontferme . . . voir mijn ziele eñ dair ic sculdich ben voir te bidden. Amen. Deo gratias.

The devotion includes 33 "Pater noster" (indicated by rubrics, not spelled out).

163r–164r: ***Sinte Augustijns ghebet van den heilighen sacrament*** . . . (163v:) (H)[5]ere ick en ben niet wairdich . . . (164r:) . . . Eñ i[n]der ewicheit mi niet en lates. Die leues eñ regneers i[n] ewicheit. Amen.

Cf. Meertens, *op. cit.* VI, ms. 23(31b).

164r–165v: ***Van den sacrament eerment ontfanget. Gebet.*** God gruet v alre heilicste lichaem ons heren . . . een salich wtganck moet ghegheuen worden Amen.

Cf. Meertens, *op. cit.* VI, ms. 23(31f). Prayer before Communion.

165v–166v: ***Alsinen sacrament ontfanghen heest Sinte machteldis ghebet:*** (O)[3] Guede Ihesu ick bid di doer die grote minne die du ons bewijste . . . op dat wi di te samen louen ewelicken. Amen.

166v; ***Sinte Augustinus gebet Ania*** O ziele xp̄i heilighe mi . . . eñ gesontmaker Amen. Deo gratias.

MS 62 The *Anima Christi* in Middle Netherlandish translation. Cf. references in Van Heel, *op. cit.*, p. 78, item 24.

* * *

Foliated in modern pencil. Preceding f. 1, free paper endleaf and 2 vellum flyleaves; at end, following f. 166, two flyleaves of vellum, one of paper, and one free endleaf also of paper. The paper is of 18th-century Dutch manufacture (watermark: coat of arms of Amsterdam, with scrolls under the stand).[6] — Written area ca. 99 × 62 mm. Frame-ruled in lead. — Script is the Netherlandish *rotunda* much used by the Brethren of the Common Life and the Windesheim canons;[7] with the 2-lobe *a* achieved by a separate dividing thin stroke. Ink brownish black, slightly bluish, more uneven than usual but free of tendency to powder. — Good-quality parchment, extraordinarily white but rather thick (ca. 19.3 mm per 100 leaves); its two sides are well distinguishable. — Rubrics in red.

Collation: 1^8 2^4 3^8(= ff. 13–19; 3_1 following f. 12 wanting, no loss of text) 4–9^8 10^8(= ff. 68–74; 10_1 following f. 67 wanting, no text loss) 11^8 12^8(= ff. 83–89; 12_4 following f. 85 wanting, no text loss) 13–20^8 21^{10} $24^{4-1?}$(= ff. 164–166; 22_4, wanting, was probably blank) — No text losses are evident but the missing leaves very likely contained full-page illustrations (introducing the Hours of Our Lady, the Penitential Psalms, and the Office for the Dead).

Surviving decoration consists of illuminated initials, some (the major ones, 7 to 9 lines in height) accompanied by fully decorated borders: on leaves 13, 60, 68, 86. In each of these, the written area is framed (except at top) by a bar with gold, blue, and light magenta segments, outlined in black. The panel borders, not outlined, are filled with winding, non-continuous vines and acanthus foliage, with some flowers, berries, and/or gold bezants. The colors are blue, red, light green, and brownish mauve, all partly in two shades. The initial letters on these four pages are blue on gold ground, infilled (except the *I* on f. 86) with rather thick vines (on f. 13, also a seed or perhaps arum flower, emphasized by color).[8] — Other illuminated initials: 6–line, on f. 157v; 5–line, on 33r, 130r, 142v (smudged), 163v; 4–line, on 23r, 37r, 40v, 44r, 47r, 53v, 61r, 62v, 63v, 64v, 65v, 66v, 115v, 148r, 151v. All these are divided letters combining gold and (velvet-texture) blue, with red penwork creating the infilling (“boxing glove” and other acanthus) and the surrounding ground and branching into the margins; small light green areas add accents and bring out the plant forms. Three-line initials (15r, 92r, 99r, 137r) are similar but the letter is gold only. — Two-line letters and versals alternately blue and red, without flourishing.

Eighteenth-century binding of brown calf; covers plain, decoratively acid-spotted; upper cover detached. Spine gold-tooled with lozenges and arabesques, also title: ROOMSCHE GETIDEN//MSS. 1477.[9]

On pastedown of upper cover, 20th-century inscriptions in pencil: Temp. no. 42; (another hand:) E. D. Neill; also pasted-on LC labels, one with “MS. 7.” — On paper endleaf formerly conjugate with the pastedown, penciled: Pre-accession 7; (in an earlier modern hand:) EX/SXX.

Former owners: Rev. Edward Duffield Neill (b. 1823, d. 1893; American clergyman, educator, historian)

2° fo.: *KL Januarius heuet xxxi daech*

Bibl.: De Ricci, *Census* (1935), p. 181, no. 7; Faye and Bond (1962), p. 117, no. 7.

NOTES

1. P. [36]–70. See *ibid.*, p. 3 on the unsolved question of the “usus” reflected in Grote’s translation. — Some details on the text of the office in present manuscript are given in our table C.

2. *Op. cit.*, p. 87–91.

3. Meertens refers to the original as *Horae canonicae Salvatoris* (?).

4. After the apostles and Innocents, the litany names 26 individual martyrs, 20 confessors, and 21 women.

5. That is of course the usual arrangement; but in Van Wijk's text and, if I am not mistaken, a number of copies of the *Officium defunctorum* from the Netherlands, the Invitatory precedes the psalms of the (first) Vespers (custom of reciting the whole office in one piece?).

6. Cf. H. Voorn, *De papiermolens in de provincie Noord-Holland* (1960) (note especially nos. 67, 69, 71).

7. It is not very round; the technical term comes from a mid-15th century advertisement of a calligrapher. Cf. *Nomenclature des écritures livresques* (1954), fig. 27, etc.

8. The overall effect is not necessarily pleasant. The work seems to be a relatively crude effort to imitate an alien (i.e., French) style; the less important initials described further are more pleasant to look at (and are probably more spontaneous).

9. Book is now in recently made box covered with brownish gray and very light brownish gray textile material.

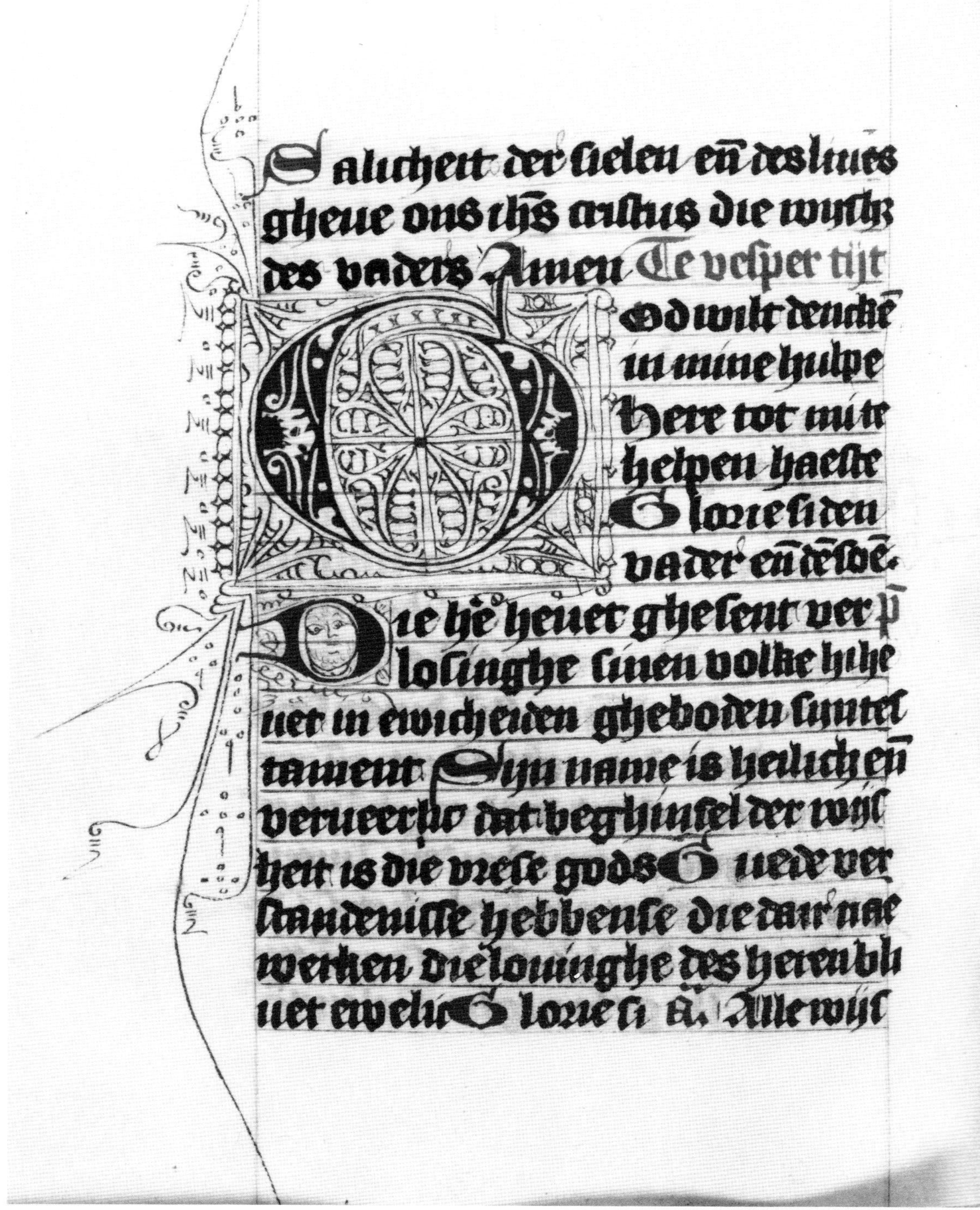

Salicheit der sielen en des liues
gheue ons ihs cristus die wijsh
des vaders Amen Te vesper tijt
God wilt dencke
in mine hulpe
Here tot mi te
helpen haeste
Glorie si den
vader en de soe.
Die he heuet ghesent ver
losinghe sinen volke hi he
uet in ewicheiden gheboden sijn tes
tament Sijn name is heilich en
verueerlijc dat beghinsel der wijs
heit is die vrese gods G uede ver
standenisse hebbense die daer nae
werken die louinghe des heren bli
uet ewelic G lorie si A. Alle wijs

MS 63, f. 91v (actual distance between the vertical ruled lines: 59 mm)

MS 63

(Collitz Hours)

BOOK OF HOURS IN NETHERLANDISH XVth c.

Netherlands. Parchment. 184 leaves,[1] 154 × ca. 111 mm (bound volume: 163 × ca. 120 mm) 1 column. 18 lines.

(ff. 1r–12v, calendar; 13r–53v, Hours of Our Lady; 54r–72v, Hours of the Holy Spirit; 73r–96v, Hours of the Eternal Wisdom; 97r–122v, Hours of the Cross; 123r–142v, Penitential Psalms with Litany; 143r–181v, Office for the Dead; 181v–184r, prayers before and after Communion)

ff. 1r–12v: ***(KL)*[3] *Januarius*** . . . **Siluester paeus.**

Full calendar (in black and red) agreeing basically with that of Utrecht; in red also Margaret, Jeron, and Willibrord; not in red, St. Mark; no *Translatio Barbarae* (not celebrated outside the city); for Oct. 1, the listing reads: Bauo ende Remigius; Ambrose (Apr. 4) is underscored in red. — Each month begins a new page.

13r–53v: ***Hier beghint die ghetide van onser lieuer vrouwen in duutsche. Dn̄e la***[2] **(H)[9]Ere du salt open doen mine lippen** . . . (ending on 53v:) . . . **en ymmer. A.M.E.N.**

The Hours of Our Lady in Geert Grote's translation. Text varies very little from that printed in N. van Wijk's edition (*Het Getijdenboek van Geert Grote*, Leiden, 1940; p. [36]–70). Grote's prologue is not included.[3]

54r–72v: ***Hier beghint die ghetide vād.h.geest*** **(H)[7]Ere du salt op doen** . . . (ending on 72v:) . . . **moeten rusten in vreden. A.M.E.N.**

The (longer) *Hours of the Holy Spirit*; text varies very little from that edited by Van Wijk *(op. cit.*, p. [71]–86).

73r–96v: ***Hier beghint die wijsheit ghetide:*** **(M)[7]Ine siele heuet di begeert in der nacht** . . . (96v:) . . . **en onse lichnamen. Amen.**

The "Hours of the Eternal Wisdom."[4] Text varies in some minor points from that given by Van Wijk (*op. cit.*, p. [92]–112).

97r–122v: ***Hier beghint die langhe cruus getide.*** **(H)[7]Ere ih[es]u criste des leuendighen godes sone ic dancke en̄ loue di** . . . **moeten rusten in vreden. Amen.**

The longer Hours of the Cross based on Bonaventura's *Officium de Passione Domini* (cf. Meertens, *Godsvrucht* I, p. 15), in Geert Grote's Middle Dutch version (printed text in Van Wijk, *op. cit.*, p. [113]–138; with introductory prayer as *ibid.*, p. [113] n. 2).[5]

123r–142v: ***Hier beghint die seuen psalmen*** (H)^{7}Ere in dijne verbolghentheit . . . van ewicheiden in ewicheiden. Amen.

Grote's version of *Septem Psalmi Poenitentiales cum Litaniis* (cf. Van Wijk, *op. cit.*, p. [139]–154); litany on ff. 133 sqq. — Additional saints not found in the Van Wijk text include Erasmus, Nicasius, Ewout (= Evrout?), Hubrecht (= Hubert?).[6]

143r–181v: ***Hier beghint die vigheli vā ix. lessē.*** (M)^{7}y hebbe[n] ombeuanghen . . . moeten rusten in vreden. Amen.

Grote's translation of the *Officium defunctorum* according to Utrecht (?) use. Cf. Van Wijk, *op. cit.*, p. 156–195.

181v–184r (beginning in 7th line of 181v): ***Dit ghebet salmen lesen als mē ten heilighen sacrame[nt] wil gaē.*** (G)^{4}od gruet alre heilichste . . . (ends on 184v, in first line:) der eynde. A.M.E.N.

Cf. Meertens, *Godsvrucht* VI, ms. 23 (31f)

184r: (lines 3–14:) ***Dit ghebet salmen*** ["lesen" omitted] ***als*** [*"ten"* written and crossed through] ***een dat sacrament heeft ontfaen.*** (A)^{3}y here coninc . . . mijnre sondigher sielen. Amen. (Line 16:) Deo gracias.

* * *

Foliated in modern pencil. Remnants of an earlier foliation, done in ink and mostly cropped in binding, appear on several leaves, beginning with "4" on what is now f. 1r; the leaf is preceded by a bifolium of two parchment leaves (with early inscriptions) which may have been included in the ink foliator's count.[7] — Two paper leaves precede the parchment material and two follow f. 184 at end, one in each case pasted to marbled free endleaf.[8]

Written area ca. 87 × 59 mm. Fully ruled in faint brownish ink; no prickings preserved. — The script is *littera textualis* of the Windesheim *rotunda* type.[9] — Ink brownish black (on some versos it shows through with a greenish cast); on some pages, signs of powdering. — Rubrics red. — Parchment of fair-to-good quality, occasionally crinkled or stained; 100 leaves add to a thickness of ca. 13.6 mm.

Collation: (bifolio of original parchment leaves; a singleton wanting?) 1^{6-1}(= ff. 1–5; 1_2 wanting, no text loss) 2^{8-1}(= ff. 6–12; 2_1 wanting, no text loss) f. 13 a singleton? 3^6(= ff. 14–19) 4^{10}(= ff. 20–29) 5^6(= ff. 30–35) 6^{10-1}(= ff. 36–44; 6_{10} wanting, no text loss) 7^8 8^{10-1}(= ff. 53–61; 8_{10} wanting, no text loss) 9^8 $10^{4-1?}$(= ff. 70–72; ff. 70.71 a bifolio; f. 72 a singleton?) $11–15^8$(= ff. 73–112) 16^{10}(= ff. 113–122) $17–18^8$ 19^4(= ff. 139–142) $20–23^8$ 24^{8+2}(= ff. 175–184; ff. 182.183 a bifolio inserted between 24_7 and 24_8). — No catchwords or signature markings preserved.

Decoration is limited to initials: Each of the six main sections begins (ff. 13r, 54r, 73r, 97r, 123r, 143r) with a 7-line (in the case of the first section, 9-line) initial in blue and red filled and surrounded by foliate designs drawn in red ink, unpainted but made to stand out by use of green in the background areas; added are red or purple penwork flourishes extending into the inner margin. — Single "hours" are introduced by mostly 4-line initials of similar character. Psalms and other minor constitutive elements begin with 2-line letters in red or blue, with purple or red flourishes running into margins; the letters are filled with forms drawn in pen and red ink: in most cases palmette or acanthus, but some are, instead, human faces (on ff. 15v, 22v, 40r, 57v, 78r, 85v, 91v, 119v, 121r, 160r, 180v). — Unlike other initials, the *I/J* is in some cases outside the written area (e.g., on 144v; a particularly interesting form on 117v). — The *KL* initials introducing each month of the calendar are 3-line, alternately blue or red, with added red or purple penwork. — Versals alternately red or blue.

Bound in 1802 by I. Versteeg;[10] covers are brown tree calf, sparingly tooled in gold. Edges sprinkled; marbled endleaves (blue and brownish).

On inside of upper cover, book label of previous owner: Hermann Collitz. (LC Rare Book Collection label tipped in.) On recto of paper flyleaf, in pencil: *Zonder nr.* — Recto of first parchment flyleaf blank; on verso, 3-line Netherlandish inscription in ornate (but hard-to-read)[11] 16th-century cursive. — On recto of the second parchment leaf, in upper right corner, in ink (Latin longhand of ca. 1900): *Versteeg* (cf. above). On verso, a 7-line Netherlandish inscription in a late 15th-century hand; it includes names and a somewhat unsatisfactory date: "op een(?) sonnendach xxxxxxx" (= [14]70?).[12]

On recto of last free endleaf, in pencil: 329; in another hand: 274; in another hand, LC note of source: "Bequest of Clara H. Collitz. Dec. 5, 1947." — In LC cataloger's handwriting: Catholic Church. Liturgy and ritual. Hours. BX 2080.A5F5/1500z (Rare Bk Coll)

Former owners: (Cornelia Theresa van Langhe? Augustinian monastery in Enkhuizen?) Hermann and Clara Collitz.

2° fo.: *(KL)³ Februarius*

Bibl.: De Ricci, *Census* (1935), p. 857, no. 4 (when in the private library of Professor Hermann Collitz in Baltimore); LC card number 62–55622.

NOTES

1. Counting the preliminary parchment flyleaves, LC catalog card (62–55622) gave the extent as "[186]" leaves.
2. The writer (or editor) was indicating the Latin initium, "Domine labia mea aperies." No mark of abbreviation with the "la."
3. For textual details see table C.
4. See note given with ff. 171r–185v of MS 60.
5. Rather extensive marginal corrections on f. 111 recto and verso, in *littera currens* of ca. 1500, partly cropped. They seem to call for changes from what resembles Van Wijk's variants mss. *B* and 185 to what is more like the text of his ms. *M* (cf. *op. cit.*, p. 126).
6. The litany names individually (after Mary, the angels, apostles, Innocents) 19 martyrs, 28 confessors, 25 women.
7. The two leaves carry, however, no remnants of foliation. In any case, at least one leaf remains unaccounted for.
8. The paper is watermarked: J. KOOL & COMP.
9. Cf. *Nomenclature des écritures livresques* (1954) , p. [25] (fig. 27); also Kruitwagen's study quoted there (on p. 24).
10. Inscription in pencil on f. 52r, tail margin: *Dit boekske is Vervaardigd door I. Versteeg inden Jare 1802 Ter glorie Van God.*
11. The last line seems to be the signature of an abbot?
12. No photocopy produced has as yet been good enough for mailing to the Netherlands; a visiting expert suggested technical processes not now available. I think the caption-like first line names En(c)huus = Enkhuizen; the next lines say more or less clearly (I will not attempt exact transcription) that the book belonged to Corneli[a?] Theresa van (Langhe?), daughter of late Lijnert (?).

MS 64

(Faye and Bond 80)

BOOK OF HOURS (Latin fragments, German additions) ca. 1500 and 17th c.

Netherlands and Cologne. Parchment and paper. 191 (xv, 177 i.e., 176) leaves, ca. 97 × ca. 58 mm[1] (bound volume: 100 × ca. 60 mm) 1 column. 17 lines (calendar, 16 lines; 17th-century additions, 16 lines)

CONTENTS (using the foliation in upper fore-edge corners):

(ff. i–xii, calendar; xiii–xv, *Tabula signorum*; 1r–29r, Hours of Our Lady (incomplete); 29v, program of *Psalmi graduales*; 30r-38r, Penitential Psalms; 38r-61r, ADDITION: prayers for a sick sister; 62r–97v, Office for the Dead (incomplete); 98r–145r, prayers for the dying (largely ADDITION); 145r–150r, ADDITION: chants for funeral service, with music; 150v–155r, ADDITION: prayers before/after meals, other community prayers; 156r–177v, ADDITION: various prayers and devotional exercises in German)

ff. i–xii^{v}: Calendar: in black, red, or blue. Major feasts originally in red or blue; later additions are all in black.

Notable among the emphasized feasts: *Rumoldi* (July 1), *Divisio Apostolorum, Augustini ep. patris nostri* (Aug. 28), *Lamberti, Nychasii.* — Pontianus (Jan. 14) is in black; Lebuinus (Nov. 12, normally) and, amazingly, Annunciation (March 25) are not included at all.[2] — As originally written, the calendar seems to have been made to serve a convent of Augustinian inspiration in the Netherlands.

To the original ca. 190 entries, later hands ADDED (sometimes erasing the original name and substituting another) ca. 70 feasts taken, largely, from the calendar of Cologne (Castoris, Justi, Euergisli, Kuniberti, Translatio Trium Regum . . .) or from the Augustinian world (Translatio scti. Augustini, Feb. 28); also included are Joseph (March 19) and some more recently canonized saints (Francis Xav.; Carlo Borromeo; François de Sales [d. 1622, canonized 1665])

(xiii^{r} blank)

xiii^{v}–xv^{r}: *"Tabula signorum"* (relating zodiac signs to the *numerus aureus*; astrological propitiousness of various periods is shown)

xv^{v}: (borders and a small Annunciation scene[3] excised from another leaf of the early book and pasted to the originally blank page; text ADDED in 2nd or 3rd hand:) *N*atiuitas tua . . . donauit nobis vitam sempiternam. Amen.[4]

1r–29r: *Incipiu[n]t hore de b[ea]ta virgine* (D)[9][omi]ne labia mea ap[er]ies . . .

Hours of Our Lady; originally, it seems, according to the use of Utrecht but later variously added to and revised.

The texts on leaves 1–4, 7[bis], 8–13, 18–22, 22[bis], and 23–29 are (basically) original; those on ff. 5–7 and 14–17, LATER ADDITIONS. — Recto of 2r formerly partly obscured by pasted-on piece of paper (54 × 41 mm) with a late engraving;[5] recto of 7[bis] at one time canceled by pasted-down, now separated f. 7. — Leaves 15–16 are wanting, with loss of most of the Prime; 22[bis] has recto blank and a large illustration on verso (Christ suffering). — F. 26r has four-side border and historiated initial: Mary Magdalen meets Christ (with hat) in the garden; the poorly visible initial letter (placed in upper right corner of the illustration field; cf. note 3) is *U/V*, to begin "Vespere aut[em] sabbati," words formerly obscured by pasted-on paper slip. The texts of the leaf seem not to belong: they are from the breviary office for Easter.[6] The original texts, as far as preserved, seem to be the (rather rarely seen) Utrecht use in Latin.[7] However, even as changed by later hands, the office corresponds to a considerable degree to the version used by Geert Grote for his 14th-century translation (which may not be pure Utrecht; cf. *Het Getijdenboek van Geert Grote*, ed. Van Wijk, Leiden, 1940, p. 3).

29v: *Incipiu[n]t quindecim gradus* . . .

Program, by means of initia, of the *Psalmi graduales* in liturgical arrangement, with formal prayers for the dead, etc., as in *Breviarium Romanum*. Text partly defaced by pasted-on paper cancel which is now missing; ends imperfectly before conclusion of the prayer *Deus cui proprium* (= last third of the whole is missing, at least one original leaf wanting).

30r–38r: (f. 30r has borders and historiated initial: David penitent) (D)[7]Omine ne i[n] furore tuo . . .

The seven Penitential Psalms, ending in 8th line of 38r. N.B. "31" of the ink foliation is verso of "30." — Leaf 38 is paper cancel[8] with end of the Ps. CXLIII in much later hand.

38r–61r (all paper; writing in LATE HAND,[9] with rubrics in German) (38r, 8th line:) *Darauff den Ps[alm]* . . . (Pss L, CXXI) (f. 40r:) . . . *An[tiphon]* *S*ana d[omi]ne infirma[m] istam . . .

Tying-in with the Penitential Psalms, prayers of a community of women (in Cologne? canonesses?) for a sick member. Litany of Saints (ff. 40r sqq.) is formulated as a litany for the sick ("Orate pro ea"); further psalms, and another litany (55r sqq.), styled as one for a departed person ("Miserere anime ejus," "Intercede pro anima ejus") follow.

The first litany has among its 30 martyrs: . . . lamberte, quirine, gorgoni, respondiastice, hermolae, theodisce, clementine, theodore, amere . . . eliphi, deonisi *[sic]* . . . ; among 16 confessors: . . . materne, . . . cuniberte, heriberte, anno . . . ; among 34 women: . . . leophania, pignosa, petronilla, . . . walbina, eufrosina, firmendina, . . . euergisla . . . ; the second litany, less rich in unusual saints, includes *Duo Ewaldi, Tres Reges,* and also Dominic and Francis, absent from the first version (which, however, has St. Clare).

(f. 61 has on verso a pasted-on baroque engraving captioned REGNV̄ TRIV̄PHANTIS CHRISTI[10])

62r–97v: *D*ilexi quoniam exaudiet dominus . . . (89r:) . . . pie peccata dilue Vt [. . . preuenti mortalitate non perdant] *Am end der vigilien* . . . (90v:) . . . *wan die leich zur Capelle soll gedrage[n] werde[n] so betten wir* . . . (92r:) . . . *Gleich vor der begräbnuss betten wir mit den priesteren die grosse Co[m]mendation* . . . (97r:) . . . *wa[n] aber der 30igste dag* . . . *Am H: Eschtag* . . . (97v:) . . . que pro peccatis nostris meremur auerte Per xp̄m dn̄m nr̄m Amen.

Office for the Dead (use of Utrecht?), followed (90v sqq.) by funeral and related *consuetudines* of the Cologne community. The office itself is imperfect, with most of

MS 64 the First Vespers and minor sections elsewhere wanting. Original parts (64v–79v, with few interruptions) include the responsories: I Domine qui creasti II Manus tuae III Memento quaeso IV Absolve V Tuam Deus piissime pater VI Rogamus te Domine VII Libera eas VIII Redemptor meus IX Deus eterne. — Invitatory, the grim *Circumdederunt me*, is in the late additions.

The ADDITIONS or substitutions (on paper, and in a 17th?-century hand) consist of f. 62, fragment numbered 63ᶜ (63ᵃ, 63ᵇ apparently excised), piece glued to and obscuring 64r, engraving pasted to and obscuring 14 lines of 69r,[11] fragment numbered 70ᵇⁱˢ, piece pasted to and obscuring 14 lines of 78r, engraving[12] obscuring 78v, cut-out piece of color border obscuring three top lines of 79r, and leaves 80–97.

97v, lower half: pasted to the paper leaf is fragment of the original parchment material with part of ornamental border and historiated initial (Coronation of the Virgin), and fragment of text: (O)⁹rtus [con]clusus es d[e]i genitrix ort[us] [con]clusus

97ᵇⁱˢ wanting? "97ᶜ", parchment leaf from the original book, attached to paper stub, is blank on recto; on verso, full-page illustration, within full border: Crucifixion.

98r–106r (LATER ADDITIONS making some use of leaves or fragments from the original book): *Cōmendacio defunct.minor* Subuenite sancti dei . . .

A *Commendatio animae* (prayers for the dying or for the just-deceased) styled for the use of the female community. — Fragments (pasted on 99v, 101r, 102v) and whole leaves (ff. 100, 103) of the early book include Psalms CXIV–CXVII and, on 102v, fragment of the original version of the text rewritten on 62r: (D)³ilexi qm̄ exaudiet . . . (= Ps. CXIV,1–5a); pasted above it, excised from another part of the original book (beginning of the Prime of Hours B.M.V.), 7-line historiated initial U/V "inhabited" by the Dove (for Holy Spirit) and scroll bearing inscription "Ueni Sancte Spūs repl[e] tuorū corda fi[delium]."

106r–145r (LATER ADDITIONS making some use of parts of the early manuscript): *Commendacio defunctoru[m]* Omnipotentis dei misericordia[m] Karissime deprecemur . . .

This seems to be the *Commendatio major.*— Fragments of leaves from the early ms. are pasted on 107v, 109r, 114v, 116r, 133v, 134r (pieces of border); whole leaves made use of are ff. 108, 110, 115, 124 (with ornamental border and initial (D)⁵), 125, 134, 135, and 136. Contents of the original parts include Psalms CXVIII, IV, CXXXIX, also (the fragment on 133v) a color miniature representing St. Andrew.[13] — The late additions include (144r–145r) the five invocations beginning "D[omi]ne Jesu Chr[ist]e adoro te in cruce[m] ascendente[m]."[14] — Pasted on 109v, a late full-page engraving (Jesus mocked and beaten by soldiers) captioned: Christi spott vnd schläg//Lehren//Der sünder schwäre. — On 113rv, major part (verses 1–15) of Psalm LVI is in printed form, i.e., excised from an incunable or early print and pasted to the leaf.

145r–150r (ALL LATER HAND, on paper): (beginning after 8th line of text) liturgical texts with music (unaccompanied melodies, square notes on 5-line staves); includes following separable items as marked by red initial letters:

Libera me domine de morte eterna (through 2nd *Quando celi)*
Quid ego miser[r]imus quid dicam
Si bona suscepimus
In omnibus his non peccavit Job
Media vita in morte sumus
Absolve Domine animas eorum
Si que illis sint
Deus eterne in cuius humana condicio potestate
Qui in cruce positus

150v–155r (ALL LATER HAND, on paper): *Dess Mittags wan wir nicht fasten:* Benedicite . . .

The *Benedictio mensae*, followed by various other formalized community prayers recited at the table or elsewhere. Prayer texts in Latin, rubrics German.

(155v blank)

(ff. 156–177 are THE MOST RECENT ADDITIONS to the volume; 3rd hand; ink foliation discontinued; texts are in German)

156r–161r: (pasted on 156r, decorative border and small illustration, Young man at prayer, from the early 16th-century ms.[15]) *Diese 7 P[ate]r n[oste]r list man dess Sondags vor die seele[n] 1p̄r̄* O Lieff Herr Jesu xp̄e diss p̄r̄. n̄r̄. opffere ich dir zu lob . . . (160r:) . . . *Dass siebende Pater N̄r̄* O lieber Herr Jesu . . . (ends 161r, 11th line:) Requiescant in pace Amen.

161r–163r: *Auffopferung dess Rosen Krantz psalters der Mutter Gottes mit diesem Gebett* Nun verehre vnd befehle ich dir . . . vnd Mutter Gottes Maria Amen

163r–164v: *Sieben Tag vor de[m] fest vnser Lieben frawe[n] hei[m]suchung . . . besuche die Kirch Maria in Capitolio* . . . O Maria die herfur bracht den baum dess lebens . . . da ich mich mach erfrewe[n] in alle ewigkeit Amen

Nuns, and later secular canonesses, lived in a community at the church *Sankt Maria im Kapitol* in Cologne through ca. 1800. Cf. Cottineau, *Répertoire*.[16]

164v–165v: *Vor dem H. Hochwurdigen sprech* O ihr heilsame wu[n]de[n] meines allersussesten . . . Jesu . . . vergebung aller meiner sunden, Amen

165v–166v: *funff p[ate]r n[oste]r* O liber heer Jesu xp̄e ich bitte dich . . . durch deine unaussprechliche Miltigkeit . . . zu Kom[m]en zu dem ewigen leben Amen

166v–176r: *Die funffzehn salue Regi[n]a am sambstag sehr Nuetzlich zu sprechc[n]* . . . Salue Regina . . . O Gnadenreiche vnd wurdige Jungfraw Maria . . . (173v:) . . . *Zum Beschlus[s] sprech also* O du allerheiligste Mutter Gottes vnd Jungfraw maria, . . . von ewigkeit zu ewigkeit Amen

176r–177v: *So wer diese 3 P̄r̄ N̄r̄ spricht . . . getrost werde[n] p̄r̄ n̄r̄* O lieff here dit p̄r n̄r opfferen ich . . . (ends on 177v, 1st line:) seligen Endt Amen

* * *

The 82 preserved leaves or fragments of leaves of the original manuscript are foliated in modern pencil in lower corner of the fore edge; an older foliation, perhaps by hand 1 of the substituted and added texts, is done in ink, in upper fore-edge corners of rectos; it begins after calendar and tables and ends with f. 155; at a later date it has been continued in pencil, through 177; same hand also added foliation in roman numerals to the preliminary leaves (the calendar and tables). While this foliation has in some cases been made incorrect by separations of parchment and paper leaves which at one time were pasted together and other irregularities, the total number of leaves, not counting some sewn-in or otherwise inserted small-size paper slips, is now 191 (xv + 176; leaves 15, 16, and 63 are wanting; "31" is verso of 30; "7bis", "22bis", and "97^{c}" make up the balance).

Written area: on undisturbed full pages of the original ms. 62 × ca. 40 mm (in the late additions, ca. 72 × 46 mm). — Original ms. fully ruled in faint red ink (highest and lowest horizontals doubled); additions partly frame-ruled in a grayish medium (lead?). No pricking marks noticed. — Script of the original book (= most of the texts on parchment) is a diminutive Netherlandish *rotunda*, clearly the work of an experienced scribe; the additions on paper are in a hybrid, generally very legible and careful but not calligraphic hand; almost certainly by several writers but all of them, rather puzzlingly, using backhand slant. — The ink of the original has faded much more, to a grayish olive color, than the brownish black of the additions (which, however, has the tendency to show through on other side of the paper). — The parchment of the original is of good quality, fairly thin, smooth on both sides. (Overall thickness of the text block, including paper parts, is ca. 22 mm.) Paper (with vertical chain lines) of medium quality.[17]

Collation: 1^{8}(= ff. i–viii) 2^{6+1}(= ff. ix–xv; xv is a singleton) 3^{8}(= ff. 1–7 and 7bis; ff. 5, 6, 7 are paper cancels) 4^{16}(= ff. 8–22; 8–13 and 18–22 parchment, 14.17 paper; 15.16 wanting; 4_{16}wanting, stub attached to f. 22bis = 5_{1}) 5^{8}(= ff. 22bis, 23–29; all are parchment, with some paper pieces attached or inserted) 6^{4}(= ff. 30–34, including "31" = 30v) 7^{12}(= parchment ff. 35–37 and paper 38–46; more compactly written original had probably 8 leaves) 8^{6}(= ff. 47–52, all paper) 9^{10}(= ff. 53–62, all paper) $10^{6?}$(= parchment ff. 64, 64bis, 65; 10_1 = f. 63^{a} and $10_2 = 63^{b}$ wanting; fragment preserved of 10_3 = f. 63^{c}) 11^{12+2} (= parchment ff. 66–79; 67 and 70 are singletons) 12^{10}(= paper ff. 80–89) 13^{8}(= paper ff. 90–97; "97^{c}" [no 97bis] is parchment singleton with illustration) $14^{6?}$(= ff. 98–106; 100, 103, and fragments [attached to 99v, 101r, and 102v] are parchment; 98, 99, 101, and 102, paper) $15^{6?}$(= ff. 107–112; 108–110 are parchment, rest paper) $16^{10?}$(= ff. 113–122; 115 and 116 parchment, the rest paper) $17^{10?}$(= ff. 123–132; 124 and 125 are parchment) $18^{10?}$(= ff. 133–142; 134, 135, and 136 are parchment) 19^{6}(= ff. 143–148, all paper) 20^{8}(= ff. 149–156, all paper except pieces pasted to 156r) 21^{6}(= ff. 157–162, all paper) 22^{10}(= ff. 163–172, all paper) 23^{4}(= ff. 173–177, all paper). — No catchwords or signature markings. Some of the paper leaves are cancels, some simply additions.

Decoration: Two full-page miniatures (22bis verso, 97^{c} verso) and nine historiated initials (on *xv* verso, 1r, 7bis verso, 26r, 30r, 97v, 102v, 133v, 156r) preserved (though often not in their proper place and used without regard for their original function) from the original book.[18] All are multicolor and some accompanied by borders of the Ghent-Bruges style. Those on xv^{v}, 26r, 133v, and 156r have the initial letter outside the illustration itself, in upper right corner of its field; due to poor color contrast (erasure?) the letter is often barely discernible. — Purely ornamental initials (phyllomorphic; letters golden yellow on blue, purple, or muted red grounds) occur on ff. 2v, 8v, 18r, 19v, 21v, 23r, 124r (all are *D*s; that on 124r is 5 lines high and accompanied by partial border). — On the original leaves, blue and red versals alternate; the parts written on paper are only black and red. — In several cases pieces excised from the original ms. have been used to decorate.

Binding: early 19th-century half-leather (spine and corners brown calf, covers dark brown paper with irregular pattern of lighter brown), severely deteriorated; upper cover detached. — Edges red. — Spine lightly tooled in gold; in gold on dark-red leather label: OFFICIVM//B.M.V.//MANVSCRPT.

On verso of front free endleaf, penciled: Temp. no. 27; MS. 80; (within a circle:) 23. On f. i recto, at top, penciled: Ac. 4560(3), no. 11; *ibid.* in tail margin, in dark blue ink: Barnheim.

Former owners: a community (or a member of a community) of women at or near the church of Sankt Maria im Capitol in Cologne; Barnheim (Prussian *Geheim-Justiz-Rat*, d. ca. 1870); Rev. E. A. Dalrymple (of Baltimore); acquired by LC with other items from the Dalrymple collection in 1916 (ms. ac. 4560, 3, 11).

2° fo.: *KL februarius habet dies . 28 . Lun 30*

Bibl.: *Bibliotheca typographica : Manuscripte, Incunabeln, Bücher . . . aus dem Nachlasse des Geh. Justiz-Rath Barnheim* (Berlin, 1873) (no. 16 in sale of May 8, 1873).[19] — De Ricci, *Census* (1935), v. I, p. 230, no. 108; Faye and Bond (1962), p. 119, no. 80.

The book, originally a fairly standard (though not uninteresting: from the Netherlands, this kind of material tends to be in Netherlandish) book of hours, was at some time carried to Cologne; more likely than not, by a displaced religious person (or a later possessor) who then proceeded to adjust the texts to local custom.

NOTES

1. This is the size of the leaves which are complete. Some of the 191 are smaller-size or fragments. The count does not include sewn-in small-size paper slips. Two leaves pasted together more or less inseparably with loss of access to the text are counted as one. Various methods of counting will produce different results. See also some observations in the contents, and the fuller description following it.

2. Conceivably omitted when black entries were being written, in order to be added in red or blue (by the rubricator), and then forgotten?

3. Originally historiated initial *A*, with the letter placed in upper right corner (cf. other instances of this practice on 26r, 133v, and 156r).

4. The text is the antiphon used in the Roman breviary with the Magnificat of the Second Vespers of the Nativity of Our Lady, September 8.

5. The engraving, in an oval frame, represents what seems to be the Deposition (of Jesus from the cross); the attendants are, however, angels (one with large candle).

6. Taken from another (office) book, uniform in script and format with the book of hours?

7. See table C for textual details. For this manuscript, the table gives, where possible, both the original and the changed text, separated by a diagonal stroke: [original]/[later]. A special difficulty occurs in the Invitatory where the "Ave Maria gratia plena Dominus tecum" of the Roman use rather clearly predated (judging from extremely abridged "A[v]e" or "Dn̄s" between verses of the psalm) the (inadequately substituted) "In Honore Dominus (-i?)" (ff. 1r-2r).

8. To accommodate changes or to substitute for lost material?

9. Seventeenth century?

10. Seventeenth century? The engraving (inside a partly cropped rectangular border) contains a coat of arms divided into 16 areas with various symbols of Christ and of his Passion. In the center, a heart. Above and around the shield, other symbols, including those of the four evangelists. Not high art.

11. Engraving represents Jesus with resurrection symbols appearing (from inside clouds) to a kneeling female saint.

12. Partly cropped, no essential content lost; the essential content is a giant heart-shaped object (cosmic door?) in the clouds with baby angels around and what may be little boy Jesus knocking on the door.

13. The apostle does not "inhabit" any letter but in the upper right corner of the miniature a small rectangular field contains the initial letter *a*. The initial is without relationship to present text of the page. (See note 3.)

14. Cf. Wilmart, *Aut. spir.*, p. 144, n. 4; Leroquais, *LH* I, p. 320.

15. Originally historiated initial *I*, with the letter placed in upper right corner (as on xv^v, 26r, 133v); letter now without relationship to the (17th-century) text.

16. It is not clear whether the advice to visit its church excludes or commends the idea that the book was held by a member of the community. N.B. The church did not, I believe, belong to the group.

17. Not clear whether identical stock all through (it looks whiter, e.g., in the sparsely written litanies); fragments of watermarks visible on ff. 6 and 160 (not identified).

18. The initial on 26r may actually be from a different book: cf. contents.

19. Not seen; information from De Ricci.

TABLE C *(SECTION 1)*—BOOKS OF HOURS:[1] Text Variations in the Hours of the Virgin

MATINS:

MS	INVITATORY	HYMN	LESSON I	RESPONSORY I	LESSON II	RESPONSORY II	LESSON III	RESPONSORY III
44	Ave Maria . . . Dominus tecum	Quem terra	In omnibus requiem	Sancta et immaculata	Et sic in Sion firmata	Beata es . . . portasti . . .	Quasi cedrus exaltata	Felix namque es
45	,,	,,	,,	,,	,,	,,	,,	,,
46	,,	,,	,,	,,	,,	,,	,,	,,
47	,,	,,	,,	,,	,,	,,	,,	,,
48	,,	,,	,,	,,	,,	,,	,,	,,
49	,,	,,	,,	,,	,,	,,	,,	,,
50	,,	,,	,,	,,	,,	,,	,,	,,
51	,,	,,	,,	,,	,,	,,	,,	,,
52	,,	,,	,,	,,	,,	,,	,,	,,
53	,,	,,	,,	,,	,,	,,	,,	,,
54	,,	,,	,,	,,	,,	,,	,,	,,
55		O quam glorifica	Surge beatissima	Beata es Virgo Maria . . . que credidisti	Cecos cordium oculos	Sancta et immaculata virginitas	O sacratissima virgo Maria nos qui	,,
56	,,	,,	Surge beatissima	,,	,,	,,	,,	,,
57	,,	Quem terra	O beata Maria quis digne	,,	Admitte piissima	Beata es	Sancta Maria succurre miseris	,,
58	,,	,,	Sancta Maria virgo virginum (rhythm.)	Beata es Virgo Maria que Dominum portasti	Sancta Maria piarum piissima	Sancta et immaculata virginitas	Sancta Dei genitrix que digne meruisti concipere	,,
59	,,	,,	,,	Sancta et immaculata	,,	Beata es	,,	,,
60	In der eerlicheit	—0—	Heilghe ioncfrouwe alre ioncfrouwen	Heilighe ende onbeulecte	Heilghe gades moeder maria die waerdelicke verdienst	Heilich bistu . . . die den heren droghes . . .	Heilighe maria doe alre hoghest gode bouen allen creaturen . . .	Selich bistu Maria
61	In der eerlicheyt	—0—	Heylige maria ioncfrouwe alre	Heylige ende onbeulecte	Heylige moeder gods die werdelic verdiendes	Salich bistu maria die den heer droochste	Heylige maria die alre goddienstichste	Salich bistu maria
62	In die eerlicheit	—0—	Heilighe maria ioncfrouwe alre	Heilighe ende onbeulecte	Heilighe maria der guedertieren alre quedertierenste	Selich bistu maria die den heren droghest	Heilighe goods moeder maria die waerdelike verdiendes . . .	Selich bistu ioncfrouwe maria
63	Inder eerlicheit	—0—	Heylighe maria ioncfrouwe alre	Heylighe ende onbeulecte	Heilighe godes moeder maria die weerdelike	Salich bistu maria die den here droghest	Heylighe maria die alre hogheste bouen alle creaturen	Salich bistu ioncfrouwe maria
64[2]	Ave . . . tecum/In honore	Quem terra//same?	? / O beata Maria quis digne	? / Sancta et immaculata.	? / Accipe itaque quascumque exiles	? / Beata es	Sancta Dei genitrix que digne /Sit per te excusabile	Felix namque/Felix namque

1. N.B. Throughout table C (as elsewhere in the tables) Latin orthography has been more or less standardized; spellings in Netherlandish follow the source. 2. Original reading / later correction.

TABLE C *(SECTION 2)*—BOOKS OF HOURS: Text Variations in the Hours of the Virgin

	MATINS (continued):			LAUDS:			
MS	TOTAL NUMBER OF LESSONS	ALTERNATE PSALM SETS?	SEASONAL VARIANTS	CAPITULUM	HYMN	ANTIPHON TO BENENEDICTUS	ORATIO ("COLLECTA")
44	Three	Yes	Advent, Xmastide, Eastertide	Viderunt eam filiae Sion	O gloriosa domina	Beata Dei genitrix . . . templum Domini . . .	Deus qui de beate . . . Mariae . . . utero . . .[1]
45	Three	No	None	"	"	"	"
46	Six (three of them for Advent)	Yes	Advent, Xmastide, Eastertide	"	"	"	"
47	Three	Yes	None	"	"	"	"
48	Three	Yes	None	"	"	"	"
49	Three	No	None	"	"	"	"
50	Six (three of them for Advent)	Yes	Advent, Xmastide	"	"	"	
51	Three	No	None	"	"	"	"
52	Six (three of them for Advent)	Yes	Advent, Xmastide	"	"	"	
53	Three	Yes	None	Maria virgo semper laetare	"	O gloriosa Dei genitrix	Deus qui corda + Concede nos + Ecclesiam tuam
54	Three	Yes	None	"	"	"	"
55	Nine	Not stated	None	Te laudant angeli	Virgo Dei genitrix quem totus . . . Vera fides	Hec est regina virginum	"
56	Three	No	None	"	"	"	"
57	Three	No	None	Maria semper uirgo laetare	O gloriosa domina	O gloriosa Dei genitrix	
58	Three	No	None	Te laudant angeli	"	"	"
59	Three	No	None	Virgo verbo concepit	"	"	Concede
60	Three	No	None	Als eyn winranck	O gloriose vrouwe bauen der sternen hoghe	Eirsame ioncfrowe godes moeder . . .	Verlene barmhertighe god [= Concede . . .]
61	Three	No	None	Als een wijnranc	O gloriose . . . bowen den ster- ren hoge	O eersame vrouwe, godes moeder . . .	Verleen ontfermhertige god
62	Three	No	None	"	None	Onder dine bescermenisse vlien wi dair die crancken . . .	Verleen here god dinen dienres des
63	Three	No	None	"	O gloriose . . . bouen den steernen hoghe	Eersame ioncfrouwe godes moeder	Verlene barmhertighe god
64	Three	No	None	In omnibus requiem/Ego quasi vitis	O gloriosa domina / ?	? / Sub tuam protectionem	? / Deus qui salutis

1. In MSS 51, 52, and perhaps others, this is followed by "commemorations" not recorded here.

TABLE C *(SECTION 3)*—BOOKS OF HOURS: Text Variations in the Hours of the Virgin

	PRIME:				TERCE:			
MS	HYMN	ANTIPHON	CAPITULUM	ORATIO	HYMN	ANTIPHON	CAPITULUM	ORATIO
44	Memento salutis auctor	Assumpta est	Quae est ista	Deus qui virginalem aulam	Memento salutis auctor	Maria virgo assumpta est	Et sic in Sion firmata sum	Deus qui virginalem aulam
45	,,	,,	,,	,,	,,	,,	,,	Deu qui salutis aeternae
46	,,	,,	,,	,,	,,	,,	,,	,,
47	-? (missing leaf)	,,	,,	,,	,,	,,	,,	,,
48	Memento salutis auctor	,,	,,	,,	,,	,,	,,	,,
49	? (missing leaf)	? (missing leaf)	? (missing leaf)	? (missing leaf)	,,	,,	,,	,,
50	Memento salutis auctor	Assumpta est	Quae est ista	Deus qui virginalem aulam	,,	,,	,,	,,
51	,,	,,	,,	,,	,,	,,	,,	,,
52	,,	,,	,,	,,	,,	,,	,,	,,
53	Veni creator (1 strophe) + Memento salutis autor	O admirabile commercium	Ab initio et ante saecula	Adsit nobis + Deus qui de beatae + Ecclesiam tuam . . . Iohannis . . .	Veni creator (1 strophe) + Memento salutis auctor	Quando natus es	,,	Deus qui apostolis + Deus qui salutis + Ecclesiam tuam
54	,,	,,	,,	,,	,,	,,	,,	,,
55	? (leaf missing)	Benedicta tu in mulieribus	Felix namque es	Deus qui apostolis tuis + Famulorum tuorum quaesumus + Ecclesiam tuam	,,	Dignare me laudare te	Paradisi porta per Euam	Adsit nobis quaesumus Domine
56	Veni creator (1 strophe) + Memento salutis auctor	,,	,,	,,	? (leaf wanting)	,,	,,	,,
57	,,	O admirabile commercium	Virgo verbo concepit	Deus qui apostolis	As in Prime	Quando natus	,,	Protege Domine famulos tuos
58	? (probably Veni creator + Memento)	,,	Sancta et immaculata	Deus qui apostolis + Famulorum tuorum + Omnium sanctorum tuorum	Veni creator (only initium given)	,,	,,	Adsit nobis + Protege Domine + Vide Domine infirmitates nostras
59	Veni creator (1 strophe) + Memento	,,	Haec est virgo sancta atque gloriosa	Famulorum tuorum	As in Prime	,,	,,	Protege Domine famulos tuos subsidiis pacis
60	Criste coninc alre guedertierenste	Doe du ontsprekelicke	Van den aenbegyn	Here god wij bidden di dat du dyne ghenaede	Criste conync (as in Prime exc.spelling)	Wij kennen dat die doernen busch	Ende aldus bin ic geuest in syon	Reike ons here dijne rechter hant
61	Criste coninc alre goedertierenste	Doe du ontsprekelic	Van aenbeghinne	Verleen ontfermhertige god help onser crancheyt	As in Prime	Wij kennen dat die dornebosch	,,	Reyke ons heer dijn recht' hant
62	,,	,,	,,	Here god wi bidden di dattu dine ghenade	As in Prime	,,	,,	Verleen ons almechtighe god een onderstant
63	,,	Doe du ontsprekelike	,,	,,	As in Prime	,,	,,	Reyke ons here
64	Section wanting	Section wanting	?	Porrige nobis Domine Deus/Protege Domine famulos tuos	Memento / ?	Rubum quem viderat / same?	Et sic in syon . . . requievi /et in Jerusalem . . . mea.	Concede misericors/Porrige nobis Domine Deus

TABLE C *(SECTION 4)*—BOOKS OF HOURS: Text Variations in the Hours of the Virgin

	SEXT:				NONE:			
MS	HYMN	ANTIPHON	CAPITULUM	ORATIO	HYMN	ANTIPHON	CAPITULUM	ORATIO
44	As in Prime	In odorem unguentorum	Et radicavi in populo honorificato	Concede misericors Deus fragilitati	As in Prime	Pulcra es et decora	In plateis sicut cinnamomum	Famulorum tuorum
45	''	''	''	''	''	''	''	''
46	''	''	''	''	''	''	''	''
47	As in Terce	''	''	''	As in Terce	''	''	''
48	''	''	''	''	''	''	''	''
49	''	''	(? missing leaf)	? (missing leaf)	? (missing leaf)	''	''	? (missing leaf)
50	As in Prime	''	Et radicavi in populo honorificato	Concede misericors Deus fragilitati	As in Prime	''	''	Famulorum tuorum
51	''	''	''	''	''	''	''	''
52	''	''	''	''	''	''	''	''
53	As in Prime	Rubum quem viderat	''	Mentes nostras + Famulorum tuorum + Ecclesiam tuam	''	Germinavit radix Jesse	Gaude Maria virgo cunctas hereses	Mentibus nostris + Concede misericors + Ecclesiam tuam
54	''	''	''	''	''	''	''	as MS 52 but erroneously "Mentes . . ."
55	As in Terce	Post partum virgo	Gaude Maria uirgo cunctas hereses	? (leaf wanting)	As in Terce	Sicut lilium inter spinas	Per te Dei genitrix est	? (missing leaf)
56	As in Prime	''	''	Mentes nostras + Concede quesumus + Ecclesiam tuam	? (leaf wanting)	''	''	Mentibus nostris + Protege nos
57	''	Rubum quem viderat	''		As in Prime	Germinavit radix Jesse	Te laudant	Concede nos famulos tuos
58	''	''	''	Mentes nostras + Beat(a)e et glorios(a)e + Infirmitatem nostram	As in Terce	''	Felix namque es	Mentibus nostris + Concede misericors
59	''	''	''	Beatae et gloriosae	As in Prime	''	Per te Dei genitrix nobis est	Adiuvet nos
60	As in Prime	Also was Jesses	Ende in dat gheeerde volke	Verlene ons	As in Prime	Sie maria heeft ons ghewonnen	Ich bijn verhoghet	God ewich ende almechtich
61	''	Yesses wortel	Ende in dat gheeerde volc	Here god wij bidden di dattu dn genade	As in Prime	Siet maria heuet ons gewonnen	Ic bin verhoghet in den berch	Wi bidden di heer dat ons moete te helpen
62	''	''	''	Bescerme ons here	As in Prime	Sie maria heeft	Ick bin verhoghet	Wi bidden di here dattu ons dat eerwairdighe gebet
63	''	''	''	Verleen ons almachtighe god	As in Prime	Sie maria heef ons ghewonnen	Ic bin verhoghet . . . berghe	God ewich ende almachtich
64	Memento / ?	Germinavit radix Jesse / same?	Et radicavi / Dilectus meus loquitur	Protege Domine famulos tuos / same?	Memento / ?	Ecce Maria genuit nobis / ?	Quasi cedrus exaltata / ?	Adiuvet nos / same?

TABLE C *(SECTION 5)*—BOOKS OF HOURS: Text Variations in the Hours of the Virgin

VESPERS:

MS	PSALM ANTIPHONS	CAPITULUM	HYMN	AD MAGNIFICAT	ORATIO
44	Five (one for each psalm)	Ab initio et ante secula	Ave maris stella	Beata mater et intacta virgo	Concede nos famulos tuos
45	,,	,,	,,	,,	,,
46	,,	,,	,,	Beata mater et et inupta virgo	,,
47	,,	,,	,,	(wanting)	(wanting)
48	,,	,,	,,	,,	Concede nos
49	,,	,,	,,	Beata mater et innupta virgo	,,
50	,,	,,	,,	,,	,,
51	,,	,,	,,	,,	,,
52	,,	,,	,,	,,	,,
53	Beata mater	Beata es Virgo Maria	Ave maria stella	Sancta Maria succurre miseris	Deus qui corda + Concede nos + Ecclesiam tuam
54	,,	,,	,,	,,	,,
55	Beatam me dicent	,,	,,	,,	Deus qui corda fidelium (+ ? (rest wanting))
56	,,	,,	,,	,,	Deus qui corda + Concede nos + Ecclesiam tuam
57	,,	,,	,,	,,	,,
58	Beata mater	,,	,,	,,	Concede nos + Deus qui corda + Ecclesiam tuam
59	,,	,,	,,	,,	Concede nos
60	Heilighe moeder ende mannes onkunndich	In allen dynghen	Ghegruet sijstu sterne	Heilige maria coem te hulpen	Verlene ons here god
61	Heilige moeder ende mannes onkundich	In allen dingen heb ic ruste gesocht	Gegruet sijstu sterre des meers	Heylige maria com te hulp	Verleen on heer god dinen dieneren des bidden
62	Heilighe moeder ende mannes oncondich	Als caneel	Ghergruet sijstu sterre	Heilige maria com te hulpe	Verleen ons here god
63	Heilighe moeder ende mannes onkundich	In allen dinghen	Ghegruet sistu sterre des meers	Heylighe maria come te hulpen	Verleen ons here god dinen dienres des bidden
64	(orig. erased)/Ecce tu pulchra es	Sicut cynamomum / same?	Ave maris stella / same?	Sancta Maria succurre / same with added "sentiant omnes . . . "	Concede nos + ? //Famulorum tuorum

TABLE C *(SECTION 6)*—BOOKS OF HOURS: Text Variations in the Hours of the Virgin

COMPLINE:

MS	PSALM ANTIPHON	HYMN	CAPITULUM	AD NUNC DIMITTIS	ORATIO	FINAL ANTIPHON
44	None	Memento salutis auctor	Ego mater pulcre dilectionis	Sub tuum pr(a)esidium	Beate et gloriose	Salve Regina + Regina coeli
45	None	"	"	"	"	Salve Regina
46	None	"	"	"	"	Salve Regina + Regina coeli
47	Section wanting	Section wanting	Section wanting	Section wanting	Section wanting	Section wanting
48	None	Memento salutis auctor	Ego mater pulcre dilectionis	Sub tuum pr(a)esidium	Beate et gloriose	Salve Regina
49	None	"	"	"	"	Salue Regina
50	None	"	"	"	"	Salve Regina + Regina coeli
51	None	"	Ego quasi pulchre delectionis [sic]	"	"	none
52	None	"	Ego mater pulchrae dilectionis	"	"	Salve Regina + Regina coeli
53	Cum iocunditate	Virgo singularis	Sicut cinamomum	Sancta Dei genitrix	Ure igne sancti Spiritus + Graciam tuam + Ecclesiam tuam	None
54	"	"	"	"	"	None
55	Beatam me dicent	Virgo Dei genitrix quem totus	Sicut cynamomum	Cum iocunditate	"	None
56	Sancta Dei genitrix uirgo semper Maria	Virgo Dei genitrix "ut supra" (= ?)	Sicut cinamomum	"	"	None
57	Sancta Dei genitrix quem totus	Virgo Dei genitrix quem totus	Sicut cynamomum	"	"	None
58	Cum iocunditate	Virgo singularis	Sicut cinamomum	Ecce completa sunt omnia	Graciam tuam + Ure igne + Consciencias nostras	None
59	"	"	"	(H)ortus conclusus	Graciam tuam (only)	None
60	Mit vrolicheit	Doer schynich open wort	Als caneel	Wij glorificiren di heilighe moeder gads	Here wijl vergheten	Ghegruet sijstu conygyne
61	Mit vroelicheyt	Doirschinich oepen wort die porte	Als caneel	Wij glorificieren di	Here wil vergeten	Ghegruet sijstu coninghinne
62	Mit vroylicheit	Doerschinich open	Coemt tot mi ghi alle die mijns begheert	Wy glorificeren di	Here wilt vergheten	"
63	Mit vrolicheit	"	Als caneel	Wi glorificieren di	Here wilt vergheten	Gegruet sijstu koninghinne
64	Cum iocunditate/Sub tuam protectionem (?)	Fit porta Christi pervia / same	Transite ad me? / Multae filiae	Glorificamus te Dei genitrix / same?	Famulorum tuorum . . . delictis . . . / same?	None

General Index

(excluding *Illustrative matter, Former owners, 2° fo.,* and *Initia)*

	MS:f.
St. Andrew	33:8r; 62:148v (suffrage in Netherlandish)
St. Anne	15:533r; 24:154v; 28 (litany); 33:74r; 39:14v (office chants); 40:62r (hymn); 41:133v (marg. add'n); 50:88r (suffrage); 58 (cal., in gold)
St. Anno (chant)	16:105v (marg. add'n)
St. Ansuerus	34 (litany)
St. Anthony, Abp. of Florence	40:115r
St. Anthony, of Padua	21:130r; 28:213r; 36 (litany); 46:198v
St. Anthony, the Hermit	47:33r; 50:86v; 51:117v; 52:108r; 53 (cal.); 54:169r
St. Antolin; *see* St. Antoninus of Apameia	
St. Antonilla	50 (cal.)
St. Antoninus of Apameia	39:61r (office chants)
St. Apollonia	30 (litany; port.); 33:116v (suffrage); 62:153v (suffrage)
St. Arnulph	17 (litany)
St. Aubert	58 (cal.)
St. Augustine (suffrage)	62:151v
St. Aurea	33:67v
St. Barbara	33:63v
St. Bartholomew	33:6v
St. Basolus	18:II,122v
St. Batildis	15:litany, 360v
St. Benignus	18:II,135v
Sts. Bercharius et Bolonia	18:II,123v
St. Birgitta, d. 1373	30; 34 (litany)
St. Blanchert	55 (cal.)
St. Bonaventura	41:130r
St. Botwidus	30 (litany); 34 (litany)
St. Brandan (May 16)	60 (cal.)
St. Brandan (May 17)	49 (cal.)
St. Brandan (No. 21)	49 (cal.)
St. Brice	39:109r (office chants)
St. Bridget (of Ireland)	34 (litany)
St. Brigidus (!?)	49 (cal.)
St. Candidus	50 (cal.)
Sts. Cantius, Cantianus, Cantianilla	15:383r
St. Caprasius	60 (cal.)
St. Catherine of Siena	40:107r (hymns)
St. Cecilia	33:58r
St. Christiana	58 (litany)
St. Christina	33:66v
St. Christopher	33:9r
St. Claudius	50:87v (suffrage)
St. Clement, Bp. of Metz	17 (cal.)
St. Clodoaldus	15:441v
St. Columba	18:I (litany)
St. Cornelius	15 (litany)

	MS:f.
St. Corona	60 (cal.)
St. Crysolius	22 (cal.)
St. Cunera	62 (litany)
St. Cyriacus & soc.	33:34v
St. Dalmatius	20:29r
St. David (of Mynyw, Wales)	49 (cal.)
St. Denis	50:86v (suffrage)
St. Dorothy	33:65v
St. Eadmundus	15 (litany)
St. Ediltruda	60 (cal.)
St. Eliphius	16:230v
St. Elizabeth	33:72r
St. Erasmus	16:134v (marg. add'n); 26:4r; 63 (litany)
St. Eric	34 (litany)
St. Eskill	34 (litany)
St. Eufraxia	33:68v
St. Evergislus	16:242r; 60 (cal.)
St. Ewout (= Evrout?)	63 (litany)
St. Extacius	57 (litany)
St. Fantinus	50 (cal.)
St. Fausta	22:344r
St. Ferreolus	18:I (litany), II:7r,91r
St. Ferrutius	18:I (litany), II:7r,91r
St. Florentius	18:I (litany)
St. Focus	60 (cal.)
St. Fortunatus	50 (cal.)
St. Gabriel; *see* Gabriel the Archangel	
St. Galdus, Bp. of Évreux	58 (cal.)
St. Gatianus	15:563v (late add'n); 57 (cal.)
St. Geneviève *des Ardents*	15:503v
St. Gengulphus	18:I (litany)
St. Gereon (chants)	16:223r
St. Germana	18:I (litany)
St. Germanus, Bp. of Paris	15:380v
St. Germanus of Auxerre	15:414v
St. Gertrude	33:119r
St. Gertrude of Nivelles	30:39v (port.)
St. Gildardus	22 (litany)
St. Gillys	62 (litany)
St. Gregory, Bp. of Langres	18:II,139r
St. Gregory *Thaumatourgos*	41:162v
St. Grondanus	50 (cal.)
St. Gudwalus	22 (cal.)
St. Guillermus Burdigalensis	15:514r
St. Guinofle	56 (cal.)
St. Hildebertus	58 (cal.)
St. Honorine	15 (cal.)
St. Hubrecht (= Hubert?)	63 (litany)
St. Hugo of Lincoln	23:202ra
St. Ianuaria	50 (cal.)
St. Ildephonsus	23:59ra
St. James's (bookbinding firm)	53
St. Jeron	62:150v (suffrage)
St. Job	26:4r

Index of Illustrative Matter

Representational elements found in many ornamental borders have not been considered for this index.

Index of Former Owners

Index of Secundo Folio

Secundo folio *refers to opening words of the second leaf, used by catalogers to identify a codex.*

Index of Initia

Concordance of Old and New Designations

Numbers in Faye & Bond	New MS numbers	Numbers in Faye & Bond	New MS numbers
2	18,I	75	15
3	18,II	79	60
7	62	80	64
8	61	81	26
9	14	84	33
10	17	85	30
18	44	86	34
19	4	87	24
20	48	91	25
32	37	92	56
34	55	93	57
45	21	126	32
47	28	127	12
52	13	128	35
53	23	130	49
70	7	139	46
71	2	150	20
72	1	169	59
73	22	172*	31
74	29	174	58

*Listed as "172" in Faye & Bond but for a long time shelved as "ms. 11" with the unnumbered Collitz Breviary and Hours.

Not in the Faye & Bond Supplement to De Ricci or Not Shelved According to the Faye & Bond Number:

Collitz Breviary (in Netherlandish): MS 27
Collitz Hours (in Netherlandish): MS 63
Hours Mrs. Carley Dawson: MS 47
Nekcsei-Lipócz Bible: MS 6
Warburg Hours: MS 46

Rosenwald Manuscripts

1977 catalog	1954 catalog	This catalog
2	5	5
3	31	3
5	28	8
9	29	51
12	11	53
14	10	52
15	33	54
16	9	50

In Music Division:

	MS
Biggers Gradual	43
117-leaf Antiphonary	38
Kelsch Gradual	41
O'Hara Hymnary	40
Stravinsky Antiphonal	39
Washington Hirmologion	9
Wilson Kyriale	42
M 2156.XII.M1/CASE	9
M 2147.XIV.M1/CASE	10
M 2147.XII.M1/CASE	11
M 2147.XIV.M3/CASE	16
M 2147.XIV.M2/CASE	19
M 2147.XV.M2/CASE	36
M 2147.XVI.M2 Folio/CASE	40
M 2147.XVI.M1 Folio/CASE	42